AutoCAD® 2009 Tutorial

Second Level: 3D Modeling

Randy H. Shih

Oregon Institute of Technology

ISBN:

978-1-58503-434-5 (Text only)

978-1-58503-442-0 (Text bundled with 180-day license AutoCAD® 2009)

SDC PUBLICATIONS

Mission, Kansas

Schroff Development Corporation
P.O. Box 1334
Mission KS 66222
(913) 262-2664
WWW.**SCHROFF**.COM

Trademarks

Examination Copies:

Electronic Files:

Shih, Randy H.
AutoCAD® 2009 Tutorial / First Level: 2D Fundamentals

Randy H. Shih

ISBN 1-58503-434-5 (Text Only)
ISBN 1-58503-442-0 (Text bundled with AutoCAD 2009)

Printed and bound in the United States of America.

Preface

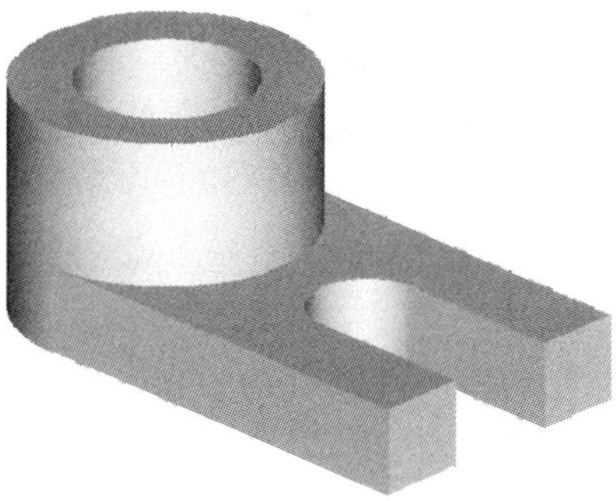

The primary goal of ***AutoCAD® 2009 Tutorial: 3D Modeling*** is to introduce the aspects of **Computer Based Three Dimensional Modeling**. This text is intended to be used as a training guide for students and professionals. This text covers *AutoCAD® 2009* and the chapters proceed in a pedagogical fashion to guide you from constructing 3D wireframe models, 3D surface models and 3D solid models to making multiview drawings. This text takes a hands-on, exercise-intensive approach to all the important 3D modeling techniques and concepts. This textbook contains a series of ten tutorial style chapters designed to introduce CAD users to 3D modeling with **AutoCAD® 2009**. This text is also helpful to AutoCAD users upgrading from a previous release of the software. The new improvements and enhancements of the software are incorporated into the tutorials. The 3D modeling techniques and concepts discussed in this text are also designed to serve as the foundation to the more advanced feature-based CAD/CAE packages such as AutoCAD® Mechanical Desktop, AutoCAD® Architectural Desktop and Autodesk Inventor®. The basic premise of this book is that the more 3D designs you create using AutoCAD® 2009, the better you learn the software. With this in mind, each tutorial introduces a new set of commands and concepts, building on previous chapters. This book does not attempt to cover all of AutoCAD® 2009's features, only to provide an introduction to the software. It is intended to help you establish a good basis for exploring and growing in the exciting field of Computer Aided Engineering.

Acknowledgments

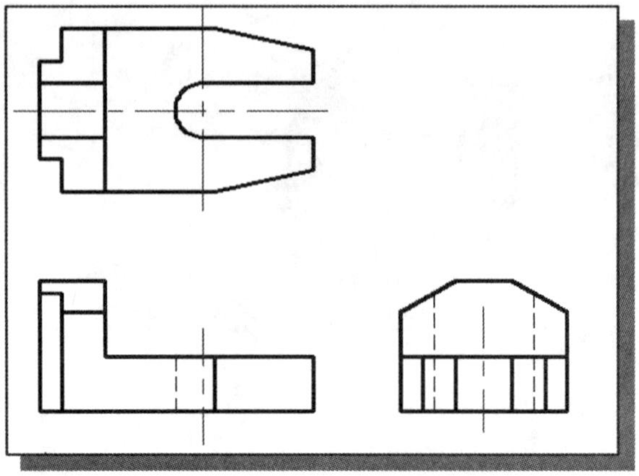

This book would not have been possible without a great deal of support. First, special thanks to two great teachers, Prof. George R. Schade of University of Nebraska-Lincoln and Mr. Denwu Lee, who taught me the fundamentals, the intrigue, and the sheer fun of Computer Aided Engineering.

The effort and support of the editorial and production staff of Schroff Development Corporation is gratefully acknowledged. I would especially like to thank Stephen Schroff and Mary Schmidt for their support and helpful suggestions during this project.

I am grateful that the Mechanical and Manufacturing Engineering Technology Department of Oregon Institute of Technology has provided me with an excellent environment in which to pursue my interests in teaching and research. I would especially like to thank Professor Brian Moravec and Emeritus Professor Charles Hermach for helpful comments and encouragement.

Finally, truly unbounded thanks are due to my wife Hsiu-Ling and our daughter Casandra for their understanding and encouragement throughout this project.

Randy H. Shih
Klamath Falls, Oregon
Spring, 2008

Table of Contents

Chapter 3
3D Wireframe Modeling

Chapter 4
UCS, Viewports and Wireframe Modeling

Chapter 7
Regions, Extrude and Solid Modeling

Chapter 8
Multiview Drawings from 3D Models

Chapter One
Getting Started

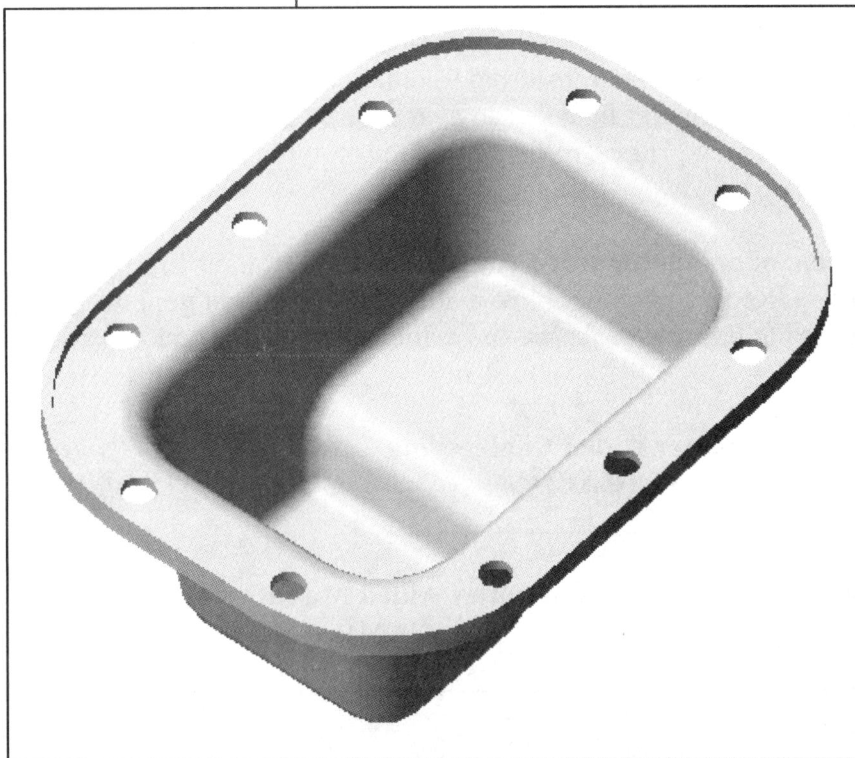

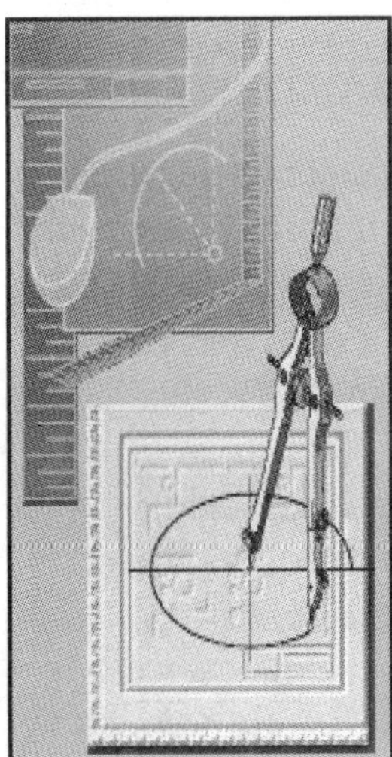

Learning Objectives

- Development of Computer Aided Design
- Why use AutoCAD 2009?
- Getting started with AutoCAD 2009
- The AutoCAD Startup dialog box and Units setup
- AutoCAD 2009 screen layout
- Mouse buttons

Introduction

Computer Aided Design (CAD) is the process of doing designs with the aid of computers. This includes the generation of computer models, analysis of design data, and the creation of the necessary drawings. **AutoCAD® 2009** is a computer-aided-design software developed by *Autodesk Inc.* The **AutoCAD® 2009** software is a tool that can be used for design and drafting activities. The two-dimensional and three-dimensional models created in **AutoCAD® 2009** can be transferred to other computer programs for further analysis and testing. The computer models can also be used in manufacturing equipment such as machining centers, lathes, mills, or rapid prototyping machines to manufacture the product.

The rapid changes in the field of **computer aided engineering** (CAE) have brought exciting advances in industry. Recent advances have made the long-sought goal of reducing design time, producing prototypes faster, and achieving higher product quality closer to a reality.

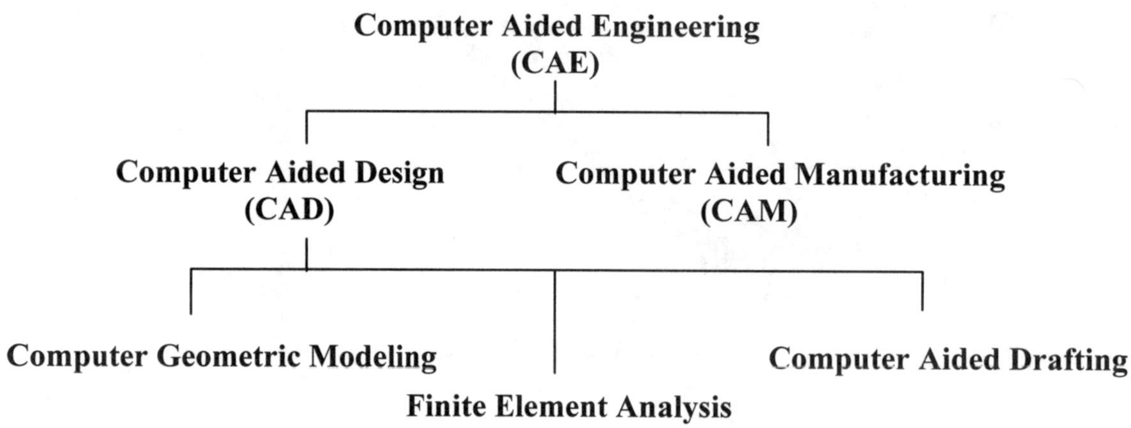

Development of Computer Geometric Modeling

Computer Aided Design is a relatively new technology and its rapid expansion in the last 50 years is truly amazing. Computer modeling technology advanced along with the development of computer hardware. The first generation CAD programs, developed in the 1950s, were mostly non-interactive; CAD users were required to create program codes to generate the desired two-dimensional (2D) geometric shapes. Initially, the development of CAD technology occurred mostly in academic research facilities. The Massachusetts Institute of Technology, Carnegie-Mellon University, and Cambridge University were the lead pioneers at that time. The interest in CAD technology spread quickly and several major industry companies, such as General Motors, Lockheed, McDonnell, IBM, and Ford Motor Co., participated in the development of interactive CAD programs in the 1960s. Usage of CAD systems was primarily in the automotive industry, aerospace industry, and government agencies that developed their own programs for their specific needs. The 1960s also marked the beginning of the development of finite element analysis methods for computer stress analysis and computer aided manufacturing for generating machine toolpaths.

The 1970s are generally viewed as the years of the most significant progress in the development of computer hardware, namely the invention and development of **microprocessors**. With the improvement in computing power, new types of 3D CAD programs that were user-friendly and interactive became reality. CAD technology quickly expanded from very simple **computer aided drafting** to very complex **computer aided design**. The use of 2D and 3D wireframe modelers was accepted as the leading edge technology that could increase productivity in industry. The developments of surface modeling and solid modeling technology were taking shape by the late 1970s; but the high cost of computer hardware and programming slowed the development of such technology. During this time period, the available CAD systems all required extremely expensive room-sized mainframe computers.

In the 1980s, improvements in computer hardware brought the power of mainframes to the desktop at less cost and with more accessibility to the general public. By the mid-1980s, CAD technology had become the main focus of a variety of manufacturing industries and was very competitive with traditional design/drafting methods. It was during this period of time that 3D solid modeling technology had major advancements, which boosted the usage of CAE technology in industry.

In the 1990s, CAD programs evolved into powerful design/manufacturing/management tools. CAD technology has come a long way, and during these years of development, modeling schemes progressed from two-dimensional (2D) wireframe to three-dimensional (3D) wireframe, to surface modeling, to solid modeling and, finally, to feature-based parametric solid modeling.

The first generation CAD packages were simply 2D **Computer Aided Drafting** programs, basically the electronic equivalents of the drafting board. For typical models, the use of this type of program would require that several to many views of the objects be created individually as they would be on the drafting board. The 3D designs remained in the designer's mind, not in the computer database. The mental translation of 3D objects to 2D views is required throughout the use of the packages. Although such systems have some advantages over traditional board drafting, they are still tedious and labor intensive. The need for the development of 3D modelers came quite naturally, given the limitations of the 2D drafting packages.

The development of the 3D wireframe modeler was a major leap in the area of computer modeling. The computer database in the 3D wireframe modeler contains the locations of all the points in space coordinates and it is sufficient to create just one model rather than multiple models. This single 3D model can then be viewed from any direction as needed. The 3D wireframe modelers require the least computer power and achieve reasonably good representation of 3D models. But because surface definition is not part of a wireframe model, all wireframe images have the inherent problem of ambiguity.

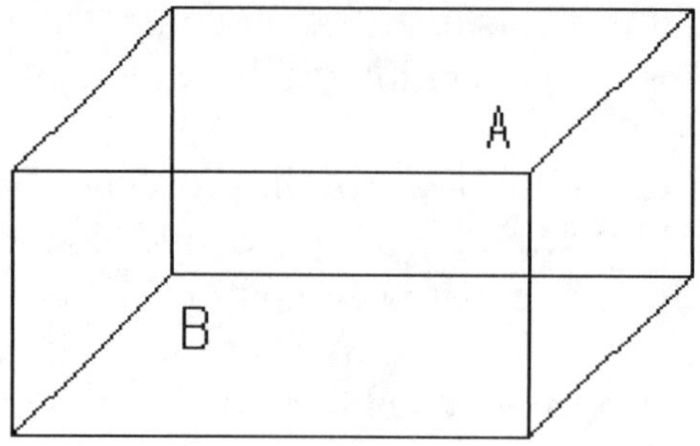

Wireframe Ambiguity: Which corner is in front, A or B?

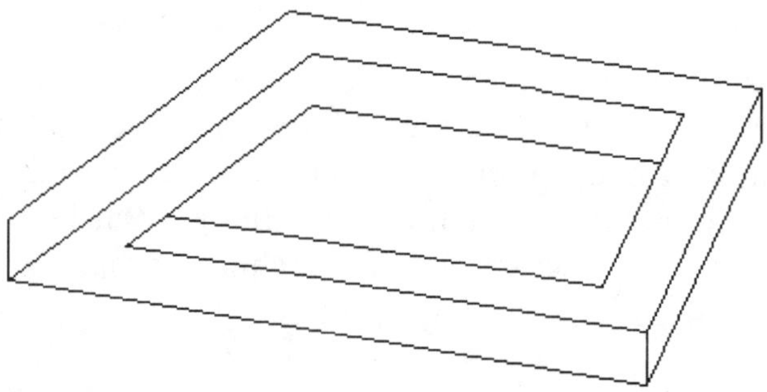

A non-realizable object: Wireframe models contain no surface definitions.

Surface modeling is the logical development in computer geometry modeling to follow the 3D wireframe modeling scheme by organizing and grouping edges that define polygonal surfaces. Surface modeling describes the part's surfaces but not its interiors. Designers are still required to interactively examine surface models to insure that the various surfaces on a model are contiguous throughout. Many of the concepts used in 3D wireframe and surface modelers are incorporated in the solid modeling scheme, but it is solid modeling that offers the most advantages as a design tool.

In the solid modeling presentation scheme, the solid definitions include nodes, edges, and surfaces, and it is a complete and unambiguous mathematical representation of a precisely enclosed and filled volume. Unlike the surface modeling method, solid modelers start with a solid or use topology rules to guarantee that all of the surfaces are stitched together properly. Two predominant methods for representing solid models are **constructive solid geometry** (CSG) representation and **boundary representation** (B-rep).

The CSG representation method can be defined as the combination of 3D solid primitives. What constitutes a "primitive" varies somewhat with the software but typically includes a rectangular prism, a cylinder, a cone, a wedge, and a sphere. Most solid modelers allow the user to define additional primitives, which can be very complex.

In the B-rep representation method, objects are represented in terms of their spatial boundaries. This method defines the points, edges, and surfaces of a volume, and/or issues commands that sweep or rotate a defined face into a third dimension to form a solid. The object is then made up of the unions of these surfaces that completely and precisely enclose a volume.

By the 1990s, a new paradigm called *concurrent engineering* had emerged. With concurrent engineering, designers, design engineers, analysts, manufacturing engineers, and management engineers all work closely right from the initial stages of the design. In this way, all aspects of the design can be evaluated and any potential problems can be identified right from the start and throughout the design process. Using the principles of concurrent engineering, a new type of computer modeling technique appeared. The technique is known as the *feature-based parametric modeling technique*. The key advantage of the *feature-based parametric modeling technique* is its capability to produce very flexible designs. Changes can be made easily and design alternatives can be evaluated with minimum effort. Various software packages offer different approaches to feature-based parametric modeling, yet the end result is a flexible design defined by its design variables and parametric features.

In this text, we will concentrate on creating designs using two-dimensional geometric construction techniques. The fundamental concepts and use of different **AutoCAD® 2009** commands are presented using step-by-step tutorials. We will begin with creating simple geometric entities and then move toward creating detailed working drawings and assembly drawings. The techniques presented in this text will also serve as the foundation for entering the world of three-dimensional solid modeling using packages such as **AutoCAD Mechanical Desktop**, **AutoCAD Architectural Desktop** and **Autodesk Inventor**.

Why use AutoCAD® 2009?

AutoCAD® was first introduced to the public in late 1982, and was one of the first CAD software products that were available for personal computers. Since 1984, **AutoCAD®** has established a reputation for being the most widely used PC-based CAD software around the world. By 2007, it was estimated that there were over 6 million **AutoCAD®** users in more than 150 countries worldwide. **AutoCAD® 2009** is the twenty-third release, with many added features and enhancements, of the original **AutoCAD®** software produced by *Autodesk Inc.*

CAD provides us with a wide range of benefits; in most cases, the result of using CAD is increased accuracy and productivity. First of all, the computer offers much higher accuracy than the traditional methods of drafting and design. Traditionally, drafting and detailing are the most expensive cost element in a project and the biggest bottleneck. With CAD systems, such as **AutoCAD® 2009,** the tedious drafting and detailing tasks are simplified through the use of many of the CAD geometric construction tools, such as *grids*, *snap*, *trim,* and *auto-dimensioning*. Dimensions and notes are always legible in CAD drawings, and in most cases, CAD systems can produce higher quality prints compared to traditional hand drawings.

CAD also offers much-needed flexibility in design and drafting. A CAD model generated on a computer consists of numeric data that describe the geometry of the object. This allows the designers and clients to see something tangible and to interpret the ramifications of the design. In many cases, it is also possible to simulate operating conditions on the computer and observe the results. Any kind of geometric shape stored in the database can be easily duplicated. For large and complex designs and drawings, particularly those involving similar shapes and repetitive operations, CAD approaches are very efficient and effective. Because computer designs and models can be altered easily, a multitude of design options can be examined and presented to a client before any construction or manufacturing actually takes place. Making changes to a CAD model is generally much faster than making changes to a traditional hand drawing. Only the affected components of the design need to be modified and the drawings can be plotted again. In addition, the greatest benefit is that, once the CAD model is created, it can be used over and over again. The CAD models can also be transferred into manufacturing equipment such as machining centers, lathes, mills, or rapid prototyping machines to manufacture the product directly.

CAD, however, does not replace every design activity. CAD may help, but it does not replace the designer's experience with geometry and graphical conventions and standards for the specific field. CAD is a powerful tool, but the use of this tool does not guarantee correct results; the designer is still responsible for using good design practice and applying good judgment. CAD will supplement these skills to ensure that the best design is obtained.

CAD designs and drawings are stored in binary form, usually as CAD files, to magnetic devices such as diskettes and hard disks. The information stored in CAD files usually requires much less physical space in comparison to traditional hand drawings. However, the information stored inside the computer is not indestructible. On the contrary, the electronic format of information is very fragile and sensitive to the environment. Heat or cold can damage the information stored on magnetic storage devices. A power failure while you are creating a design could wipe out the many hours you spent working in front of the computer monitor. It is a good habit to save your work periodically, just in case something might go wrong while you are working on your design. In general, one should save one's work onto a storage device at an interval of every 15 to 20 minutes. You should also save your work before you make any major modifications to the design. It is also a good habit to periodically make backup copies of your work and put them in a safe place.

Getting started with AutoCAD® 2009

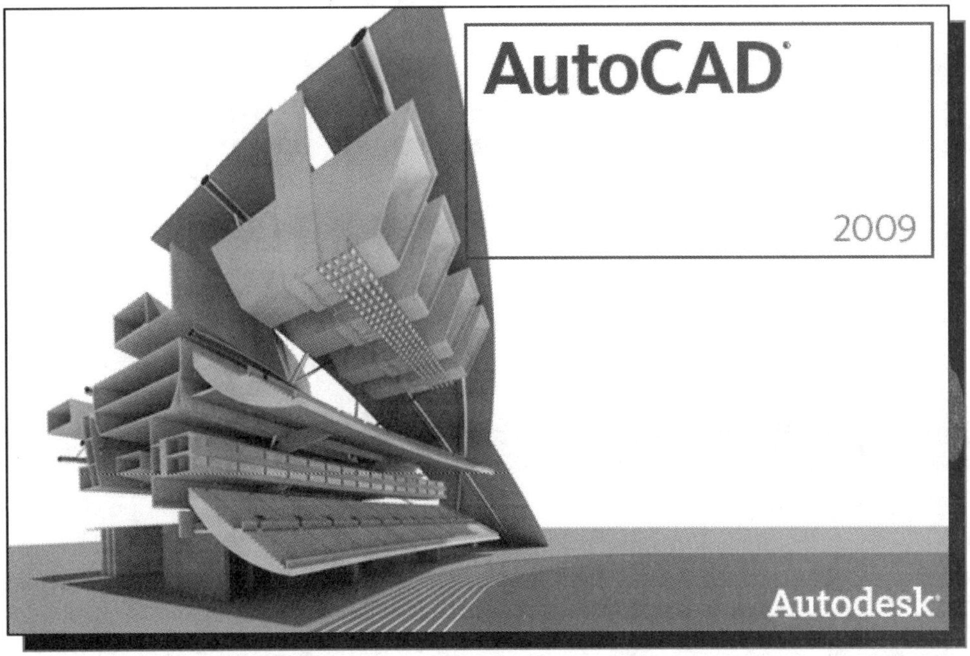

How to start **AutoCAD® 2009** depends on the type of workstation and the particular software configuration you are using. With most *Windows* systems, you may select the **AutoCAD 2009** option on the *Start* menu or select the **AutoCAD 2009** icon on the *Desktop*. Consult with your instructor or technical support personnel if you have difficulty starting the software.

The program takes a while to load, so be patient. Eventually the **AutoCAD® 2009** main *drawing screen* will appear on the screen. The tutorials in this text are based on the assumption that you are using **AutoCAD® 2009**'s default settings. If your system has been customized for other uses, some of the settings may not work with the step-by-step instructions in the tutorials. Contact your instructor and/or technical support personnel to restore the default software configuration.

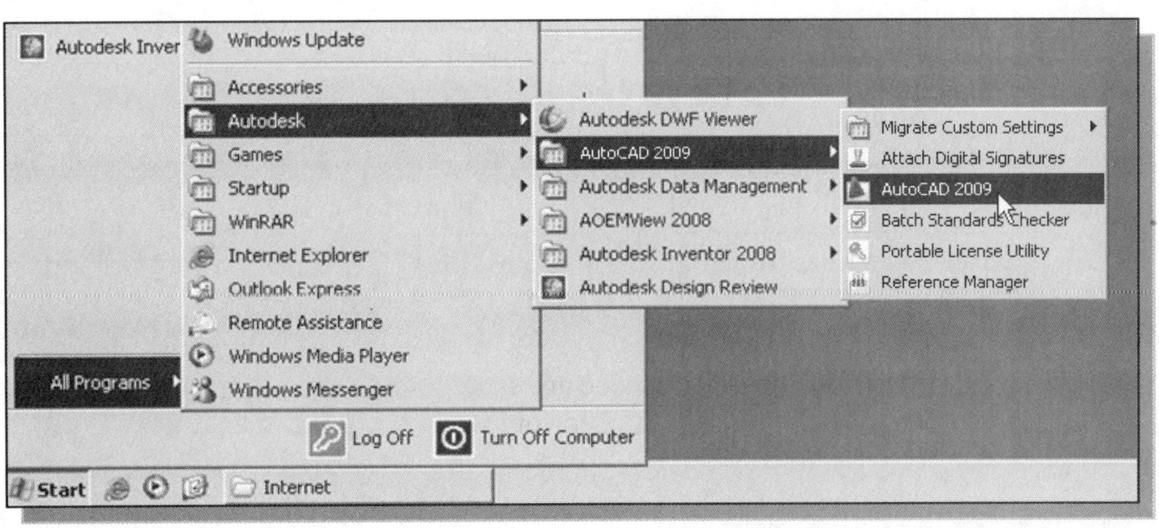

AutoCAD® 2009 Screen Layout

The default **AutoCAD® 2009** *drawing screen* contains the *pull-down* menus, the *Standard* toolbar, the *InfoCenter Help system,* the *scrollbars,* the *command prompt area*, the *Status Bar* and the *Ribbon Tabs and Panels* that contains several *control panels* such as the *Draw and Modify* panel and the *Annotation Panel*. You may resize the **AutoCAD® 2009** drawing window by click and drag at the edges of the window, or relocate the window by click and drag at the window title area.

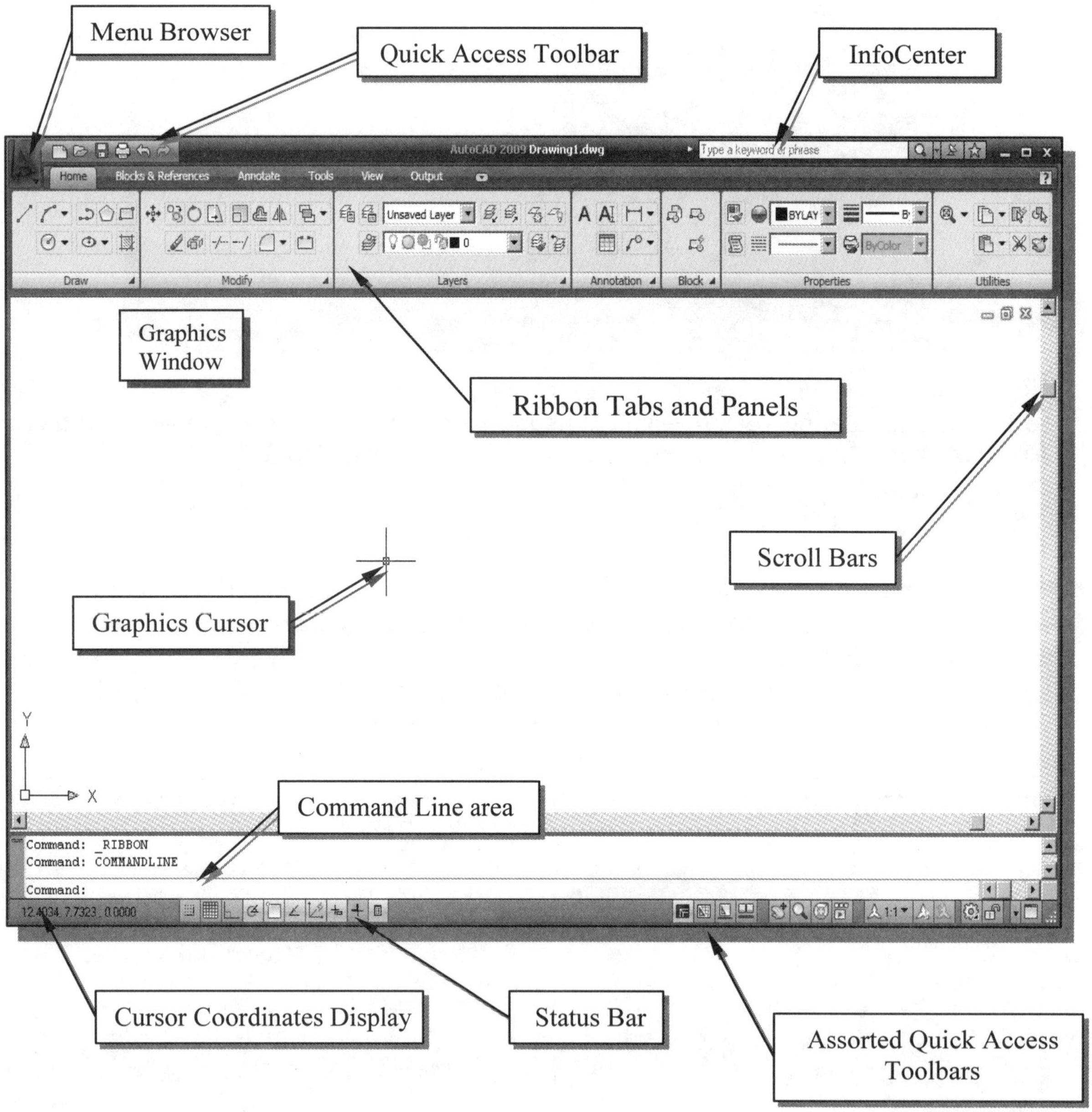

- **Menu Browser**
  The *Menu Browser* at the top of the main window contains operations that you can use for all modes of the system.

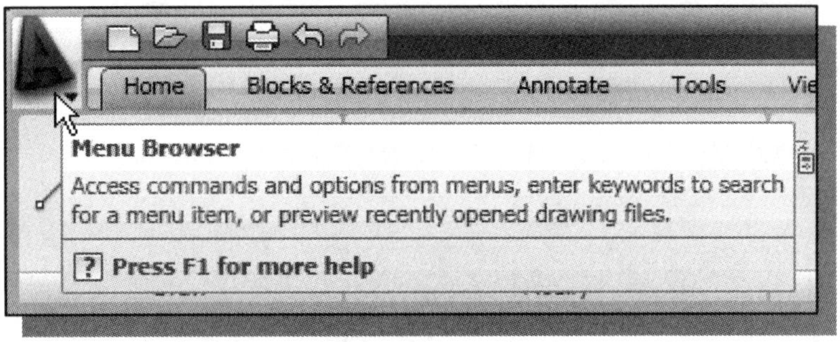

- **Quick Access Toolbar**
  The *Quick Access* toolbar at the top of the *AutoCAD* window allows us quick access to frequently used commands, such as Qnew, Open, Save and also the Undo command. Note that we can customize the quick access toolbar by adding and removing sets of options or individual commands.

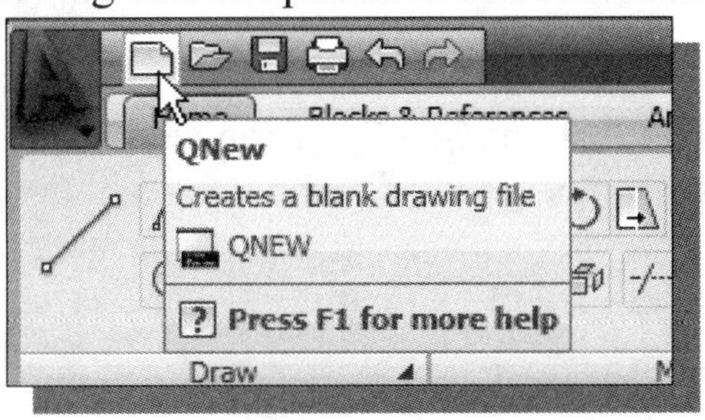

- **Graphics Window**
  The *graphics window* is the area where models and drawings are displayed.

- **Graphics Cursor or Crosshairs**
  The *graphics cursor*, or *crosshairs*, shows the location of the pointing device in the graphics window. The coordinates of the cursor are displayed at the bottom of the screen layout. The cursor's appearance depends on the selected command or option.

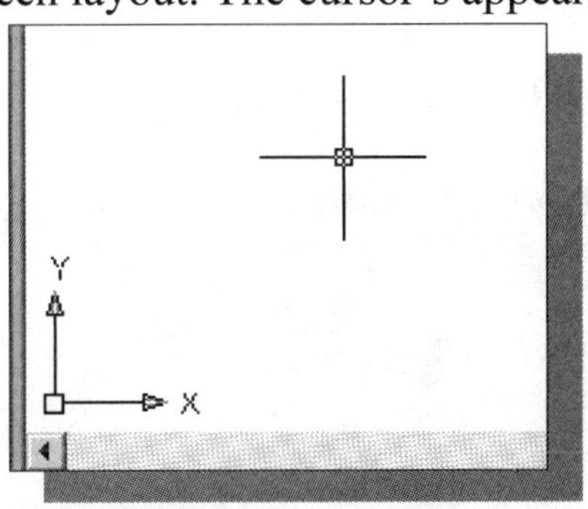

- **Command Prompt Area**
  The bottom section of the screen layout provides status information for an operation and it is also the area for data input.

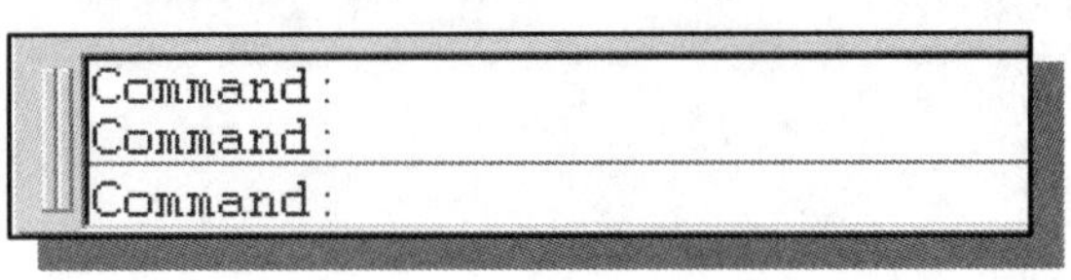

- **Cursor Coordinates**
  The bottom left section of the screen layout displays the coordinate information of the cursor.

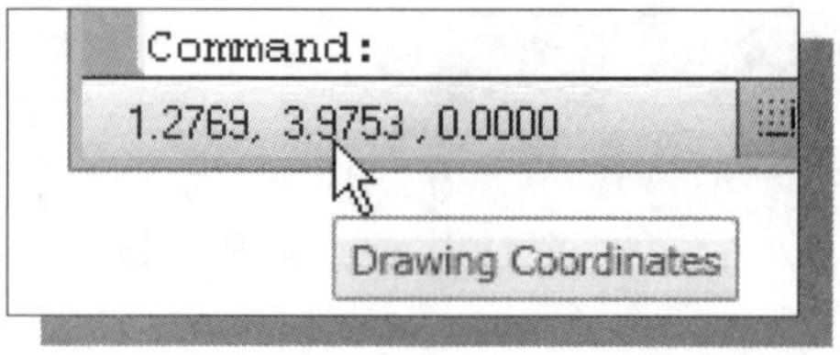

- **Status Toolbar**
  Next to the Cursor Coordinate display is the status toolbar, showing the status of several commonly used Display and Construction options.

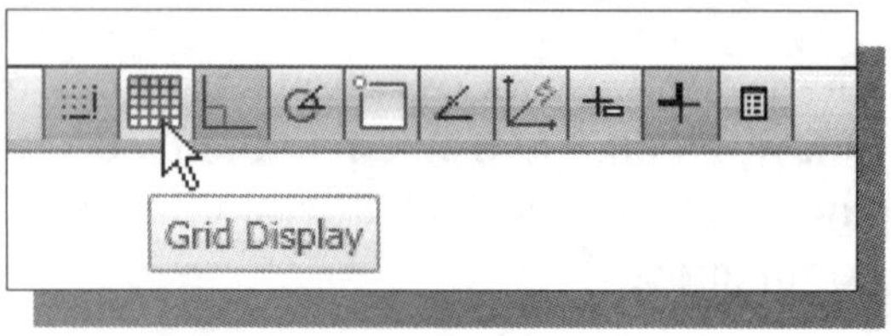

- **Ribbon Tabs and Panels**
  The top section of the screen layout contains customizable icon panels, which contain groups of buttons that allow us to pick commands quickly, without searching through a menu structure. These panels allow us to quickly access the commonly used commands available in AutoCAD.

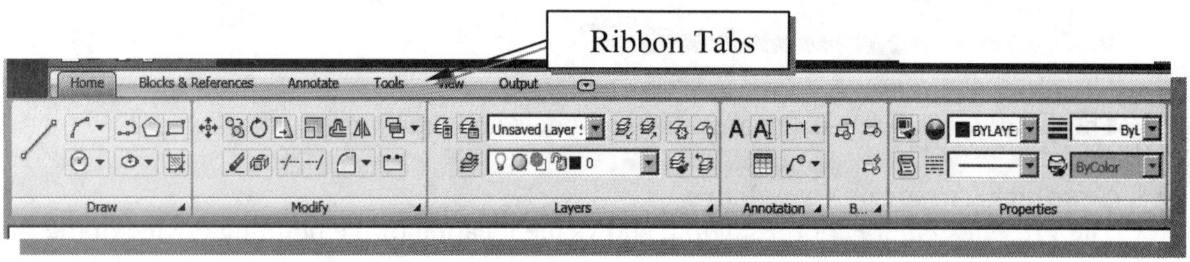

- **Draw and Modify Toolbar Panels**
  The *Draw* and *Modify* toolbar Panel contain icons for basic draw and modify commands.

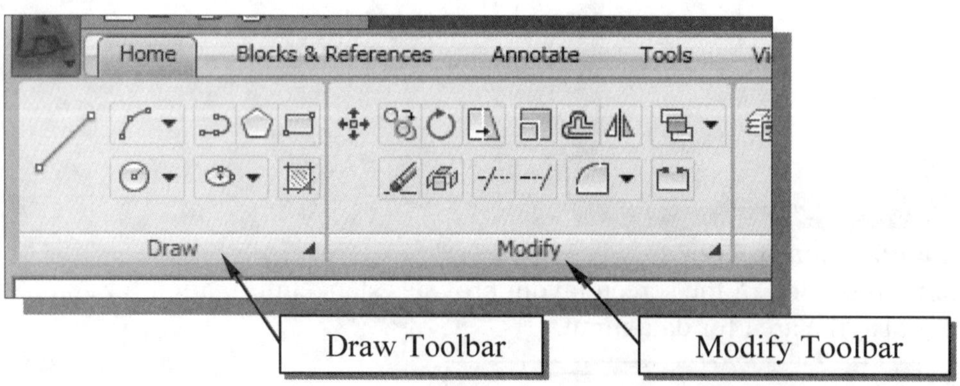

- **Layers Control Toolbar Panel**
  The *Layers Control* Toolbar Panel contains tools to help manipulate the properties of graphical objects.

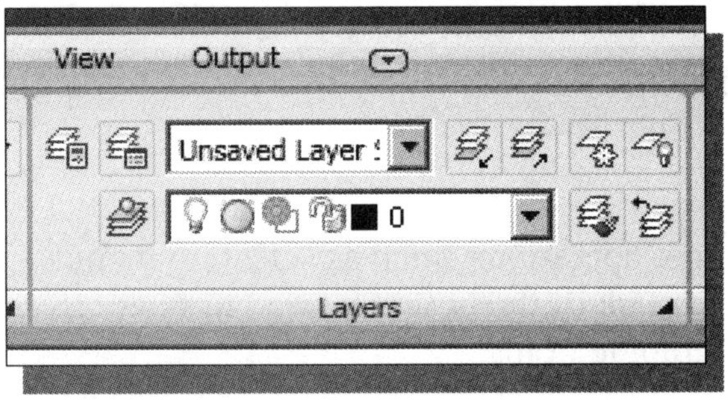

- **Annotation Toolbar Panel**
  The *Annotation Toolbar* Panel contains tools for creating and editing dimensions.

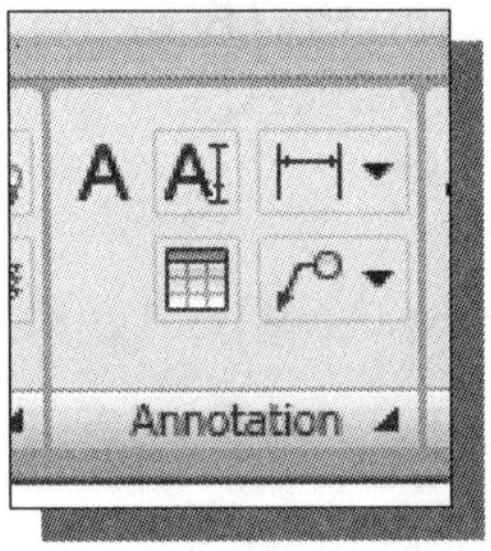

- **Layout/Model Toolbar**
  The *Layout/Model Toolbar* contains tools for creating and editing layouts.

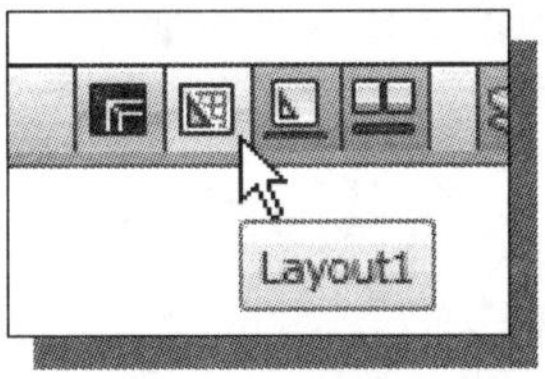

- **Viewing Toolbar**
  The *Viewing Toolbar* contains tools for viewing commands, such as Zoom and Pan.

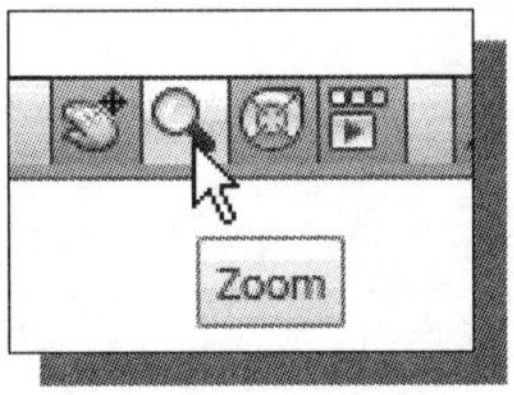

- **Workspace switching**
  The *Workspace Switching Icon* allows us to switch in between different system settings.

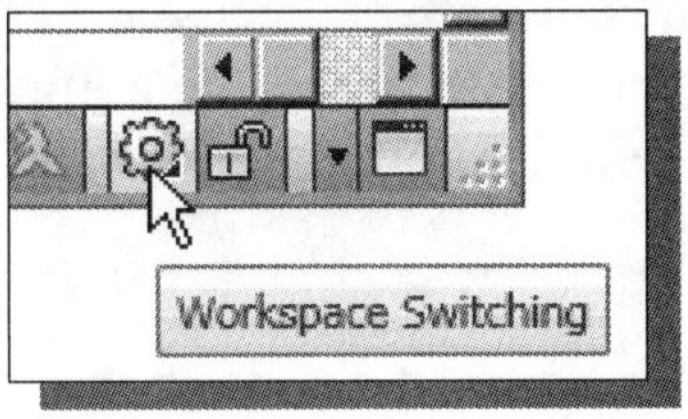

Mouse Buttons

AutoCAD® 2009 utilizes the mouse buttons extensively. In learning **AutoCAD® 2009**'s interactive environment, it is important to understand the basic functions of the mouse buttons. It is highly recommended that you use a mouse or a tablet with **AutoCAD® 2009** since the package uses the buttons for various functions.

- **Left mouse button**
  The **left-mouse-button** is used for most operations, such as selecting menus and icons, or picking graphic entities. One click of the button is used to select icons, menus and form entries, and to pick graphic items.

- **Right mouse button**
  The **right-mouse-button** is used to bring up additional available options. The software also utilizes the **right-mouse-button** as the same as the **ENTER** key, and is often used to accept the default setting to a prompt or to end a process.

- **Middle mouse button/wheel**
  The middle mouse button/wheel can be used to Pan (hold down the wheel button and drag the mouse) or Zoom (rotate the wheel) realtime.

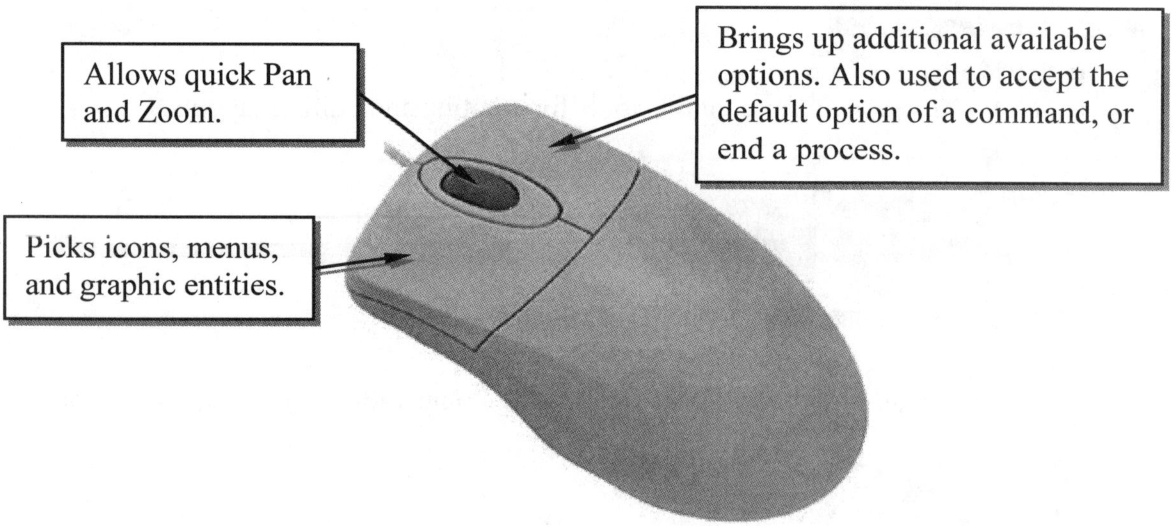

[Esc] – Canceling Commands

The [**Esc**] key is used to cancel a command in **AutoCAD® 2009**. The [**Esc**] key is located near the top-left corner of the keyboard. Sometimes, it may be necessary to press the [**Esc**] key twice to cancel a command; it depends on where we are in the command sequence. For some commands, the [**Esc**] key is used to exit the command.

On-Line Help

❖ Several types of on-line help are available at any time during an **AutoCAD® 2009** session. The **AutoCAD® 2009** software provides many on-line help options:

- **InfoCenter**:
  The **InfoCenter** option provides an instant search to the AutoCAD help system to find information related to the question entered in the input box. The guidance from the **Help** system enables users to quickly get started on performing desired tasks. In the **InfoCenter** list, links to different group of information can be activated by clicking on the items.

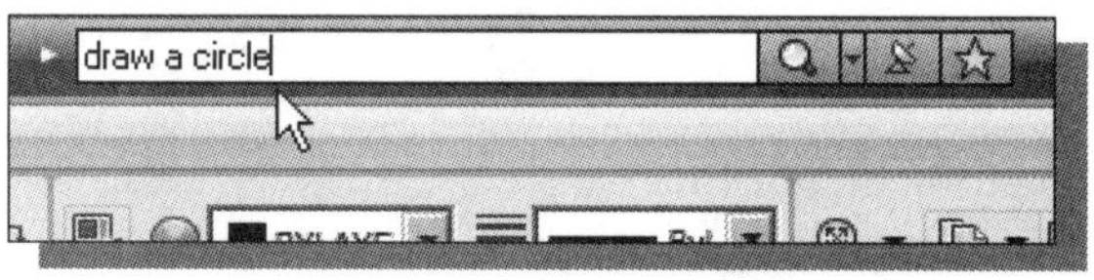

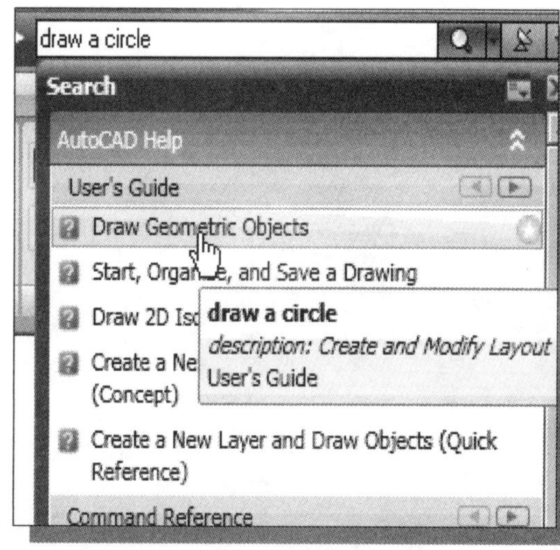

- To use the *InfoCenter*, simply type in a question in the *input box* to search through the AutoCAD's Help system as shown in the above figure.

- A list of the search results will appear on the screen and we can choose to display the associated information.

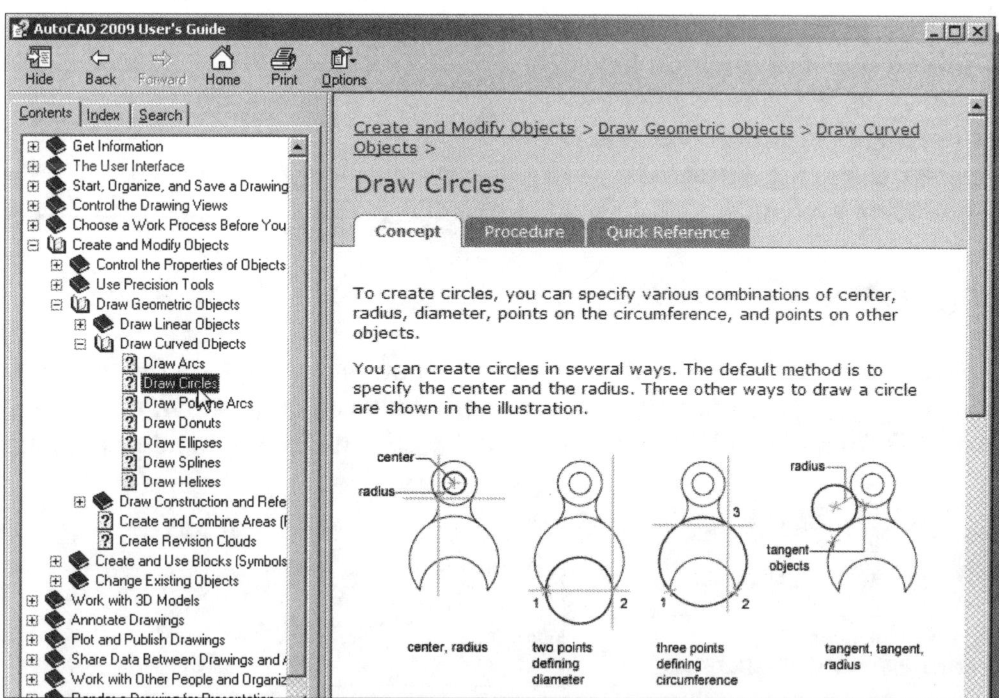

- **Info Center menu**: Click on the **InfoCenter** option menu, as shown in the below figure, to access the available **AutoCAD® 2009 help system**.

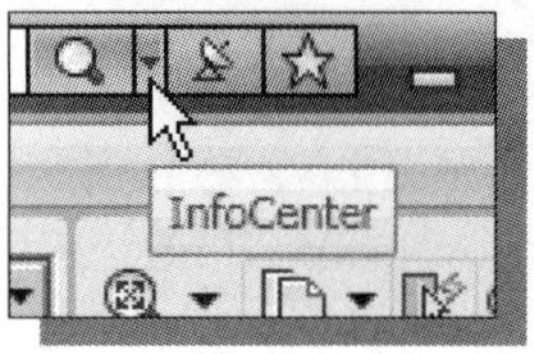

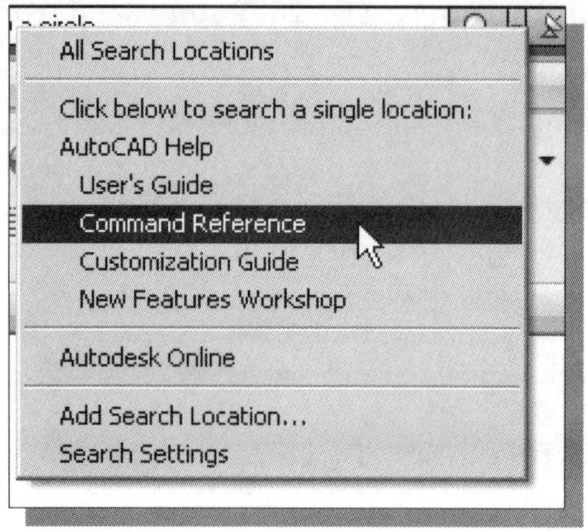

- **Help Icon**: Click on the **[?]** icon in the top right corner of the main AutoCAD window to access Autodesk On-line Help.

- **Command line and function key [F1]**: Press the [**F1**] key or enter a question mark [**?**] at the command prompt to access the **AutoCAD On-line Help system**.

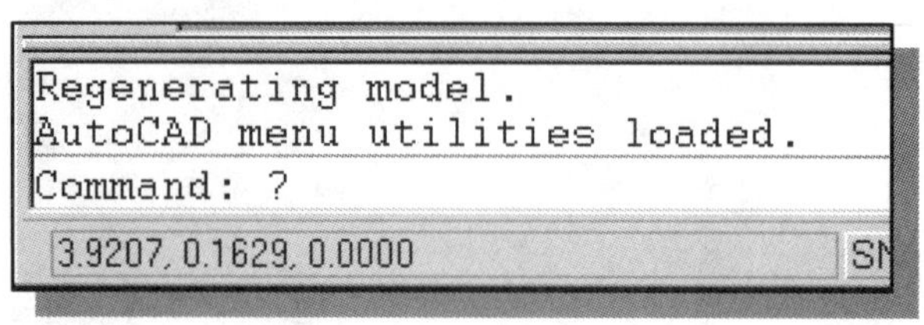

Leaving AutoCAD® 2009

➢ To leave **AutoCAD® 2009**, use the left-mouse-button and click on **Menu Browser** button at the top left corner of the **AutoCAD® 2009** screen window, then choose **Exit AutoCAD** from the pull-down menu or type ***QUIT*** in the command prompt area.

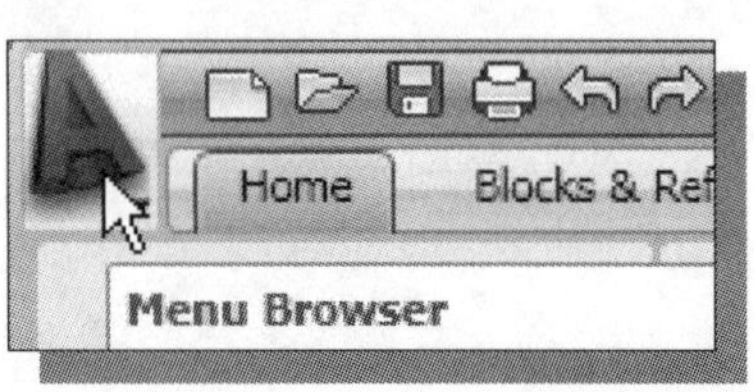

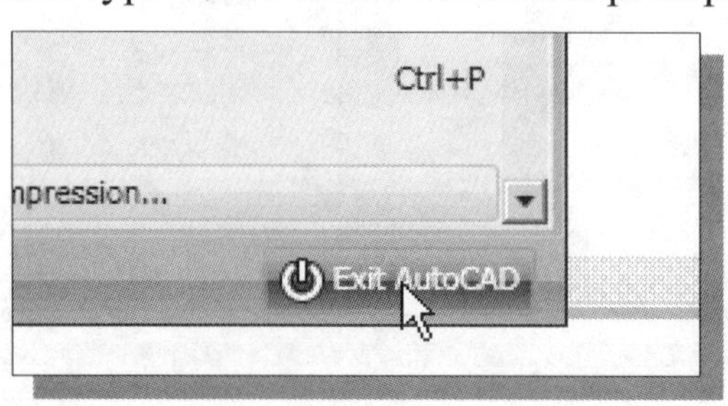

Creating a CAD File Folder

❖ It is a good practice to create a separate folder to store your CAD files. You should not save your CAD files in the same folder where the **AutoCAD® 2009** application is located. It is much easier to organize and backup your project files if they are in a separate folder. Making folders within this folder for different types of projects will help you organize your CAD files even further. When creating CAD files in **AutoCAD® 2009**, it is strongly recommended that you *save* your CAD files on the hard drive. However, if you do want to save your files on a floppy drive, be sure to exit the **AutoCAD® 2009** program before removing the diskette from the drive. The better alternative is to save the files on the hard drive and then copy the files onto a floppy diskette under the operating system.

➢ To create a new folder in the Windows environment:

1. In *My Computer*, or the ***Windows Explorer*** under the *Start* menu, open the folder in which you want to create a new folder.

2. On the **File** menu, point to **New**, and then click **Folder**. The new folder appears with a temporary name.

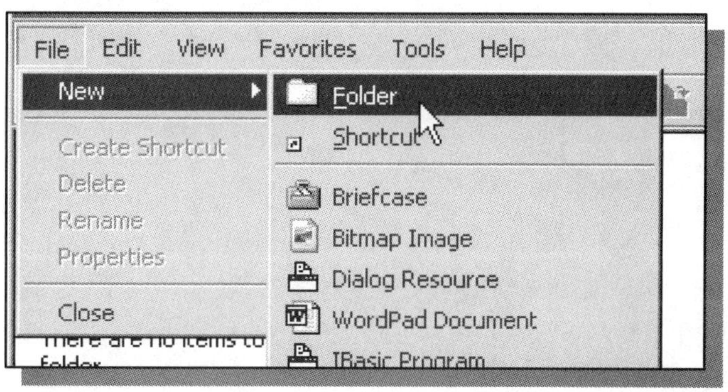

3. Type a name for the new folder, and then press **ENTER**.

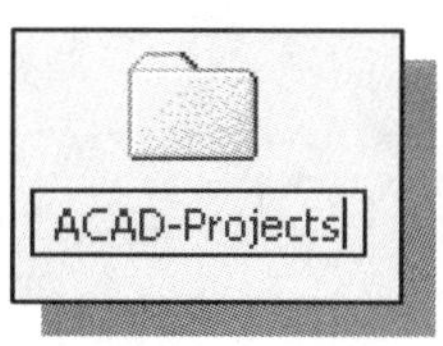

Notes:

Chapter 2
User Coordinate Systems and the Z-Axis

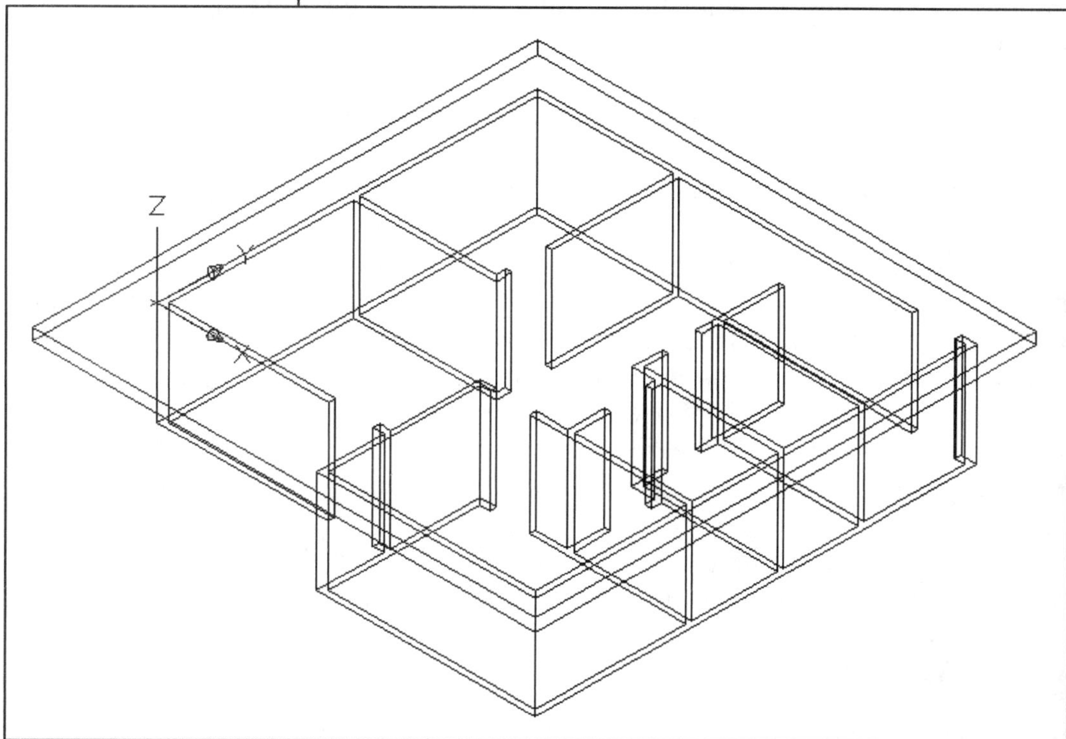

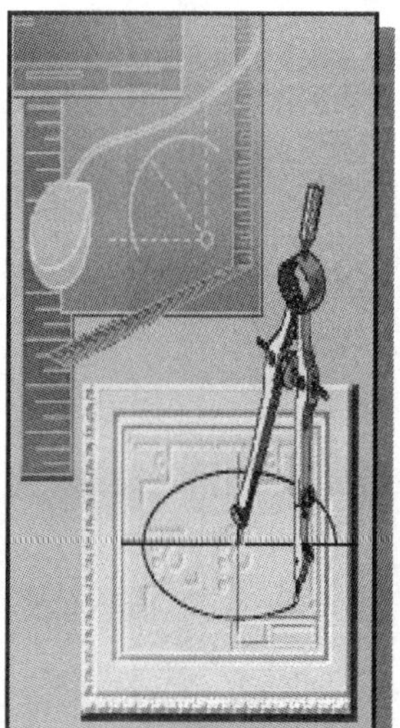

Learning Objectives

- Using the Drawing Units and Drawing Limits Commands
- Understand and Use the THICKNESS Option
- Understand the AutoCAD UCS
- Be able to Switch to Predefined Views
- Pre-selection of Objects
- Controlling Object Properties
- Viewing with the Visual Styles Option

Introduction

Creating three-dimensional models on a CAD system provides us a means to check the integrity of a design. Creating realistic three-dimensional models helps us visualize our final design much more clearly than we can with 2D representations of the design. Several different approaches are available in AutoCAD that allow us to quickly create 3D models. The simplest approach is to use the *Thickness* variable to perform an extrusion in the third dimension of 2D geometries. In AutoCAD, the *Thickness* variable can make certain 2D objects look like 3D objects. It is important to realize that this approach is somewhat limited and that the objects created are not true solids. This approach allows us to start considering the complexity involved in creating 3D models.

In this chapter, we will explore the virtual 3D environment in AutoCAD. Understanding how to maneuver in the virtual 3D environment and the use of a *User Coordinate System* (UCS) are the foundations and perhaps the most difficult parts of 3D modeling. We will also examine the basic viewing and rendering options that are available in AutoCAD. Specifically, we will use the **Hide** options to create hidden-line-removed images. The hidden-line-removed image makes it easier to visualize the model because the back faces are not displayed.

In this chapter, we will begin with the construction of a 2D floor plan design. This tutorial will also serve as a review of some of the 2D CAD construction techniques. The main goal of this chapter is to provide you with a basic understanding of the 3D environment of AutoCAD.

The *Floor Plan* Design

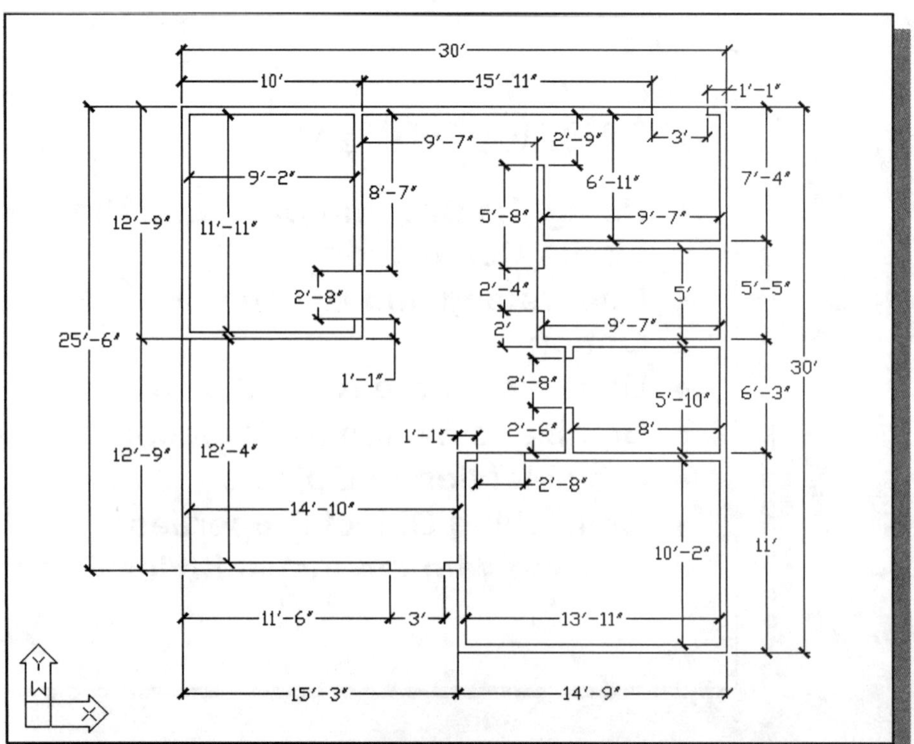

Starting Up AutoCAD® 2009

1. Select the **AutoCAD 2009** option on the *Program* menu or select the **AutoCAD 2009** icon on the *Desktop*. Once the program is loaded into memory, the **AutoCAD® 2009** drawing screen will appear on the screen.

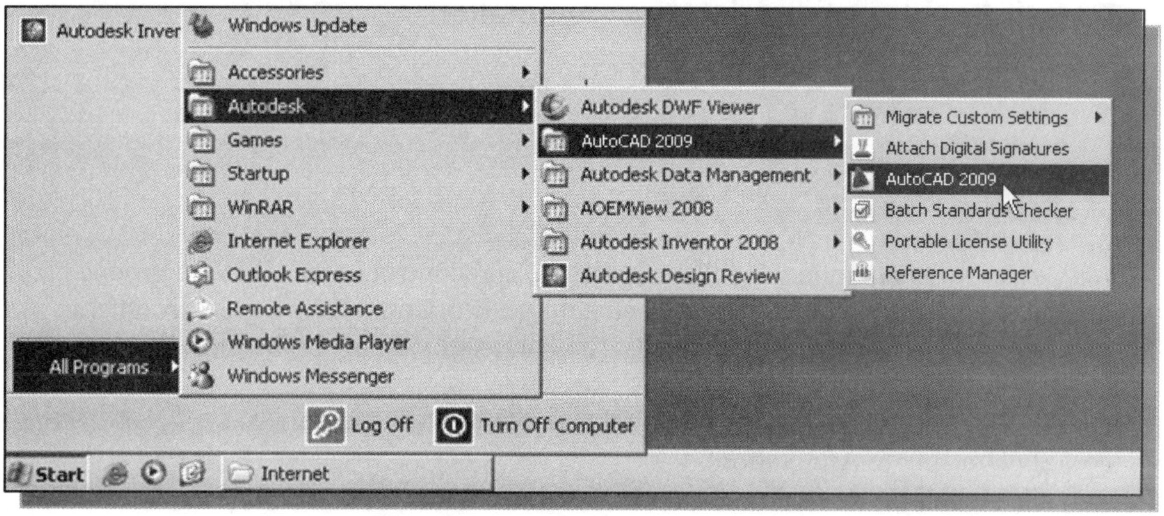

➢ Note that AutoCAD automatically assigns generic name, *Drawing X*, as new drawings are created. In our example, AutoCAD opened the graphics window using the default system units and assigned the drawing name *Drawing1*.

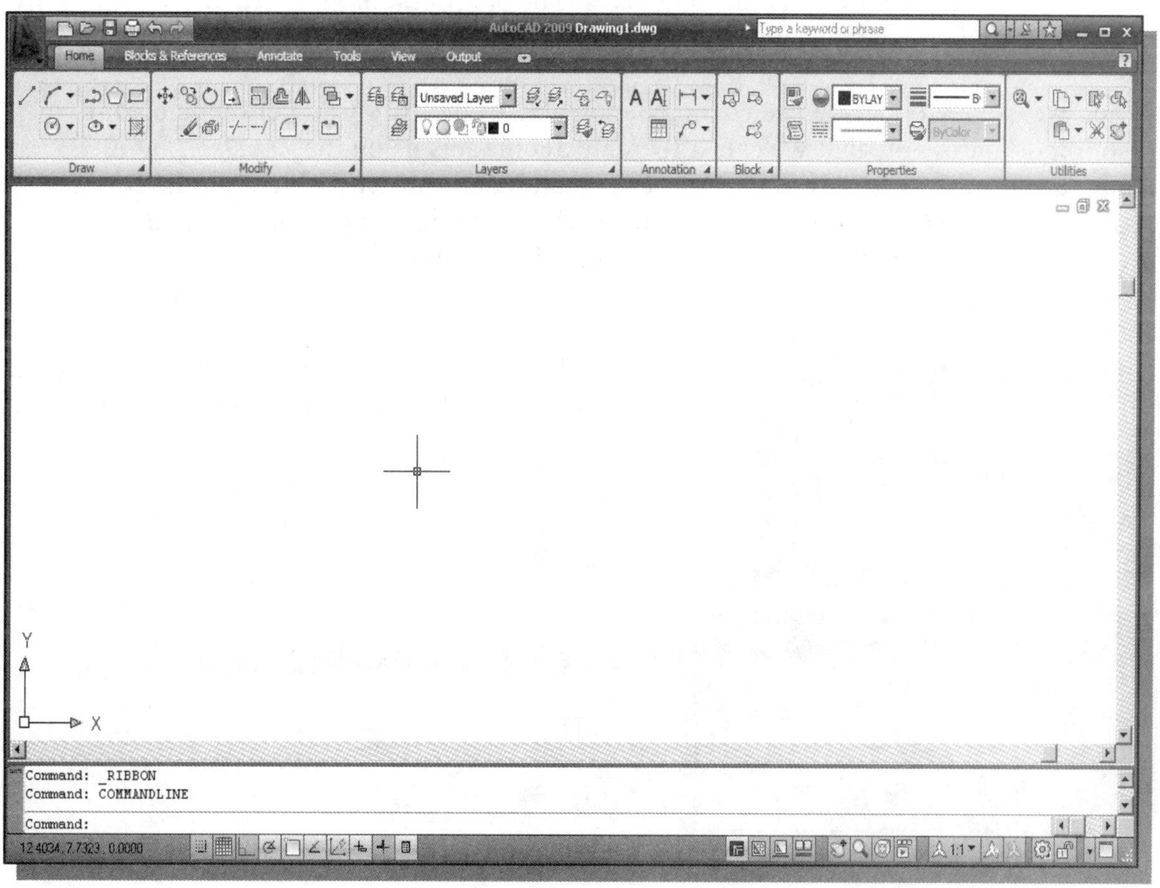

3D Modeling WorkSpace

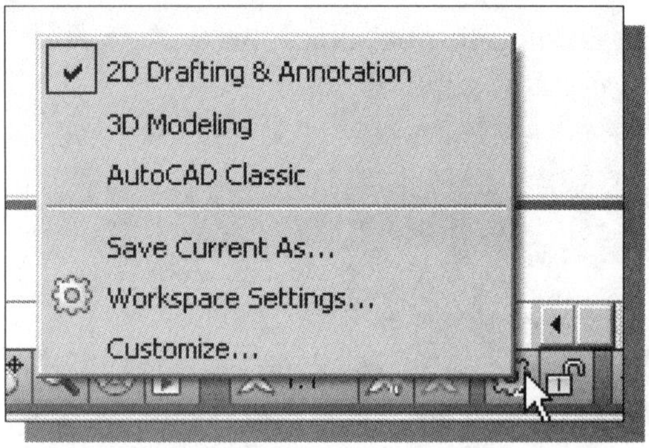

➢ Note that the default AutoCAD 2009 *workspace* setting is set to **2D Drafting & Annotation**.

Workspaces are sets of menus, toolbars, palettes, and control panels that are grouped and organized so that the user can work in a custom, task-oriented drawing environment. Workspaces control the display of menus, toolbars, and palettes in the drawing area.

AutoCAD 2009 provides three pre-defined task-based workspaces:

- 2D Drafting & Annotation
- 3D Modeling
- AutoCAD Classic

For example, the *2D Drafting & Annotation workspace* displays most of the toolbars and menus commonly used for 2D drafting tasks. The *3D Modeling* workspace contains only 3D-related toolbars, menus, and palettes.

When we use a workspace, we change the display of the AutoCAD drawing area. It is also important to note that we can still create 3D models using the *2D Drafting & Annotation workspace*. All of the AutoCAD commands are available regardless which workspace we use. Using the workspaces is one of the many options available in AutoCAD 2009 that can help simplify our drafting/modeling tasks.

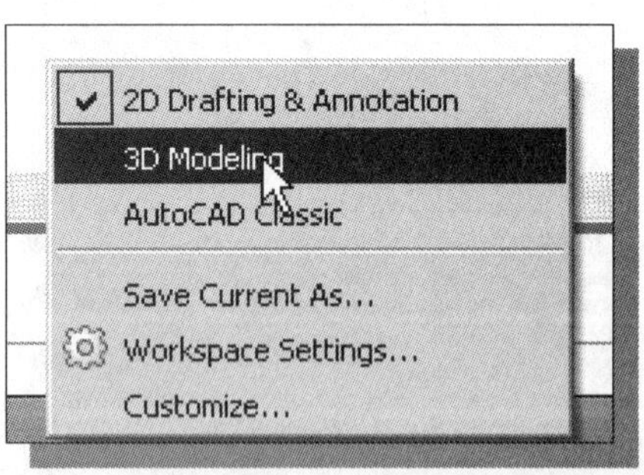

1. Click on the *Workspaces list* in the workspace toolbar and choose to use the **3D Modeling** workspace as shown.

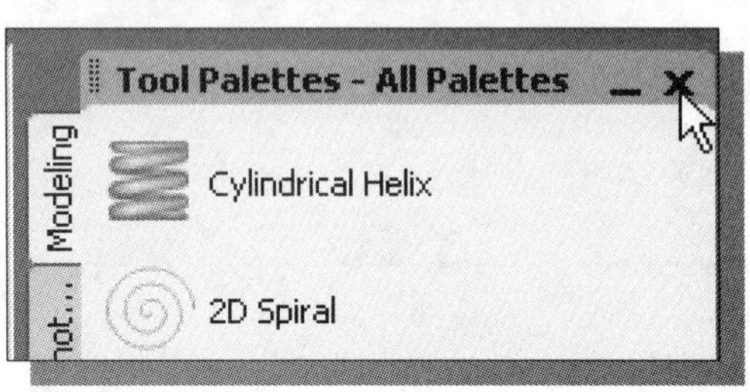

2. Close the **Tool Palettes** panel as shown.

Drawing Units Setup

➢ Every object we construct in a CAD system is measured in **units**. We should determine the value of the units within the CAD system before creating the first geometric entities.

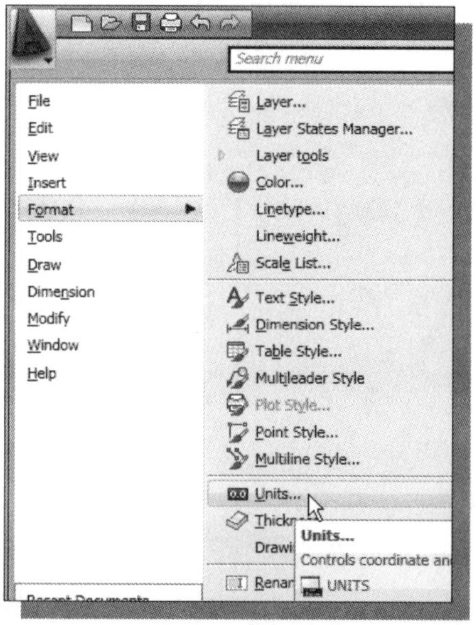

1. In the *Menu Browser*, select: **[Format] → [Units]**

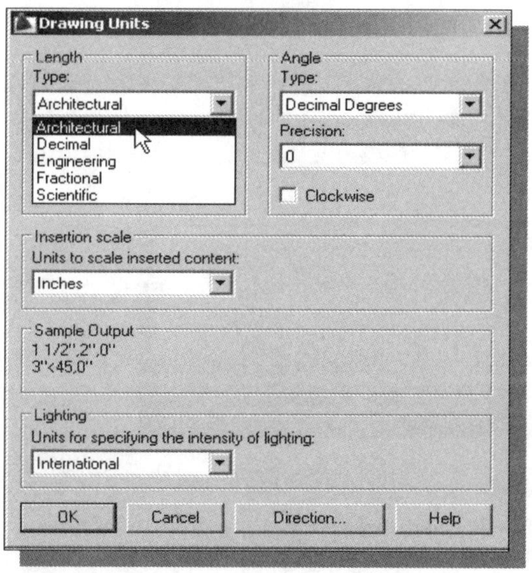

2. In the *Drawing Units* dialog box, set the *Length Type* to **Architectural**. This will set the measurement to the default Architectural units, feet and inches.

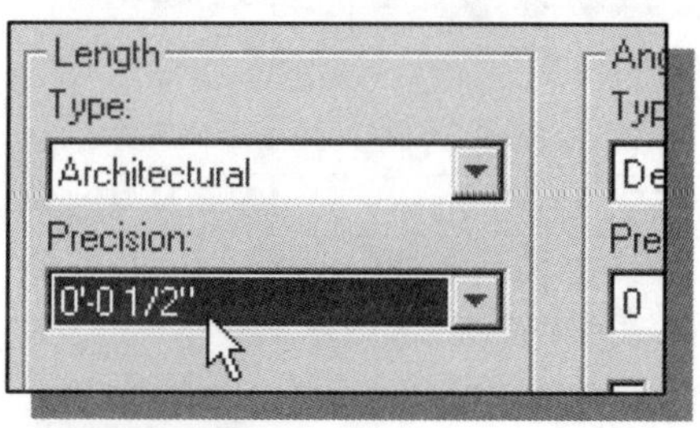

3. Set the *Precision* to **half-an-inch** as shown in the figure.

4. Click **OK** to exit the *Drawing Units* dialog box.

Drawing Area Setup

❖ Next, we will setup the **Drawing Limits**; setting the Drawing Limits controls the extents of the display of the *grid*. It also serves as a visual reference that marks the working area. It can also be used to prevent construction outside the grid limits and also as a plot option that defines an area to be plotted/printed. Note that this setting does not limit the region for geometry construction.

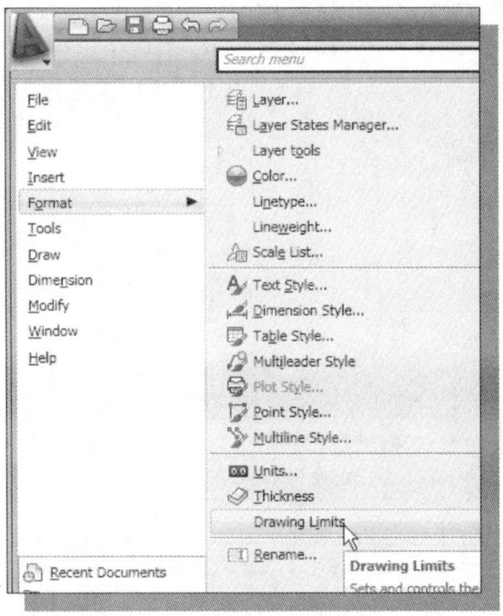

1. In the *Menu Browser*, select:
   [Format] → [Drawing Limits]

2. In the *command prompt* area, near the bottom of the AutoCAD drawing screen, the message "*Reset Model Space Limits: Specify lower left corner or [On/Off] <0'-0",0'-0">:*" is displayed. Press the **ENTER** key once to accept the default coordinates **<0'-0",0'-0">**.

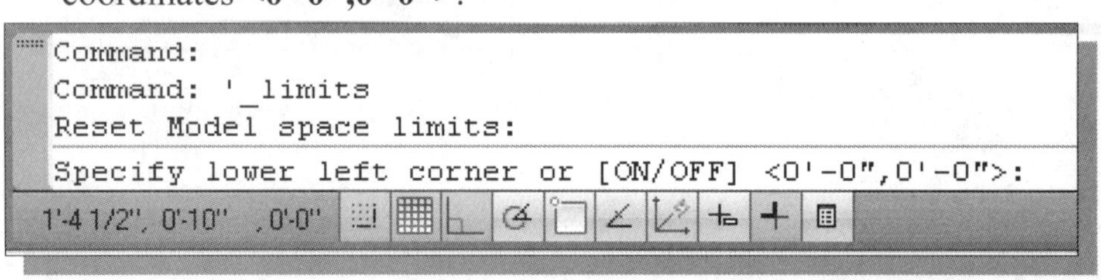

3. In the *command prompt* area, the message "*Specify upper right corner <1'-0", 0'-9">:*" is displayed. Enter **60',40'** to change the upper right coordinates to **<60',40'>**.

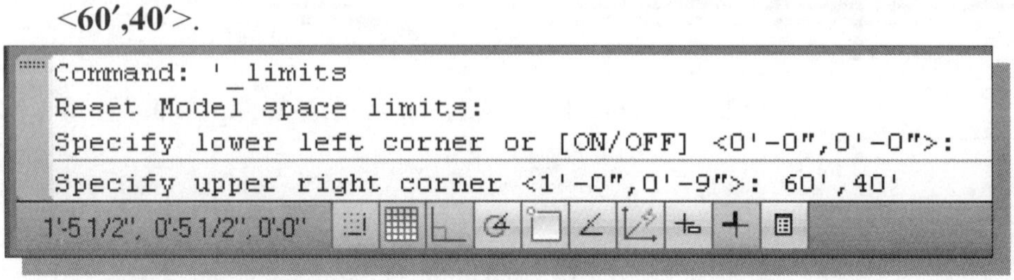

4. On your own, move the graphic cursor near the upper right corner inside the drawing area and note that the drawing area is unchanged. (The drawing limits command is used to set the drawing area; but the display will not be adjusted until a display command is used.)

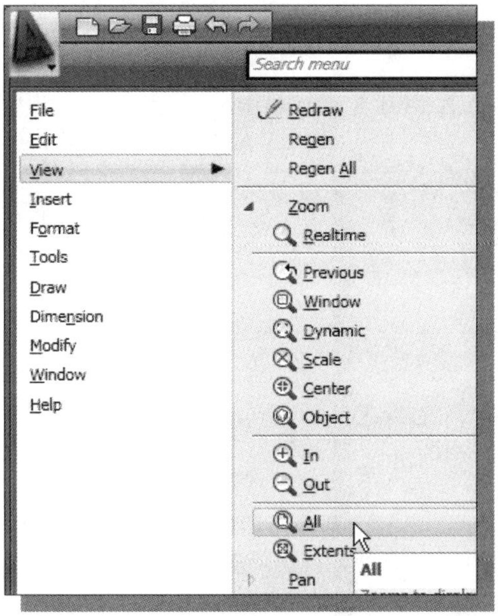

5. In the *Menu Browser*, select:
   [View] → [Zoom] → [All]

❖ The **Zoom All** command can be used to adjust the display so that all objects in the drawing are displayed to be as large as possible. If no objects are constructed, the Drawing Limits are used to adjust the current viewport.

6. Move the graphic cursor near the upper right corner inside the drawing area and note that the display area is updated.

GRID and *SNAP* Intervals Setup

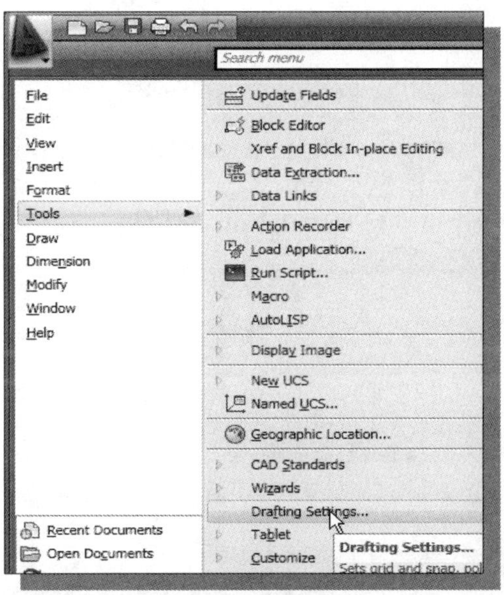

1. In the *Menu Browser*, select:
   [Tools] → [Drafting Settings]

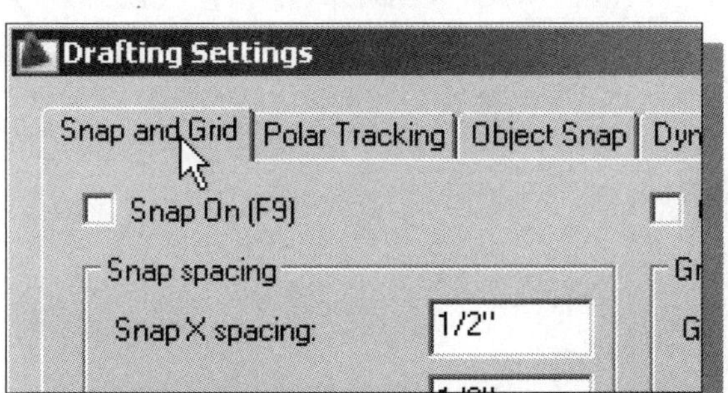

2. In the *Drafting Settings* dialog box, select the **SNAP and GRID** tab if it is not the page on top.

3. Change *Grid Spacing* to **6"** for both X and Y directions.

4. Also adjust the *Snap Spacing* to **6"** for both X and Y directions.

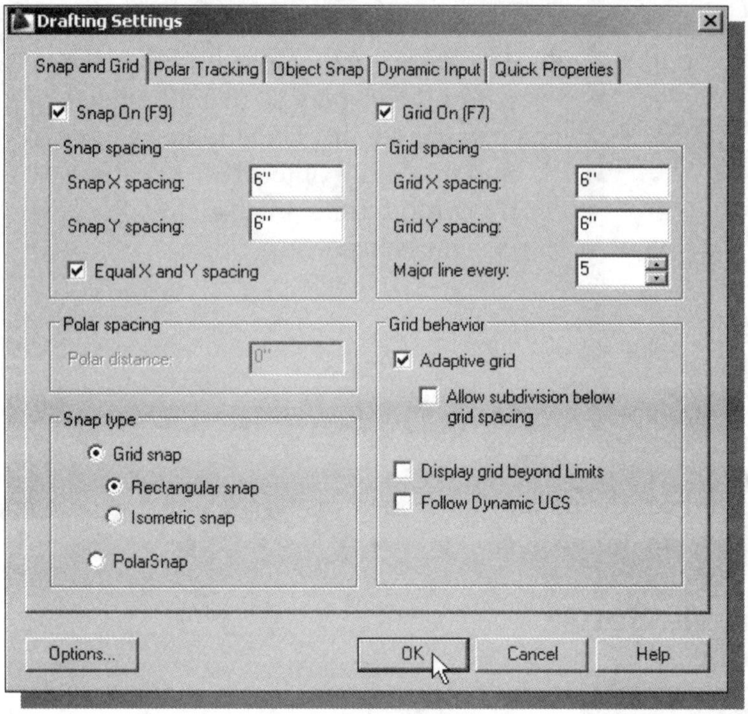

5. Pick **OK** to exit the *Drafting Settings* dialog box.

6. Move the cursor on top of the icons in the status toolbar and read the description of each icon. Note these icons act as toggle switches, which can be used to control the status of several commonly used Display and Construction options.

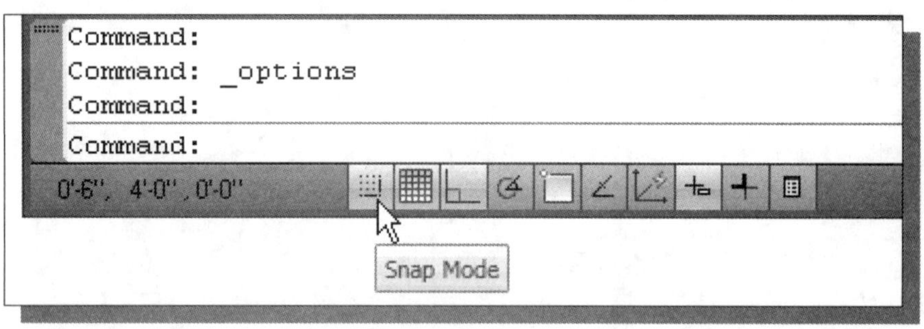

7. On your own, reset the option buttons so that *SNAP, GRID, ORTHO* and *Dynamic Input* are switched ***ON***.

Drawing Polylines

❖ In this tutorial, we will first create a 2D floor plan. The 2D floor plan will be converted into a 3D model with the **Thickness** command. In AutoCAD, a **polyline** is a connected sequence of line segments created as a single object. A polyline can contain straight line segments, arc segments, or a combination of the two.

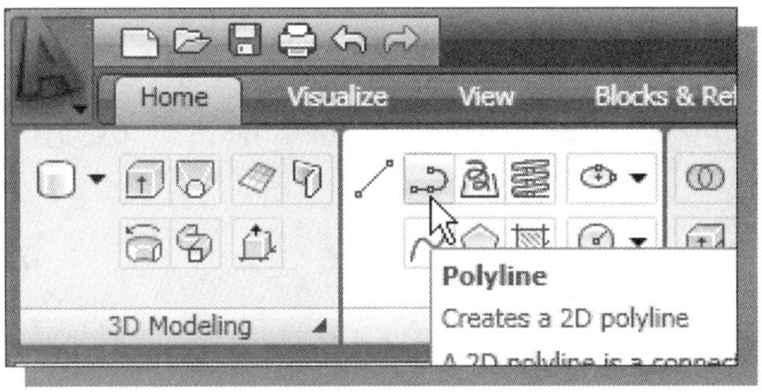

1. Select the **Polyline** command icon in the *Draw* toolbar.

2. In the command prompt area, the message "*Specify start point:*" is displayed. Select a location that is near the coordinates (**25′-0″, 10′-0″**) as the **starting point** of the polyline.

3. In the command prompt area, create a horizontal line by using the *relative rectangular coordinates entry method*, relative to the last point we specified
 Specify next point: **@-11′6″,0 [ENTER]**

4. In the command prompt area, create a vertical line by using the *relative rectangular coordinates entry method*, relative to the last point we specified
 Specify next point: **@0,25′6″ [ENTER]**

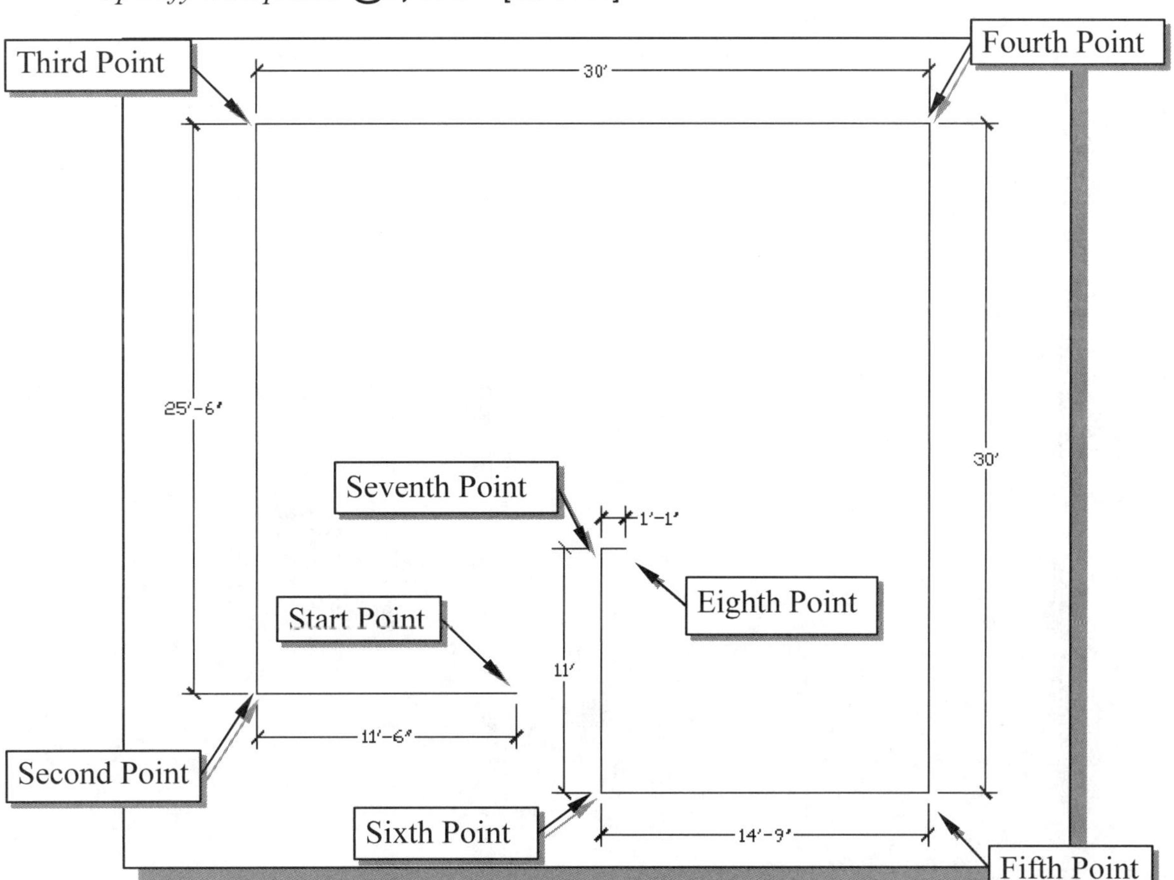

5. On your own, complete the polyline by specifying the rest of the points, *point four* through *point eight*.

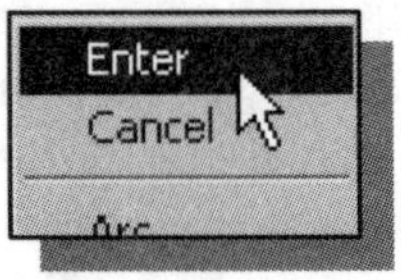

6. Inside the graphics window, right-mouse-click and select **Enter** to end the **Polyline** command.

Creating an Offset Polyline

- The **Offset** command creates a new object at a specified distance from an existing object or through a specified point.

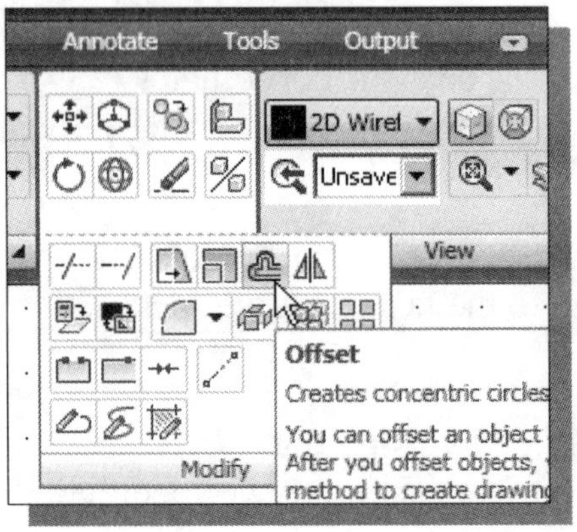

1. Select the **Offset** command icon in the *Modify* toolbar. In the command prompt area, the message "*Specify offset distance or [Through]:*" is displayed.

   Specify offset distance or [Through]:
   6" [ENTER]

2. In the command prompt area, the message "*Select object to offset or <exit>:*" is displayed. Pick the polyline on the screen. (Note that all line segments of the polyline are automatically selected.)

3. AutoCAD next asks us to identify the direction of the offset. Pick a location that is ***inside*** the polyline.

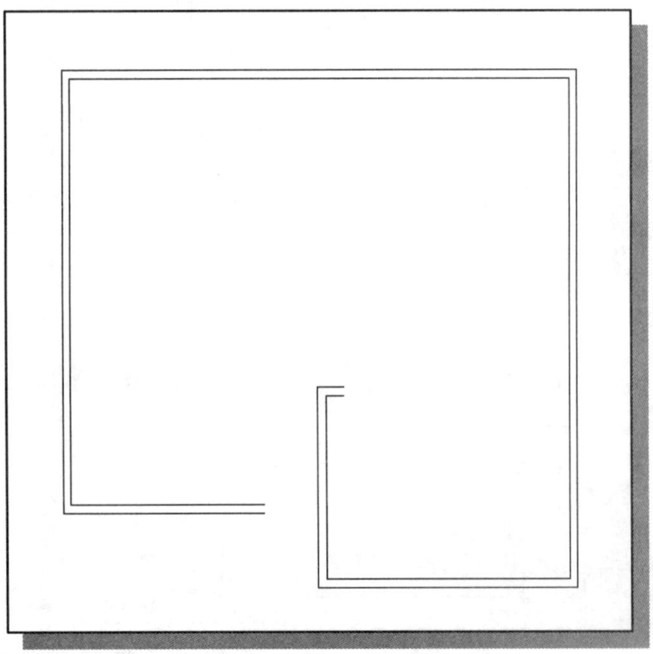

4. Inside the graphics window, **right-mouse-click** and select **Enter** to end the **Offset** command.

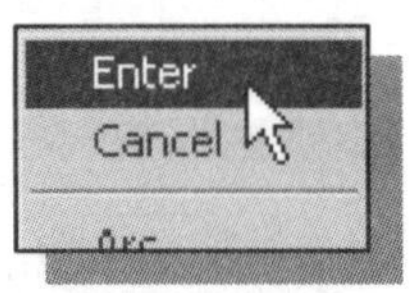

Creating Interior Walls

1. Move the cursor on any icon in the *Standard* toolbar area and **right-mouse-click** once to display a list of options. Select **Toolbars → AutoCAD**.

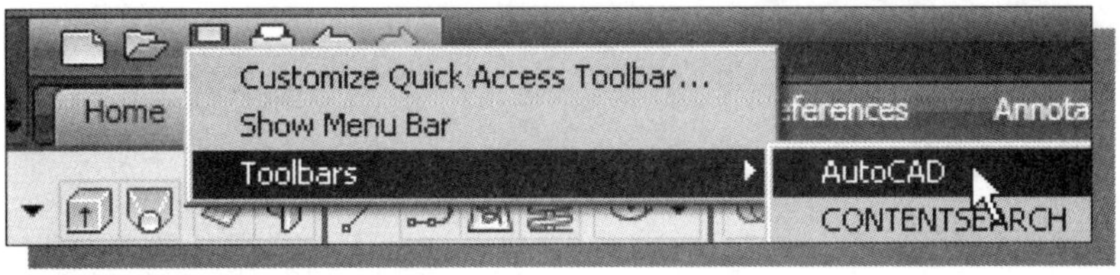

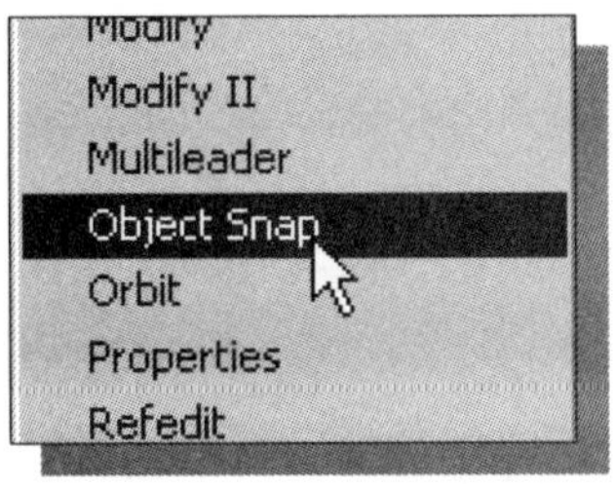

2. Select **Object Snap**, with the left-mouse-button, to display the *Object Snap* toolbar on the screen to assist the construction of the floor plan.

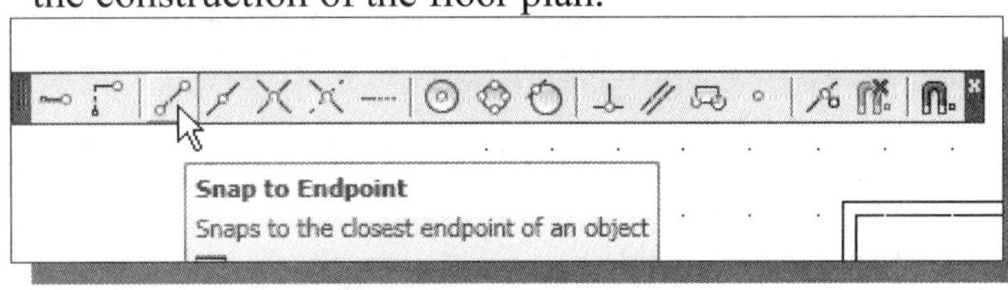

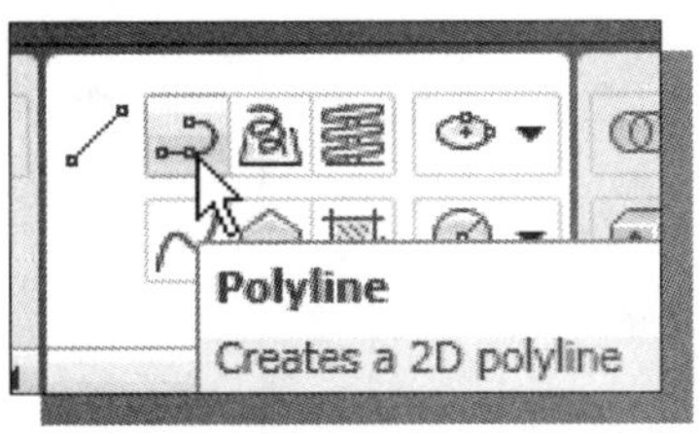

3. Select the **Polyline** command icon in the *Draw* toolbar. In the command prompt area, the message "*Specify start point or [Justification/Scale/Style]:*" is displayed.

4. In the *Object Snap* toolbar, pick **Snap to Midpoint**. In the command prompt area, the message "*_mid of*" is displayed. AutoCAD now expects us to select a geometric entity on the screen.

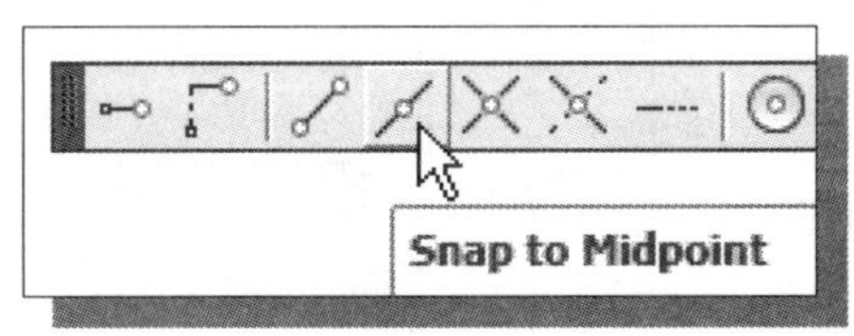

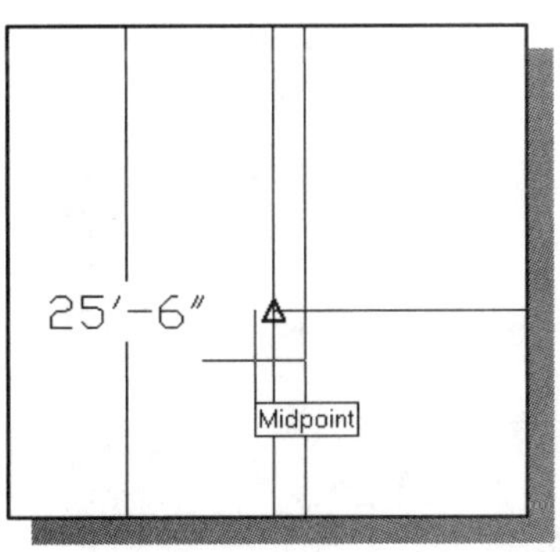

5. Select the vertical line on the left as shown.

6. At the command prompt, enter **@10',0 [ENTER]**.

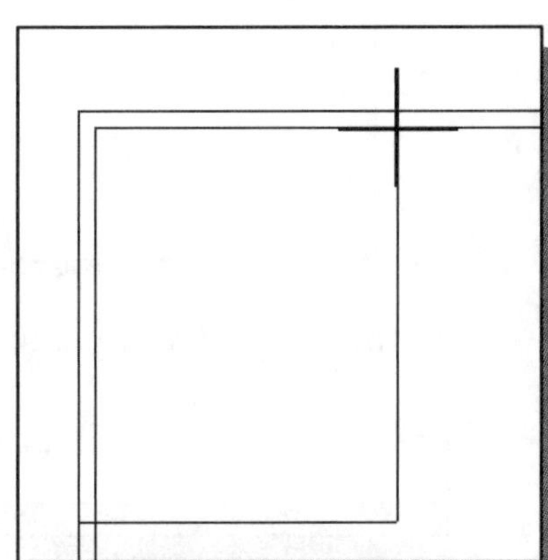

7. On your own, define a vertical line at the location as shown in the figure.

8. Inside the graphics window, **right-mouse-click** and select **Enter** to end the Polyline command.

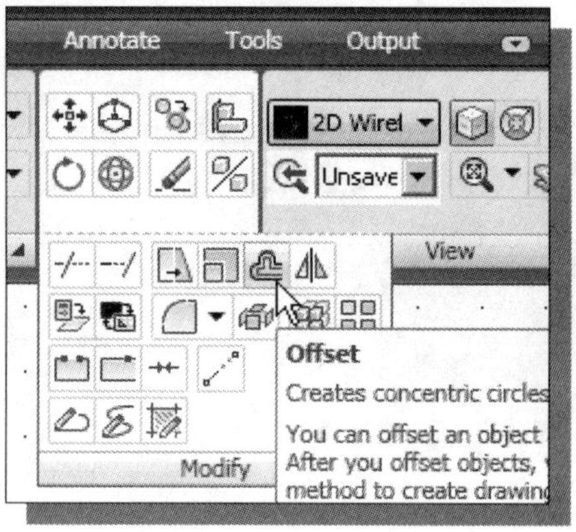

9. Select the **Offset** command icon in the *Modify* toolbar. In the command prompt area, the message "*Specify offset distance or [Through]:*" is displayed.

   Specify offset distance or [Through]:
   6" [ENTER]

10. In the command prompt area, the message "*Select object to offset or <exit>:*" is displayed. Pick the polyline we just created.

11. AutoCAD next asks us to identify the direction of the offset. Pick a location that is toward the upper left corner of the design.

12. Inside the graphics window, **right-mouse-click** to end the Offset command.

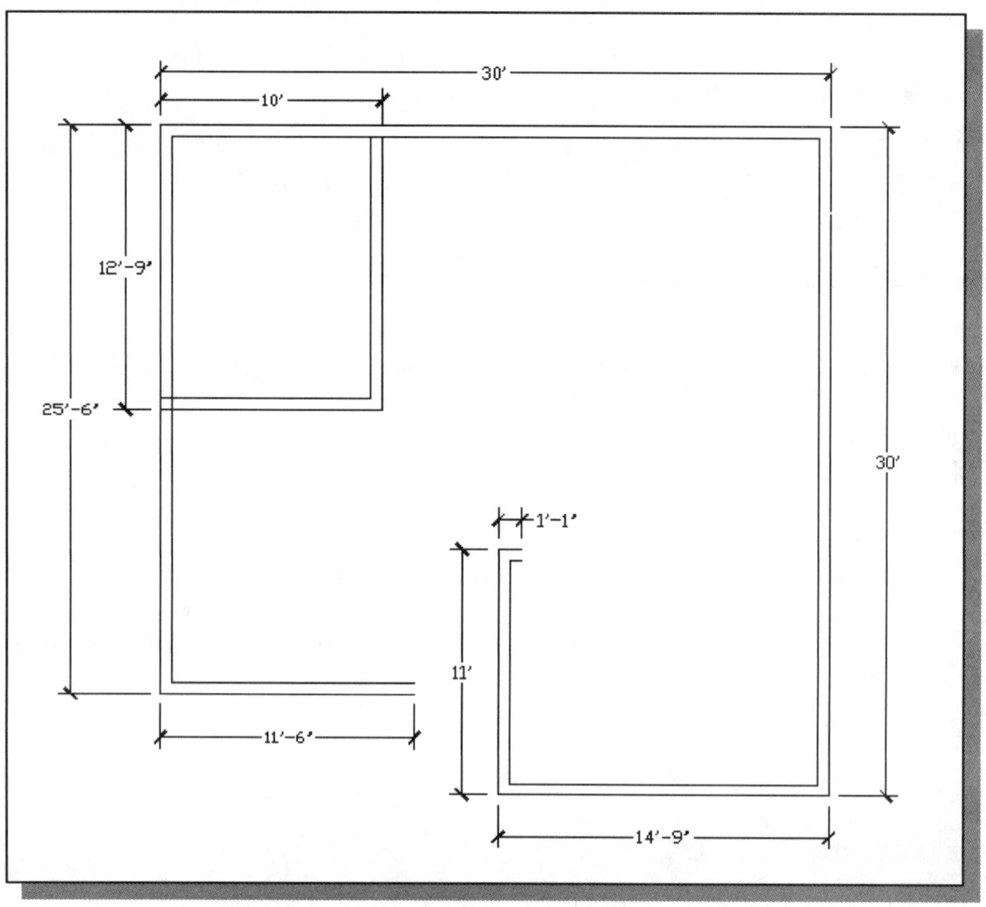

➤ In the *Status Bar* area, reset the option buttons and switch ***OFF*** all options.

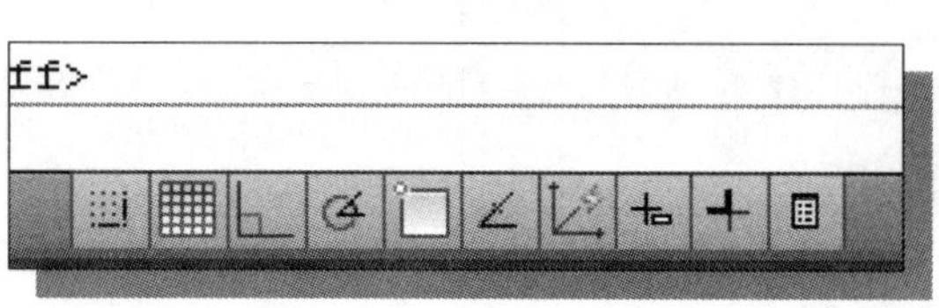

- Next, we will create a 2′-8″ doorway.

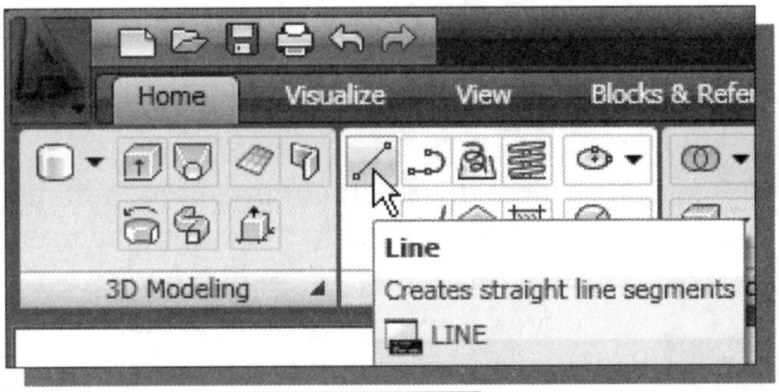

13. Select the **Line** command icon in the *Draw* toolbar. In the command prompt area, the message "*_line Specify first point:*" is displayed.

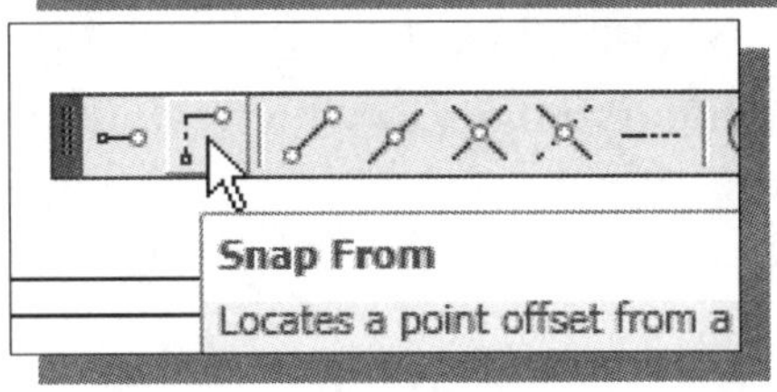

14. In the *Object Snap* toolbar, pick **Snap From**. In the command prompt area, the message "*_from Base point*" is displayed. AutoCAD now expects us to select a geometric entity on the screen.

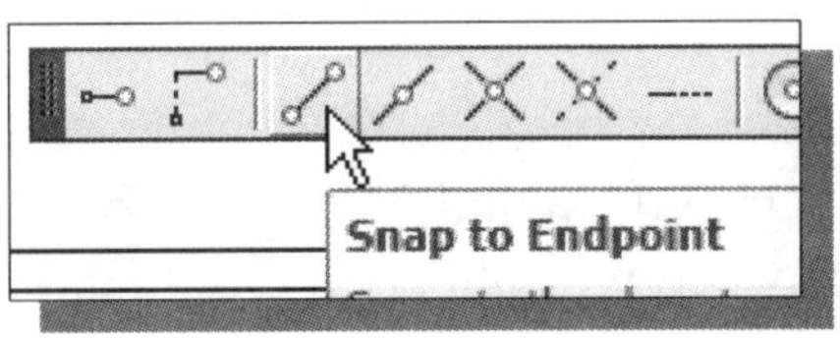

15. We will measure relative to the lower left corner of the interior wall. In the *Object Snap* toolbar, pick **Snap to Endpoint**.

16. In the command prompt area, the message "*_from Base point:_endp of*" is displayed. Pick the **lower right corner** as shown.

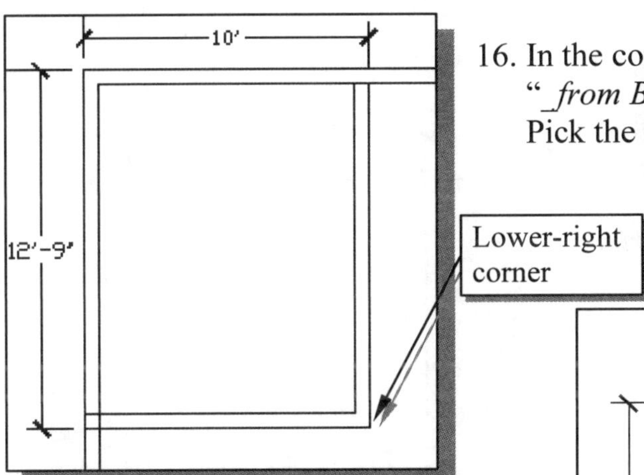

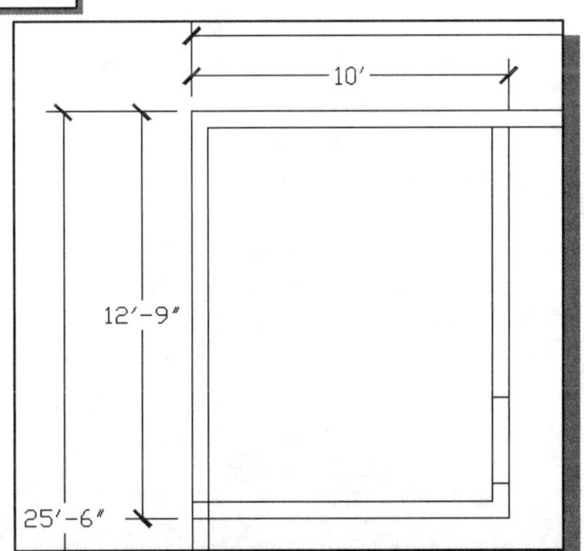

17. At the command prompt, enter **@0,1′-1″ [ENTER]**.

18. At the command prompt, enter **@-6″,0 [ENTER]**.

19. Inside the graphics window, right-mouse-click once and select **Enter** to end the Line command.

20. On your own, use the **Offset** command to create a parallel line that is **2′-8″** above the line we just created.

Completing the Doorway Using the *Trim* Command

- The **Trim** command shortens an object so that it ends precisely at a selected boundary.

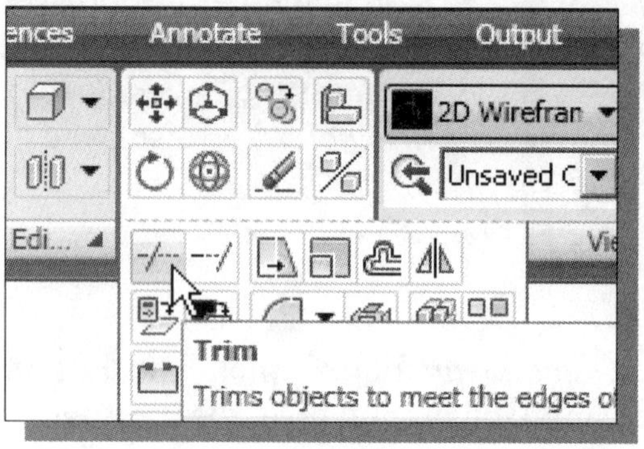

1. Select the **Trim** command icon in the *Modify* toolbar. In the command prompt area, the message "*Select boundary edges... Select objects:*" is displayed.

- First we will select the objects that define the boundary edges to which we want to trim the object.

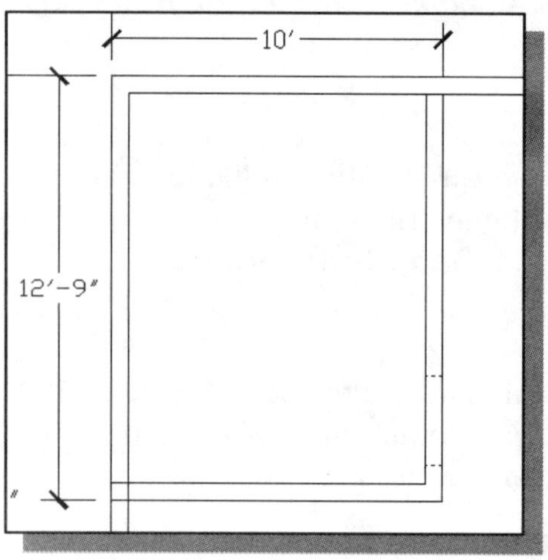

2. Pick the **two horizontal lines** we just created as the *boundary edges*.

3. Inside the graphics window, right-mouse-click to proceed with the Trim command.

4. The message "*Select object to trim or shift-select object to extend or [Project/ Edge/ Undo]:*" is displayed in the command prompt area. Pick the vertical sections bound by the two selected horizontal lines.

5. Inside the graphics window, right-mouse-click to activate the option menu and select **Enter** with the left-mouse-button to end the Trim command.

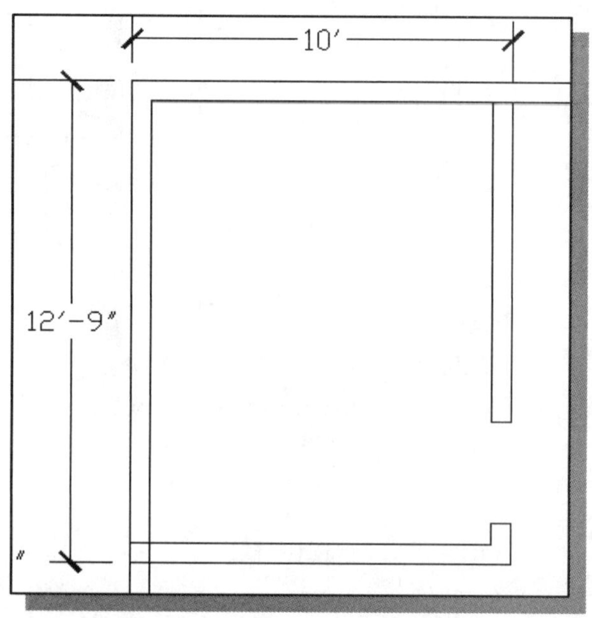

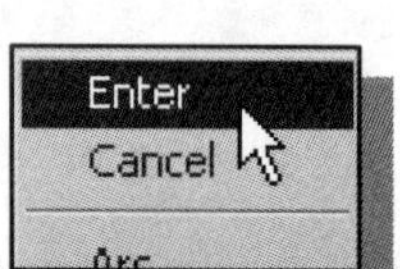

- Using the **Polyline** and **Line** commands, create the additional walls and doorways as shown.

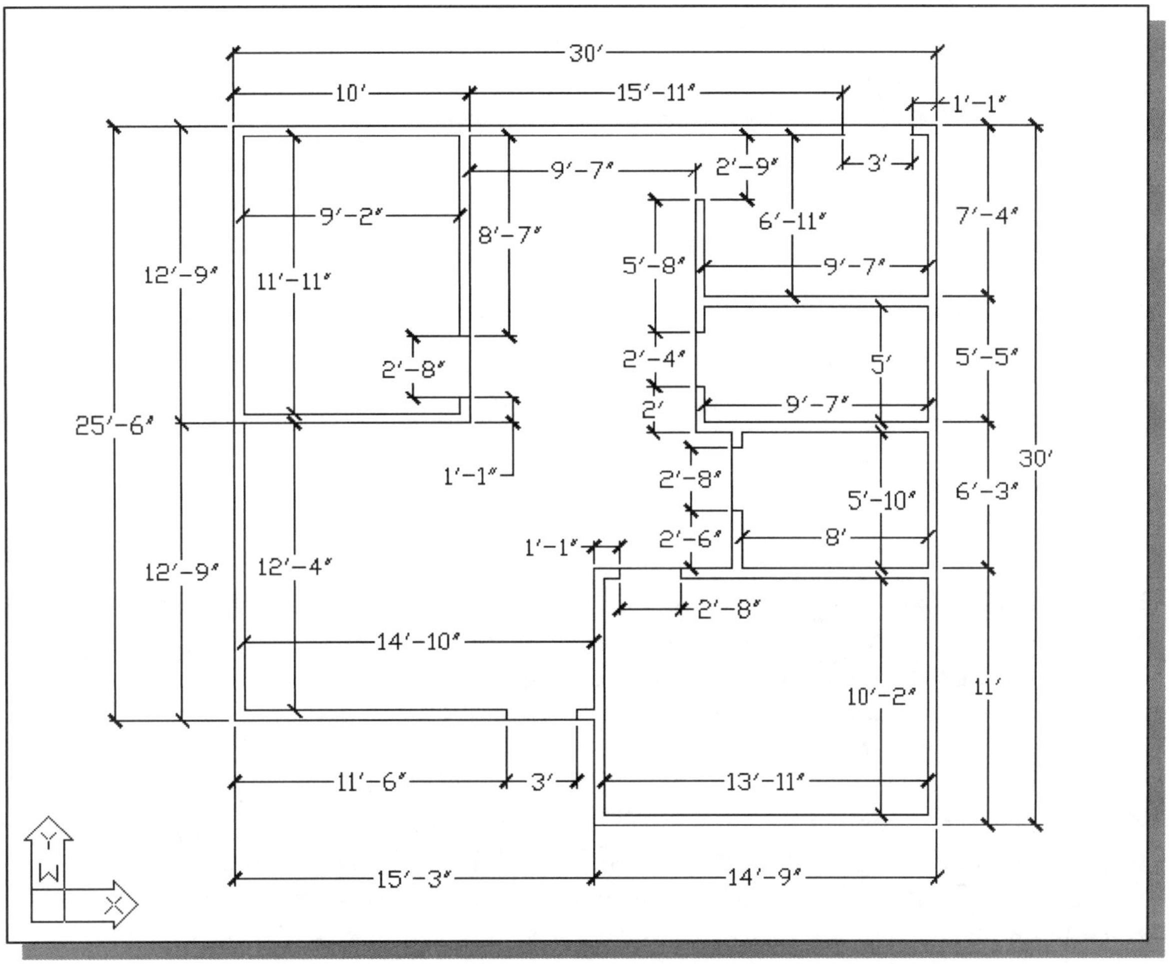

❖ Hints: Use the **Trim/Extend**, **Undo** and **Erase** commands to assist the construction of the floor plan.

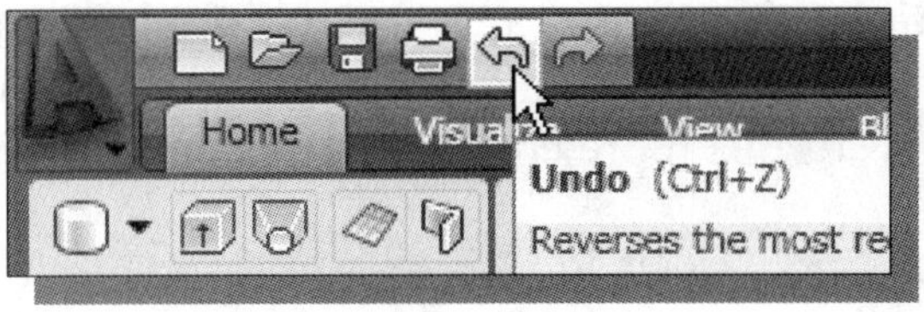

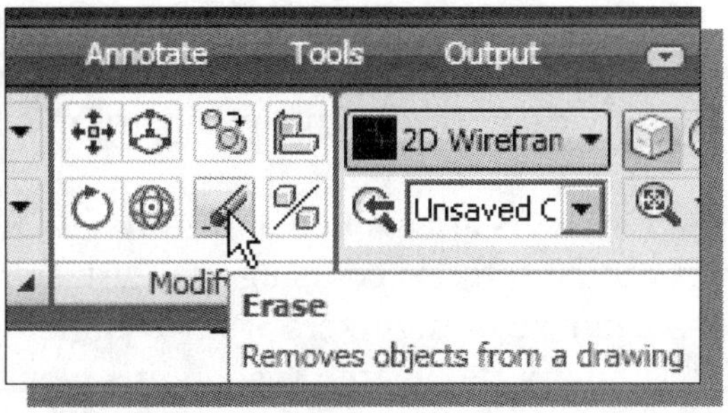

- Now is a good time to save the design. Select **[File] → [Save As]** in the pull-down menu and use ***FloorPlan*** as the *File name.*

User Coordinate System – It is an XY CRT, but an XYZ World

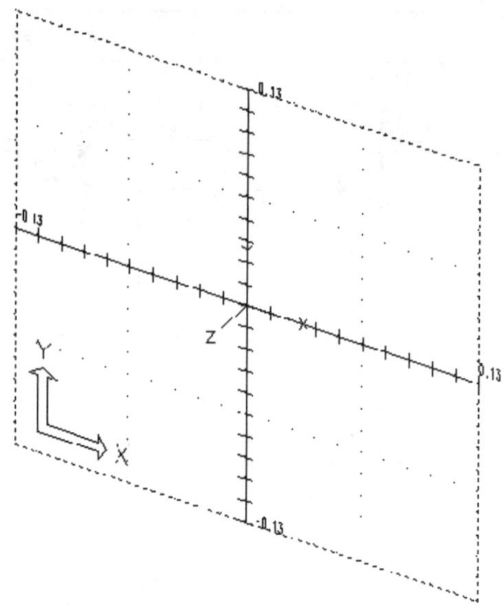

Design modeling software is becoming more powerful and user friendly, yet the system still does only what the user tells it to do. When using a geometric modeler, we therefore need to have a good understanding of what the inherent limitations are. We should also have a good understanding of what we want to do and what to expect, as the results are based on what is available.

In most 3D geometric modelers, 3D objects are located and defined in what is usually called **world space** or **global space**. Although a number of different coordinate systems can be used to create and manipulate objects in a 3D modeling system, the objects are typically defined and stored using the world space. The world space is usually a **3D Cartesian coordinate system** that the user cannot change or manipulate.

In most engineering designs, models can be very complex, and it would be tedious and confusing if only the world coordinate system were available. Practical 3D modeling systems allow the user to define **Local Coordinate Systems (LCS)** or **User Coordinate Systems (UCS)** relative to the world coordinate system. Once a local coordinate system is defined, we can then create geometry in terms of this more convenient system.

Although objects are created and stored in 3D space coordinates, most of the geometry entities can be referenced using 2D Cartesian coordinate systems. Typical input devices such as a mouse or digitizers are two-dimensional by nature; the movement of the input device is interpreted by the system in a planar sense. The same limitation is true of common output devices, such as CRT displays and plotters. The modeling software performs a series of three-dimensional to two-dimensional transformations to correctly project 3D objects onto a 2D picture plane.

The AutoCAD's **User Coordinate System (UCS)** is a special construction tool that enables the planar nature of the 2D input devices to be directly mapped into the 3D coordinate system. The ***UCS*** is a local coordinate system that can be aligned to the world coordinate system, an existing face of a part, or a predefined plane. By default, the UCS is aligned to the XY plane of the world coordinate system.

Think of the UCS as the surface on which we can sketch the 2D profiles of designs. It is similar to a piece of paper, a white board, or a chalkboard that can be attached to any planar surface. In the previous sections, we created the 2D design of a floor plan using the default settings where the UCS is aligned to the XY plane of the world coordinate system.

Viewing the 2D Design in 3D Space

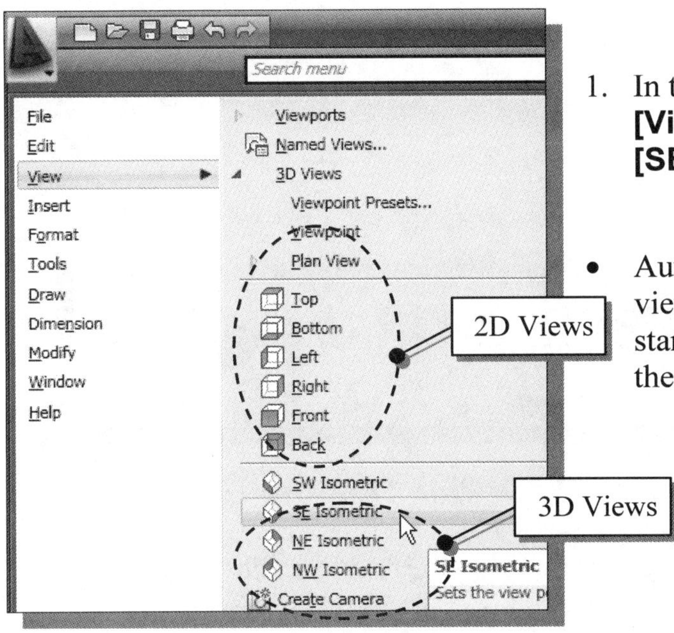

1. In the *Menu Browser*, select:
   [View] → [3D Views] →
   [SE Isometric]

- AutoCAD provides a set of pre-defined views, which contains most of the standard 2D and 3D views as shown in the figure.

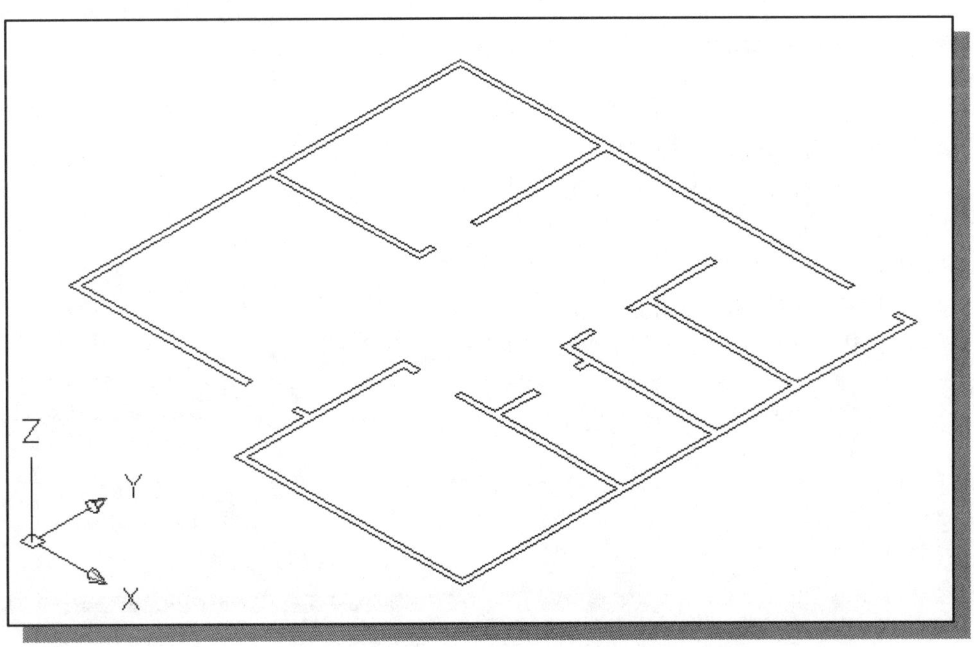

- The orientations of the preset 2D and 3D views are based on the world coordinate system as shown below. Note that the positive Y-axis direction is also identified as pointing toward **North** and the preset 3D views are oriented using the **North**, **East**, **South** and **West** directions.

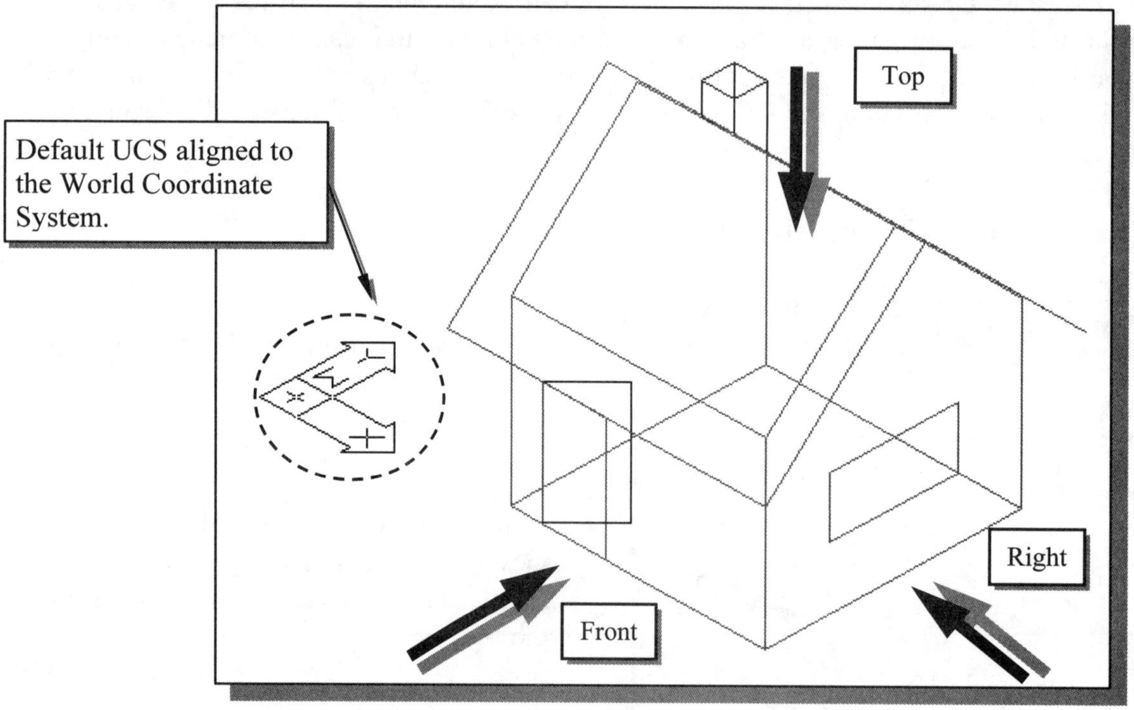

Adding the 3rd Dimension to the *Floor Plan* Design

❖ **AutoCAD® 2009** provides a flexible graphical user interface that allows users to select graphical entities **BEFORE** the command is selected (*Pre-selection*), or **AFTER** the command is selected (*Post-selection*). We can preselect one or more objects by clicking on the objects at the command prompt (**Command:**). To deselect the selected items, press the **[Esc]** key twice.

1. Inside the *graphics window*, pre-select all objects by enclosing all objects inside a **selection window** as shown.

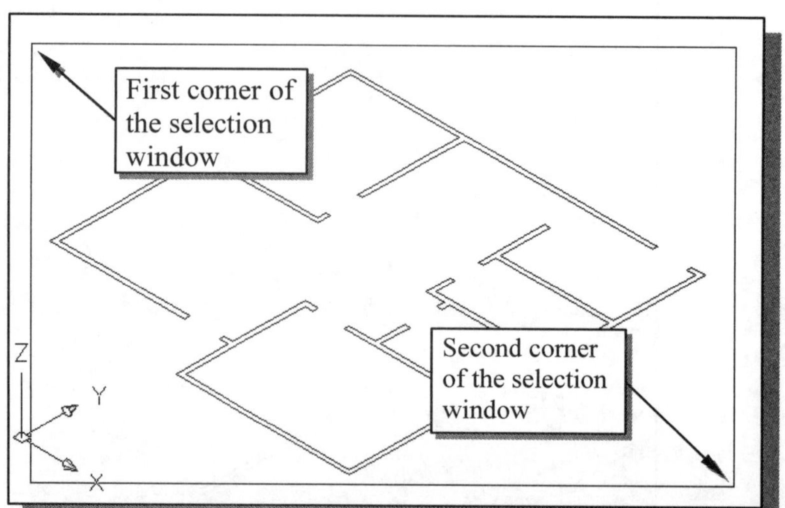

2. Inside the graphics window, right-mouse-click once to bring up the option list and select **Properties** as shown.

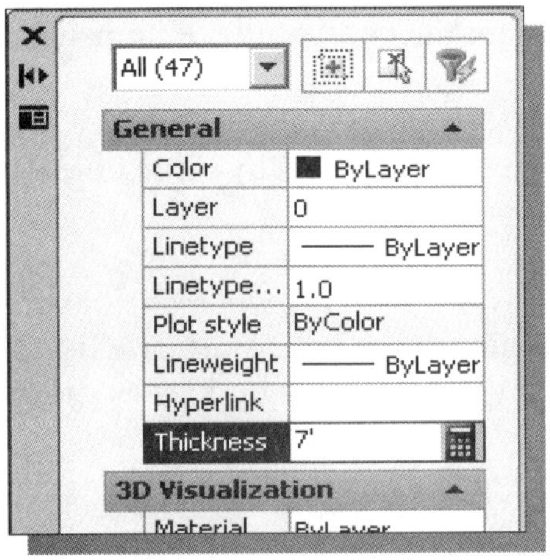

3. In the *Properties* dialog box, properties of the highlighted entities are displayed. Notice the current *Thickness* is set to 0″.

4. **Left-click** the *Thickness* box and enter a new value: **7′ [ENTER]** as the new thickness value.

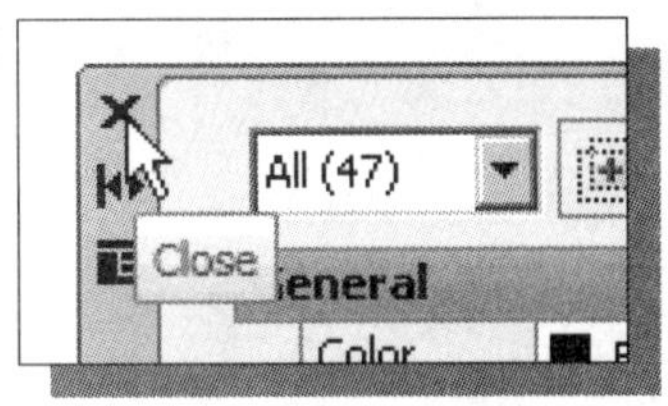

5. Click on the [**X**] button to exit the *Properties* dialog box.

In AutoCAD, the *thickness* of an object determines the distance that the object is extruded above or below its current Z-elevation. Positive thickness will extrude the objects upward (positive Z), negative thickness extrudes downward (negative Z), and zero thickness means no extrusion. The Z direction is determined by the orientation of the UCS at the time the object was created.

Changing the *thickness* of objects changes the appearance of certain geometric objects, such as circles, lines, polylines, arcs, 2D solids and points. Note that the *Thickness* property is not available on certain geometric objects, such as *Splines* and *Multilines*. We can set the *thickness* of an object with the ***Thickness*** variable. AutoCAD applies the extrusion uniformly to an object. A single object cannot have different thickness for its various points.

Changing the thickness of objects simulates a simple Z-extrusion of creating solid objects in AutoCAD. The main advantage of using the object thickness to create the Z-elevation instead of creating a true solid is that the operation is quick and easy. In AutoCAD, objects with thickness can be hidden, shaded, and rendered as if they are three-dimensional solids. Once an object's thickness is set, we can visualize the results in any view other than the plan view.

This method is also known as the **2½D solid modeling approach**. This modeling technique was first invented in the 1970s and was adopted by several of the first-generation solid-modeling packages. This approach requires no additional 3D construction tools and only minimum computing power is needed. Note that this modeling approach does not create true 3D solids and objects can only be extruded in one direction. This modeling approach is considered to be less flexible and its application is somewhat limited.

Viewing the Design Using the Hide Option

- By default, AutoCAD produces a wireframe image of the constructed 2D/3D design on the screen. All geometric entities are present, including those that should be hidden by other objects. Several options are available in AutoCAD to create more realistic images of 3D designs. In this section, we will introduce the Hide option, which can be used to adjust the display of the design; the Hide option eliminates the hidden lines on the screen.

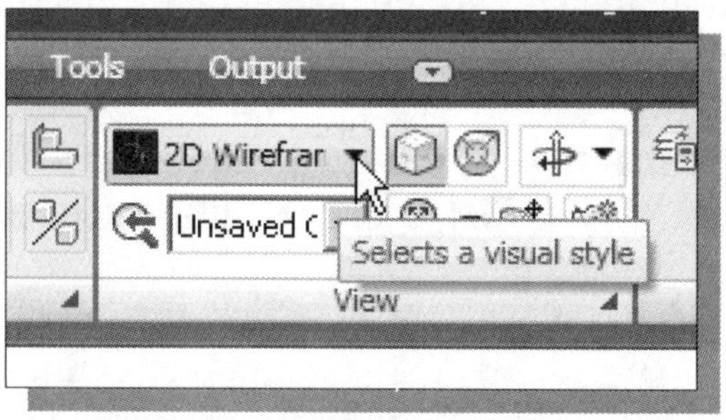

1. Deselect any objects by hitting the [**Esc**] key once.

2. In the *View toolbar panel*, click on the **triangle** next to the *visual style* list to display the available options as shown.

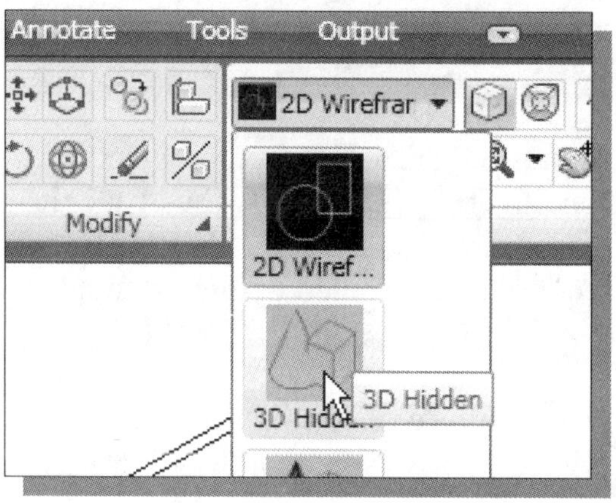

3. Select the [**3D Hidden**] option, the 2nd option from the top, as shown.

4. To redisplay the wireframe image, select the 1st option: **[2D WireFrame]**

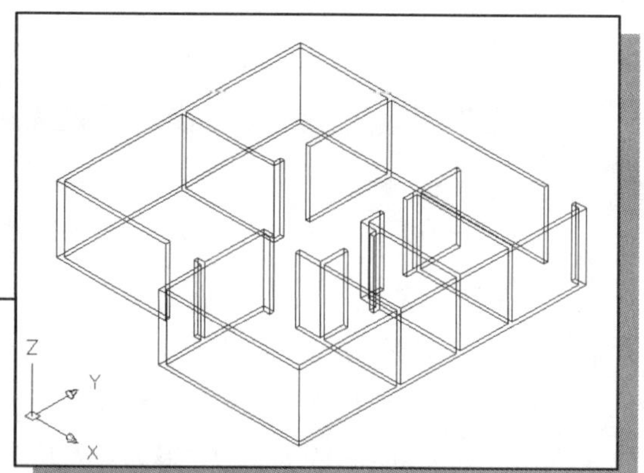

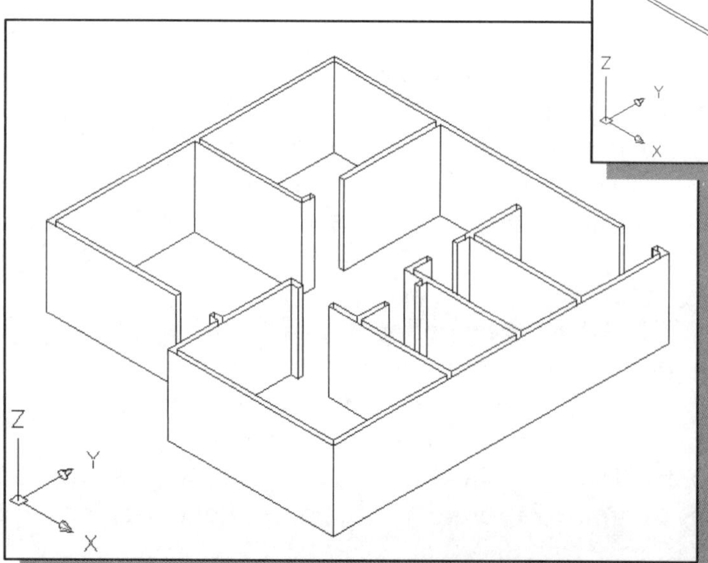

Adding New Layers

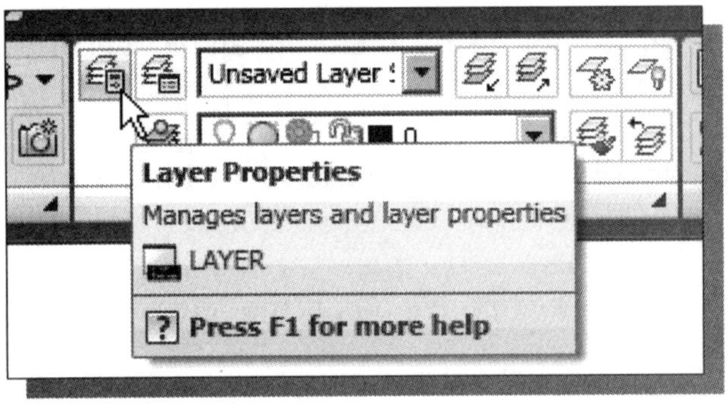

1. Pick **Layers Properties Manager** in the *Layers* toolbar.

❖ The *Layer Properties Manager* dialog box appears. AutoCAD creates a default layer, *layer 0*, which we cannot rename or delete. *Layer 0* has special properties used by the system.

❖ In AutoCAD, we always construct entities on a layer. It may be the default layer or a layer that we create. Each layer has associated properties such as the visibility setting, color, linetype, lineweight and plot style.

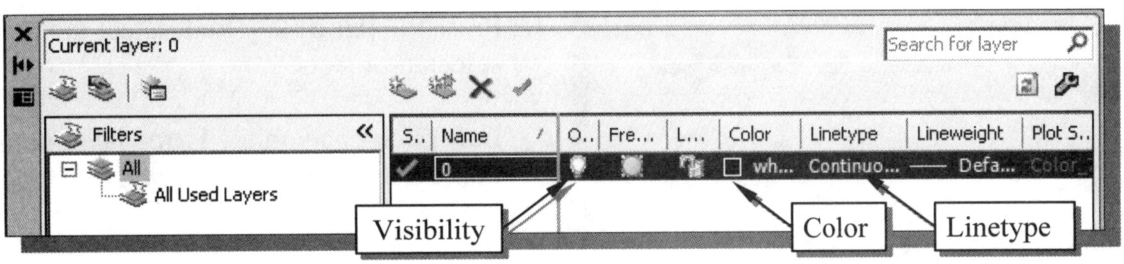

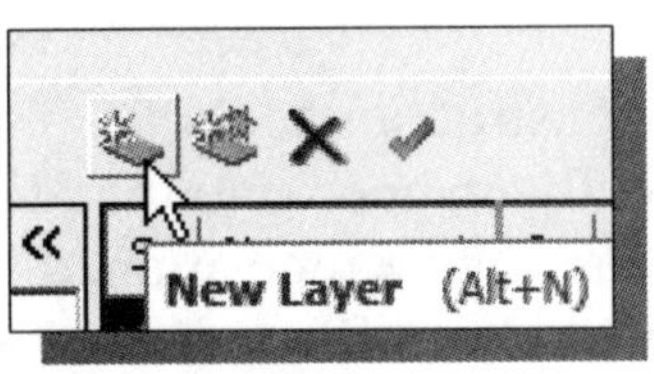

2. Click on the **New** button. Notice a layer is automatically added to the list of layers.

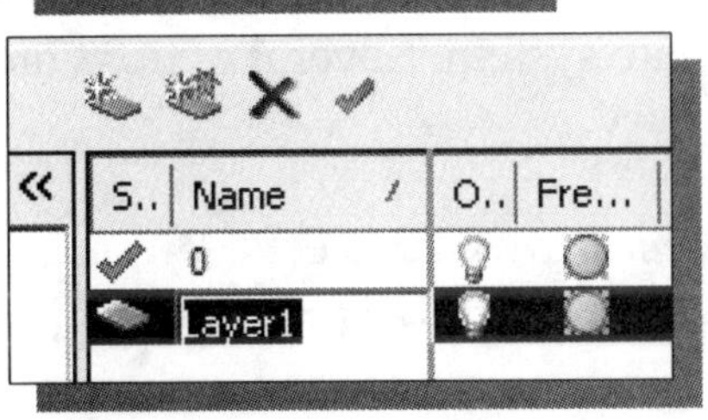

3. AutoCAD will assign a generic name to the new layer (*Layer1*). Enter ***Walls*** as the name of the new layer and change the layer color to ***Green*** as shown in the below figure.

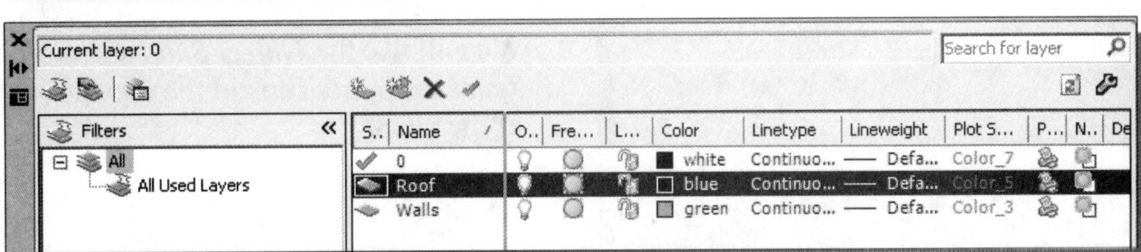

4. On your own, create another layer (layer name: ***Roof***) and change the layer color to ***Blue***.

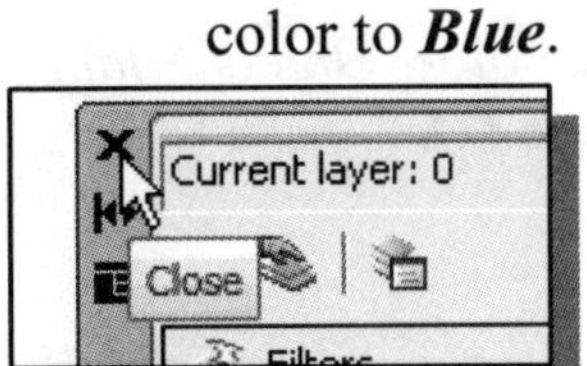

5. Click on the **Close** button to accept the settings.

Moving Entities to a Different Layer

1. Inside the graphics window, pre-select all objects by enclosing all objects inside a **selection window**.

2. On the *Object Properties* toolbar, choose the ***Layer Control*** box with the left-mouse-button.

❖ Notice the layer name displayed in the *Layer Control* box is the selected object's assigned layer and layer properties.

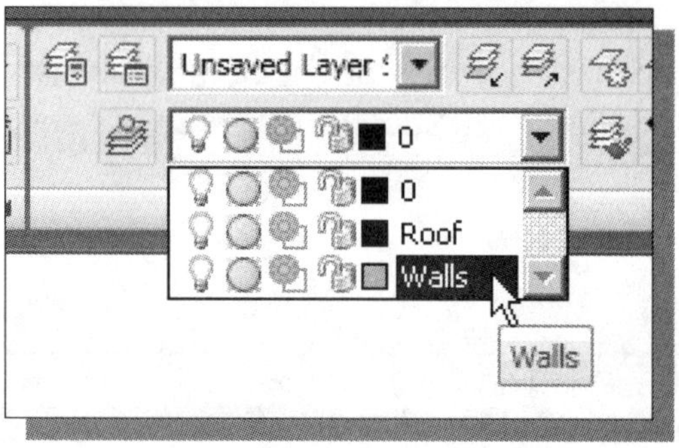

3. In the *Layer Control* box, click on the ***Walls*** layer name. The selected objects are now moved to the *Walls* layer.

4. Press the [**Esc**] key to deselect the pre-selected objects.

5. Left-click once on the **Roof** layer name to set it as the ***Current Layer***.

Moving the UCS

- AutoCAD's **User Coordinate System (UCS)** is a special construction tool that enables the planar nature of the 2D input devices to be directly mapped into the 3D coordinate system. The **UCS** is a local coordinate system that can be repositioned and/or reoriented to an existing face of a part, or a predefined plane. By default, the UCS is aligned to the XY plane of the world coordinate system. Several options are available to reposition and reorient the UCS in 3D space.

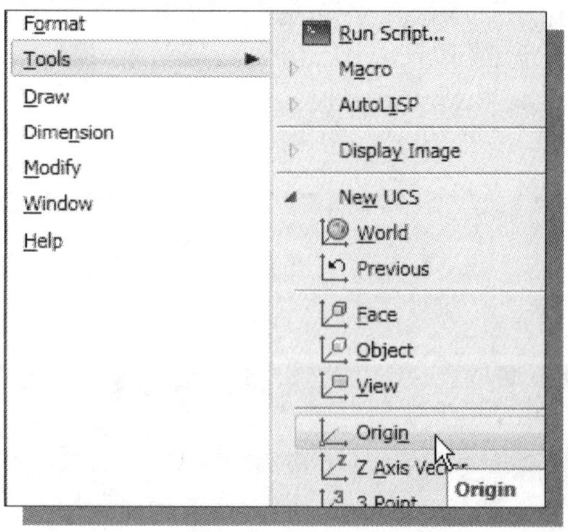

1. In the *Menu Browser*, select:
   [Tools] → [New UCS] → [Origin]

2. We will use the *Object Snap* and *Object Tracking* options to aid the repositioning of the UCS.

3. In the *Status Bar* area, reset the option buttons so that the *Polar, Object Snap, Object Snap Tracking, Dynamic Input* options are switched ***ON***.

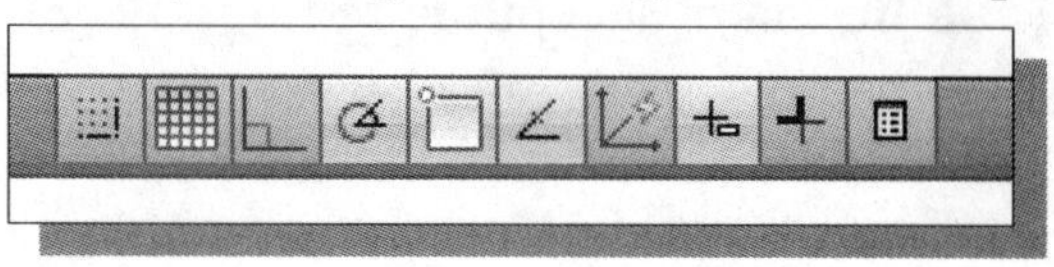

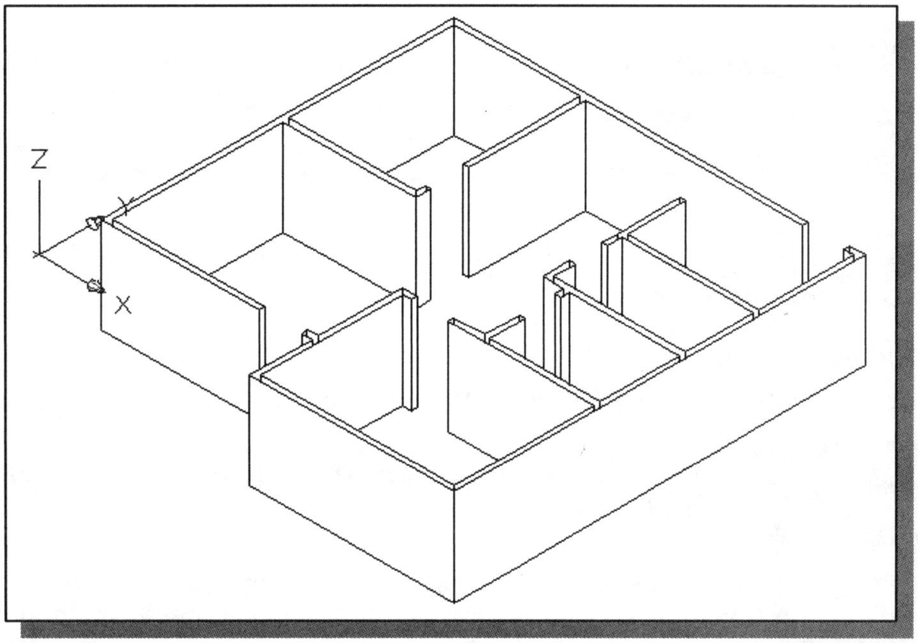

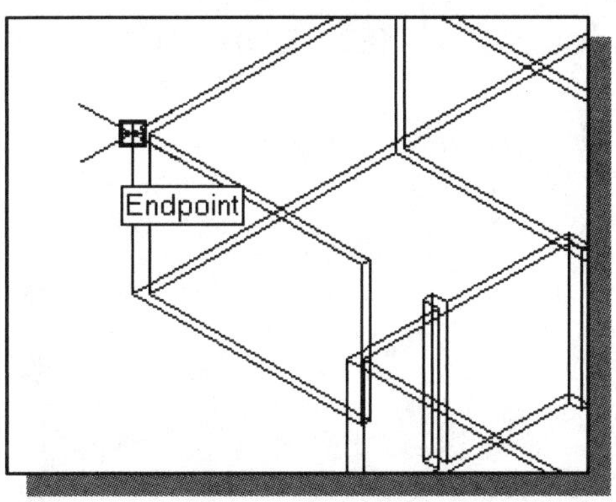

- We will reposition the UCS at the intersection of the left wall and the front wall; the intersection can be found by using the AutoCAD object tracking options.

4. Move the cursor on the top left corner of the external wall as shown; pause for a few seconds to activate the *OTRACK* option.

5. Move the cursor on the top front corner of the external wall as shown; pause for a few seconds to activate the *OTRACK* option.

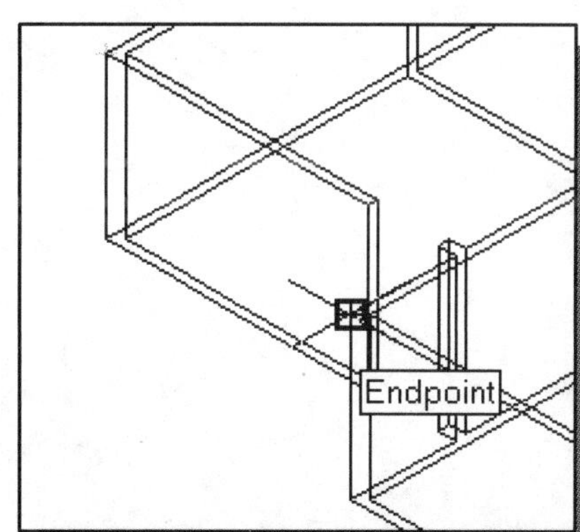

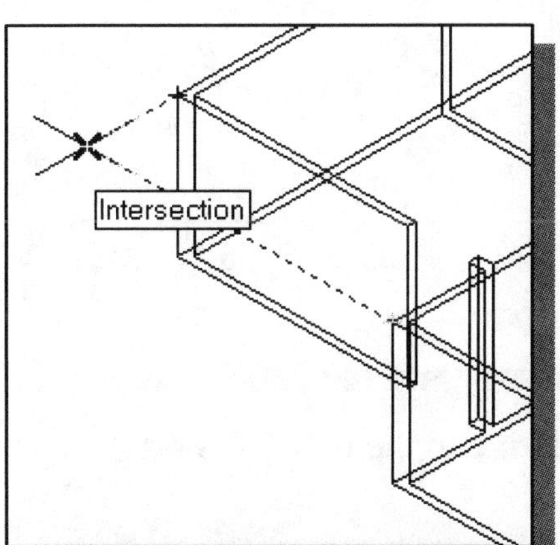

6. Left-click once when the cursor is aligned to the intersection of the left wall and the front wall as shown.

- The UCS is repositioned to the new location as shown. This location is the new origin for any geometric constructions.

Creating the Roof

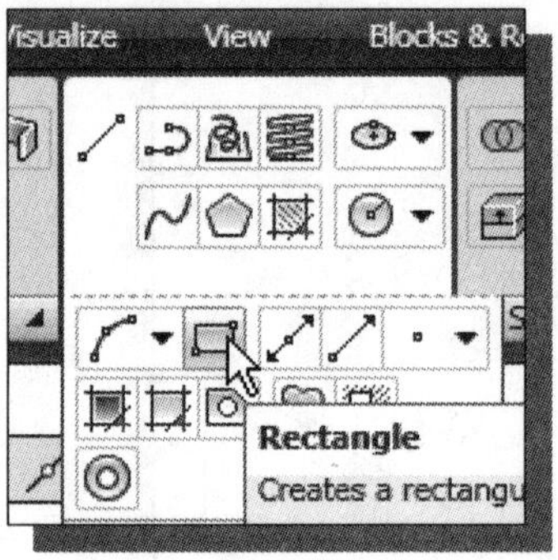

1. Select the **Rectangle** command icon in the *Draw* toolbar as shown.

2. In the command prompt area, the message "*Specify first corner point or [Chamfer/Elevation/Fillet/ Thickness/Width]:*" is displayed. Move the cursor inside the graphics window and right-mouse-click to display the option menu.

- The thickness of certain geometry entities can be set as they are being created.

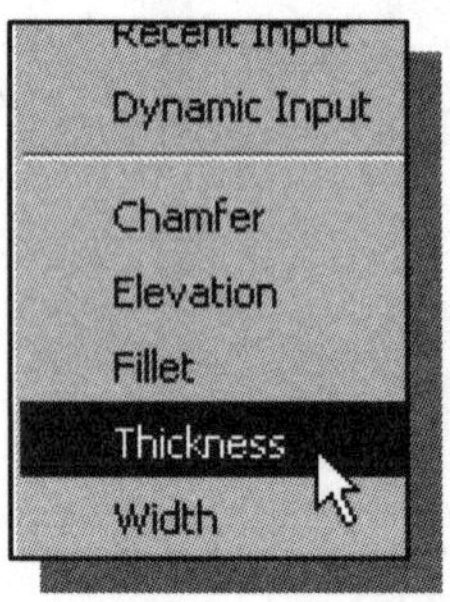

3. In the option menu, select **Thickness** by clicking once with the left-mouse-button.

4. In the command prompt area, the message "*Specify thickness for rectangles <0'-0">:*" is displayed. Enter **10"** **[ENTER]**.

5. At the command prompt, enter **-2',-2'** **[ENTER]**.

6. In the command prompt area, the message "*Specify other corner point or [Dimensions]:*" is displayed. Enter **@34',34'** **[ENTER]**.

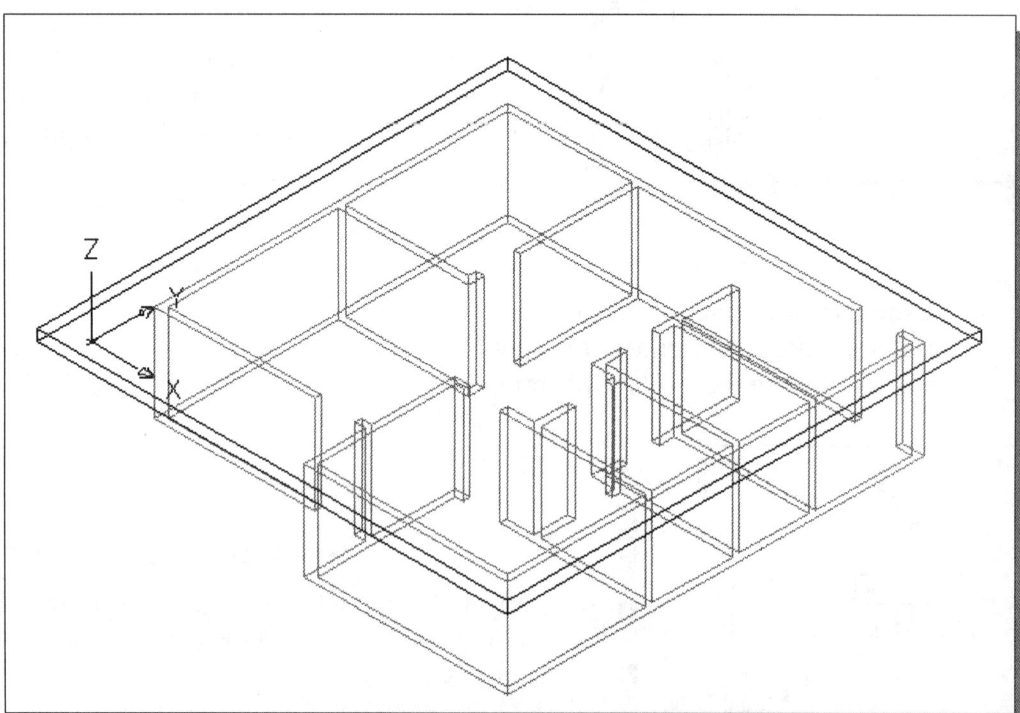

- Note that the coordinates entered are measured relative to the new UCS origin.

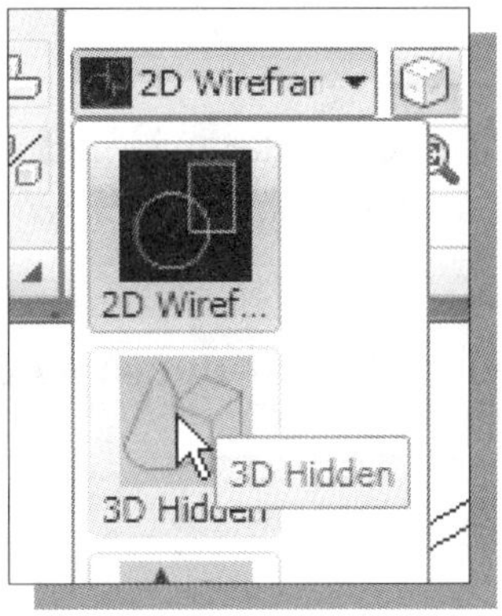

7. In the *Visual Styles* toolbar panel, select:
   [3D Hidden]

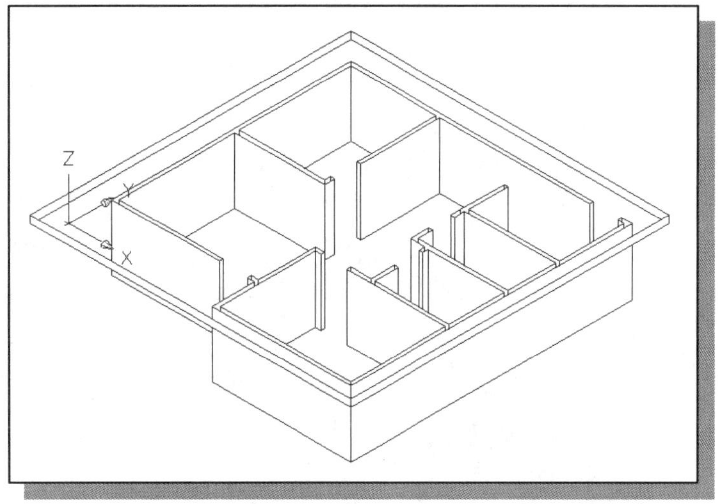

- The **Thickness** option extrudes the 2D design in the positive Z-direction relative to the current UCS, which is at the same Z-elevation of the plane of the 2D design. Note that the **Thickness** option only makes 2D objects look like 3D solids; only surfaces perpendicular to the plane of the 2D design are created. No top or bottom surfaces are created with the **Thickness** option.

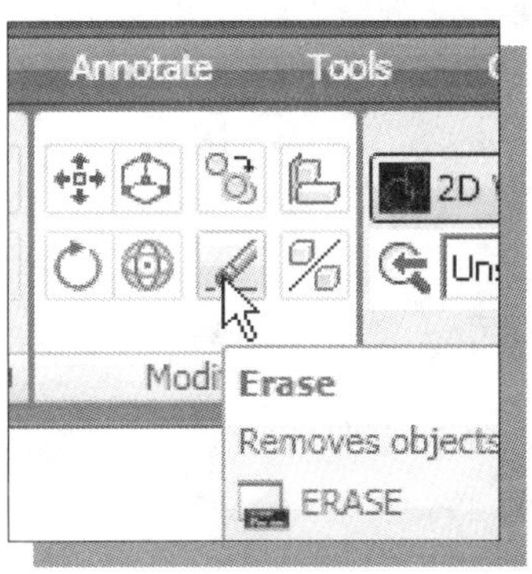

8. Pick **Erase** in the *Modify* toolbar. (The icon is the first icon in the *Modify* toolbar.) The message "*Select objects*" is displayed in the command prompt area and AutoCAD awaits us to select the objects to erase.

9. Pick any edge of the rectangle we just created.

10. **Right-mouse-click** inside the graphics window to accept the selection.

11. Reset the display to the 2D wireframe image by using the *menu browser*:
    [View] → [Visual Styles] → [2D wireframe]

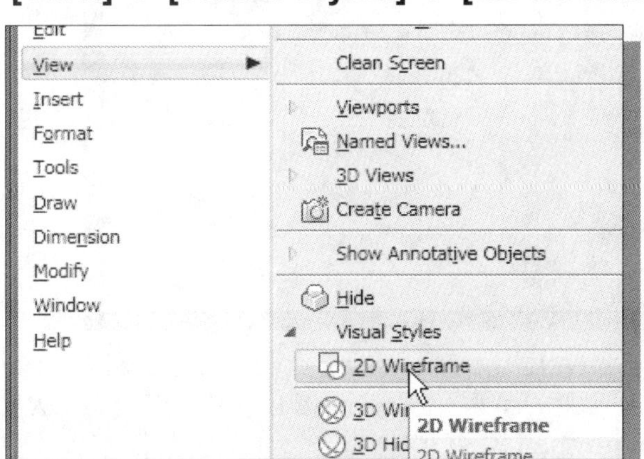

Rotating the UCS

- AutoCAD's **User Coordinate System (UCS)** can be repositioned and reoriented in 3D space. All of the UCS options are organized and can be found in the *Standard* toolbar.

1. Move the cursor on any icon in the *Standard* toolbar area and **right-mouse-click** once to display the option list. Select **Toolbars → AutoCAD**.

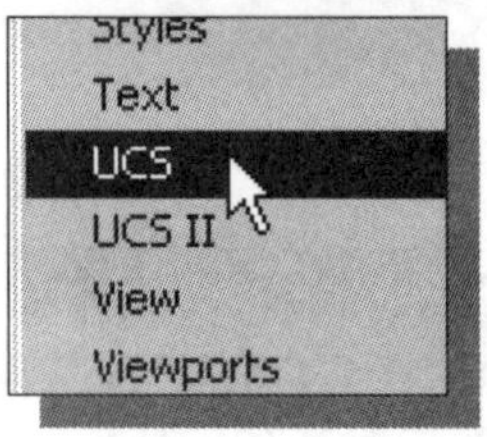

2. Select **UCS**, with the left-mouse-button, to display the *UCS* toolbar on the screen to assist the construction of the *Roof*.

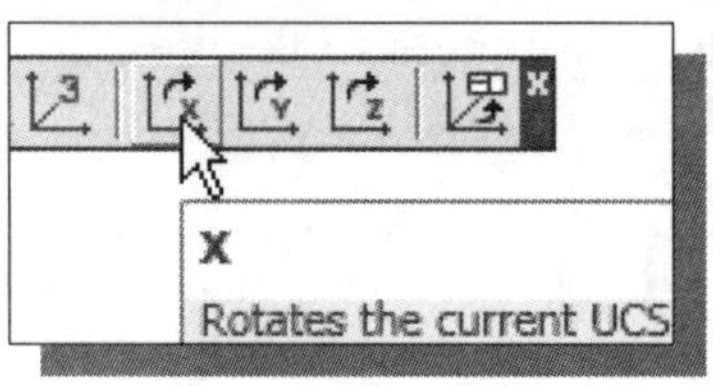

3. Select the **X Axis Rotate** option in the *UCS* toolbar as shown.

4. In the command prompt area, the message "*Specify rotation angle about X axis<90>:*" is displayed. Enter: **90 [ENTER]**.

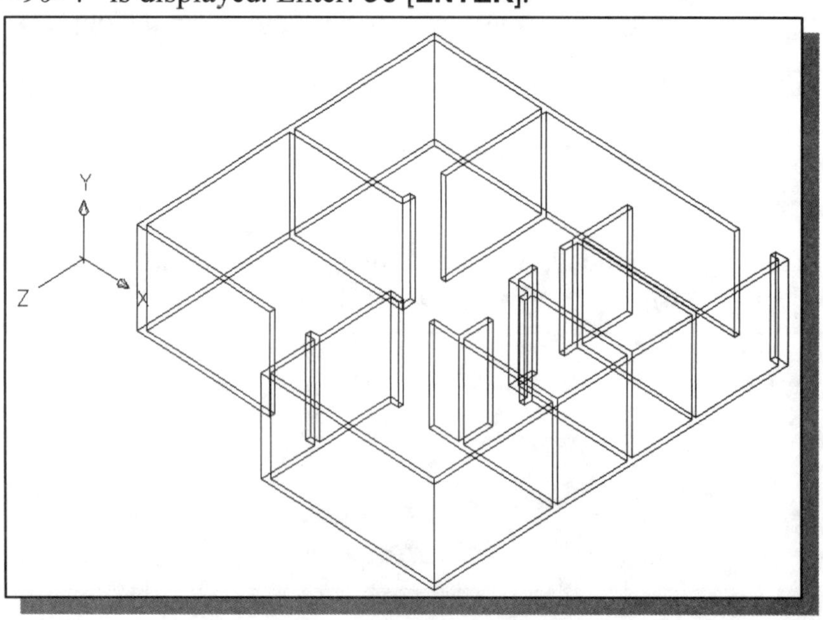

- The UCS rotation is done using the standard engineering convention, where positive values are treated as rotating counter-clockwise. Also note that the *SNAP*, *GRID* and *ORTHO* options all rotate in line with the UCS.

Sketching on the Rotated UCS

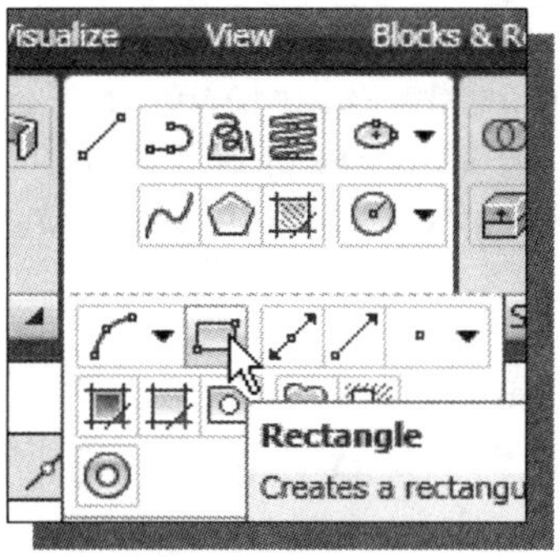

1. Select the **Rectangle** command icon in the *Draw* toolbar as shown.

2. In the *command prompt* area, the message "*Specify first corner point or [Chamfer/Elevation/Fillet/Thickness/ Width]:*" is displayed. Move the cursor inside the graphics window and right-mouse-click to display the option menu.

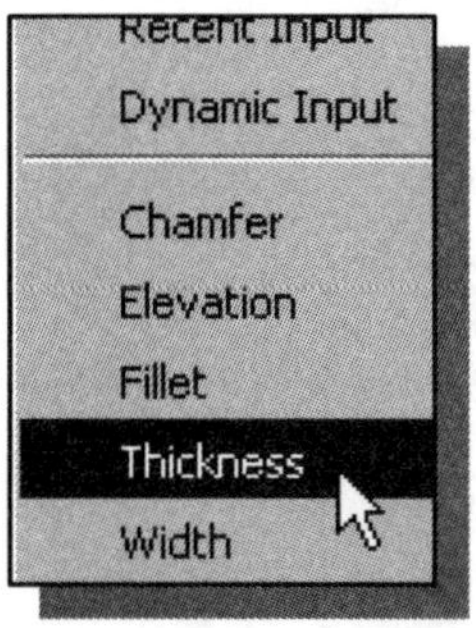

3. In the *option menu*, select **Thickness** by clicking once with the left-mouse-button.

4. In the *command prompt* area, the message "*Specify thickness for rectangles <0'-10">:*" is displayed. Enter **-30'** **[ENTER]**.

5. At the *command prompt*, enter **-2',0'** **[ENTER]** as the first corner of the rectangle.

6. In the *command prompt* area, the message "*Specify other corner point or [Dimensions]:*" is displayed. Enter **@34',10"** **[ENTER]**.

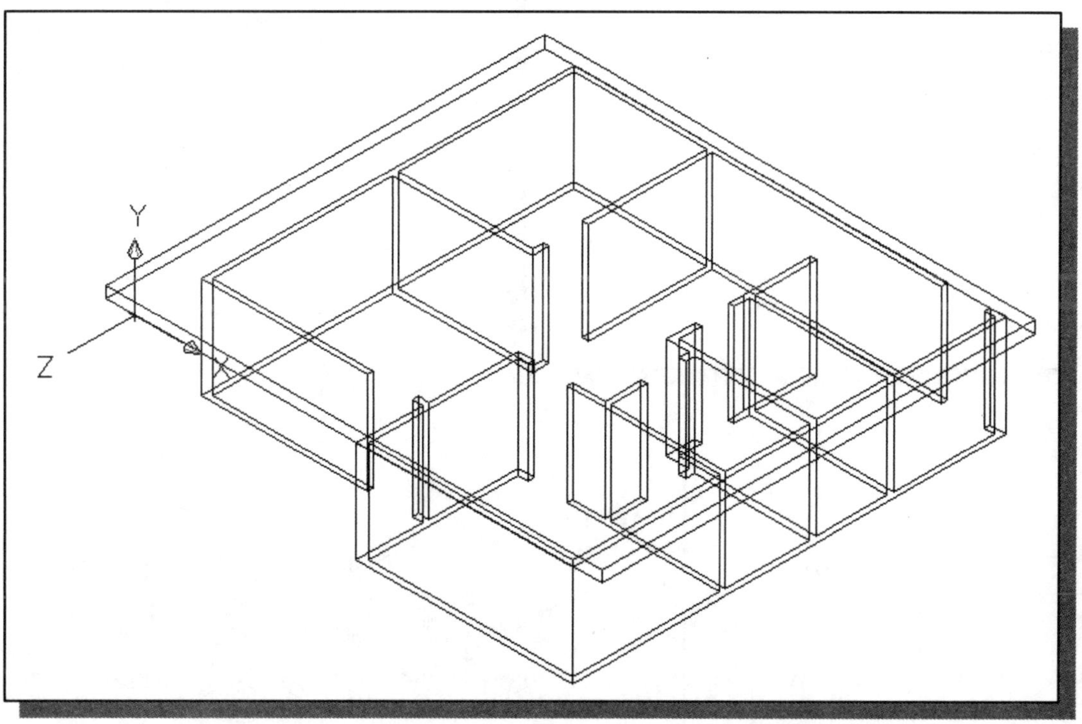

- The negative thickness extrudes the rectangle in the negative Z-direction of the current UCS.

Viewing the Design Using the Hidden Option

- Several options are available in AutoCAD to create more realistic images of 3D designs. The **Visual Styles – Hidden** option can also be used to eliminate the hidden lines on the screen. The **Visual Styles – 3D Hidden** option performs a more complicated calculation of the display and usually produces a better image than the **Hide** option.

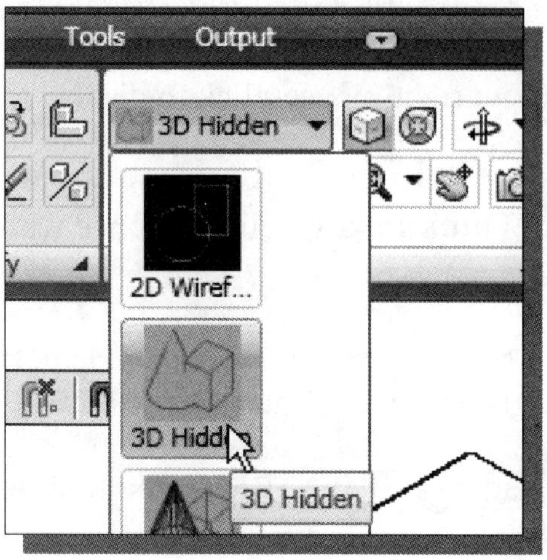

1. In the dashboard panel, select:
   [Visual Styles] → [3D Hidden]

2. To display the 2D wireframe image, select:
   [Visual Styles] → [2D Wireframe]

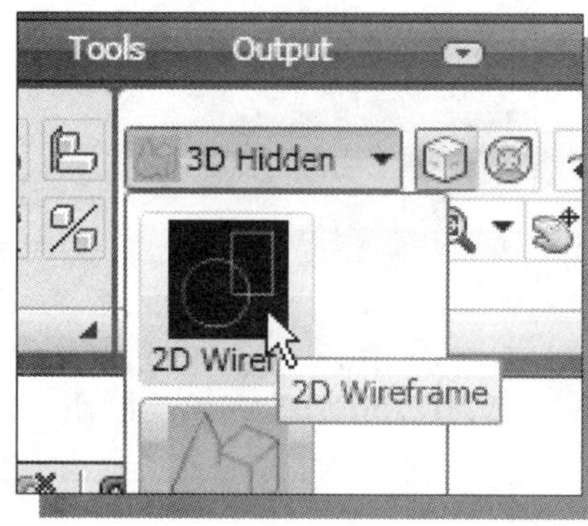

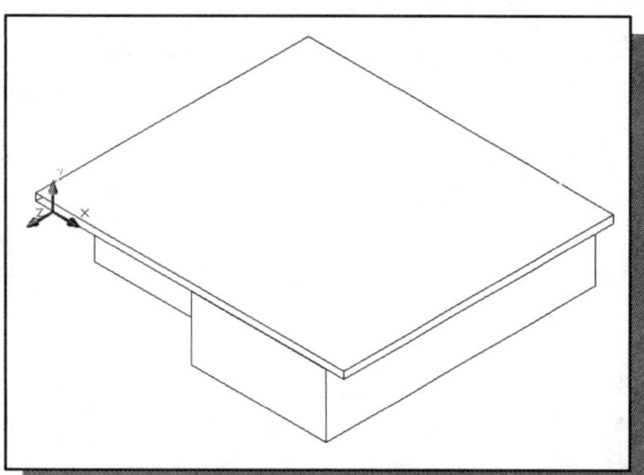

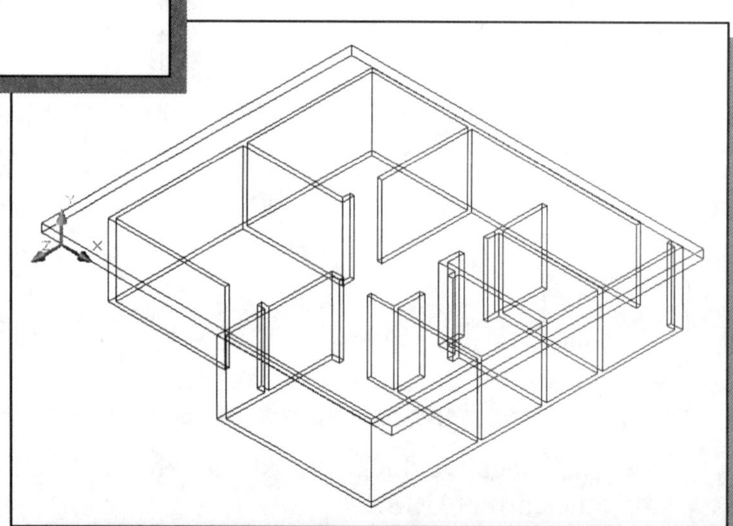

Questions:

1. What is the difference between *WCS* and *UCS*?

2. List and describe two available options to manipulate the UCS.

3. Describe some of the advantages of using the AutoCAD **Thickness** option over creating 2D or 3D models.

4. In the tutorial, which commands were used to eliminate the hidden lines on the screen?

5. What is the difference between a **Polyline** and a **Line**?

6. Identify the following commands:

(a)

(b)

(c)

(d)

Exercises:

1. Dimensions are in inches. Thickness: 0.5 & 0.75

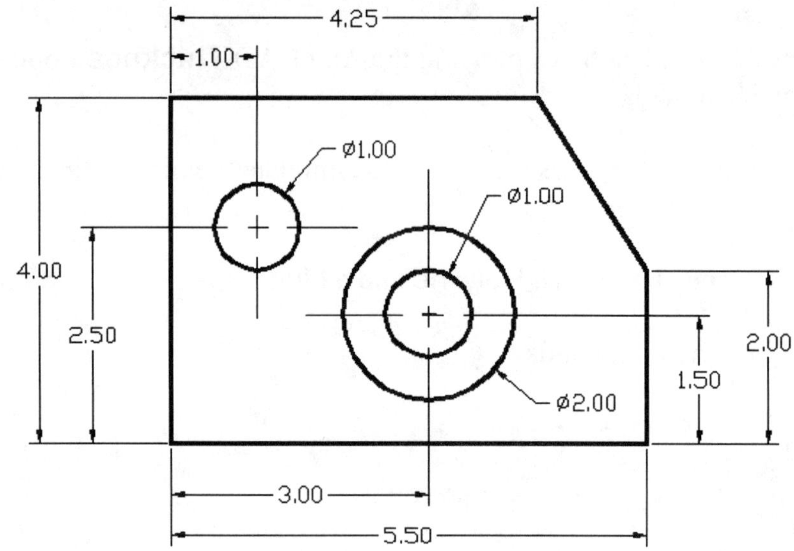

2. Wall thickness: 5 inch; height: 7 feet

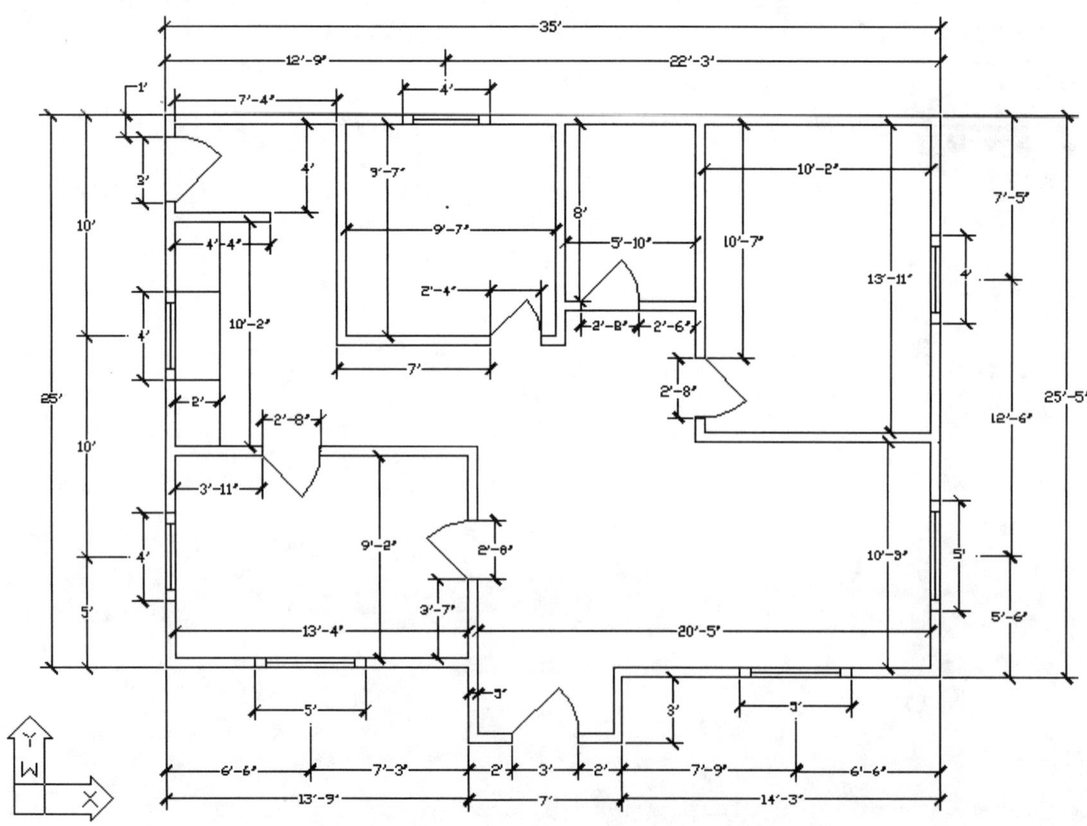

3. Dimensions are in inches. Thickness: 0.25

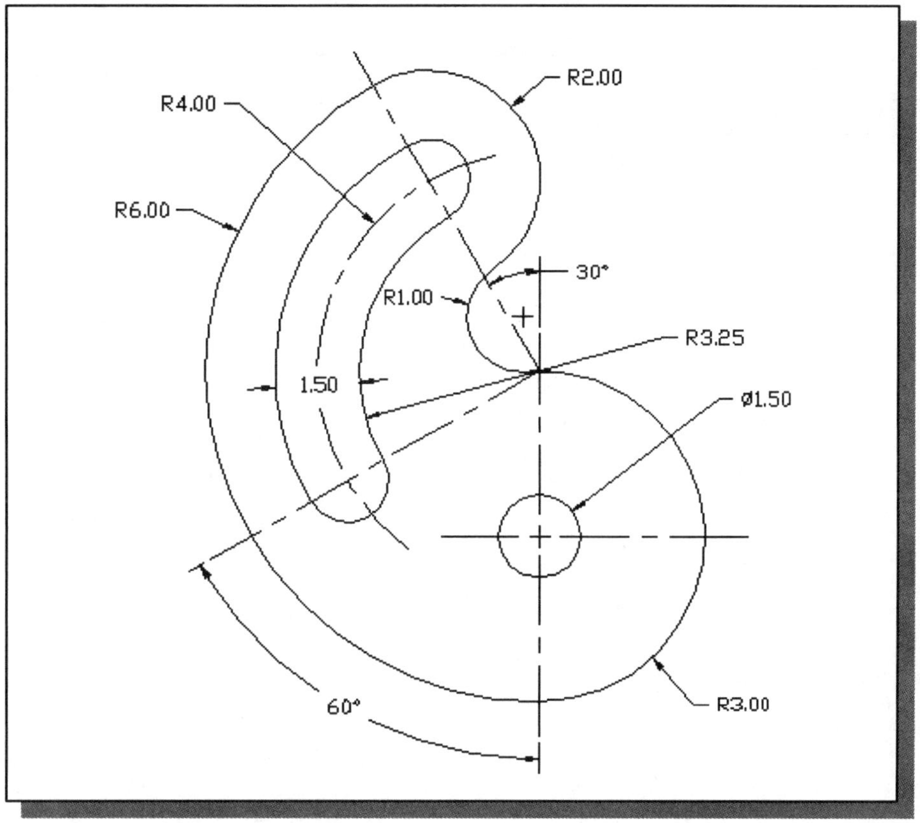

4. Dimensions are in inches. Thickness: 0.25

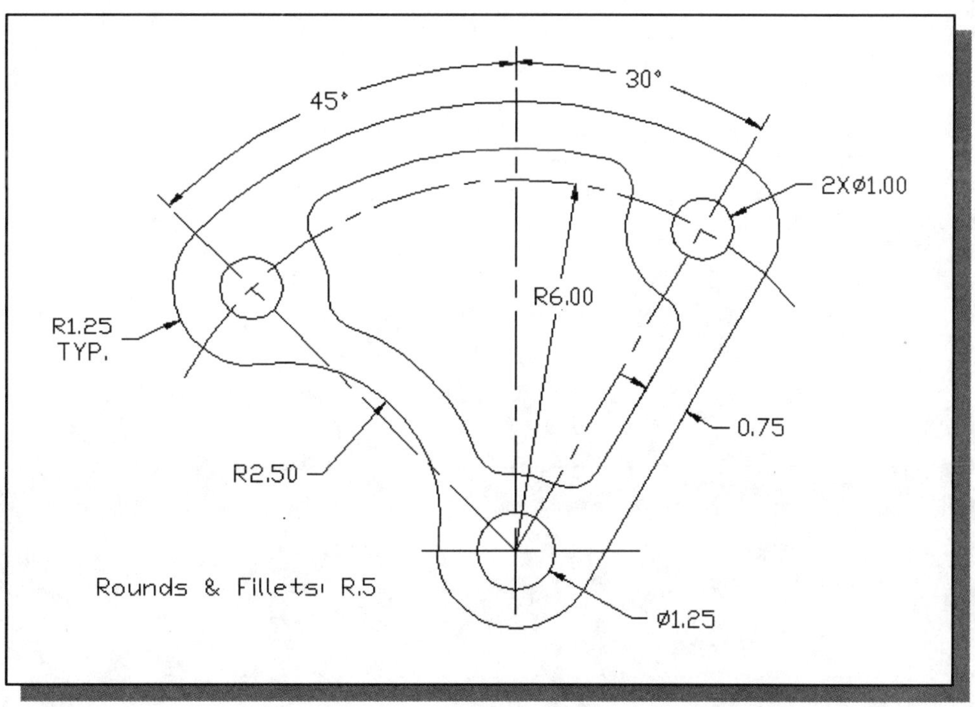

Notes:

Chapter 3
3D Wireframe Modeling

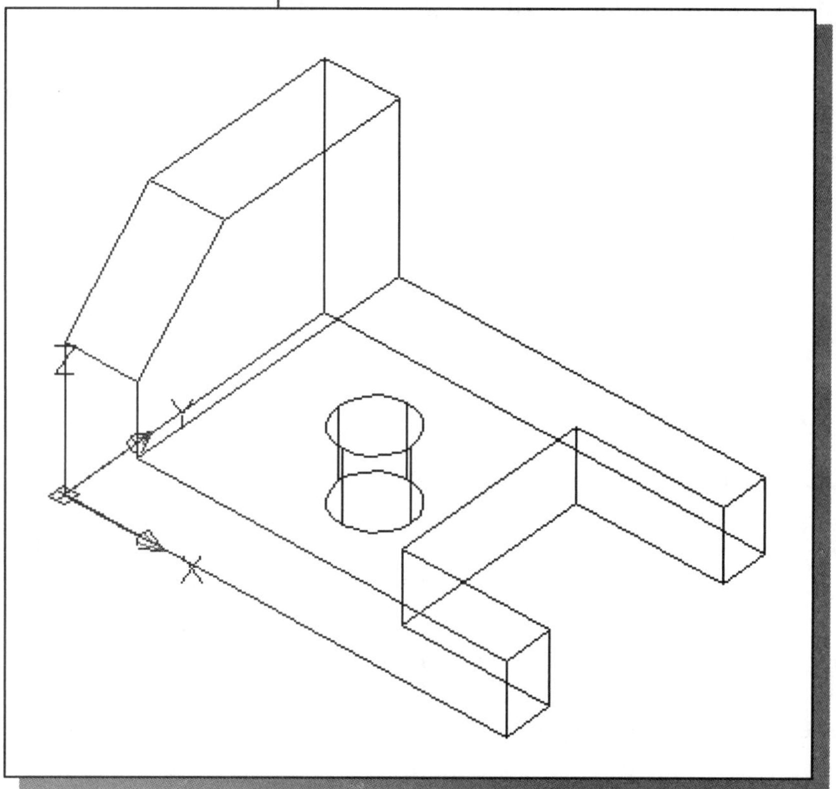

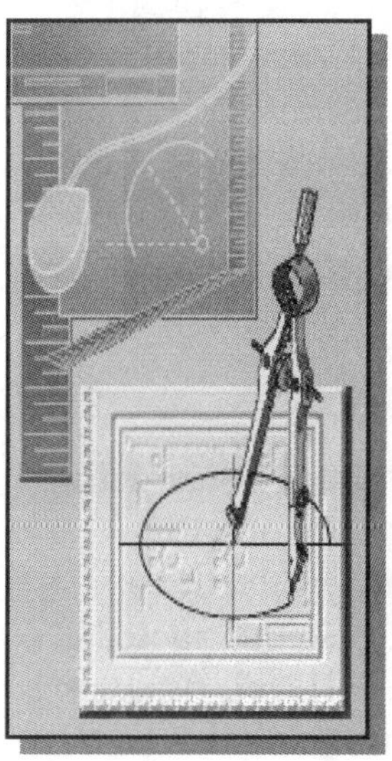

Learning Objectives

- Using the Setup Wizard
- Create Wireframe Models
- Apply the Box Method in Creating Models
- Construct with the Copy Command
- Understand the Available 3D Coordinates Input Options
- Using the View Toolbar
- Setup and Using the TRIM options

Introduction

The first true 3D computer model created on CAD systems in the late 1970s was the 3D wireframe model. Computer generated 3D wireframe models contain information about the locations of all the corners and edges in space coordinates. The 3D wireframe models can be viewed from any direction as needed and are in general reasonably good representations of 3D design. But because surface definition is not part of a wireframe model, all wireframe images have the inherent problem of ambiguity. For example, in the figure displayed below, which corner is in front, corner A or corner B? The ambiguity problem becomes much more serious with complex designs that have many edges and corners.

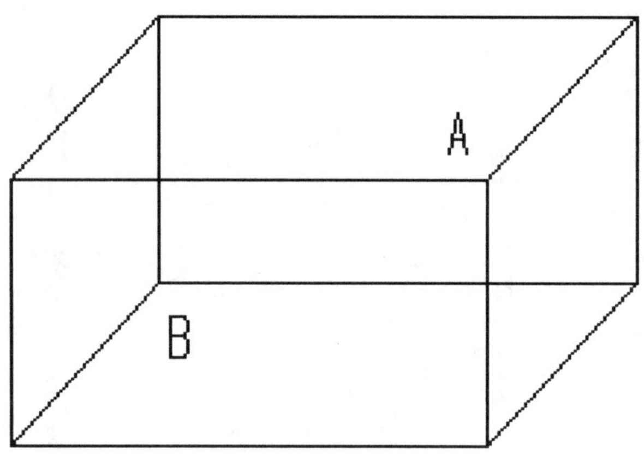

Wireframe Ambiguity: Which corner is in front, A or B?

The main advantage of using a 3D wireframe modeler to create 3D models is its simplicity. The computer hardware requirements for wireframe modelers are typically much lower than the requirements for surface and solid modelers. A 3D wireframe model, also known as a stick-figure model or a skeleton model, contains only information about the locations of all the corners and edges of the design in space coordinates. You should also realize that, in some cases, it could be quite difficult to locate some of the corner locations while creating a 3D wireframe model. Note that 3D wireframe modelers are usually used in conjunction with surfacing modelers, which we will discuss in the later chapters of this text, to eliminate the problem of ambiguity.

With most CAD systems, creating 3D wireframe models usually starts with constructing 2D entities in 3D space. Two of the most commonly used methods for creating 3D wireframe models are the **Box method** and the **2D Extrusion method**. As the name implies, the *Box method* involves the creation of a 3D box with the edges constructed from the overall height, width and depth dimensions of the design. The 3D wireframe model is typically completed by locating and connecting corners within the box.

The *2D Extrusion method* involves making copies of 2D geometries in specific directions. This method is similar to the 2½D extrusion approach illustrated in the previous chapter (Chapter 2) with several differences. First of all, we do not really extrude the wireframe entities; instead we simply make copies of wireframe entities in the desired directions. Secondly, constructed wireframe entities have true 3D space coordinates, while the *thickness* approach creates entities with no true 3D coordinates. And lastly, no surfaces are created in the 3D wireframe models.

In this chapter, we will illustrate the general procedure to construct a 3D wireframe model using both the box method and the 2D extrusion method. To illustrate the AutoCAD 3D construction environment, we will create the wireframe model using only the default UCS system, which is aligned to the world coordinate system. Repositioning and/or reorienting the User Coordinate System can be useful in creating 3D models. But it is also feasible to create 3D models referencing only a single coordinate system. One important note about creating wireframe models is that the construction techniques mostly concentrate on locating the space coordinates of the individual corners of the design. The ability to visualize designs in the form of 3D wireframe models is extremely helpful to designers and CAD operators. It is hoped that the experience of thinking and working on 3D wireframe models, as outlined in this chapter, will enhance one's 3D visualization ability.

The *Locator* Design

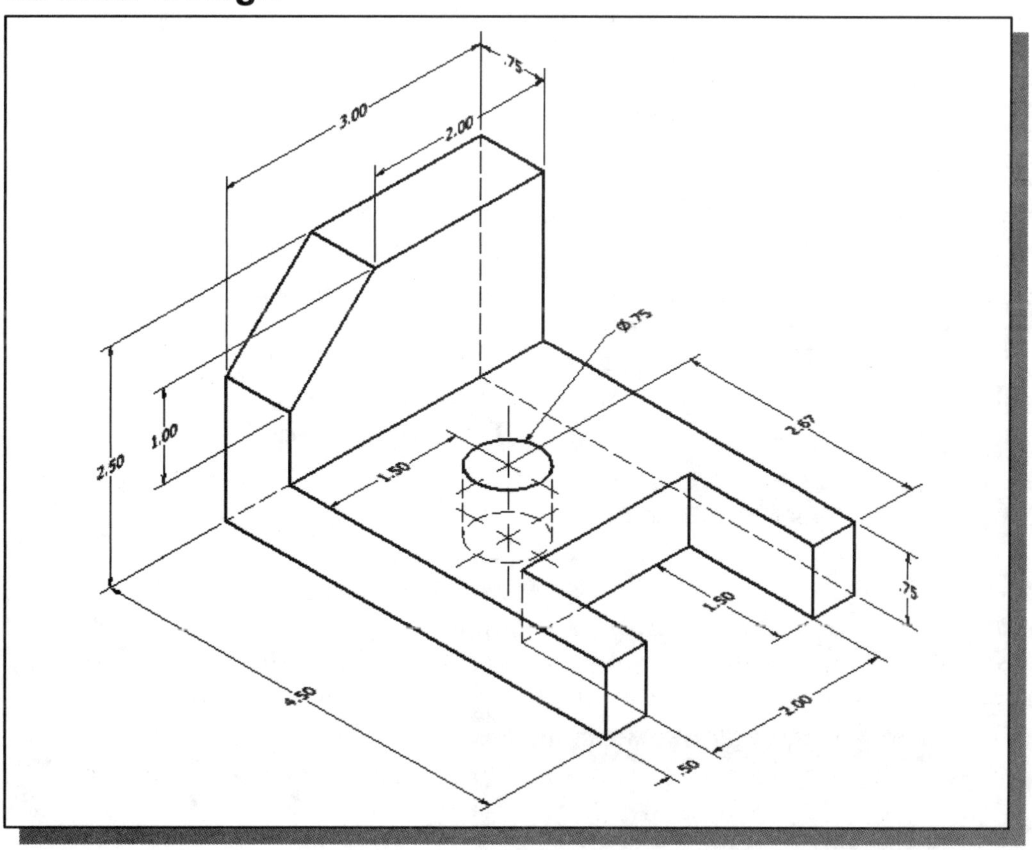

Starting Up AutoCAD® 2009

1. Select the **AutoCAD 2009** option on the *Program* menu or select the **AutoCAD 2009** icon on the *Desktop*. Once the program is loaded into the memory, the **AutoCAD® 2009** drawing screen will appear on the screen.

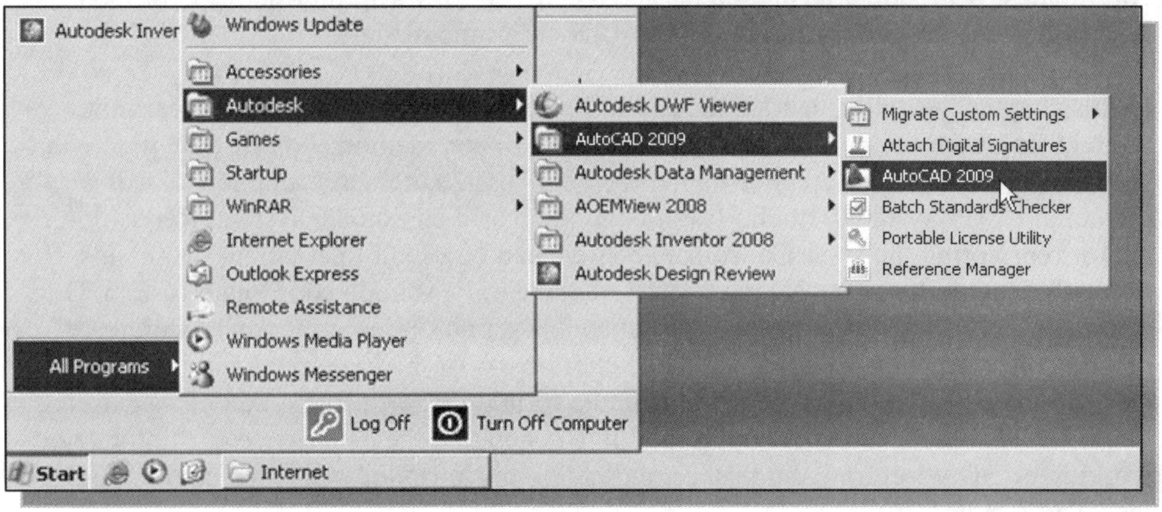

Using the Startup Options

❖ In **AutoCAD® 2009**, we can use the *Startup* dialog box to establish different types of drawing settings. The startup dialog box can be activated through the use of the **STARTUP** system variable.

The STARTUP system variable can be set to either 0 or 1:

- 1: displays the **Create New Drawing** dialog box.
- 0: displays the **Select Template** dialog box (default).

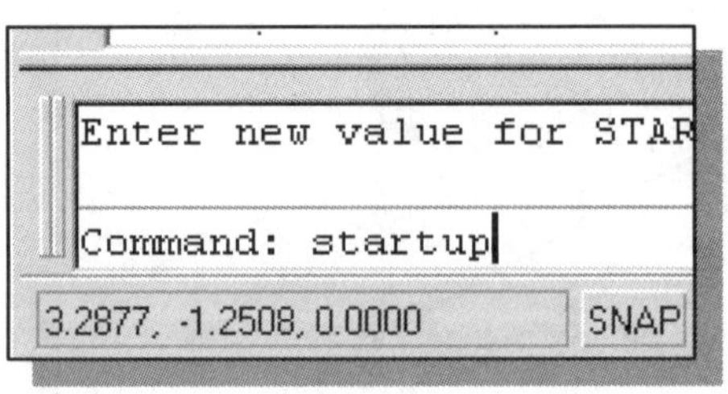

1. In the command prompt area, enter the system variable name:
   STARTUP [**ENTER**]

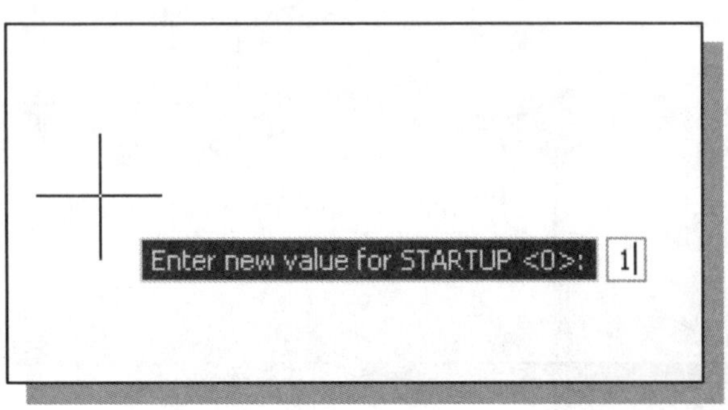

2. Enter **1** as the new value for the startup system variable.

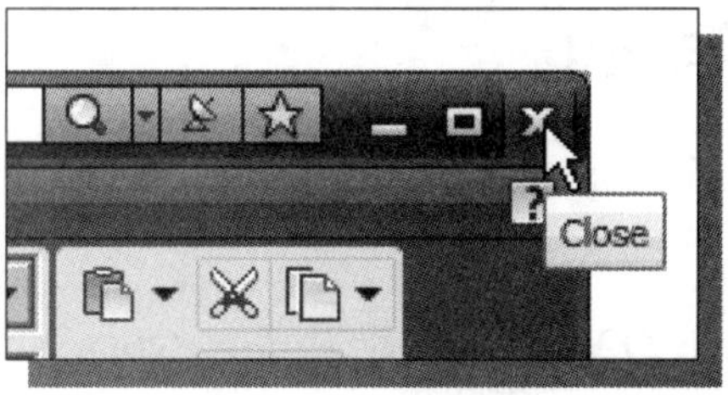

3. To show the effect of the *Startup* option, **exit** AutoCAD by clicking on the **Close** icon as shown.

4. Restart AutoCAD by selecting the **AutoCAD 2009** option through the *Start* menu.

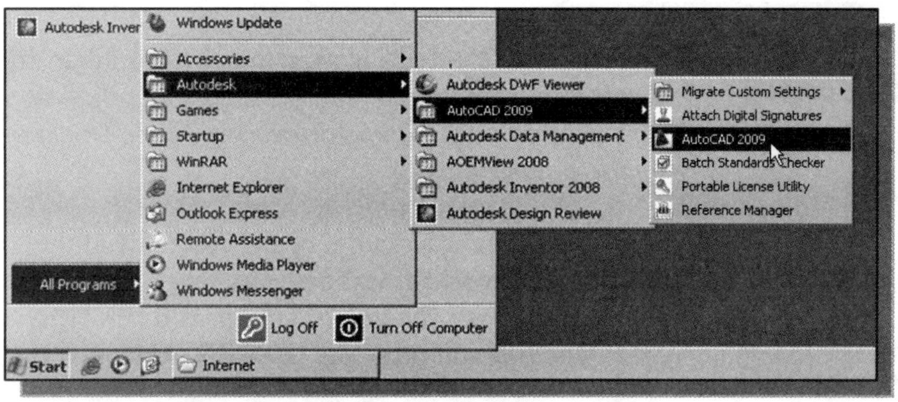

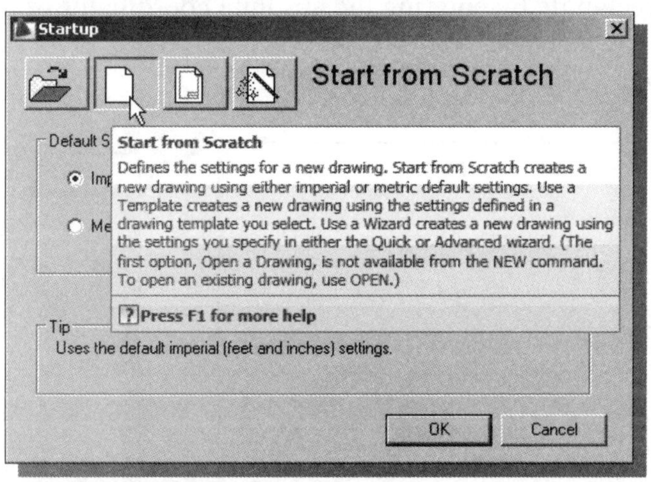

5. The *Startup* dialog box appears on the screen with different options to assist the creation of drawings. Move the cursor on top of the four icons and notice the four options available:
(1) **Open a Drawing**
(2) **Start from Scratch**
(3) **Use a Template** and
(4) **Use a Setup Wizard**.

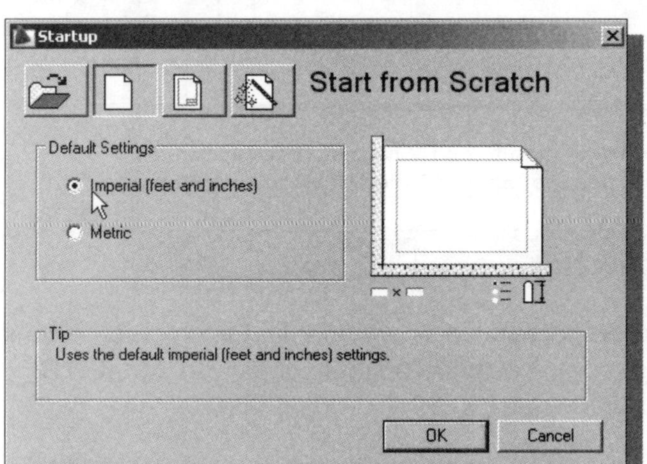

6. In the *Startup* dialog box, select the **Start from Scratch** option as shown in the figure.

7. Choose **Imperial** to use the *Standard English* units setting.

8. Click **OK** to accept the setting.

Creating the Rectangular Base of the Design

➢ We will first construct the wireframe geometry defining the rectangular base of the design.

1. In the *Status Bar* area, reset the options and turn ***ON*** the *Grid, Polar, Object Snap, Object Snap Tracking, Dynamic Input* and *Line Weight* options.

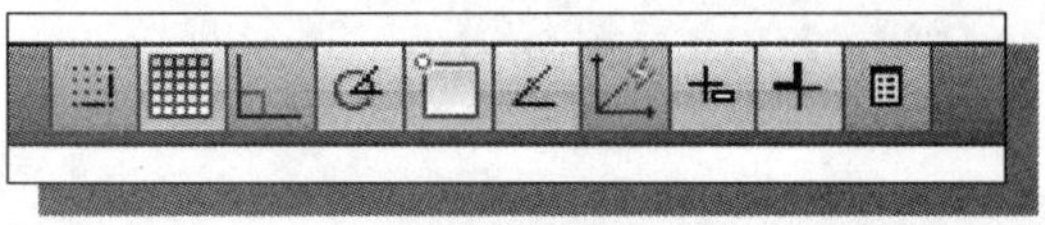

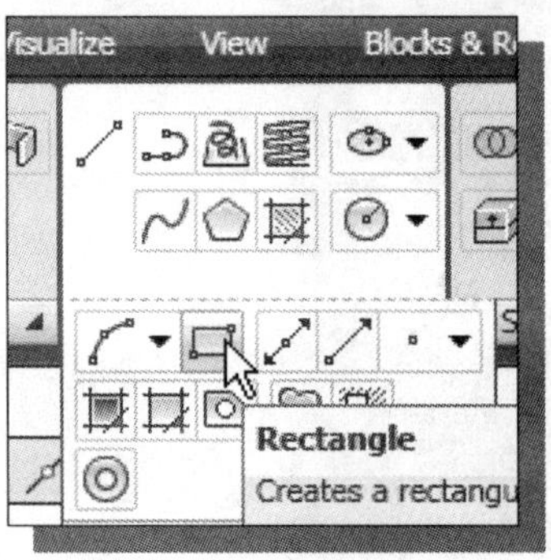

2. Select the **Rectangle** icon in the *Draw* toolbar. In the command prompt area, the message "*Specify first corner point or [Chamfer/Elevation/Fillet/Thickness/ Width]:*" is displayed.

3. Place the first corner-point of the rectangle at the origin of the world coordinate system.
   Command: _line Specify first point: **0,0 [ENTER]**
   (Type **0,0** and press the **[ENTER]** key once.)

4. We will create a 4.5″ × 3.0″ rectangle by entering the absolute coordinates of the second corner.
   Specify other corner point or [Dimension]: **4.5,3 [ENTER]**

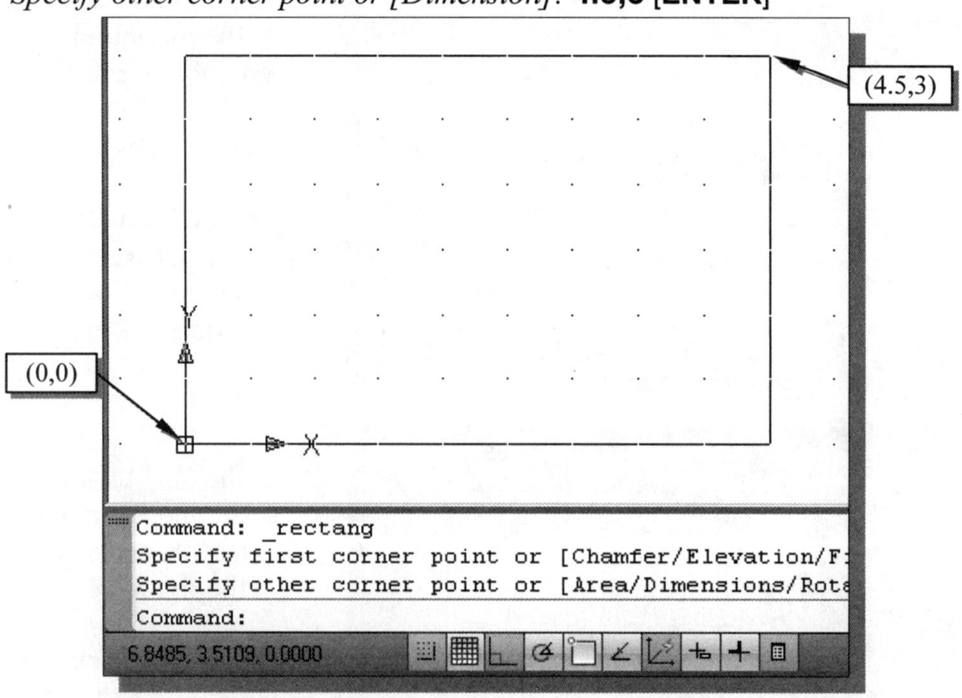

- The **Rectangle** command creates rectangles as *polyline* features, which means the four segments of a rectangle, are created as a single object. In AutoCAD, rectangles are wireframe entities.

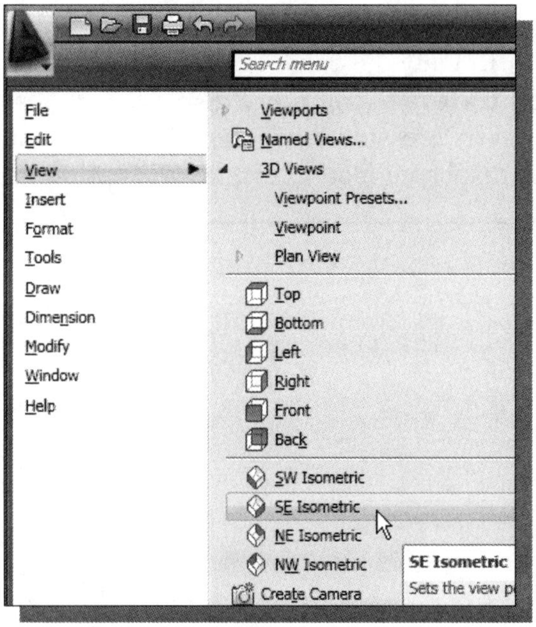

5. In the Menu Browsers, select: **[View] → [3D Views] → [SE Isometric]**

- Notice the orientation of the sketched 2D rectangle in relation to the displayed AutoCAD user coordinate system. By default, the 2D sketch-plane is aligned to the XY plane of the world coordinate system.

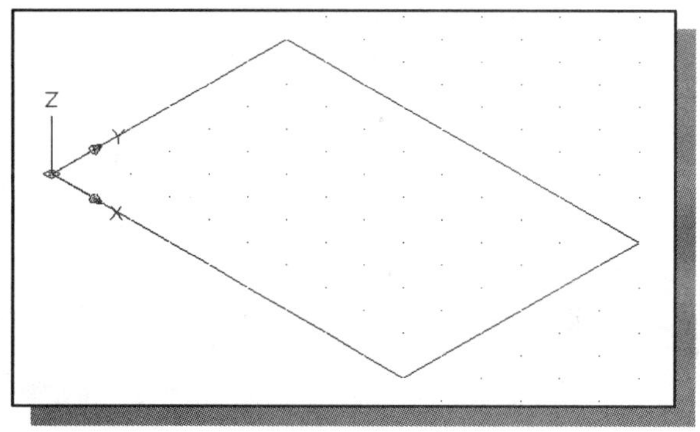

Create a 3D Box

- We will create a 3D box to define the 3D boundary of the design. We will do so by placing a copy of the base rectangle at the corresponding height elevation of the design. The dimensions of the 3D box are therefore based on the height, width and depth dimensions of the design.

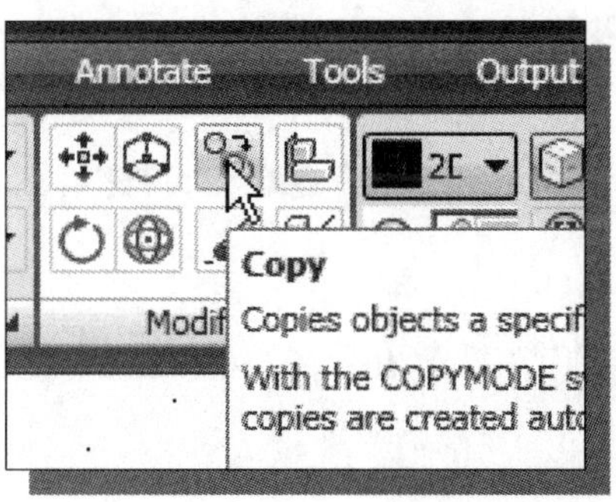

1. Click on the **Copy Object** icon in the *Modify* toolbar.

2. In the command prompt area, the message "*Select objects:*" is displayed. Pick any edge of the sketched rectangle.

3. Inside the graphics window, right-mouse-click once to accept the selection.

4. In the command prompt area, the message "*Specify base point or displacement, or [Multiple]:*" is displayed. Pick any corner of the sketched rectangle as a base point to create the copy.

5. In the command prompt area, the message "*Specify second point of displacement or <use first point as displacement>:*" is displayed.
   Enter: **@0,0,2.5 [ENTER]**
   (The three values are the X, Y and Z coordinates of the new location.)

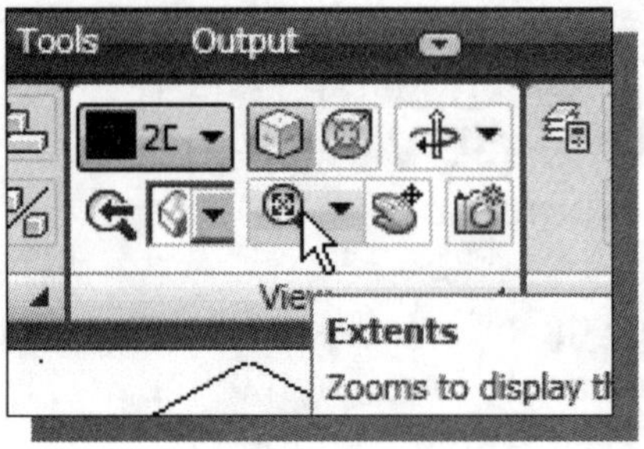

6. Select the **Zoom Extents** icon in the *Standard* toolbar to view the constructed geometry. If the **Zoom Extents** icon is not displayed, choose the icon by pressing down the left-mouse-button on the displayed icon to display the option list.

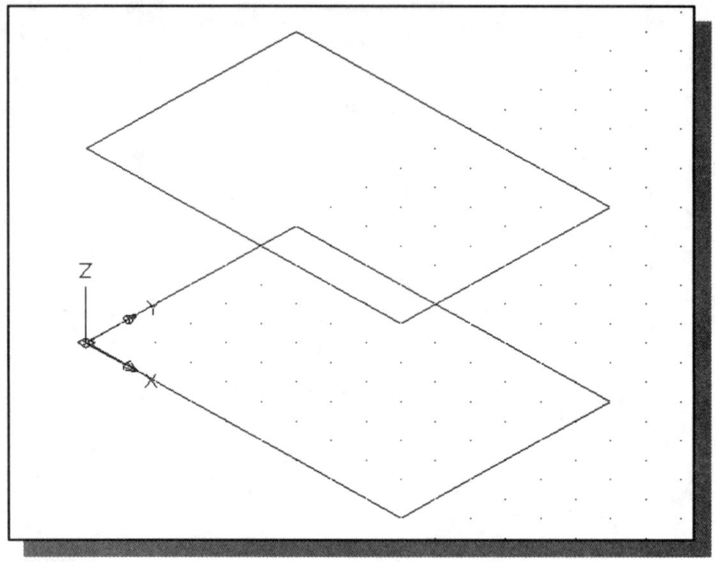

❖ The two rectangles represent the top and bottom of a 3D box defining the 3D boundary of the design. Note that the construction of the second rectangle was independent of the UCS, User Coordinate System; the UCS is still aligned to the world coordinate system.

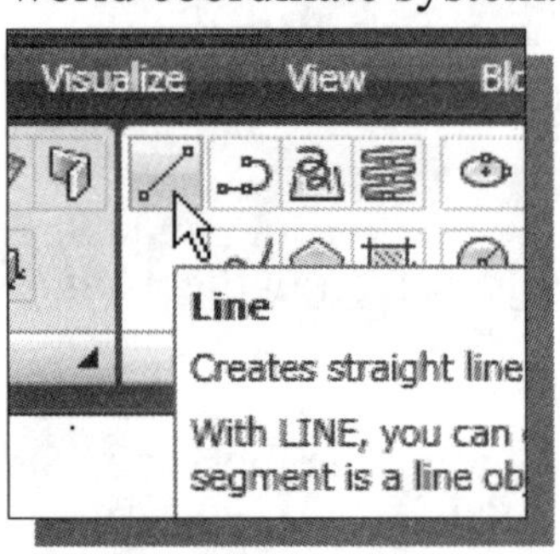

7. Select the **Line** icon in the *Draw* toolbar.

8. In the command prompt area, the message "*_line Specify first point:*" is displayed.

   Command: _line Specify first point: **0,0 [ENTER]**

9. In the command prompt area, the message "*Specify next point or [Undo]:*" is displayed.

   Command: _line Specify first point: **0,0,2.5 [ENTER]**

❖ Notice the Line command correctly identified the entered 3D coordinates of the second point. The default Z-coordinate, which is set by the AutoCAD UCS, is applied automatically whenever the Z-coordinates are omitted.

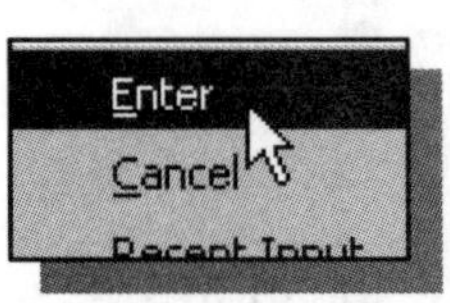

10. Inside the graphics window, right-mouse-click to activate the option menu and select **Enter** with the left-mouse-button to end the Line command.

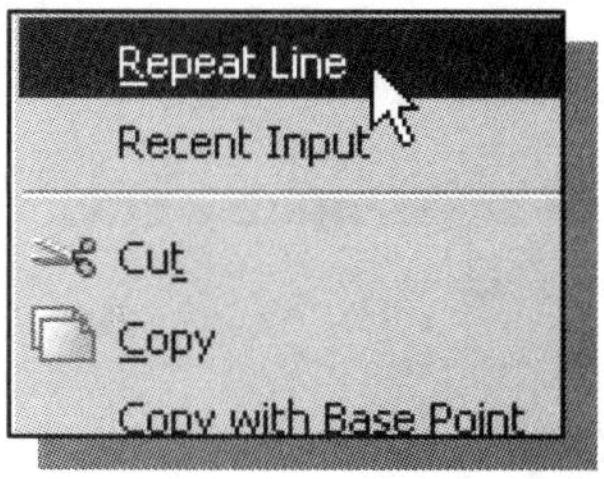

11. Inside the graphics window, **right-mouse-click** to bring up the popup option menu.

12. Pick **Repeat Line** with the left-mouse-button in the popup menu to repeat the last command.

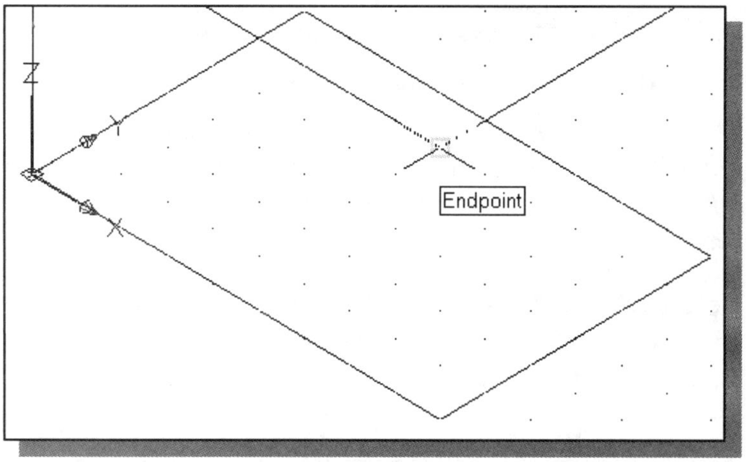

13. Move the cursor on top of the top front corner as shown. Note that the AutoCAD's *Object Snap* and *Object Snap Tracking* features identify geometric features, such as endpoints, automatically.

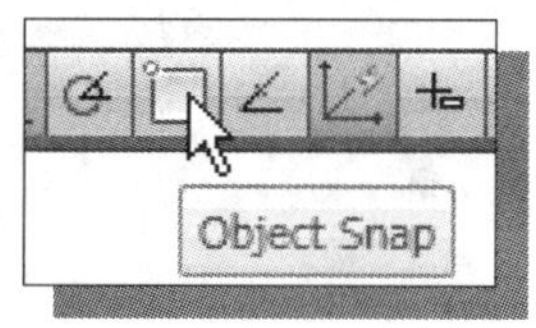

14. Left-click once to select the endpoint as shown.

15. Create a line connecting to the endpoint directly below the previously selected point.

16. On your own, complete the 3D box by creating the two lines connecting the back corners of the 3D box as shown.

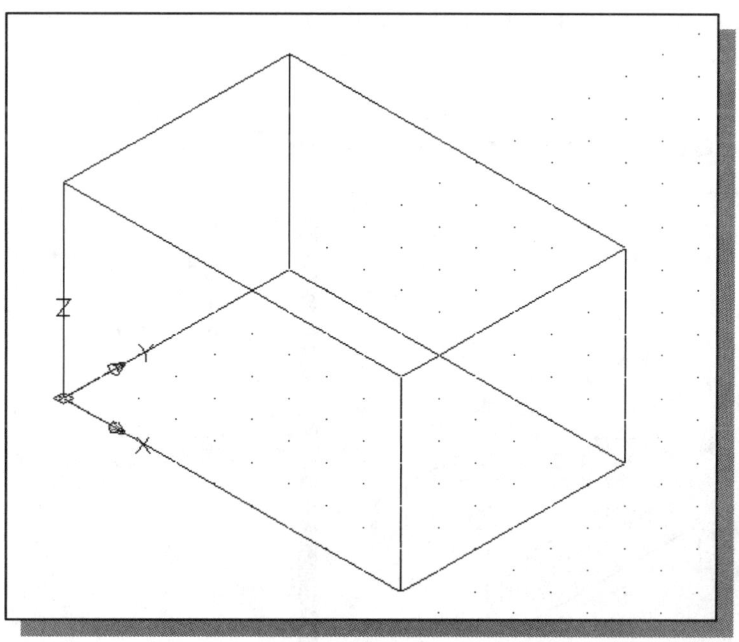

Object Snap Toolbar

1. Move the cursor on any icon in the *Standard* toolbar area and **right-mouse-click** once to display a list of options. Select **Toolbars → AutoCAD**.

❖ AutoCAD provides many toolbars for access to frequently used commands, settings, and modes. The *Standard*, *Object Properties*, *Draw*, and *Modify* toolbars are displayed by default. The *check marks* in the list identify the toolbars that are currently displayed on the screen.

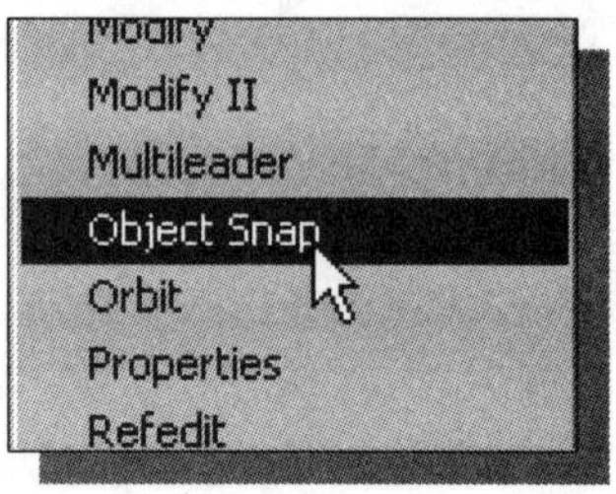

2. Select **Object Snap**, with the left-mouse-button, to display the *Object Snap* toolbar on the screen to assist the construction of the floor plan.

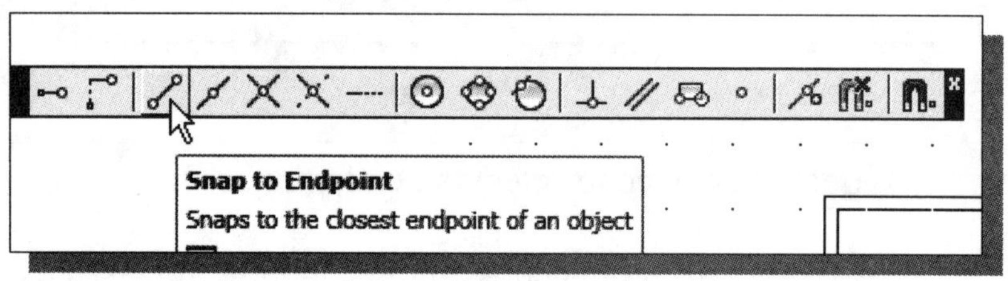

❖ ***Object Snap*** is an extremely powerful construction tool available on most CAD systems. During an entity's creation operations, we can snap the cursor to points on objects such as endpoints, midpoints, centers, and intersections. For example, we can turn on ***Object Snap*** and quickly draw a line to the center of a circle, the midpoint of a line segment, or the intersection of two lines.

Using the Snap Options to Locate the Top Corners

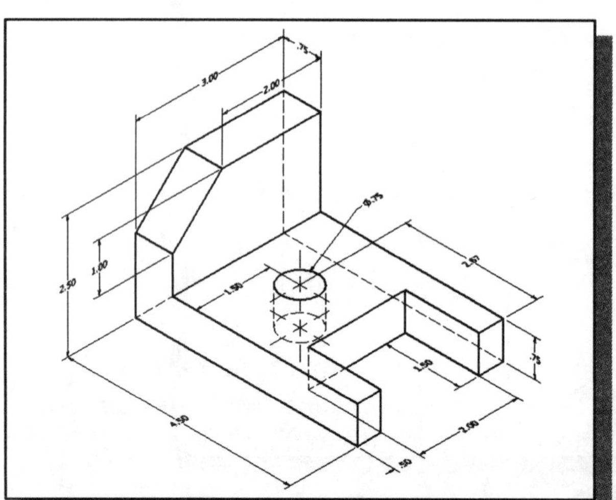

❖ We will use the *Object Snap* options to identify the locations of the top corners of the model.

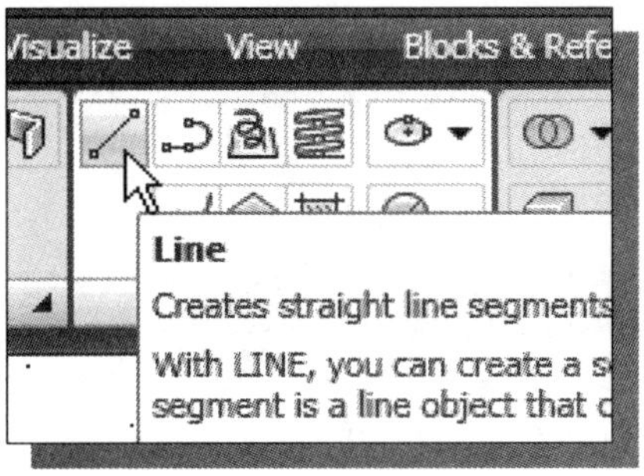

1. Select the **Line** icon in the *Draw* toolbar.

2. In the command prompt area, the message "*_line Specify first point:*" is displayed. Select **Snap From** in the *Object Snap* toolbar.

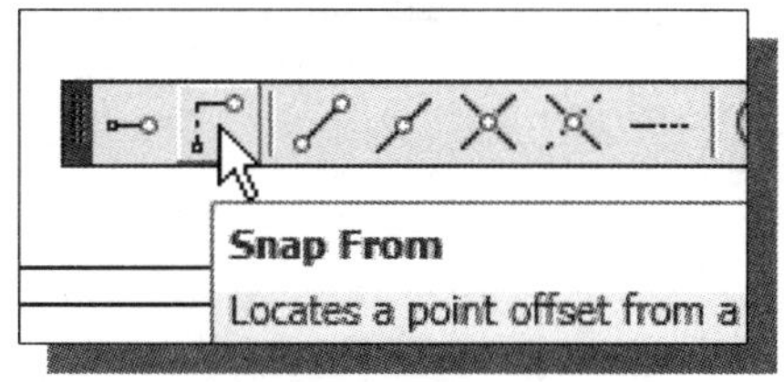

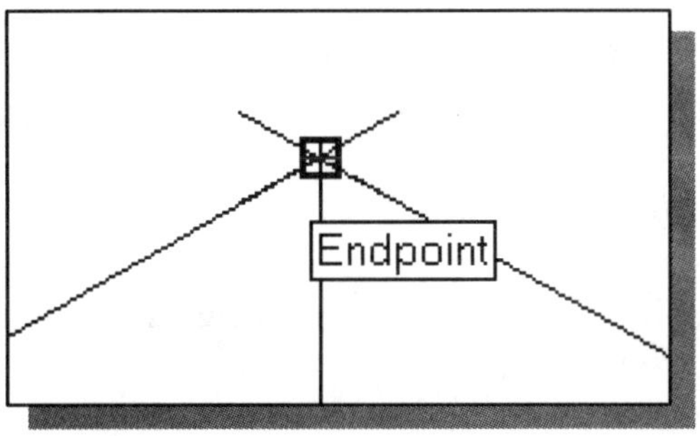

3. Select the **top back corner** as the reference point as shown.

4. In the command prompt area, the message "*_line Specify first point: from Base point:<Offset>:*" is displayed.

   Command: **@0.75,0,0 [ENTER]**

❖ By using the relative coordinate input method, we can locate the position of any point in 3D space. Note that the entered coordinates are measured relative to the current UCS.

5. In the command prompt area, the message " *Specify next point or [Undo]:*" is displayed.

   Command: Specify next point or [Undo]: **@0,-2,0 [ENTER]**

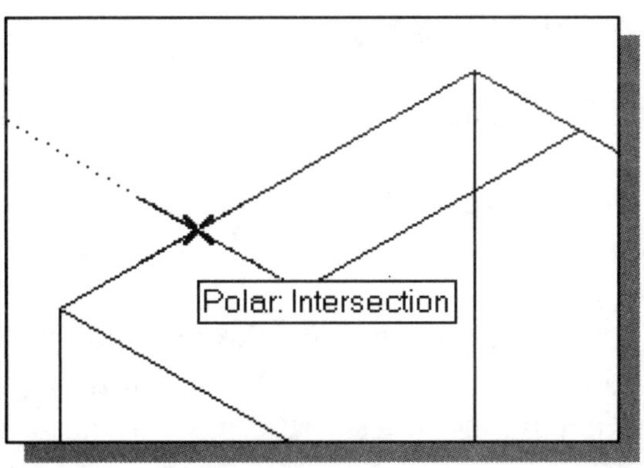

6. Move the cursor toward the left to create a perpendicular line. Select a location that is on the back line as shown, notice the displayed *Object Snap/Tracking* tips: **Polar: Intersection.**

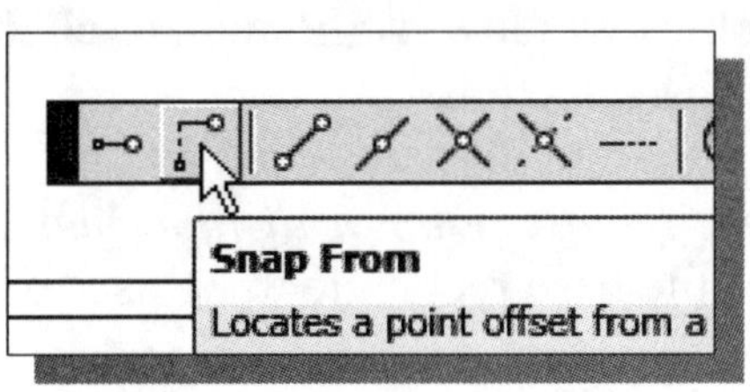

7. In the command prompt area, the message "*Specify next point or [Undo]:*" is displayed. Select **Snap From** in the *Object Snap* toolbar.

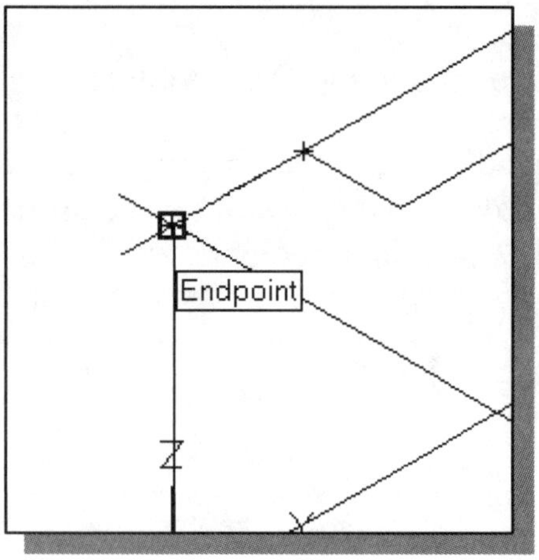

8. Select the **top front corner** as the reference point as shown.

9. In the command prompt area, the message "*Specify next point or [Close/Undo]:_from Base point <Offset>:*" is displayed.

   Command: **@0,0,-1 [ENTER]**

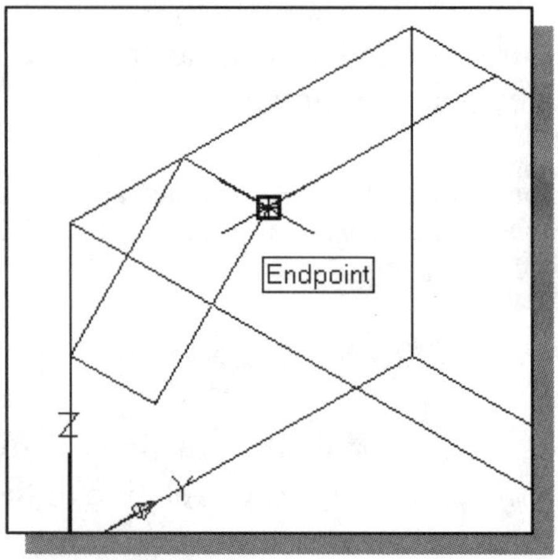

10. In the command prompt area, the message "*Specify next point or [Undo]:*" is displayed.

    Command: **@0.75,0,0 [ENTER]**

11. Move the cursor to the top corner as shown in the figure.

❖ Using the *Object Snap* options and the *relative coordinate input method* allow us to quickly locate points in 3D space.

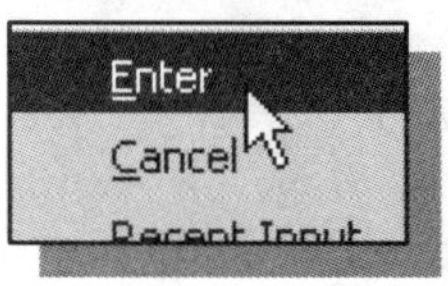

12. Inside the graphics window, right-mouse-click to activate the option menu and select **Enter** with the left-mouse-button to end the Line command.

Using the *Copy* Option to Create Additional Edges

❖ The Copy option can also be used to create additional edges of the wireframe model.

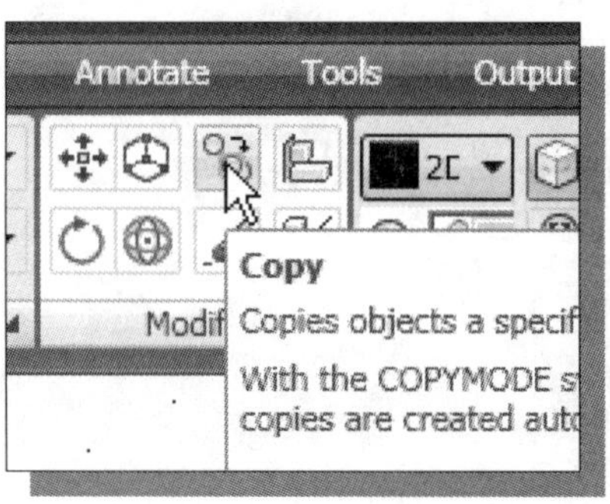

1. Click on the **Copy Object** icon in the *Modify* toolbar.

2. In the command prompt area, the message "*Select objects:*" is displayed. Pick any edge of the bottom rectangle.

3. Inside the graphics window, **right-mouse-click** once to accept the selection.

4. In the command prompt area, the message "*Specify base point or displacement, or [Multiple]:*" is displayed. Pick any corner of the base rectangle to be used as a base point to create the copy.

5. In the command prompt area, the message "*Specify second point of displacement or <use first point as displacement>:*" is displayed. Enter: **@0,0,0.75 [ENTER]**

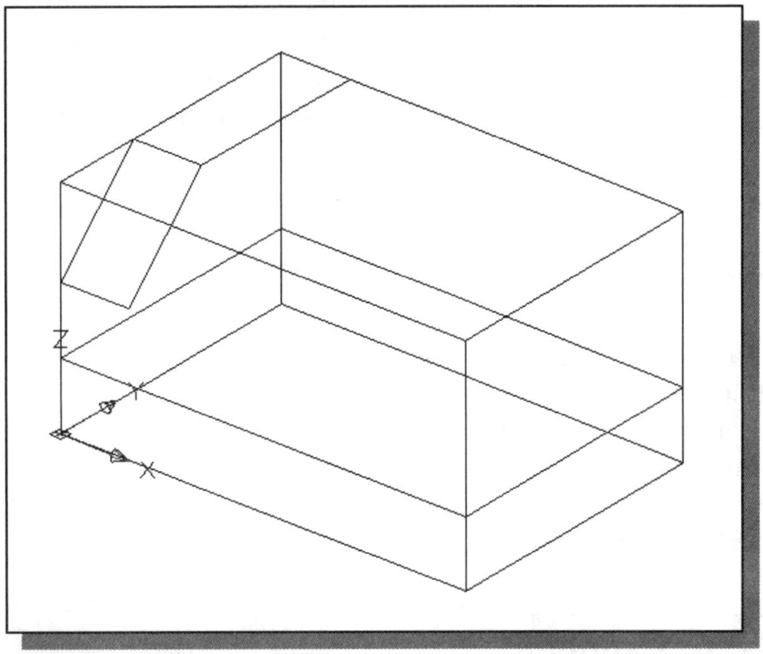

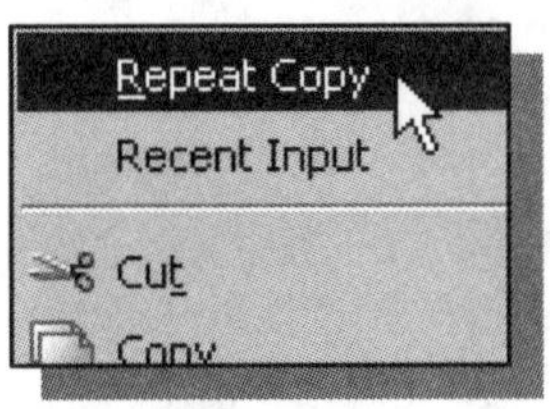

6. Inside the graphics window, right-mouse-click to bring up the popup option menu.

7. Pick **Repeat Copy Object** with the left-mouse-button in the popup menu to repeat the last command.

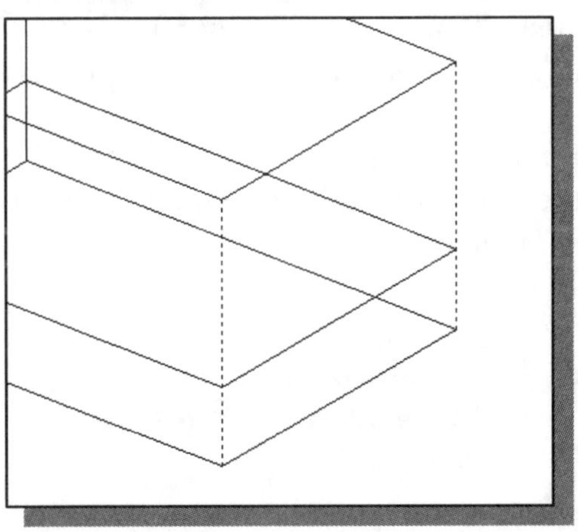

8. Pick the two **vertical lines** on the right side of the 3D box as shown.

9. Inside the graphics window, **right-mouse-click** once to accept the selection.

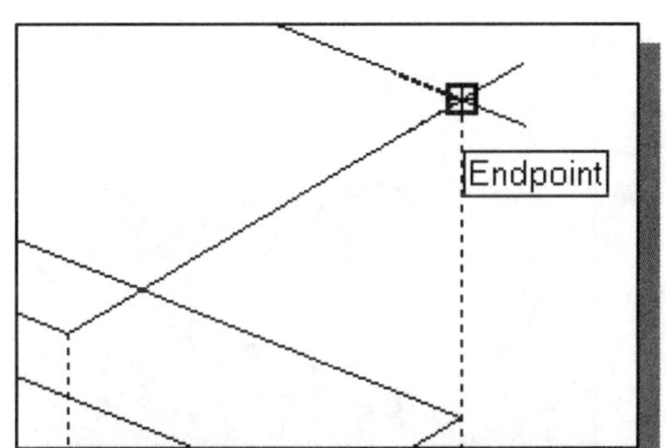

10. In the command prompt area, the message "*Specify base point or displacement, or [Multiple]:*" is displayed. Pick the **top back corner** of the wireframe as a base point to create the copy.

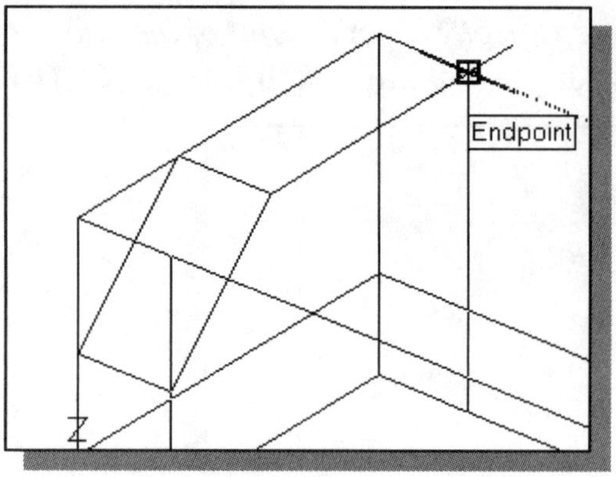

11. In the command prompt area, the message "*Specify second point of displacement or <use first point as displacement>:*" is displayed. Pick the **top back corner** of the wireframe model as shown.

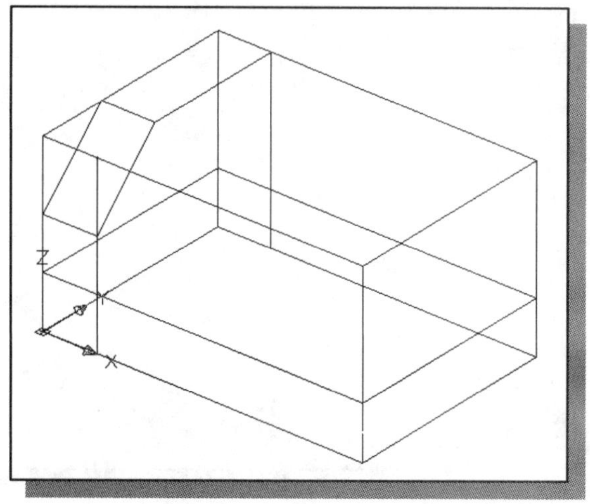

❖ The copy option is an effective way to create additional edges of wireframe models, especially when multiple objects are involved. With wireframe models, the emphasis is placed on the corners and edges of the model.

Using the Trim Command

❖ The Trim command can be used to shorten objects so that they end precisely at selected boundaries.

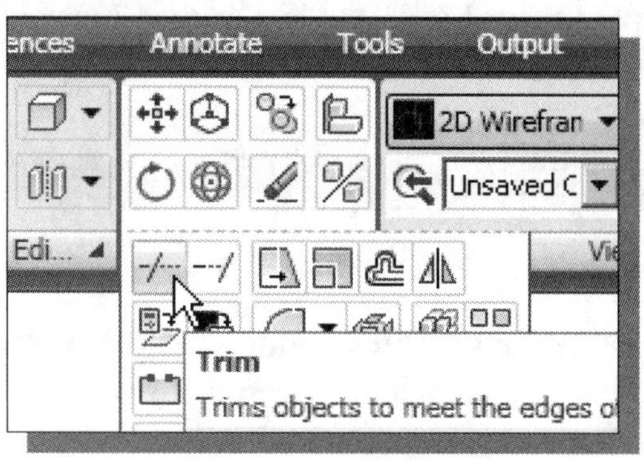

1. Select the **Trim** command icon in the *Modify* toolbar. In the command prompt area, the message "*Select boundary edges... Select objects:*" is displayed.

❖ First we will select the objects that define the boundary edges to which we want to trim the object.

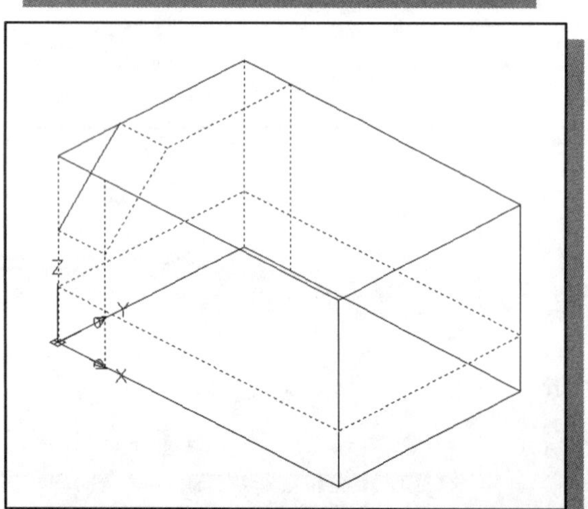

2. Pick the highlighted edges as shown in the figure; these edges are the *boundary edges*.

3. Inside the graphics window, **right-mouse-click** once to accept the selection of boundary edges and proceeds with the Trim command.

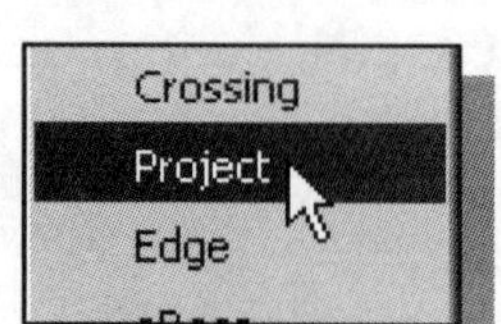

4. Inside the graphics area, right-mouse-click once to bring up the option menu and select **Project** as shown.

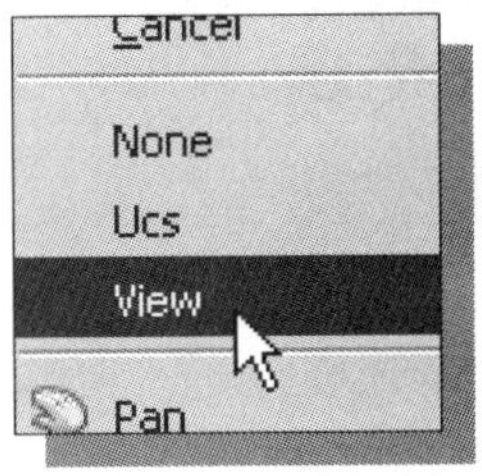

5. Inside the graphics area, right-mouse-click once to bring up the option menu and select **View** to allow trimming option based on the displayed view.

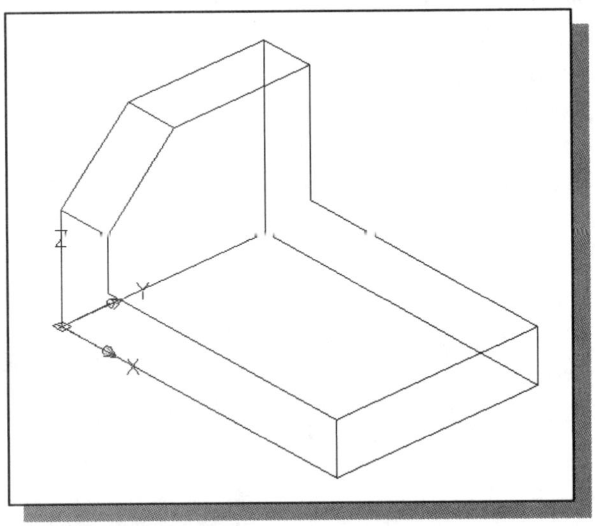

6. The message "*Select object to trim or shift-select object to extend or [Project/Edge/Undo]:*" is displayed in the command prompt area. Pick the portions of the entities to be trimmed so that the model appears as shown.

❖ Note that in AutoCAD 2009, the default AutoCAD trim projection setting is set to **UCS**, which allows us to trim objects that are perpendicular to the **UCS plane**.

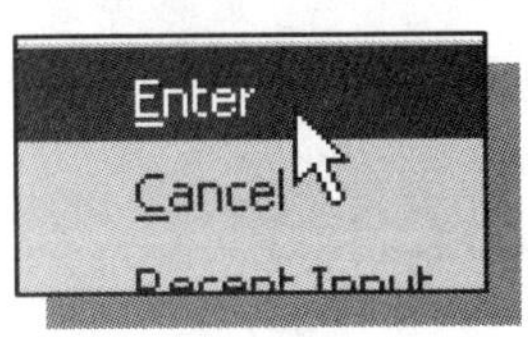

7. Inside the graphics window, right-mouse-click to bring up the option menu and select **Enter** to end the Trim command.

8. On your own, use the Line command to complete the inside corner of the wireframe model as shown.

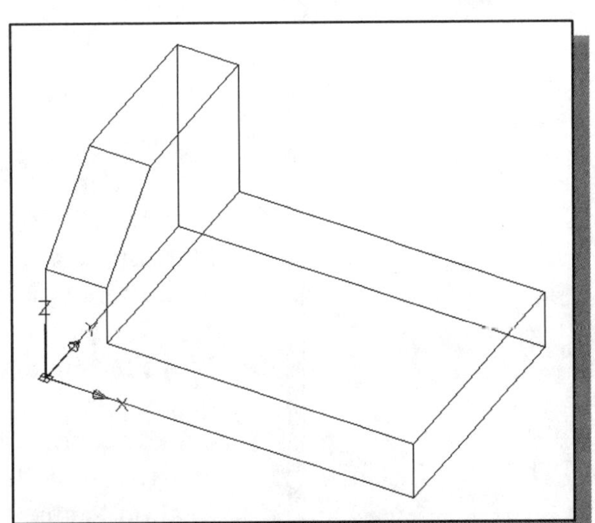

Using the View Toolbar

1. Move the cursor on any icon in the *Standard* toolbar area and **right-mouse-click** once to display a list of options. Select **Toolbars → AutoCAD**.

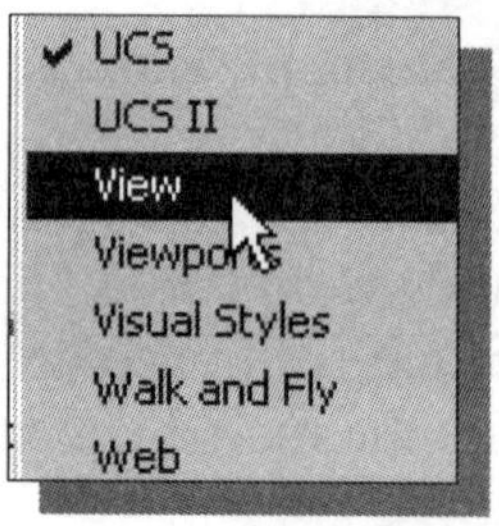

2. Select **View**, with the left-mouse-button, to display the *View* toolbar on the screen.

➢ The *View* toolbar contains two sections of icons that allow us to quickly switch to standard 2D and 3D views.

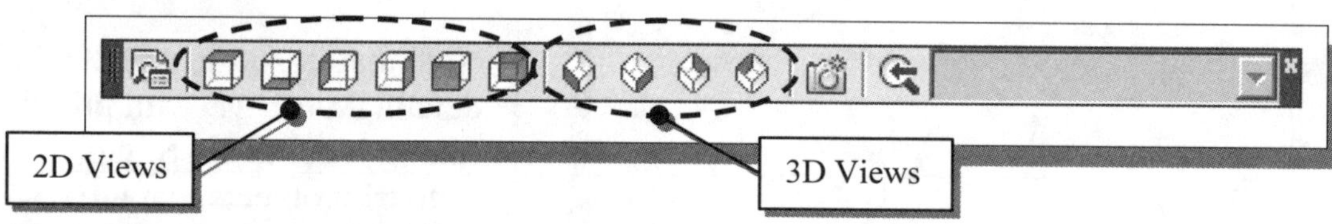

Dynamic Rotation – Free Orbit

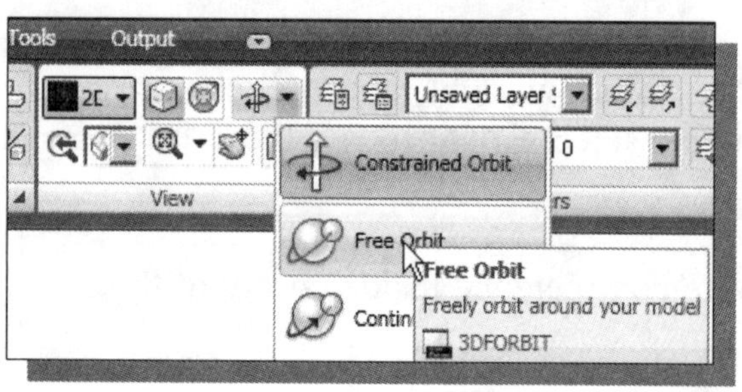

1. Select **Free Orbit** in the *View Toolbar panel.*
   [Orbit] → [Free Orbit]

❖ The Free Orbit view displays an ***arcball***, which enables us to manipulate the view of 3D objects by clicking and dragging with the left-mouse-button.

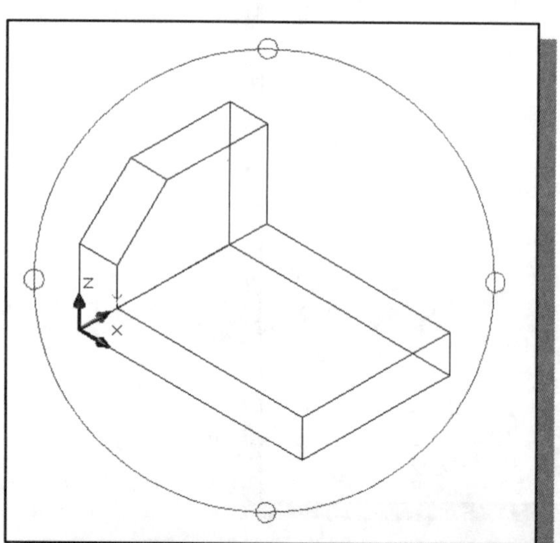

2. Inside the *arcball*, press down the left-mouse-button and drag it up and down to rotate about the screen X-axis. Dragging the mouse left and right will rotate about the screen Y-axis.

3. Move the cursor to different locations on the screen, outside the *arcball* or on one of the four small circles, and experiment with the real-time dynamic rotation feature of the Free Orbit command.

Using the *Offset* Command to Create Parallel Edges

❖ The AutoCAD **Offset** option can also be used to create edges that are at specific distances to existing 3D wireframe edges. Prior to creating the parallel edges, we will first convert one of the polylines to individual line segments.

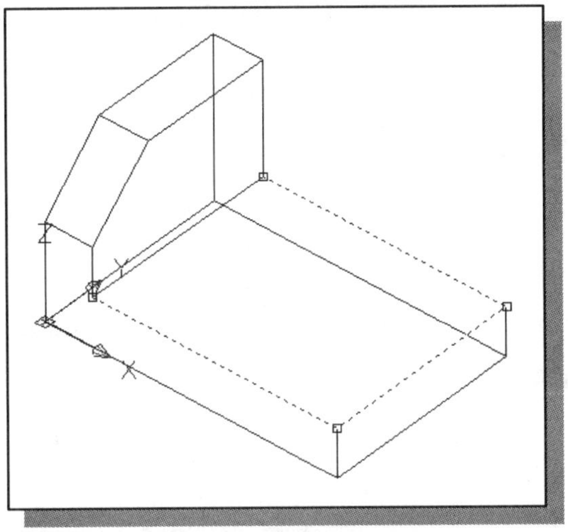

1. Pick the top right edge of the wireframe model.

- **AutoCAD® 2009** provides a flexible graphical user interface that allows users to select graphical entities BEFORE the command is selected (*Pre-selection*), or AFTER the command is selected (*Post-selection*). The polyline we have pre-selected consists of three line-segments.

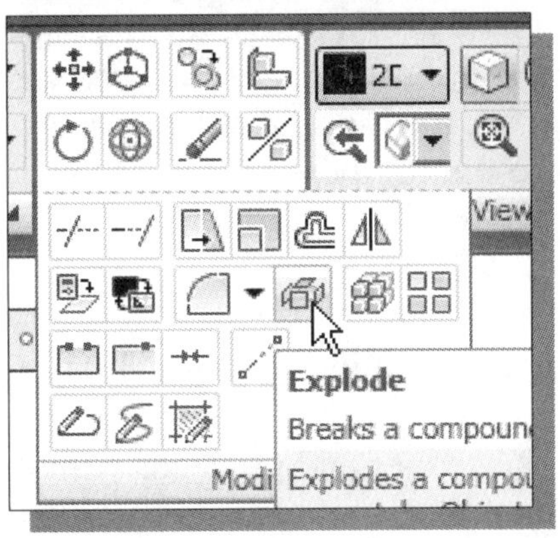

2. Select the **Explode** command icon in the *Modify* toolbar as shown.

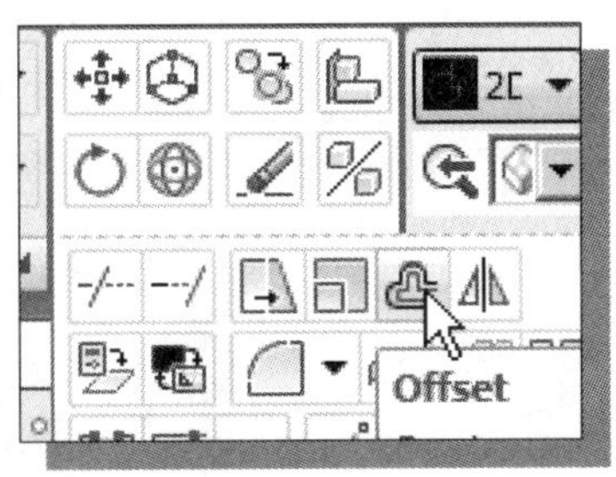

3. Pick **Offset** in the *Modify* toolbar as shown.

4. In the command prompt area, the message "*Specify offset distance or [Through] <Through>:*" is displayed.
   Enter: **0.5 [ENTER]**

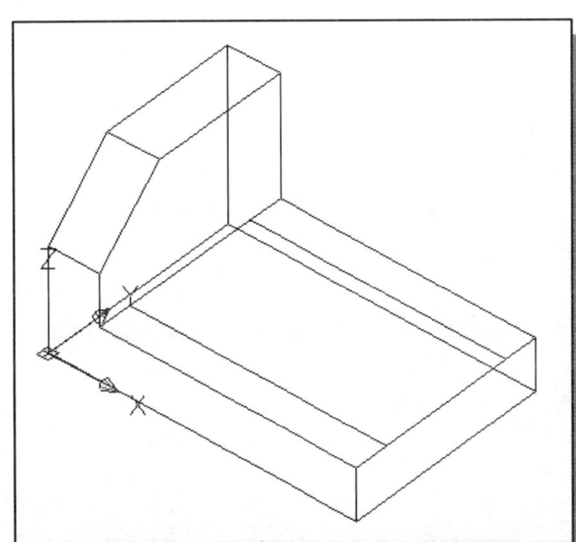

5. Select the front line segment of the polyline we just exploded.

6. In the command prompt area, the message "*Specify point on side to offset:*" is displayed. Pick a location that is above the line to create the first parallel line.

7. Select the back line segment of the polyline we exploded and create another parallel line as shown.

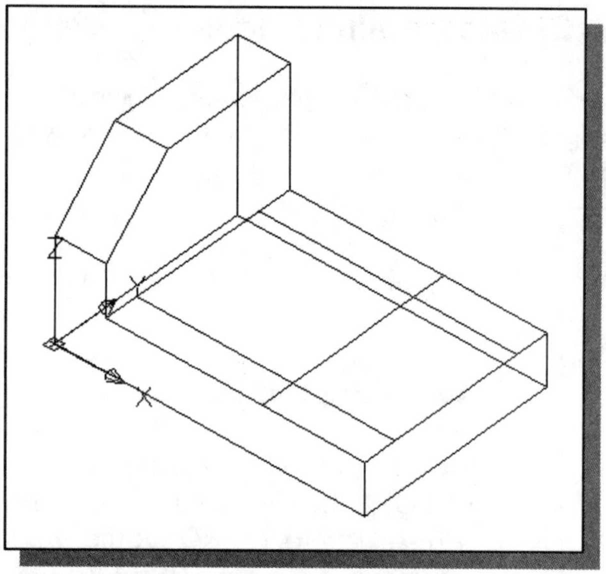

8. On your own, repeat the above steps and create another parallel line (distance: **1.5**) as shown.

- In creating parallel edges, the **Offset** command can be viewed as an alternative to the **Copy** command. In 3D wireframe modeling, the focus is on identifying the edges and corners of the model. Most of the 2D construction tools are also applicable in 3D environment.

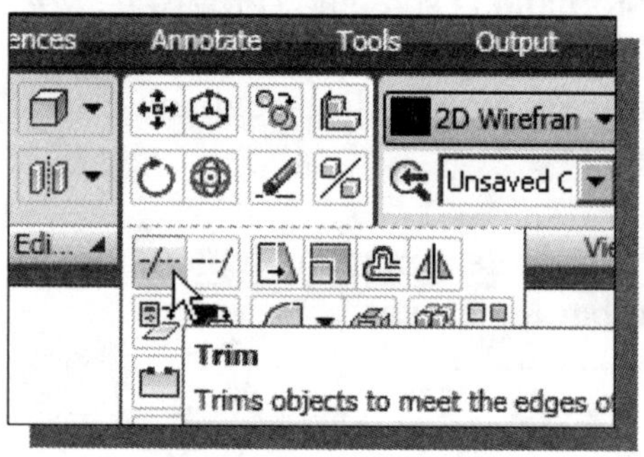

9. Select the **Trim** command icon in the *Modify* toolbar.

10. In the command prompt area, the message "*Select boundary edges... Select objects:*" is displayed. Pick the highlighted edges as shown in the figure; these edges are the *boundary edges*.

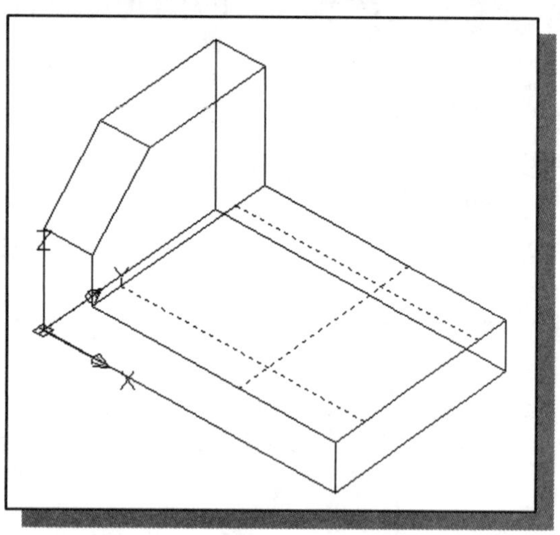

11. Inside the graphics window, right-mouse-click to accept the selection of boundary edges and proceeds with the **Trim** command.

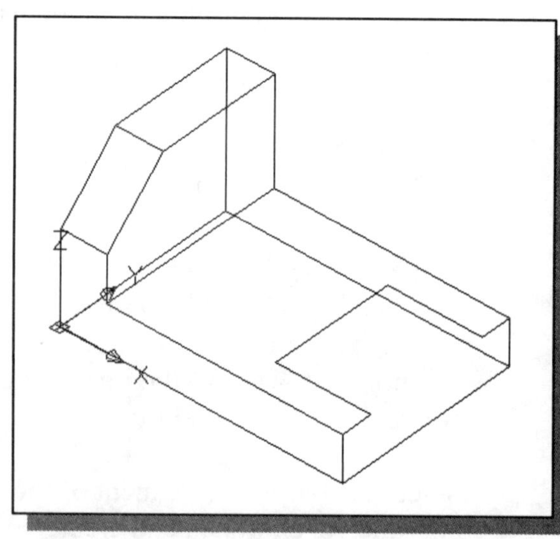

12. On your own, trim the line segments so that the wireframe model appears as shown.

Creating a Circle Above the UCS Sketch Plane

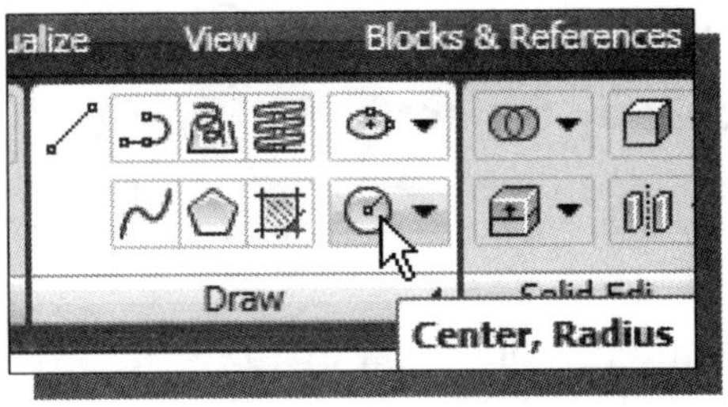

1. Select the **Circle** command icon in the *Draw* toolbar.

- By default, the XY plane of the UCS defines the sketching plane for constructing 2D geometric entities.

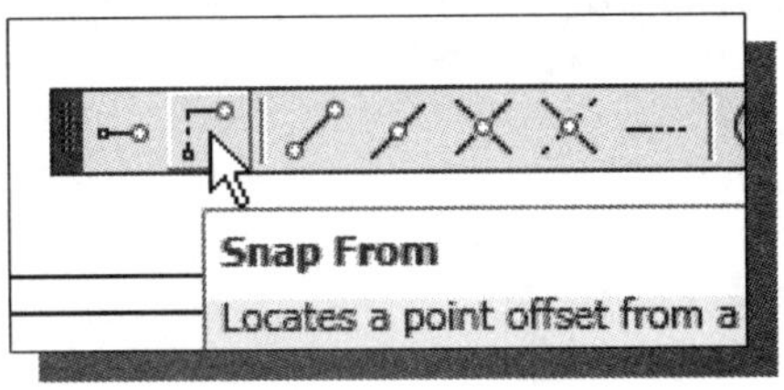

2. In the command prompt area, the message "*_circle Specify center point for circle or[3P/2P/Ttr (tan tan radius)]:*" is displayed. Select **Snap From** in the *Object Snap* toolbar.

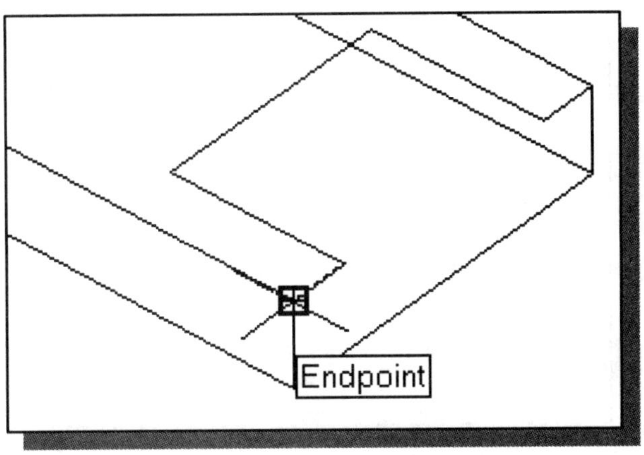

3. Select the **top right corner** as the reference point as shown.

4. In the command prompt area, the message "*Specify next point or [Close/Undo]:_from Base point <Offset>:*" is displayed.

   Command: **@-2.67,1.5 [ENTER]**

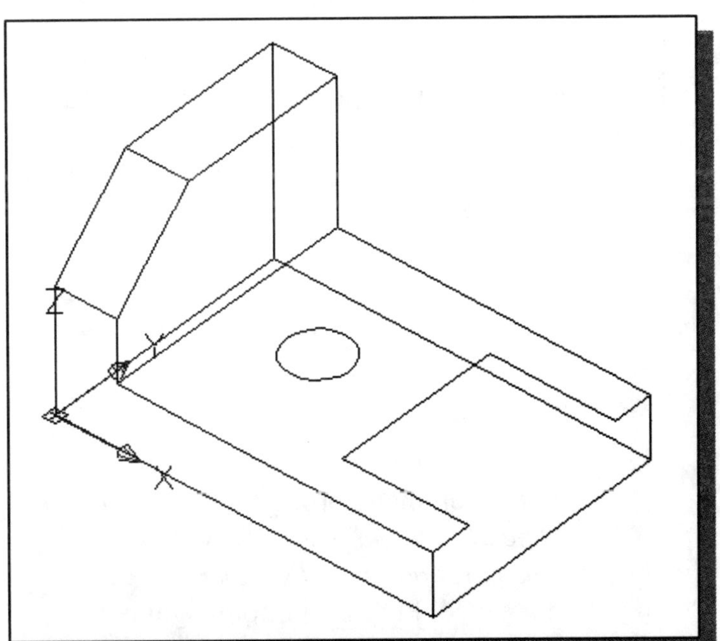

5. In the command prompt area, the message "*Specify radius of circle or [Diameter]:*" is displayed.

   Command: **0.375 [ENTER]**

- The circle is created above the sketching plane with the **Snap From** option.

Completing the Wireframe Model

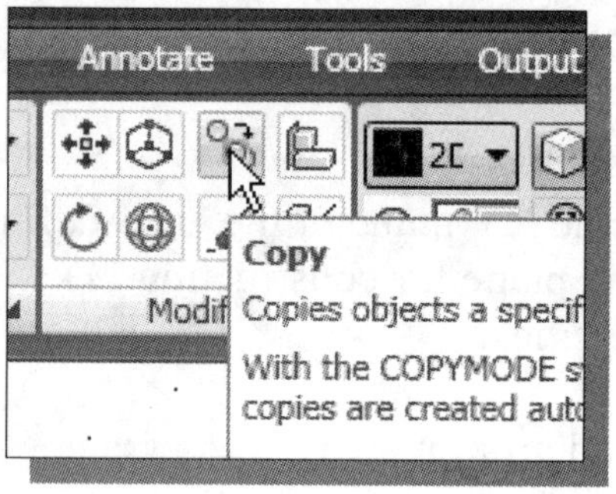

1. Click on the **Copy Object** icon in the *Modify* toolbar.

2. In the command prompt area, the message "*Select objects:*" is displayed. Pick the edges and the circle as shown in the figure.

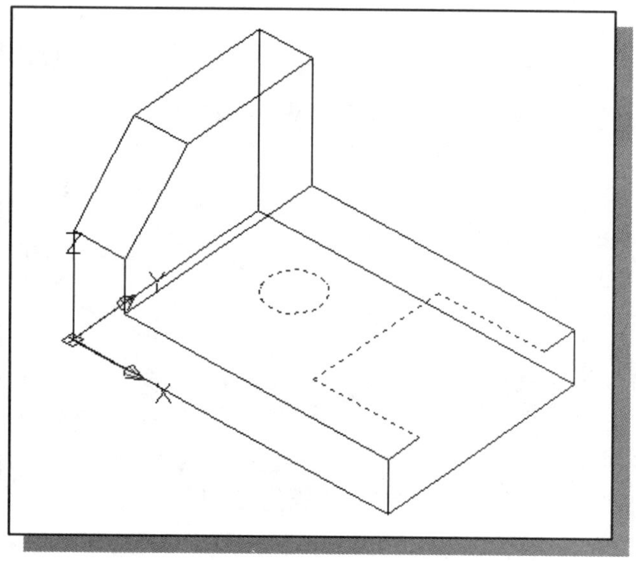

3. Inside the graphics window, right-mouse-click once to accept the selection.

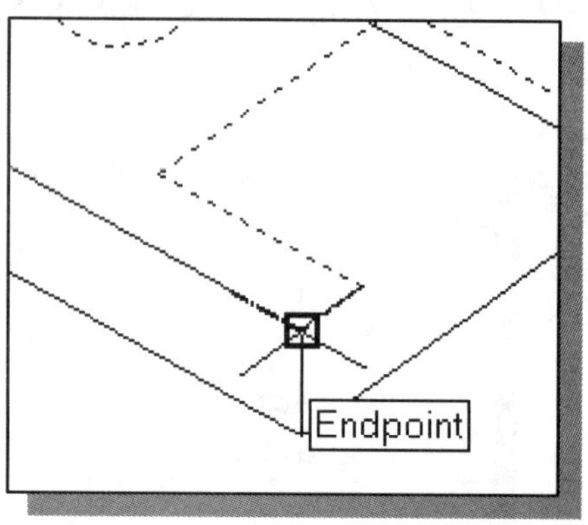

4. In the command prompt area, the message "*Specify base point or displacement, or [Multiple]:*" is displayed. Pick the front right corner as shown.

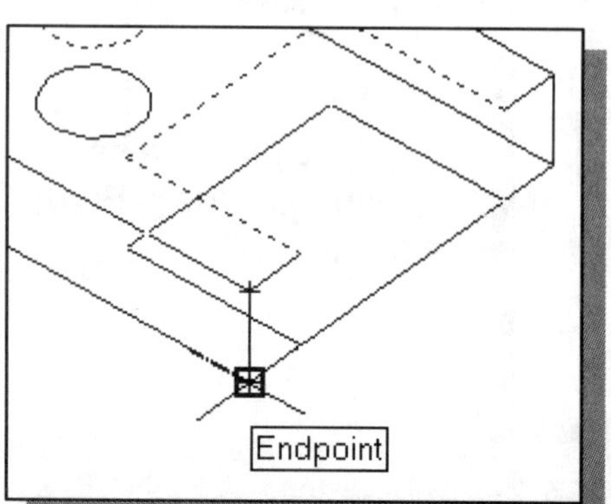

5. In the command prompt area, the message "*Specify second point of displacement or <use first point as displacement>:*" is displayed. Pick the bottom-right corner as shown.

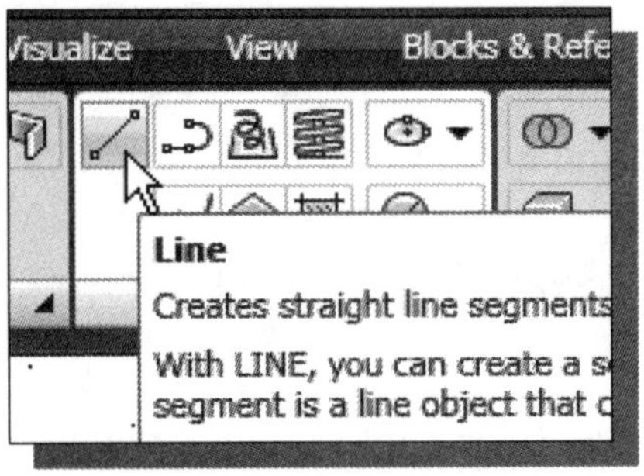

6. Select the **Line** icon in the *Draw* toolbar.

7. On your own, create the lines connecting the corners of the created edges as shown in the below figure.

8. Use the **Snap to Quadrant** option to create edges in between the two circles.

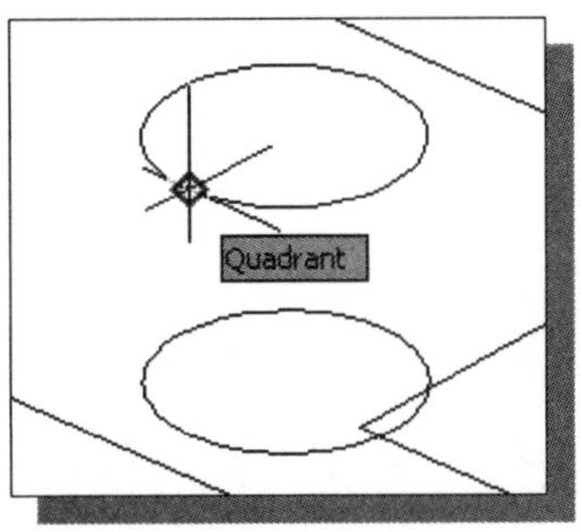

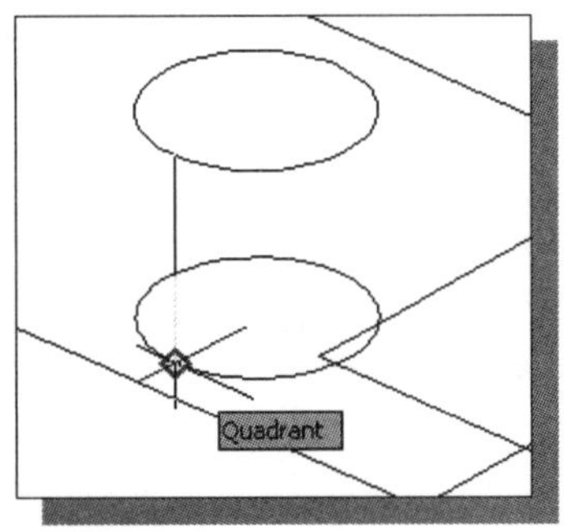

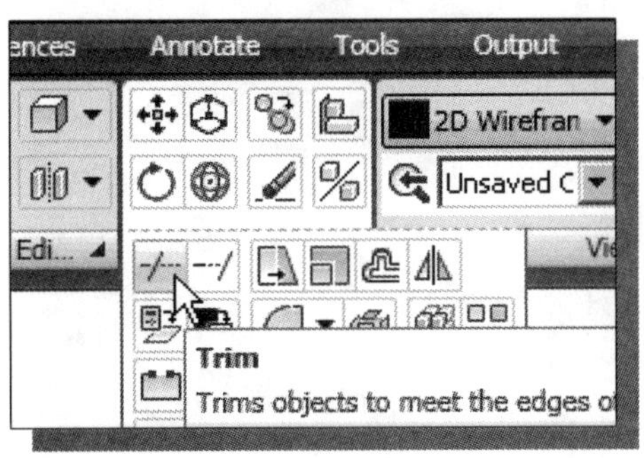

9. Select the **Trim** command icon in the *Modify* toolbar.

10. On your own, trim the center portion of the bottom right edge and complete the wireframe model as shown.

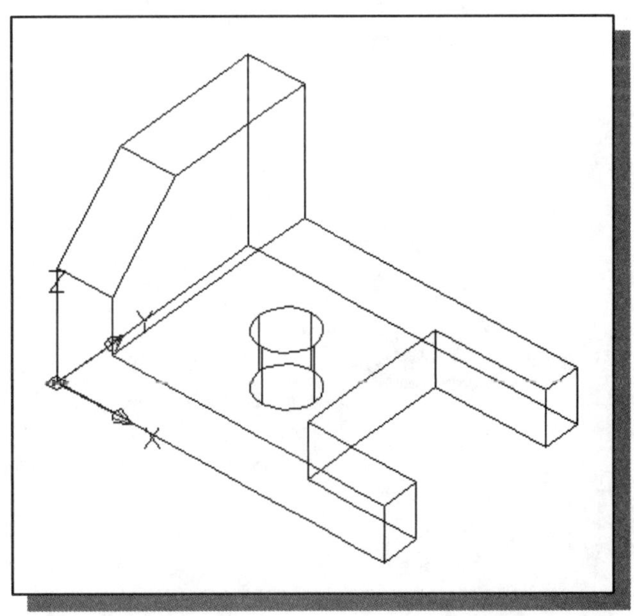

❖ On your own, save the ***Locator*** design (Locator.dwg), this model will be used again in the Surface Modeling Chapter.

Questions:

1. Describe some of the control options available with the **Free Orbit** command.

2. List and describe two different methods to create 3D edges from existing 3D edges in **AutoCAD® 2009**.

3. How many of the UCS options were used to create the 3D model in this chapter and how many were used to create the model in the previous chapter?

4. When and why would you use the **Trim-Project-View** option?

5. Identify the following commands:

(a)

(b)

(c)

(d)

Exercises: All dimensions are in inches.

1.

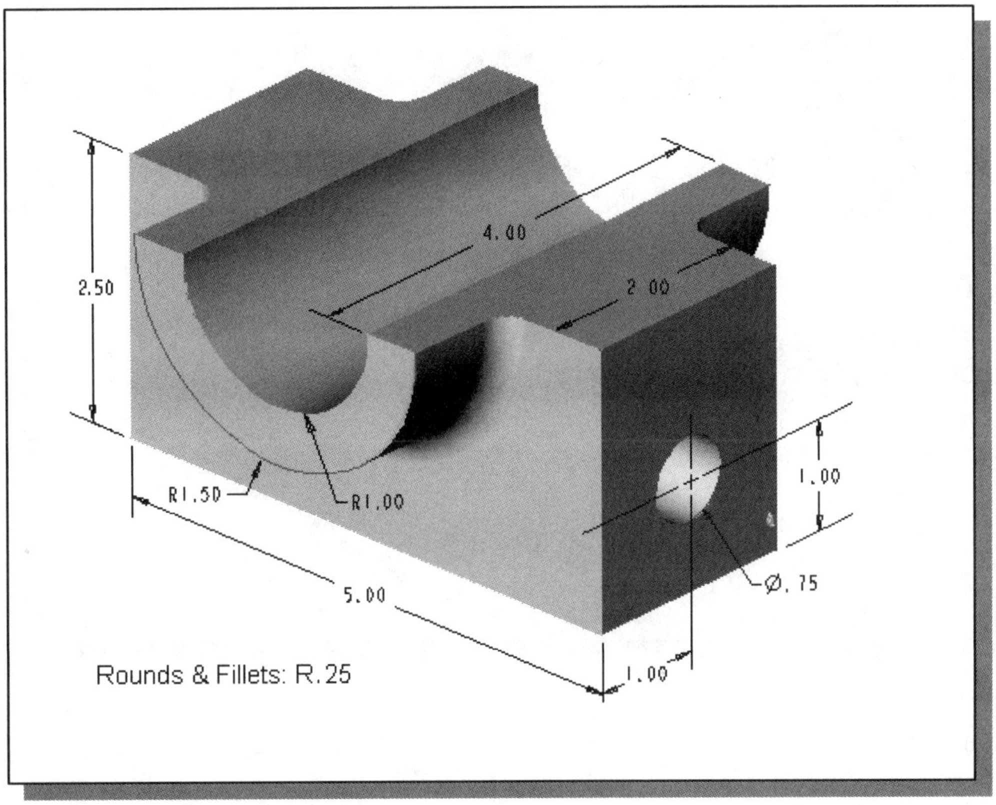

2.

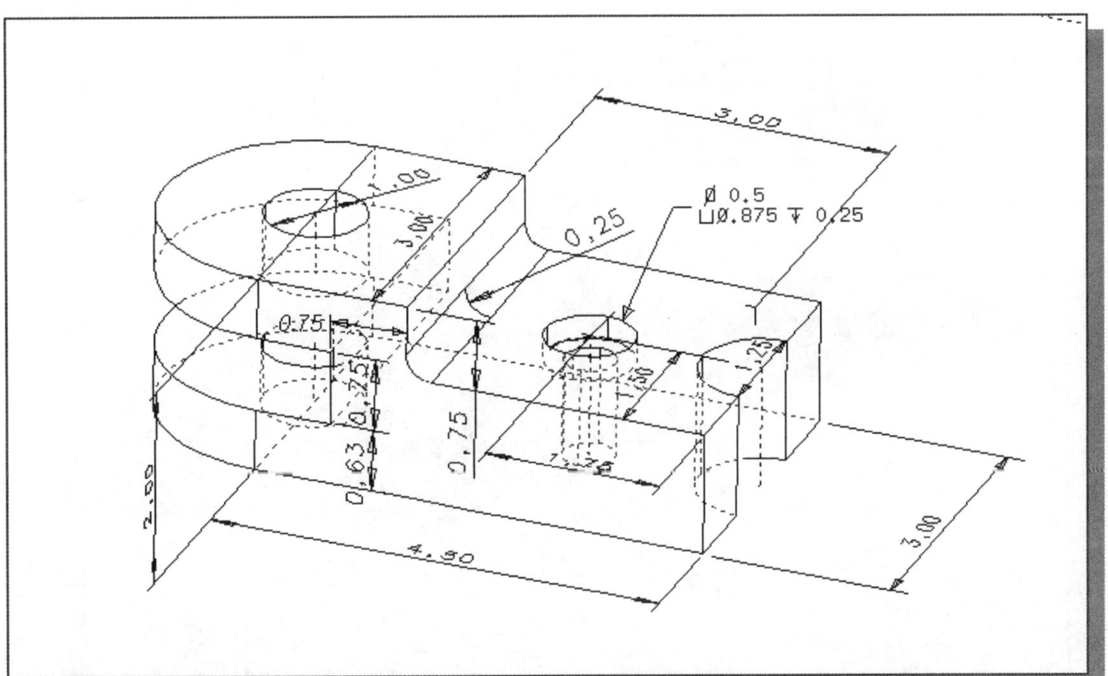

3.

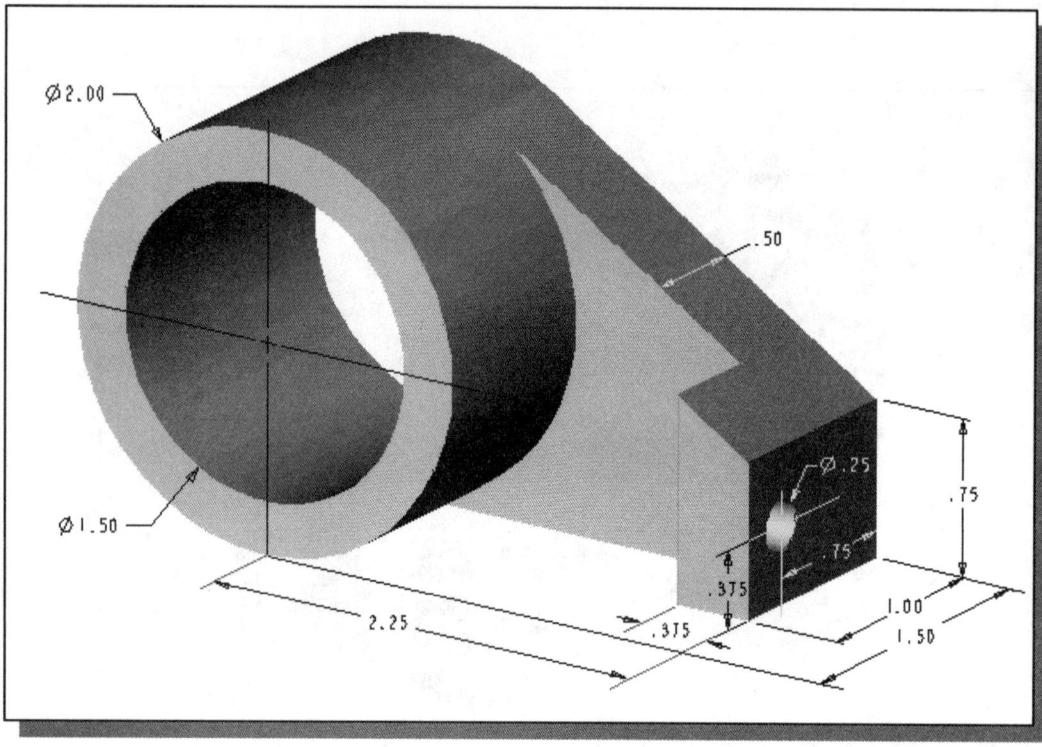
Ø2.00
.50
Ø.25
.75
Ø1.50
.75
.375
1.00
2.25
.375
1.50

4.

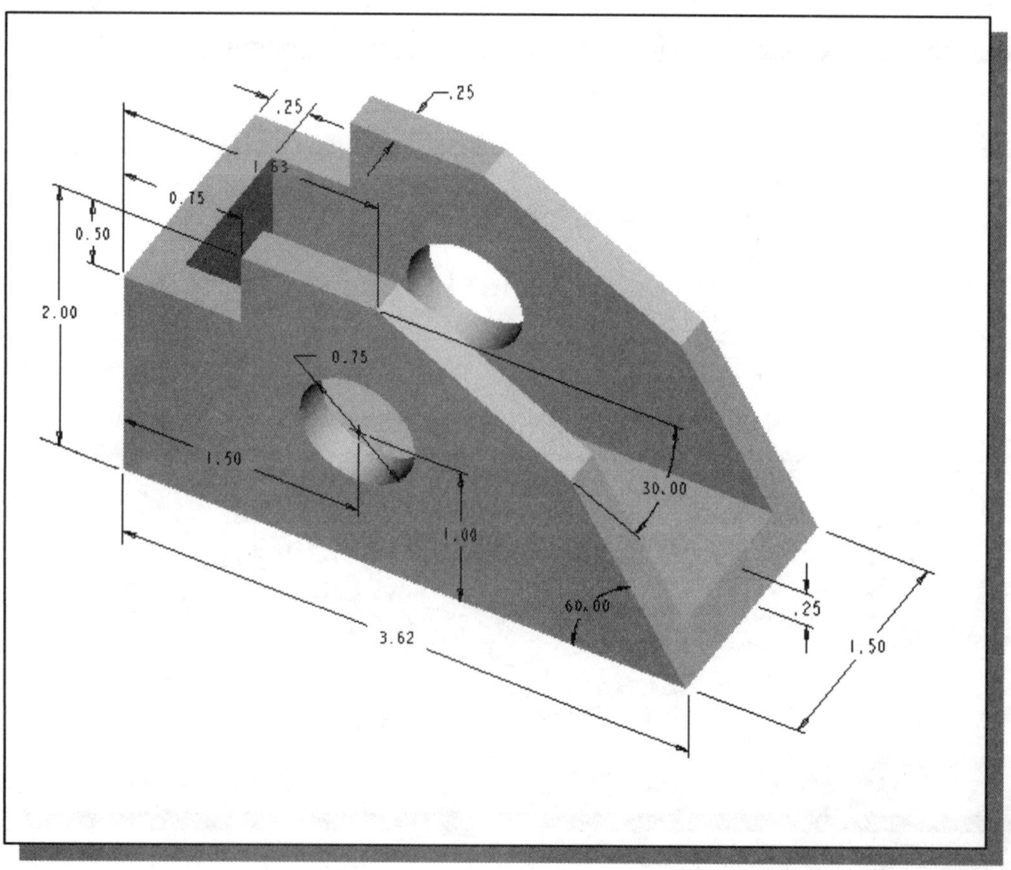
.25
.25
1.63
0.75
0.50
2.00
0.75
1.50
30.00
1.00
60.00
.25
3.62
1.50

Chapter 4
UCS, Viewports and Wireframe Modeling

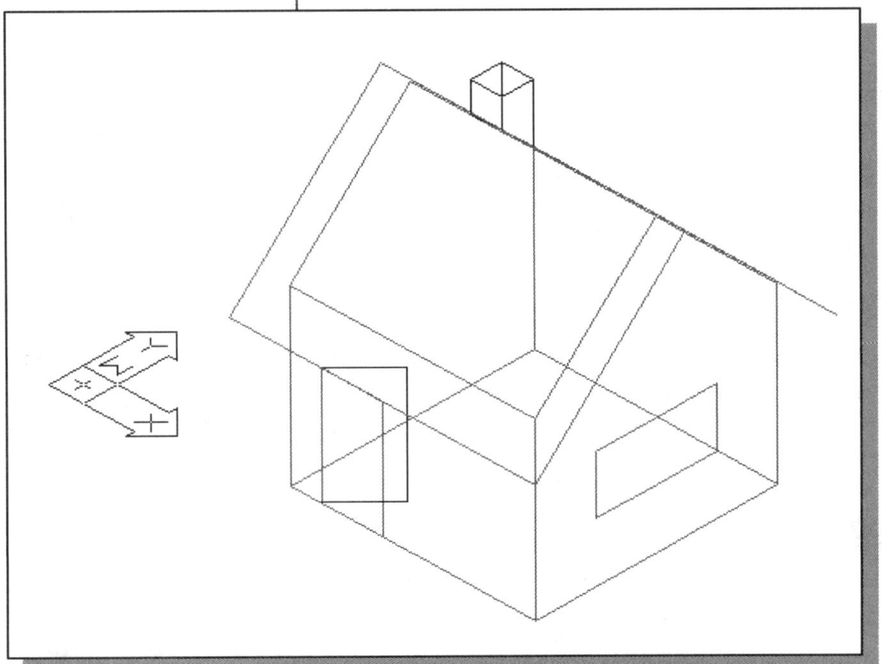

Learning Objectives

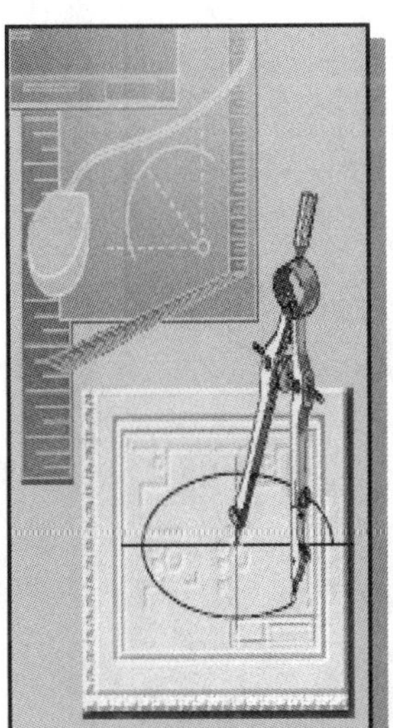

- ♦ **Understand the Use of UCS on More Complex Designs**
- ♦ **Display and Orient 3D Views**
- ♦ **Apply and Expand the Basic Wireframe Construction Techniques**
- ♦ **Using Additional Tools to Assist the Creation of 3D Wireframe Models**
- ♦ **Use the Named Views Option**

Introduction

In the previous chapter, we examined some of the basic techniques to create 3D wireframe models. Again, a wireframe model is a skeletal description of a 3D object. There are no surfaces in a wireframe model; it consists only of points, lines, and curves that describe the edges of the object.

In this chapter, we will further discuss the techniques and wireframe modeling tools available in AutoCAD. Instead of creating the corners and edges of wireframe models by entering the precise 3D coordinates, the use of construction lines and referencing techniques are illustrated. The construction of edges in 3D space can be simplified by using the AutoCAD User Coordinate System. We will also use the multiple viewports option, which is available in most CAD systems, to aid the construction of 3D wireframe models.

It is important to point out that most of the construction tools used in creating 2D designs, such as *Object Snap* and *Polar Tracking*, as well as the Copy, Mirror and Array commands, are also applicable to the constructions of 3D wireframe models.

The *V-Block* Design

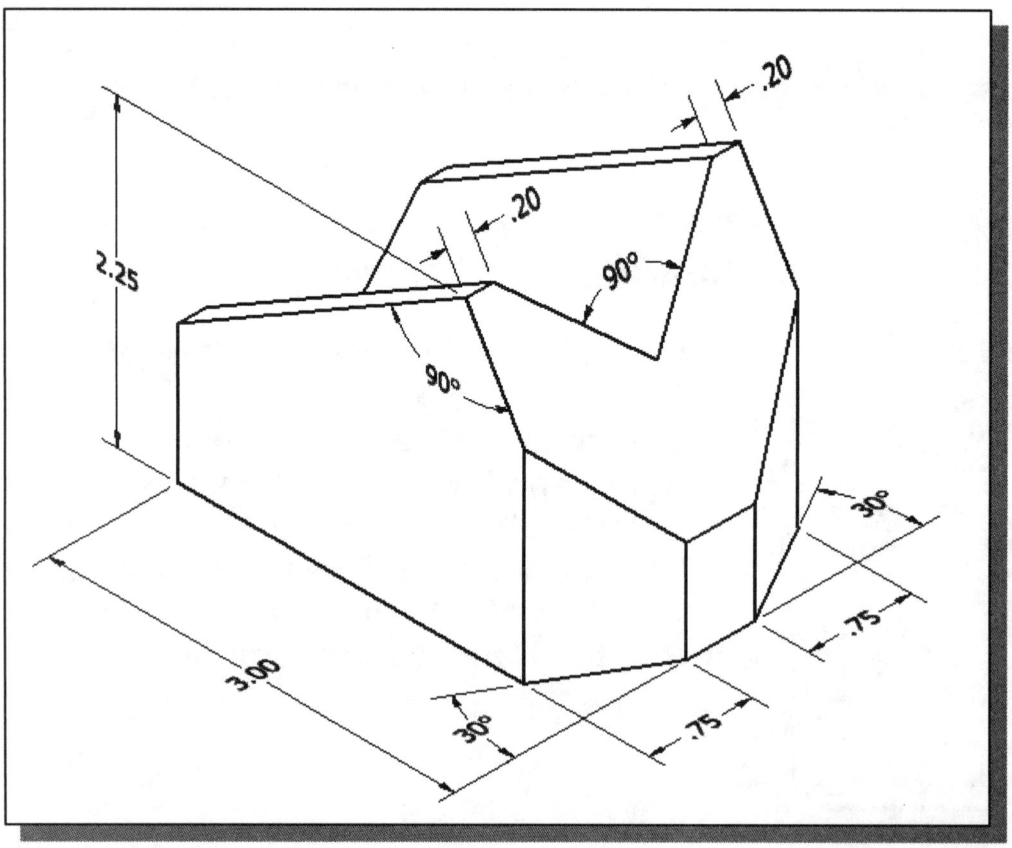

Starting Up AutoCAD® 2009

1. Select the **AutoCAD 2009** option on the *Program* menu or select the **AutoCAD 2009** icon on the *Desktop*.

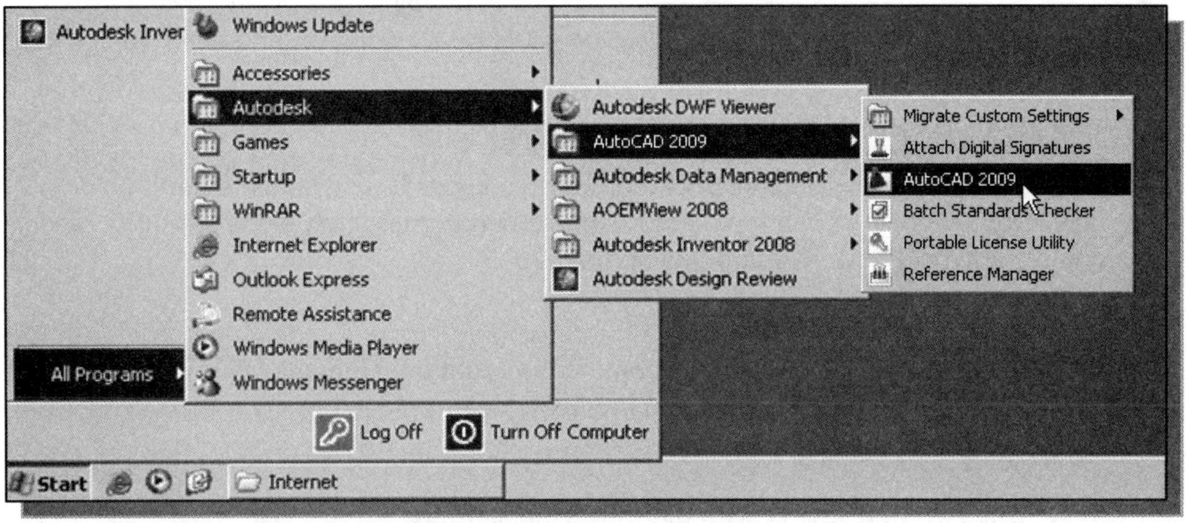

2. In the startup window, select **Start from Scratch**, as shown in the figure below.

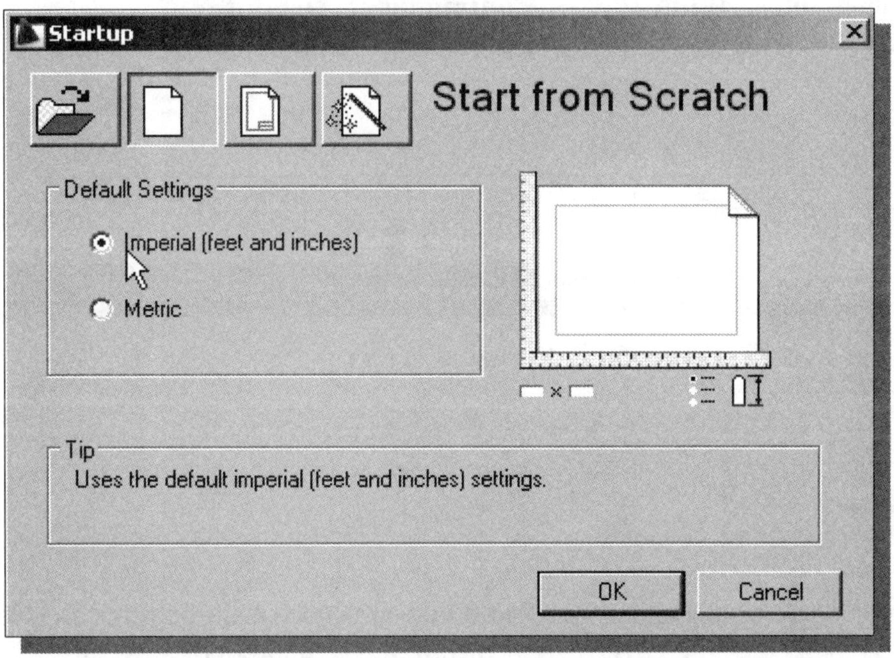

3. In the *Default Settings* section, pick **Imperial (feet and inches)** as the drawing units.

4. Pick **OK** in the startup dialog box to accept the selected settings.

Layers Setup

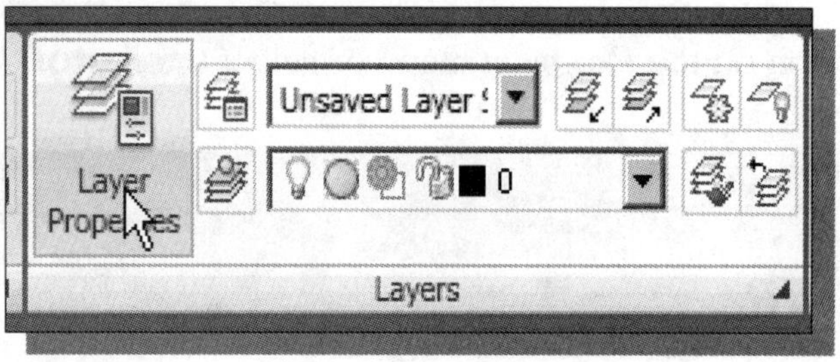

1. Click **Layers Properties Manager** in the *Layers* toolbar.

❖ In AutoCAD, we always construct entities on a layer. It may be the default layer or a layer that we create. Each layer has associated properties such as the visibility setting, color, linetype, lineweight and plot style.

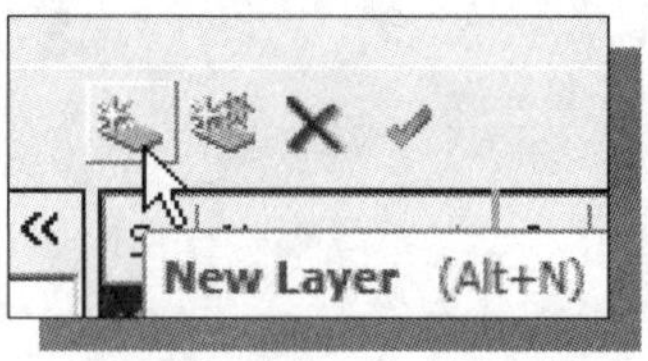

2. Click on the **New** button. Notice a layer is automatically added to the list of layers.

3. Create **two new layers** with the following settings:

Layer	*Color*	*LineType*	*LineWeight*
Construction	**White**	**Continuous**	**Default**
Object	**Cyan**	**Continuous**	**0.30mm**

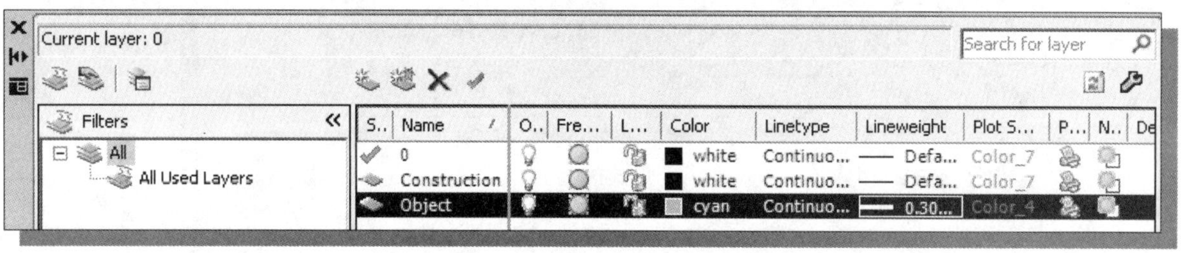

4. Highlight the layer *Construction* in the list of layers.

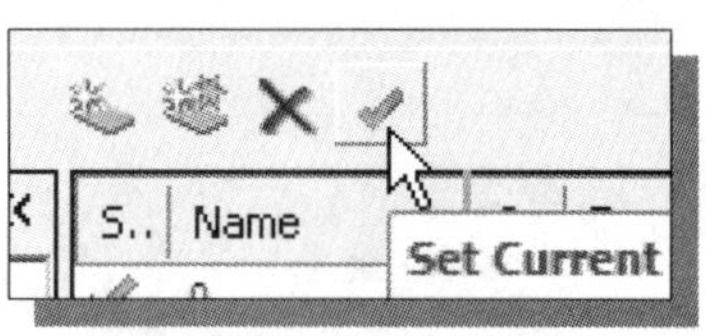

5. Click on the **Current** icon to set layer *Construction* as the *Current Layer*.

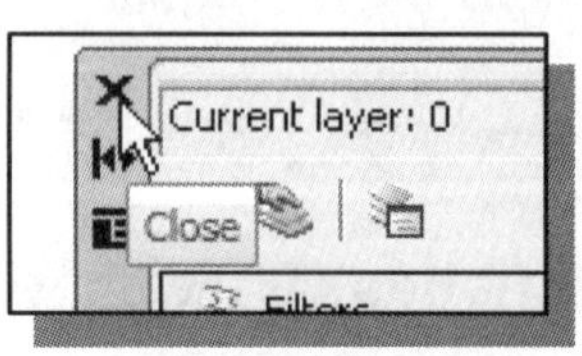

6. Click on the **Close** button to accept the settings and exit the *Layer Properties Manager* dialog box.

7. In the *Status Bar* area, reset the options and turn ***ON*** the *Grid, Polar, Object Snap, Object Snap Tracking, Dynamic Input* and *Line Weight* options.

This package includes

AutoCAD 2009 Tutorial – Second Level: 3D Modeling

bundled with

AutoCAD 2009 Student Version Software

180-day license

The AutoCAD 2009 Student Version Software is visible on the front of this book.

DO NOT PURCHASE if you do not see the software!!

The **Autodesk Student Version** software enclosed is for purchase by students and faculty for personal use for education purposes and is not for professional use or for use by an institution for classroom instruction. The **Autodesk Student Version** includes a 180-day term learning license for use in the US or Canada only.

AutoCAD Student Version System Requirements:

For 32-bit AutoCAD 2009:

- Intel® Pentium® 4 processor or AMD Athlon®, 2.2 GHz or greater
  or
  intel or AMD Dual Core processor, 1.6 Ghz or greater
- Microsoft® Windows® Vista, Windows XP SP2 operating systems

For Microsoft Windows XP SP2:

- 1 GB RAM
- 750 MB free disk space for installation
- 1024 x 768 VGA display with true color
- Microsoft® Internet Explorer® 6.0 (SP1 or higher)

For Microsoft Windows Vista or 3D modeling:

- Intel® Pentium® 4 processor or AMD Athlon®, 3.0 GHz or greater
  or
  intel or AMD Dual Core processor, 2.0 Ghz or greater
- 2 GB RAM or greater
- 2 GB free hard disk space available (not including installation)
- 1280 x 1024 VGA 32-bit color vide display adapter (true color) 128 MB or greater,
- OpenGL or Direct 3D capable workstation class graphics card.

***For Windows Vista**, a Direct 3D capable workstation class graphics card with 128 MB or greater is required.*

INSTALLATION SUPPORT: If you encounter any problems installing the Autodesk Student Version software, you will find solutions in the Support Knowledge Base at http://www.autodesk.com.

SDC
PUBLICATIONS

Offering a wide variety of

CAD, FEA and Engineering Graphics Books

ISBN 978-1-58503-442-0

9 781585 034420

Schroff Development Corporation
www.schroff.com

Better Textbooks. Lower Prices.

Creating the Rectangular Base of the Design

➢ We will first use construction geometry to define the outer edges of the design.

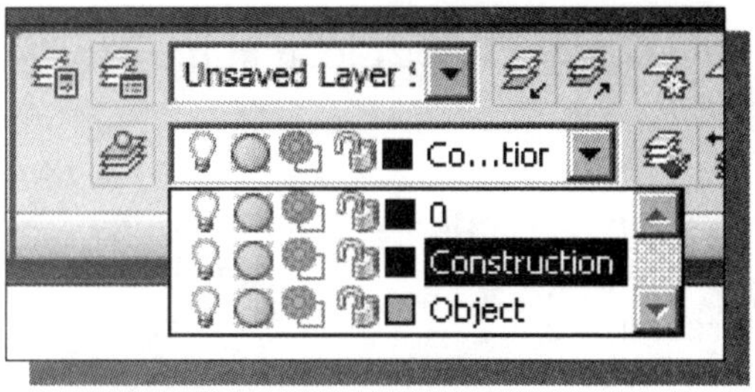

1. In the *Layer Control* box, confirm that layer *Construction* is set as the *Current Layer*.

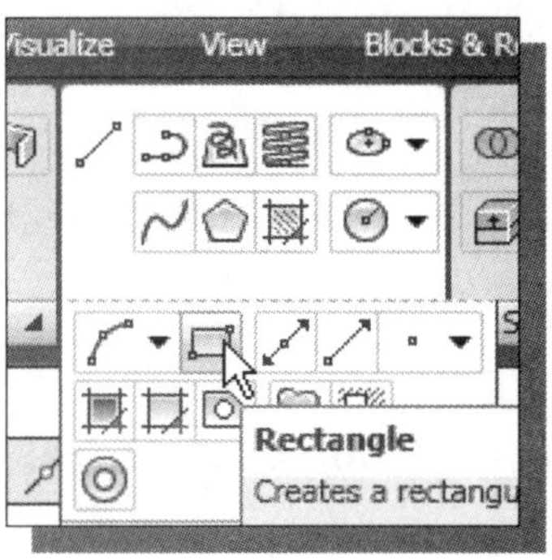

2. Select the **Rectangle** icon in the *Draw* toolbar. In the command prompt area, the message "*Specify first corner point or [Chamfer/Elevation/Fillet/Thickness/Width]:*" is displayed.

3. Place the first corner point of the rectangle near the lower left corner of the screen. Do not be overly concerned about the actual coordinates of the location; the drawing space is as big as you can imagine.

4. We will create a 3″ × 2″ rectangle by entering the coordinates of the second corner using the relative coordinates input method.
   Specify other corner point or [Dimension]: **@3,2 [ENTER]**

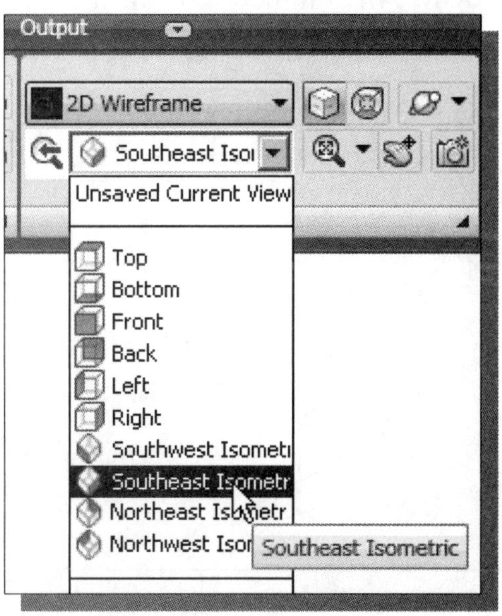

5. In the *View* toolbar, select:
   [View] → [SouthEast Isometric]

- Notice the orientation of the sketched 2D rectangle in relation to the displayed AutoCAD user coordinate system. By default, the 2D sketch-plane is aligned to the XY plane of the world coordinate system.

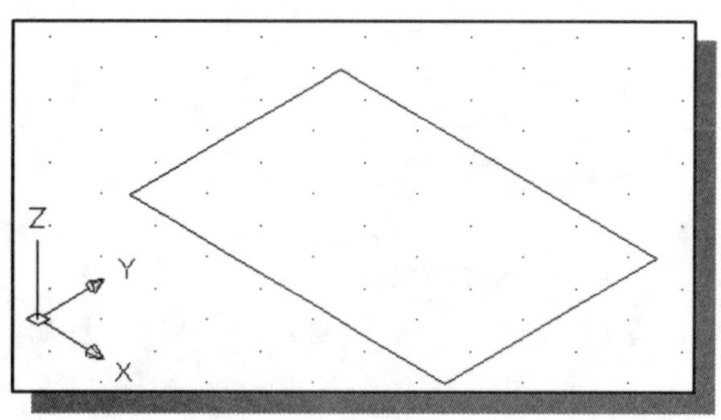

Creating a Wireframe Box

- Next, we will use the Copy command to define the 3D boundary of the design.

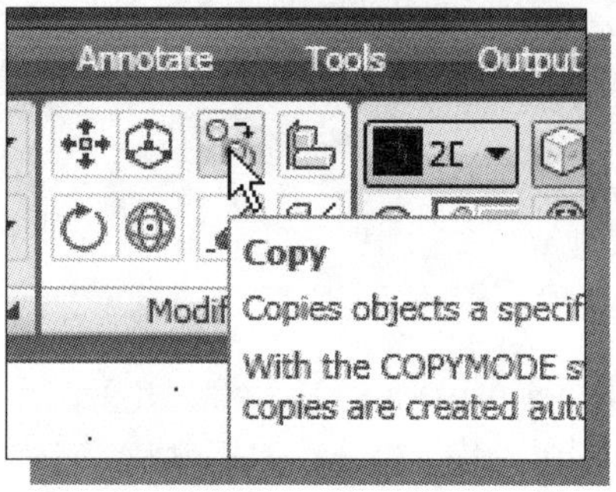

1. Click on the **Copy Object** icon in the *Modify* toolbar.

2. In the command prompt area, the message "*Select objects:*" is displayed. Pick any edge of the sketched rectangle.

3. Inside the graphics window, right-mouse-click once to accept the selection.

4. In the command prompt area, the message "*Specify base point or displacement, or [Multiple]:*" is displayed. Pick any corner of the sketched rectangle as a base point to create the copy.

5. In the command prompt area, the message "*Specify second point of displacement or <use first point as displacement>:*" is displayed.
   Enter: **@0,0,2.25 [ENTER]**

➢ Note that the three values represent the distance measured in the X, Y and Z directions relative to the current UCS.

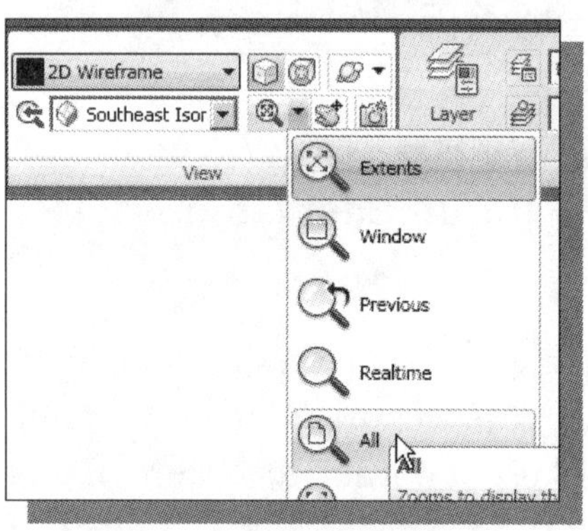

6. Use the **Zoom All** command to adjust the display.

7. On your own, use the Line command to create the four lines connecting the four-corners of the two rectangles as shown.

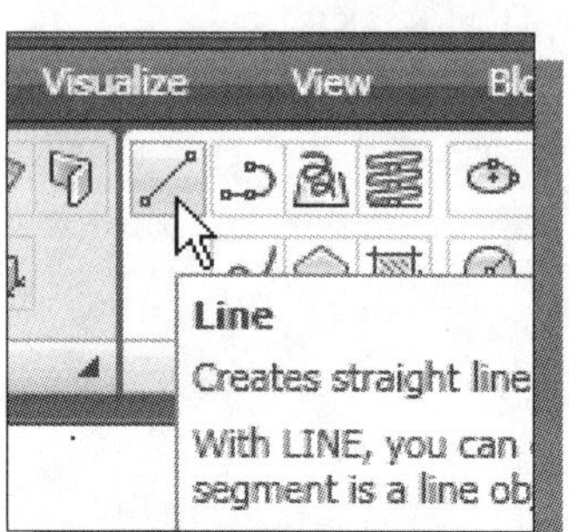

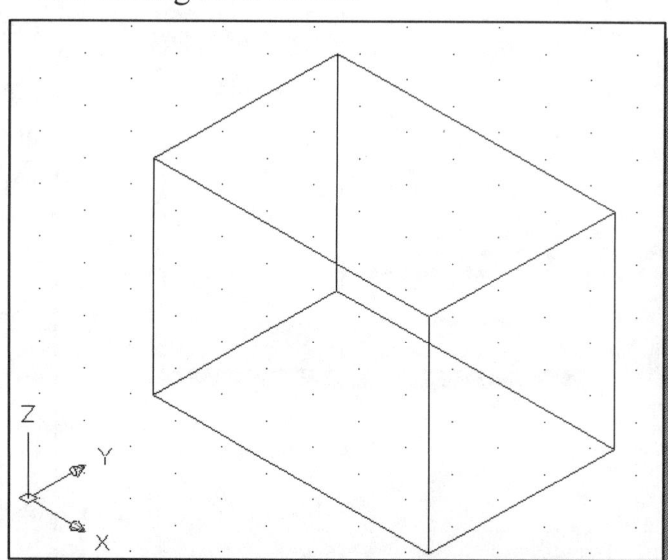

Using the View and the UCS Toolbars

1. Move the cursor on any icon in the *Standard* toolbar area and **right-mouse-click** once to display a list of options. Select **Toolbars → AutoCAD**.

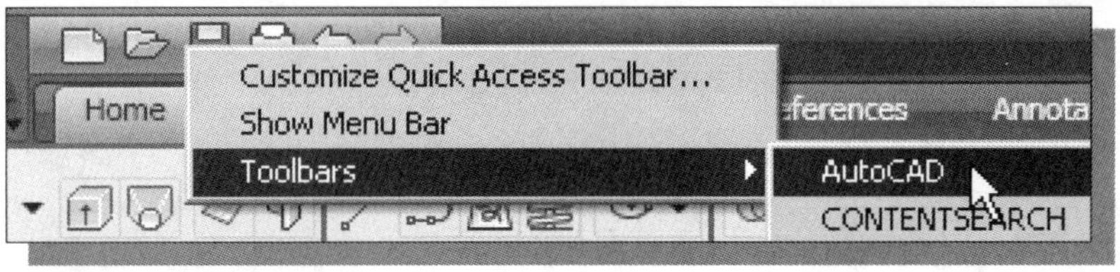

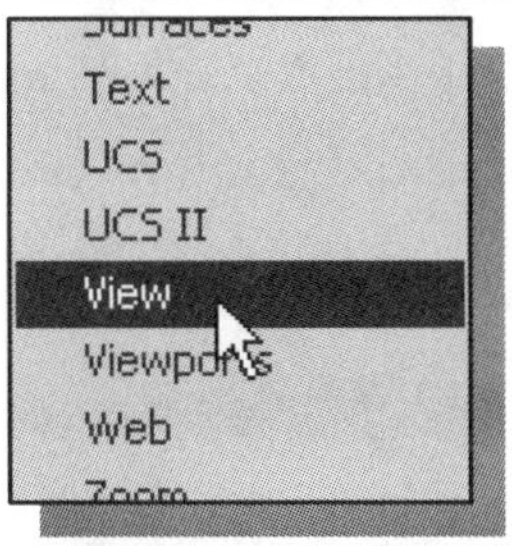

2. Select **View**, with the left-mouse-button, to display the *View* toolbar on the screen.

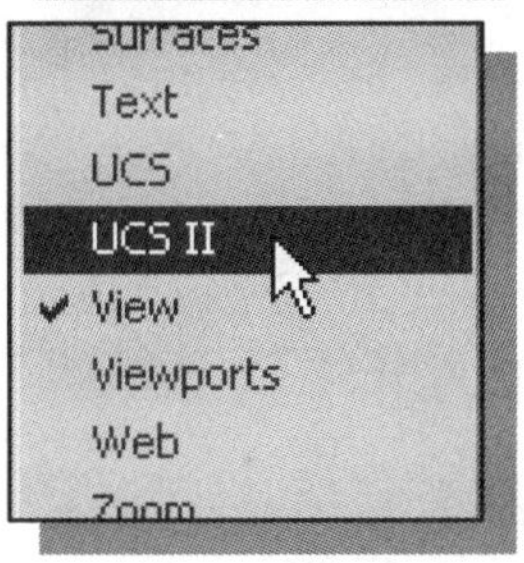

3. Move the cursor to the *Standard* toolbar area and **right-click** on any icon of the *Standard* toolbar to display a list of toolbar menu groups.

4. Select **UCS II**, with the left-mouse-button, to display the *UCSII* toolbar on the screen.

➤ The options available in *UCS II* toolbar allow us quickly align the UCS to the preset standard 2D views.

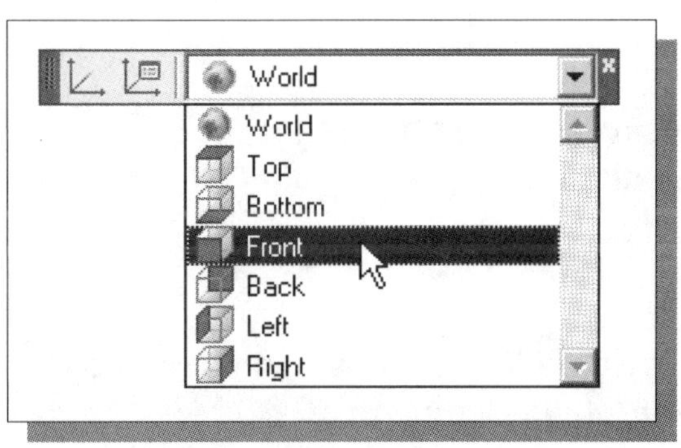

5. Note that the current *UCS* is aligned to the *World Coordinate System*. Select **Front** in the *UCS II* toolbar as shown.

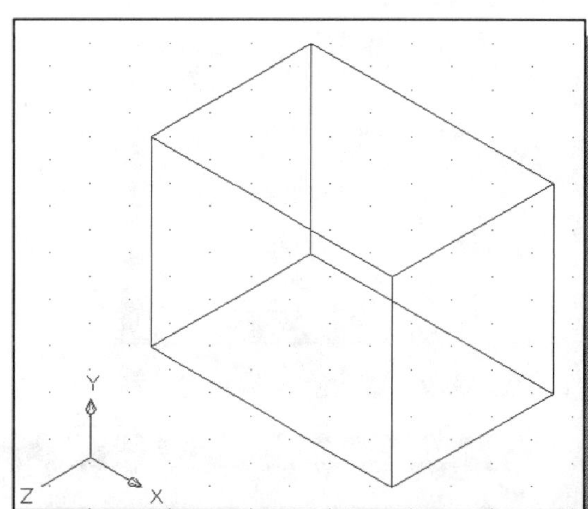

➤ Note that the UCS has been adjusted and it is now aligned parallel to the front view of the wireframe box as shown in the figure.

Creating Construction Lines in the Front View

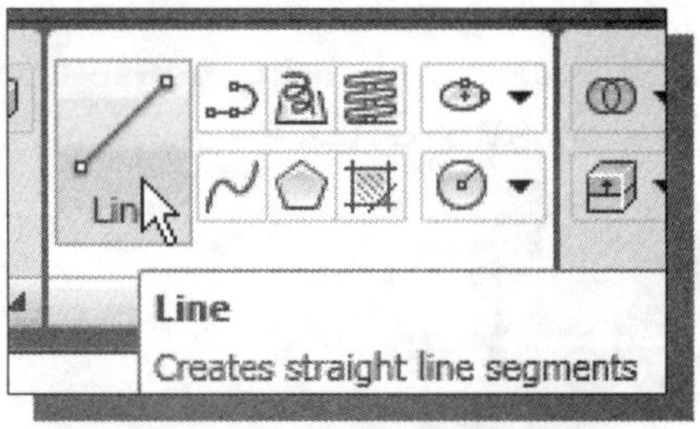

1. Select the **Line** command icon in the *Draw* toolbar. In the command prompt area, the message "*_line Specify first point:*" is displayed.

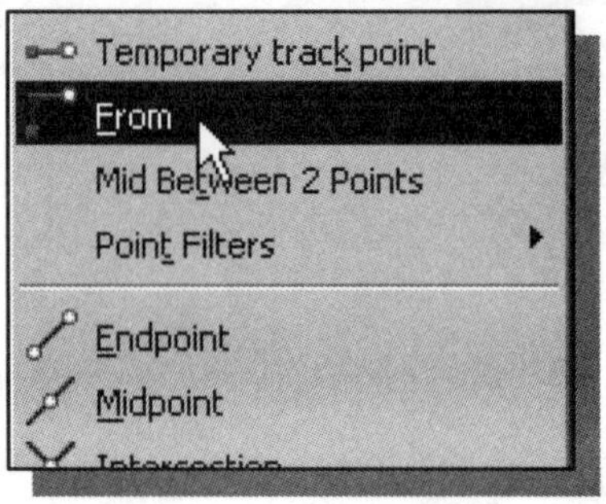

2. Inside the graphics window, hold down the [**SHIFT**] key and **right-mouse-click** once to bring up the *Object Snap* shortcut menu.

3. Select the **From** option in popup window.

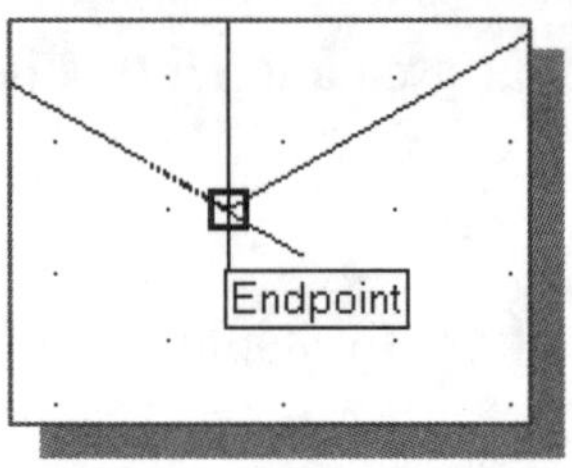

4. Pick the lower right corner of the bottom horizontal line in the front view as the base point.

5. In the command prompt area, the message "*Specify next point or [Undo]:*" is displayed. Enter: **@0,0.75 [ENTER]**

6. We will set up the *Polar Tracking* option to assist the creation of the next corner. **Right-mouse-click** once on the *POLAR* option located at the bottom of the graphics window.

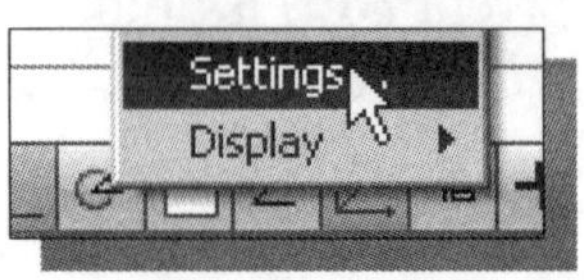

7. In the option menu, select **Settings** by clicking once with the left-mouse-button.

8. In the *Drafting Settings* dialog box, set the *Polar Increment Angle* setting to **30** degrees.

9. Click on the **Object Snap** tab to switch to the *Object Snap* option settings.

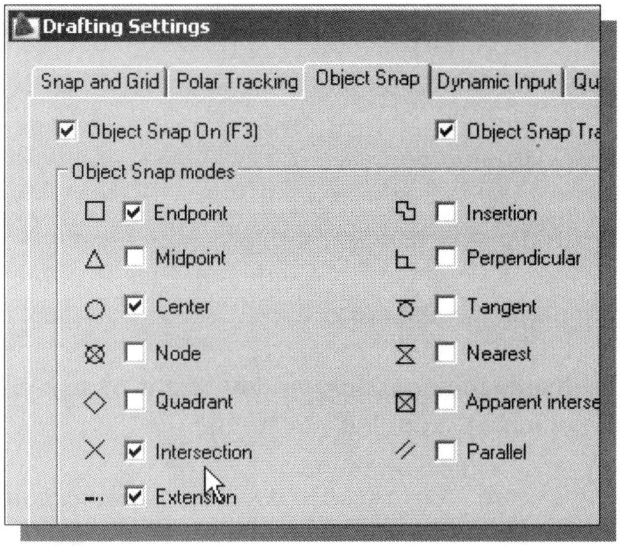

10. Confirm that the *Intersection* and *Extension* options are switched *ON* as shown.

11. Click on the **OK** button to accept the settings.

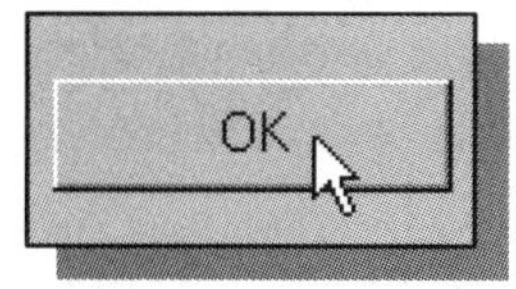

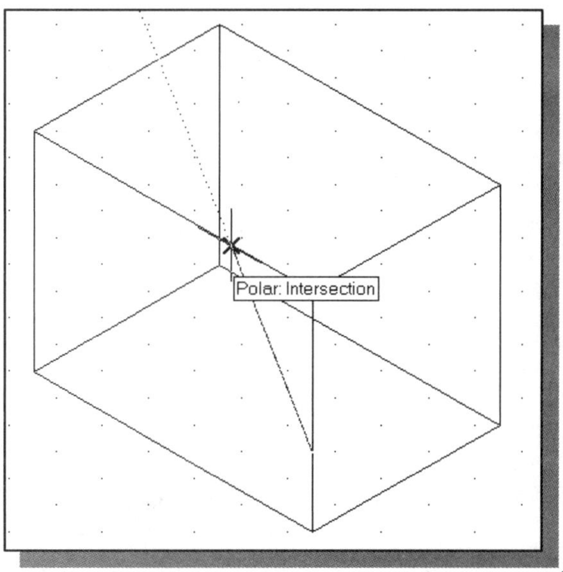

12. In the command prompt area, the message "*Specify next point or [Undo]:*" is displayed. Using the *Polar Tracking* option (30 degrees increment), create a line as shown in the figure.

13. Move the cursor near the left vertical edge of the front view and create the second line perpendicular to the last line we created.

14. Inside the graphics window, **right-mouse-click** to activate the option menu and select **Enter** with the left-mouse-button to end the **Line** command.

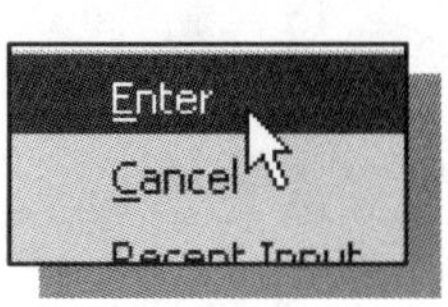

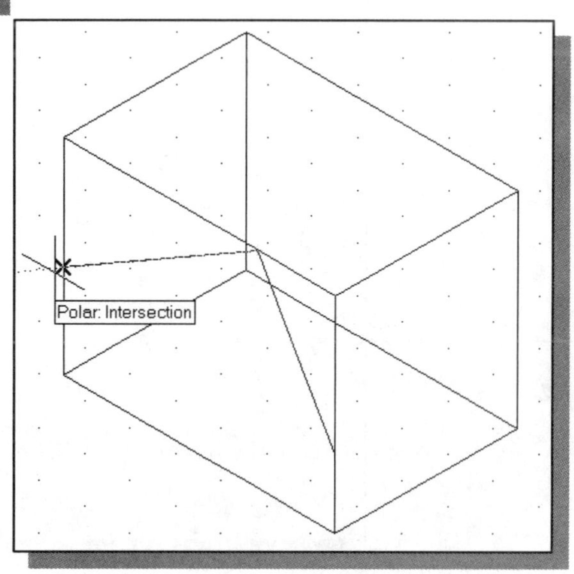

Copying in the Negative Z Direction

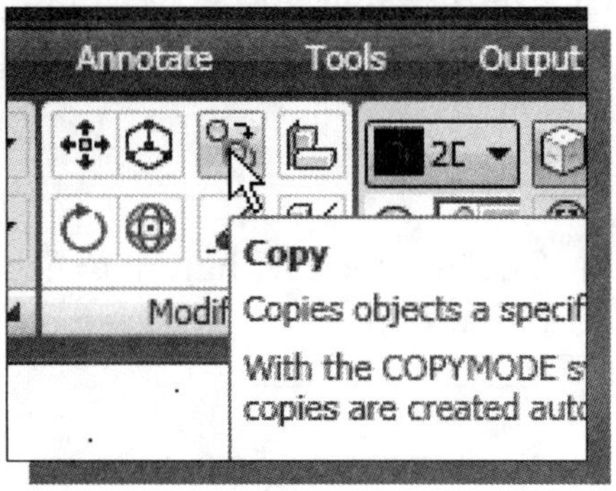

1. Click on the **Copy Object** icon in the *Modify* toolbar.

2. In the command prompt area, the message "*Select objects:*" is displayed. Pick the two edges we just created.

3. Inside the graphics window, right-mouse-click once to accept the selection.

4. In the command prompt area, the message "*Specify base point or displacement, or [Multiple]:*" is displayed. Pick any corner of the wireframe mode to use as a base point to create the copy.

5. In the command prompt area, the message "*Specify second point of displacement or <use first point as displacement>:*" is displayed.

   Enter: **@0,0,-2.0 [ENTER]**

➢ Note that the negative value represents the distance measured in the negative Z direction relative to the current UCS.

6. On your own, create three lines to connect the corners of the two sets of lines we just created, as shown below.

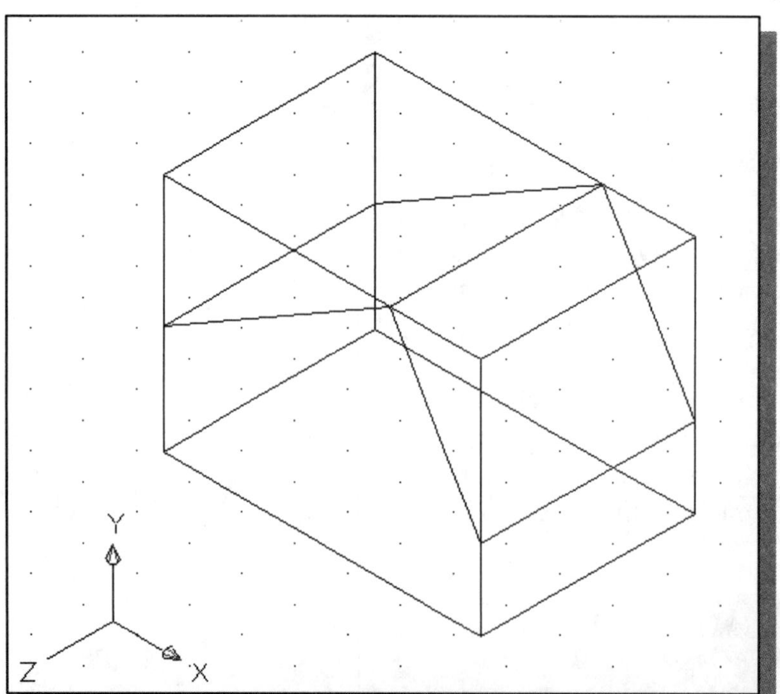

Creating an Inclined Line at the Base of the Model

1. Select **Top** in the *UCS II* toolbar as shown.

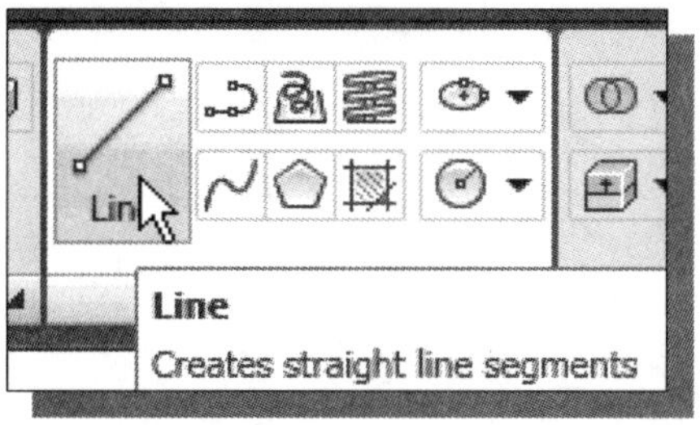

2. Select the **Line** command icon in the *Draw* toolbar. In the command prompt area, the message "*_line Specify first point:*" is displayed.

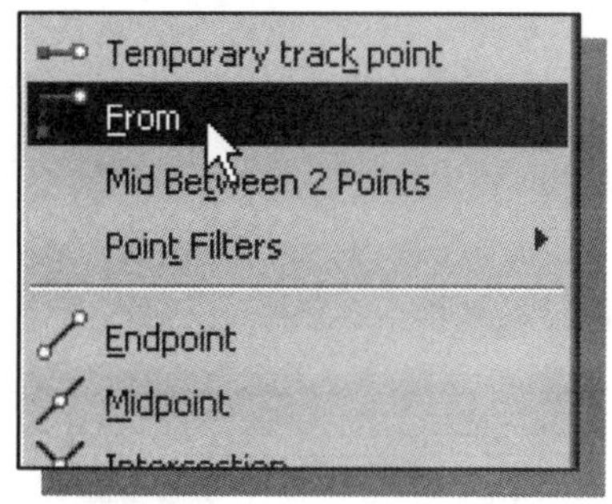

3. Inside the graphics window, hold down the **[SHIFT]** key and **right-mouse-click** once to bring up the *Object Snap* shortcut menu.

4. Select the **From** option in popup window.

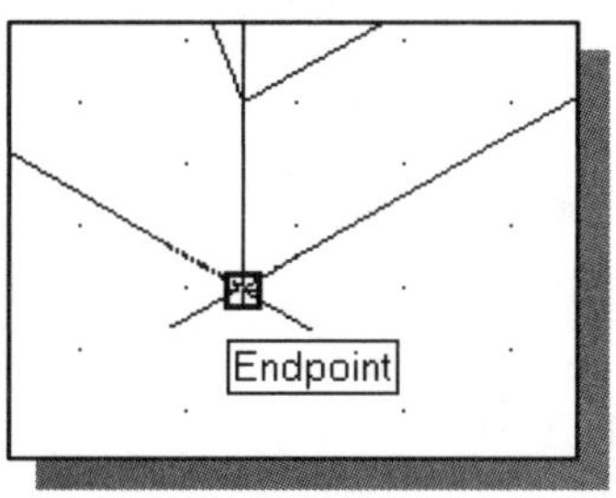

5. Pick the lower right corner of the bottom horizontal line as the base point as shown in the figure.

6. We will place the first point above the selected corner. Enter: **@0,0.75 [ENTER]**

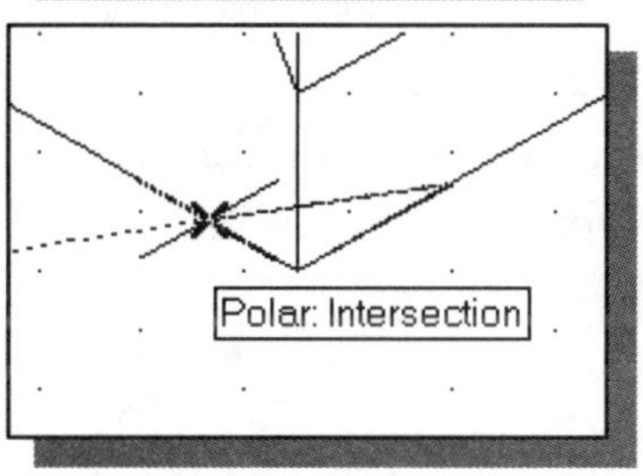

7. In the command prompt area, the message "*Specify next point or [Undo]:*" is displayed. Using the *Polar Tracking* option (30 degrees increment), create a line as shown in the figure.

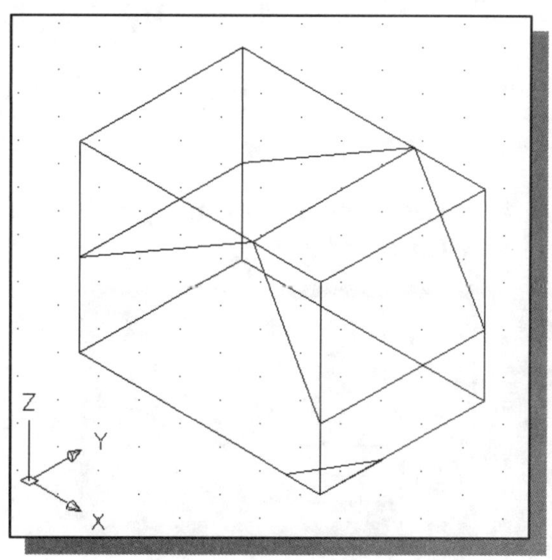

8. Inside the graphics window, right-mouse-click to activate the option menu and select **Enter** with the left-mouse-button to end the **Line** command.

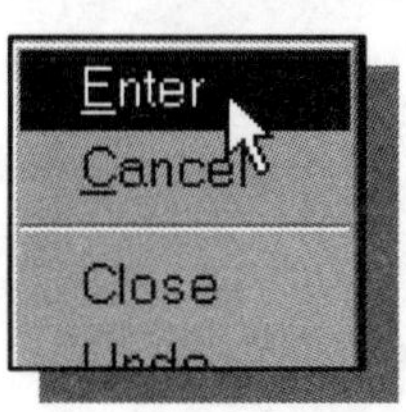

➢ On your own, use the **Copy** and **Line** commands to create additional edges so that the wireframe model appeared as shown below.

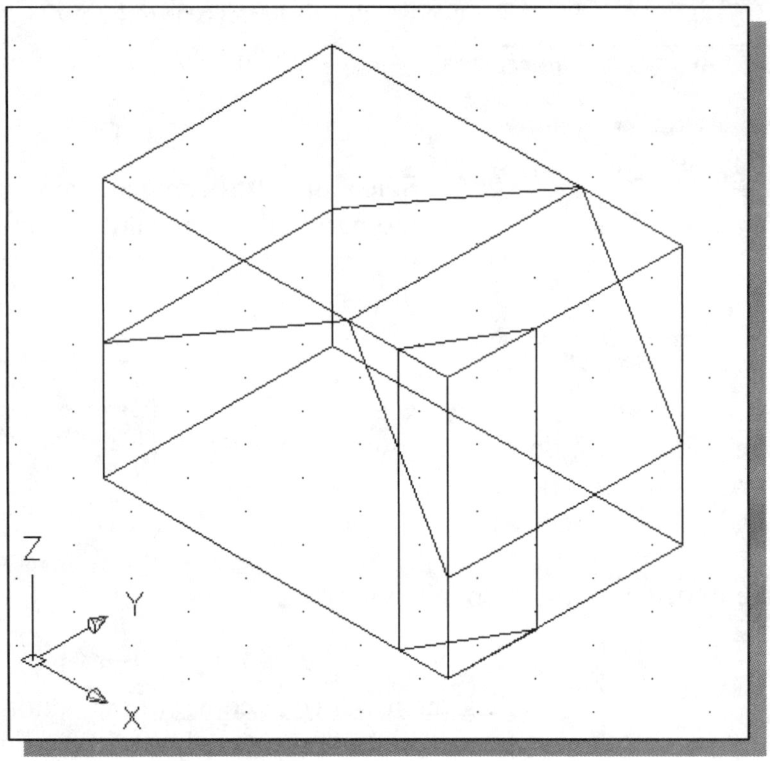

Creating Object Lines

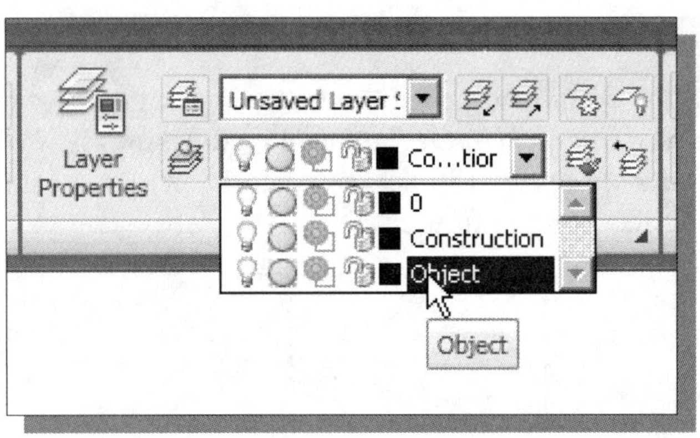

1. On the *Object Properties* toolbar, choose the ***Layer Control*** box with the left-mouse-button.

2. Move the cursor over the name of layer ***Object***; the tool tip "*Object*" appears.

3. **Left-mouse-click once** on the layer name and now layer *Object* is set as the *Current Layer*.

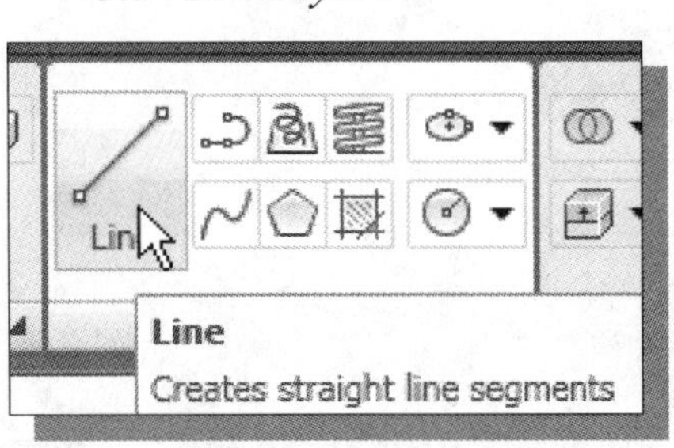

4. Select the **Line** command icon in the *Draw* toolbar. In the command prompt area, the message "*_line Specify first point:*" is displayed.

5. Pick the lower left corner of the bottom of the wireframe model as the starting point and create the four line segments as shown.

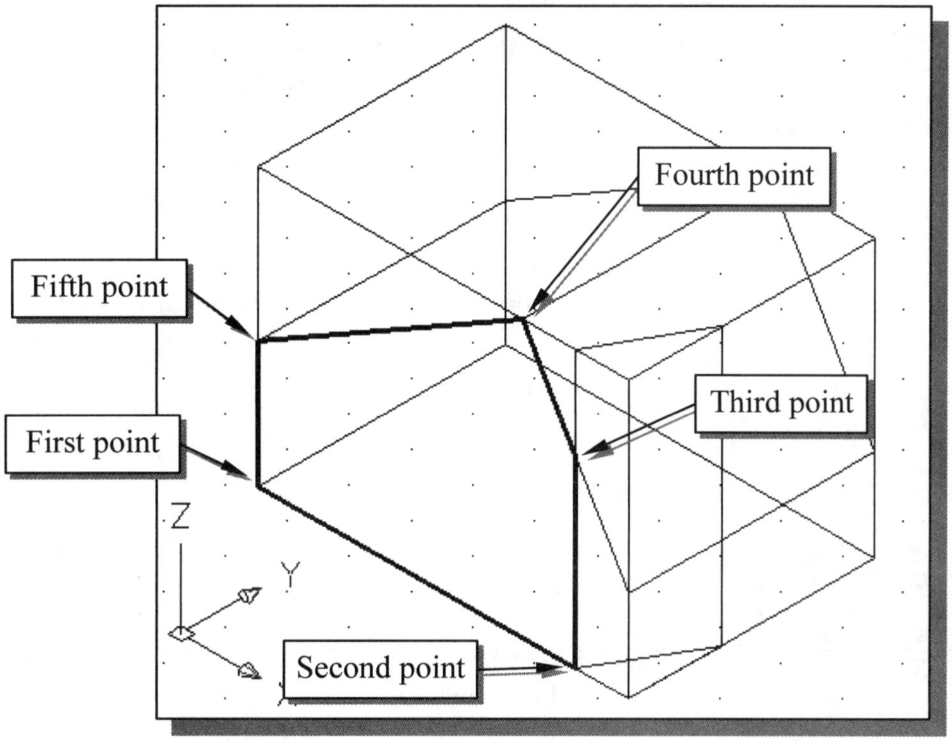

- Note that even though the UCS is aligned to the base plane of the model, the *Object Snap* option enables us to select points on the front plane of the model.

➢ On you own, create three additional lines representing the edges of the inclined face of the design as shown.

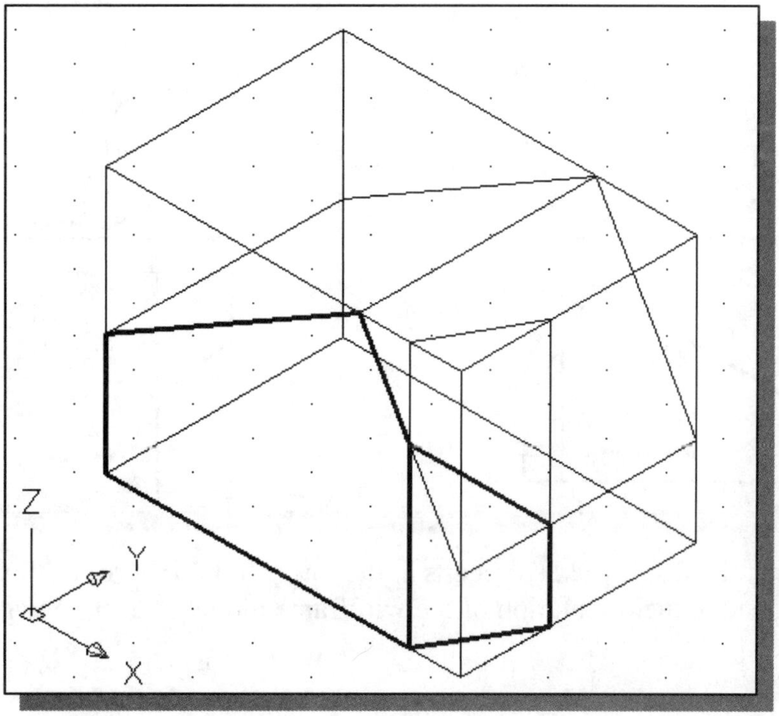

Multiple Viewports

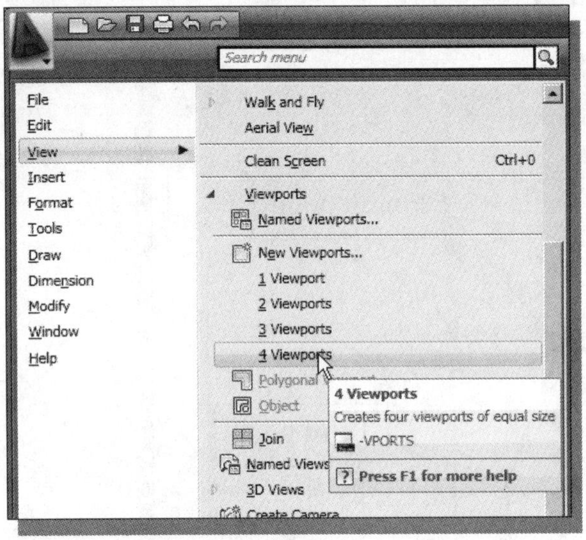

1. In the Menu Browser, select:
   [View] → [Viewports] → [4 viewports]

➢ AutoCAD allows us to display different VIEWS of the model simultaneously. Only one viewport is activated at one time. The viewport with the darker border is the active viewport. Move the cursor inside each viewport and notice the different cursor-display inside the active viewport.

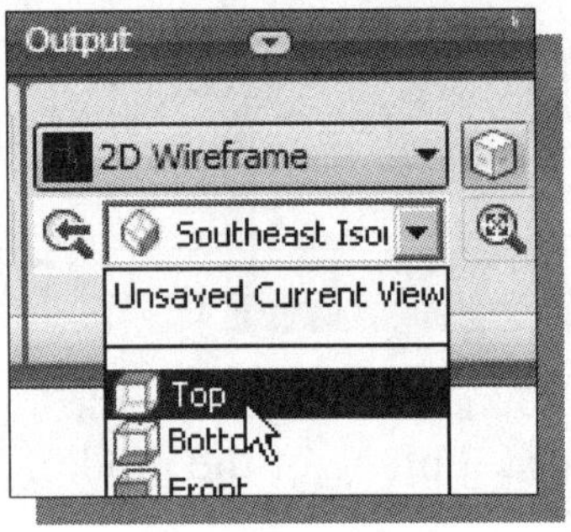

2. Activate the top **left viewport** by left-clicking once inside the viewport.

3. Select **Top View** in the *View* toolbar to change the display of the viewport.

4. On your own, repeat the above steps and use the **Realtime Zoom** command to set and adjust the displays of the viewports as shown below.

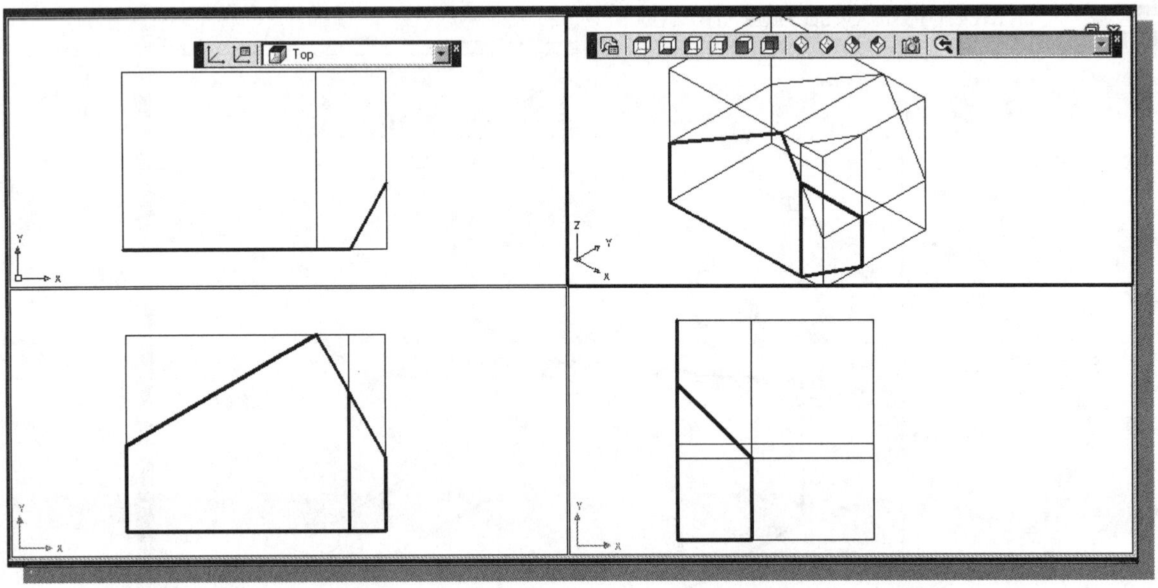

➢ Note that the displayed UCS icons at the lower left corner of each viewport correspond to the orientation of the wireframe model in each viewport.

Using the Mirror Command

1. Activate the top left viewport by left-clicking once inside the viewport.

2. ***Pre-select*** all the objects in the active viewport by using a selection window.

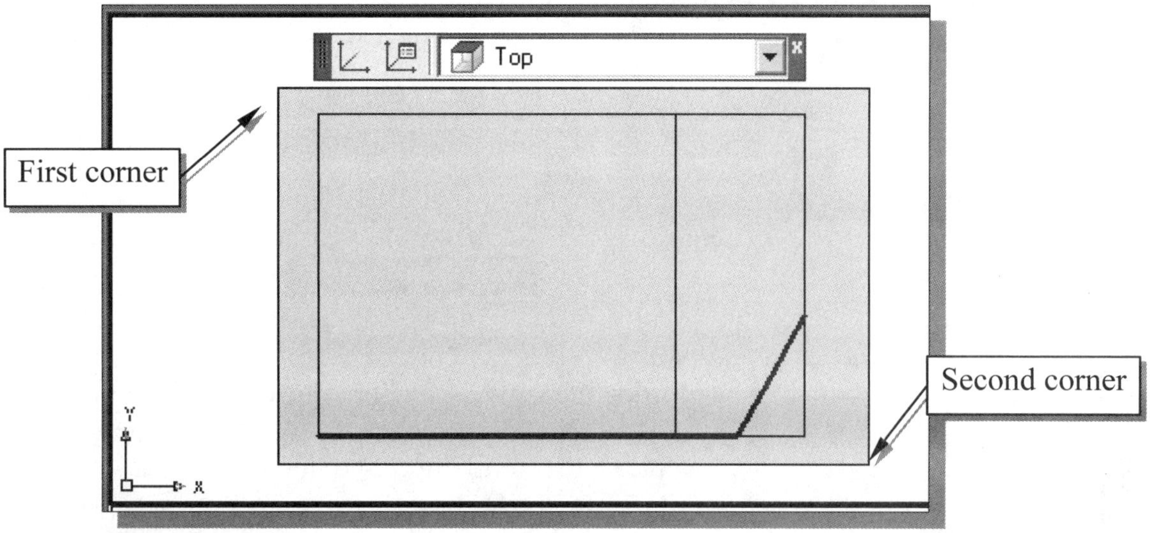

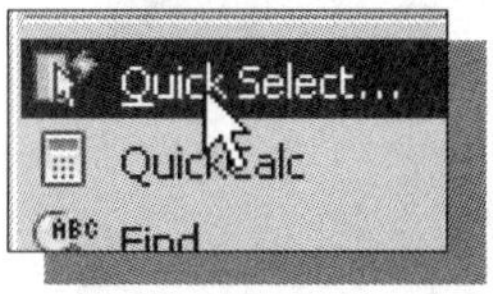

3. Inside the *active viewport*, **right-mouse-click** to bring up the popup option menu and select the **Quick Select** option.

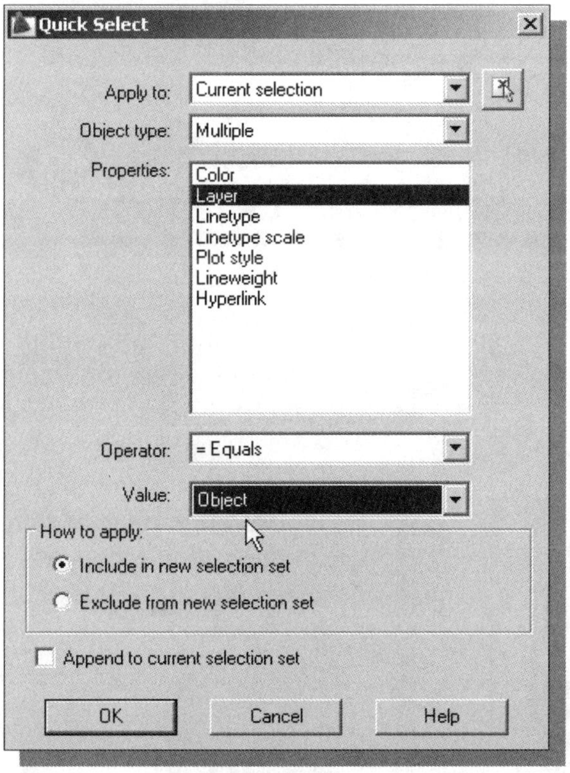

4. In the *Quick Select* dialog box, select **Layer** from the *Properties* list.

5. Set the *Value* box to **Object_Lines**.

6. In the *How to apply* section, confirm the ***Include in new selection set*** option is selected.

7. Switch *OFF* the *Append to current selection set*.

8. Click on the **OK** button to accept the settings.

- AutoCAD will now **filter out** objects that are not on layer *Object*.

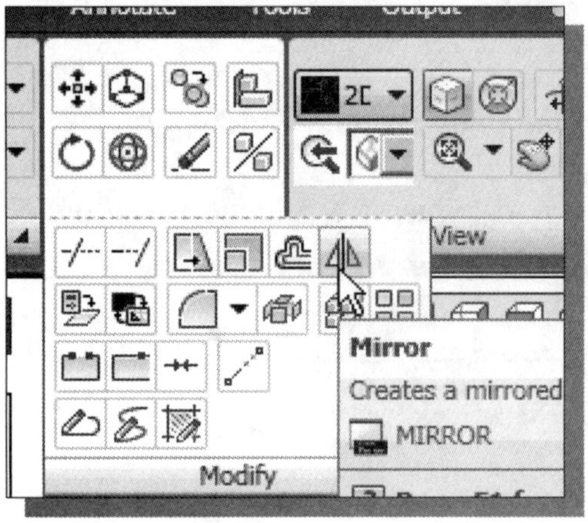

9. Click on the **Mirror** icon in the *Modify* toolbar.

10. Inside the graphics window, hold down the **[SHIFT]** key and **right-mouse-click** once to bring up the *Object Snap* shortcut menu.

11. Select the **Midpoint** option in popup window.

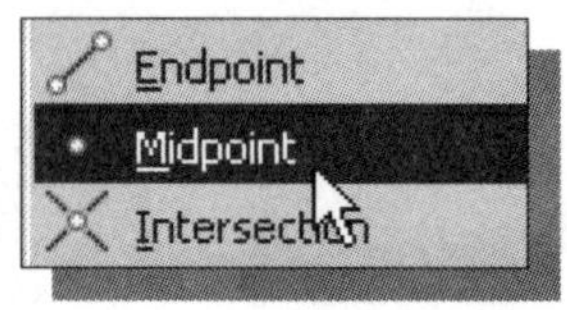

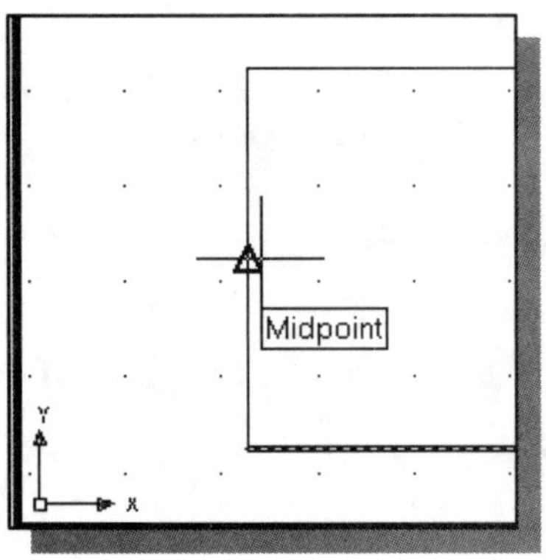

12. Inside the active viewport, click on the left vertical line of the wireframe model. With the *Midpoint* snap option, the midpoint of the line is selected

13. Move the cursor toward the right vertical line in the active viewport, left-click once when the **Intersection** symbol is displayed as shown.

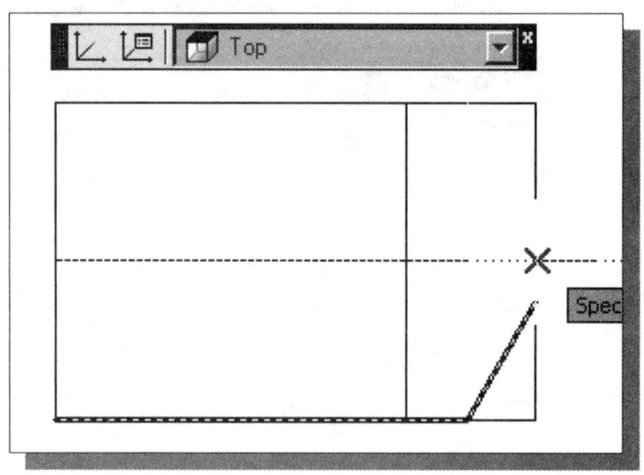

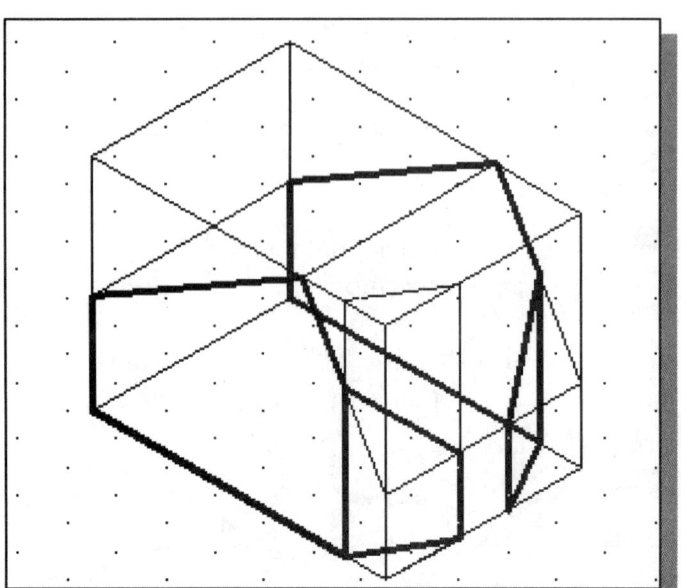

14. In the command prompt area, the message "*Delete Source Objects? [Yes/No] <N>:*" is displayed. Inside the graphics window, right-mouse-click once to bring up the option menu and select **No** to keep both sets of objects.

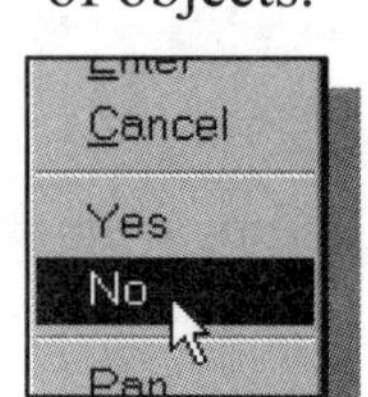

Turn *OFF* the Construction Lines

1. On the *Object Properties* toolbar, choose the ***Layer Control*** box with the left-mouse-button.

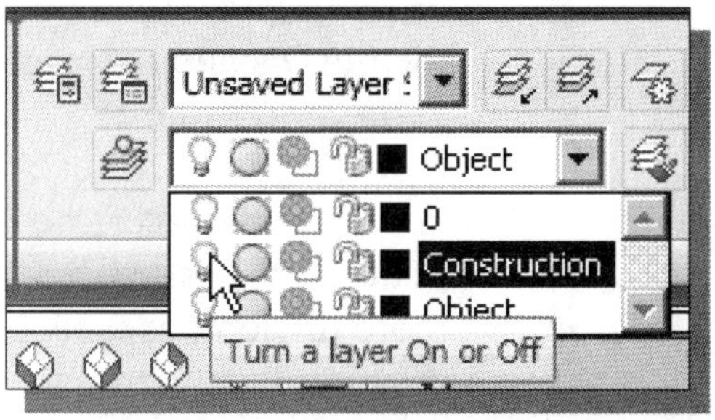

2. Move the cursor over the **light-bulb** icon for layer *Construction*, **left-mouse-click once**, and notice the icon color is changed to a gray tone color, representing the layer (layer *Construction*) is turned *OFF*.

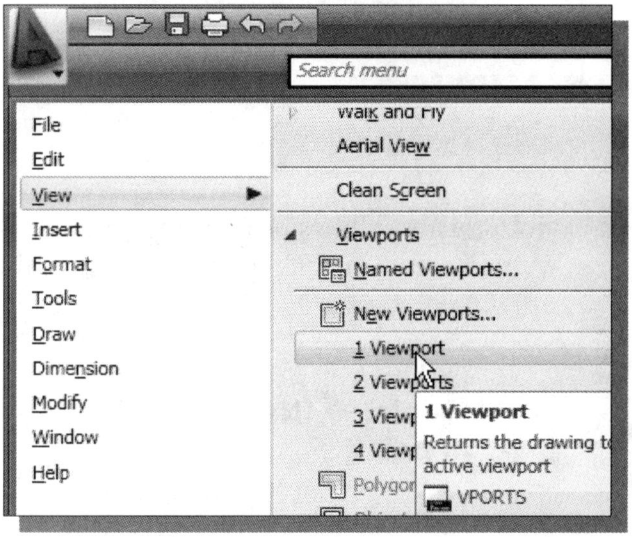

3. In the *Menu Browser*, select: **[View] → [Viewports] → [1 viewport]**

- Viewports can also be used as a way of checking the integrity of the constructed 3D models. Feel free to switch to multiple viewports in the following sections of this tutorial.

4. On your own, create the additional **object lines** connecting the two sets of objects as shown below.

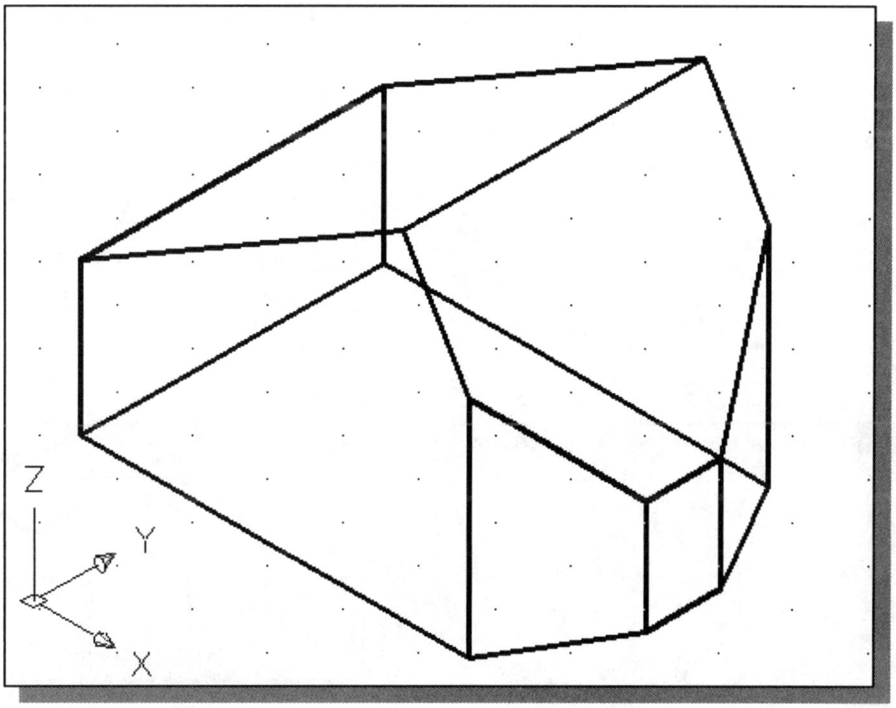

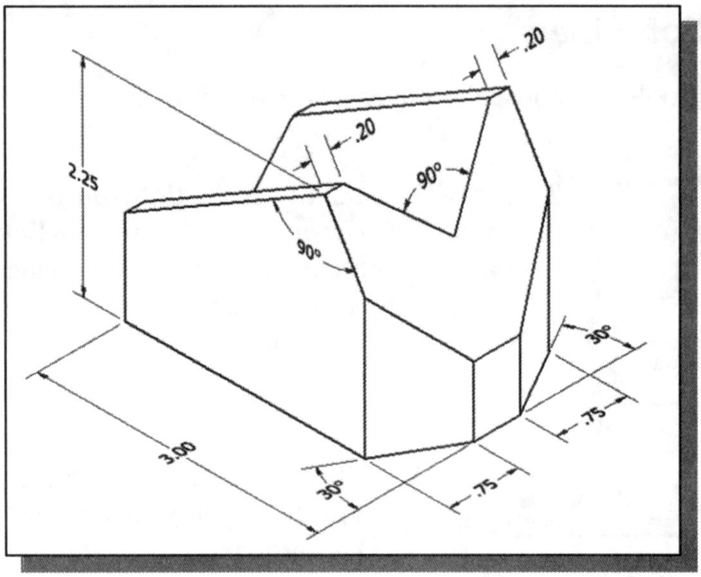

➤ The V-cut feature of the design is the last feature, and perhaps the most difficult one, to create in the CAD system. Based on your knowledge of modeling with AutoCAD, how would you create this feature? What are the more difficult aspects of creating this feature?

Creating a New UCS

➤ Besides using the preset UCS planes, AutoCAD also allows us to change our viewpoint and create new UCS planes. We will create an UCS plane aligning to the inclined plane of the design.

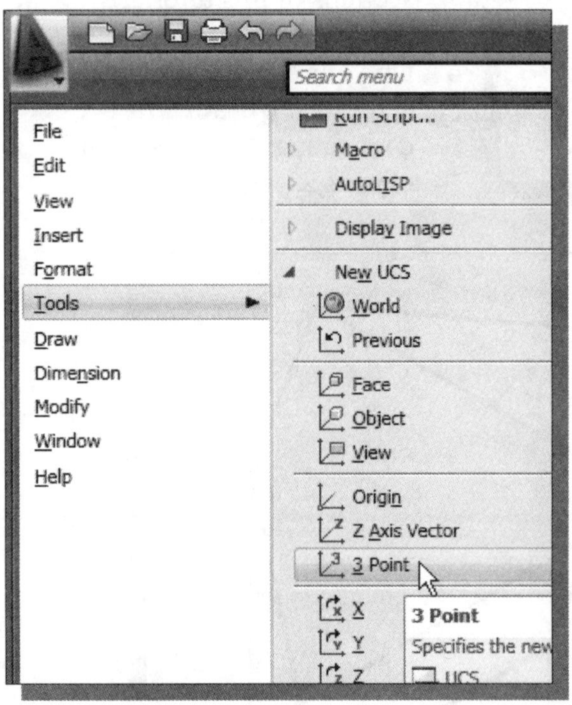

1. In the *Menu Browser*, select: **[Tools] → [New UCS] → [3 point]**

• Note that other options are also available to aid the creation of new UCS planes.

2. In the command prompt area, the message "*Specify New Origin point <0,0,0>:*" is displayed. Pick the lower-left corner of the inclined plane as shown.

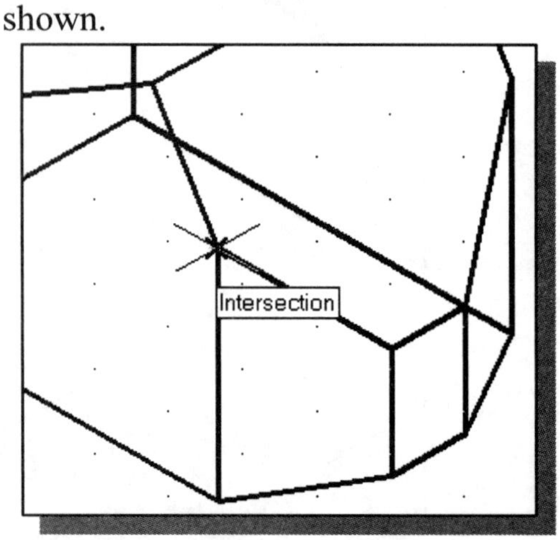

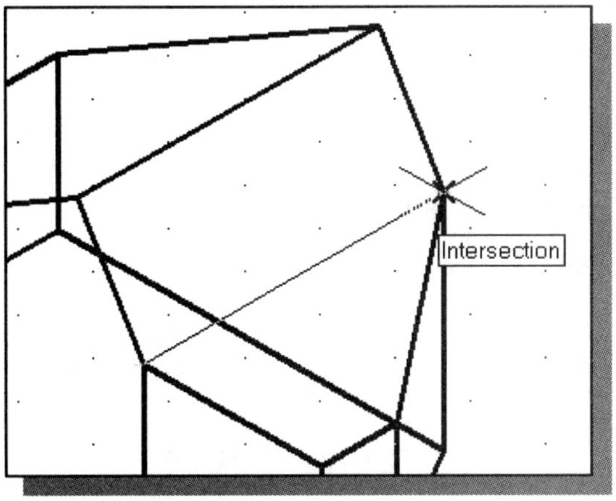

3. In the command prompt area, the message "*Specify point on positive portion of X-axis:*" is displayed. Pick the lower right corner of the inclined plane as shown.

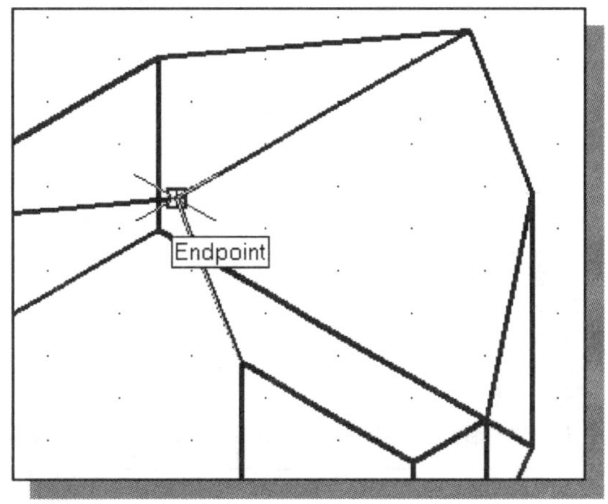

4. In the command prompt area, the message "*Specify point on positive portion of X-axis:*" is displayed. Pick the top left corner of the inclined plane as shown.

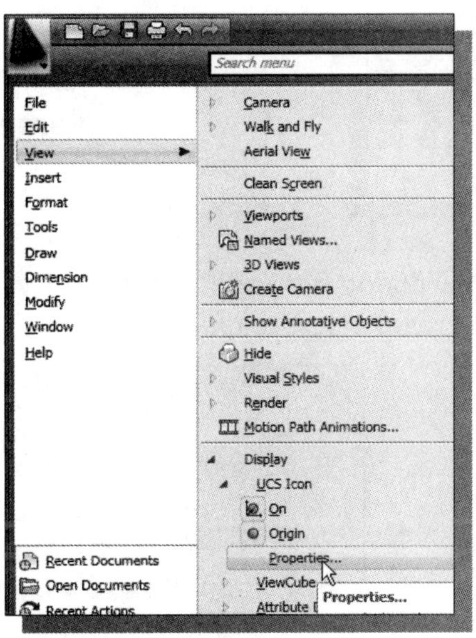

5. In the *Menu Browser*, select **[View] → [Display] → [UCS Icon] → [Properties]**

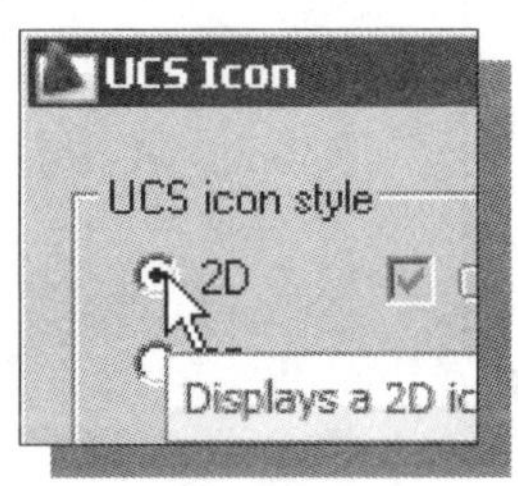

6. In the *UCS Icon* window, switch the *UCS icon style* to ***2D*** as shown.

7. Click on the **OK** button to accept the settings.

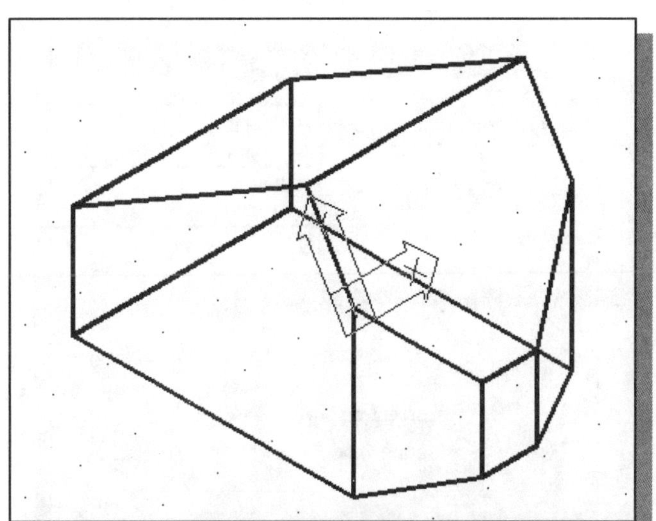

Creating a New Named View

- Besides using the preset views, AutoCAD also allows us to change our viewpoint and create new views, which can be saved and restored by name for convenient access. We will create a new view aligned to the new UCS plane we just created.

1. In the *Menu Browser*, select **[View] → [3D Views] → [Plan View] → [Current UCS]**

- The graphics window is now adjusted to display the current UCS plane.

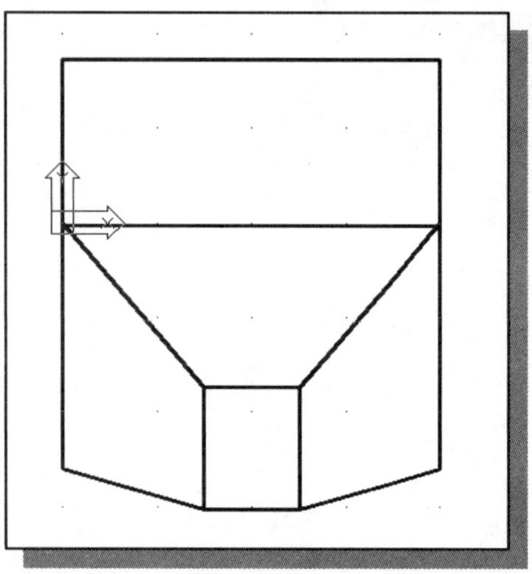

2. Click on the **Named Views** icon in the *View* toolbar.

3. In the *View* dialog box, click on the **New** button to create a new named view.

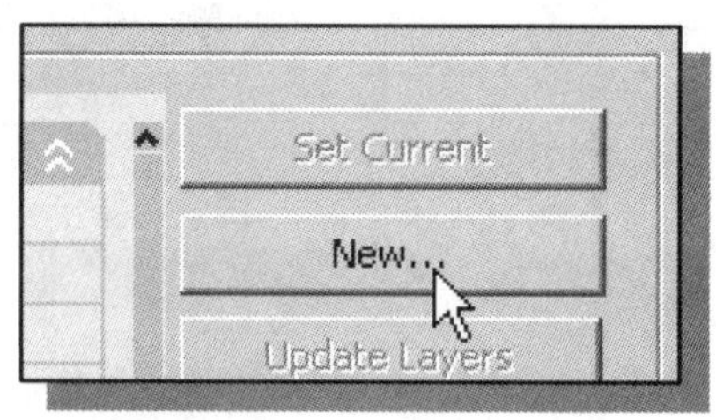

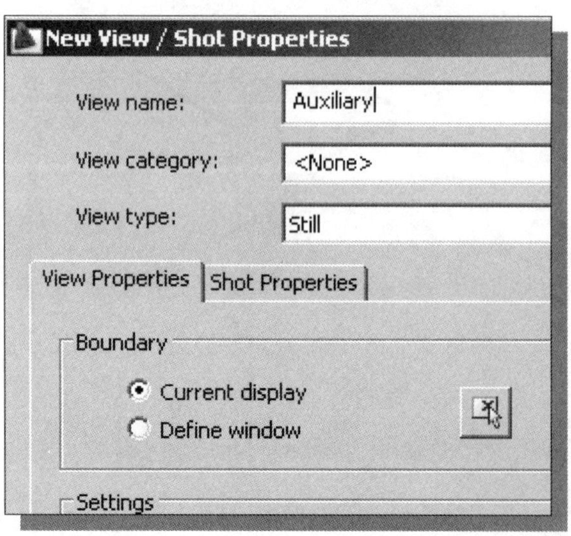

4. In the *New View* dialog box, enter **Auxiliary** as the new *View name* and confirm the ***Current display*** option and the ***Save layer Snapshot with view*** option are switched ***ON*** and the *UCS option* is set to ***Unnamed*** as shown.

5. Click on the **OK** button to accept the settings and create the named view.

6. In the *View* dialog box, the new named view (*Auxiliary*) is added to the *Named Views* list. Note that we can always switch to this view by using the **Set Current** option.

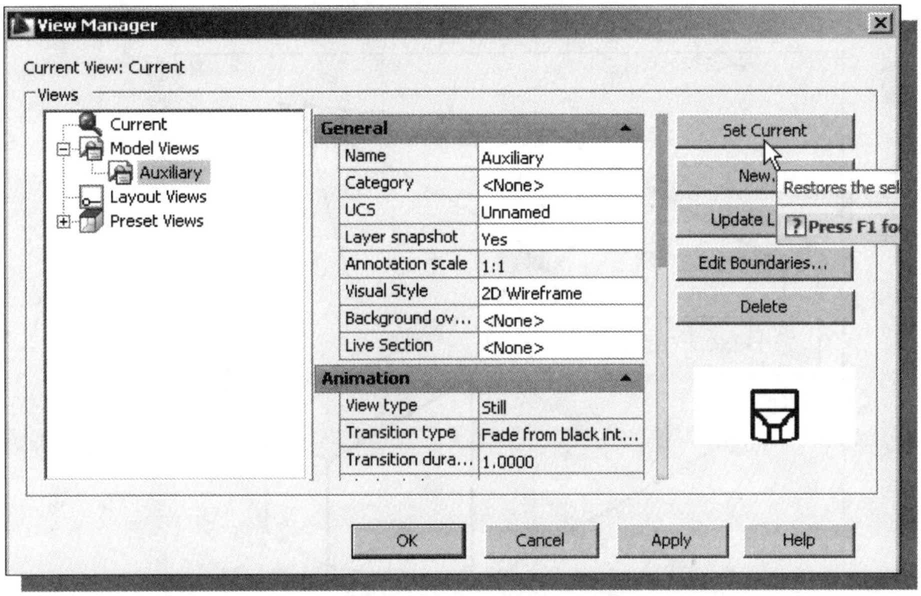

7. Click on the **OK** button to accept the settings.

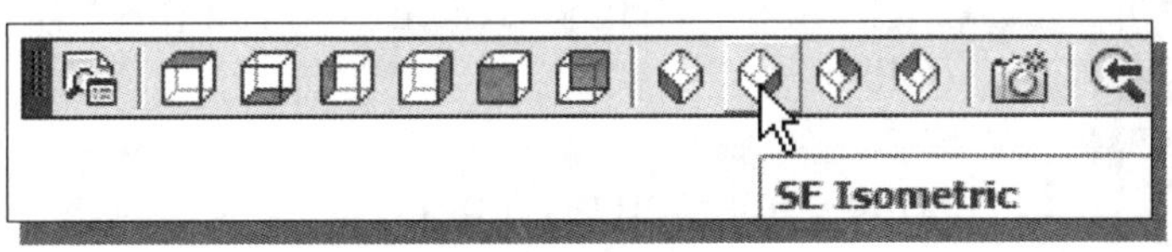

8. In the *View* toolbar, select **SE Isometric View**.

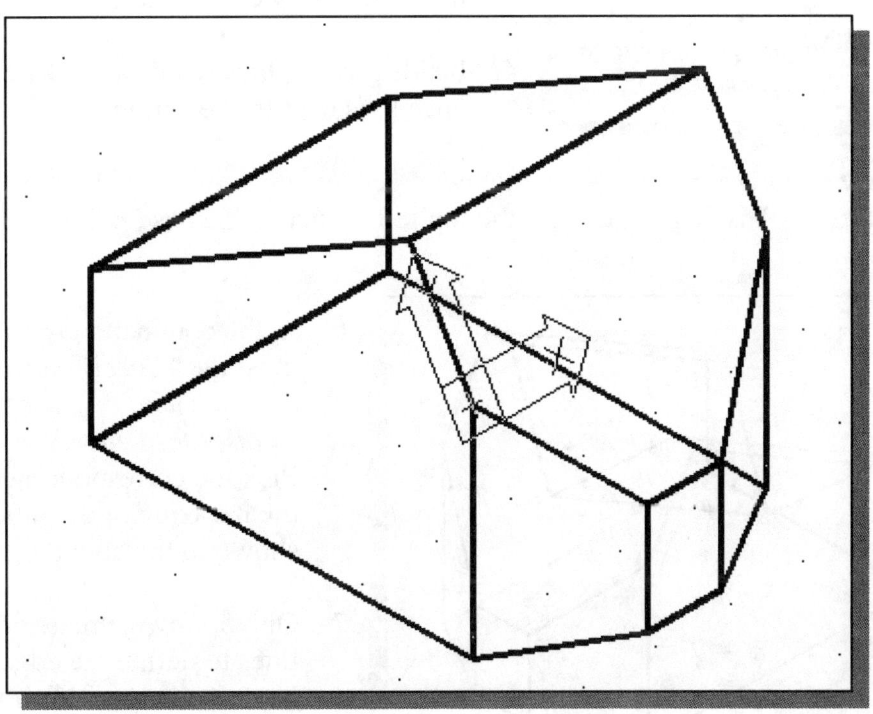

Creating the V-Cut Feature on the Inclined Plane

1. On your own, create two lines that are **0.2″** away from the top corners of the model, which are also rotated **45 degrees** relative to the top edge of the model.

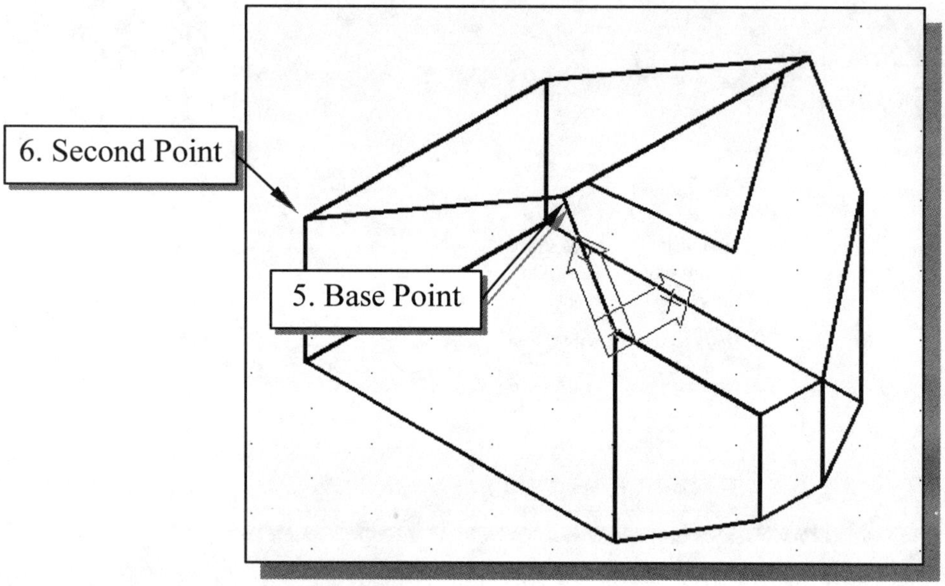

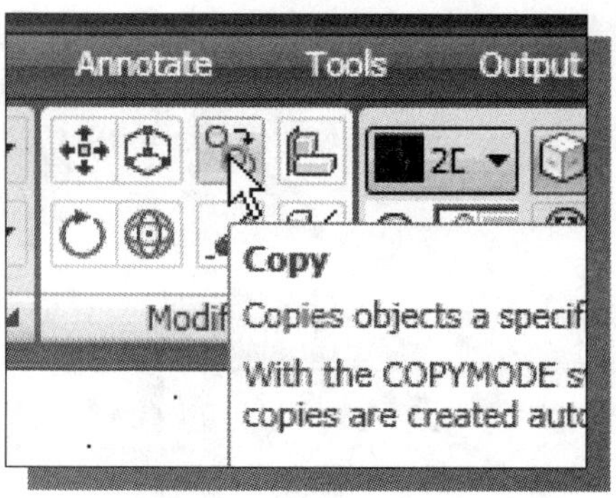

2. Click on the **Copy Object** icon in the *Modify* toolbar.

3. In the command prompt area, the message "*Select objects:*" is displayed. Pick the two inclined lines we just created.

4. Inside the graphics window, **right-mouse-click** once to accept the selections.

5. In the command prompt area, the message "*Specify base point or displacement, or [Multiple]:*" is displayed. Pick the top left corner as the base point to create the copy.

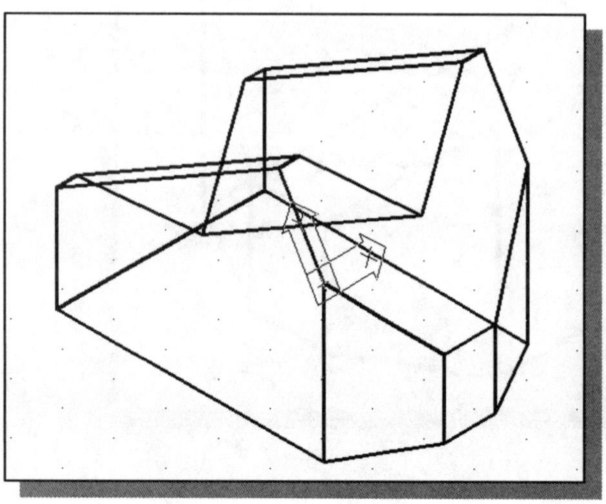

6. In the command prompt area, the message *"Specify second point of displacement or <use first point as displacement>:"* is displayed. Pick the corresponding corner on the backside of the model as shown in the above figure.

7. On your own, create addition lines to define the edges of the V-cut and use the **Trim** command to complete the model as shown.

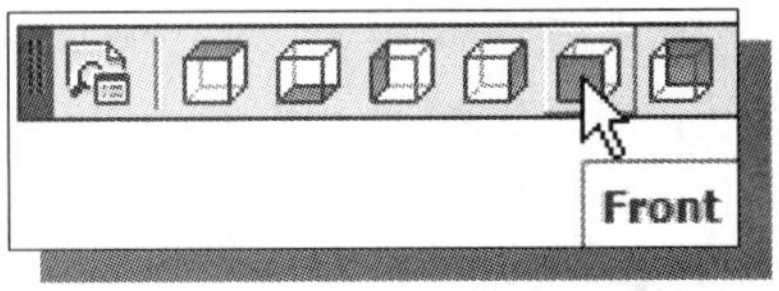

8. Click on the **Front View** icon in the *View* toolbar.

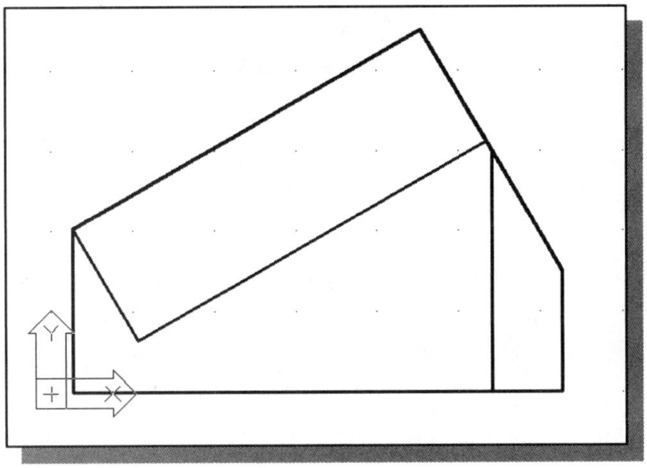

➢ Note that the V-cut we created, using the Copy command, does not represent a cut that passes through the entire block.

Extend the Cut and GRIP Editing

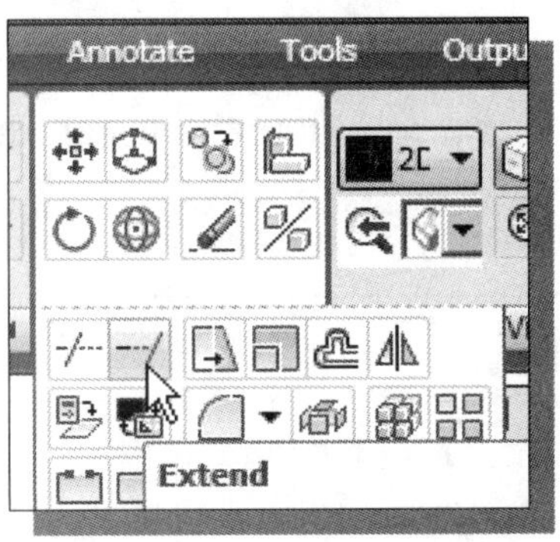

1. Select the **Extend** command icon in the *Modify* toolbar.
2. In the command prompt area, the message "*Select boundary edges... Select objects:*" is displayed. Pick the left vertical line as the *boundary edge*.
3. Inside the graphics window, **right-mouse-click** to accept the selection.

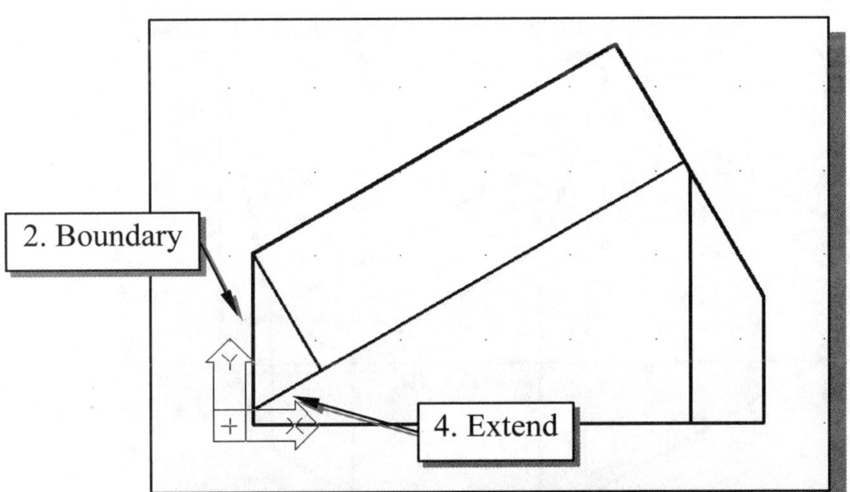

4. The message "*Select object to Extend or [Project/Edge/Undo]:*" is displayed in the command prompt area. Pick the bottom edge of the V-cut to extend.

5. Inside the graphics window, **right-mouse-click** to activate the option menu and select **Enter** with the left-mouse-button to end the Extend command.

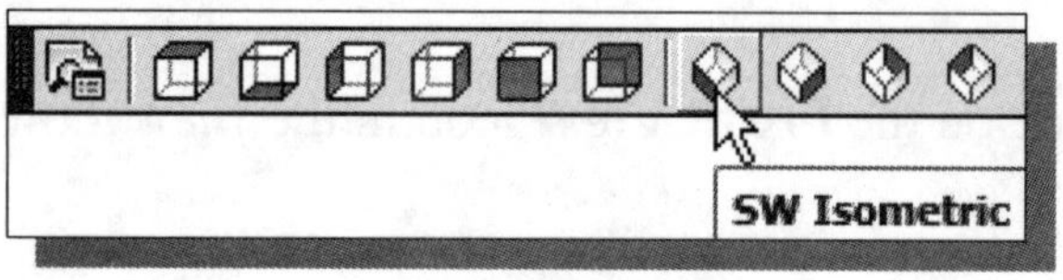

6. Click on the **SW Isometric View** icon to reset the display to the preset isometric view.

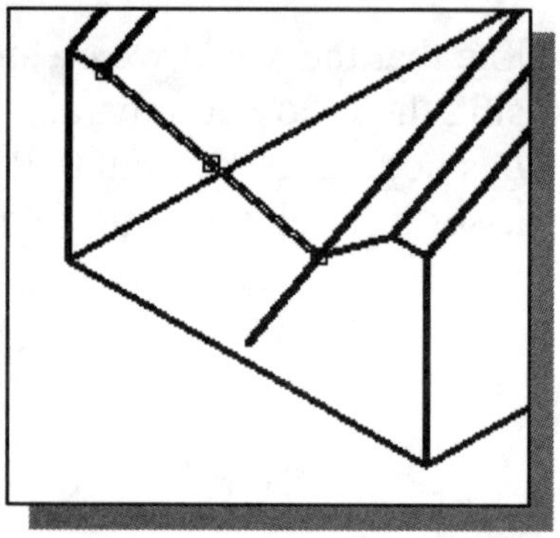

7. ***Pre-select*** the top edge of the *V-block* as shown.

8. Left-click once on the lower right grip point on the selected line.

- Selecting the grip points located at the end of the line or arc allows us to STRETCH the selected line.

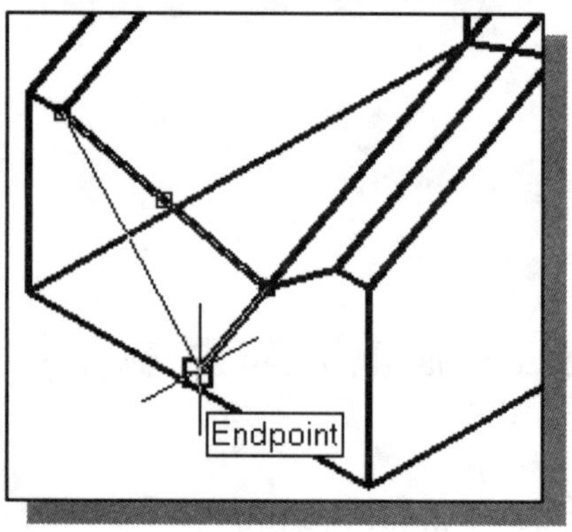

9. Move the cursor toward and select the lower corner of the V-cut as shown.

➢ On your own, repeat the above steps and use the grip editing options and complete the wireframe model as shown below.

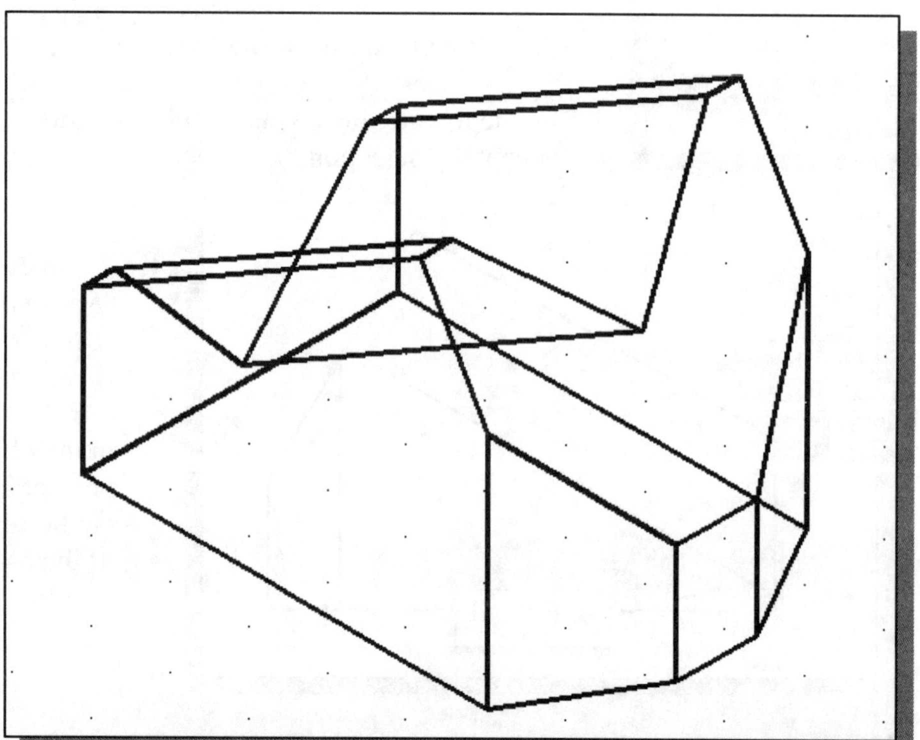

Questions:

1. List and describe three different types of 3D computer geometric modeling software available today?

2. What is a *Named View*?

3. What is the difference between Stretch and Extend?

4. List and describe the methods available in AutoCAD to create a new UCS plane.

5. What is the difference between Copy and Mirror in AutoCAD?

6. Identify and describe the following commands:

   a)

   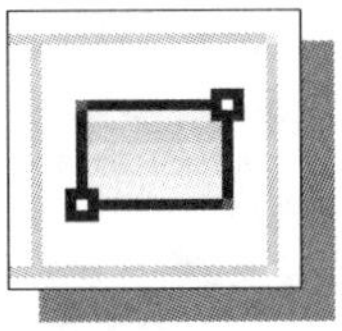

   b)

   c)

   d)

   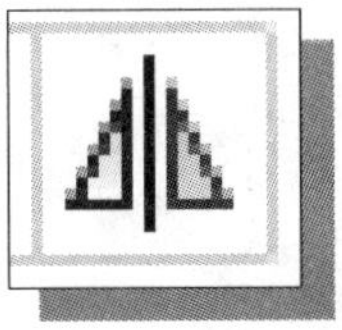

Exercises: (Unless otherwise specified, dimensions are in inches.)

1.

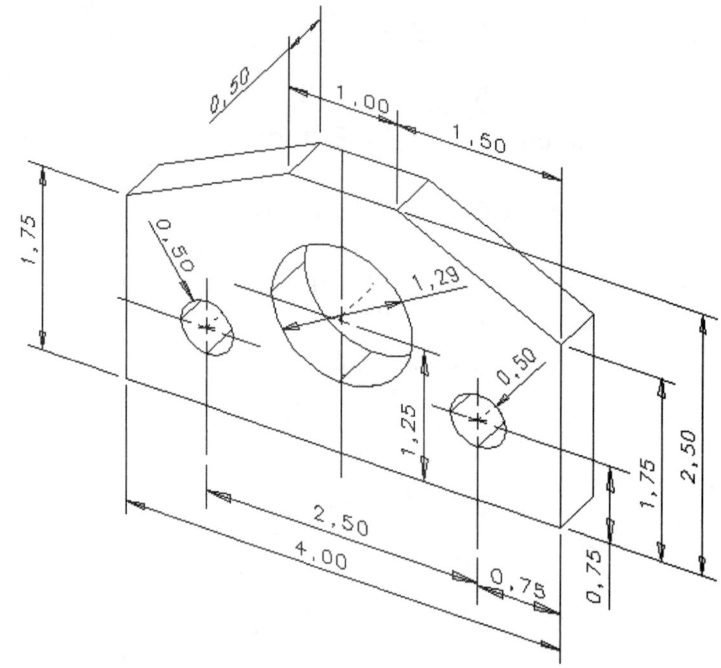

2.

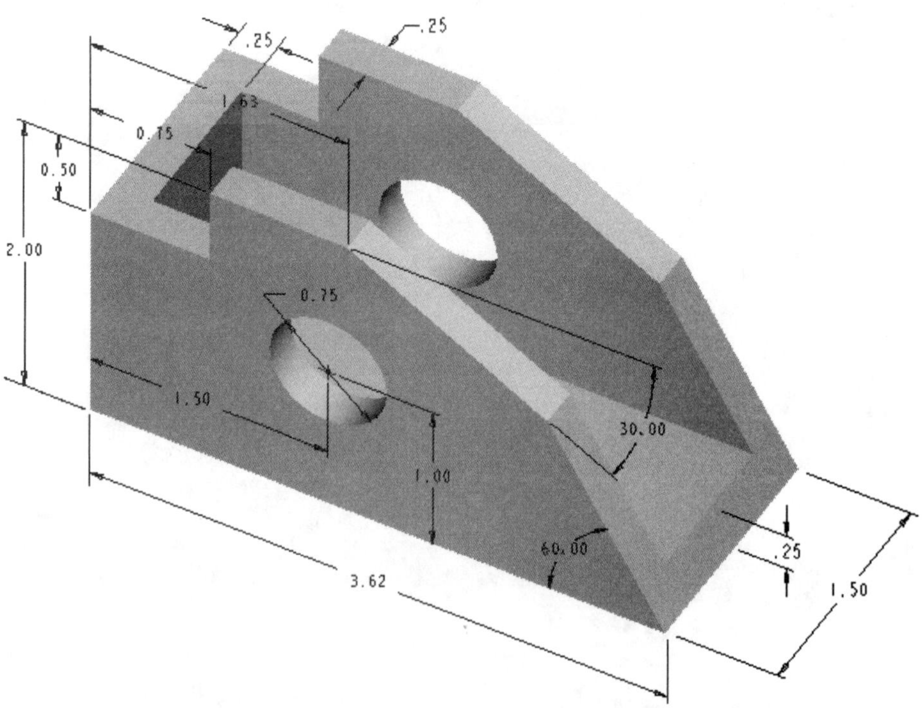

3.

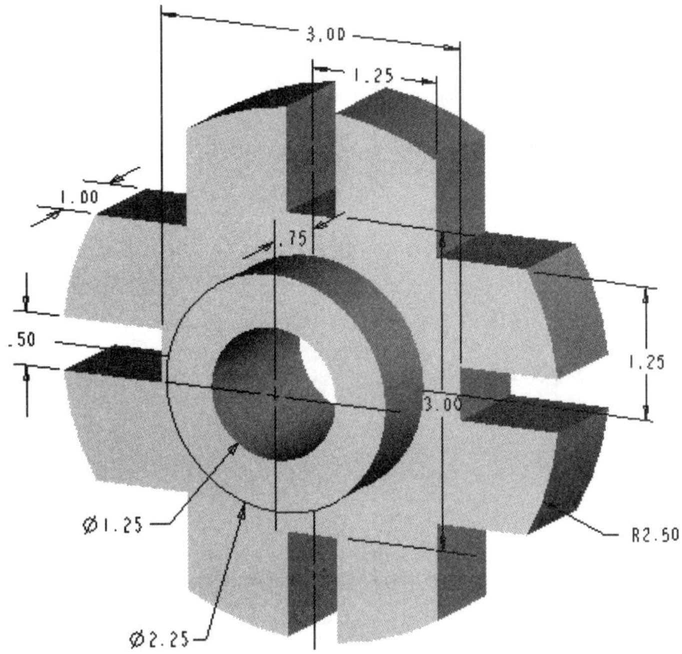
3.00
1.25
1.00
.75
.50
1.25
3.00
Ø1.25
R2.50
Ø2.25

4.

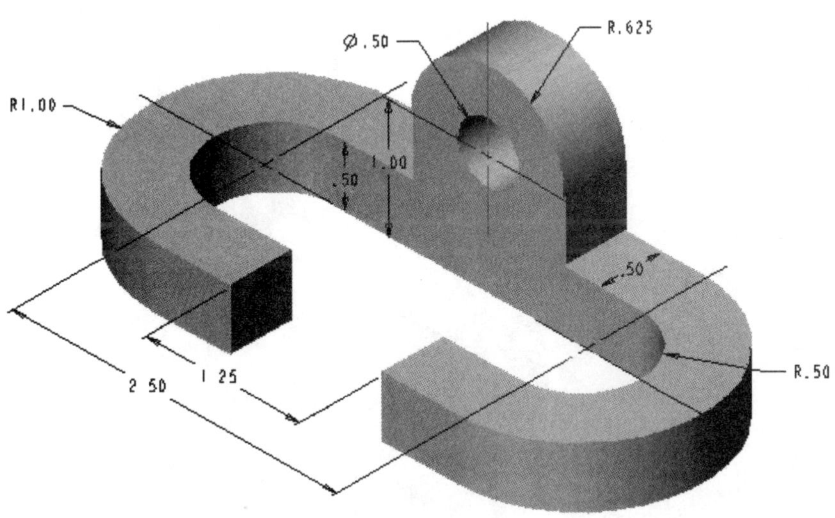
Ø.50
R.625
R1.00
1.00
.50
.50
R.50
2.50
1.25

NOTES:

Chapter 5
3D Surface Modeling

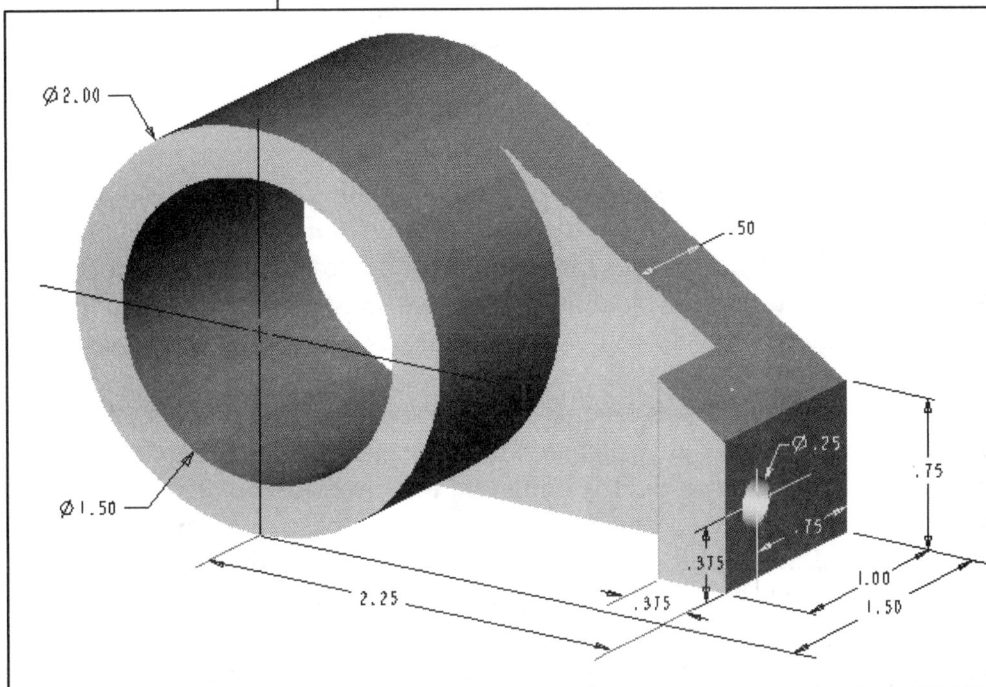

Learning Objectives

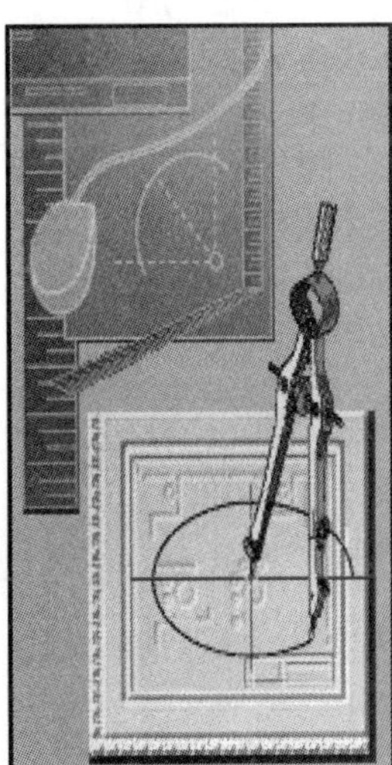

- Create 3D Surface Models
- Understand and Apply the Different Surface Modeling Techniques
- Understand the Use of the 2D SOLID Command
- Understand the Use of 3D FACE Command
- Use the Hidden Edge Option

Introduction

As illustrated in the previous chapters, there are no surfaces in a wireframe model; it consists only of points, lines and curves that describe the edges of the object. Surface modeling was developed to provide the surface information that is missing in wireframe modeling. Essentially, defining the skin of a design creates a surface model. Although it is possible to create a surface model without using a wireframe model, in most cases it is much easier to create a surface model on top of a wireframe model. In surface modeling, a wireframe model can be used to provide information about the edges and corners so that the desired faces can be easily positioned and placed.

Surface modeling is more sophisticated than wireframe modeling in that surface modelers define not only the edges of 3D objects, but also the surfaces. Surface modeling provides hiding, shading, and rendering capabilities that are not available in wireframe modeling. Surface models do not provide the physical properties that solid models provide, such as mass, weight, center of gravity, and so on.

The AutoCAD surface modeler defines faceted surfaces using a filled polygon. The created faces of surface models are only planar, which means the surface models can only have approximate curved surfaces. It is important to note that the AutoCAD surface modeler does not create true curved surfaces. To differentiate these two types of surfaces, faceted surfaces are called **meshes** in AutoCAD. Because of the use of faceted approximation on true curved surfaces, the computer requirements of most faceted surface modelers are typically much less than that of solid modelers. Faceted surface modeling usually provides reasonably good representations of 3D designs with fast rendering and shading capabilities. Faceted surface models are also useful for creating geometry with unusual surface patterns, such as a 3D topographical model of mountainous terrain.

AutoCAD® 2009 provides three basic methods for creating surfaces – the **2D Solid**, **3D Face** and **Region** commands. The three commands were developed parallel to the historical development of the different types of computer modelers.

- **2D Solid**: The first generation surface command available in AutoCAD. Used mostly to fill an area in the sketch plane of the current UCS. This type of surface is not a true 3D surface.

- **3D Face**: Creates a true 3D planar surface (allowing X, Y and Z coordinates) of three-sided or four-sided shape. This is the type of surface developed primarily for creating faceted surface models.

- **Region**: Creates a 2D surface of arbitrary shape from existing 2D entities. This command creates the most flexible and the most complicated type of surface available in AutoCAD. This command was developed to allow manipulation of 2D surfaces using one of the solid modeling construction techniques, namely, the **Constructive Solid Geometry** method.

Although all three commands can be used to create planar surfaces, the resulting surfaces are not equal. In fact, the three commands are developed for specific tasks in mind. The **2D Solid** command is mostly used in 2D drawings to create 2D filled area and the **Region** command is designed so that general 2D shapes can be easily transformed into solid models. The **3D Face** command is the only one that is designed specifically for surface modeling and therefore it is the most suitable for such tasks. The use of the **2D Solid** and **Region** commands in 3D surface modeling can be somewhat awkward and at times very difficult. Note that the use of the **Region** command will be focused on in the solid modeling chapters of this text.

As one can imagine, sketching each surface manually can be very time consuming and tedious. AutoCAD also provides additional tools for more advanced surface modeling, such as **Tabulated surfaces**, **Ruled surfaces** and **Revolved surfaces**. These tools are basically automated procedures, which can be used to define and create multiple copies of planar surfaces in specific directions. The principles and concepts used by these tools are also used in creating solid models, which are covered in chapter six through chapter eight of this text. You are encouraged to re-examine these commands after you have finished the solid modeling chapters.

In this chapter, the general procedures to create surface models are illustrated. The use of the **2D Solid** and **3D Face** commands are illustrated and differences discussed. We will also demonstrate the use of the more advanced surface modeling tools. Two wireframe models, which were created in the previous chapters, will be converted into surface models.

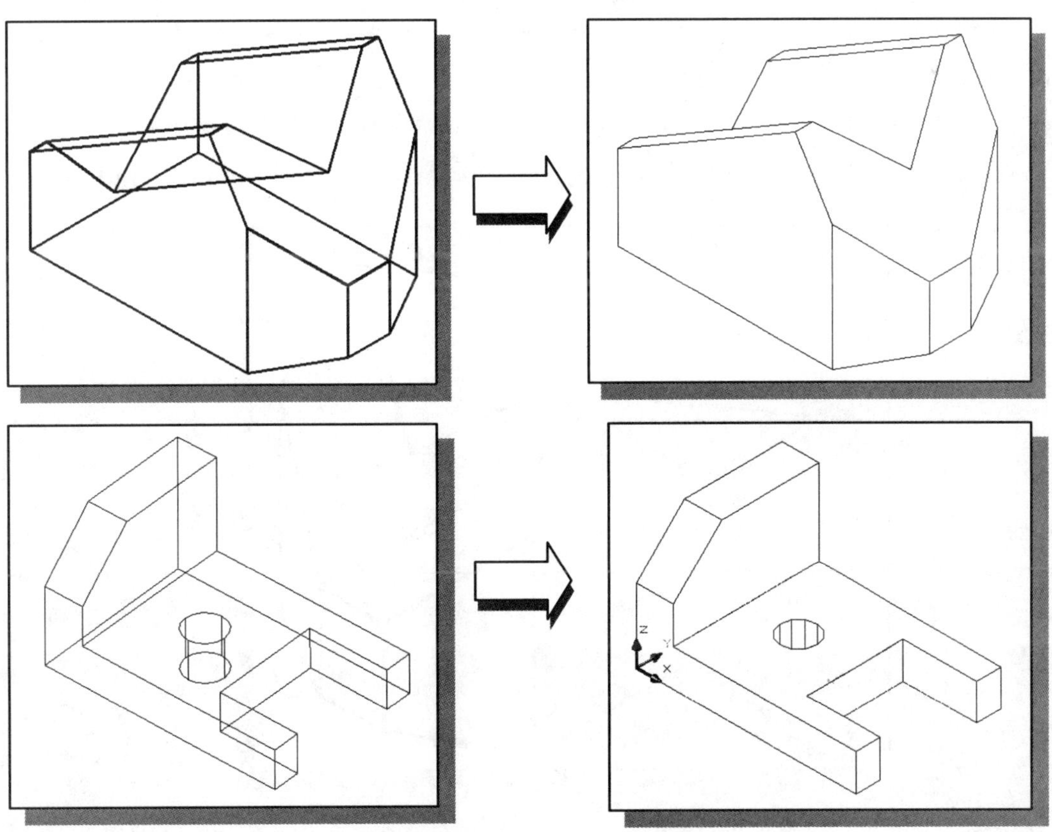

Starting Up AutoCAD® 2009

1. Select the **AutoCAD 2009** option on the *Program* menu or select the **AutoCAD 2009** icon on the *Desktop*.

2. In the *AutoCAD Today* startup dialog box, select the **Open a Drawing** icon with a single click of the left-mouse-button.

3. Click on the ***V-block.dwg*** filename to open the *V-block* wireframe model that was created in the previous chapter. (Use the Browse option to locate the file if it is not displayed.)

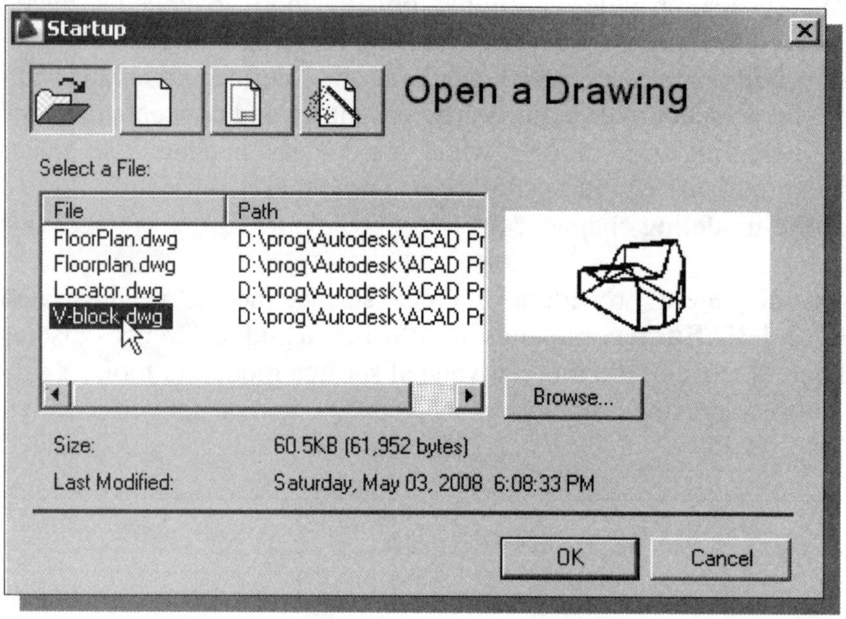

- The *V-block* wireframe model is retrieved and displayed in the graphics window.

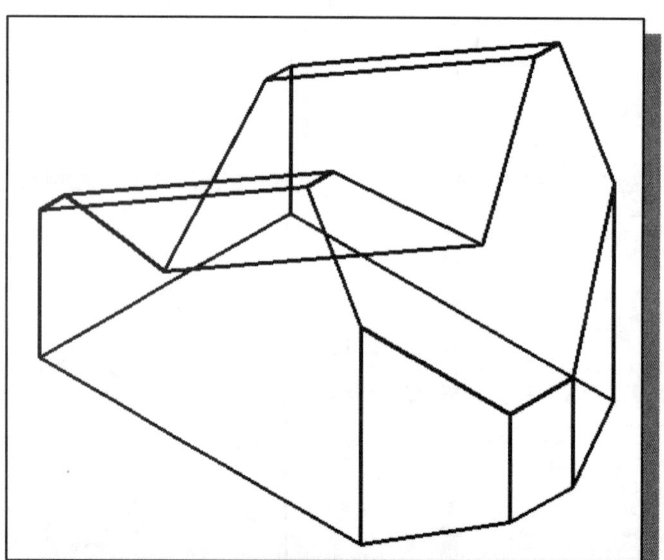

The UCS Toolbar and the Meshes Commands

1. Move the cursor on any icon in the *Standard* toolbar area and **right-mouse-click** once to display a list of options. Select **Toolbars → AutoCAD**.

2. Select **UCS**, with the left-mouse-button, to display the *UCS* toolbar on the screen.

➢ The options available in the *UCS* toolbar allow us to quickly orient and align the UCS.

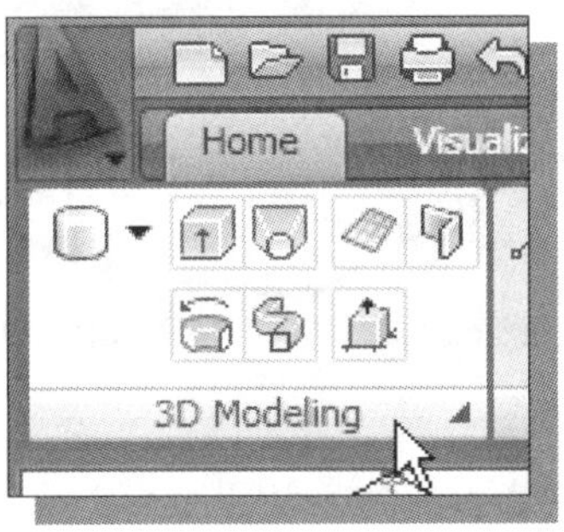

3. Click on the Title area of the *3D Modeling Toolbar* to show the addition commands available

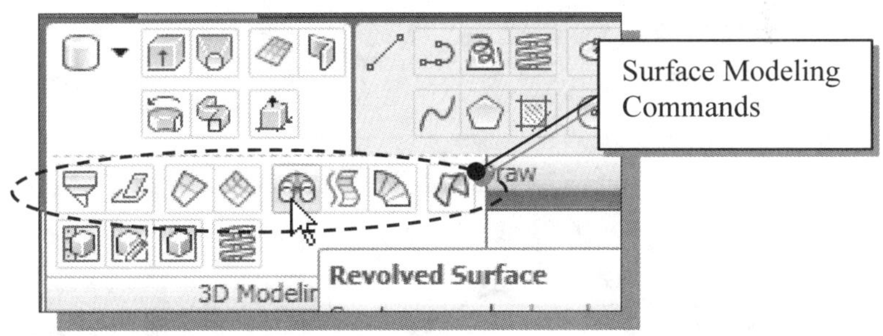

- Note that eight surface modeling commands are available to create Meshes. On your own, move the cursor on top of the different commands and read the brief description of the commands.

Creating a Surface Using the 2D Solid Command

➢ The first generation surface available in AutoCAD is used to fill an area in the sketch plane of the current UCS. It is therefore necessary to properly orient the UCS prior to using the 2D Solid command.

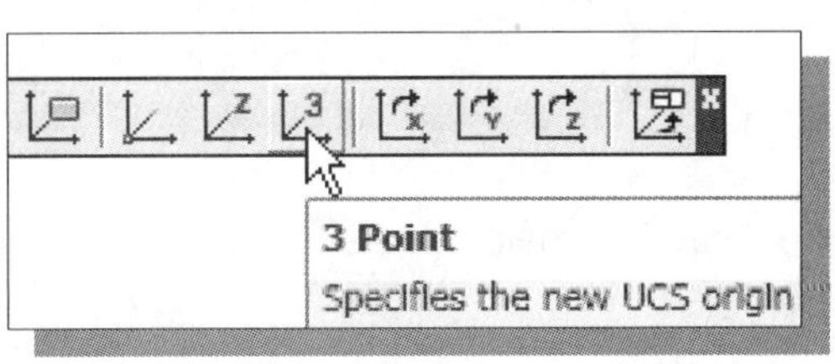

1. Select the **3 Point UCS** icon in the *UCS* toolbar.

- The **3 Point UCS** option allows us to specify the new X-axis and Y-axis directions to align the UCS.

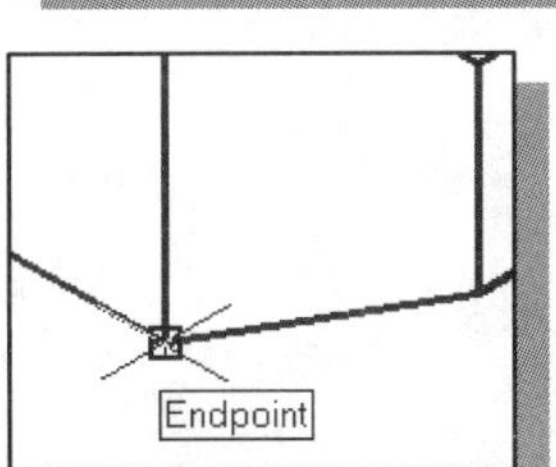

2. In the command prompt area, the message "*Specify new origin point<0,0,0>:*" is displayed. Pick the **lower right corner** of the front face of the wireframe model as shown.

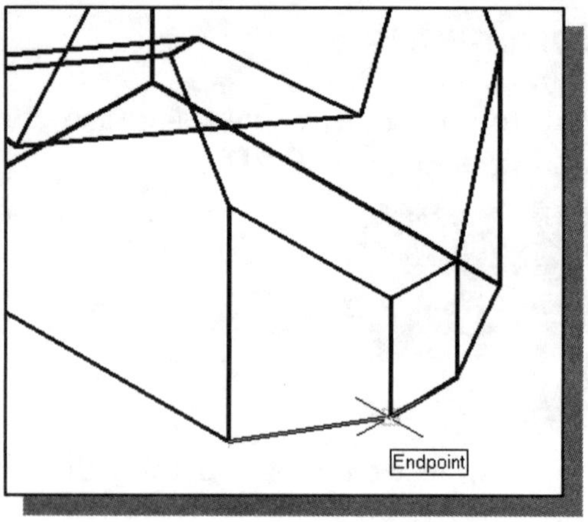

3. In the command prompt area, the message "*Specify point on positive portion of X-axis:*" is displayed. Pick the adjacent corner toward the right side of the model as shown.

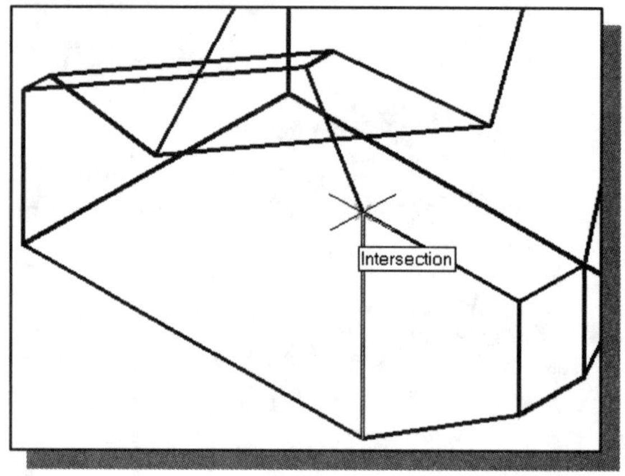

4. In the command prompt area, the message "*Specify point on positive portion of X-axis:*" is displayed. Pick the right corner of the inclined plane as shown.

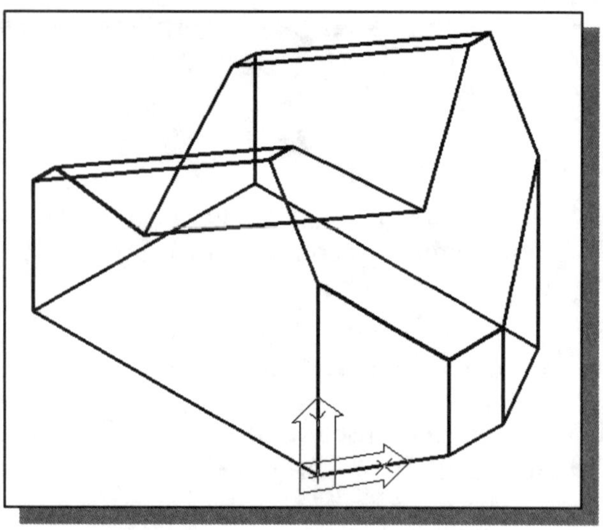

- The new UCS is aligned to the vertical inclined plane as shown.

5. In the *3D Modeling* toolbar, select **2D Solid** as shown.

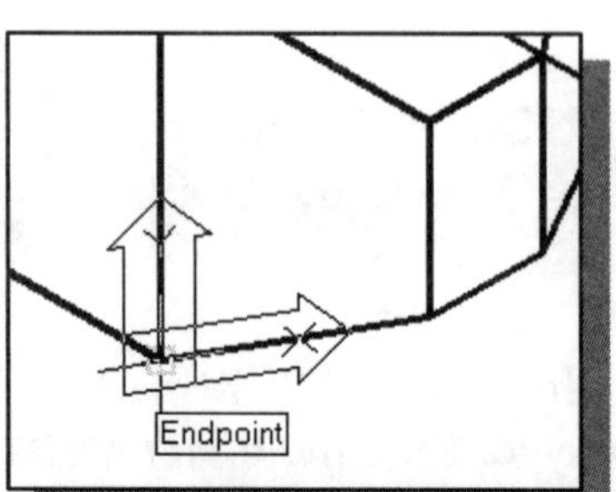

6. Place the first corner point of the 2D solid at the origin of the new UCS.

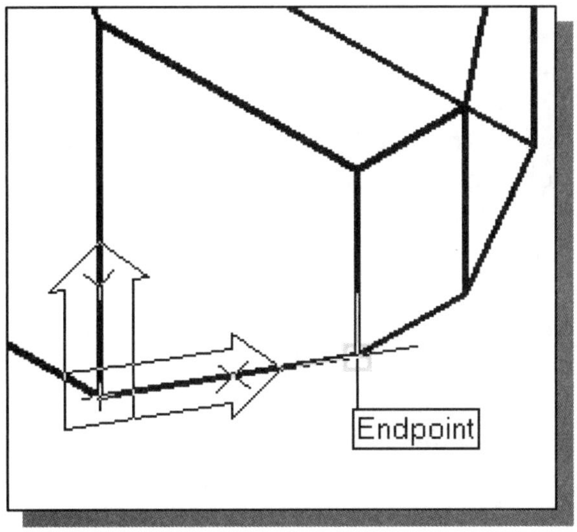

7. In the command prompt area, the message "*Specify second point:*" is displayed. Pick the bottom right corner of the inclined plane as shown.

8. In the command prompt area, the message "*Specify third point:*" is displayed. Pick the corner directly above the origin of the UCS as shown.

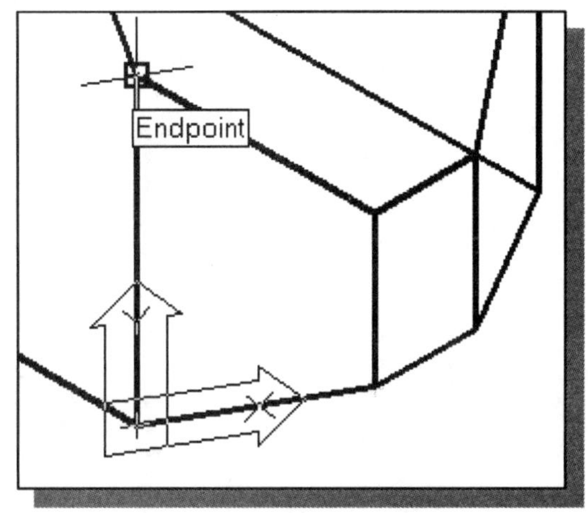

- The **2D Solid** command requires the third point to be specified diagonally opposite to the second point. This seemly strange way of specifying the third corner was established when the **2D Solid** command was first introduced back in the mid-1980s. Note that the **3D Face** command, the second-generation surface command in AutoCAD, does not follow this convention.

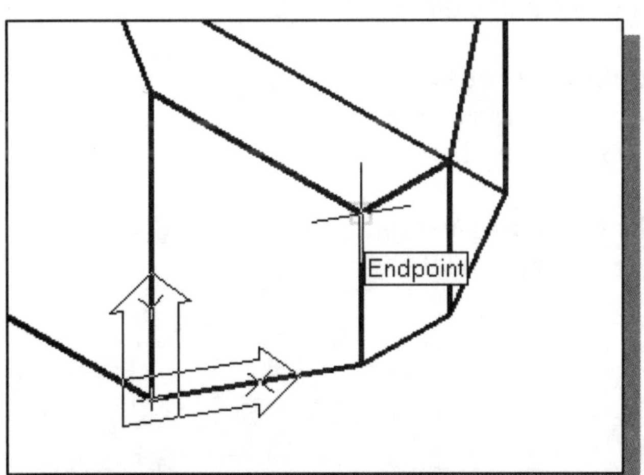

9. In the command prompt area, the message "*Specify fourth point or [Exit]:*" is displayed. Pick the corner directly above the second point we selected as shown in the figure.

10. Inside the graphics window, **right-mouse-click once** to end the **2D Solid** command.

- The **2D Solid** command allows the creation of three-sided or four-sided filled polygons, which can be used to represent faces of surface models. Note that in the above steps, we could accept the three-sided polygon after defining the third corner.

Using the Visual Styles Toolbar

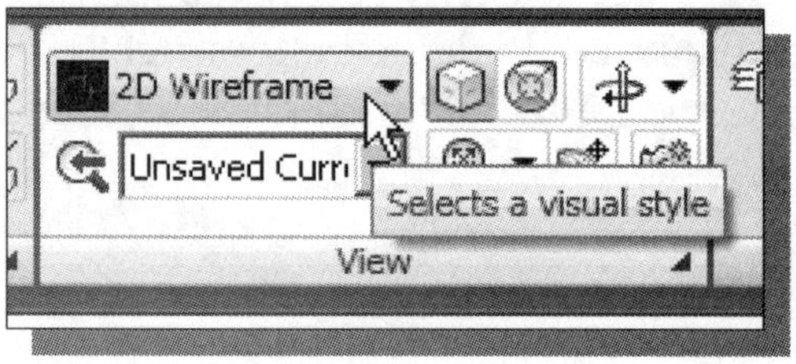

1. Move the cursor to the *View* toolbar panel and **left-click** on the downward triangle to display a list of available options.

   ❖ Five visual styles are available.

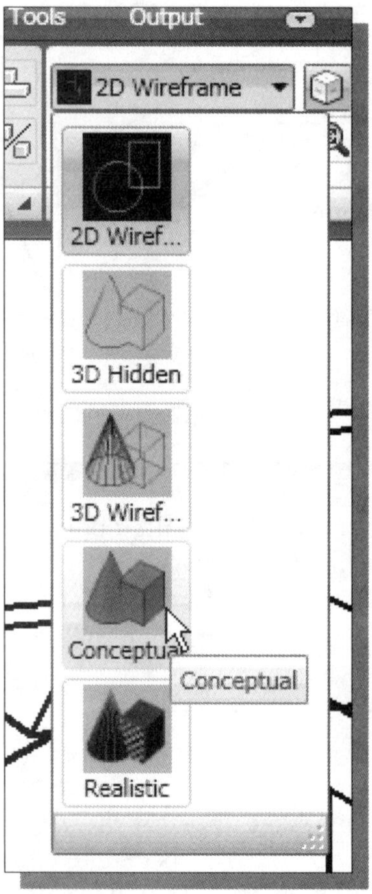

- **2D Wireframe**: Displays the objects using lines and curves to represent the boundaries of objects created. Linetypes and lineweights are visible with this option. Note that this is the default AutoCAD display mode.
- **3D Hidden**: Displays the objects using the 3D wireframe representation with lines that are located behind surfaces and solids removed.
- **3D Wireframe**: Displays the objects using lines and curves to represent the boundaries of objects created. Displays a shaded 3D user coordinate system (UCS) icon. Note that linetypes and lineweights are not visible with this option.
- **Conceptual Visual Style**: Creates a shaded image of polygon faces and solids that uses the Gooch face style, a transition between cool and warm colors rather than dark to light. The effect is less realistic, but it can make the details of the model easier to see.
- **Realistic Visual Style**: Creates a shaded image of polygon faces and solids that gives the objects a smooth and realistic appearance.

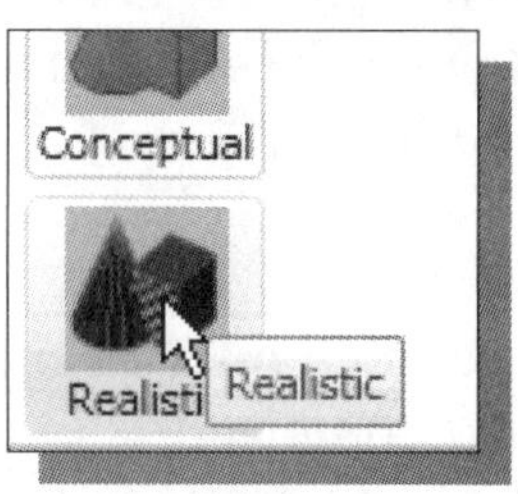

2. Click on the **Realistic Visual Style** icon to display the shaded image of the model.

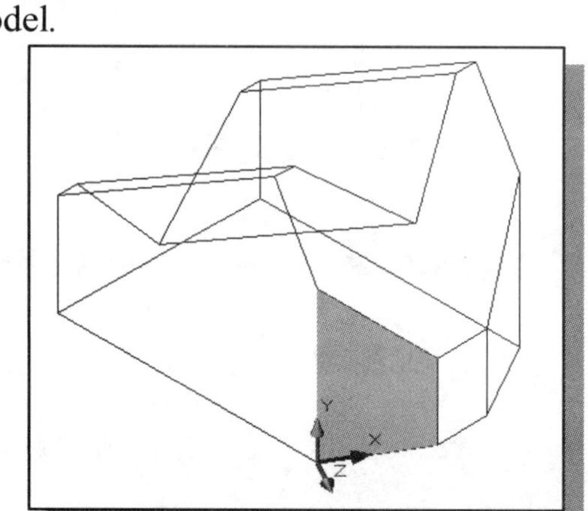

❖ There exists only one surface in our model. The surface was created with the 2D Solid command.

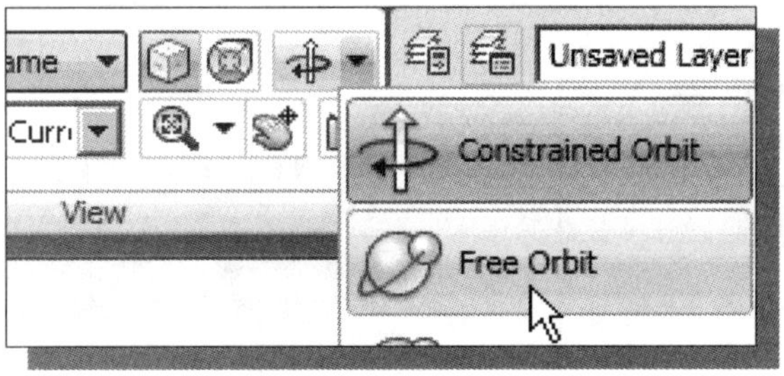

3. Select **Free Orbit** in the *View* toolbar as shown.

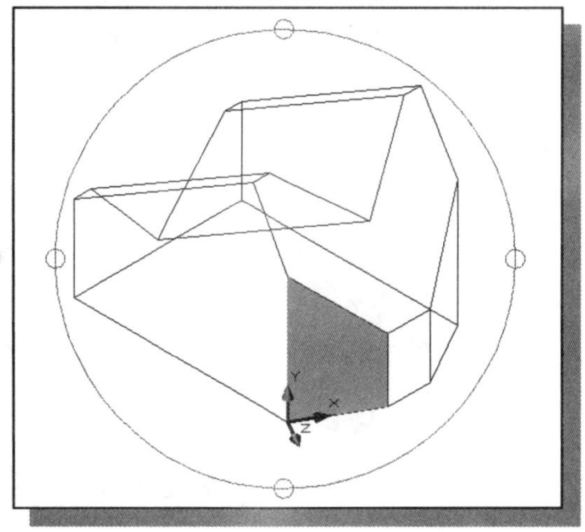

4. Inside the *arcball*, press down the left-mouse-button and drag it to rotate the model freely in 3D space. Observe the display of the shaded surface in contrast to the 3D wireframe edges that are located behind it.

5. In the *UCS* toolbar, select the **World UCS**. This option resets the UCS to align to the world coordinate system.

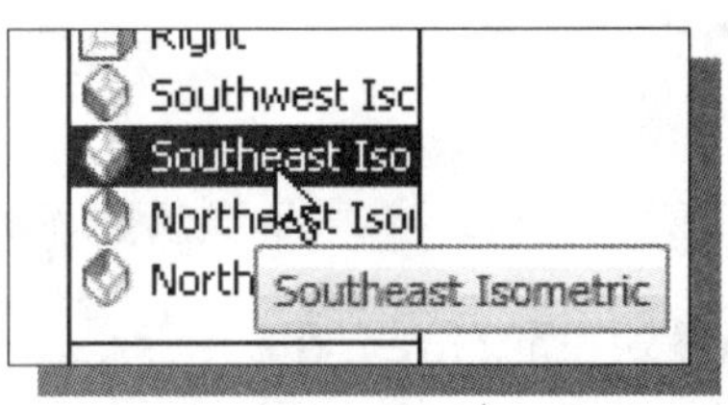

6. On your own, reset the display to the **SE Isometric View** before continuing to the next section.

Creating a Surface Using the 3D Face Command

- The second generation of surface command made available in AutoCAD was the **3D Face** command. The **3D Face** command can be used to create true 3D planar surfaces by allowing the X, Y and Z coordinates of the corners to be selected independently of the current UCS. The created polygon can be a three-sided or four-sided shape. This command is the primary construction tool for surface modeling in AutoCAD.

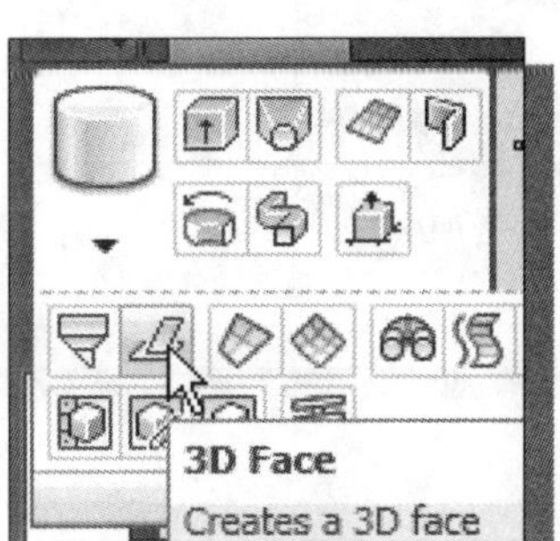

1. In the *3D Modeling* toolbar, select **3D Face** as shown.

2. In the command prompt area, the message "*_3dface Specify first point or [invisible]:*" is displayed. Pick the lower right corner of the vertical inclined face of the model as shown.

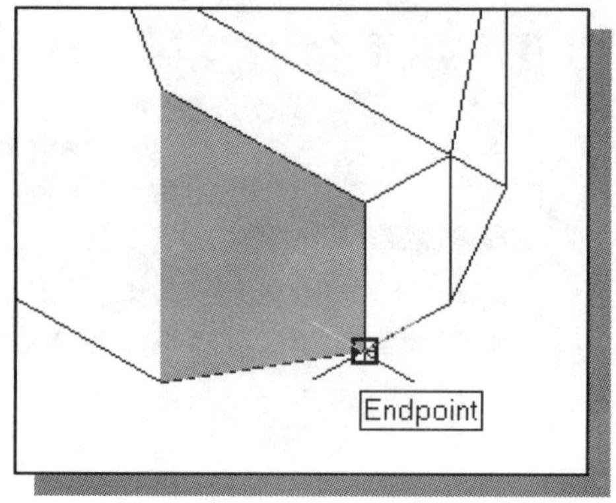

3. In the command prompt area, the message "*Specify second point or [invisible]:*" is displayed. Pick the adjacent corner above the previous selected corner of the vertical inclined face as shown.

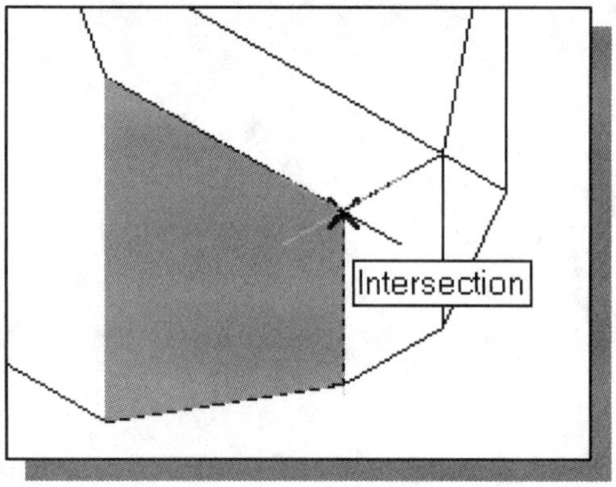

4. In the command prompt area, the message "*Specify third point or [invisible]:*" is displayed. Pick the adjacent corner of the right vertical face of the model as shown.

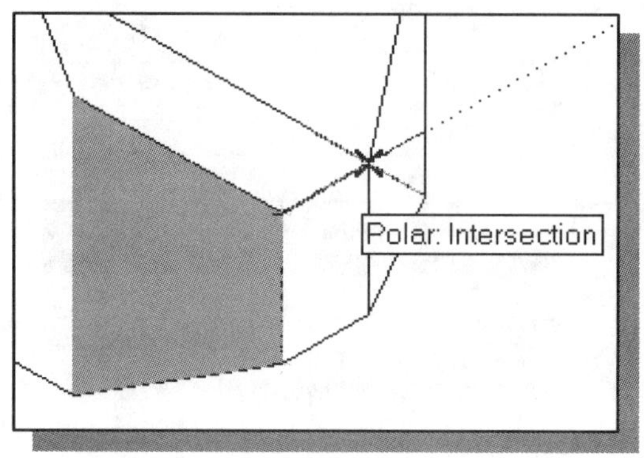

5. In the command prompt area, the message "*Specify fourth point or [invisible] <Create three-sided face>:*" is displayed. Pick the corner below the last selected corner as shown.

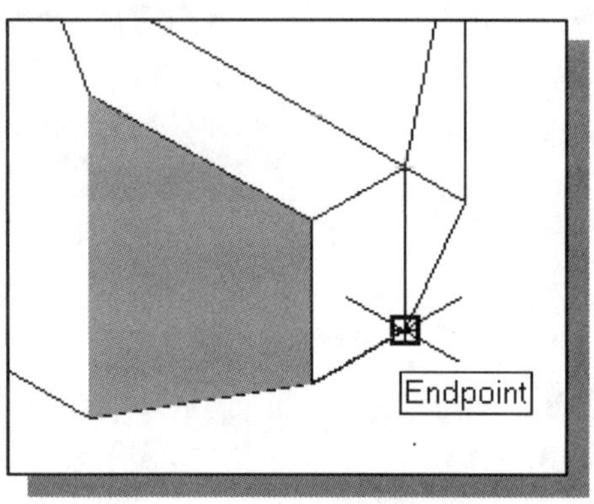

6. In the command prompt area, the message "*Specify third point or [invisible] <exit>:*" is displayed. Pick the back corner of the model as shown.

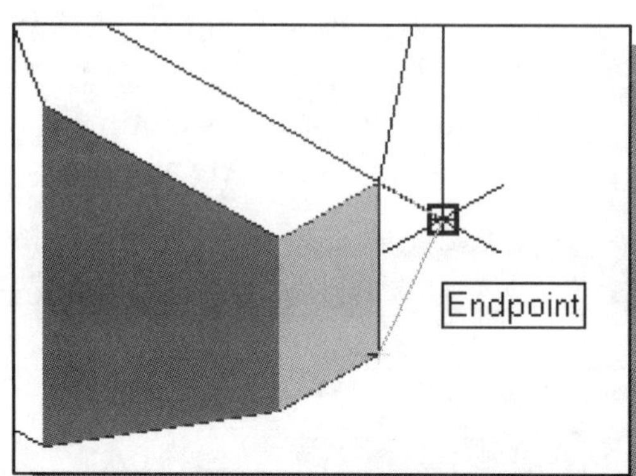

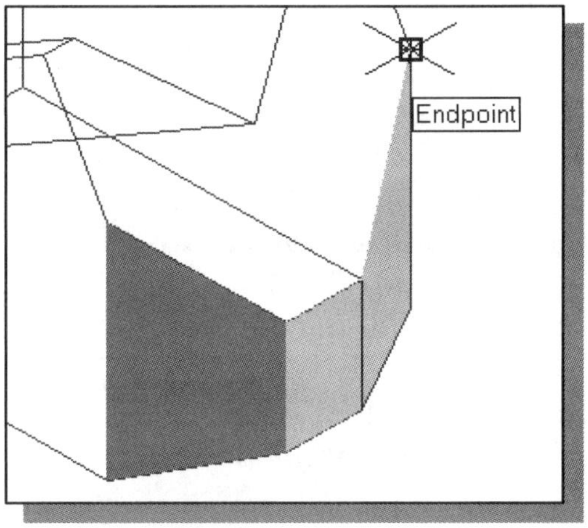

7. In the command prompt area, the message "*Specify fourth point or [invisible] <Create three-sided face>:*" is displayed. Pick the back corner of the model as shown.

- Note that this surface is created independent of the UCS and two corners of the previous face were used to position this face.

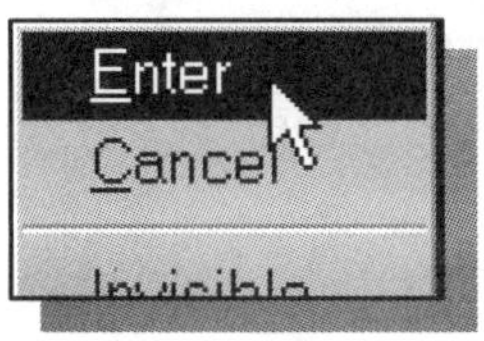

8. Inside the graphics window, right-mouse-click to activate the option menu and select **Enter** with the left-mouse-button to end the **3D Face** command.

The ViewCube

The *ViewCube* is a 3D navigation tool that appears when the 3D graphics system is enabled. With the *ViewCube*, you can switch between standard and isometric views.

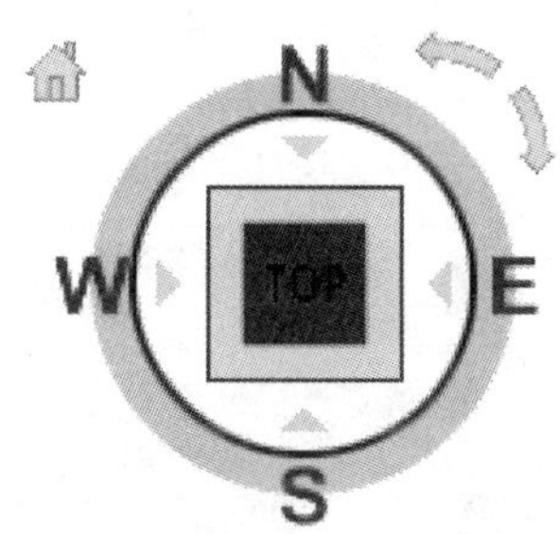

Once the ViewCube is displayed, it is shown in one of the corners of the graphics window over the model in an inactive state. The ViewCube also provides visual feedback about the current viewpoint of the model as view changes occur. When the cursor is positioned over the ViewCube, it becomes active and allows you to switch to one of the available preset views, roll the current view, or change to the Home view of the model.

1. Move the cursor over the ViewCube and noticed the different sides of the ViewCube become highlighted and can be activated.

2. Single left-mouse-click when the Front Side is activated as shown. The current view is set to viewing the Front side.

3. Move the cursor over the Counter Clockwise Arrow of the ViewCube and noticed the orbit option become highlighted.

4. Single left-mouse-click to activate the Counter Clockwise option as shown. The current view is orbitd 90 degrees, we are still viewing the Front side.

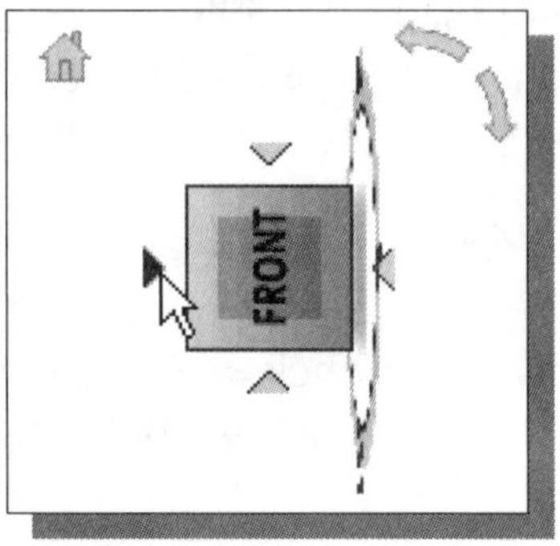

5. Move the cursor over the Left Arrow of the ViewCube and noticed the orbit option become highlighted.

6. Single left-mouse-click to activate the Left Arrow option as shown. The current view is now set to viewing the Top side.

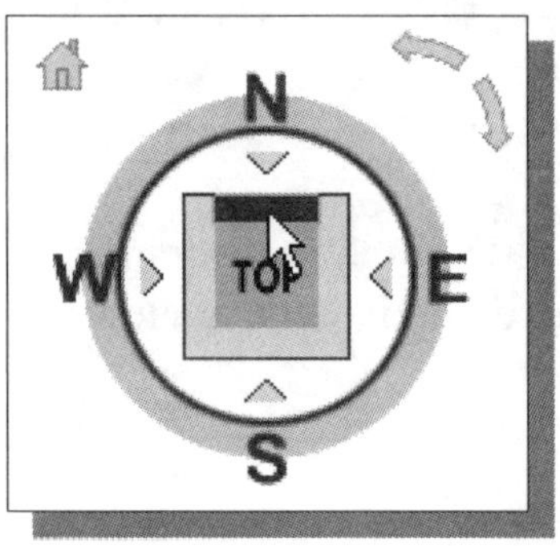

7. Move the cursor over the Top Edge of the ViewCube and noticed the roll option become highlighted.

8. Single left-mouse-click to activate the Roll option as shown. The view will be adjusted to roll 45 degrees.

9. Move the cursor over the *ViewCube* and drag with the left-mouse-button to activate the **Free Rotation** option.

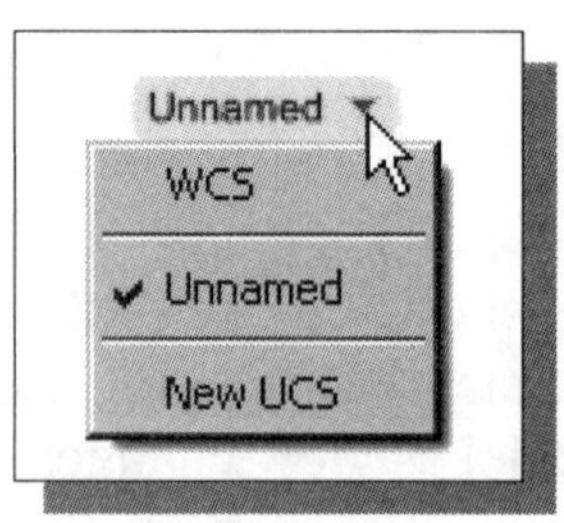

➢ The orientation of the model can also be changed to base on either the UCS or the WCS by clicking on the coordinate setting option below the ViewCube as shown.

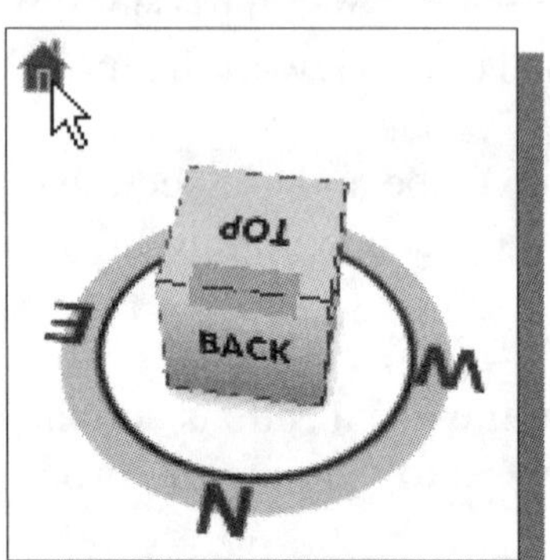

10. Move the cursor over the Home icon of the *ViewCube* and noticed the Home View option become highlighted.

11. Single left-mouse-click to activate the **Home View** option as shown. The view will be adjusted back to the default ***SW Isometric View***.

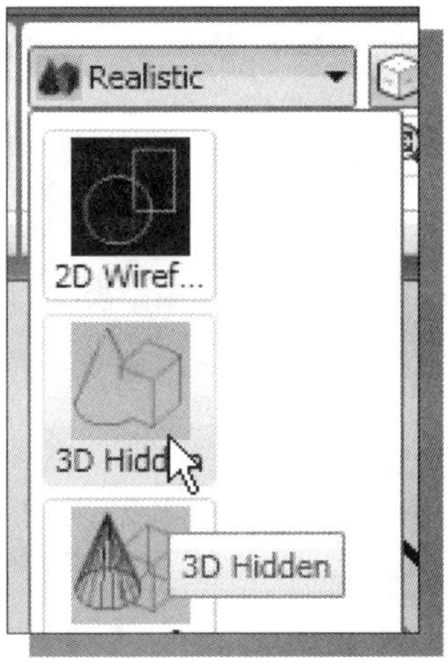

11. In the *Visual Styles* toolbar, click on the **3D Hidden** icon to display the model with hidden lines removed.

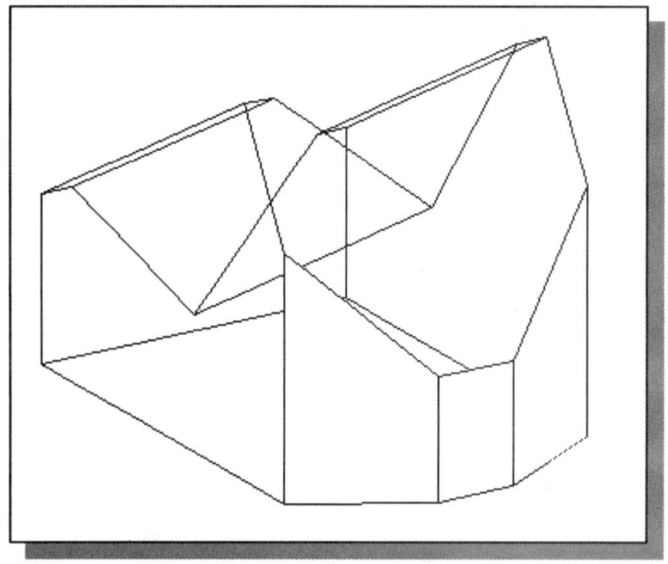

12. On your own, use the **ViewCube** to rotate the model and examine the constructed surface model.

- Reset the display to SE Isometric View before proceed to the next section.

Creating a Surface of Irregular Shape

- The **3D Face** command allows us to create three-sided or four-sided polygons. For surfaces of irregular shape, the Invisible Edge option is available in conjunction with the 3D Face command. Note that the Invisible Edge option cannot be applied to polygons created by the 2D Solid command.

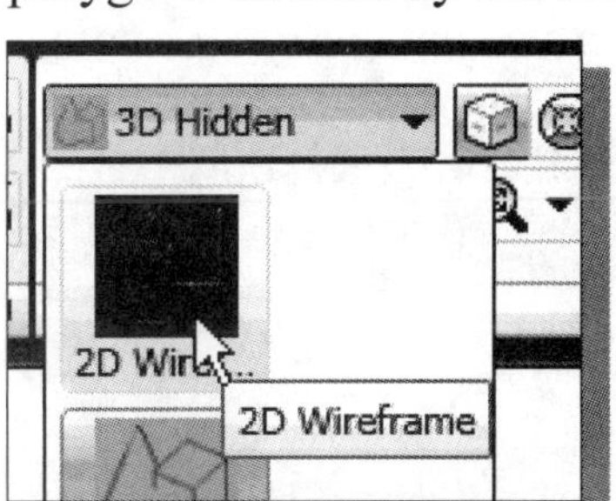

1. Select the **2D Wireframe** in the *Visual Styles* toolbar.

- The 2D Wireframe command resets the display to the default AutoCAD display mode

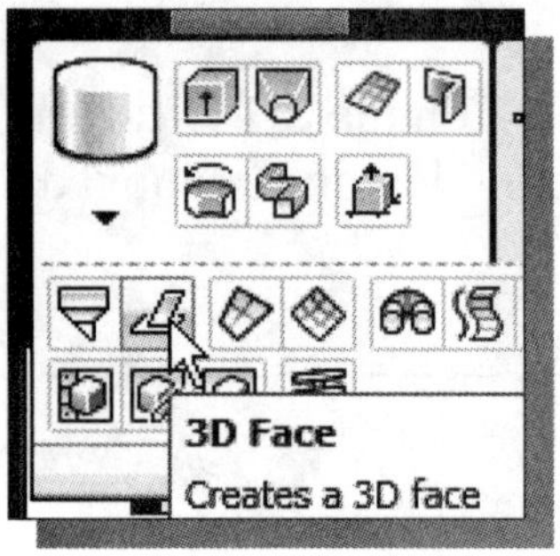

2. In the *3D Modeling* toolbar, select **3D Face**.

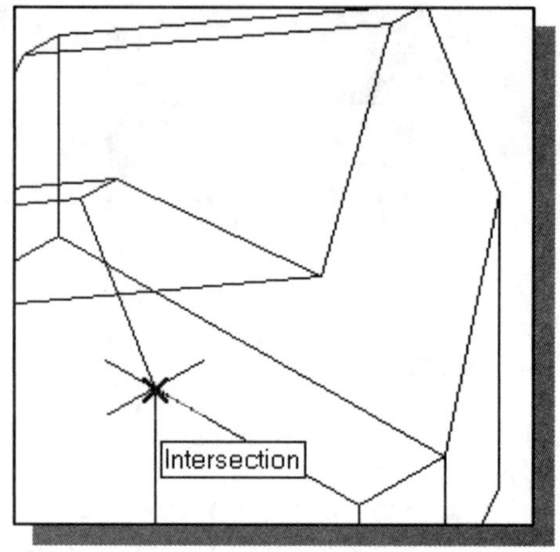

3. In the command prompt area, the message "*_3dface Specify first point or [invisible]:*" is displayed. Pick the top right corner of the model as shown.

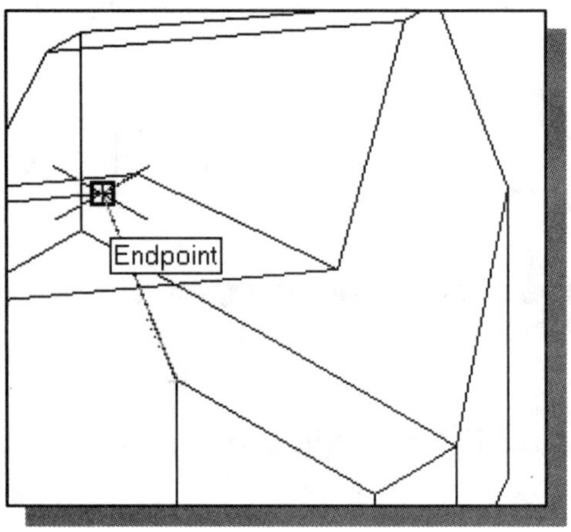

4. In the command prompt area, the message "*Specify second point or [invisible]:*" is displayed. Pick the top front corner of the model as shown.

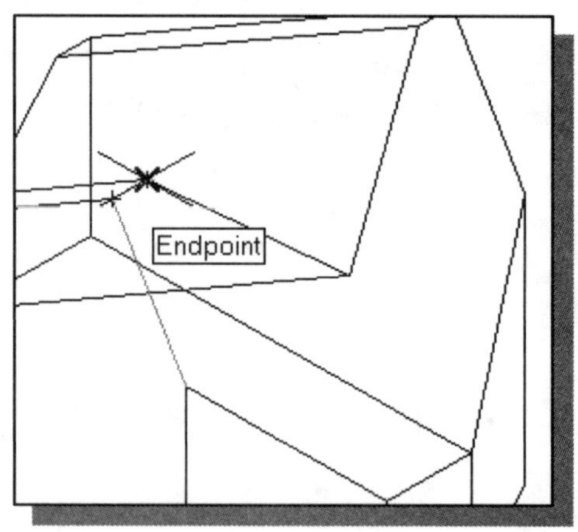

5. In the command prompt area, the message "*Specify third point or [invisible] <exit>:*" is displayed. Pick the top corner of the model adjacent to the previously selected corner as shown.

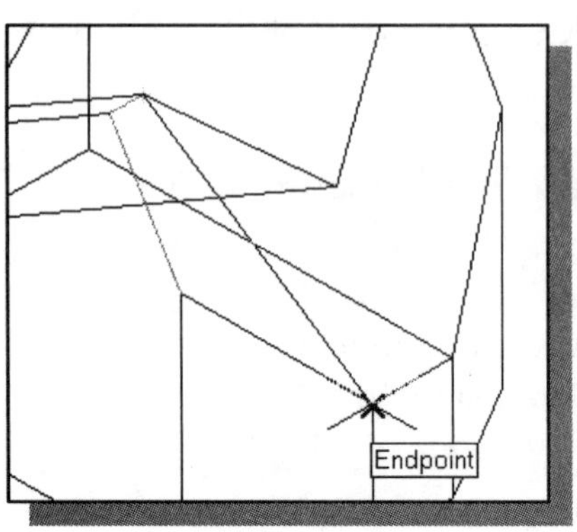

6. In the command prompt area, the message "*Specify fourth point or [invisible] <Create three-sided face>:*" is displayed. Pick the corner below the last selected corner as shown.

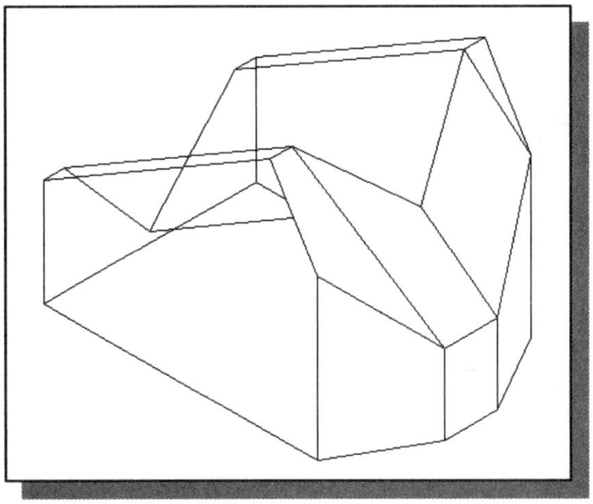

7. On your own, repeat the zigzagging pattern to define polygons until all corners of the inclined surface have been selected and additional polygons are created as shown in the figure. Note that the last polygon we created is a three-sided polygon.

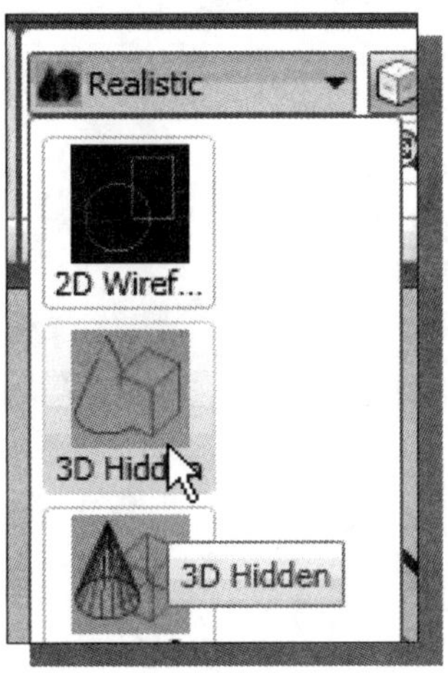

8. In the *Visual Styles* toolbar, click on the **3D Hidden** icon to display the model with hidden lines removed. Note that the edges of the polygons are displayed as shown.

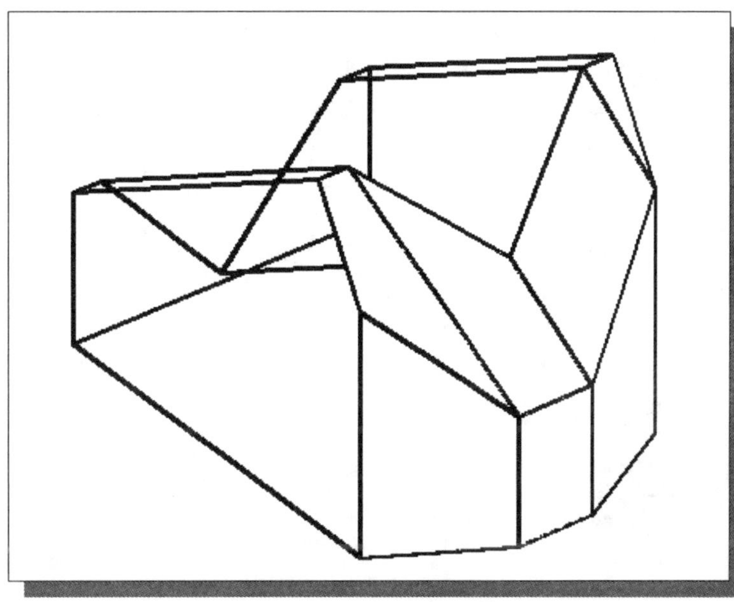

9. On your own, examine the model by selecting the different *Visual Styles*.

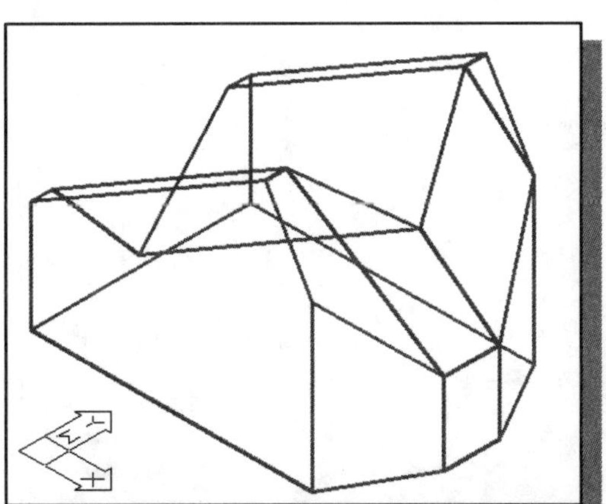

10. Rest the *Visual Styles* toolbar to **2D Wireframe,** the default AutoCAD display mode.

Using the Invisible Edge Option

- The Invisible Edge option is used to turn off the display of selected edges and therefore allow the adjacent polygons, created by the 3D Face command, to appear as being joined together.

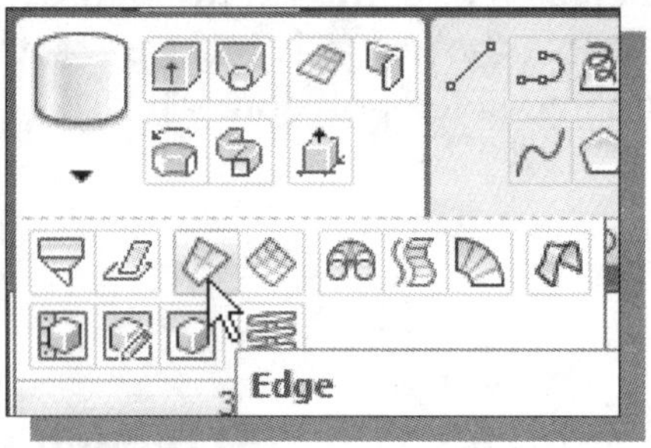

1. In the 3D Modeling toolbar, select **Edge** as shown in the figure.

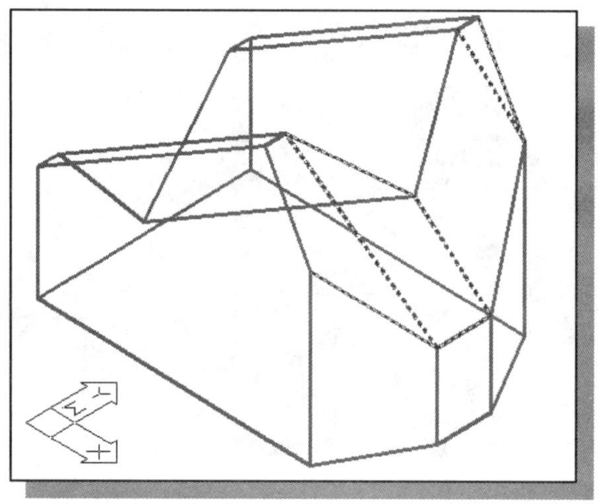

2. In the command prompt area, the message "*Specify edge of 3dface to toggle visibility or [Display]:*" is displayed. Pick the three edges inside the inclined surface as shown.

3. Inside the graphics window, right-mouse-click to activate the option menu and select **Enter** to end the Edge command.

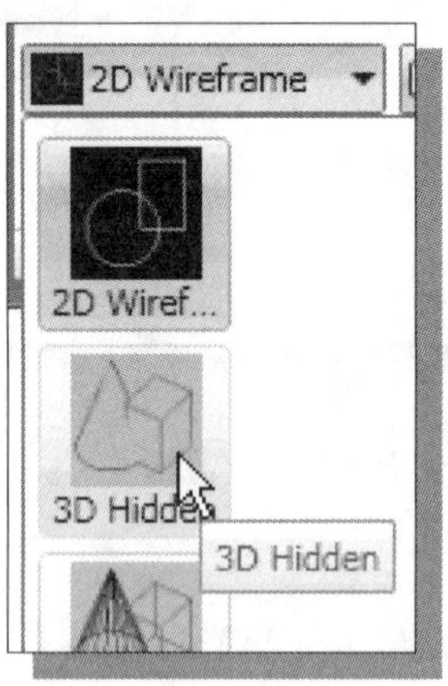

4. Set the *Visual Style* toolbar to **3D Hidden**.

5. On your own, examine the model by selecting the different *Visual Styles.*

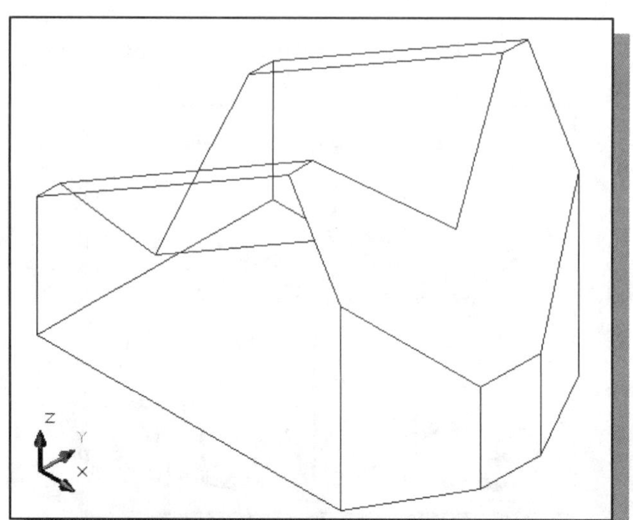

- The selected edges are removed from the display so that the face of the inclined surface of the model appears to be more realistic.

Moving with the Grip Editing Tools

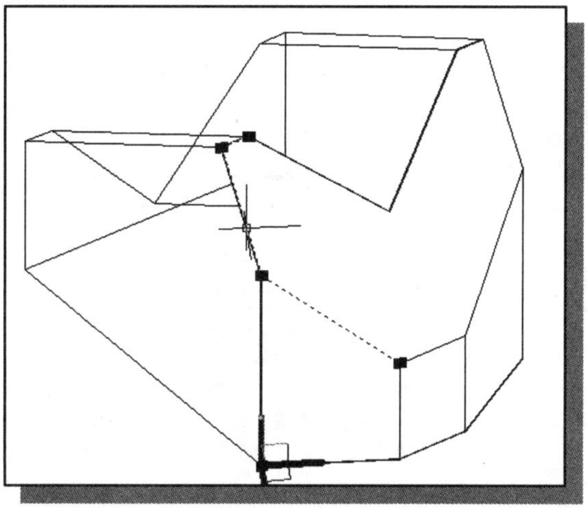

1. Select one of the 3D face we created by clicking on the front edge of the inclined surface as shown.

- Four grip points, the small rectangles displayed at the corners of the highlighted polygon, can be used to adjust the size and shape of the highlighted polygon.

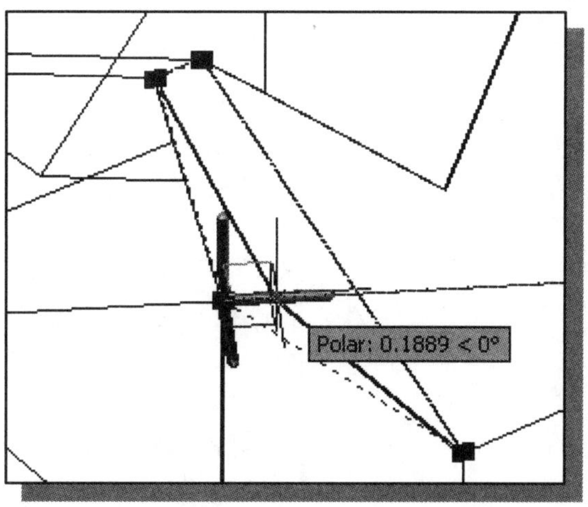

2. Move the cursor on one of the grip points. Notice the grip editing axes is automatically aligned to the grip point.

3. Click on one of the axes and drag with the left-mouse-button to move the grip point. (Clicking on the axis constrain the movement to the selected axis.)

4. Press the **[Esc]** key to deselect the highlighted entities.

➢ On your own, repeat the above steps and complete the surface model of the design.

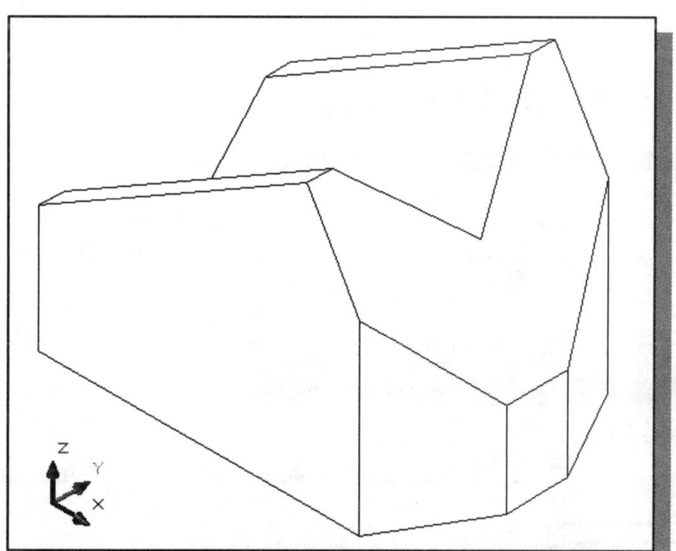

The *Locator* Wireframe Model

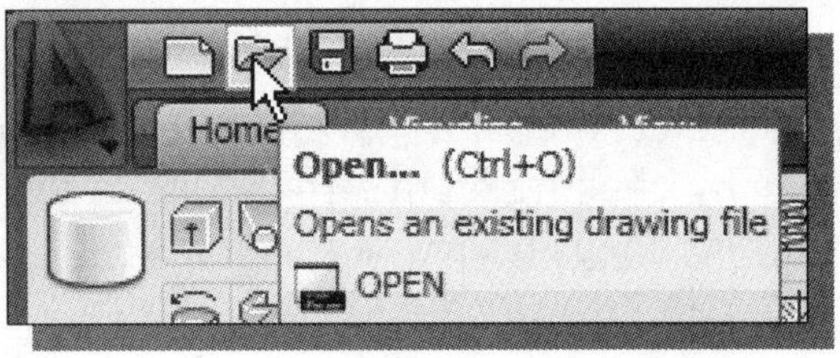

1. Click on the **Open** icon in the *Standard* toolbar.

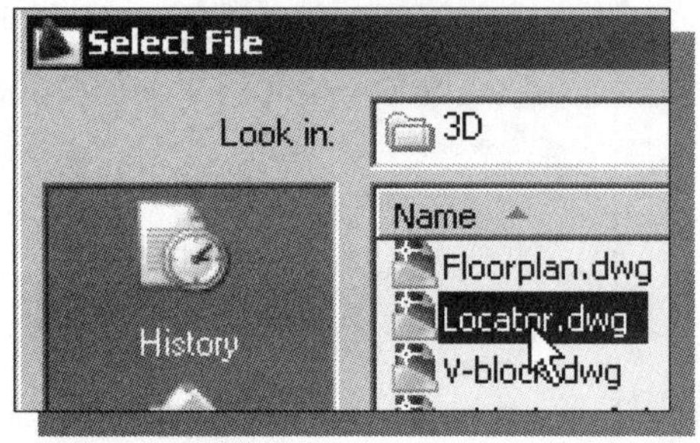

2. In the *Select File* window, pick the ***Locator*** file that was created in Chapter 3.

3. Click **Open** to open the model file.

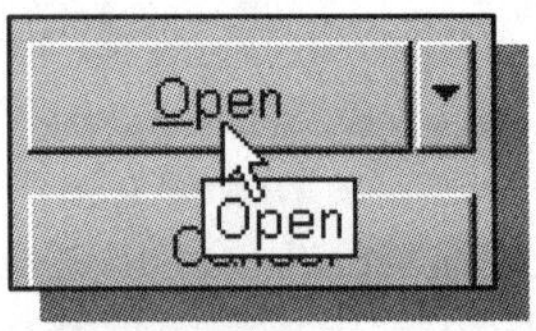

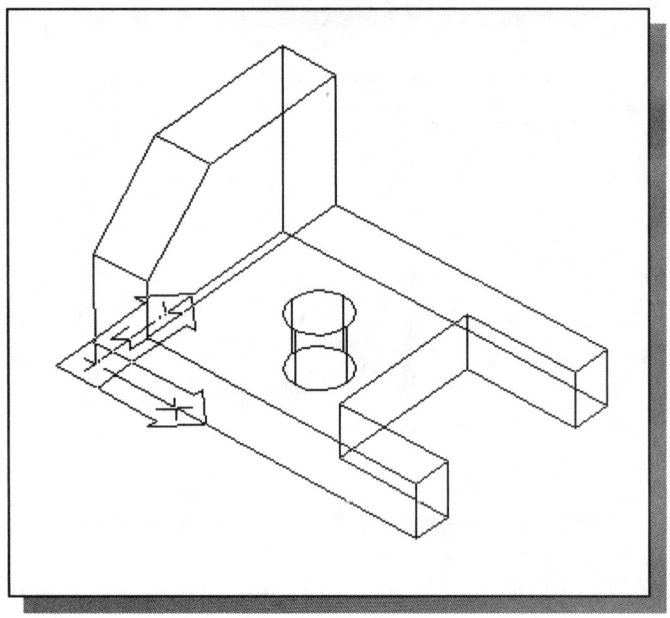

Moving Objects to a Different Layer

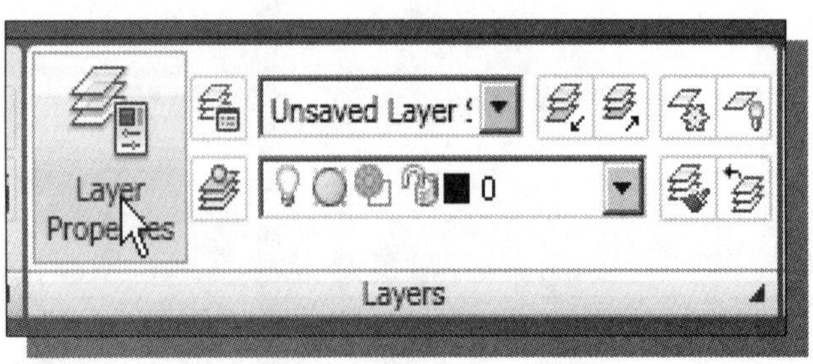

1. Click **Layers Properties Manager** in the *Layers* toolbar.

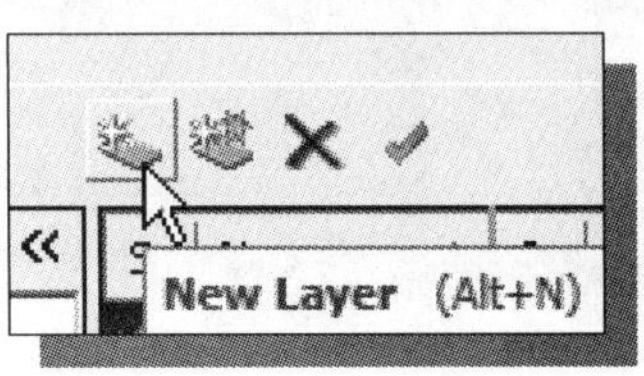

2. Click on the **New** button to create new layers.

3. Create **three new layers** with the following settings:

Layer	*Color*	*LineType*	*LineWeight*
Construction	**White**	**Continuous**	**Default**
Wireframe	**Blue**	**Continuous**	**0.30mm**
Surface	**Cyan**	**Continuous**	**Default**

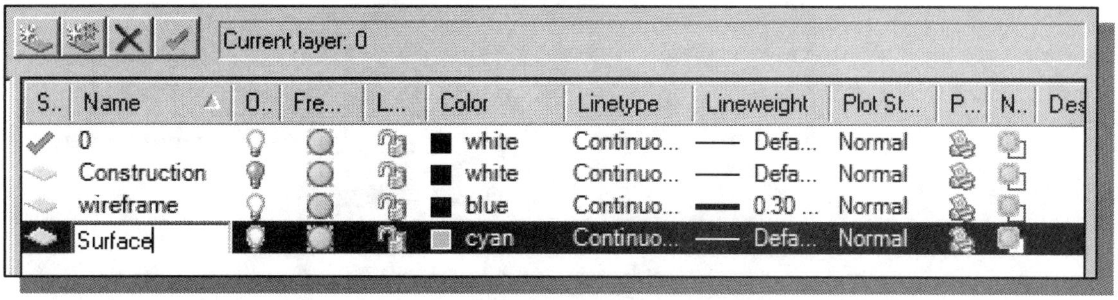

4. Click on the **Close** button to accept the settings and exit the *Layer Properties Manager* dialog box.

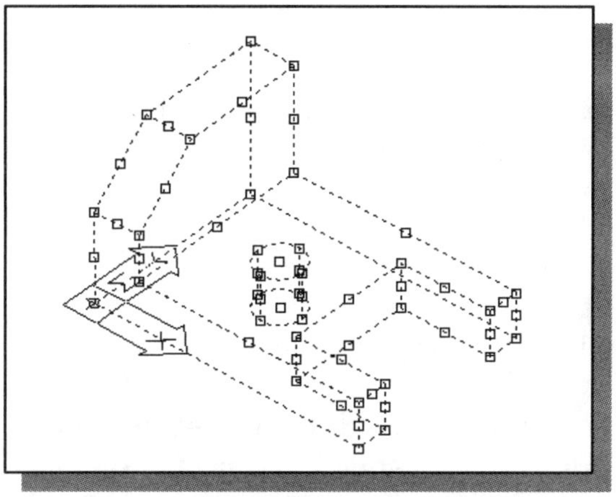

5. Inside the graphics window, pre-select all entities by using the left-mouse-button to create a *selection window* enclosing all entities.

- Note that all selected entities are highlighted.

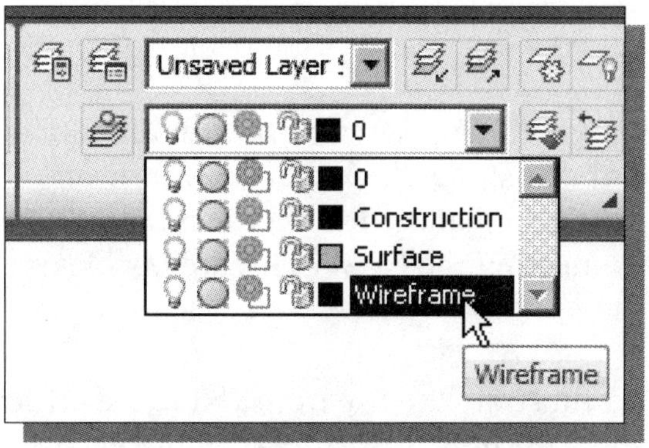

6. On the *Object Properties* toolbar, choose the ***Layer Control*** box with the left-mouse-button.

- Notice the layer name displayed in the *Layer Control* box is the selected object's assigned layer and layer properties.

7. In the *Layer Control* box, click on the ***Wireframe*** layer name as shown.

❖ All entities of the *Locator* model are moved to the *Wireframe* layer.

8. Press the **[ESC]** key twice to deselect all highlighted entities.

Advanced Surface Modeling Commands

❖ Several of the advanced surface-modeling commands are displayed in the last group of the *Surfaces Modeling* toolbar. These commands allow us to quickly create and duplicate surfaces in specific manners.

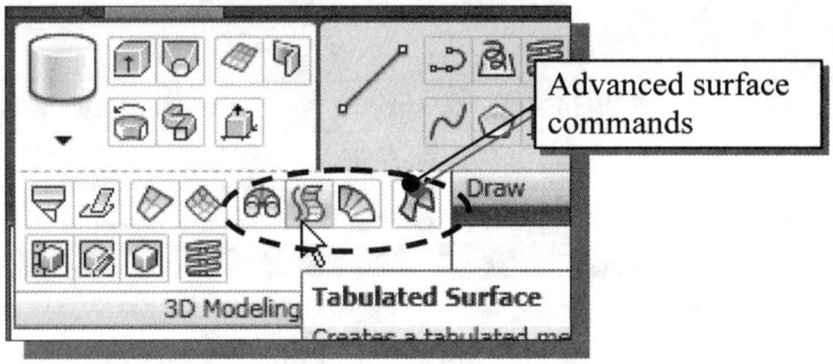

- **Revolved Surface**: Creates a surface mesh by rotating a group of objects about an axis.

- **Tabulated Surface**: Creates a surface mesh representing a general tabulated surface defined by a path curve and a direction vector. The resulting mesh is a series of parallel polygons running along a specified path.

- **Ruled Surface**: Creates a surface mesh between two objects.

- **Edge Surface**: Creates a surface patch mesh from four edges.

SurfTab1 & SurfTab2 system variables: These two variables are used to set the number of increments used by the Ruled Surface and Tabulated Surface commands. The default values are set to six, which means any curve will be approximated with six straight lines.

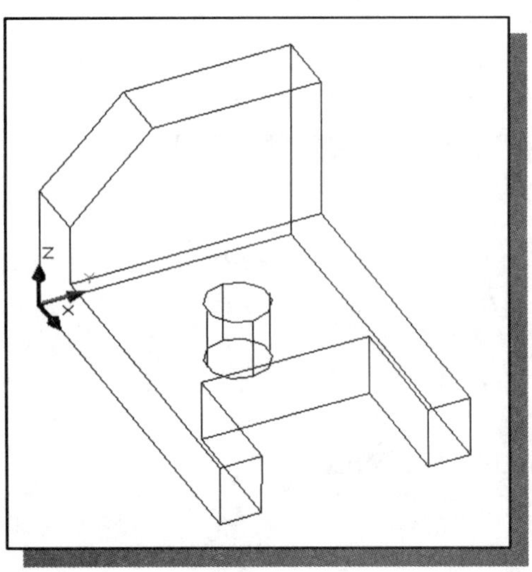

1. On your own, use the **Free Orbit** command and adjust the display of the wireframe model so that the four vertical lines connecting the two circles are visible as shown.

- To illustrate the use of the Ruled Surface and Tabulated Surface commands, we will first split the top circle into two arcs. Note that these surfacing commands allow us to construct a polygon mesh for different situations and regions. The split of the circle is necessary in creating a mapped surface on the top plane of the model.

2. Select **Break** in the *Modify* toolbar.

- The **Break** command can be used to erase parts of objects or split an object in two. Note that we can only erase parts of a circle. We will therefore erase a portion of the circle and then split the circle into two arcs.

3. Select the top circle as shown. Note that the portion defined by two points will be erased.

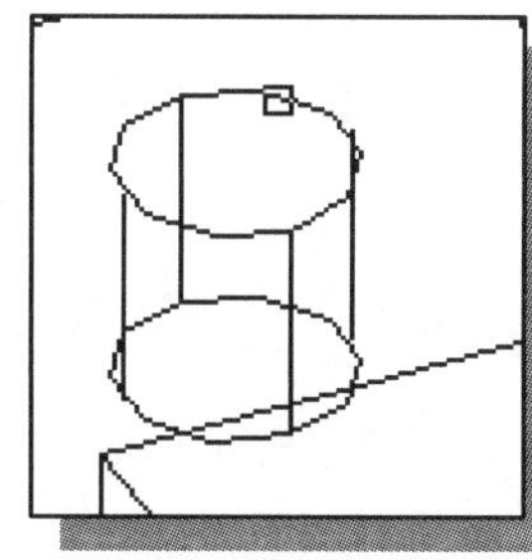

- By default, AutoCAD treats the selection point as the first break point. We can override the first point by choosing **First point** in the option menu.

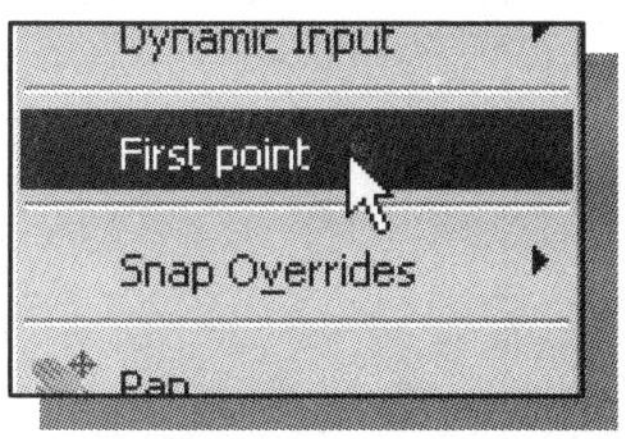

4. In the command prompt area, the message "*Specific second break point or [First point]:*" is displayed. Right-mouse-click once and select **First point** in the option menu.

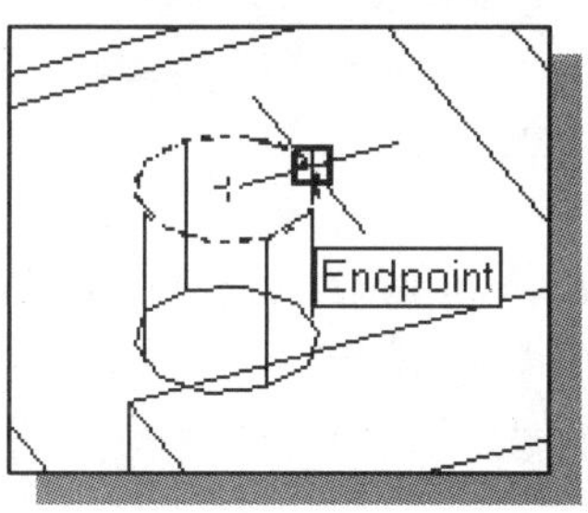

5. In the command prompt area, the message "*Specific first break point:*" is displayed. Choose the top endpoint of the vertical line as shown.

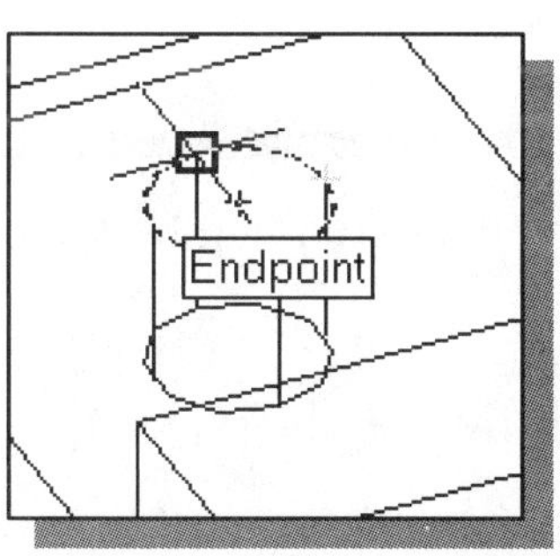

6. In the command prompt area, the message "*Specific second break point:*" is displayed. Choose the top endpoint of the vertical line as shown.

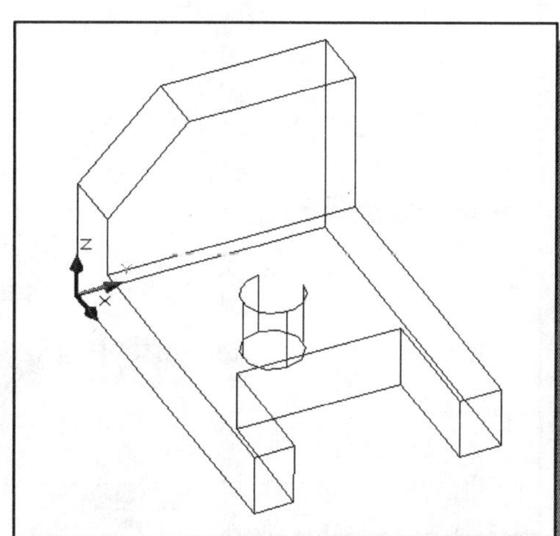

- One quarter of the circle has been erased. We will next split the arc into two arcs, again using the **Break** command.

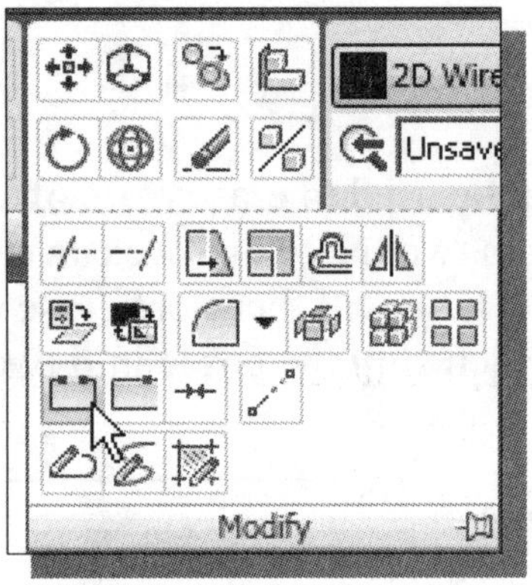

7. Select **Break** in the *Modify* toolbar.

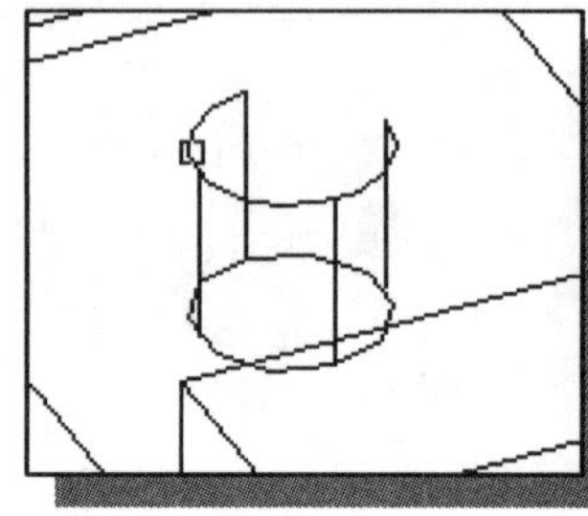

8. Select the top arc as shown.

- By default, AutoCAD treats the selection point as the first break point. We can override the first point by choosing **First point** in the option menu.

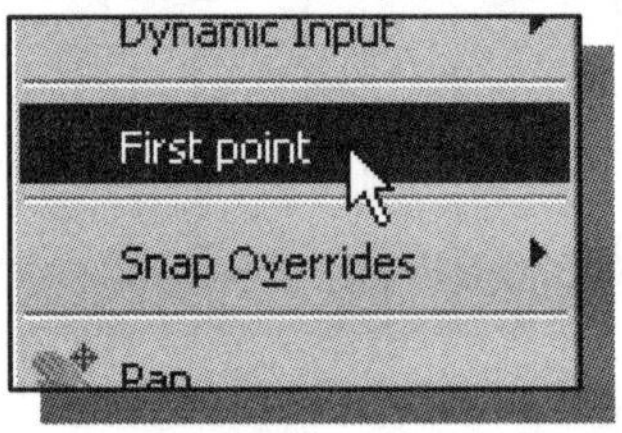

9. In the command prompt area, the message "*Specific second break point or [First point]:*" is displayed. Right-mouse-click once and select **First point** in the option menu.

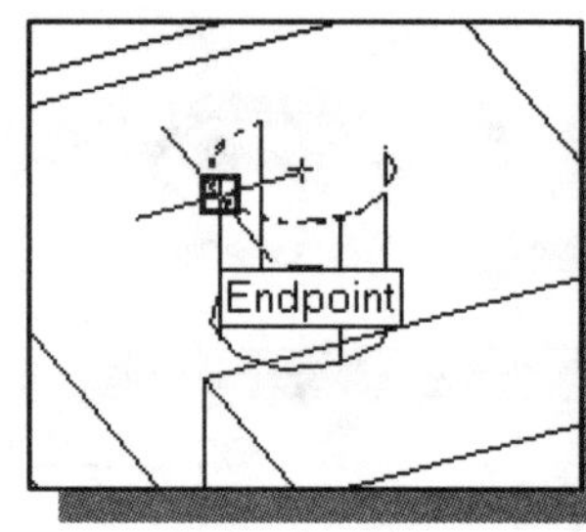

10. In the command prompt area, the message "*Specific first break point:*" is displayed. Choose the top endpoint of the left vertical line as shown.

11. In the command prompt area, the message "*Specific second break point:*" is displayed. To split an object, choose the **same endpoint** that was chosen as the first endpoint.

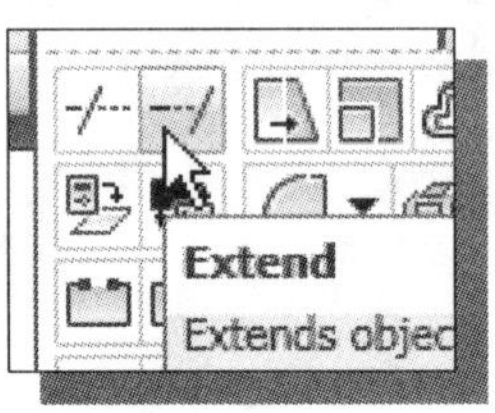

12. Select **Extend** in the *Modify* toolbar. Note the *Projection* type is set to **View**, as shown in the prompt window.

```
Command: _extend
Current settings: Projection=View, Edge=None
Select boundary edges ...
Select objects or <select all>:
```

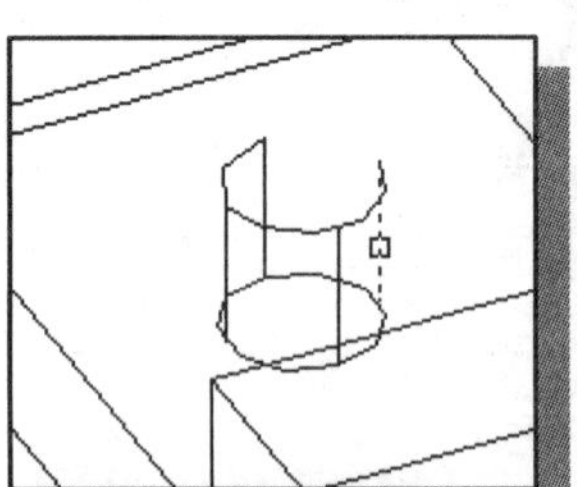

13. Select the right vertical edge to be the extending boundary as shown.

14. Inside the graphics window, right-mouse-click once to accept the selection.

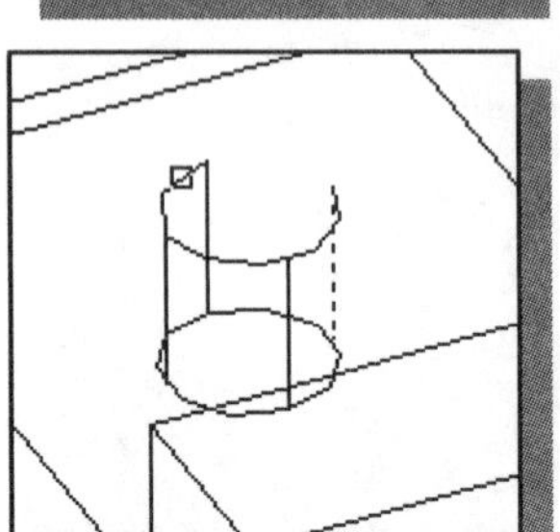

15. Pick the shorter arc near the right endpoint to extend the arc in that direction.

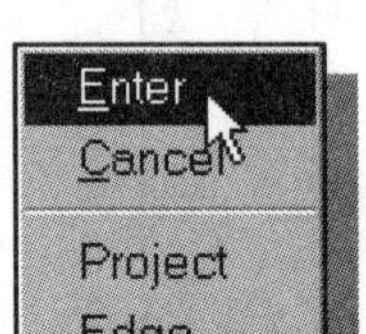

16. Inside the graphics window, right-mouse-click once to display the option menu and select **Enter** to end the **Extend** command.

Using the Tabulated Surface Option

- In AutoCAD, the **TABSURF** command allows us to construct a polygon mesh representing a general tabulated surface defined by a path curve and a direction vector.

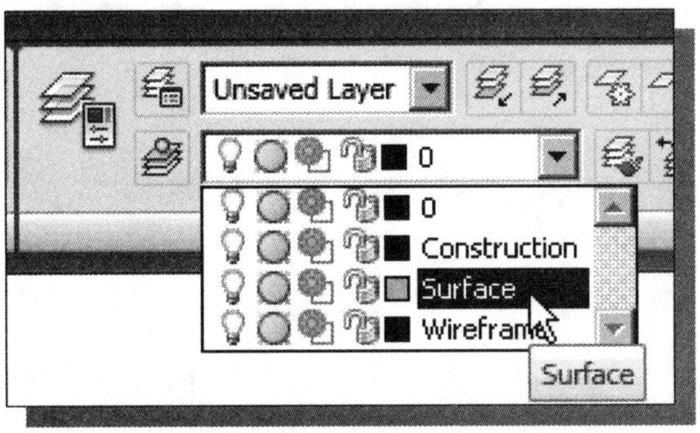

1. Set the ***Surface*** layer as the *Current Layer* by choosing the layer name in the *Layer Control* box as shown.

- We will place the surface model on a different layer than the wireframe model.

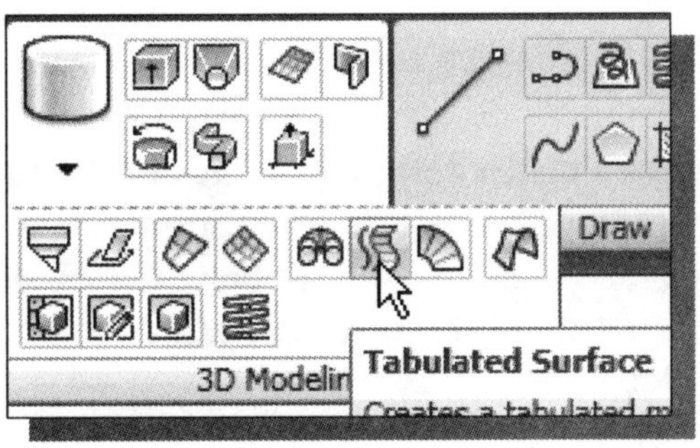

2. Click **Tabulated Surface** in the *3D Modeling* Toolbar.

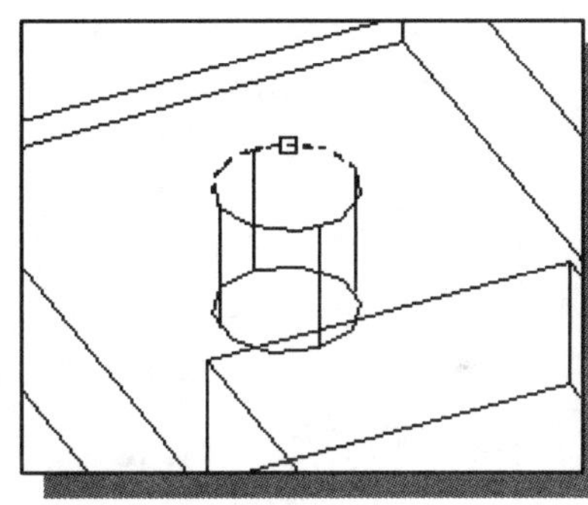

3. In the command prompt area, the message "*Select object for path curve:*" is displayed. Choose the upper arc as shown.

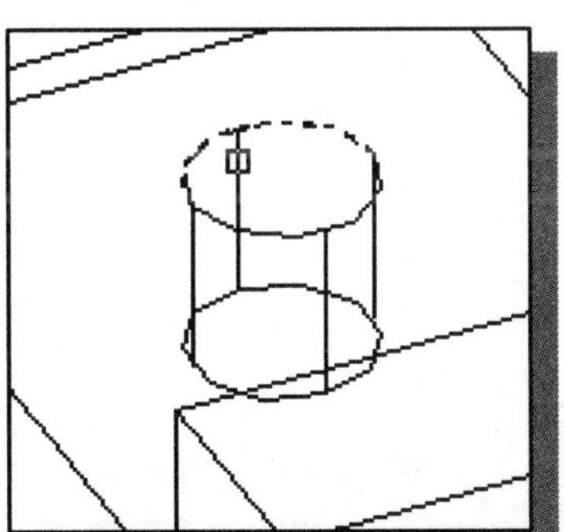

4. In the command prompt area, the message "*Select object for direction vector:*" is displayed. Choose the vertical line near the top endpoint as shown. Note that the endpoint of the line is used as a reference point to determine the direction of the polygon mesh.

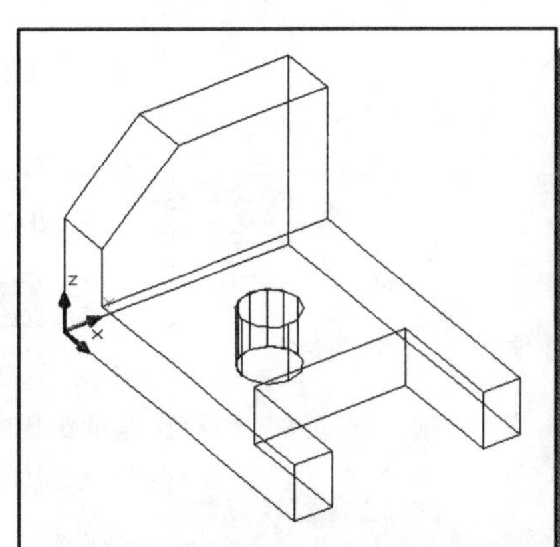

5. On your own, use the **Orbit** and **Visual Styles** commands to examine the constructed polygons.

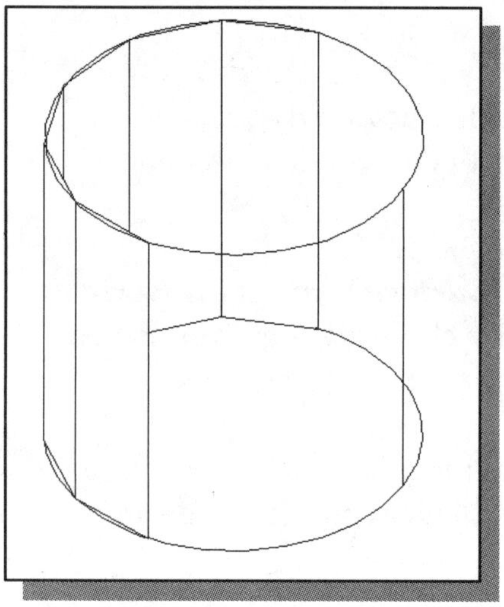

- Exactly six polygons are created and positioned along the selected *path curve*, the upper arc, with the Tabulated Surface command. This is set by the **SurfTab1** variable. We can adjust number of segments to use by typing the word, **surftab1**, at the command prompt.

❖ Note that a surface modeler using polygons to approximate true curves is called a *faceted surface modeler*.

Using the Ruled Surface Option

- In AutoCAD, the **RULESURF** command allows us to construct a polygon mesh between two objects. We can use two different objects to define the edges of the ruled surface: lines, points, arcs, circles, ellipses, elliptical arcs, polylines or splines. The two objects to be used as the *rails* of a ruled surface mesh must both be either open or closed. For open curves, AutoCAD starts construction of the ruled surface based on the locations of the specified points on the curves.

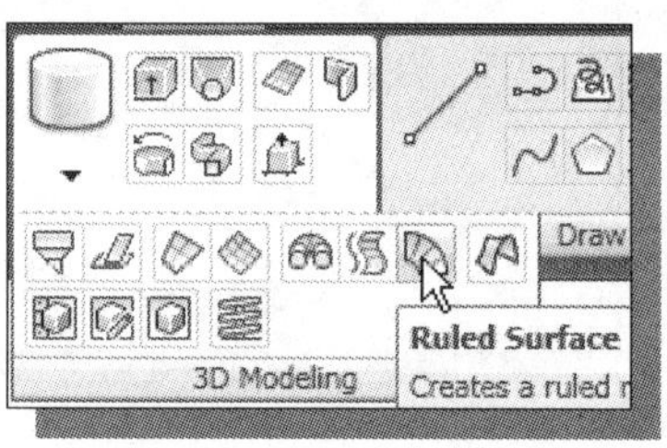

1. Pick **Ruled Surface** in the *Draw* pull-down menu.

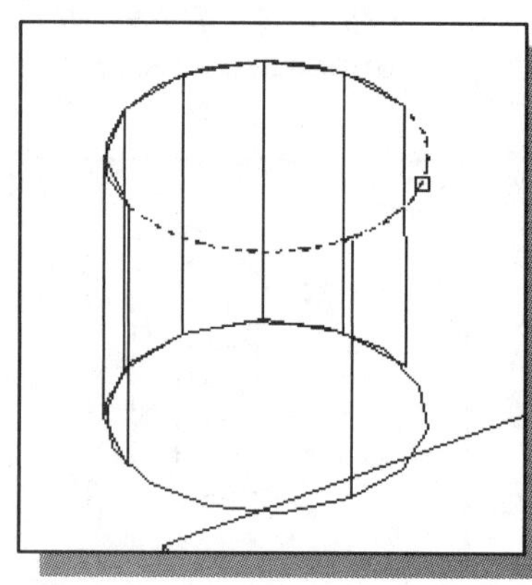

2. In the command prompt area, the message "*Select first defining curve:*" is displayed. Choose the lower arc by clicking on the right side as shown.

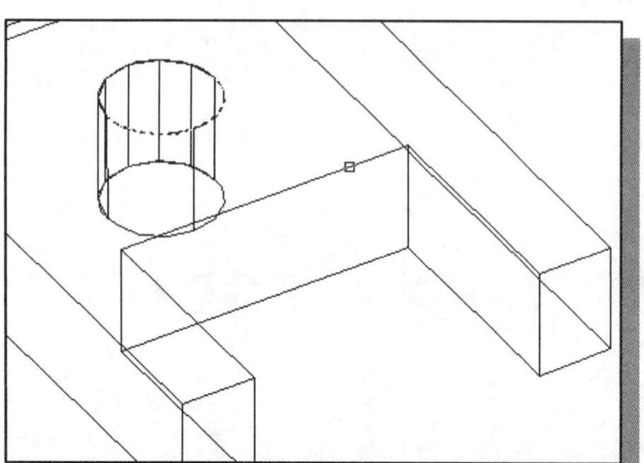

3. In the command prompt area, the message "*Select second defining curve:*" is displayed. Choose the inside straight edge on the right side as shown.

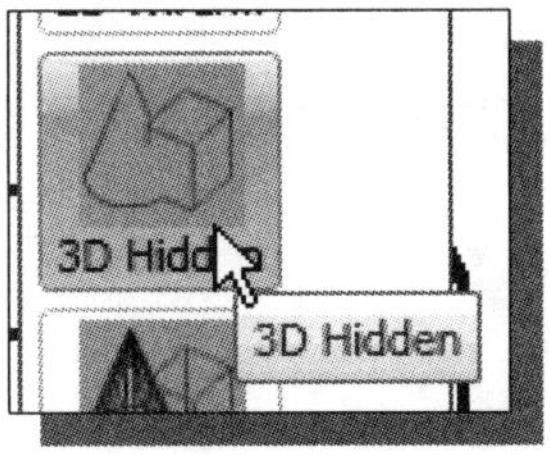

4. In the *Visual Styles* toolbar, click on the **3D Hidden** icon to display the model with hidden lines removed.

- The selected edges are removed from the display so that the face of the ruled surface appears to be more realistic.

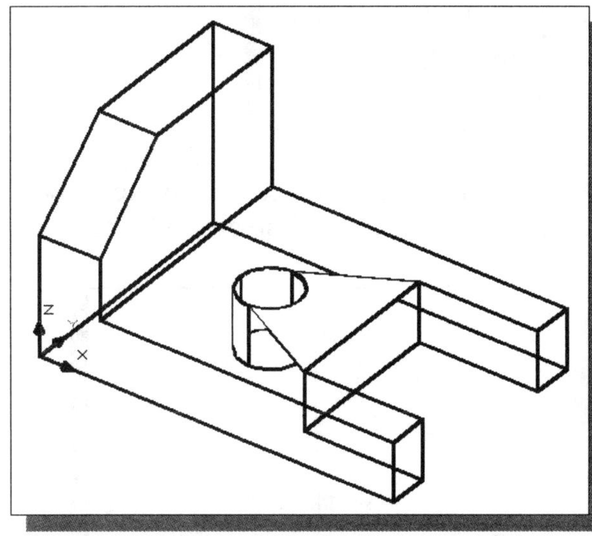

5. On your own, repeat the above steps and create another ruled surface as shown. (Hint: Use the **Realtime Zoom** function to assist the selection of the arc.)

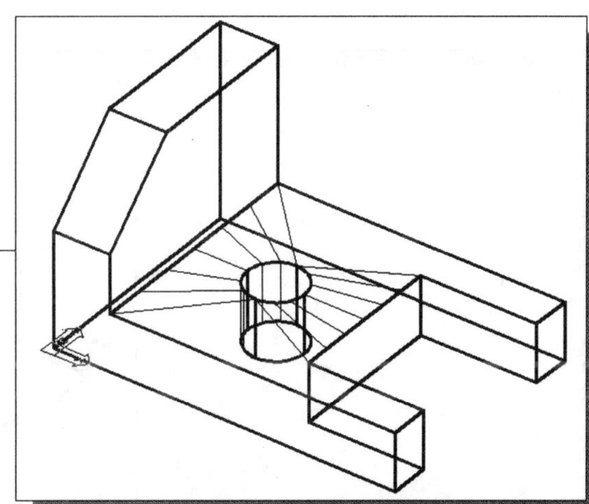

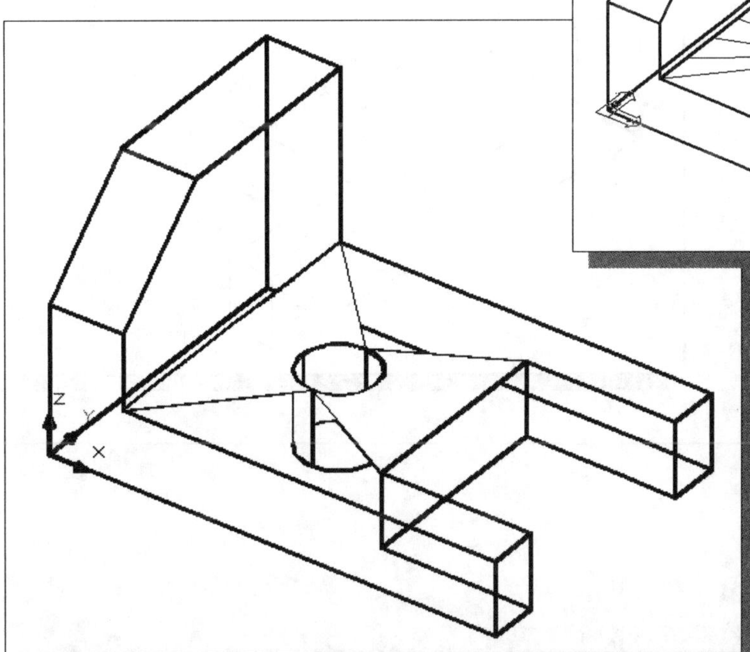

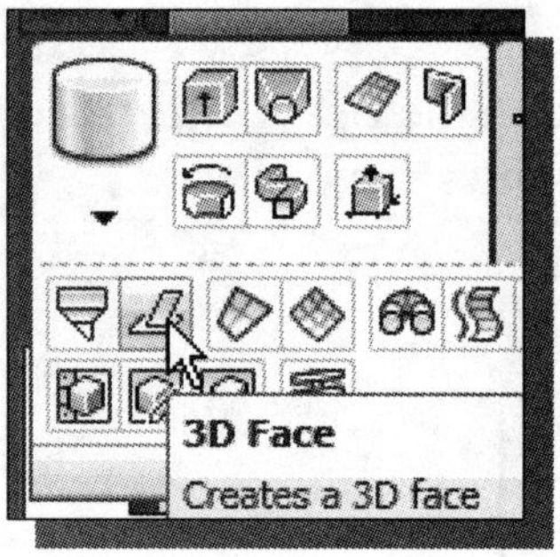

6. In the *3D Modeling* toolbar, select **3D Face**.

- On your own, complete the surface model as shown. (Hint: Use the [**Edge**] command to hide the edges of the created faces.)

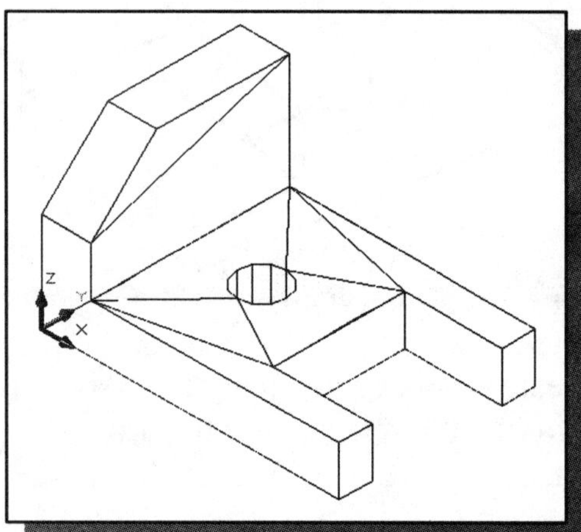

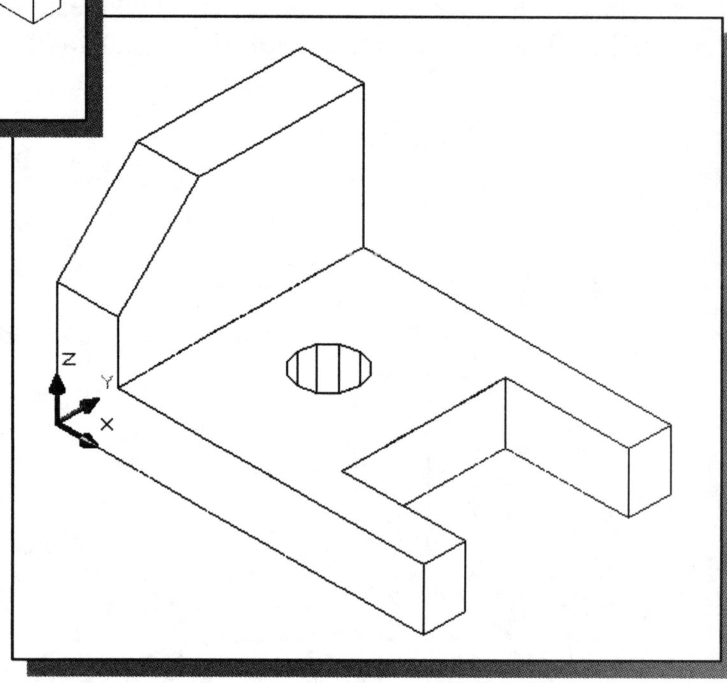

Questions:

1. List and describe three differences between *Wireframe models* and *Surface models*.
2. List and describe the three types of surfaces available in AutoCAD.
3. List and describe two different shading options in AutoCAD.
4. What is the difference between the **2D Solid** and **3D Face** commands in AutoCAD?
5. What is the difference between **Tabulated Surface** and **Ruled Surface** in AutoCAD?
6. Identify and describe the following commands:

a)

b)

c)

d)

Exercises: All dimensions are in inches.

1.

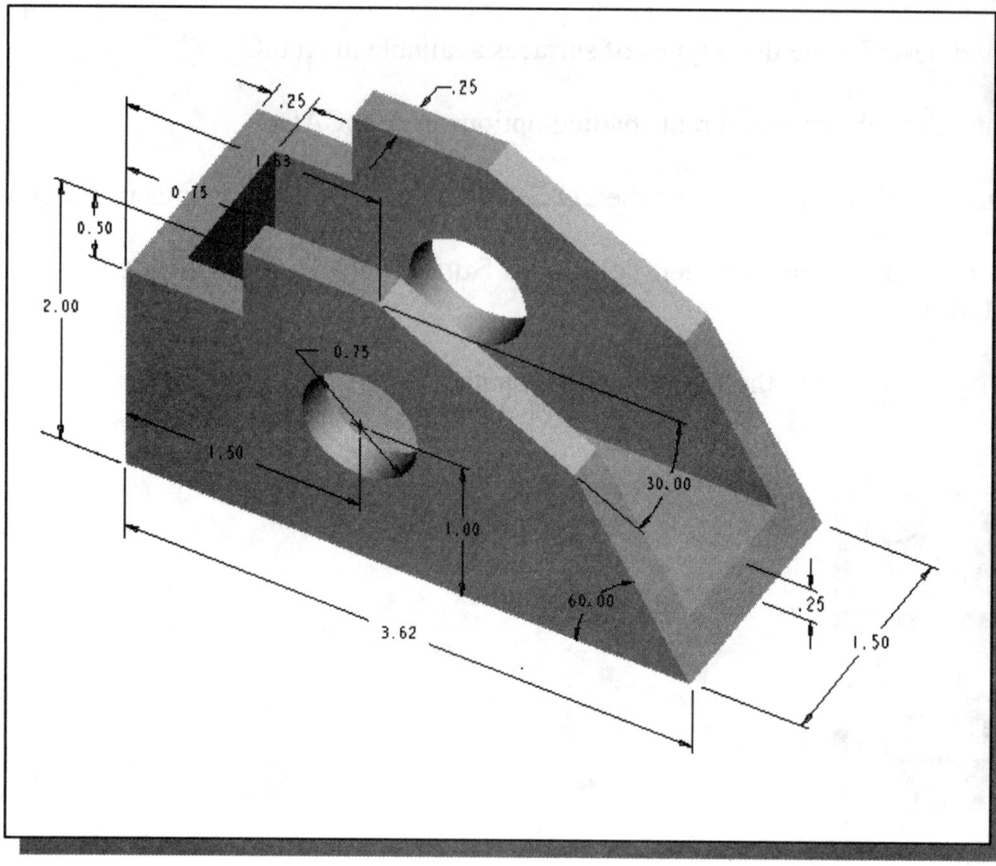

2.

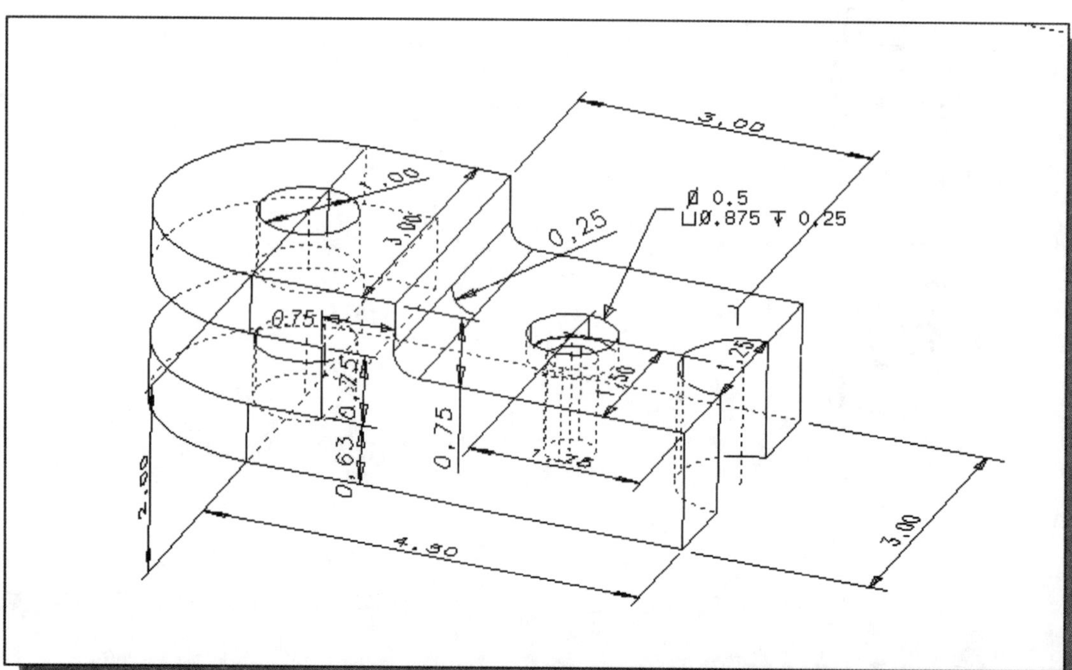

3.

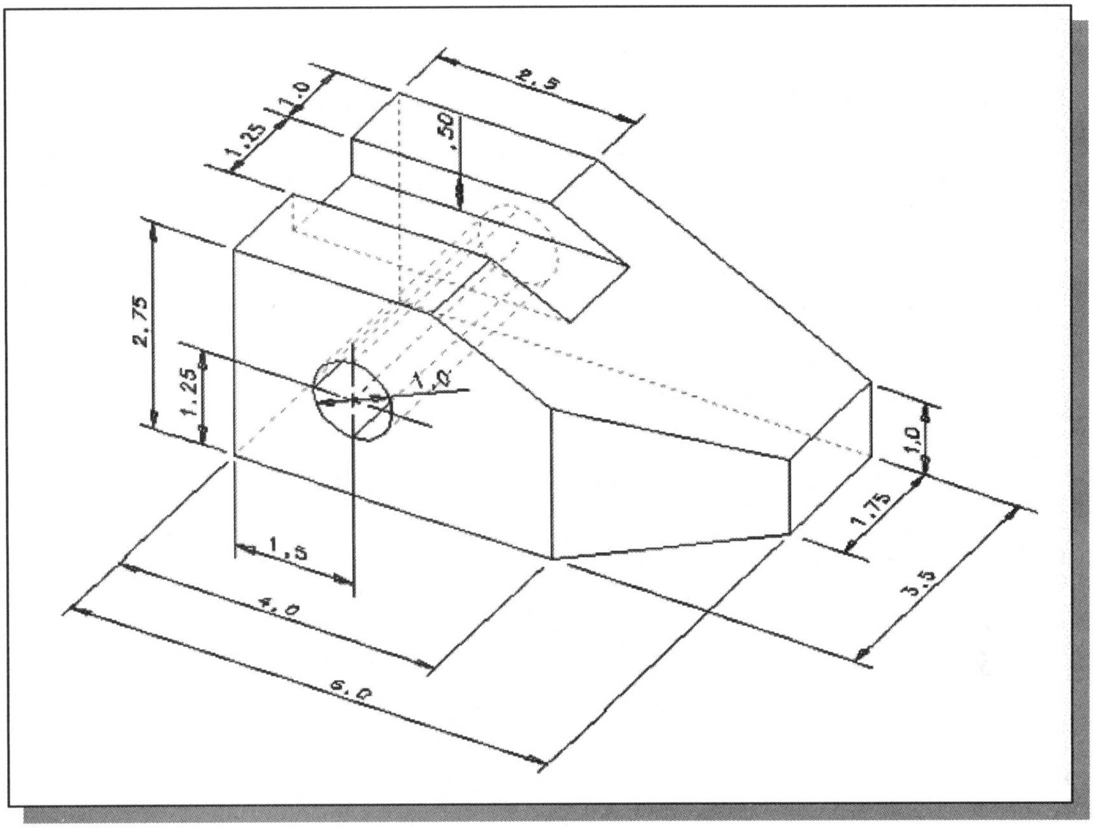
2.5
.50
1.25
1.0
2.75
1.25
1.0
1.5
4.0
6.0
1.0
1.75
3.5

4.

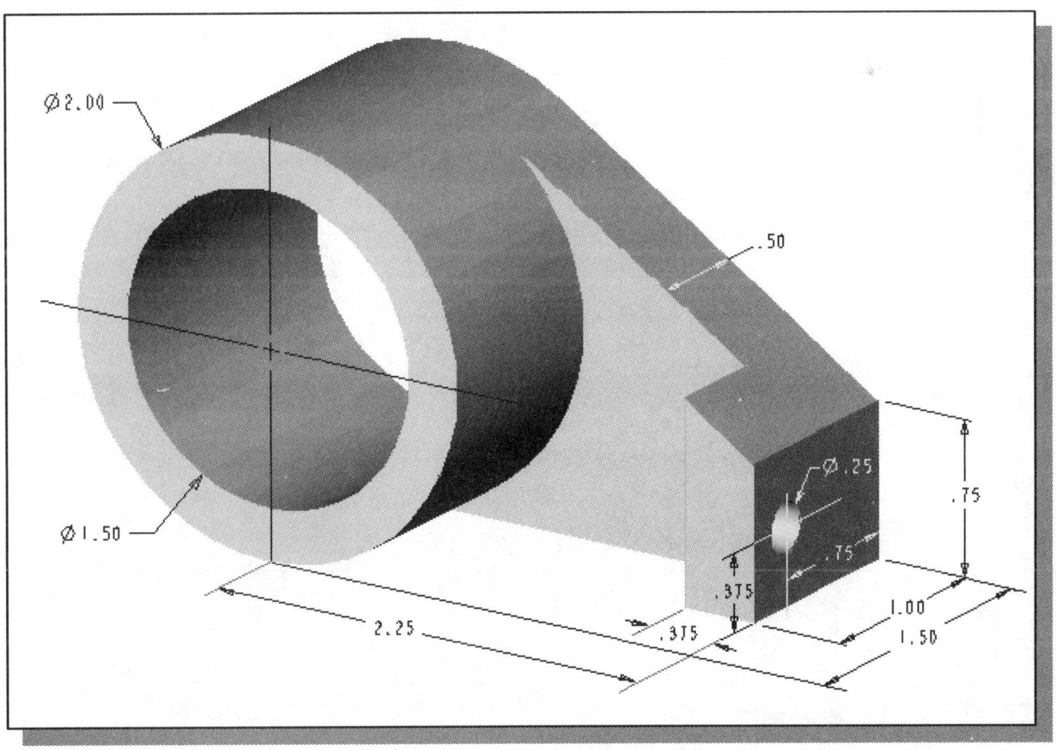
Ø2.00
.50
Ø.25
.75
Ø1.50
.75
.375
1.00
1.50
2.25
.375

NOTES:

Chapter 6
Solid Modeling – Constructive Solid Geometry

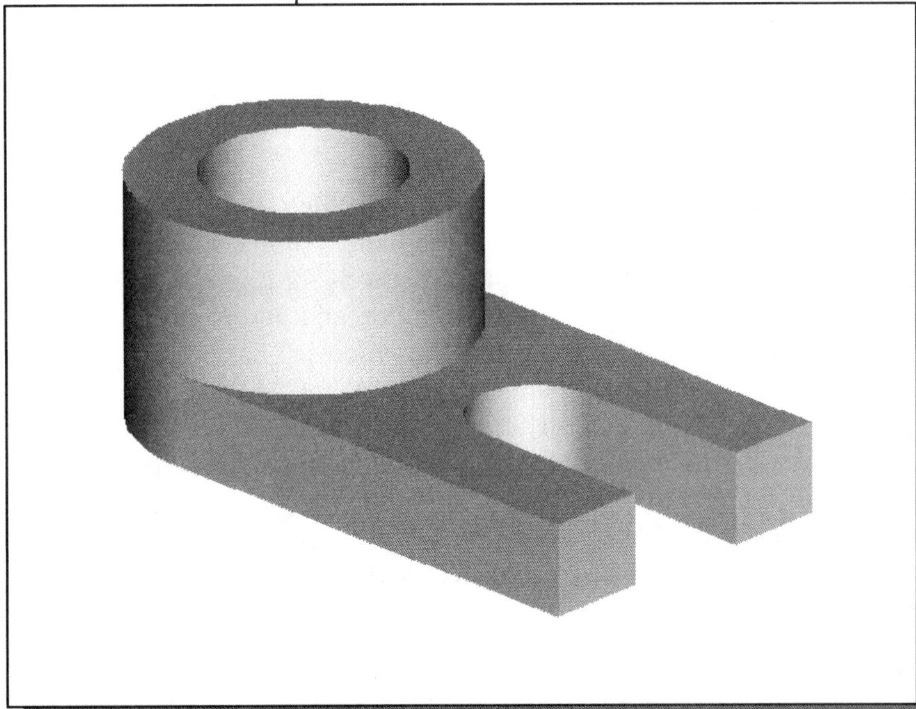

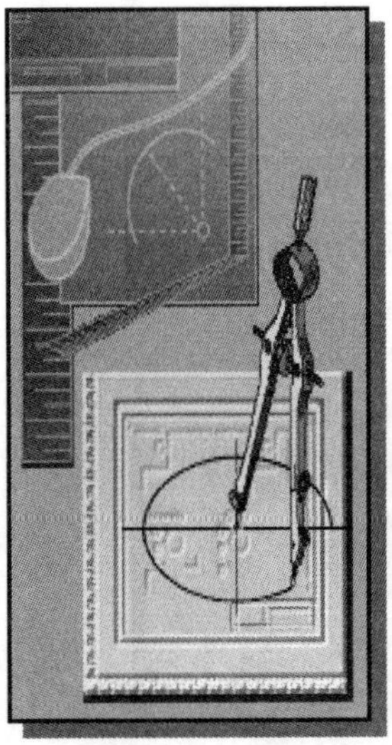

Learning Objectives

- **Understand the Constructive Solid Geometry Concept**
- **Create a Binary Tree**
- **Understand the Basic Boolean Operations**
- **Create Solids Using AutoCAD Primitive Solids**
- **Generate Shaded SOLID Images**
- **Using Steeringwheels**

Introduction

In the previous chapters, we have looked at wireframe modeling and surface modeling. Wireframe modeling describes only the corners and edges of designs. Surface modeling describes part surfaces but not interiors. Although surface models are fairly good representations of the actual designs, designers are still required to interactively examine surface models to insure that the various surfaces on a model are contiguous throughout. Many of the concepts used in 3D wireframe and surface modelers are incorporated in the solid modeling scheme, but it is solid modeling that offers the most advantages as a design tool.

In the solid modeling presentation scheme, the solid definitions include nodes, edges and surfaces, and it is a complete and unambiguous mathematical representation of a precisely enclosed and filled volume. Two predominant methods for representing solid models are **constructive solid geometry** (CSG) representation and **boundary representation** (B-rep). CSG defines a model in terms of combining basic solid shapes and B-rep defines a model in terms of its edges and surfaces. AutoCAD's solid modeler is a hybrid modeler; the user interface and construction techniques are CSG-based, whereas the B-rep capabilities are invoked automatically and are transparent to the user.

In this chapter, we will discuss the fundamental concepts of solid modeling. We will demonstrate the procedure required to construct a solid model using AutoCAD's CSG-based user interface.

The *Guide-Block* Design

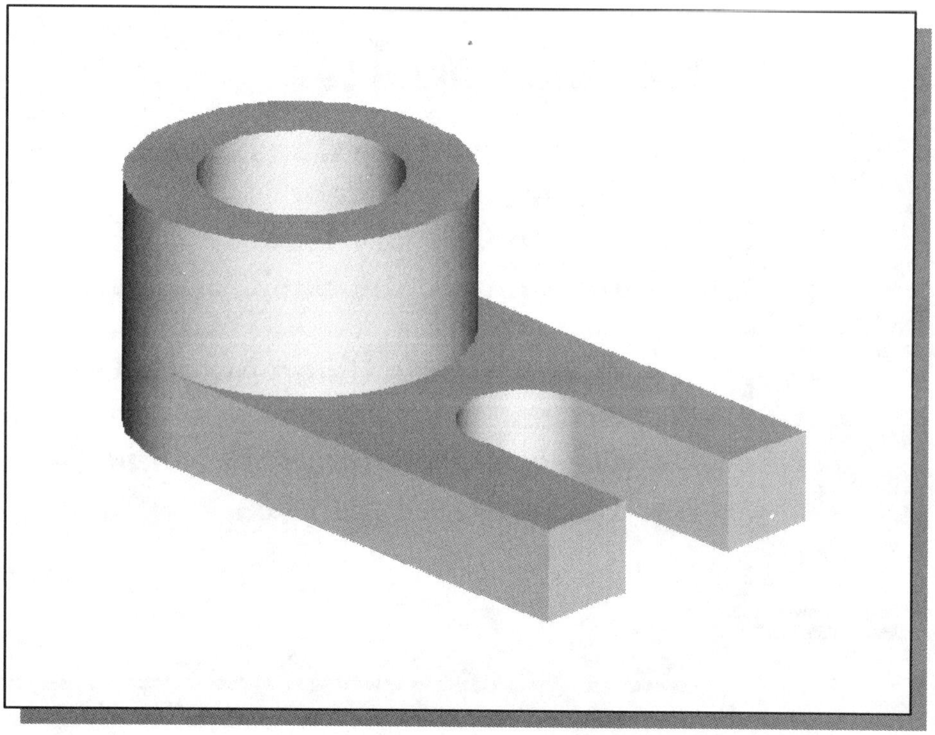

Constructive Solid Geometry Concept

In the 1980s, one of the main advancements in **Solid Modeling** was the development of the **Constructive Solid Geometry** (CSG) method. CSG describes the solid model as the combination of basic three-dimensional shapes (**primitive solids**). The basic primitive solid set typically includes: Rectangular-prism (Block), Cylinder, Cone, Sphere and Torus (Donut). Two solid objects can be combined into one object in various ways, these operations are known as **Boolean operations**. There are three basic Boolean operations: **UNION (Join)**, **SUBTRACT (Cut)**, and **INTERSECT**. The UNION operation combines the two volumes included in the different solids into a single solid. The SUBTRACT operation subtracts the volume of one solid object from the other solid object. The INTERSECT operation keeps only the volume common to both solid objects. The CSG method is also known as the **Machinist's Approach**, as the method is parallel to machine shop practices.

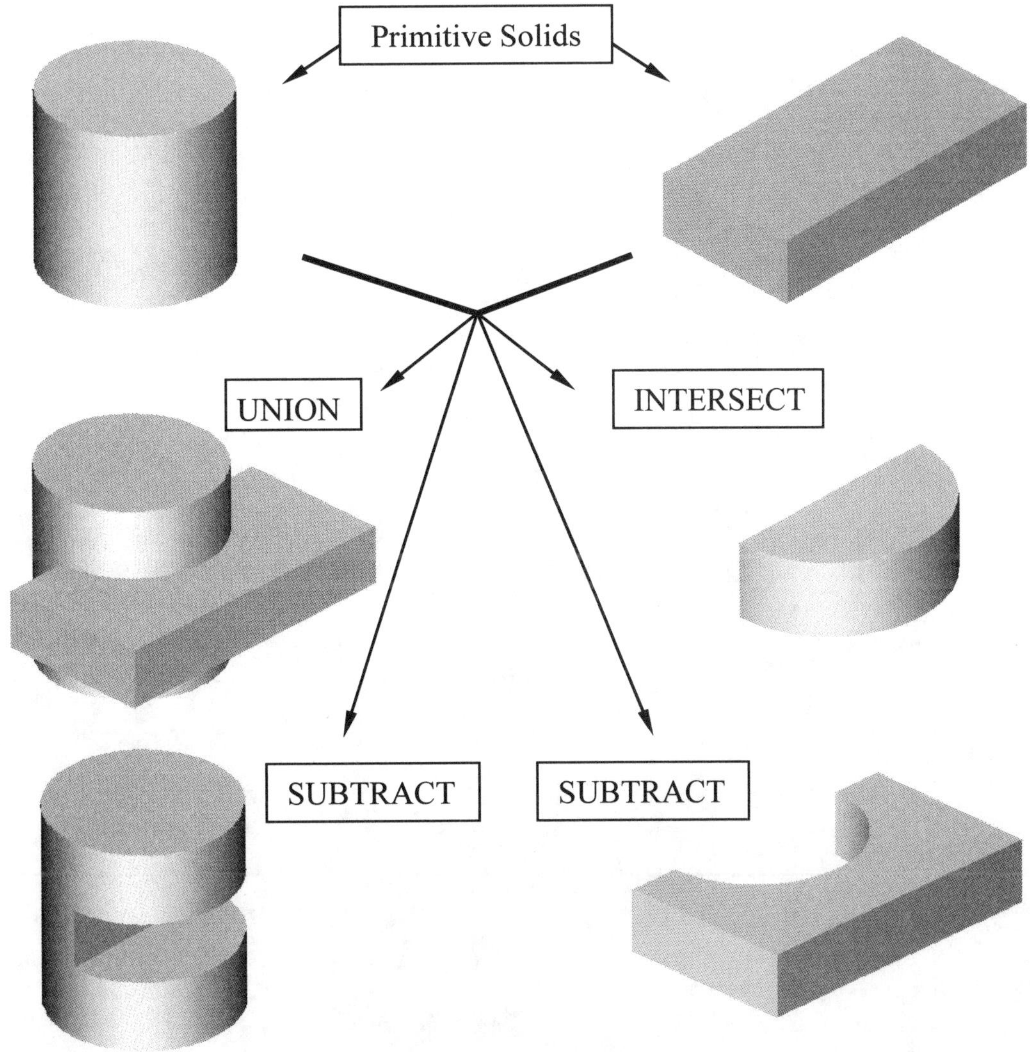

Binary Tree

CSG is also referred to as the method used to store a solid model in the database. The resulting solid can be easily represented by what is called a **binary tree**. In a binary tree, the terminal branches (leaves) are the various primitives that are linked together to make the final solid object (the root). The binary tree is an effective way to represent the steps required to construct the solid model. Complicated solid models can be modeled by considering the different combinations of Boolean operations required in the binary tree. This provides a convenient and intuitive way of modeling that imitates the manufacturing process. A binary tree is an effective way to plan your modeling strategy before you start creating anything.

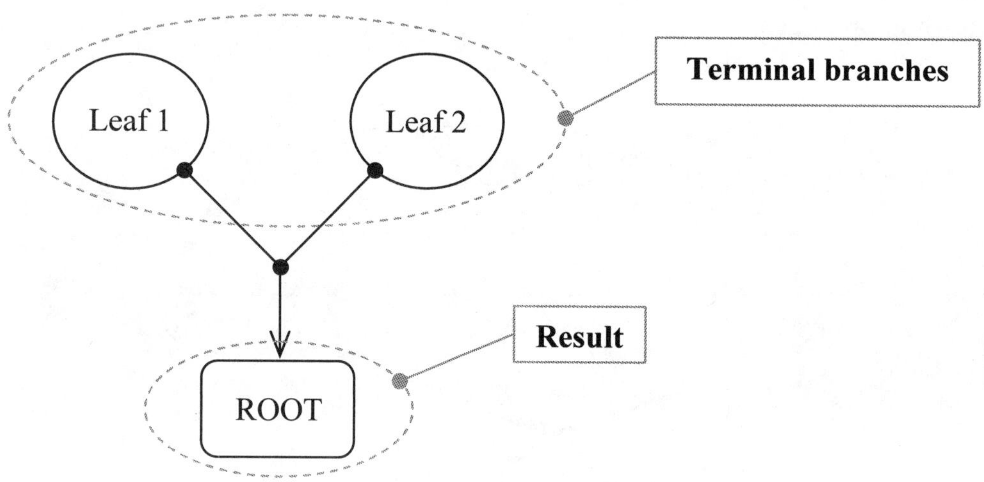

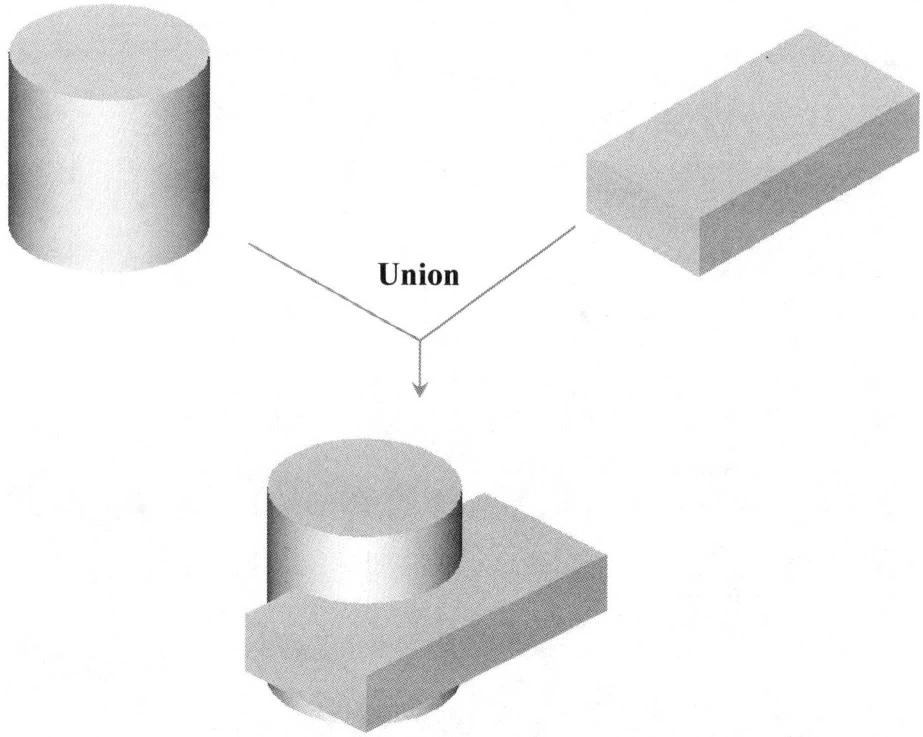

The *Guide-Block* CSG Binary Tree

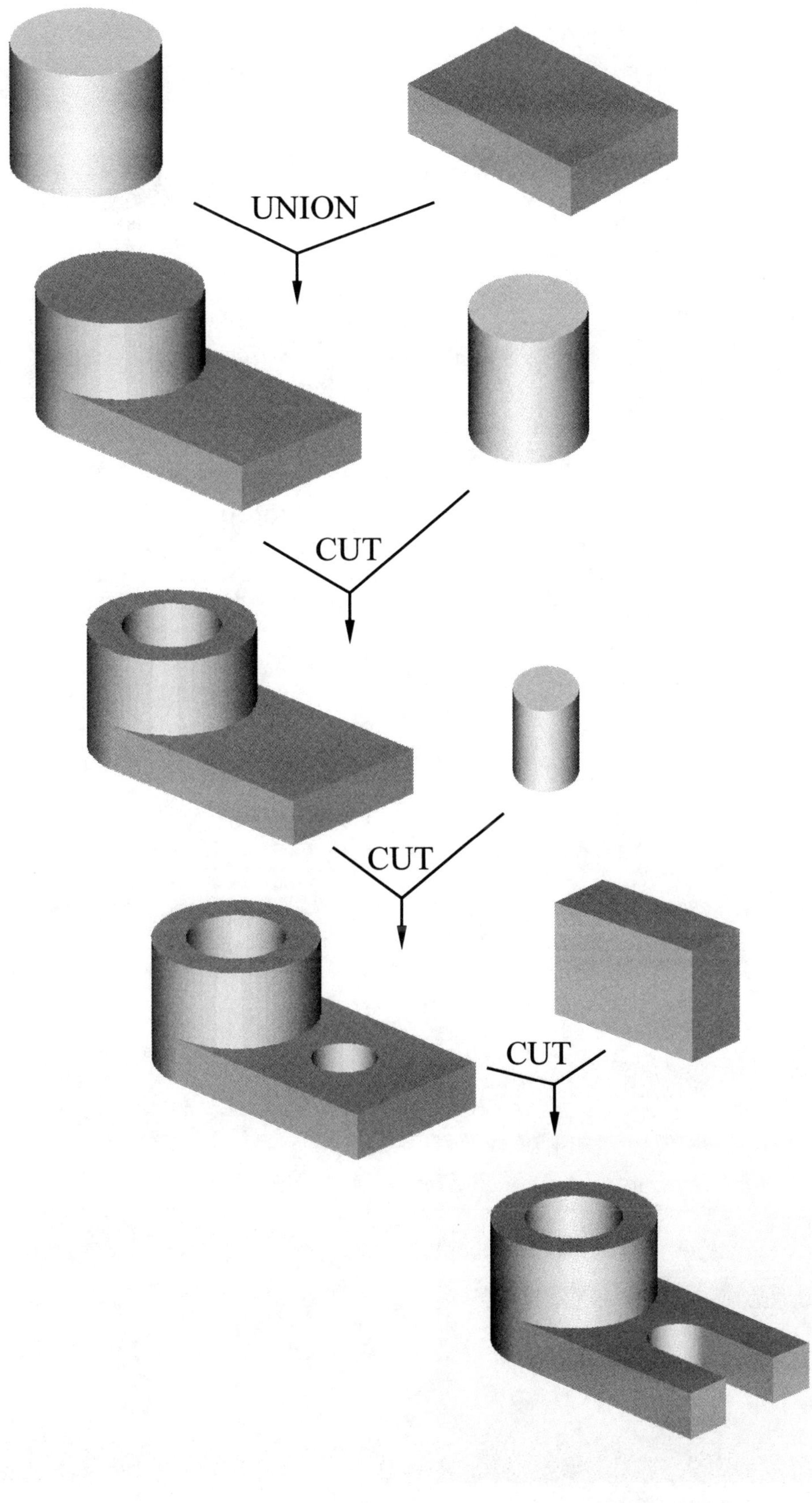

Starting Up AutoCAD 2009

1. Select the **AutoCAD 2009** option on the *Program* menu or select the **AutoCAD 2009** icon on the *Desktop*.

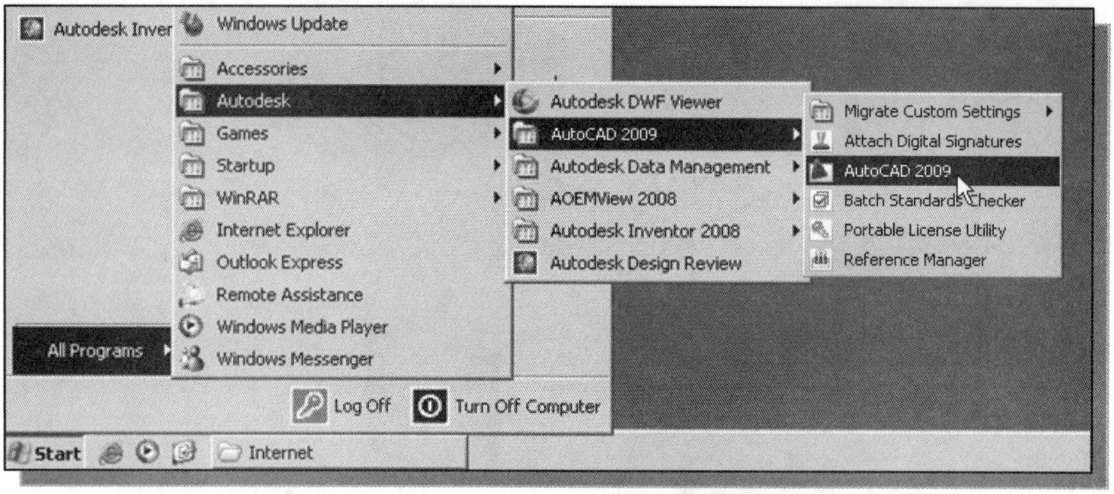

2. In the startup dialog box, select the **Start from Scratch** option with a single click of the left-mouse-button.

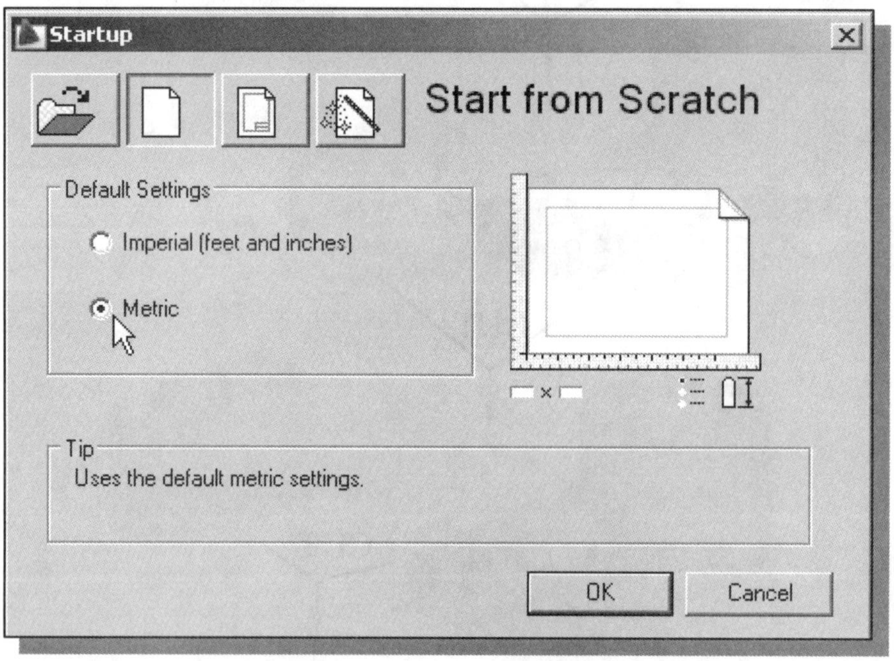

3. In the *Default Settings* section, pick **Metric** as the drawing units.

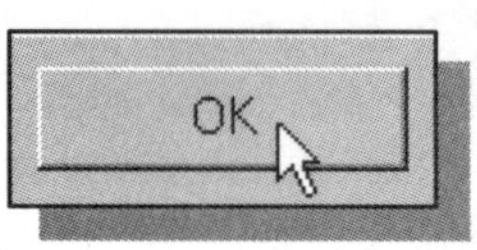

4. Click **OK** to accept the settings and exit the *Startup* window.

Layers Setup

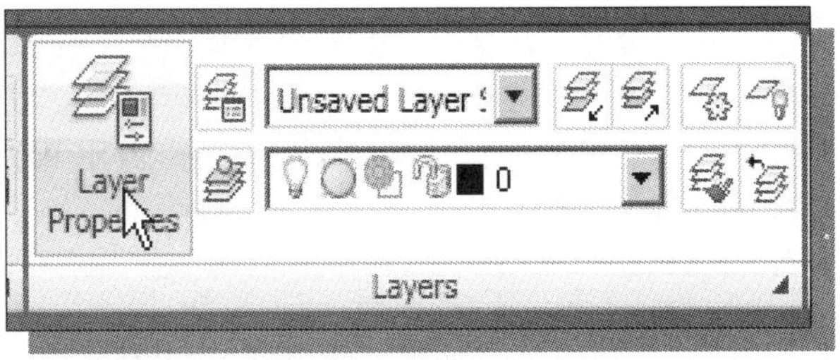

1. Click **Layers Properties Manager** in the *Layers* toolbar.

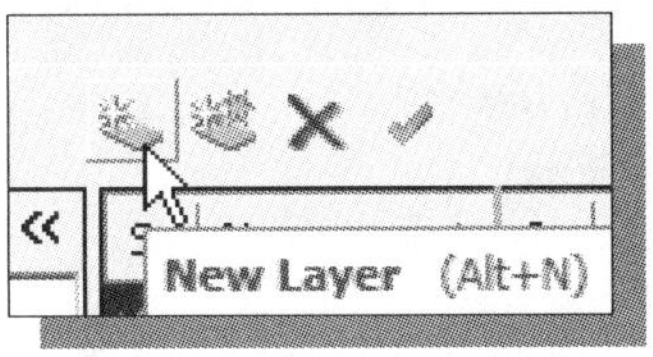

2. Click on the **New** button. Notice a layer is automatically added to the list of layers.

3. Create a **new layer** with the following settings:

Layer	*Color*	*LineType*
Solid_Objects	**Cyan**	**Continuous**

4. Set layer ***Solid_Objects*** as the *Current Layer*.

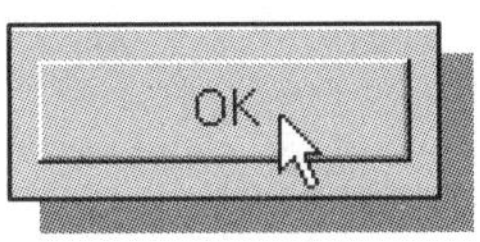

5. Click on the **Close** button to accept the settings and exit the *Layer Properties Manager* dialog box.

Creating the First 3D Object

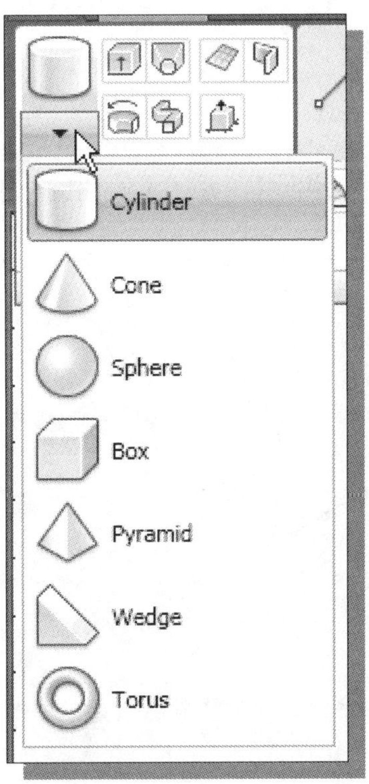

1. Click on the down arrow below the first icon of the 3D Modeling toolbar as shown.

❖ Note that the first icon of the *3DModeling toolbar* contains the basic set of pre-defined solids, primitive solids, available in **AutoCAD® 2009**.

2. On your own, move the cursor on top of the different icons and examine the available options.

➢ Also note that the typical basic primitive solid set includes: **Rectangular-prism** (Block), **Cylinder**, **Cone**, **Sphere** and **Torus** (Donut).

- We will first create a **75 × 50 × 15** rectangular block.

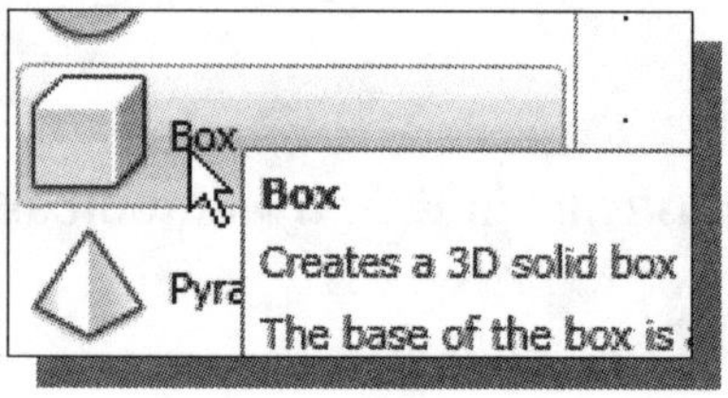

3. In the *Modeling toolbar*, click on the **Box** icon. In the command prompt area, the message "*Specify corner of box or [Center] <0,0,0>:*" is displayed.

4. Pick a location that is near the lower left corner of the graphics window.

5. In the command prompt area, the message "*Specify corner or [Cube/Length]:*" is displayed. Enter: **@75,50 [ENTER]**.

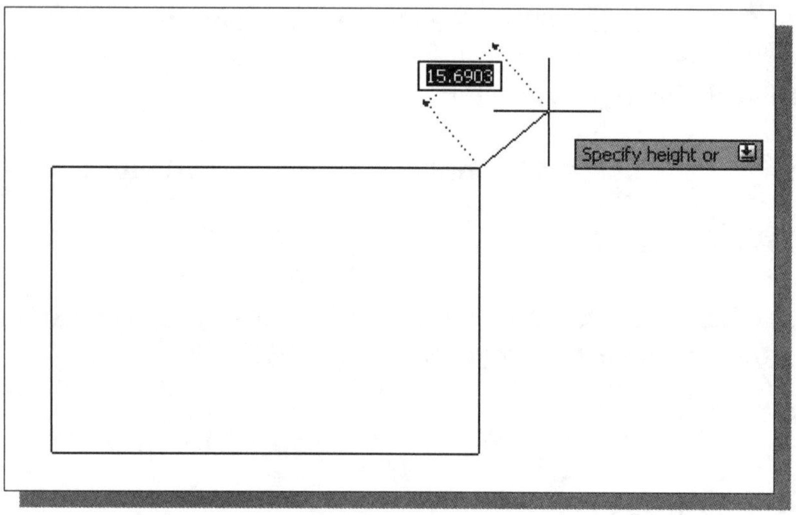

6. In the command prompt area, the message "*Specify Height:*" is displayed. Enter: **15 [ENTER]**.

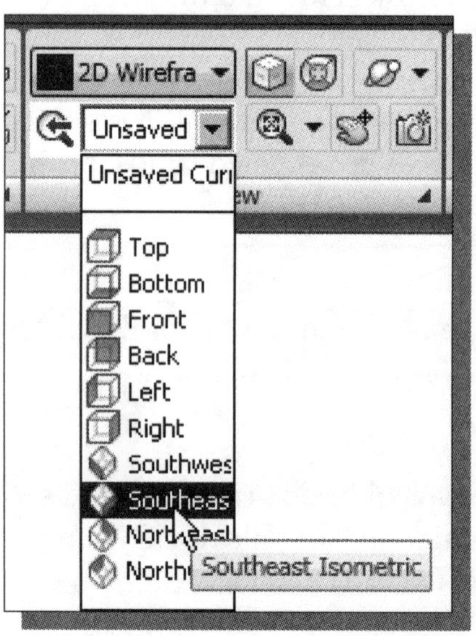

7. In the *View* toolbar, click on the **SE Isometric View** icon to set the display of the solid model.

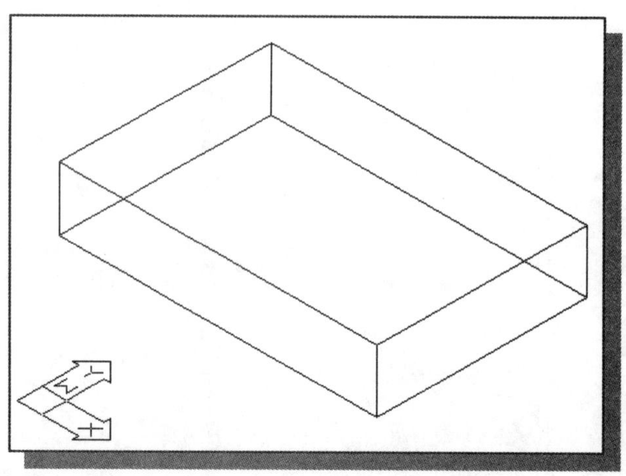

Creating the Second Solid Feature

- We will next create a cylinder block as the second solid feature.

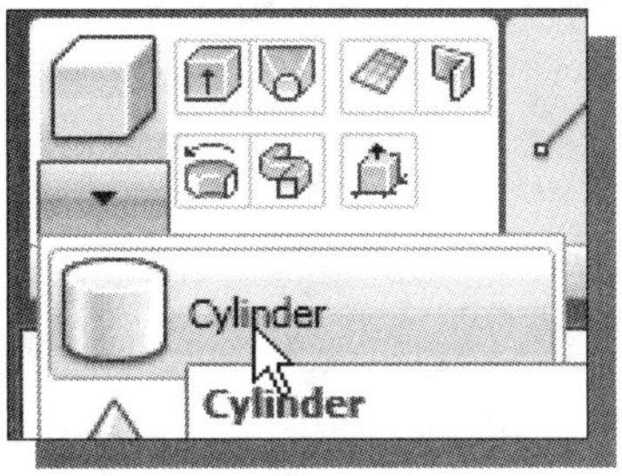

1. In the *3D Modeling toolbar*, click on the **Cylinder** icon. In the command prompt area, the message "*Specify center point for base cylinder or [Elliptical] <0,0,0>:*" is displayed.

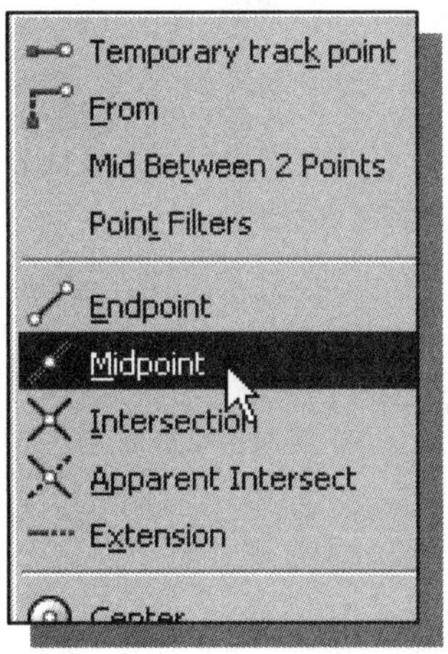

2. Inside the graphics window, press down the **[SHIFT]** key and **right-mouse-click** once to bring up the *Object Snap* shortcut menu.

3. Select the **Midpoint** option in the shortcut menu. Snap to and select the midpoint of the bottom-left edge of the rectangular block as shown in the below figure.

4. In the command prompt area, the message "*Specify radius for base of cylinder or [Diameter]:*" is displayed. Snap to and select one of the **endpoints** of the bottom edge of the rectangular block.

5. In the command prompt area, the message "*Specify height of cylinder or [Center of other end]:*" is displayed. Move the cursor up to set the height direction and enter: **40 [ENTER]**.

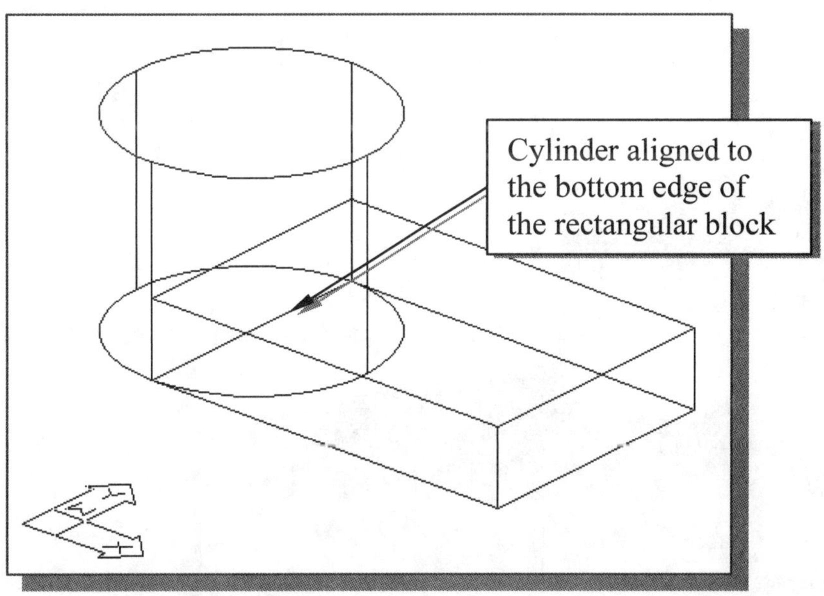

- We have created **two solid objects**, one rectangular box and one cylinder, that are displayed on the screen.

Boolean Operation – *UNION*

1. Move the cursor on top of the third group of icons in the *Modeling* toolbar, which contains the basic set of Boolean operation icons. On your own, read the brief description of each Boolean commands.

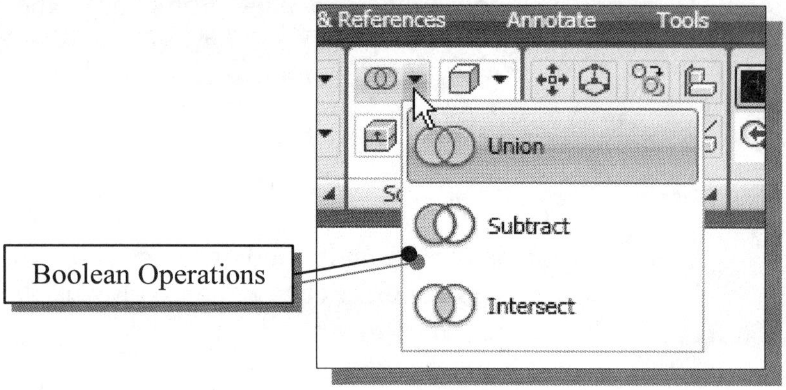

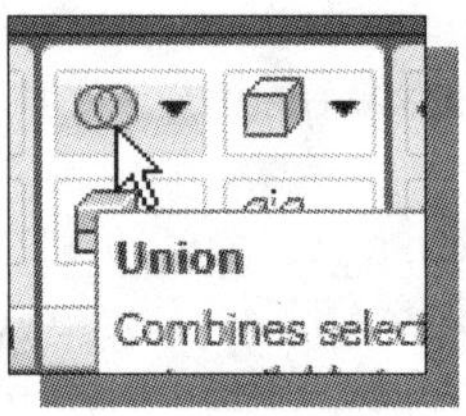

2. In the *Modeling* toolbar, click on the **Union** icon. In the command prompt area, the message "*Select Objects:*" is displayed.

3. Pick both solids by clicking on their edges.

4. Inside the graphics window, right-mouse-click to accept the selection and proceed with the Union command.

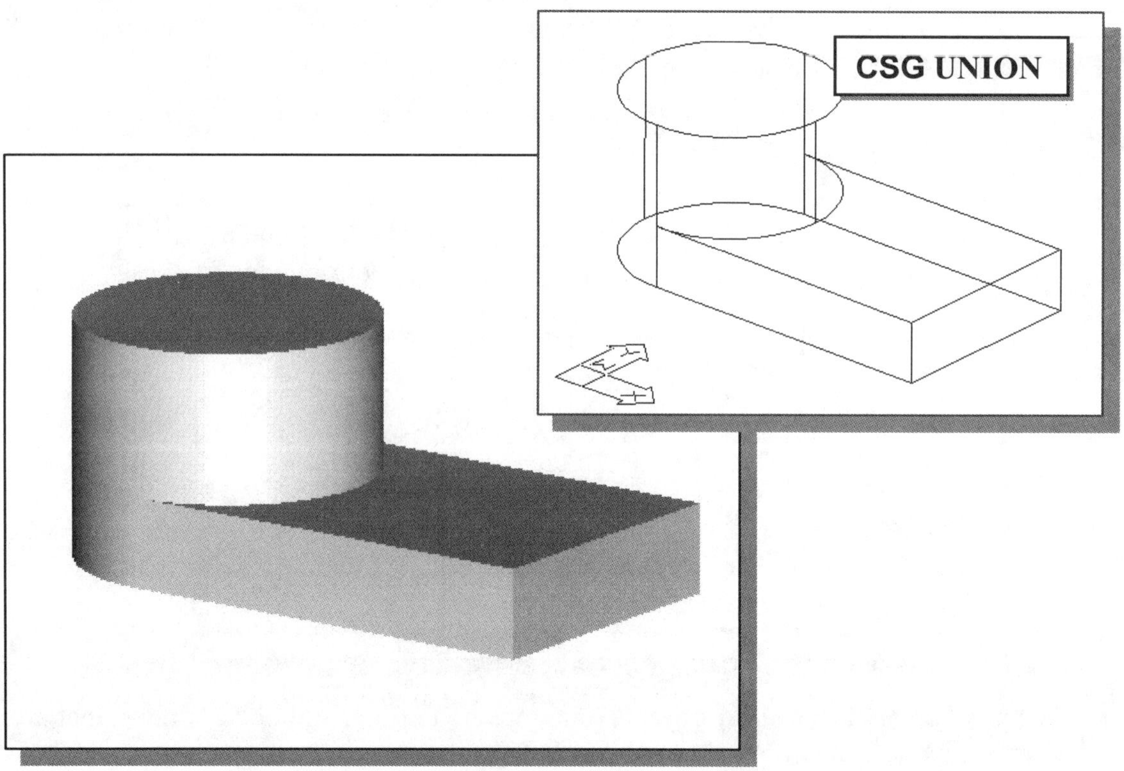

Creating the Second Cylinder Feature

- We will create another cylinder as the next solid feature.

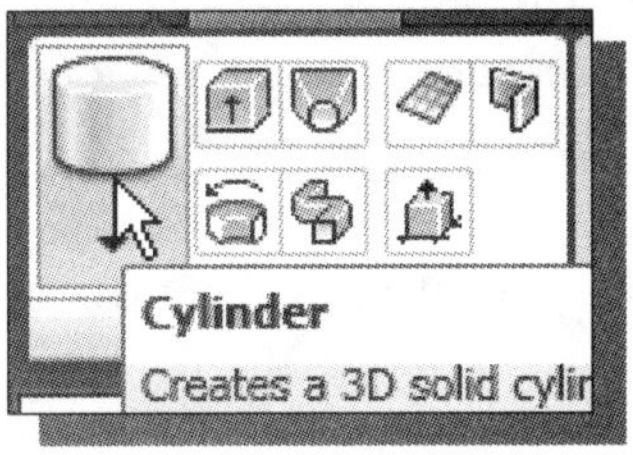

1. In the *Modeling toolbar*, click on the **Cylinder** icon. In the command prompt area, the message "*Specify center point for base cylinder or [Elliptical] <0,0,0>:*" is displayed.

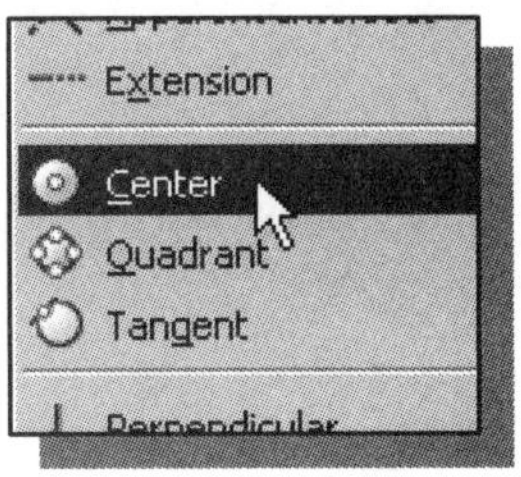

2. Inside the graphics window, press down the **[SHIFT]** key and **right-mouse-click** once to bring up the *Object Snap* shortcut menu.

3. Select the **Center** option in the shortcut menu.

4. Snap to and select the **center of the circle** that is at the **top** of the solid block.

5. In the command prompt area, the message "*Specify radius for base of cylinder or [Diameter]:*" is displayed. Enter 15 as the radius value: **15 [ENTER]**.

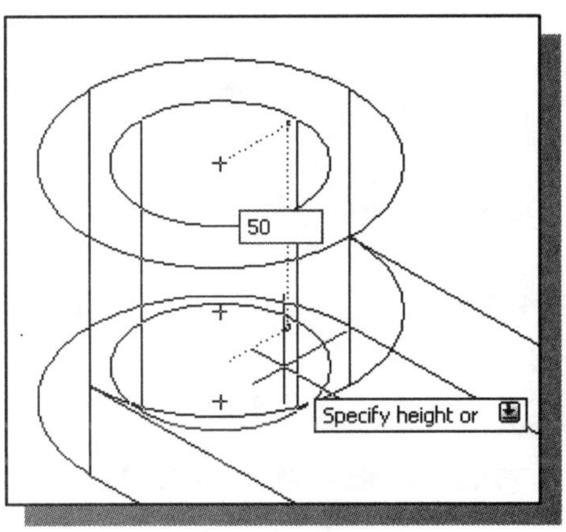

6. In the command prompt area, the message "*Specify radius for base of cylinder or [Diameter]:*" is displayed. Move the cursor **downward** to set the height direction and enter 50 as the height value: **50 [ENTER]**.

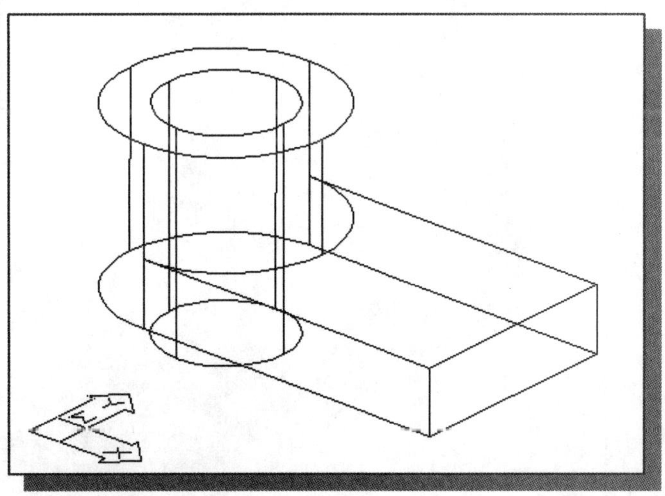

- Two solid objects, the base block and a cylinder, are displayed on the screen. On your own, use the available **Views** options to confirm the top of the two solids are aligned. (Before continuing, set the view as shown in the above figure.)

Boolean Operation – *SUBTRACT*

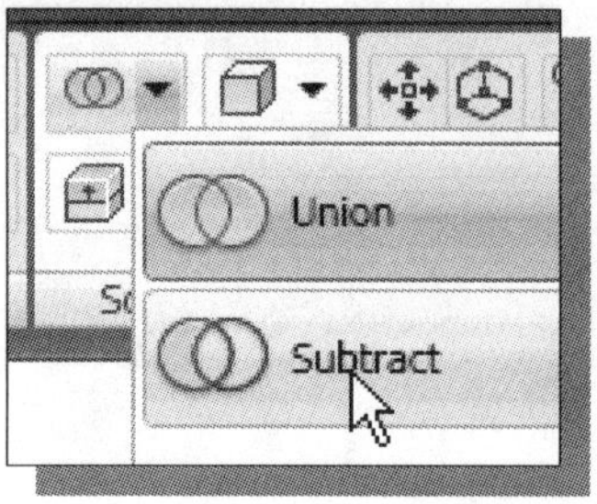

1. In the *Modeling* toolbar, click on the **Subtract** icon. In the command prompt area, the message "*_subtract Select solids and regions to subtract from .. Select Objects:*" is displayed.

2. Pick the **base block** solid by clicking on one of the straight edges.

3. Inside the graphics window, **right-mouse-click** to accept the selection and proceed with the Subtract command.

4. In the command prompt area, the message "*Select solids and regions to subtract .. Select Objects:*" is displayed.

5. Pick the cylinder block by clicking on one of the circular edges.

6. Inside the graphics window, **right-mouse-click** to accept the selection and proceed with the Subtract command.

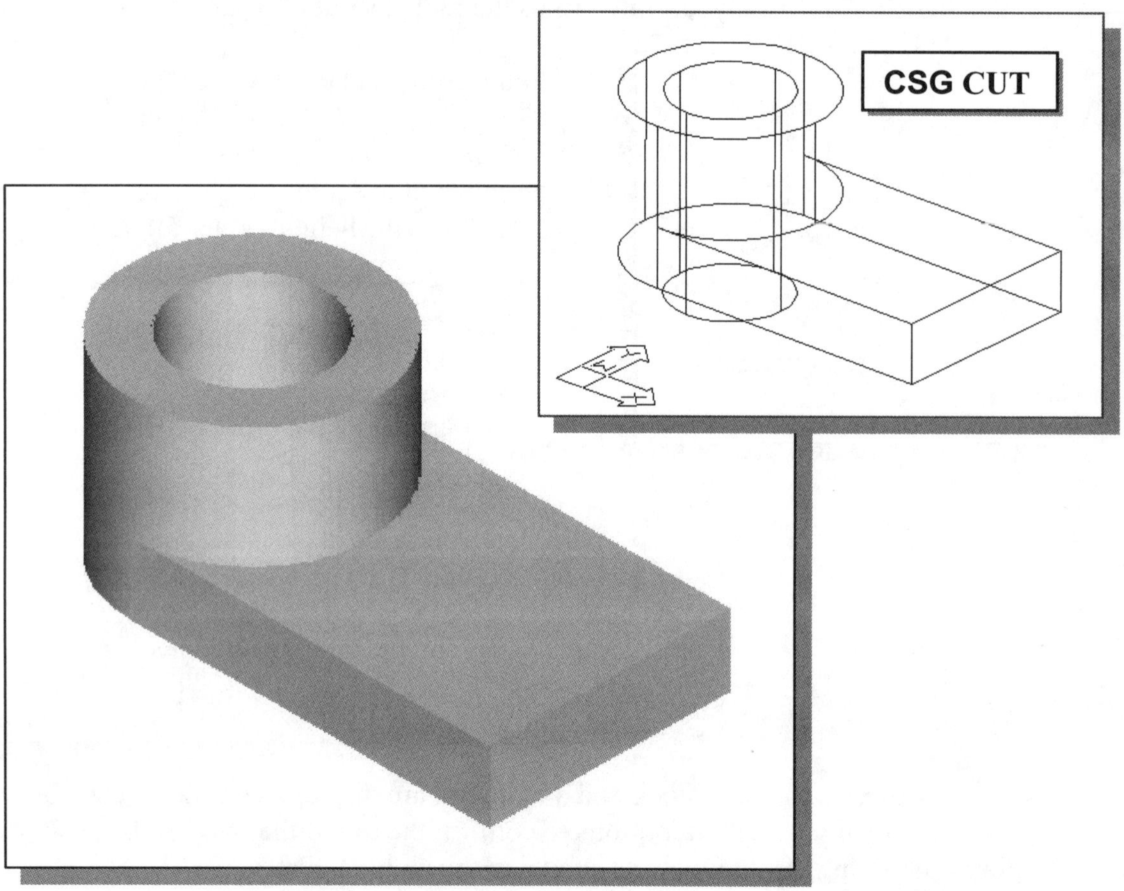

Creating Another Solid Feature

- As can be seen, the CSG construction approach is quite straightforward. The main task is in positioning and aligning the solid blocks prior to applying a Boolean operation.

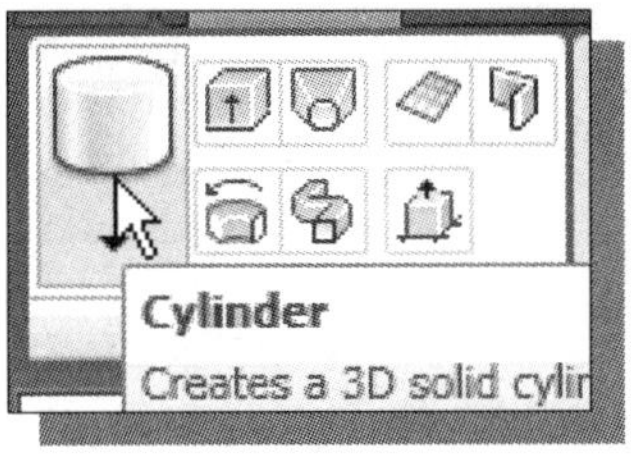

1. In the *Modeling toolbar*, click on the **Cylinder** icon. In the command prompt area, the message "*Specify center point for base cylinder or [Elliptical] <0,0,0>:*" is displayed.

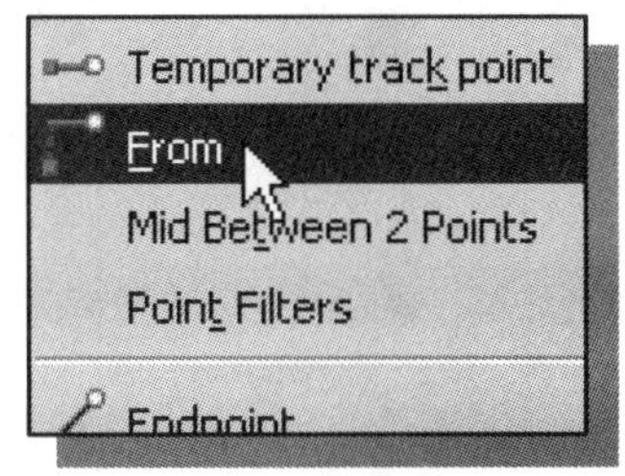

2. Inside the graphics window, press down the **[SHIFT]** key and **right-mouse-click** once to bring up the *Object Snap* shortcut menu.

3. Select the **From** option in the shortcut menu.

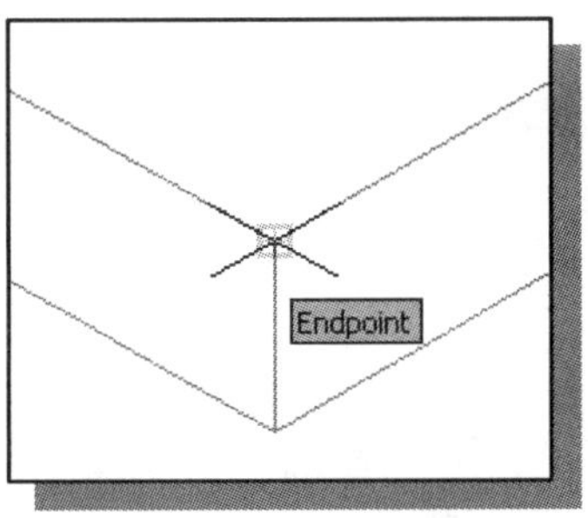

4. Snap to the **top front** corner of the base block and enter: **@-30,25 [ENTER]**.

5. In the command prompt area, the message "*Specify radius for base of cylinder or [Diameter]:*" is displayed. Enter: **10 [ENTER]**.

6. Move the cursor **downward** and create a cylinder that is longer than the height of the horizontal base as shown.

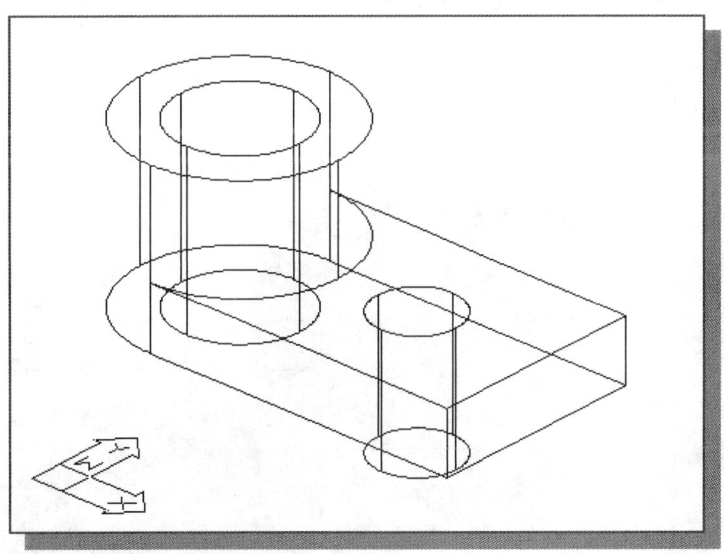

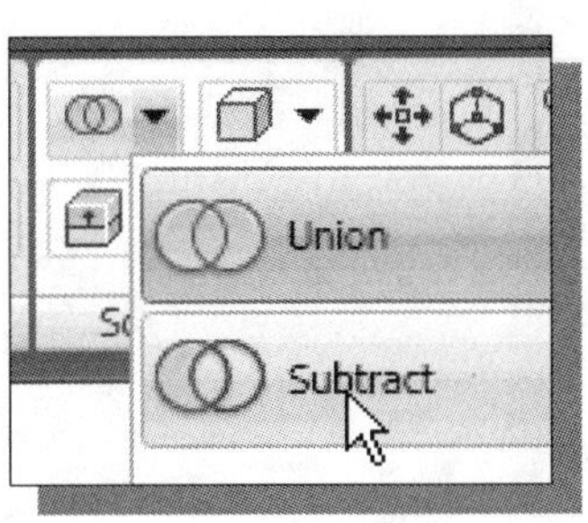

7. On your own, perform the Boolean **Subtract** operation.

Visual Styles Options

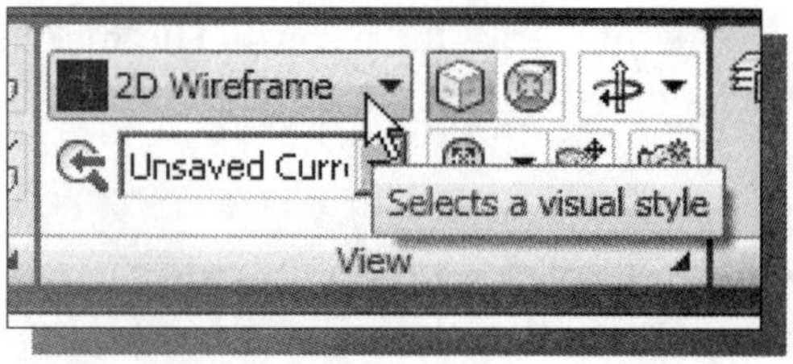

1. Move the cursor to the *View* toolbar panel and **left-click** on the downward triangle to display a list of available options.

   ❖ Five Visual Styles are available.

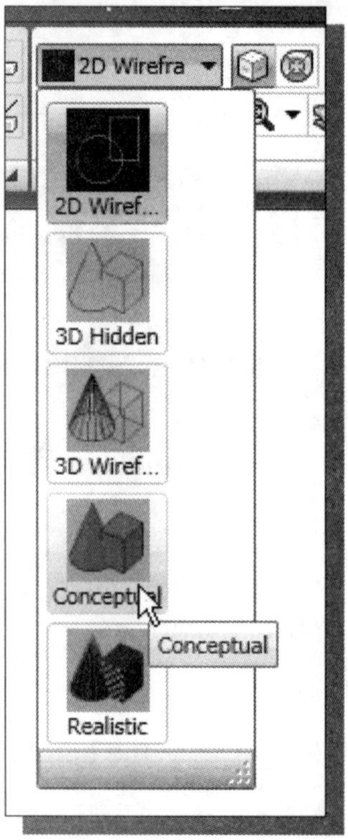

2. In the *Visual Styles* toolbar, click on the **Conceptual Visual Style** icon to display the shaded image of the solid model. A solid model contains both surfaces and volume.

➢ On your own, examine the solid model by using the **ViewCube**.

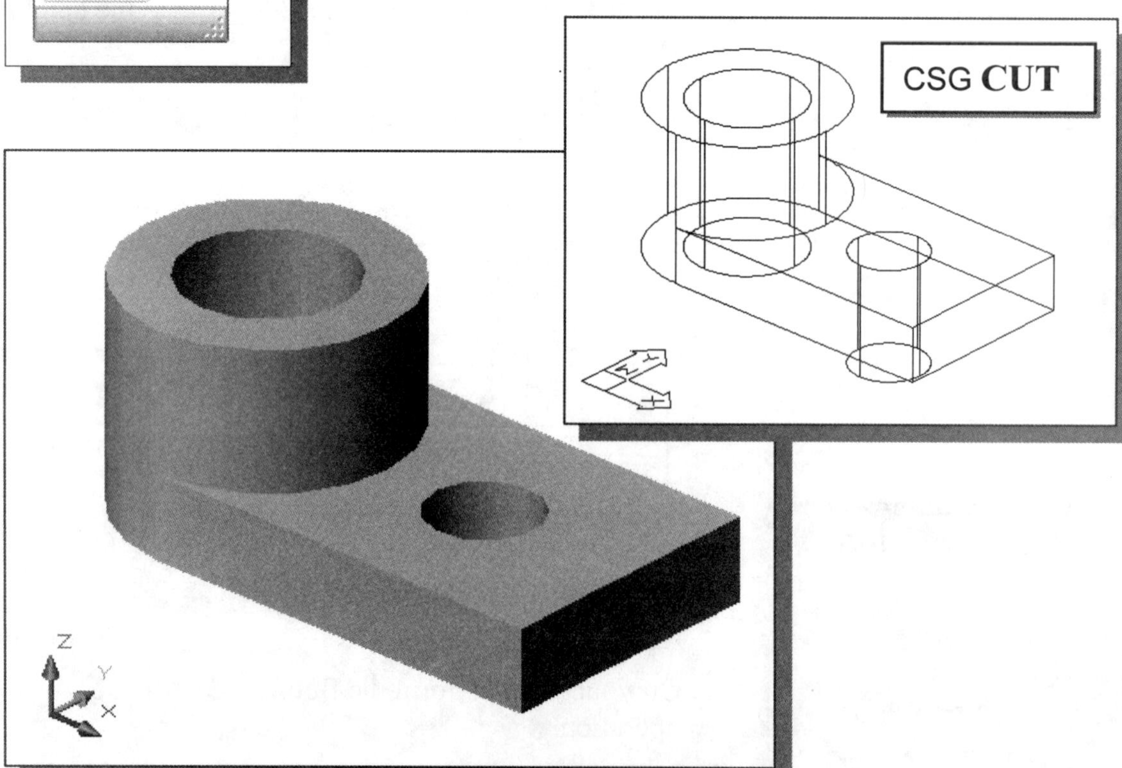

Creating the Final Feature

- We will create a rectangular cut as the final solid feature of the part. In the previous sections, with some careful planning, we positioned the solid blocks at the correct space locations while we were creating the solids. It is also possible to take a more general approach to orient and position solid blocks in space coordinates.

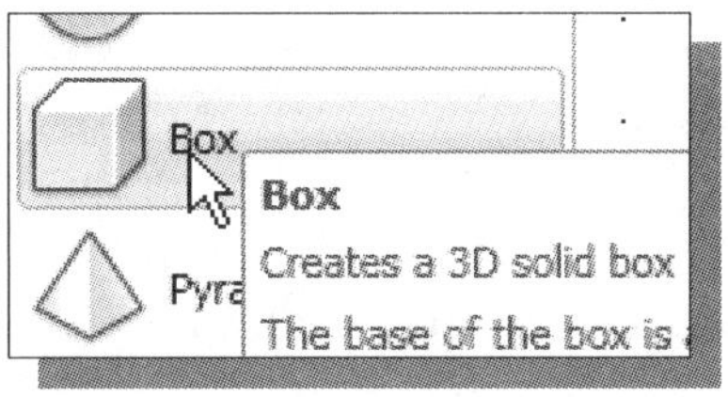

1. In the *Modeling toolbar*, click on the **Box** icon. In the command prompt area, the message "*Specify corner of box or [Center] <0,0,0>:*" is displayed.

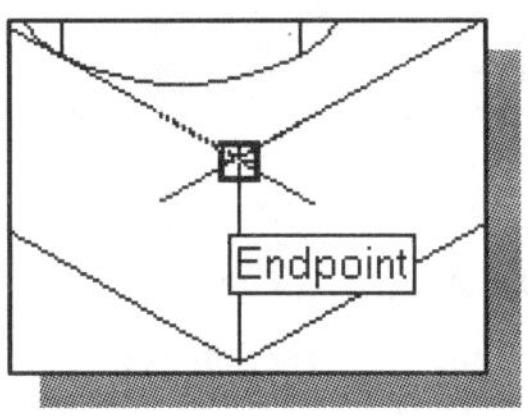

2. Snap to and select the **top front corner** of the base block.
3. In the command prompt area, the message "*Specify corner or [Cube/Length]:*" is displayed. Enter: **@-30,30 [ENTER]**.
4. In the command prompt area, the message "*Specify height:*" is displayed. Move the cursor **downward** to set the height direction and enter a value to extrude in the negative Z direction.
   Enter: **20 [ENTER]**.

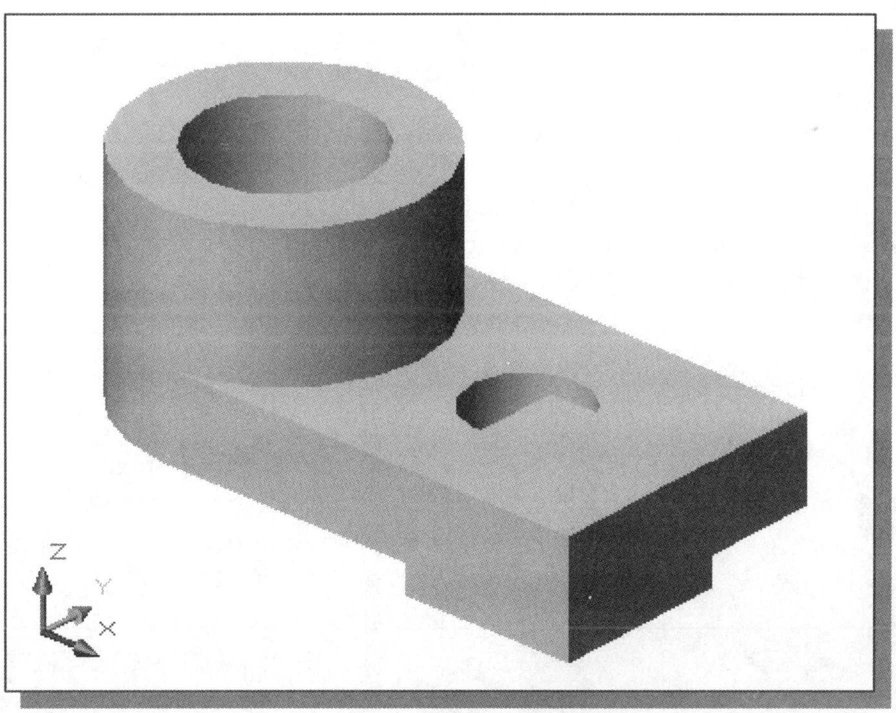

➢ Two overlapping solids appear on the screen. We will use the *editing tools* to orient the cutter, the newly created rectangular block, to its correct location.

Rotating the Rectangular Block

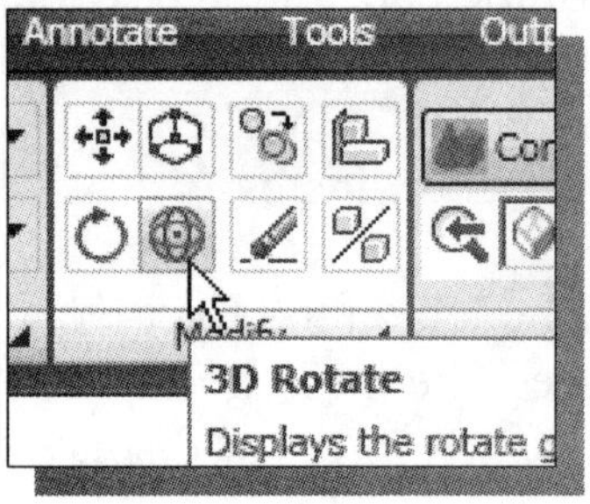

1. Select **3D Rotate** in the *Modify* toolbar as shown.

2. In the command prompt area, the message "*Select objects:*" is displayed. Select the **rectangular block** by clicking on any of the displayed edges of the model.

3. Inside the graphics window, right-mouse-click to accept the selection and proceed with the **3D Rotate** command.

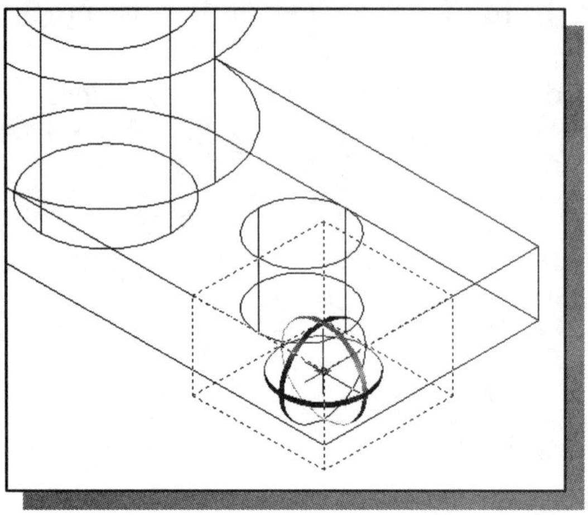

4. In the command prompt area, the message "*Specify base point:" is displayed.* Select the top front corner of the rectangular box as shown.

- Note that the **3D Rotate** command requires the definition of a *base point, a rotation axis and the angle of rotation.*

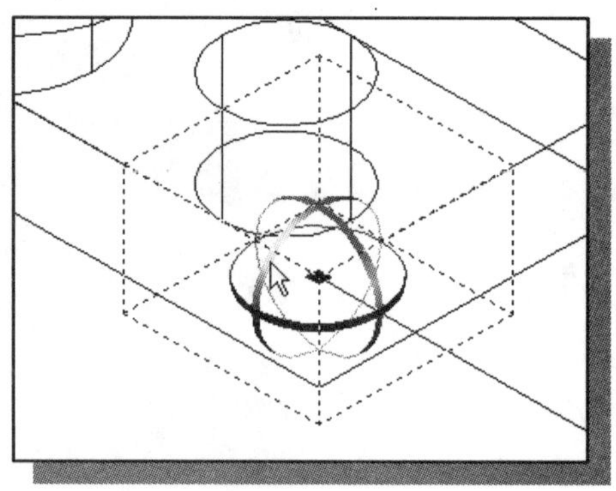

5. In the command prompt area, the message "*Pick a rotation axis:*" is displayed. Select the X-axis by clicking once on the **RED grip rotate handle** as shown.

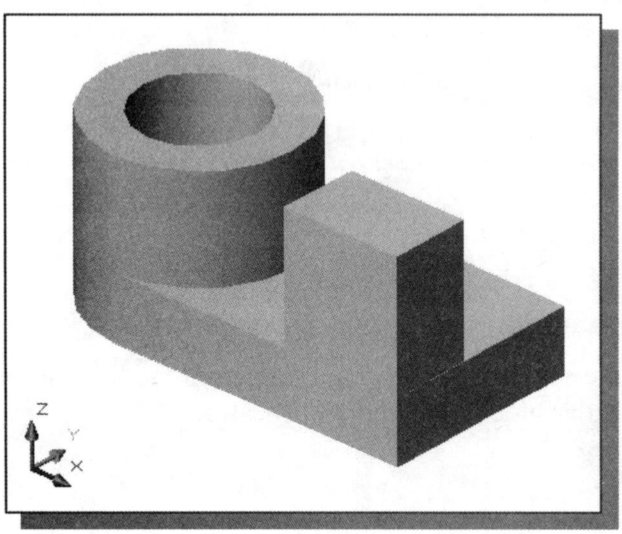

6. In the command prompt area, the message "*Specify angle start point:*" is displayed. Enter: **90** **[ENTER]**

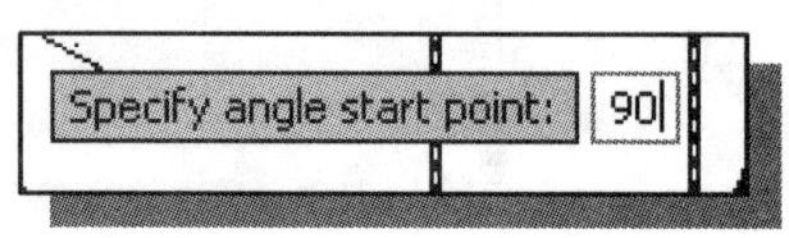

Moving the Rectangular Block

1. **Pre-select** the rectangular block by left-clicking on any edge of the block.

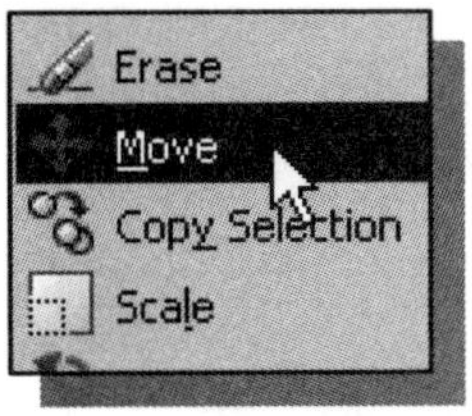

2. Inside the graphics window, right-mouse-click and select **Move** in the popup menu. In the command prompt area, the message "*Specify base point or displacement:*" is displayed.

3. Snap to and select the **top front corner** of the rectangular block as the reference point.

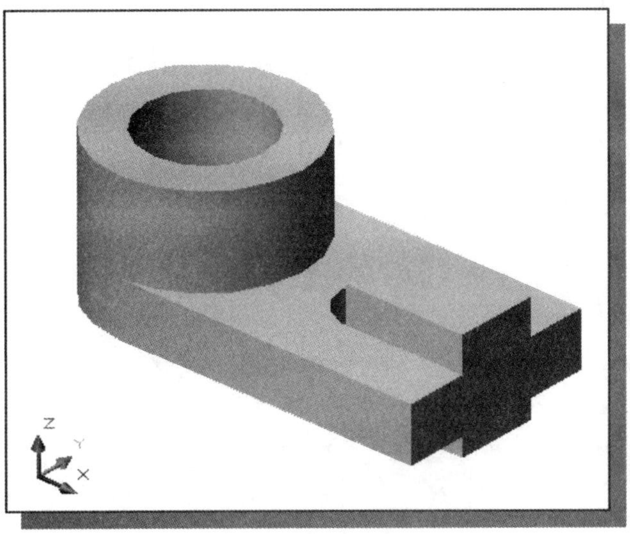

4. In the command prompt area, the message "*Specify second point of displacement or <use first point as displacement>:*" is displayed. Enter: **@0,15,-20 [ENTER]**.

5. On your own, use the **Free Orbit** command to examine the constructed objects.

6. On your own, perform the Subtract Boolean operation and complete the model.

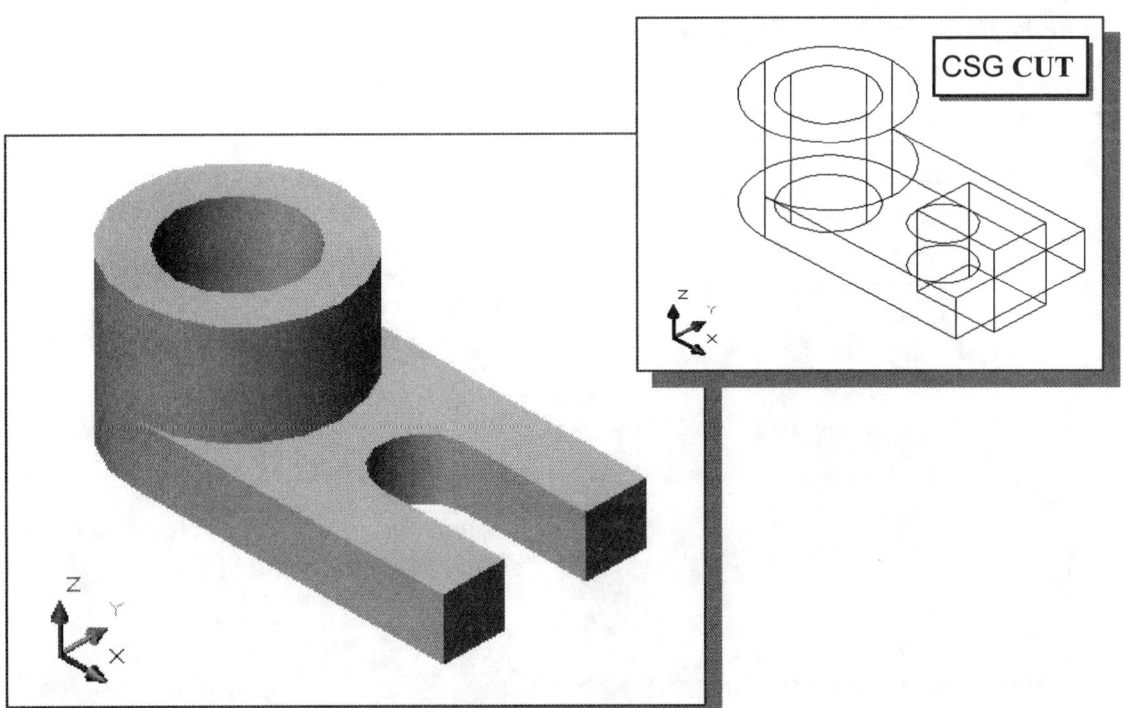

The SteeringWheels

The SteeringWheels are tracking menus that are divided into different sections known as wedges. Each wedge on a wheel represents a single navigation tool. You can pan, zoom, or manipulate the current view of a model in different ways. The *3D SteeringWheel* and *2D SteeringWheel* (mostly used in the 2D drawing mode) some or all of the following options:

Zoom – Adjusts the magnification of the view.
Center – Centers the view based on the position of the cursor over the wheel.
Rewind – Restores the previous view.
Forward – Increases the magnification of the view.
Orbit – Allows 3D free rotation with the left-mouse-button.
Pan – Allows panning with the dragging of the left mouse-button.
Up/Down – Allows panning with the use of a scroll control.
Walk – Allows the *walking*, which linear motion perpendicular to the screen, through the model space.
Look – Allows rotate the current view vertically and horizontally

3D Steering Wheel

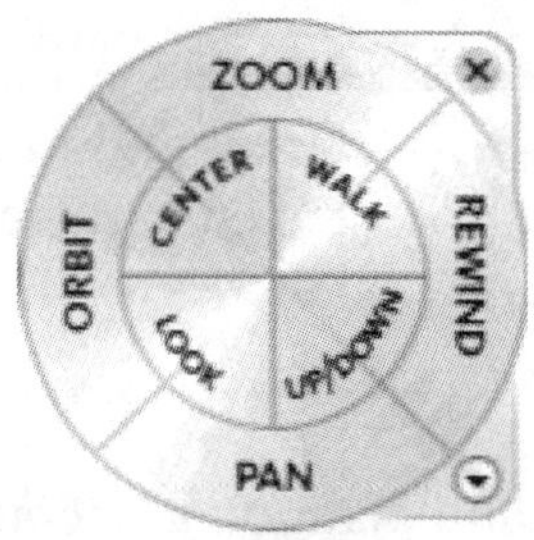

2D Steering Wheel

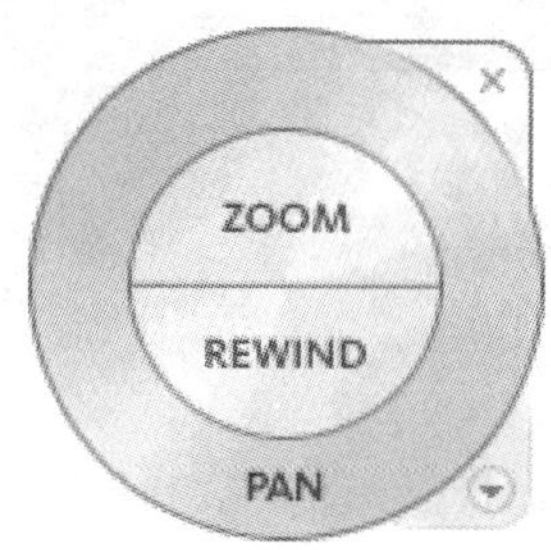

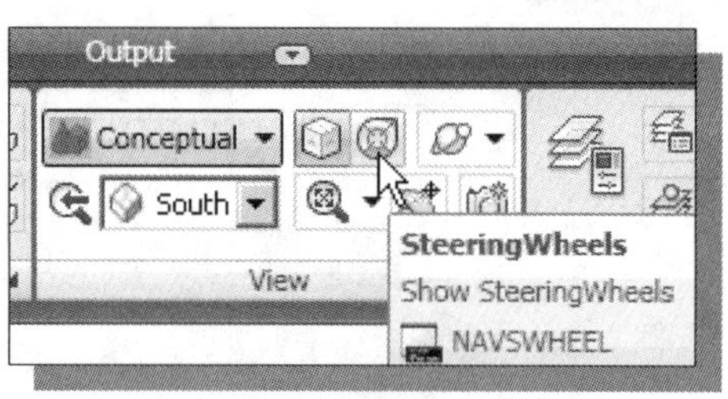

1. Activate the SteeringWheels, by clicking on the icon as shown.

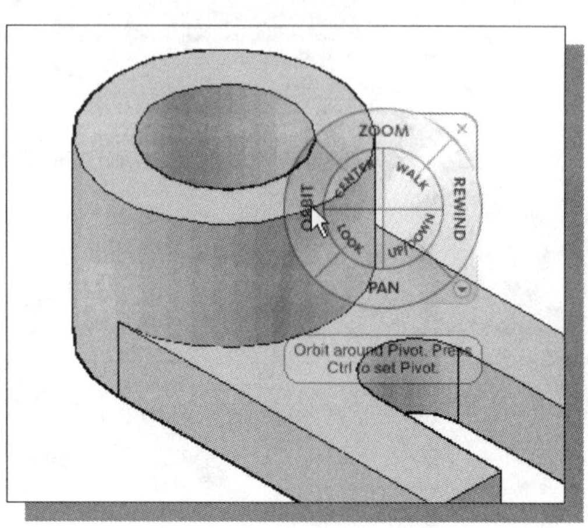

2. Move the cursor in the graphics window and notice the 3D Steering wheel menu follows the cursor on the screen.

3. Move the cursor on the **Orbit** option to highlight the option.

4. Click and drag with the left-mouse-button to activate the **Free Rotation** option.

5. Drag with the left-mouse-button and notice the *ViewCube* also reflects the model orientation.

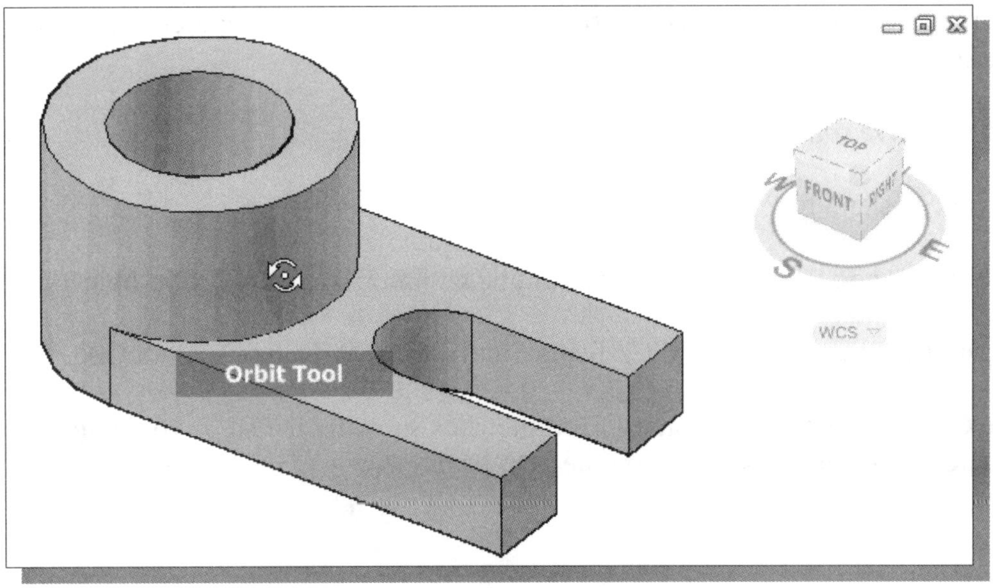

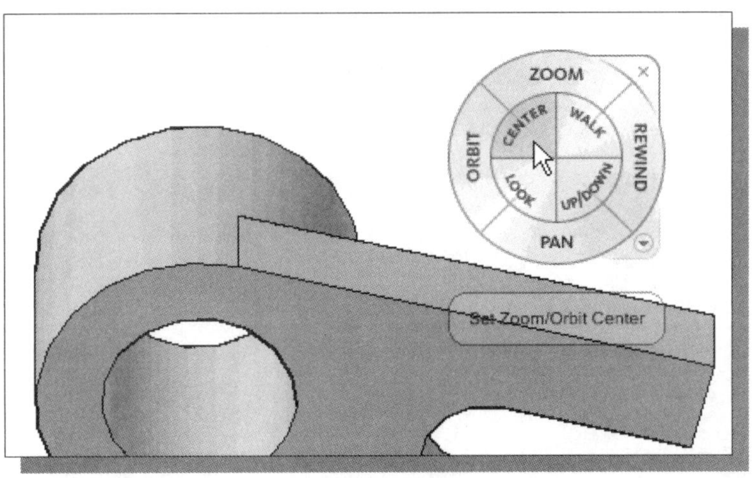

6. Move the cursor to the left side of the model and click the Center option as shown. The display is adjusted so the selected point is the new Zoom/Orbit center.

7. On your own, experiment with the other available options.

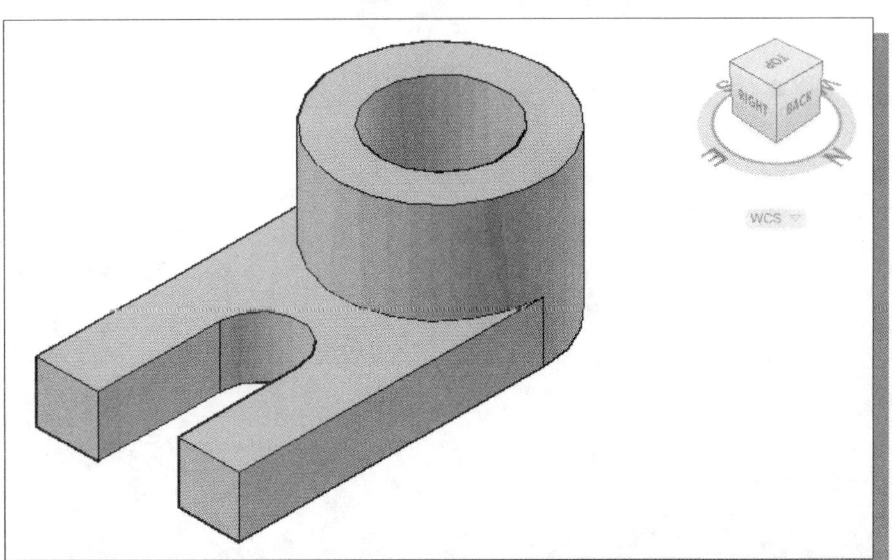

Questions:

1. What are the three basic Boolean operations commonly used in computer geometric modeling software?

2. What is a *primitive solid*?

3. What does *CSG* stand for?

4. Which Boolean operation keeps only the volume common to the two solid objects?

5. What is the difference between a *CUT* feature and a *UNION* feature in AutoCAD?

6. Using the CSG concept, create Binary Tree sketches showing the steps you plan to use to create the two models shown on the next page:

Ex.1)

Ex.2)

Exercises: All dimensions are in inches.

1.

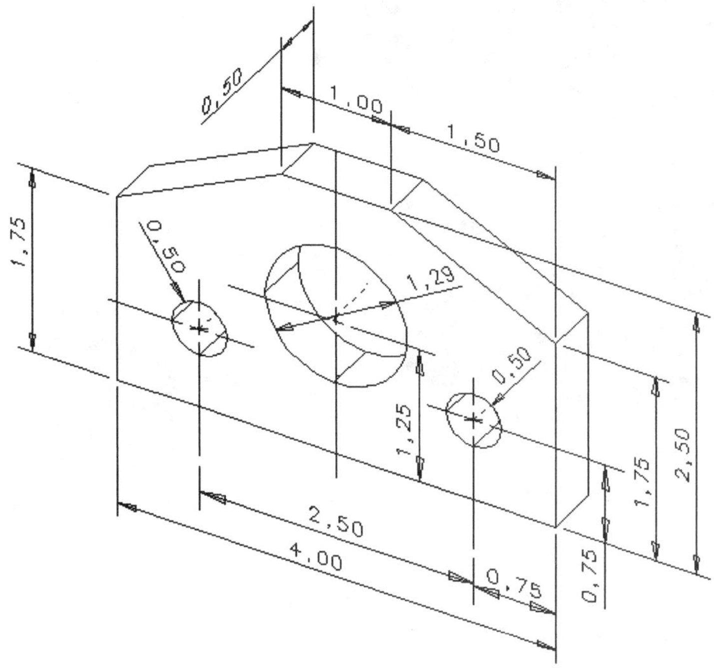

2.

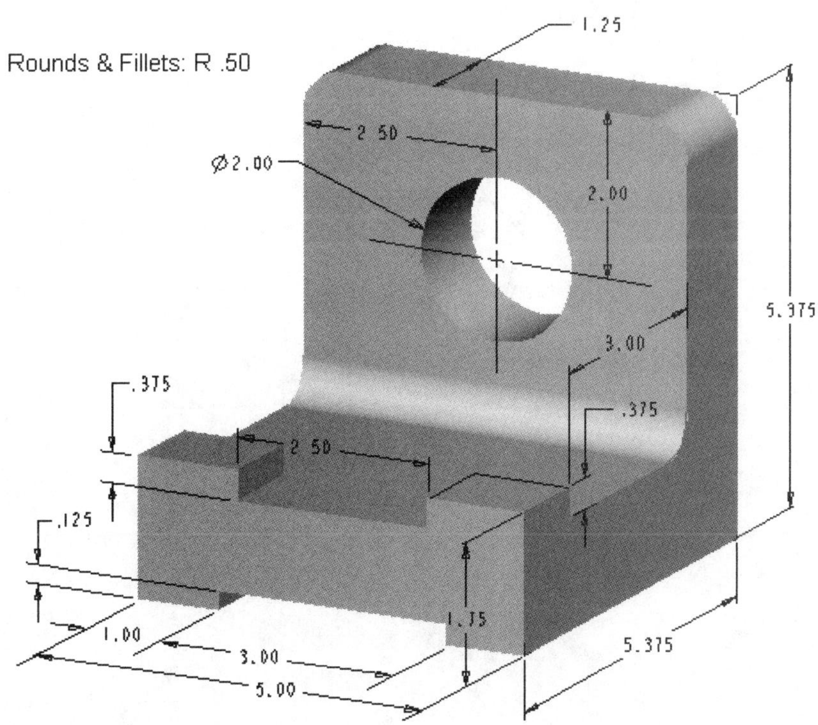

3.

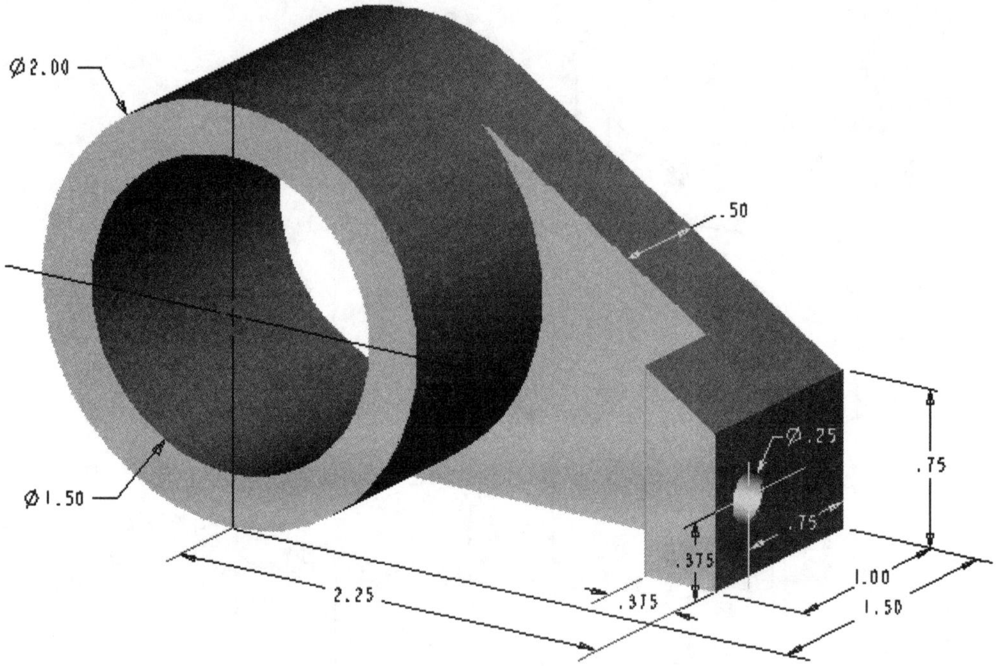
Ø2.00
.50
Ø.25
.75
Ø1.50
.75
.375
2.25
.375
1.00
1.50

4.

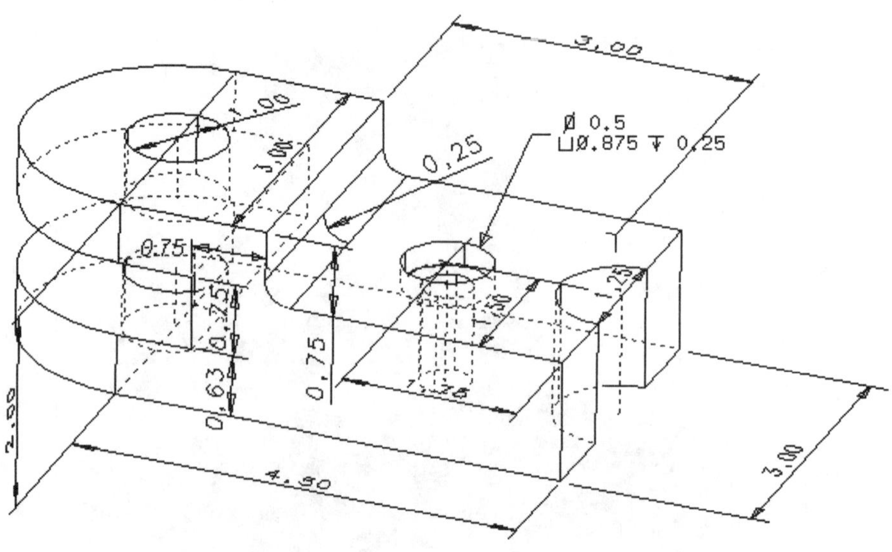
3.00
1.00
3.00
Ø 0.5
⌴Ø.875 ↧ 0.25
0.25
0.75
0.375
1.50
1.25
0.63
0.75
2.00
1.75
4.50
3.00

Chapter 7
Regions, Extrude and Solid Modeling

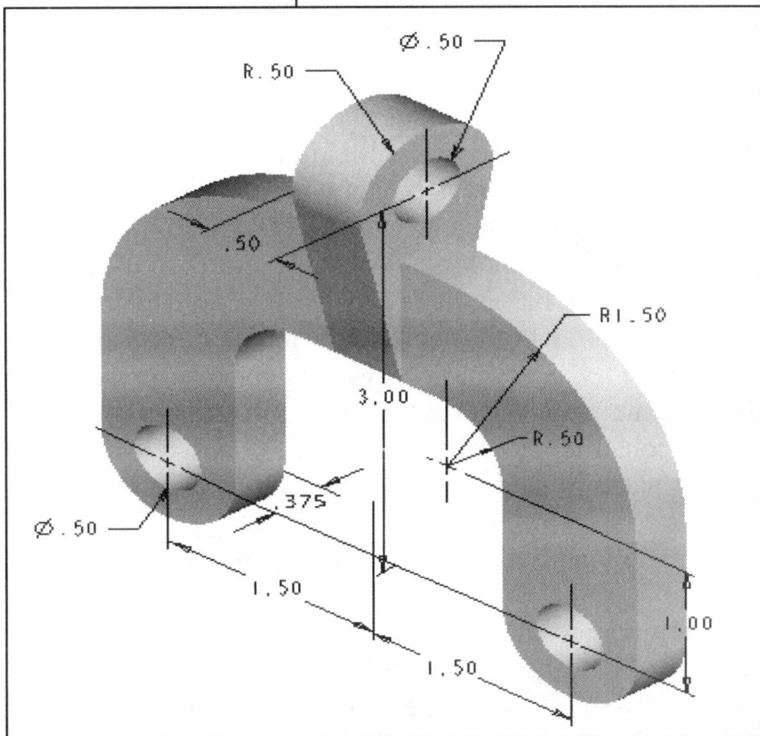

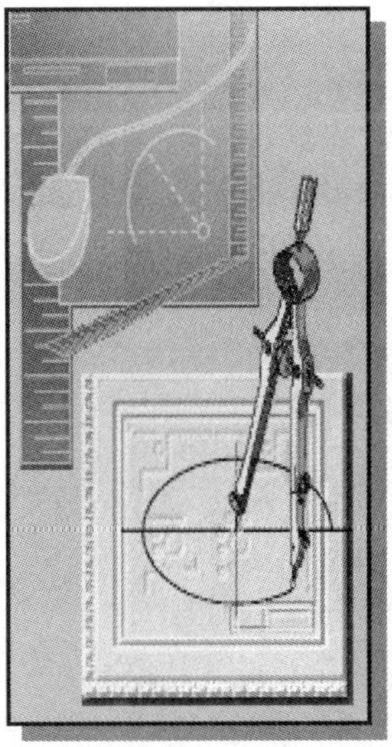

Learning Objectives

- Use 2D Extrusion Method to Create Solid Models
- Understand and Create Regions
- Edit 3D Geometry with the Rotate and Move Commands
- Examine the Mass Properties of Solids
- Understand the Concept of Boundary-Representation Modeling Approach

Introduction

AutoCAD provides many powerful modeling and design-tools, and there are many different approaches to accomplish solid modeling tasks. The CSG approach, as illustrated in the previous chapter, allows designers to create solid models by using a set of predefined shapes to simulate the manufacturing process. Using only a limited set of predefined solids becomes less efficient as more complex geometric definitions are involved. Another solid modeling method, parallel to the development of the CSG approach, is the **Boundary Representation (B-rep)** approach. CSG defines a model in terms of combining basic solid shapes and B-rep defines a model in terms of its edges and surfaces. Two of the most important solid construction operations based on the B-rep approach are **Extrude** and **Revolve**. The Extrude and Revolve options can be used to convert two-dimensional filled polygons into 3D solid models. This concept of using two-dimensional sketches of the three-dimensional features proves to be an effective way to construct solid models. Many designs are in fact the same shape in one direction. Computer input and output devices we use today are largely two-dimensional in nature, which makes this modeling technique quite practical. AutoCAD's solid modeler is a hybrid modeler; the user interface and construction techniques are CSG-based, whereas the B-rep capabilities are invoked automatically and are transparent to the user.

It is important to point out that solid modeling provides us with very powerful design tools. With the abundant tools available in solid modeling software, the modeling techniques are limited only to the imagination of the designer. Instead of the individual 2D views, one should concentrate on the 3D features of designs. In this chapter, the *V-Block* design from chapter four is revisited to introduce the solid modeling tools available in *A*utoCAD. The procedure to creating solid models using the **Extrude** command is demonstrated.

The *V-BlockSolid* Design

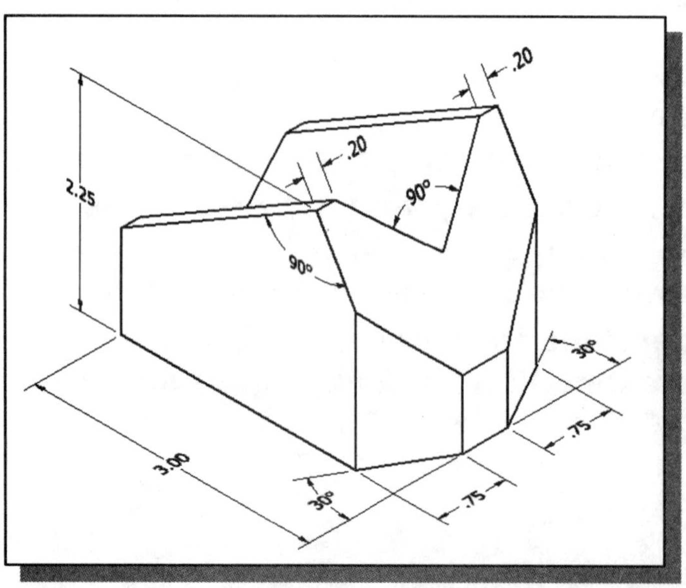

➢ Make a rough sketch of a CSG binary tree showing the steps that can be used to construct the design. What are the advantages and limitations of using the CSG approach in creating the design? What other tools could be helpful to the modeling task at hand? Take a few minutes to consider these questions and you are encouraged to construct the design on your own prior to going through the tutorial.

Starting Up AutoCAD® 2009

1. Select the **AutoCAD 2009** option on the *Program* menu or select the **AutoCAD 2009** icon on the *Desktop*.

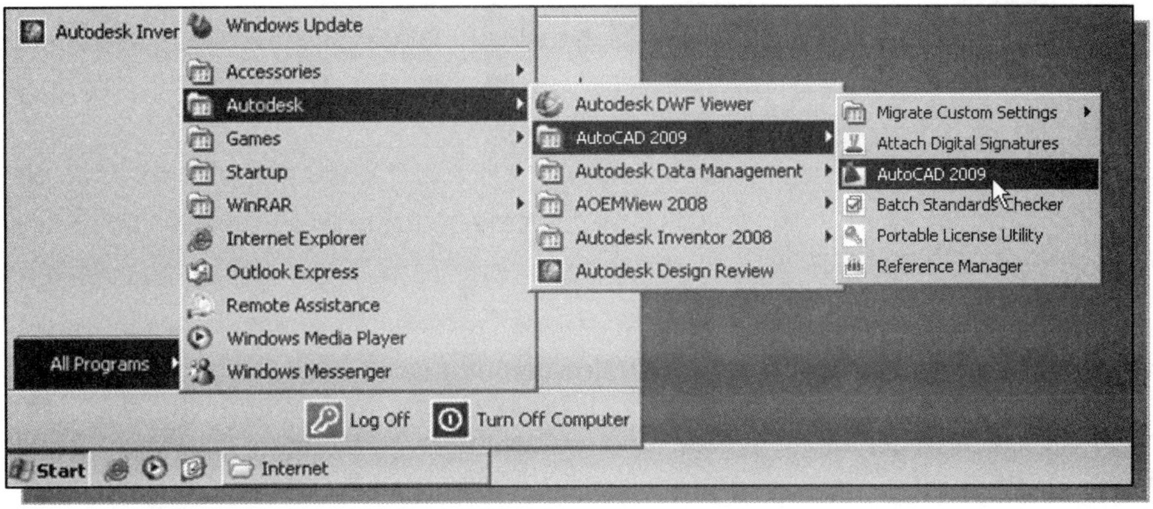

2. In the startup window, select **Start from Scratch**, as shown in the figure below.

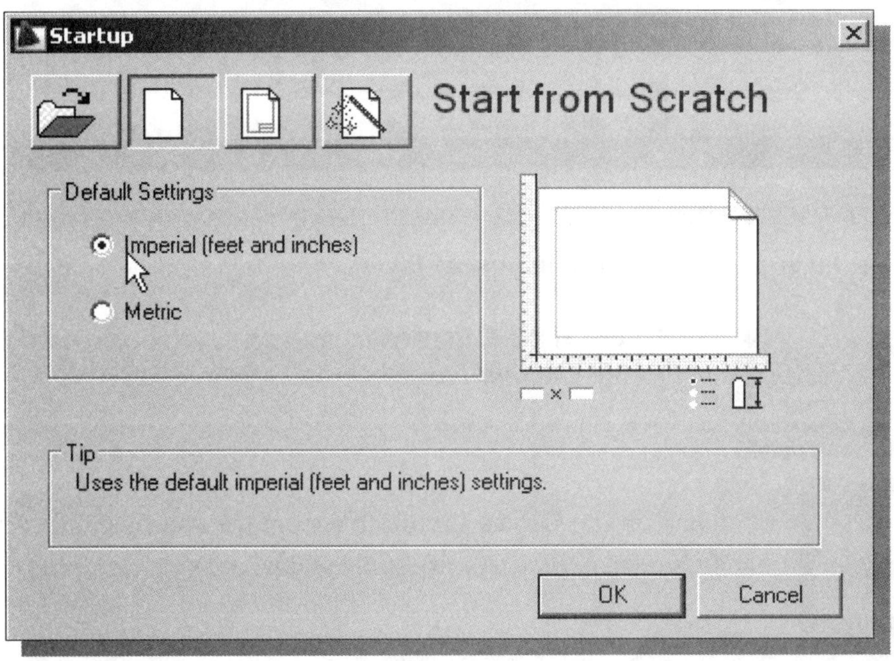

3. In the *Default Settings* section, pick **Imperial (feet and inches)** as the drawing units.

4. Pick **OK** in the startup dialog box to accept the selected settings.

Layers Setup

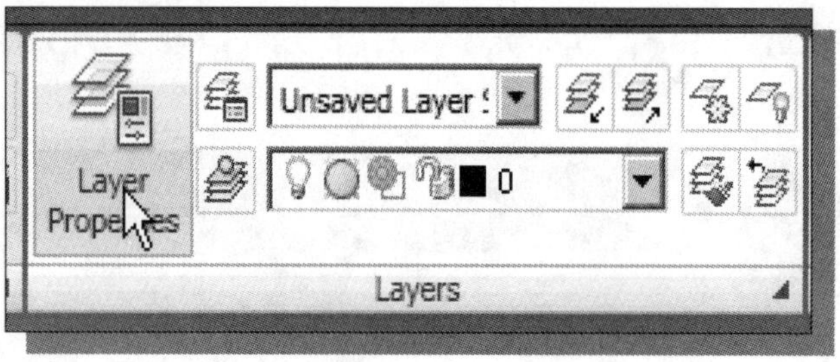

1. Click **Layers Properties Manager** in the *Layers* toolbar.

2. Click on the **New** button to create new layers.

3. Create **two new layers** with the following settings:

Layer	*Color*	*LineType*	*LineWeight*
Construction	**White**	**Continuous**	**Default**
Object	**Cyan**	**Continuous**	**0.30mm**

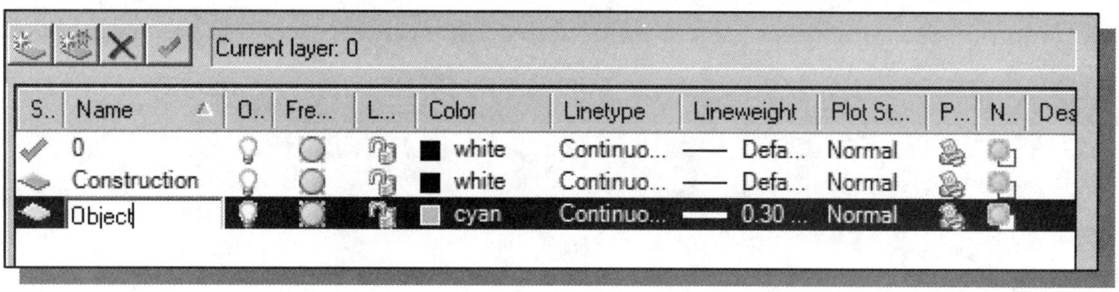

4. Highlight the layer ***Construction*** in the list of layers.

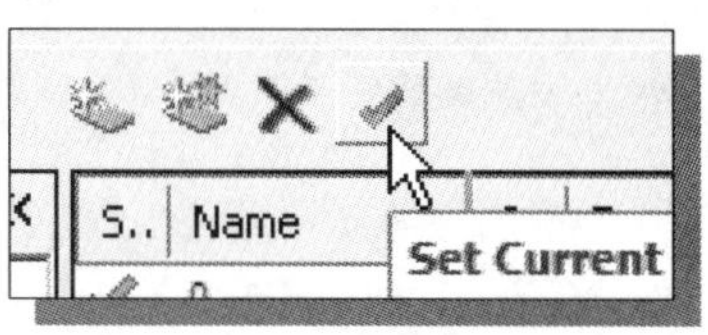

5. Click on the **Current** icon to set layer ***Construction*** as the *Current Layer*.

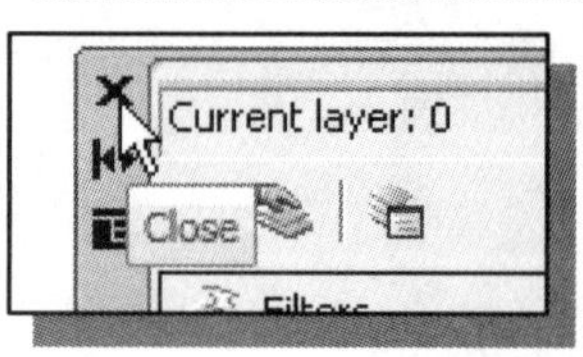

6. Click on the **Close** button to accept the settings and exit the *Layer Properties Manager* dialog box.

7. In the *Status Bar* area, reset the options and turn ***ON*** the *Polar, Object Snap, Object Snap Tracking, Dynamic Input* and *Line Weight* options.

Setting Up a 2D Sketch

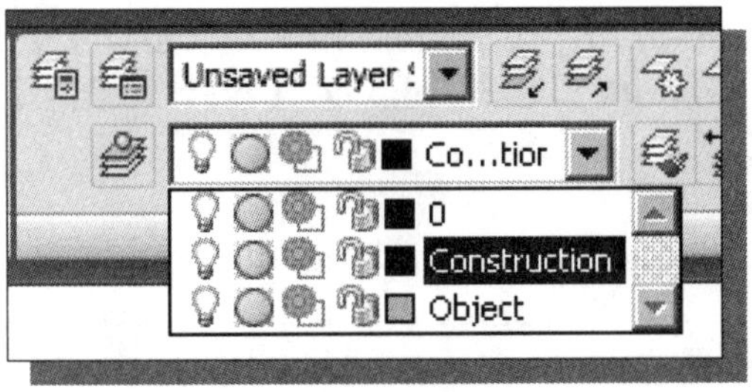

1. In the *Layer Control* box, confirm layer *Construction* is set as the *Current Layer*.

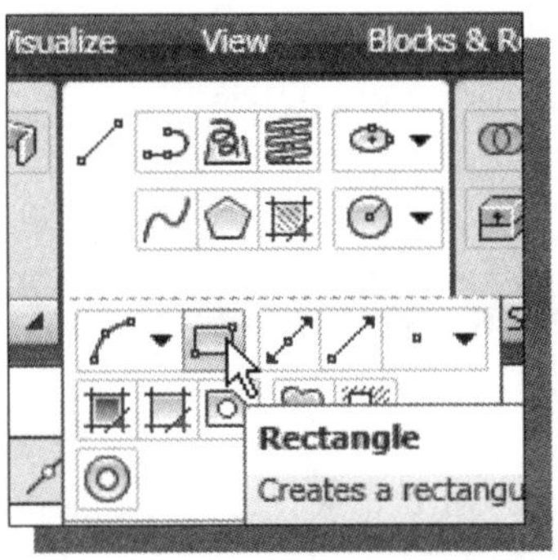

2. Select the **Rectangle** icon in the *Draw* toolbar. In the command prompt area, the message "*Specify first corner point or [Chamfer/Elevation/Fillet/Thickness/Width]:*" is displayed.

3. Place the first corner point of the rectangle near the lower left corner of the screen. Do not be overly concerned about the actual coordinates of the selected location; the CAD drawing space is as big as you can imagine.

4. We will create a 3″ × 2.25″ rectangle. Enter **@3,2.25 [ENTER]**.

❖ The Rectangle command creates rectangles as *polyline* features, which means all segments of a rectangle are created as a single object.

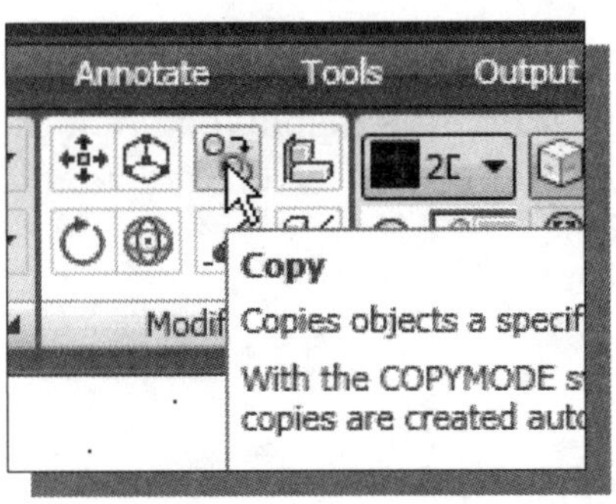

5. We will next make a copy of the rectangle. Pick **Copy Object** in the *Modify* toolbar.

6. Pick any edge of the rectangle we just created.

7. Inside the graphics window, **right-mouse-click** to accept the selection.

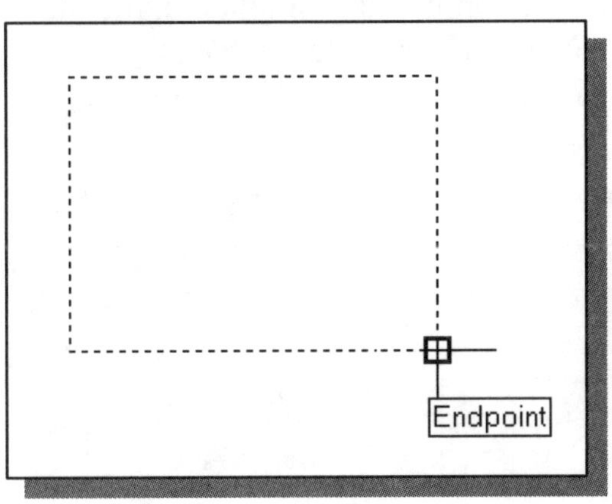

8. In the command prompt area, the message "*Specify base point or displacement, or [Multiple]:*" is displayed. Pick the lower right corner of the rectangle as the base point. A copy of the rectangle is attached to the cursor at the selected base point.

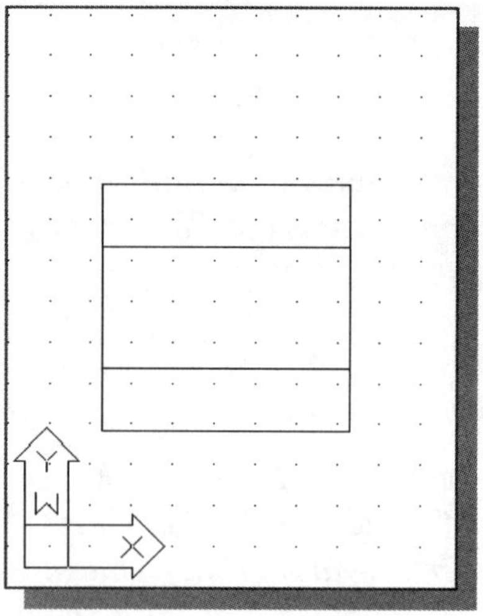

9. In the command prompt area, the message "*Specify second point of displacement, or <use first point as displacement>:*" is displayed. Enter: **@0,0.75 [ENTER]**.

❖ This will position the second rectangle at the location for the 30-degree angle that is needed in the design.

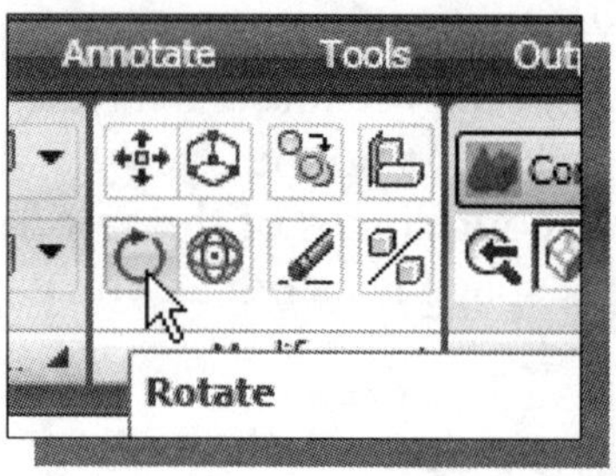

10. Pick **Rotate** in the *Modify* toolbar as shown.

11. Pick the top horizontal line on the screen. The second rectangle, the copy we just created, is selected.

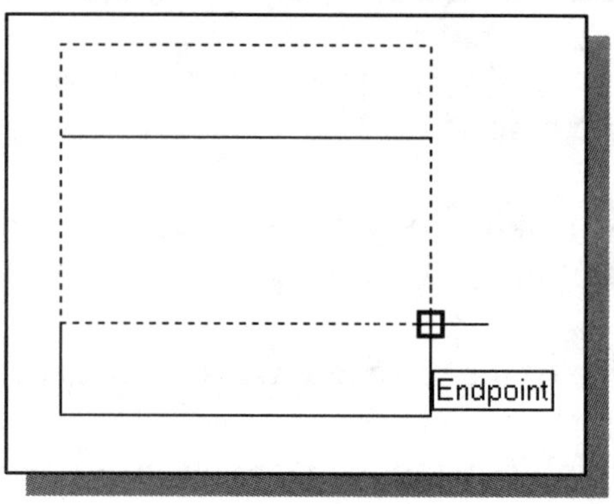

12. Inside the graphics window, right-mouse-click to accept the selection.

13. In the command prompt area, the message "*Specify base point:*" is displayed. Pick the lower right corner of the selected rectangle as the base point.

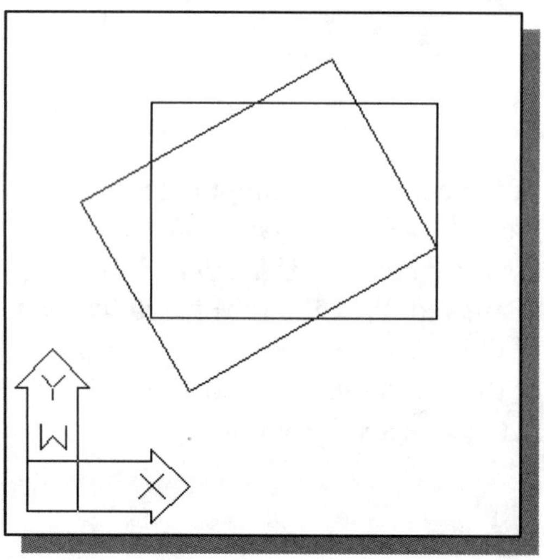

14. In the command prompt area, the message "*Specify the rotation angle or [Reference]:*" is displayed. Enter: **30 [ENTER]**.

Defining the Front Edges of the Design

1. In the *Status Bar* area, right-mouse-click on the *POLAR* option to bring up the option menu.

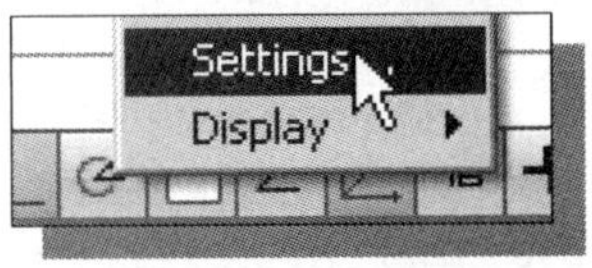

2. Select **Settings** in the option menu as shown.

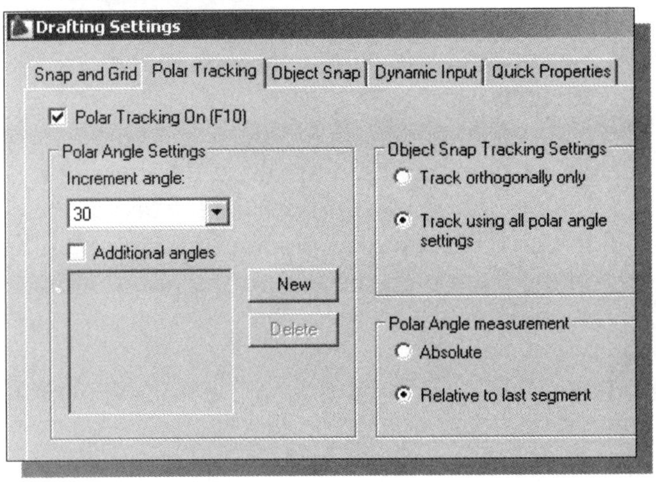

3. In the *Drafting Settings* window, confirm the *Increment angle* is set to **30** in the *Polar Angle Settings* area.

4. Switch **on** the ***Track using all polar angle settings*** and ***Relative to last segment*** options as shown.

5. In the *Drafting Settings* window, click on the **Object Snap** tab to display and set the *Object Snap* options.

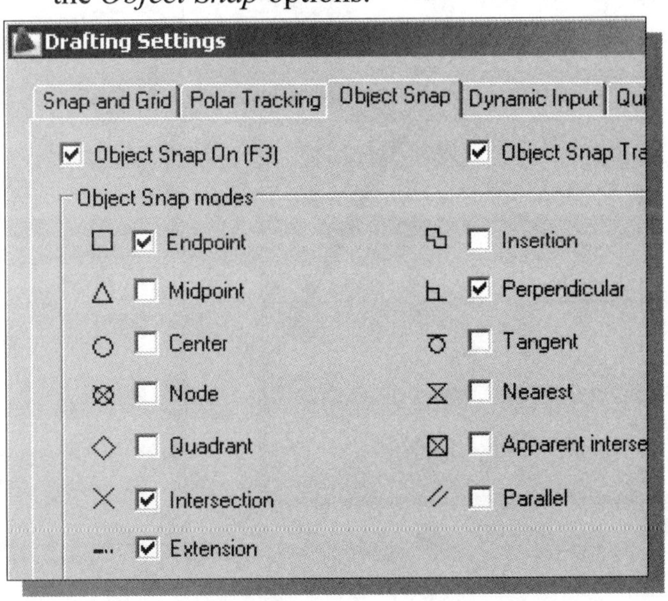

6. On your own, reset the *Object Snap modes* so that only the *Endpoint*, *Extension*, *Intersection* and *Perpendicular* are switched ***ON*** as shown in the figure.

7. In the *Drafting Settings* window, click **OK** to accept the settings.

- The AuotCAD *AutoTrack*™ feature includes two tracking options: *POLAR* tracking and *OBJECT SNAP* tracking. When these options are turned on, alignment markers are displayed to help us create objects at precise positions and angles.

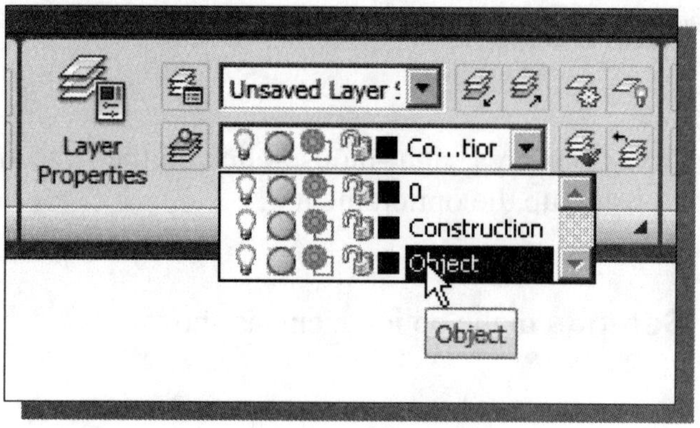

8. On the *Object Properties* toolbar, choose the *Layer Control* box with the left-mouse-button.

9. Move the cursor over the name of layer *Object*; the tool tip "*Object*" appears.**Left-mouse-click once** and layer *Object* is set as the *Current Layer*.

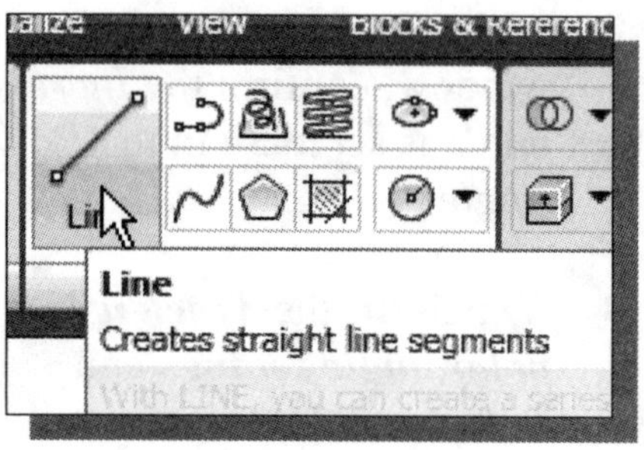

10. Select the **Line** command icon in the *Draw* toolbar.

11. In the command prompt area, the message "*_line Specify first point:*" is displayed. Pick the **lower left corner** of the bottom horizontal line in the front view as the starting point of the line segments.

12. Pick the **lower right corner** of the bottom horizontal line in the front view as the second point.

13. Select the **third** and **fourth** points as shown in the figure below.

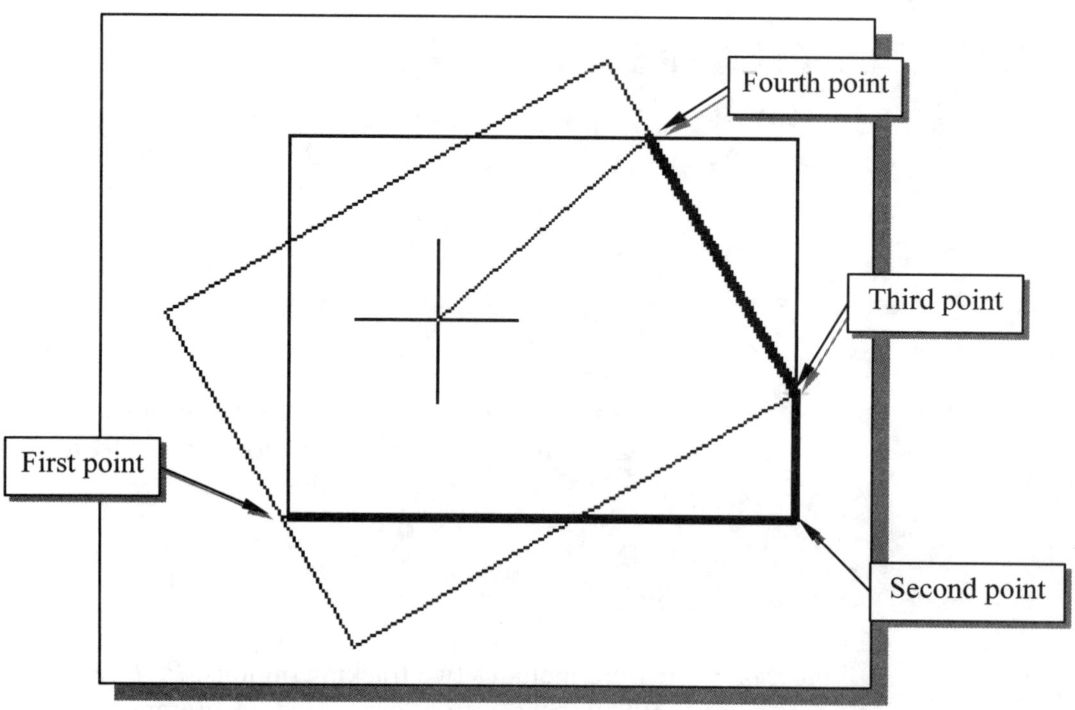

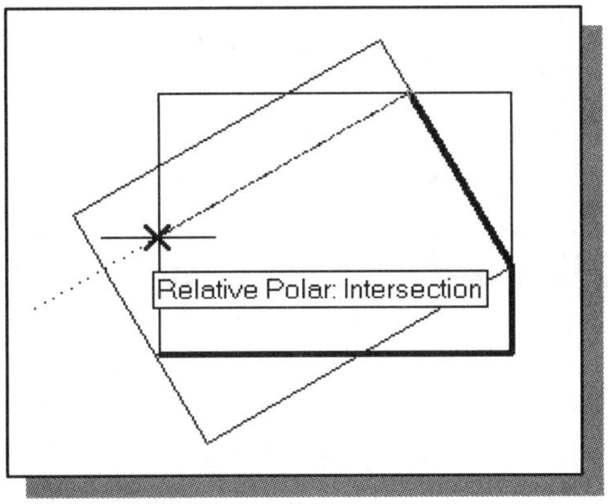

14. Move the cursor near the left vertical line and notice the *AutoTrack* feature automatically snaps the cursor to the intersection point.

15. Left-click at the intersection point as shown.

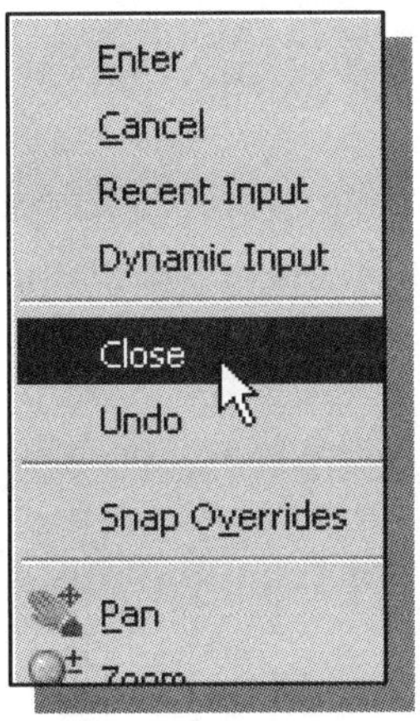

16. Inside the graphics window, right-mouse-click once to bring up the popup menu.

17. Pick **Close** in the popup menu. The Close option will create a line segment connecting the last point to the first point of the line sequence.

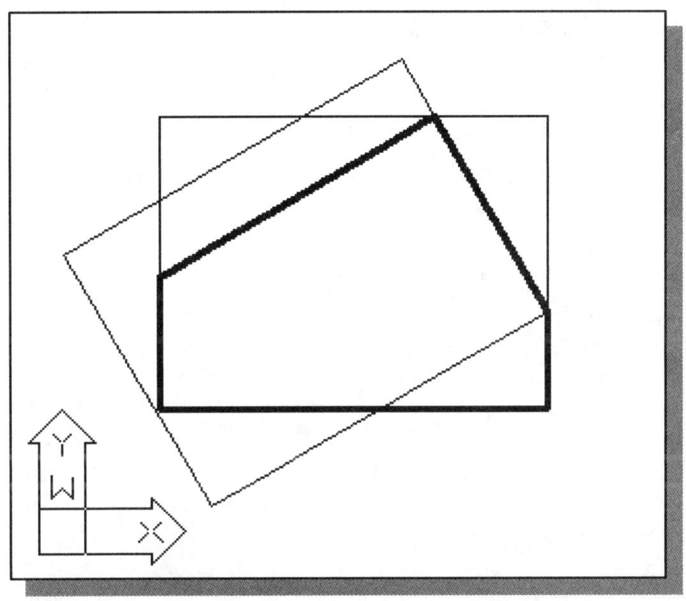

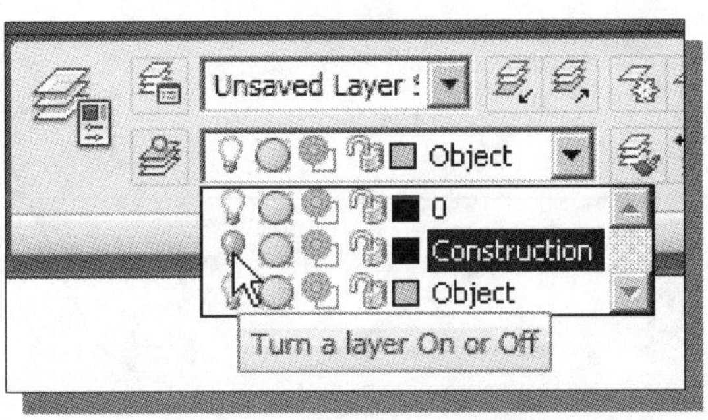

18. On your own, turn ***OFF*** the display of the **Construction Layer** by using the left-mouse-button.

19. Move the cursor into the graphics window and **left-mouse-click once** to accept the layer control settings.

Creating a Region

- In AutoCAD, **regions** are 2D enclosed areas, which can be created from one or more closed shapes called **loops**. A *loop* is a curve or a sequence of connected curves that defines an area on a plane with a boundary that does not intersect itself. *Loops* can be combinations of lines, polylines, circles, arcs, ellipses, elliptical arcs, splines, 3D faces, traces and solids. The objects that make up the loops must either be closed or form closed areas by sharing endpoints with other objects. The objects must also be coplanar, which means they must be on the same plane. We can create regions out of multiple loops and out of open curves whose endpoints are connected. Objects that intersect with themselves or with other objects cannot form regions; for example, intersecting lines, intersecting arcs or self-intersecting curves. Once a region is created, we can analyze properties such as its area and moments of inertia.

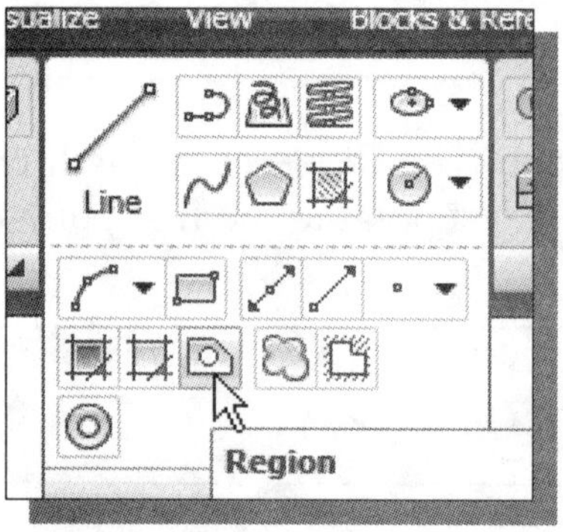

1. Select the **Region** command icon in the *Draw* toolbar.

2. In the command prompt area, the message "*Select objects:*" is displayed. Select displayed entities by creating a selection window enclosing **all objects**.

3. Inside the graphics window, **right-mouse-click** to accept the selection and create a region.

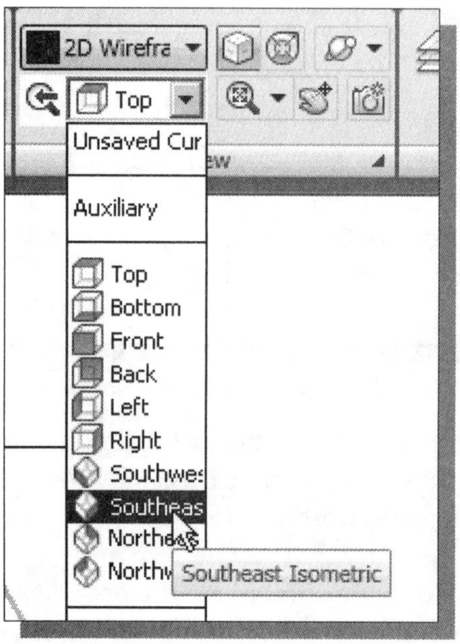

4. In the *View* toolbar, select: **[SouthEast Isometric]**

- Notice the orientation of the 2D region in relation to the displayed AutoCAD user coordinate system. By default, the 2D sketch-plane is aligned to the XY plane of the world coordinate system.

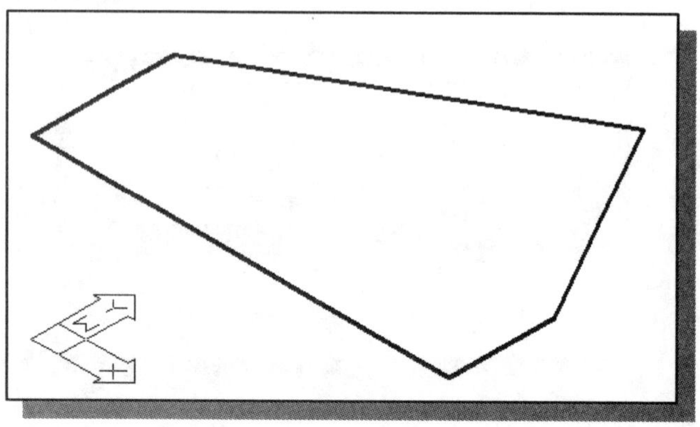

Extruding the Created Region

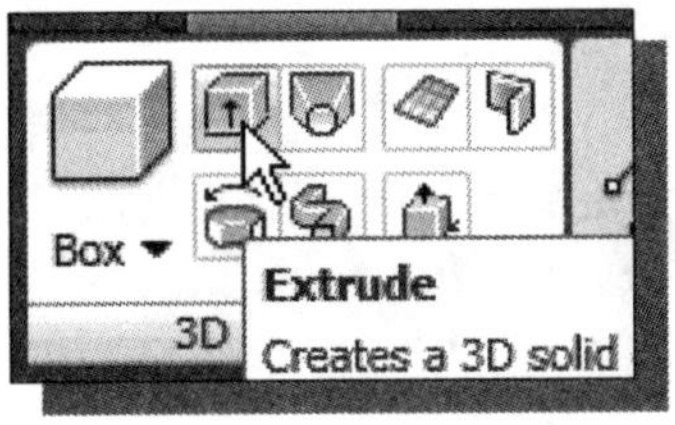

1. Select **Extrude** in the *3D Modeling* toolbar as shown.

2. In the command prompt area, the message "*Select objects:*" is displayed. Select the region by clicking on any of the displayed segments.

3. Inside the graphics window, **right-mouse-click** to accept the selection and proceed with the extrude command.

4. In the command prompt area, the message "*Specify height of extrusion or [path]:*" is displayed. We will extrude the region in the upward direction, enter: **2.0** [**ENTER**].

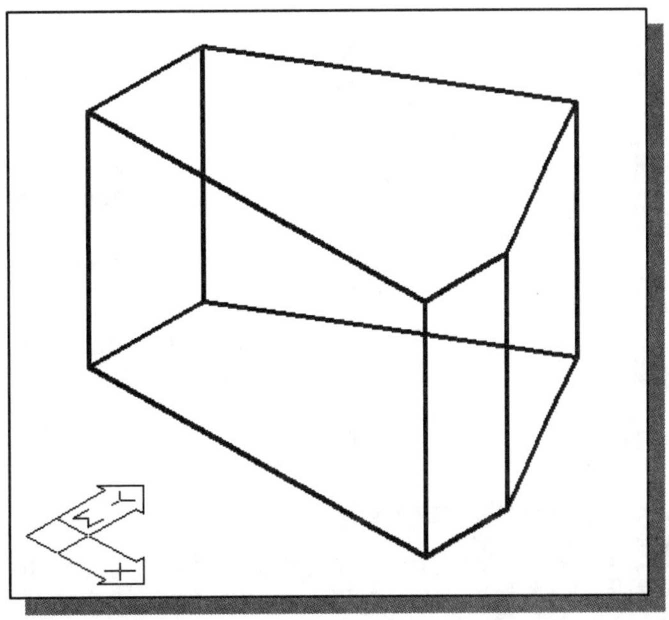

- Note that the orientation and position of solid models, in relation to the world coordinate system, can be adjusted using the Move and 3D Rotate commands.

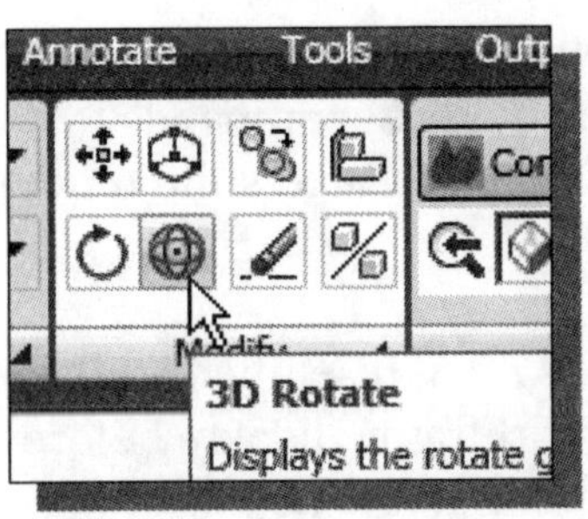

5. Select **3D Rotate** in the *Modify* toolbar as shown.

6. In the command prompt area, the message "*Select objects:*" is displayed. Select the solid model by clicking on any of the displayed edges of the model.

7. Inside the graphics window, right-mouse-click to accept the selection and proceed with the **3D Rotate** command.

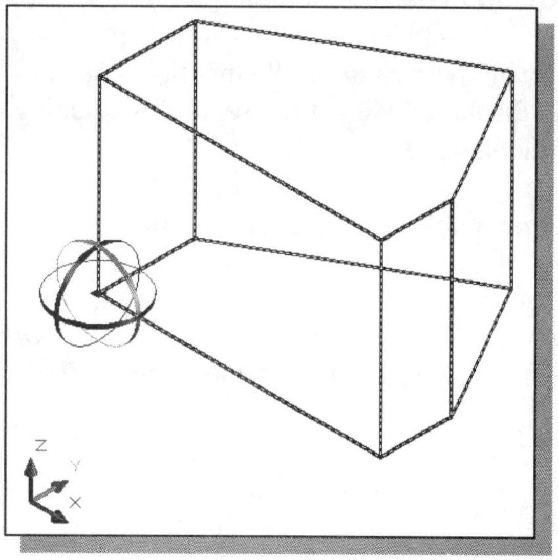

8. In the command prompt area, the message *"Specify base point:" is displayed.* Select the lower left corner of the model as shown.

- Note that the **3D Rotate** command requires the definition of a *base point, a rotation axis and the angle of rotation.*

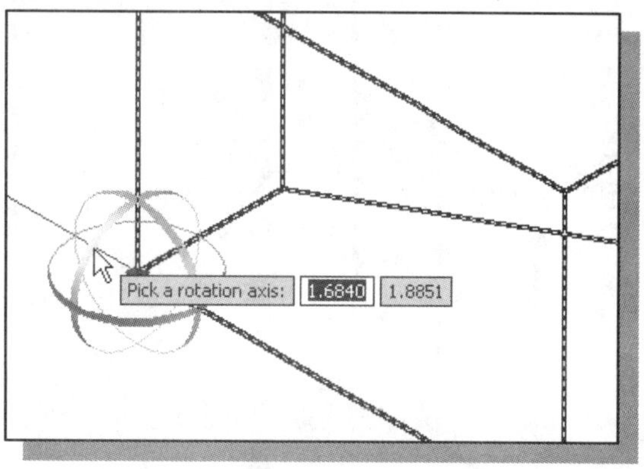

9. In the command prompt area, the message "*Pick a rotation axis:*" is displayed. Select the X-axis by clicking once on the **red grip rotate handle** as shown.

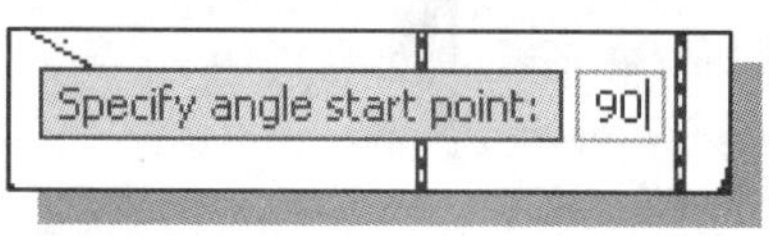

10. In the command prompt area, the message "*Specify angle start point:*" is displayed. Enter: **90** [**ENTER**]

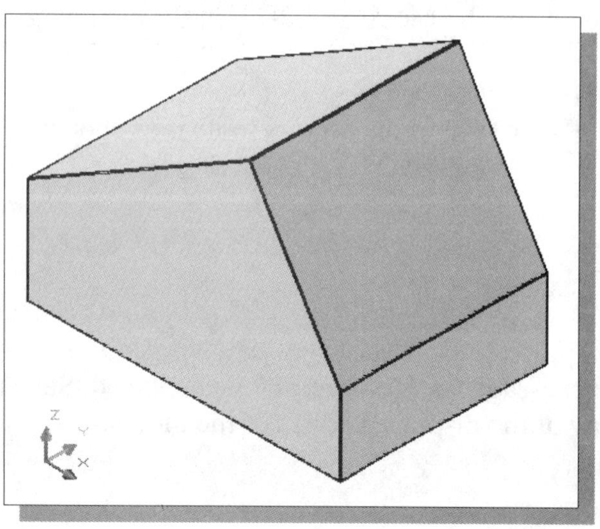

11. On your own, use the available **Visual Styles** commands to examine the created solid object.

12. On your own, reset the display to 2D wireframe display before proceeding to the next section.

Creating a 2D Sketch at the Base of the Model

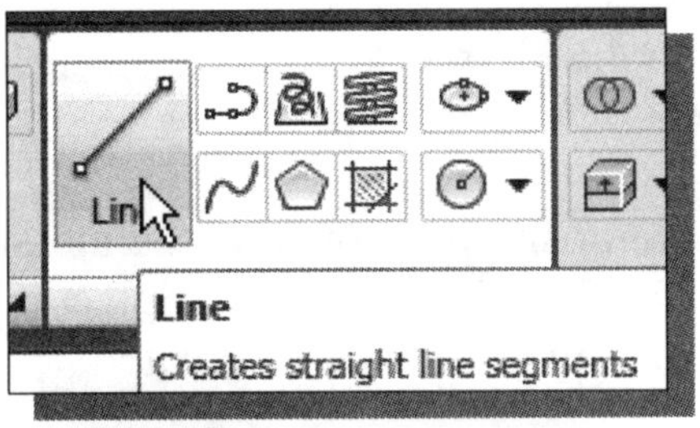

1. Select the **Line** command icon in the *Draw* toolbar. In the command prompt area, the message "*_line Specify first point:*" is displayed.

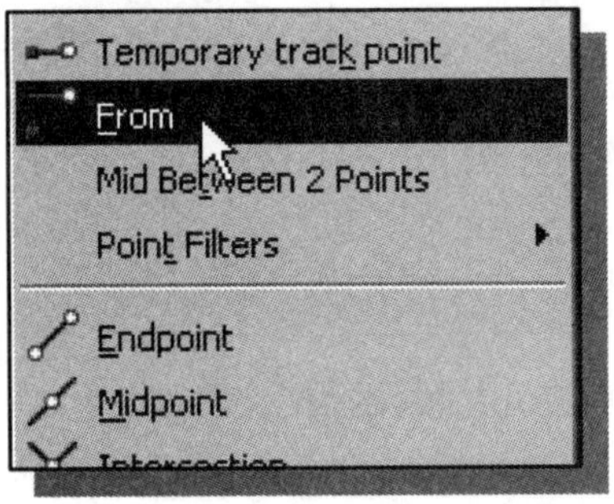

2. Inside the graphics window, hold down the **[SHIFT]** key and **right-mouse-click** once to bring up the *Object Snap* shortcut menu.

3. Select the **From** option in popup window.

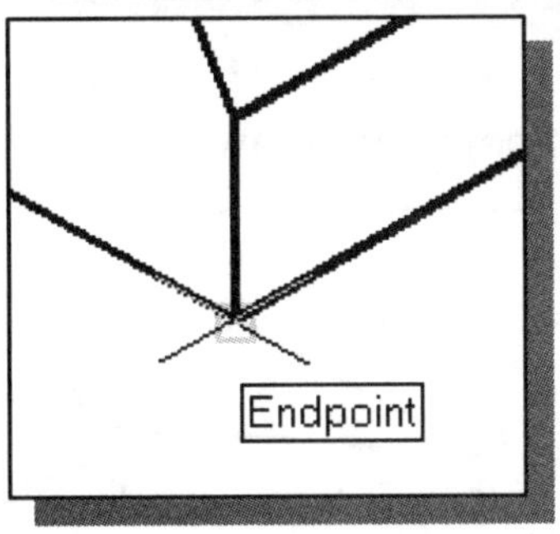

4. Pick the lower right corner of the solid model as the base point as shown in the figure.

5. We will place the first point above the selected corner. Enter: **@0,0.75 [ENTER]**

- Note the orientation of the world XY plane.

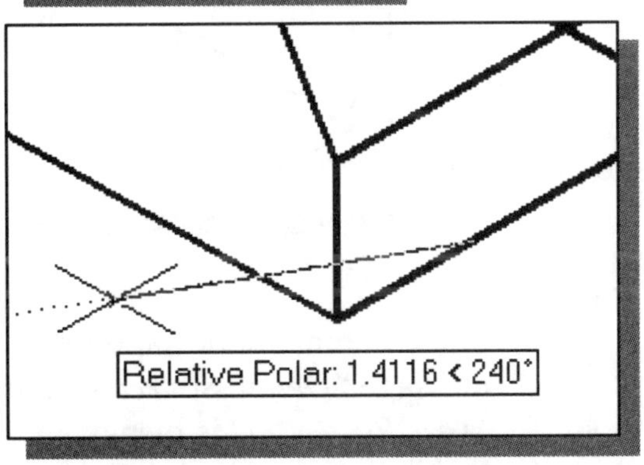

6. In the command prompt area, the message "*Specify next point or [Undo]:*" is displayed. Using the *POLAR Tracking* option (30 degrees increment), create a line that is about 1.4 inches long, as shown in the figure.

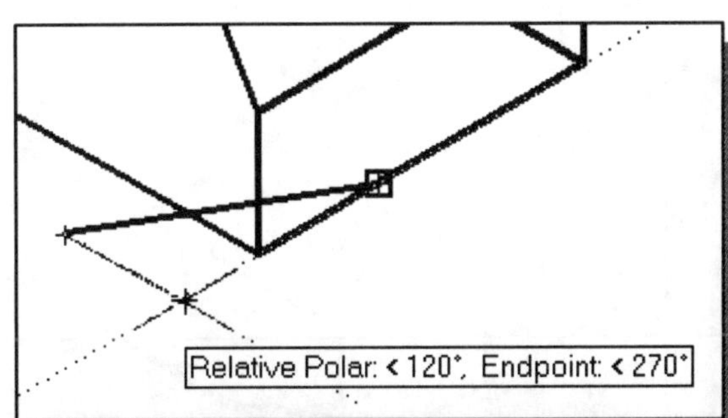

7. Move the cursor on top of the starting point of the last line to activate the *OTRACK* option and select the location that forms a 90-degrees angle as shown.

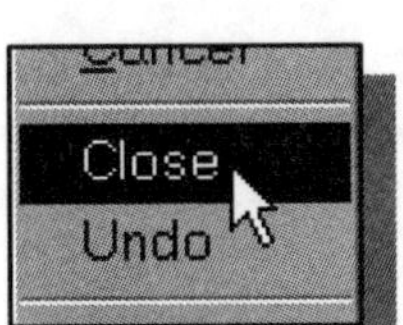

8. Inside the graphics window, right-mouse-click to activate the option menu and select **Close** with the left-mouse-button to create a line connecting to the starting point and end the **Line** command.

Creating a Copy of the 2D Sketch

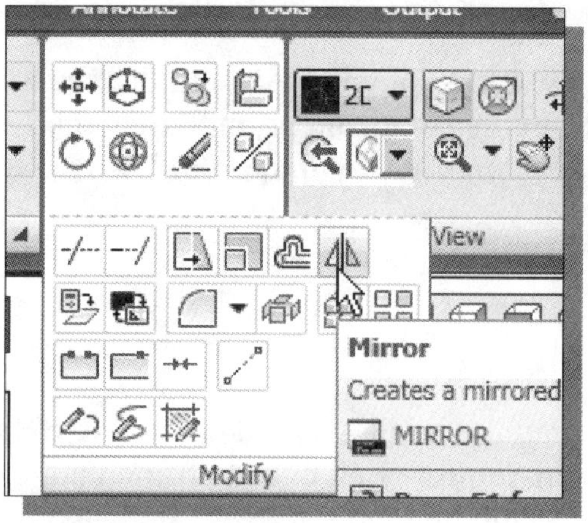

1. Click on the **Mirror** icon in the *Modify* toolbar.

2. In the command prompt area, the message "*Select objects:*" is displayed. Select the three line segments we just created.

3. Inside the graphics window, right-mouse-click to accept the selection and proceed with the **Extrude** command.

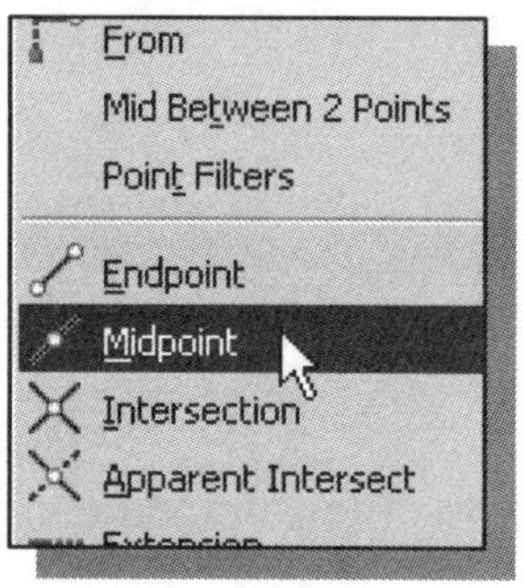

4. Inside the graphics window, hold down the [**SHIFT**] key and **right-mouse-click** once to bring up the *Object Snap* shortcut menu.

5. Select the **Midpoint** option in popup window.

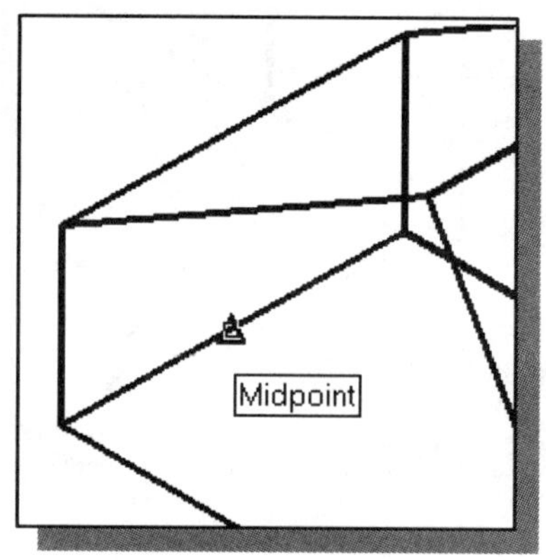

6. Click on the bottom left edge of the model. With the *Midpoint SNAP* option, the midpoint of the edge is selected.

7. Move the cursor toward the right vertical line in the active viewport, and left-click once when the ***Perpendicular*** tooltip is displayed as shown in the below figure.

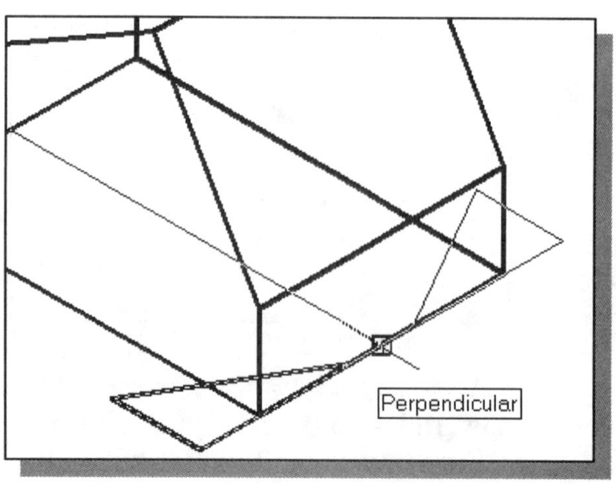

8. In the command prompt area, the message "*Delete Source Objects? [Yes/No] <N>:*" is displayed. Inside the graphics window, right-mouse-click once to bring up the option menu and select **No** to keep both sets of objects.

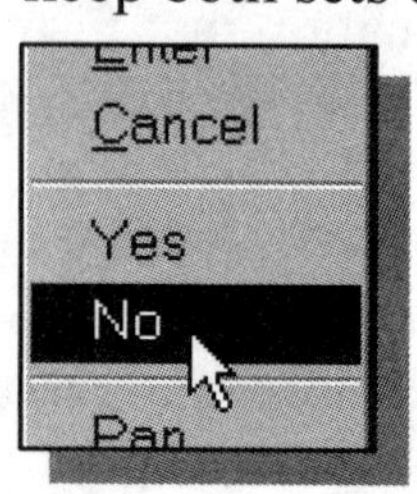

Creating the Cutter Solids

- The two triangular shapes will be the extruded in the Z-direction to form two solids that can be used to create the two vertical cuts.

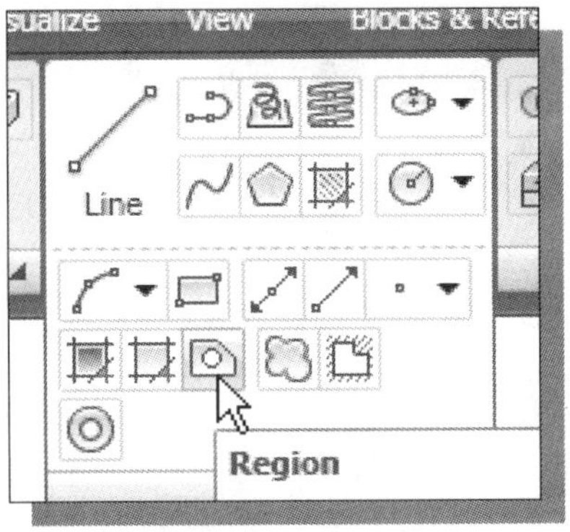

1. Select the **Region** command icon in the *Draw* toolbar.

2. In the command prompt area, the message "*Select objects:*" is displayed. Select the **six line segments** we just created.

3. Inside the graphics window, right-mouse-click to accept the selection and create two regions.

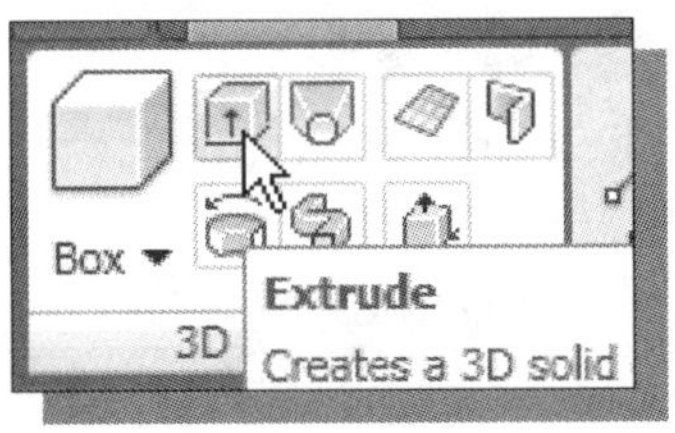

4. Select **Extrude** in the *3D Modeling* toolbar as shown.

5. In the command prompt area, the message "*Select objects:*" is displayed. Select the **two regions** by clicking on the two triangular regions.

6. Inside the graphics window, right-mouse-click to accept the selection and proceed with the Extrude command.

7. In the command prompt area, the message "*Specify height of extrusion or [path]:*" is displayed. We will extrude the regions in the upward direction, enter: **2.5** [**ENTER**].

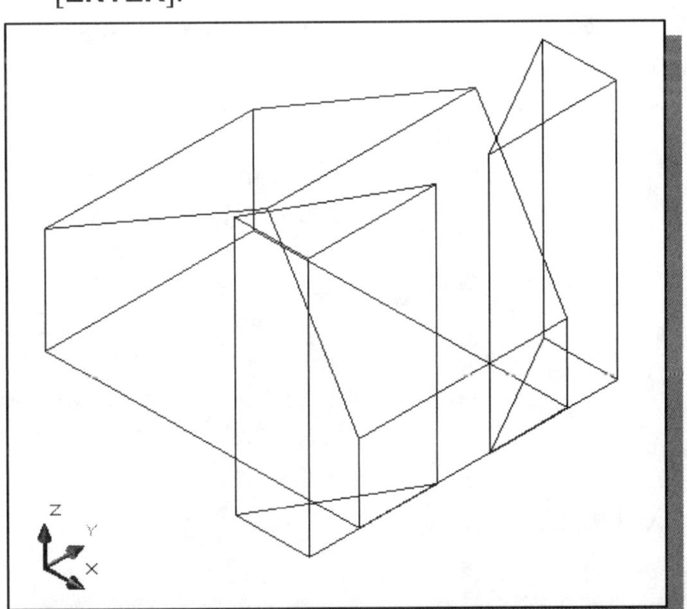

- Note that the two cutters were intentionally made larger than the dimensions shown on the design. In fact, we could create a single cutter, instead of the two we have created, provided the two triangular shapes are included and positioned at the proper locations.

Boolean Operation – *Subtract*

1. Move the cursor on top of the third group of icons in the Modeling toolbar, which contains the basic set of Boolean operation icons. On your own, read the brief description of each Boolean commands.

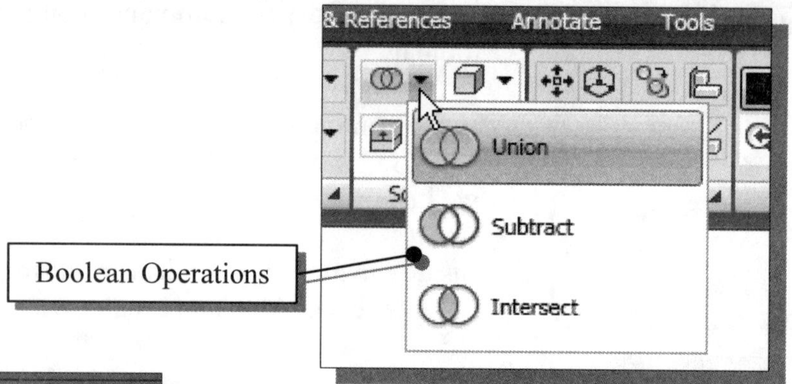

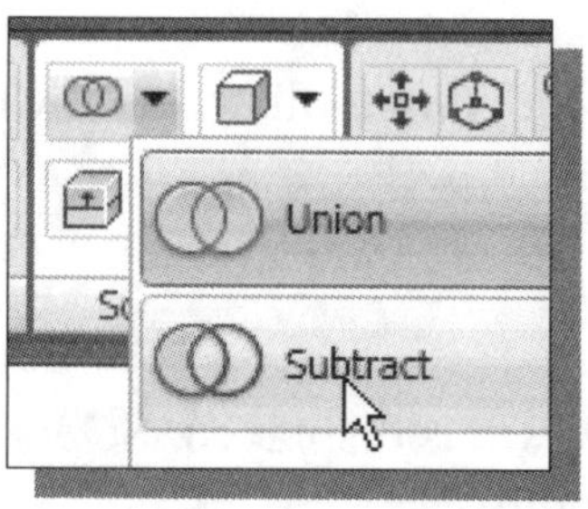

2. In the*Solid Editing* toolbar, click on the **Subtract** icon. In the command prompt area, the message "*_subtract Select solids and regions to subtract from .. Select Objects:*" is displayed.

3. Pick the base block solid by clicking on one of the edges.

4. Inside the graphics window, right-mouse-click to accept the selection and proceed with the Subtract command.

5. In the command prompt area, the message "*Select solids and regions to subtract .. Select Objects:*" is displayed. Pick the two triangular blocks by clicking on the edges of the two cutters.

6. Inside the graphics window, right-mouse-click to accept the selection and proceed with the Subtract command.

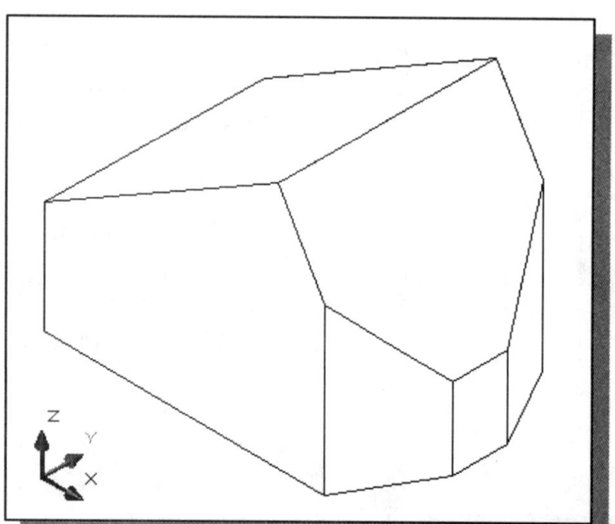

- Note that the two cut features are created fairly quickly. In comparison to the wireframe or surface models created in the previous chapters, the solid modeling approach is much more straightforward and parallel to the manufacturing processes.

Mass Properties of the Solid Model

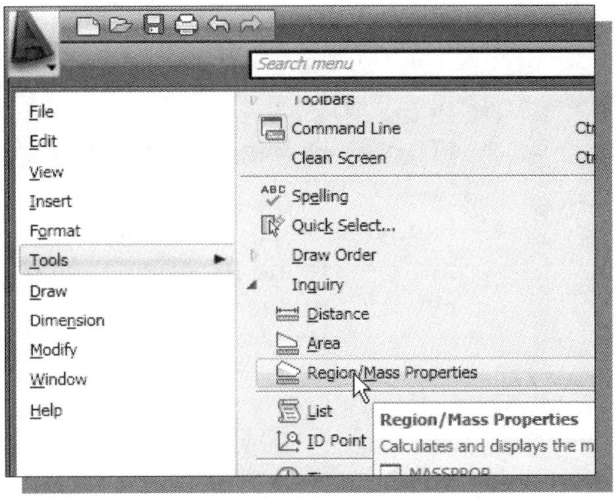

1. In the *Menu Browser*, select: **[Tools] → [Inquiry] → [Region/Mass Properties]**

2. In the command prompt area, the message "*Select objects:*" is displayed. Select the solid model by clicking on any of the displayed edges of the model.

3. Inside the graphics window, right-mouse-click to accept the selection and proceed with the Region/Mass Properties command.

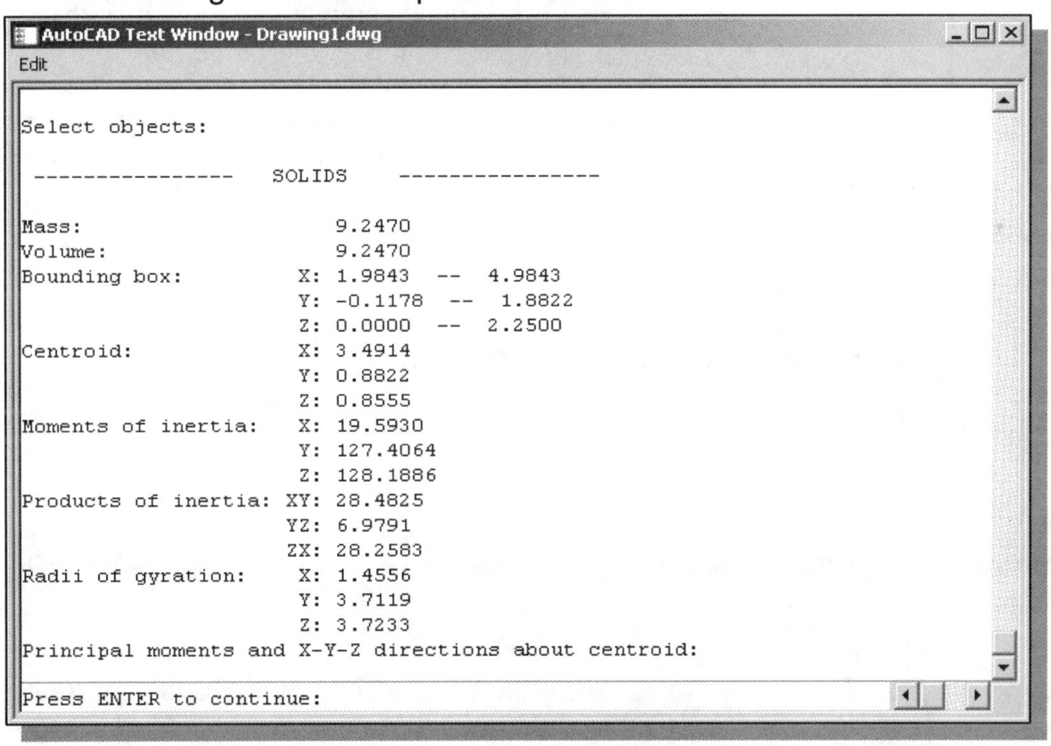

- In the *AutoCAD Text Window*, a list of properties related to the created solid model is displayed. The *Mass* and *Volume* properties are listed as the same since a mass density of one is used for the calculation.

4. Press the **ENTER** key twice to close the *AutoCAD Text Window.*

Align the UCS to the Inclined Face

➢ We will create an UCS plane aligning to the inclined face of the design.

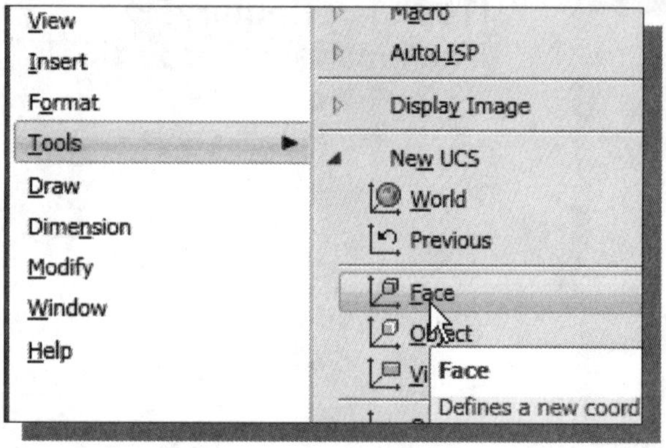

1. In the *Menu Browser*, select: **[Tools] → [New UCS] → [Face]**

- Note that other options are also available to aid the orientation of new UCS planes.

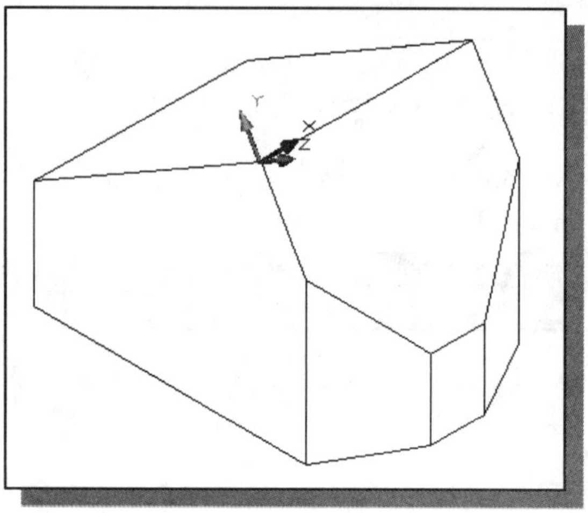

2. In the command prompt area, the message "*Select face of solid object:*" is displayed. Pick the **inclined face** by clicking on the inside of the surface and near the upper left corner.

3. In the command prompt area, the message "*Enter an option [Next/Xflip/Yflip] <accept>:*" is displayed. Press the **[ENTER]** key to accept the new UCS positioned as shown.

4. On your own, bring up the ***UCS*** toolbar.

5. In the *UCS* toolbar, select the **Z Axis Rotate** command icon as shown.

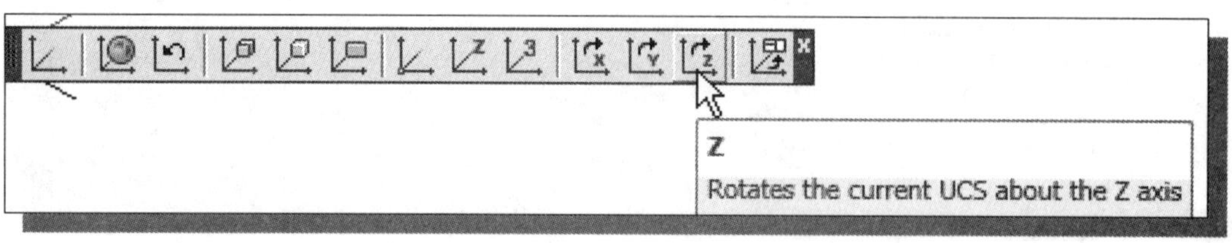

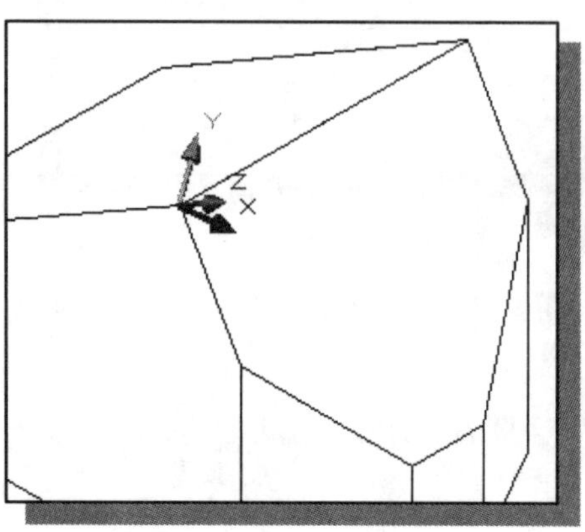

6. In the command prompt area, the message "*Specify rotation angle about Z-axis <90>:*" is displayed. Enter: **-45 [ENTER]**.

- The negative value entered rotates the UCS clockwise about the current UCS Z-axis.

Creating the *V-cut*

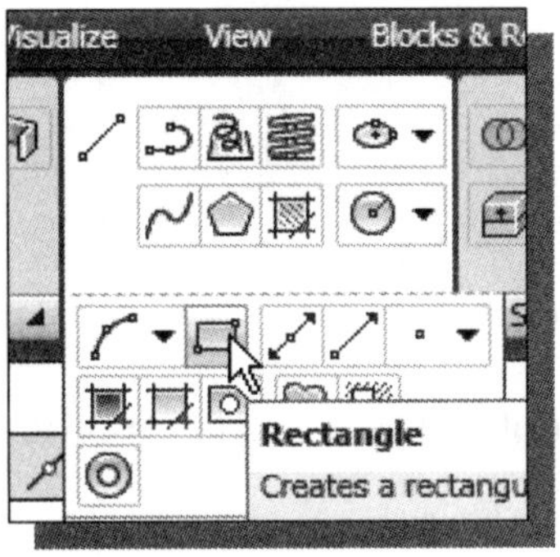

1. Select the **Rectangle** icon in the *Draw* toolbar. In the command prompt area, the message "*Specify first corner point or [Chamfer/Elevation/Fillet/Thickness /Width]:*" is displayed.

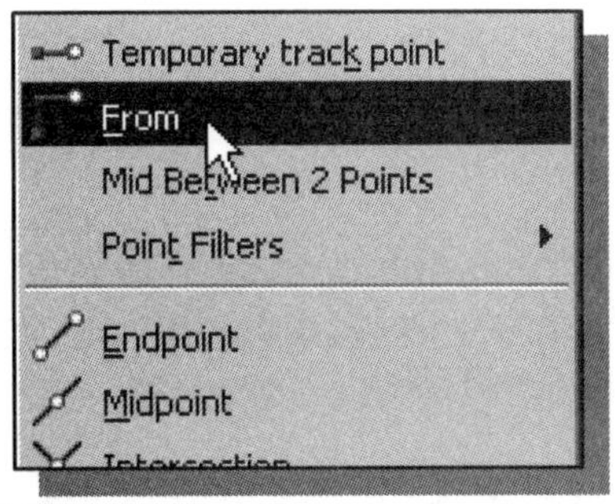

2. Inside the graphics window, hold down the [**SHIFT**] key and **right-mouse-click** once to bring up the *Object Snap* shortcut menu.

3. Select the **From** option in popup window.

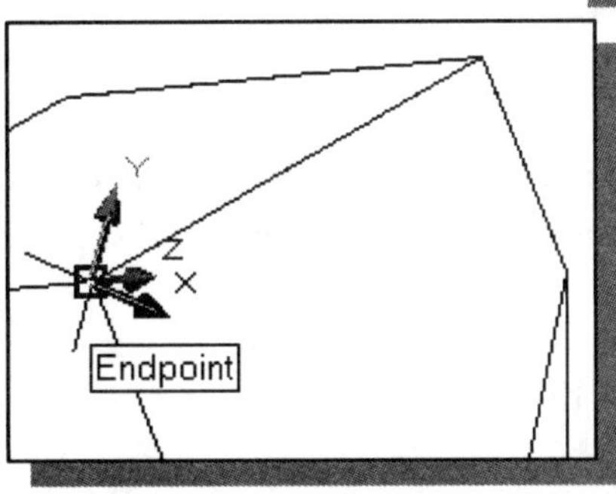

4. Pick the upper left corner of the inclined surface as the base point as shown in the figure.

5. We will place the first point above the selected corner. Enter: **@0.2<45 [ENTER]**

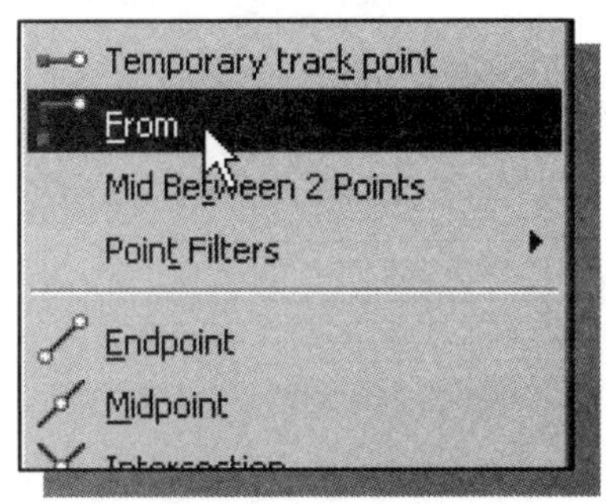

6. Inside the graphics window, hold down the [**SHIFT**] key and right-mouse-click once to bring up the *Object Snap* shortcut menu.

7. Select the **From** option in popup window.

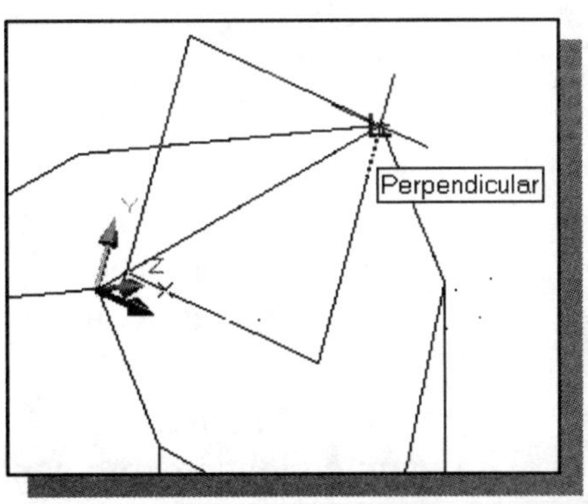

8. Pick the upper right corner of the inclined surface as the base point as shown in the figure.

9. We will place the first point above the selected corner. Enter: **@0.2<-135 [ENTER]**

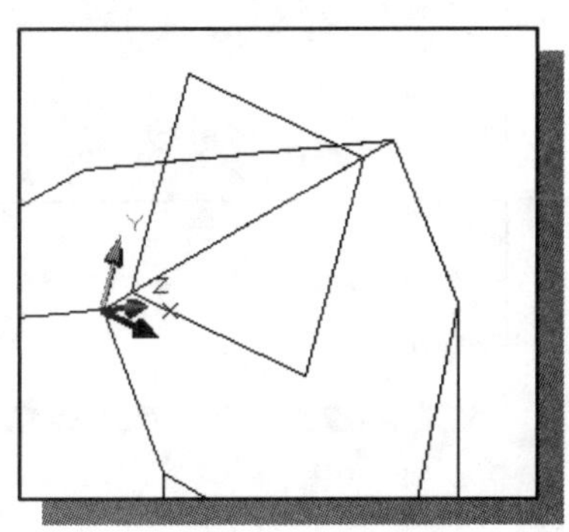

- The above procedure of creating the rectangle at the proper location is simplified by first orienting the UCS.

❖ Note that a rectangle is a valid filled polygon and therefore can be extruded into a solid object.

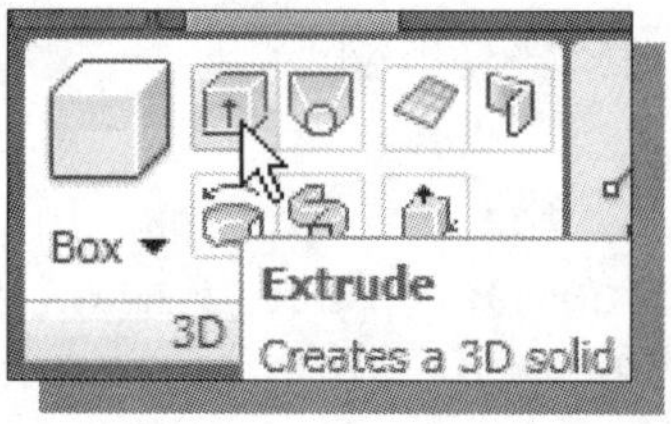

10. Select **Extrude** in the *Modeling* toolbar as shown.

11. In the command prompt area, the message "*Select objects:*" is displayed. Select the rectangle by clicking on the any edges of the created rectangle.

12. Inside the graphics window, right-mouse-click to accept the selection and proceed with the Extrude command.

13. In the command prompt area, the message "*Specify height of extrusion or [path]:*" is displayed. Move the cursor toward the left side of the model to set the extrusion direction and enter: **4.5** [**ENTER**].

- The negative number indicates the extrusion direction, which needs to be in the negative Z-direction of the current UCS.

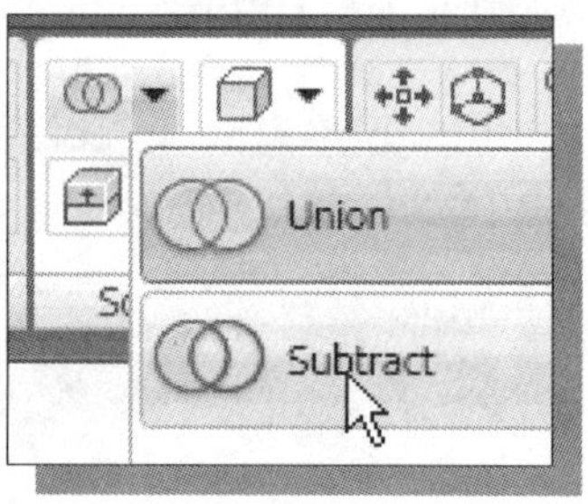

14. In the *Modeling* toolbar, click on the **Subtract** icon. In the command prompt area, the message "*_subtract Select solids and regions to subtract from .. Select Objects:*" is displayed. Pick the base solid block by clicking on one of the edges.

15. Inside the graphics window, right-mouse-click to accept the selection and proceed with the Subtract command.

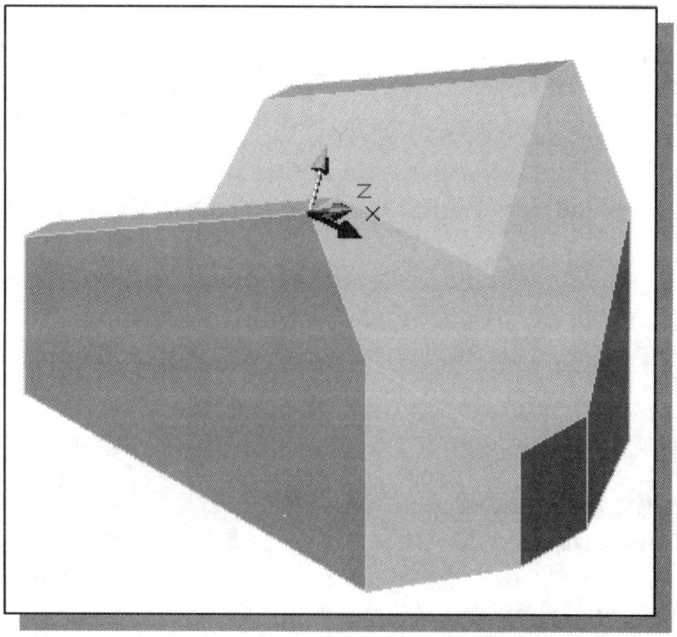

16. In the command prompt area, the message "*Select solids and regions to subtract .. Select Objects:*" is displayed. Pick the rectangular block.

17. Inside the graphics window, right-mouse-click to accept the selection and proceed with the Subtract command.

- On your own, use the dynamic viewing commands to examine the completed solid model.

18. In the *UCS* toolbar, select the **World UCS** command icon as shown.

- The World UCS command aligns the UCS to the world coordinate system.

19. In the Menu Browser, select:
    [Tools] → [Inquiry] → [Region/Mass Properties]

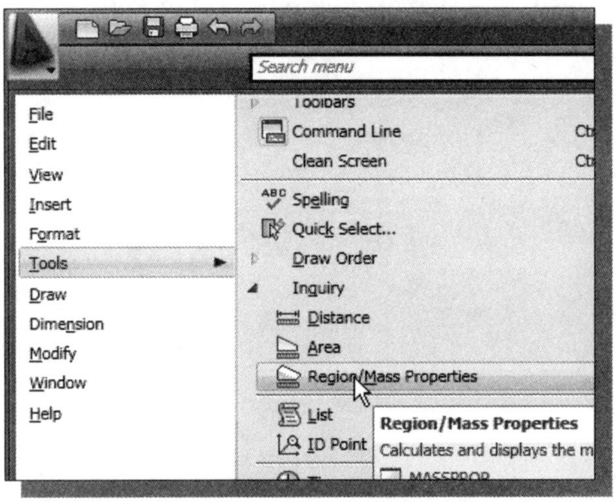

20. In the command prompt area, the message *"Select objects:"* is displayed. Select the solid model by clicking on any of the displayed edges of the model.

21. Inside the graphics window, right-mouse-click to accept the selection. On your own, compare the displayed values to those shown on page 7-17.

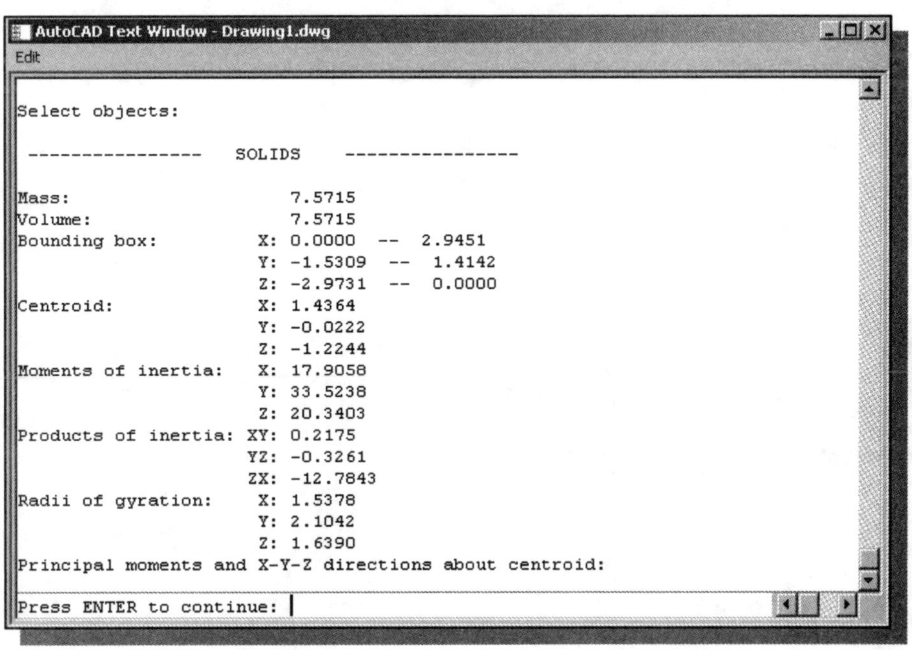


```
Select objects:

 ----------------    SOLIDS    ----------------

Mass:                     7.5715
Volume:                   7.5715
Bounding box:          X: 0.0000  --  2.9451
                       Y: -1.5309  --  1.4142
                       Z: -2.9731  --  0.0000
Centroid:              X: 1.4364
                       Y: -0.0222
                       Z: -1.2244
Moments of inertia:    X: 17.9058
                       Y: 33.5238
                       Z: 20.3403
Products of inertia:  XY: 0.2175
                      YZ: -0.3261
                      ZX: -12.7843
Radii of gyration:     X: 1.5378
                       Y: 2.1042
                       Z: 1.6390
Principal moments and X-Y-Z directions about centroid:

Press ENTER to continue:
```

Questions:

1. What is an auxiliary view and why would it be important?

2. When is a line viewed as a point? When is a surface viewed as true size and shape?

3. How do we define a **Region** in AutoCAD? What are the advantages of using the Regions?

4. How is a **Solid Model** different from a **Surface Model**?

5. List some of the different mass properties that are available with 3D models in AutoCAD.

6. Identify the following commands:

(a)

(b)

(c)

(d)

Exercises: All dimensions are in inches.

1.

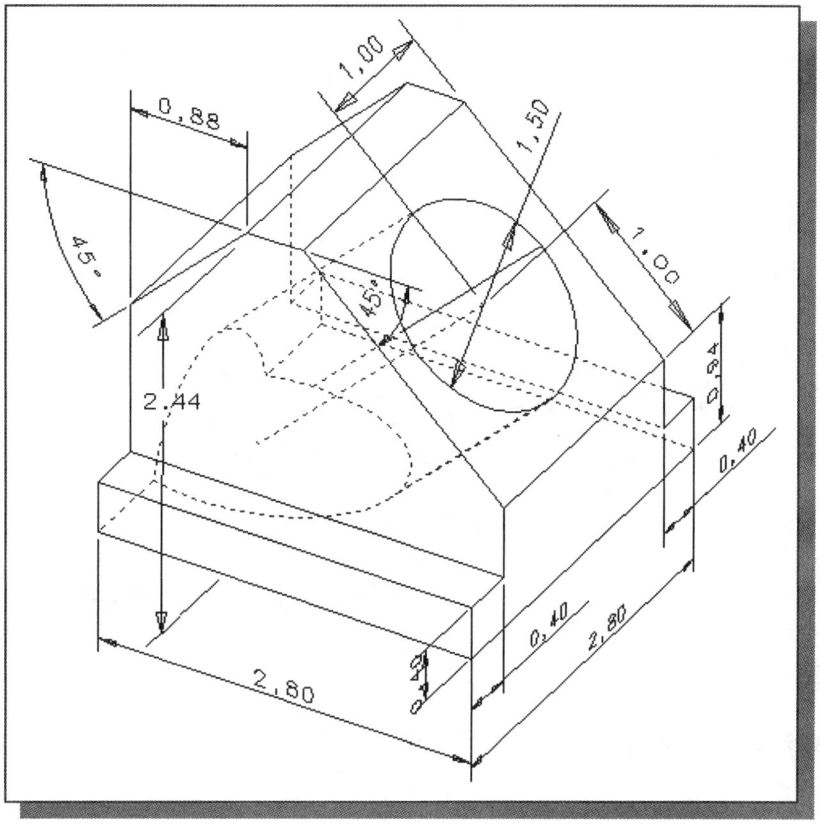

2.

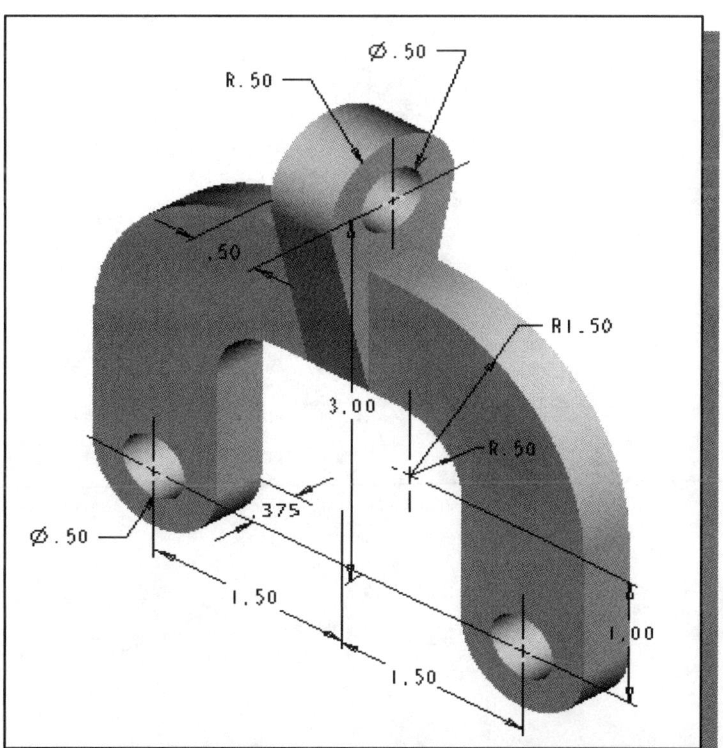

3.

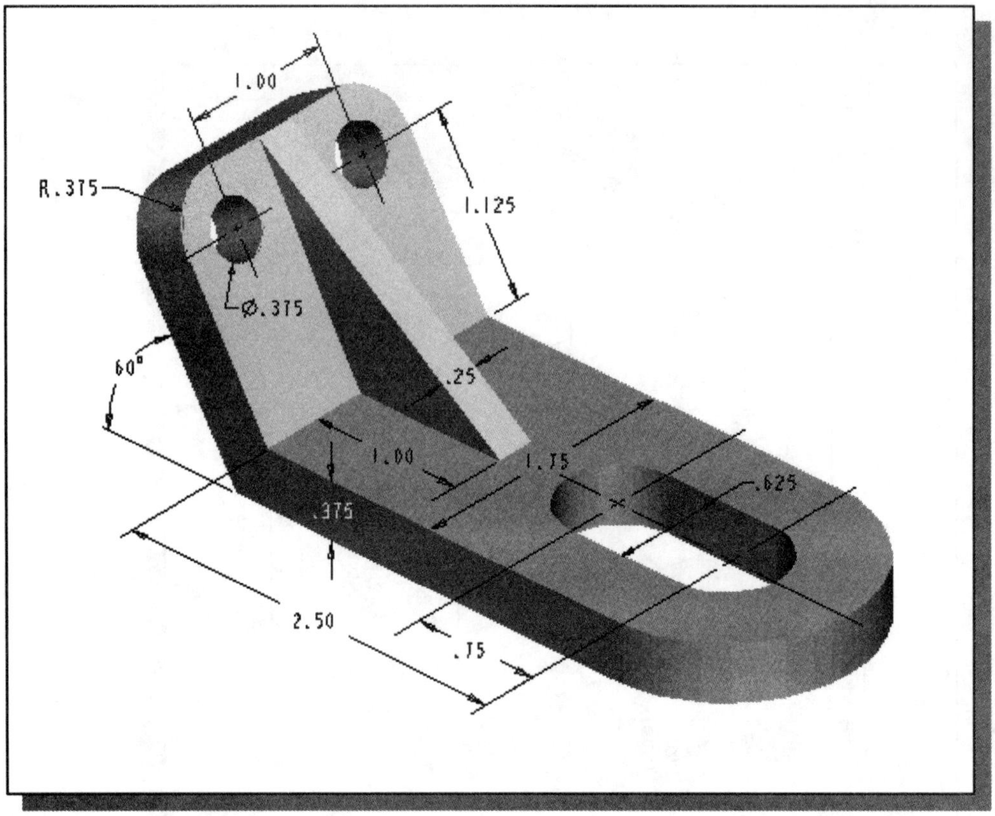

Chapter 8
Multiview Drawings from 3D Models

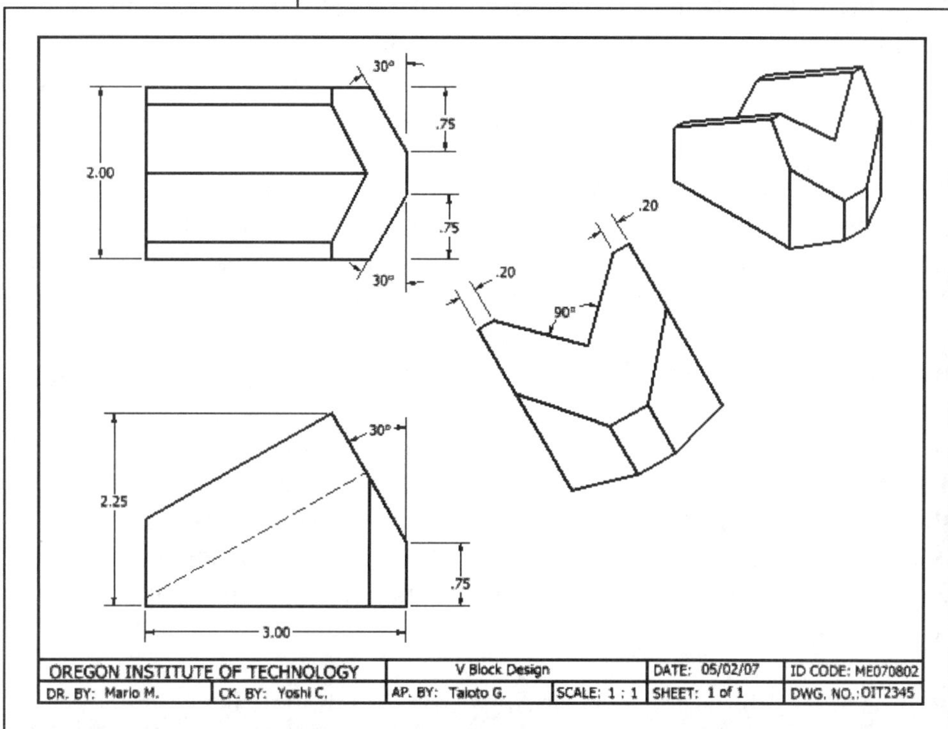

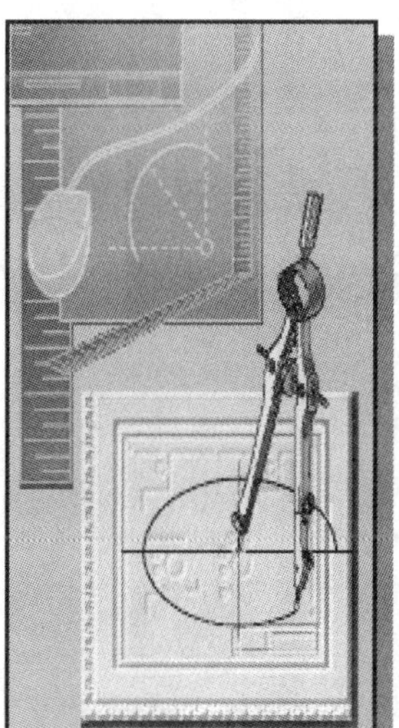

Learning Objectives

- ♦ Create Multiview Drawings from 3D Models
- ♦ Create Borders and Title Block in the Layout Mode
- ♦ Create 2D Projections from 3D Models
- ♦ Create Multiple Viewports in Paper Space
- ♦ Align and Position 2D Projected Views in Layout Mode

Introduction

With the capabilities of solid modeling software, the importance of two-dimensional drafting is decreasing. Drafting is now considered as one of the downstream applications of using solid modeling. In many production facilities, solid models are being used to generate machine tool paths for *computer numerical control* (CNC) machine tools. Solid models can also used in *rapid prototyping* to create 3D physical models out of plastic resins, powdered metal, etc. Ideally, the solid model database should be used directly to generate the final product. However, many organizations still require the use of two-dimensional drawings for the applications in their production facilities. In AutoCAD, model views can be used to automatically create 2D views in AutoCAD *paper space*. Using the 3D model as the starting point for a design, 3D modeling tools can easily create all the necessary two-dimensional views. In this sense, 3D modeling tools are making the process of creating two-dimensional drawings more efficient and effective.

An important rule concerning multiview drawings is to create enough views to accurately describe the design. This usually requires two or three of the regular views, such as a front view, a top view and/or a side view. Many designs have features located on inclined surfaces that are not parallel to the regular planes of projection. To truly describe the feature, the true shape of the feature must be shown using an **auxiliary view**. An *auxiliary view* has a line of sight that is perpendicular to the inclined surface, as viewed looking directly at the inclined surface. An *auxiliary view* is a supplementary view that can be constructed from any of the regular views.

In this chapter, the procedure of creating 2D drawings from 3D models is presented. We will create orthographic views, including an auxiliary view, of the *V-block* design.

The *V-Block* Design

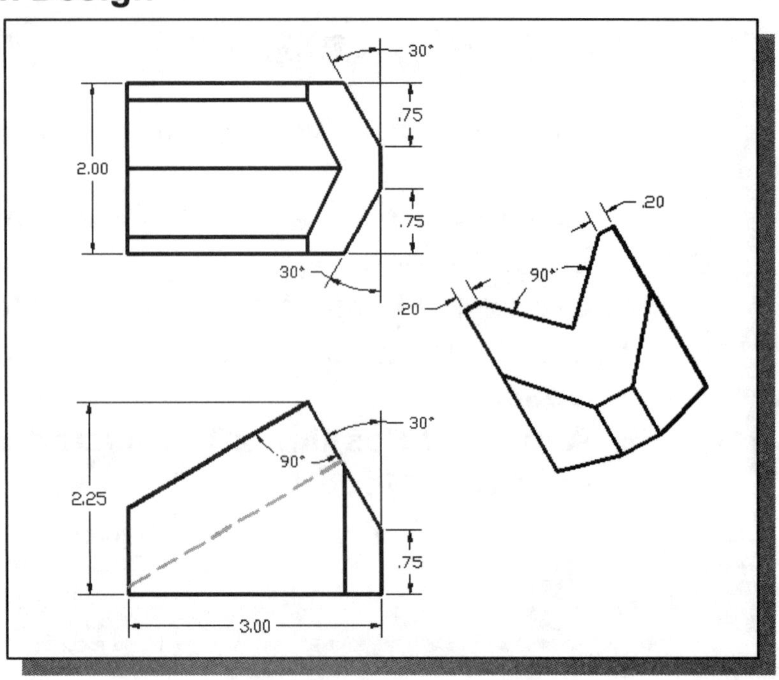

Starting Up AutoCAD® 2009

1. Select the **AutoCAD 2009** option on the *Program* menu or select the **AutoCAD 2009** icon on the *Desktop*.

2. In the *AutoCAD* startup dialog box, select the **Open a Drawing** option with a single click of the left-mouse-button.

3. Open the *V-BlockSolid* solid model created in the previous chapter by clicking on the corresponding filename. (Use the Browse option to locate the solid model file if it is not displayed.)

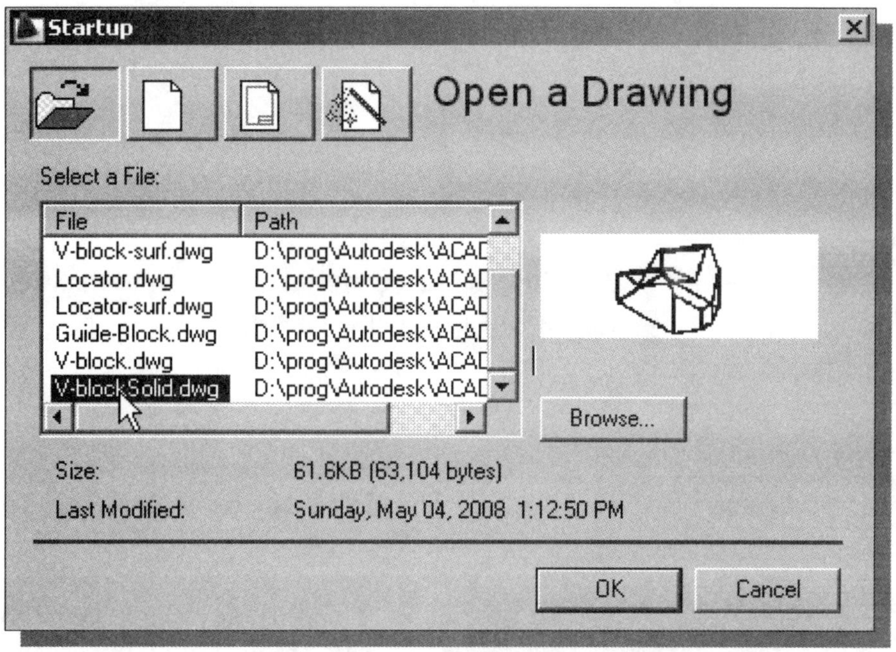

- The *V-BlockSolid* solid model is retrieved and displayed in the graphics window.

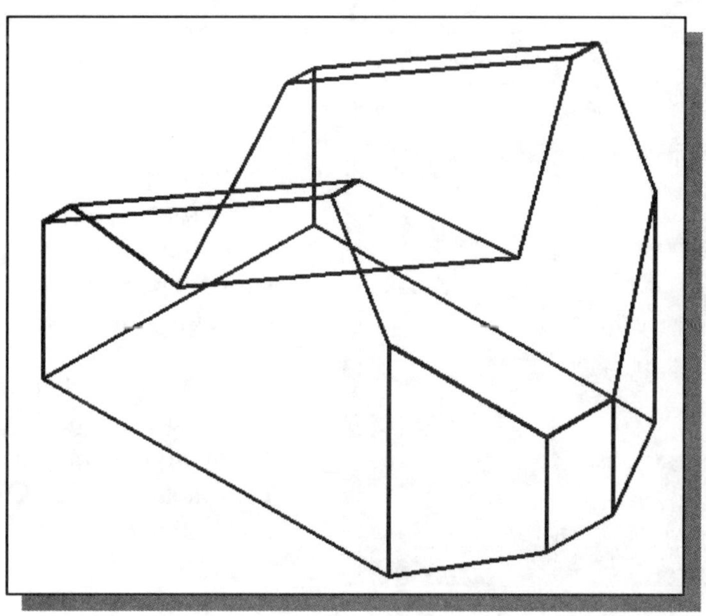

AutoCAD Paper Space

- Until now, we have been working in ***model space*** to create our design in **full size**. Once the 3D model is constructed, we can arrange our design on a two-dimensional sheet of paper so that the plotted hardcopy is exactly what we want. This two-dimensional sheet of paper is known as ***paper space*** in AutoCAD. We can place borders and title blocks, the objects that are less critical to our design, on *paper space*.

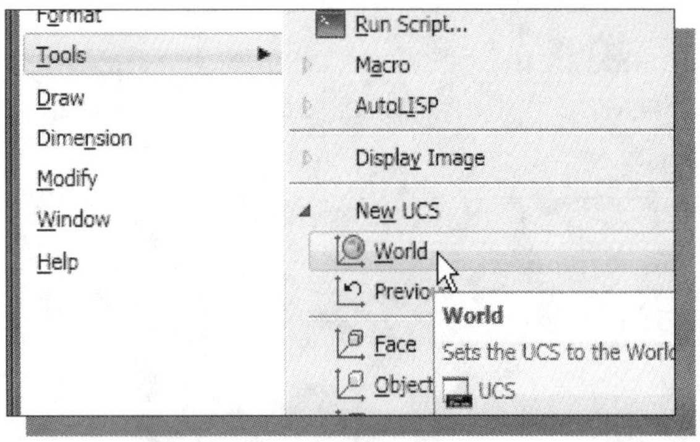

1. Set the UCS to the ***World UCS*** by selecting:
   [Tools] → [New UCS] → [World]

- The default 2D views generated in *paper space* are oriented based on the *World Coordinate System*. It is always a good idea to align the UCS to the WCS prior to entering the AutoCAD *paper space*.

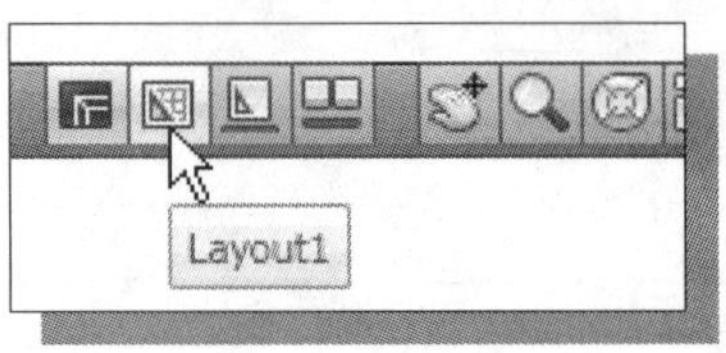

2. Click the **Layout1** tab to switch to the two-dimensional paper space.

3. Right-mouse-click once on the Layout tab and select **Display Layout and Model Tabs**.

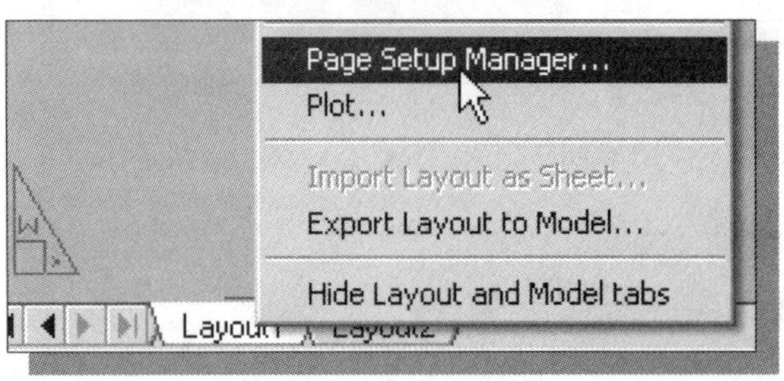

4. To adjust any *Page Setup* options, right-mouse-click once on the Layout1 tab and select **Page Setup Manager**.

5. Choose the default layout in the *Page Setup Manager*.

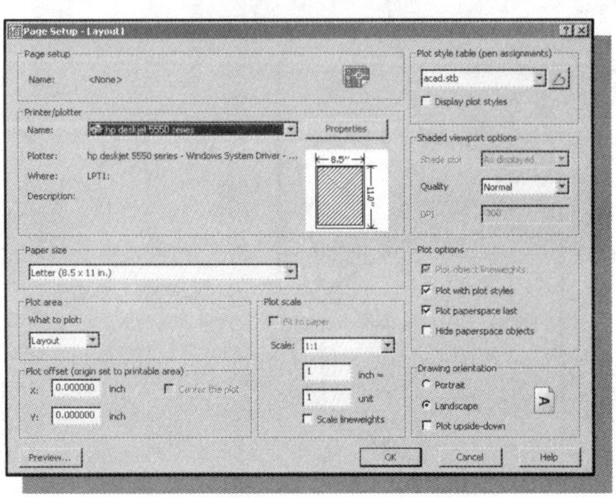

6. In the *Page Setup* dialog box, select a plotter/printer that is available to your system. Consult with your technical support personnel if you have difficulty identifying the hardware.

7. Confirm the *Paper size* is set to **Letter** or equivalent (8.5″ by 11″) and the *Drawing orientation* is set to **Landscape**. Click **OK** button to accept the settings.

❖ In the graphics window, a rectangular outline on a gray background indicates the paper size. The dashed lines displayed within the paper indicate the *printable area.* The 3D model appears inside a solid rectangle, which is known as a **viewport**. Note that the orientation of the model is identical to that of the model space.

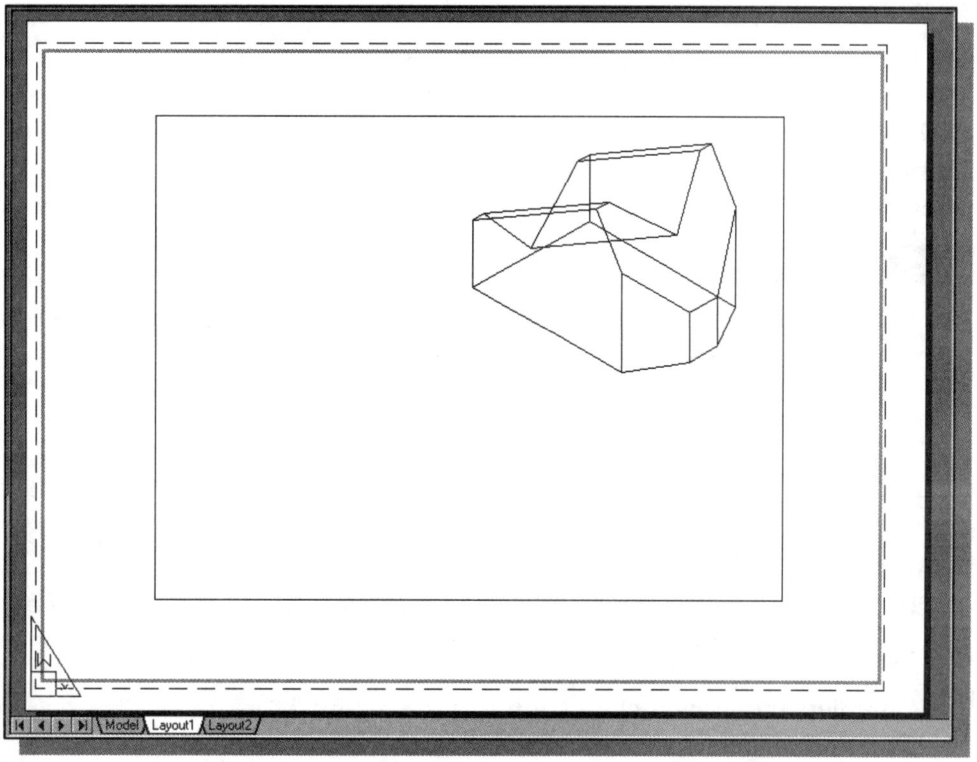

Deleting the Displayed Viewport

- Viewports can be considered as objects with a view into model space that we can move and resize. Floating viewports can be overlapping or separated from one another. We can also create new viewports, as well as delete them.

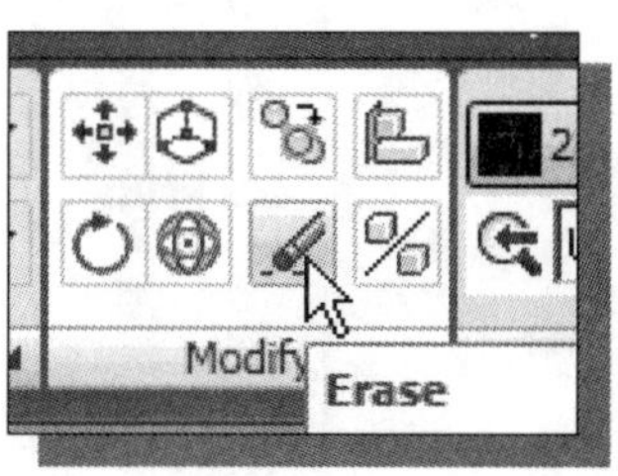

1. Pick **Erase** in the *Modify* toolbar.

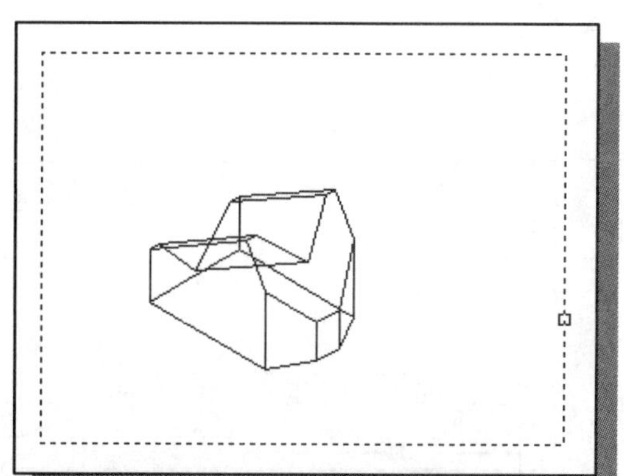

2. Pick the viewport by clicking on one of the edges of the viewport border.

3. Inside the graphics window, **right-mouse-click** to accept the selection and delete the viewport.

Adding Borders and Title Block in the Layout

➢ **AutoCAD® 2009** allows us to create plots/prints to any exact scale on the paper. We can place borders and title blocks, the objects that are less critical to our design, on *paper space*.

1. On your own, create three new layers and set *Title_Block* as the *Current Layer*.

Layer	***Color***	***LineType***	***Lineweight***	***PlotStyle***
Title_Block	**Green**	**Continuous**	**1.2mm**	**Normal**
Dimensions	**Magenta**	**Continuous**	**Default**	**Normal**
Viewport	**White**	**Continuous**	**Default**	**Normal**

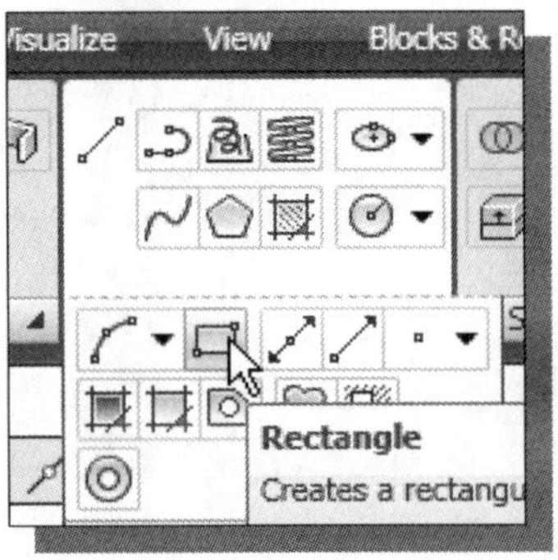

2. Select the **Rectangle** icon in the *Draw* toolbar. In the command prompt area, the message "*Specify first corner point or [Chamfer/Elevation/Fillet/Thickness/Width]:*" is displayed.

3. Pick a location that is on the inside and near the lower left corner of the dashed rectangle.

4. In the command prompt area, use the *relative coordinate entry method* and create a **10.25" × 7.75"** rectangle.

5. Complete the title block as shown in the below figure. (Place the ***text*** in the *Dimensions* layer.)

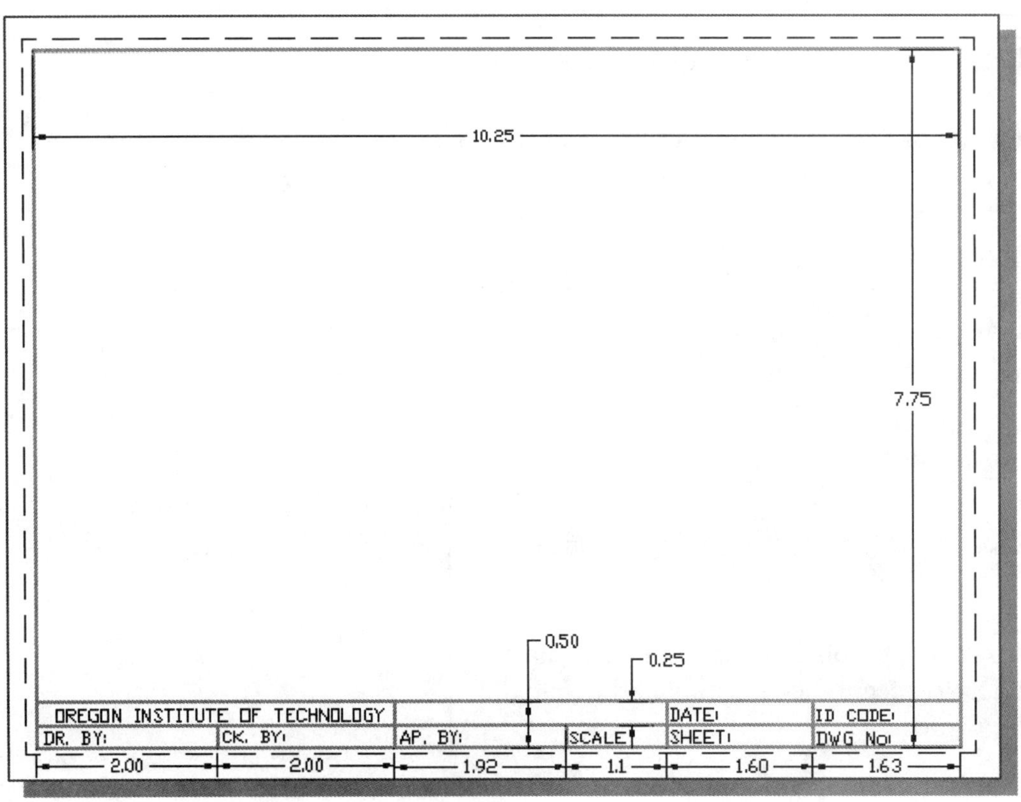

Setting Up Viewports inside the Titleblock

- Viewports can be used in both model mode and in layout mode. In *model mode*, only *tiled viewports* (viewports cannot overlap each other) can be created. In *layout mode*, *floating viewports* (viewports can overlap each other) can be created to set up standard 2D views from 3D models.

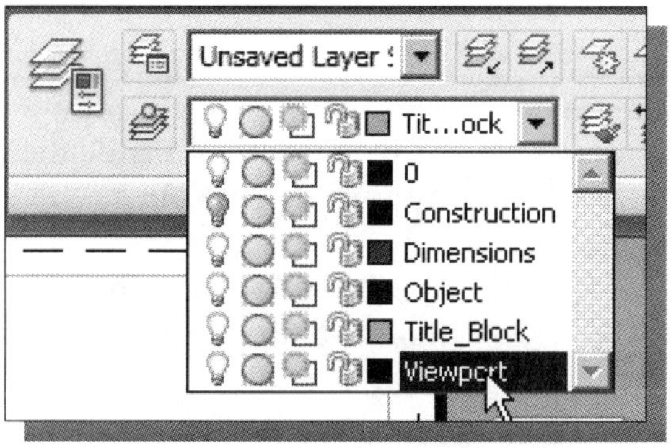

1. In the *Object Properties* toolbar area, select the *Layer Control* box and set layer ***Viewport*** layer as the *Current Layer*.

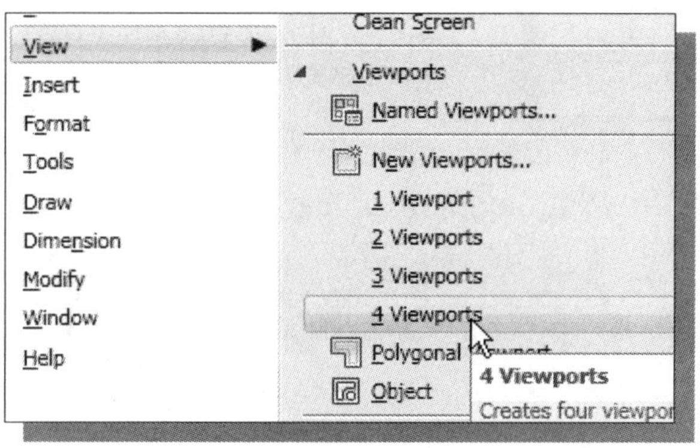

2. In the *Menu Browser*, select: **[View] → [Viewports] → [4 viewports]**

3. In the command prompt area, the message "*Specify first corner of viewport or [Fit] <Fit>:*" is displayed. Pick a location near the lower left corner of the created border.

4. In the command prompt area, the message "*Specify opposite corner:*" is displayed. Pick a corner near the upper right corner of the border as shown.

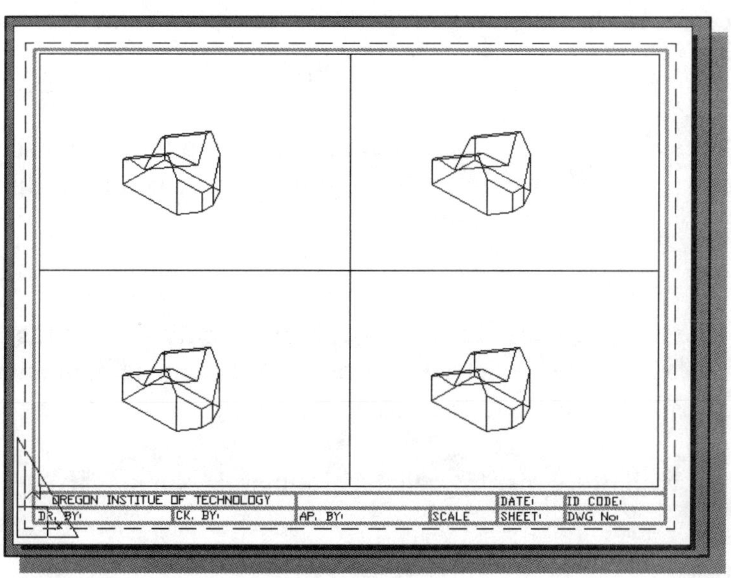

- Four viewports, with rectangular viewport borders, displaying the same isometric view are created.

Setting Up the Standard Views

➢ AutoCAD allows us to control the display of the model inside the created viewports. This is accomplished by switching to *model mode* within each viewport. In *layout mode*, either the *paper space* is activated or one of the created viewports is activated at one time. When a viewport is activated, the *model space* of the viewport is opened, and the model mode commands become available within the viewport. The viewport with the darker border is the active viewport.

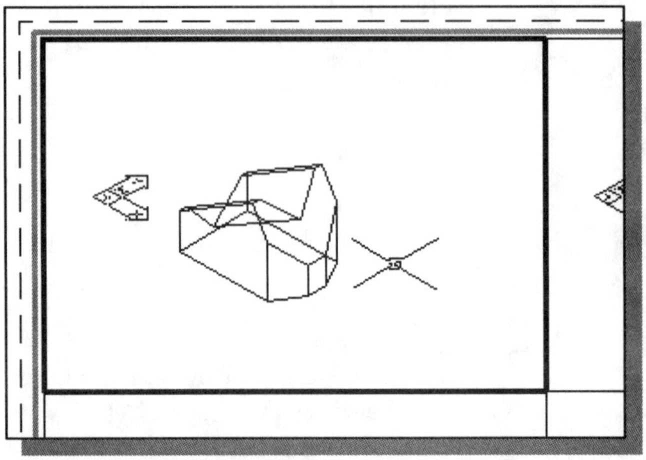

1. Move the cursor inside the **upper left viewport**.
2. **Double-click** with the left-mouse-button to activate the viewport.

- Note the darker border and the cursor display of the active viewport.

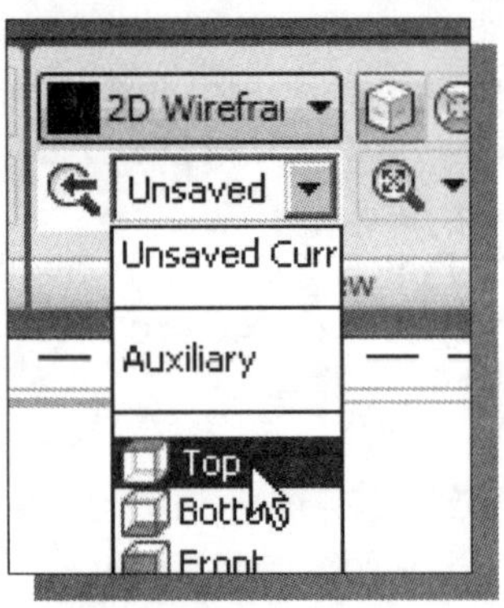

3. Pick **Top View** in the *View* toolbar as shown.

- The display is changed to the top view based on the current User Coordinate System, which is aligned to the WCS.

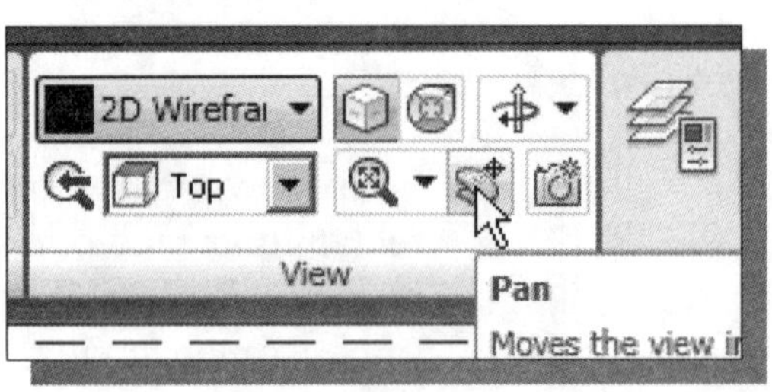

4. Pick **Pan** in the *View* toolbar as shown.
5. On your own, reposition the model so that it is roughly near the center of the viewport.

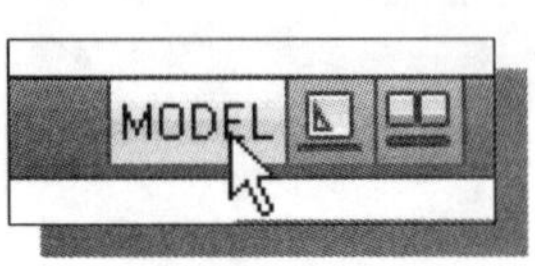

- Note that the **Pan Realtime** command only adjusts the display within the active viewport. Model space commands are only available in the active viewport.

- On your own, experiment with other display related commands, such as Free Orbit and Zoom.

6. Move the cursor inside the lower right viewport. Left-click once inside the viewport to activate it.

7. On your own, repeat the above steps and set the four viewports to display the standard four engineering views, as shown in the figure below. (The standard four engineering views are: **top**, **front**, **right**, and **isometric**)

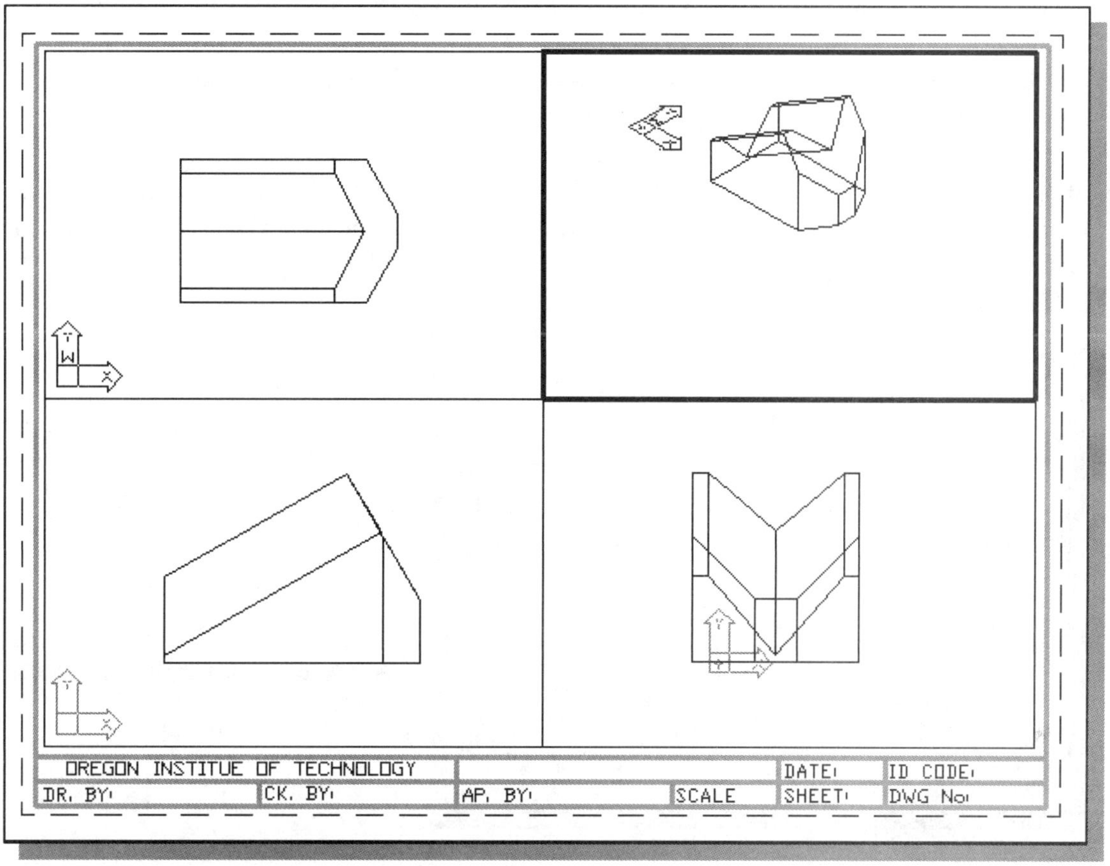

8. In the status bar area, switch back to the ***paper space*** by left-clicking once on ***MODEL***.

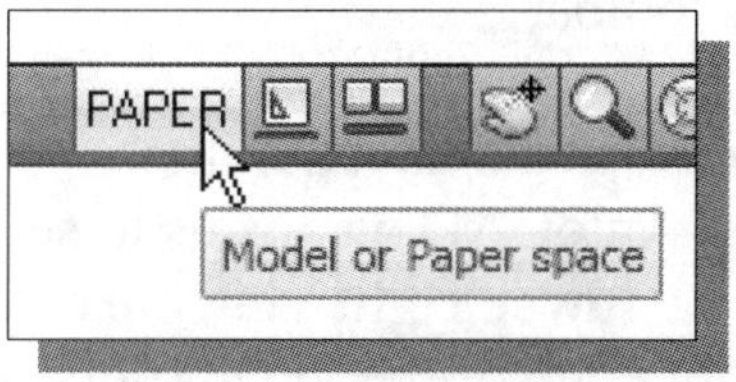

9. Click on ***PAPER*** to switch back to *model space* and note the last active viewport is activated again.

- The 3D model is displayed in all viewports; note that there is only one 3D model. The multiple viewports simply allow us to view the same model from different angles simultaneously. This approach assures the correctness and accuracy of the 2D views of the model since the views are generated from the database of the same 3D model.

Determining the Necessary 2D Views

- Multiview drawings usually require two or three of the regular views, such as a front view, a top view and/or a side view. Many designs have features located on inclined surfaces that are not parallel to the regular planes of projection. For the ***V-block*** design, to truly describe the V-cut feature, the true shape of the feature must be shown using an **auxiliary view**. An *auxiliary view* has a line of sight that is perpendicular to the inclined surface, as viewed looking directly at the inclined surface. An *auxiliary view* is a supplementary view that can be constructed from any of the regular views.

➢ Examining the current four standard views, we can conclude that the right side view provides no crucial information on the design. Instead, an *auxiliary view* is needed to truly describe the V-cut feature.

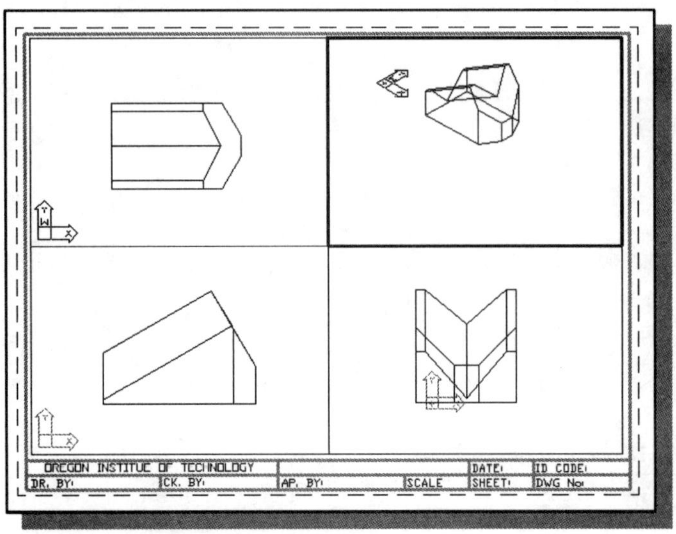

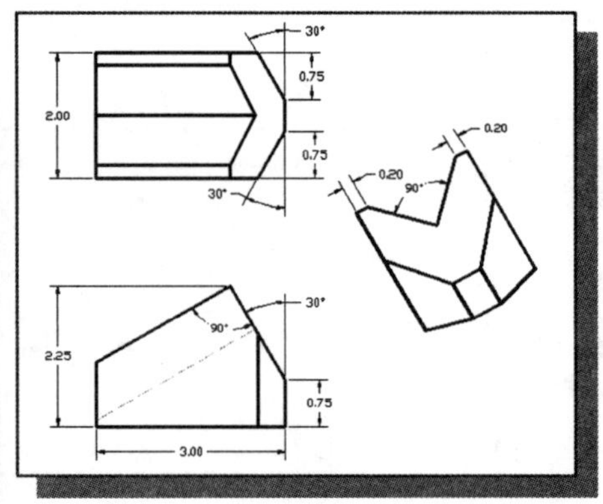

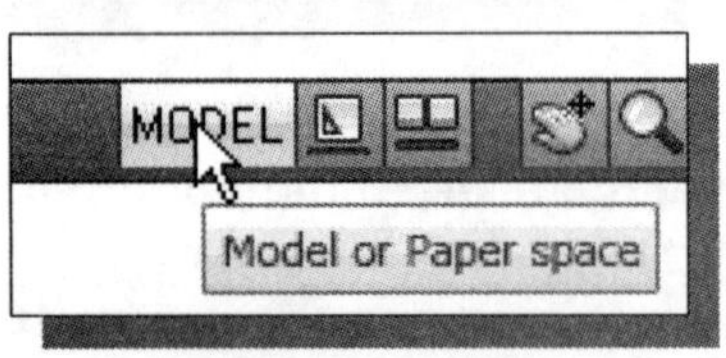

1. In the *Status Bar* area, switch back to the ***paper space*** by left-clicking once on ***MODEL***.

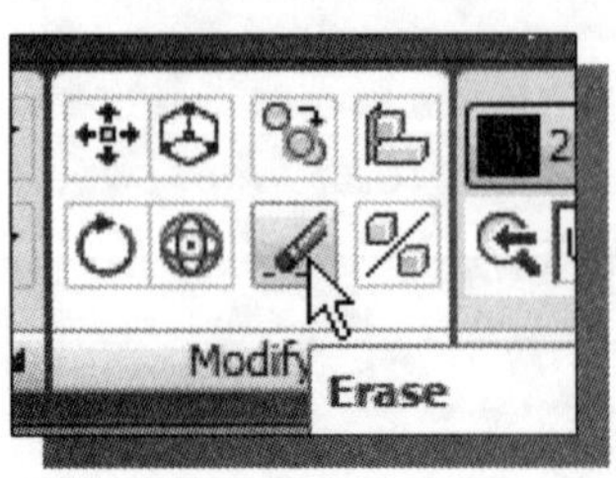

2. Pick **Erase** in the *Modify* toolbar.

3. The message "*Select objects*" is displayed in the command prompt area and AutoCAD awaits us to select the objects to erase. Pick the **lower right viewport** by clicking on the bottom-right edge of the viewport border.

4. Inside the graphics window, **right-mouse-click** to accept the selection and delete the viewport.

Establishing an Auxiliary View in Model Mode

➢ AutoCAD provides us with many options to establish new viewpoints. The easiest approach is to create a new UCS aligned to the inclined plane of the design and then adjust the display view to the UCS.

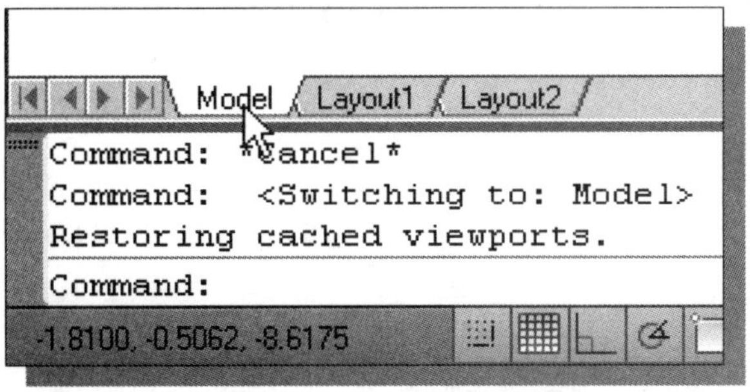

1. Pick the **Model** tab to switch back to *model space.*

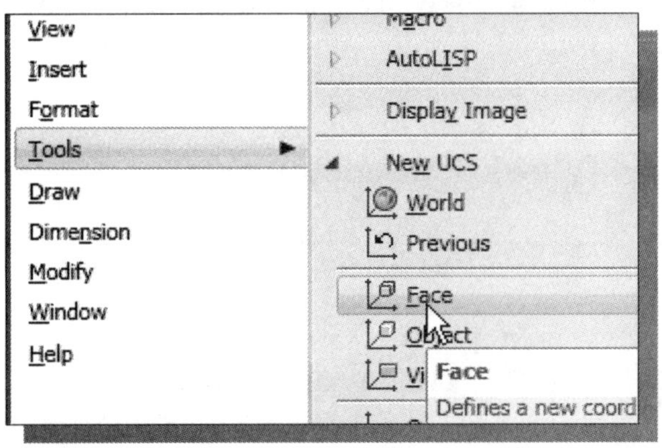

2. In the *Menu Browser*, select: **[Tools] → [New UCS] → [Face]**

3. In the command prompt area, the message "*Select face of solid object:*" is displayed. Pick the **inclined face** by clicking on the surface near the **bottom horizontal edge** of the surface.

4. In the command prompt area, the message "*Enter an option [Next/Xflip/Yflip] <accept>:*" is displayed. Press the [**ENTER**] key once to accept the new UCS positioned as shown.

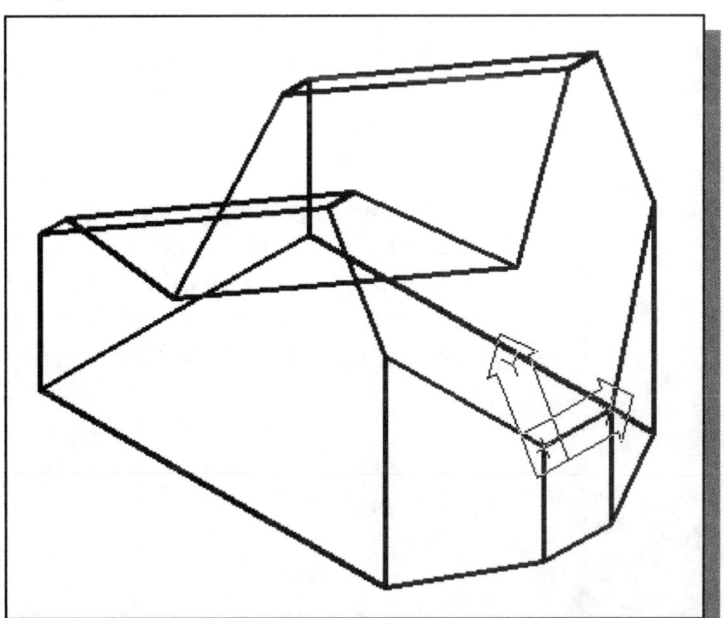

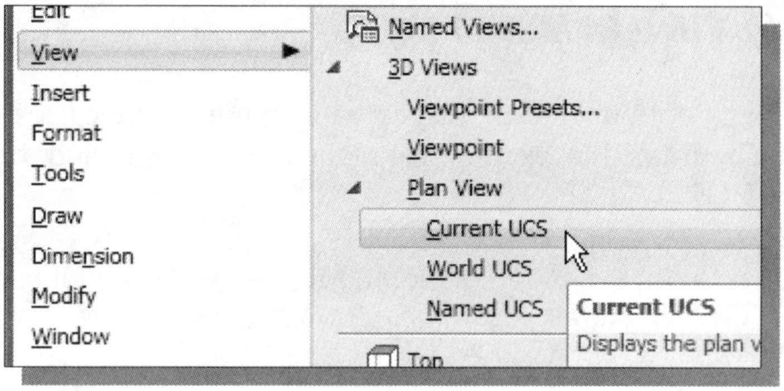

5. In the *Menu Browser*, select **[View] → [3D Views]→ [Plan View] → [Current UCS]**

- The graphics window is now adjusted to display the current UCS plane.

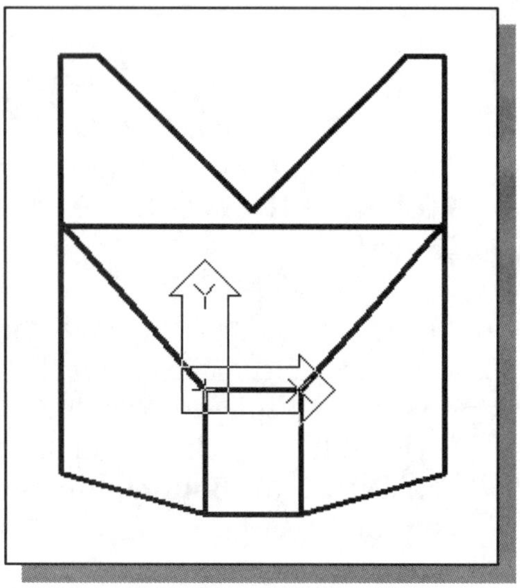

- Note the orientation of the UCS in the display view. This is the auxiliary view that is needed in the multiview drawing.

6. In the *Menu Browser*, select: **[View] → [Named Views]**

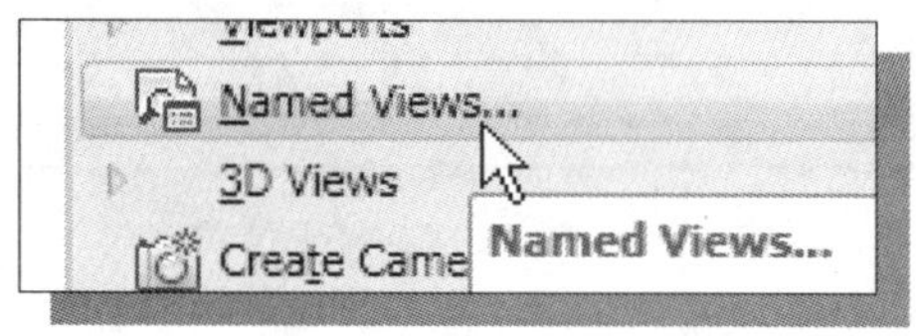

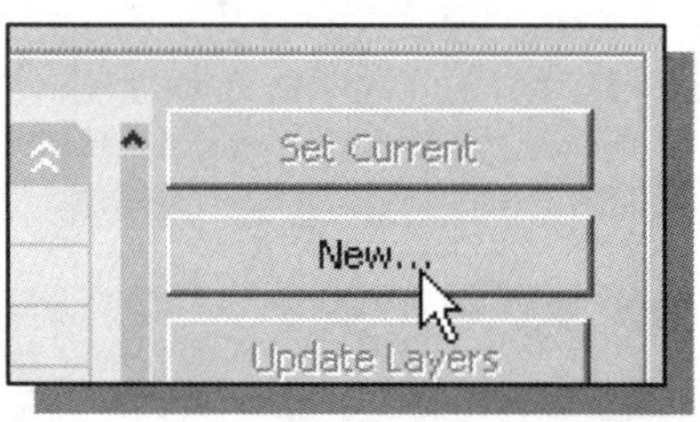

7. In the *View* dialog box, click on the **New** button to create a new named view.

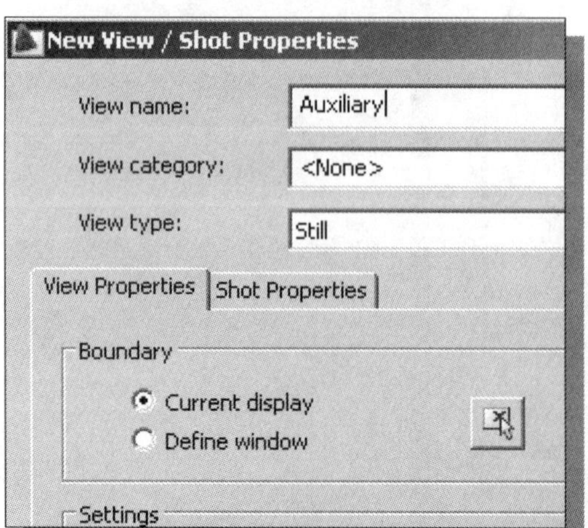

8. In the *New View* dialog box, enter **Auxiliary** as the new *View name* and confirm the ***Current display*** option and the ***Save layer Snapshot with view*** option are switched ***ON*** and the *UCS option* is set to ***Unnamed*** as shown.

9. Click on the **OK** button to accept the settings and create the named view.

10. In the *View* dialog box, the new named view (*Auxiliary*) is added to the *Named Views* list. (Note that we can also switch to this view by using the **Set Current** option.)

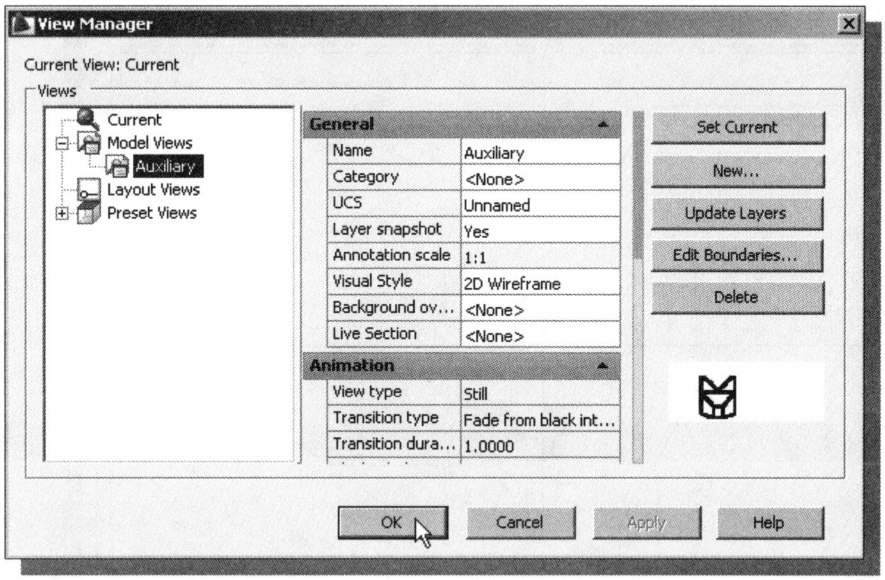

11. Click on the **OK** button to accept the settings.

Adding a Viewport for an Auxiliary View

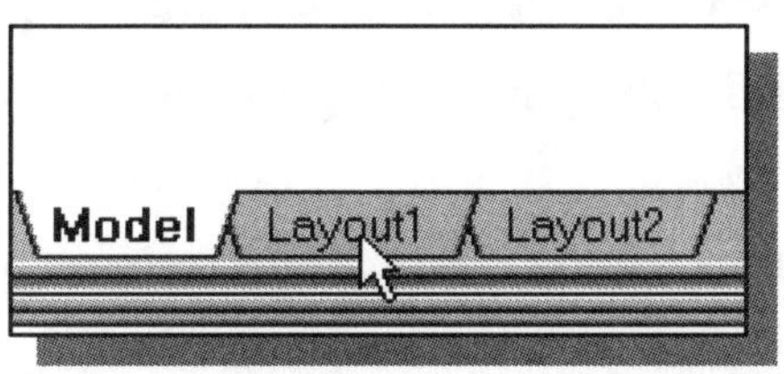

1. Pick the **Layout1** tab to switch back to the two-dimensional paper space.

2. In the status bar area, reset the option buttons so that only *Line Weight* is switched ***ON***.

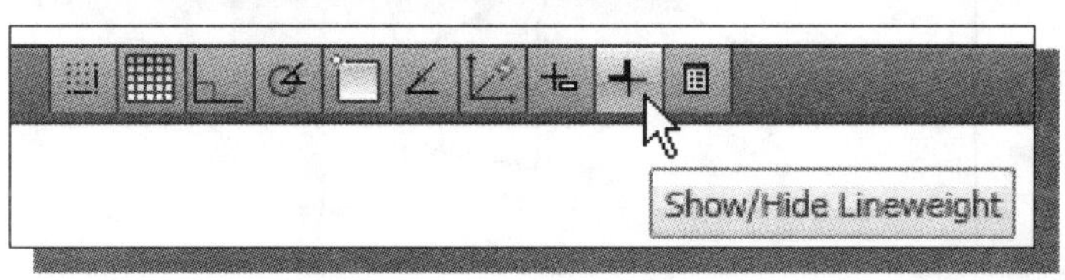

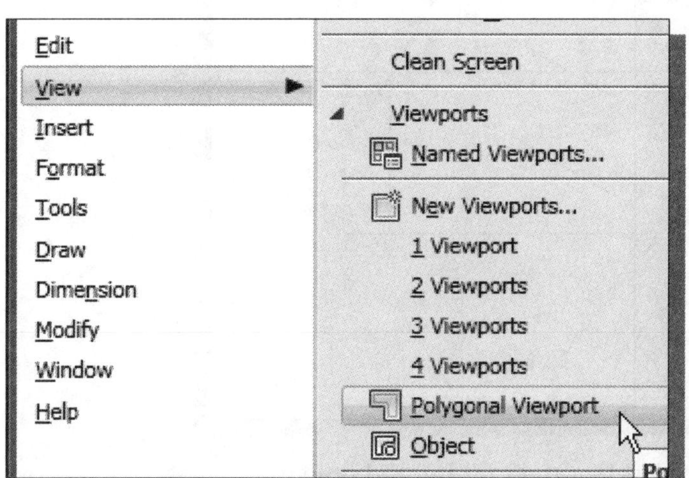

3. In the *Menu Browser*, select **[View] → [Viewports] → [Polygonal Viewport]**

- In **AutoCAD® 2009**, viewports can be of arbitrary polygonal shapes. In the layout mode, the viewports can also overlap each other. We will create a four-sided viewport overlapping the other viewports.

4. In the command prompt area, the message "*Specify start point:*" is displayed. Create **a** ***four-sided shape*** as shown. (Hint: use the **Close** option to assure the last segment is connected to the start point.)

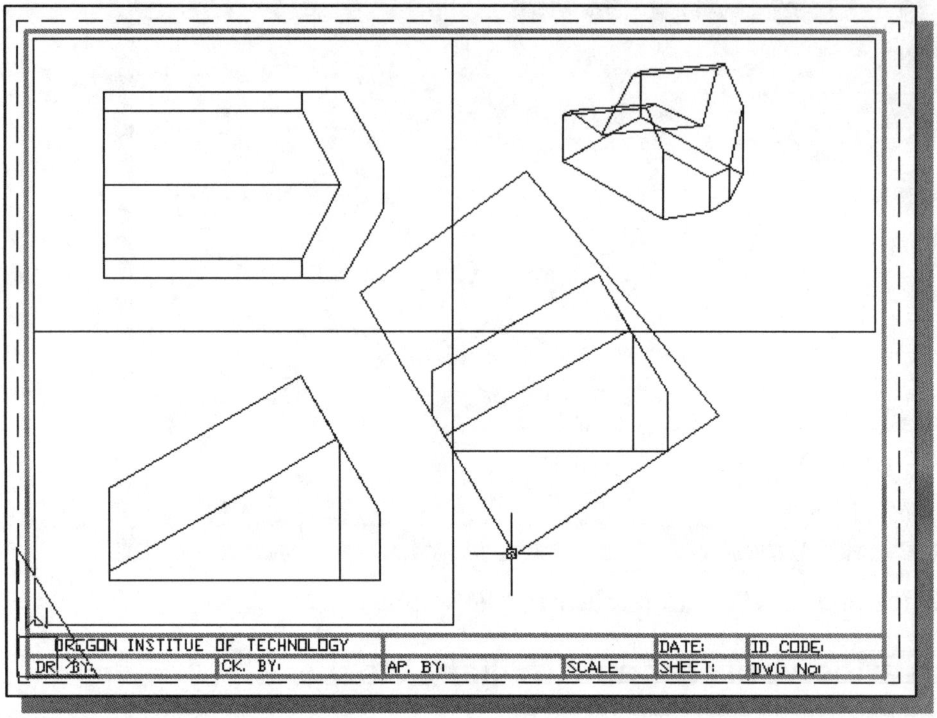

5. Pick one of the edges of the viewport border and notice that four grip points are displayed.

6. Adjust the size and shape of the viewport by dragging the grip points.

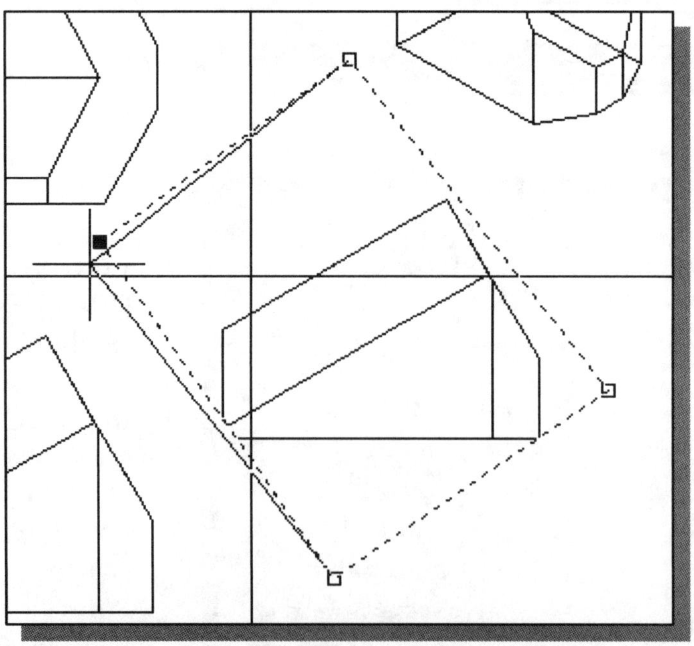

7. Press the **[Esc]** key once to deselect the highlighted objects.

8. Double-click inside the viewport we just created to activate the new viewport.

9. In the Menu Browser, select:
[View] → [Named Views]

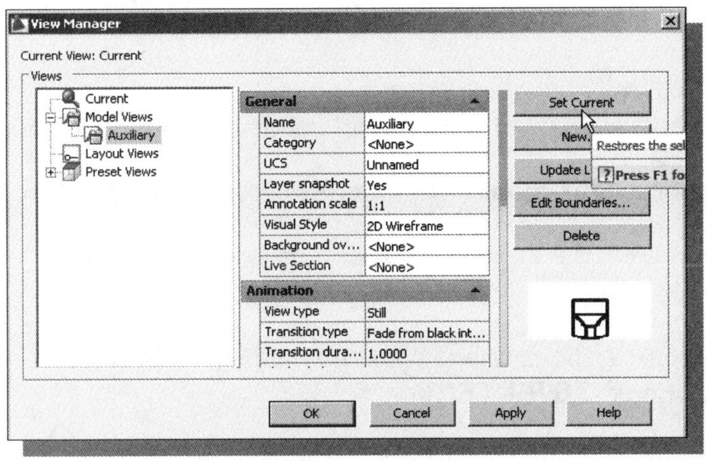

10. Pick the ***Auxiliary*** view in the *Named Views* list as shown.

11. Click on the **Set Current** to change the current display to the saved *Auxiliary* view.

12. Click **OK** to accept the settings.

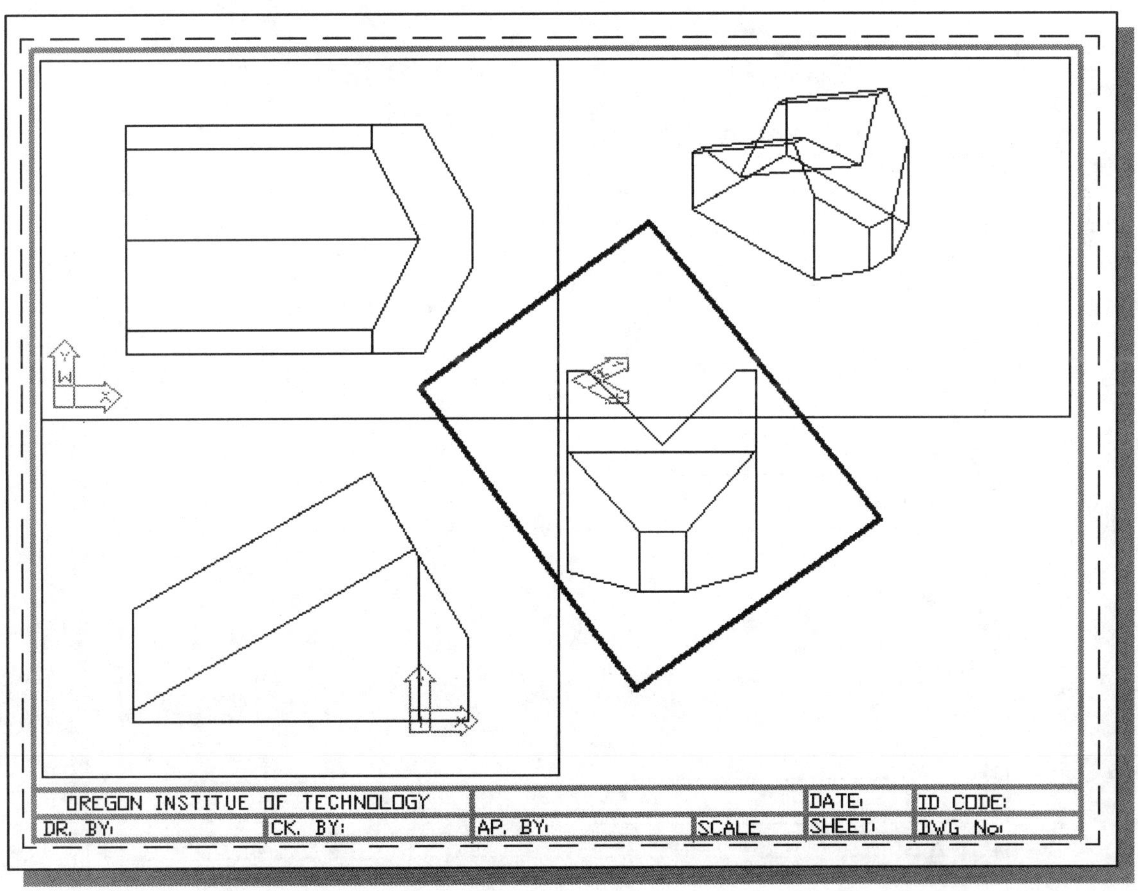

Using the DVIEW Command

- The DVIEW command can be used to zoom, pan, and twist views. We can also use DVIEW to remove objects from in front of and behind a clipping plane and to remove hidden lines during a dynamic viewing operation.

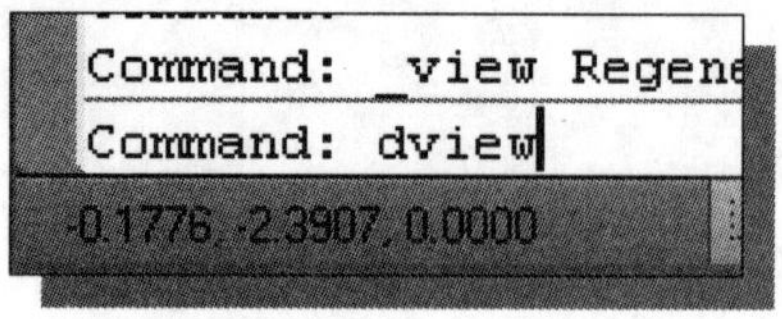

1. At the command prompt, enter: **dview** [**ENTER**]

2. In the command prompt area, the message "*Select objects or <use DVIEWBLOCK>:*" is displayed. Pick the solid model inside the active viewport.

3. Inside the active viewport, **right-mouse-click** once to accept the selection.

4. In the command prompt area, the message "*Enter option:*" is displayed. Choose the **Twist** option by entering: **TW** [**ENTER**]

5. In the command prompt area, the message "*Specify the view twist angle <0.00>:*" is displayed. Enter: **30** [**ENTER**]

6. Press the [**ENTER**] key once to end the DVIEW command.

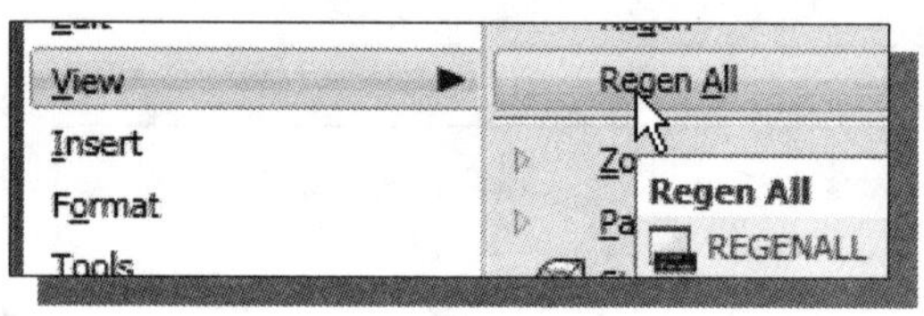

7. In the Menu Browser, select: **[View] → [Regen All]**

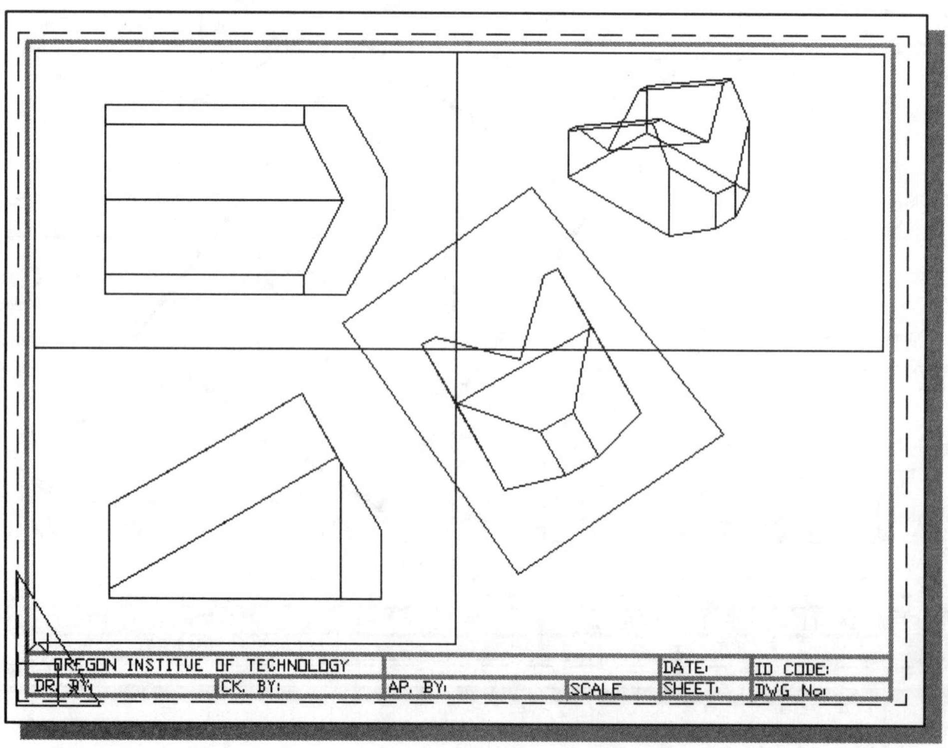

Adjusting the Viewport Scale

- A uniform scale for the 2D views is necessary for view alignments and dimensioning the features.

1. Left-mouse-click in the status bar area, switch back to the ***paper space*** mode.

2. Pre-select all entities by using a selection window.

3. Right-mouse-click once to display the option menu.

4. Pick **Properties** in the *Standard* toolbar as shown.

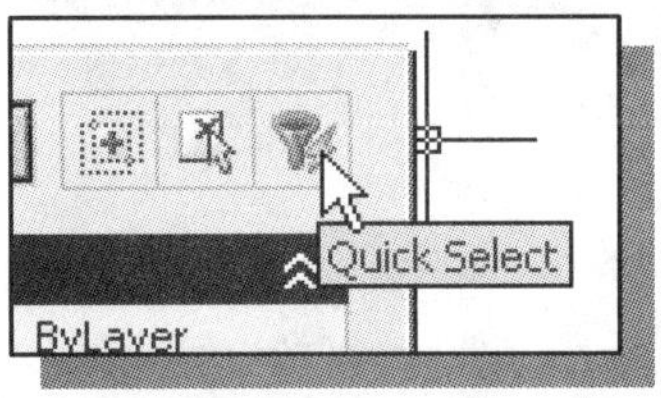

5. In the *Properties* window, click on the **Quick Select** icon.

- The Quick Select option allows us to select items based on the object properties.

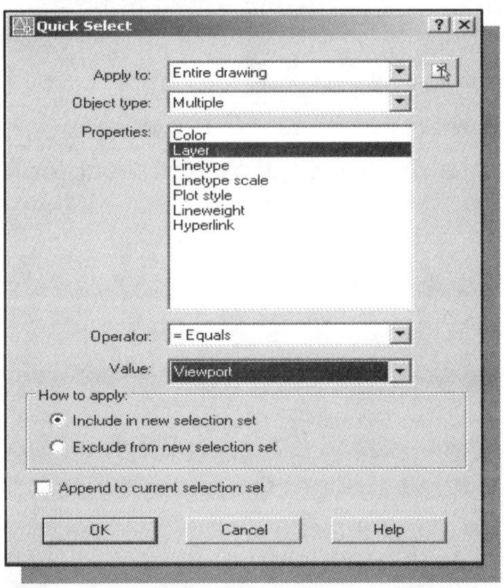

6. In the *Quick Select* window, choose **Layer** in the *Properties* list and set the selection operation to **Equal Viewport** as shown in the figure.

7. Click **OK** to accept the setting and proceed to select objects matching the quick select settings.

8. Choose the **4 viewports** in the selection list as shown.

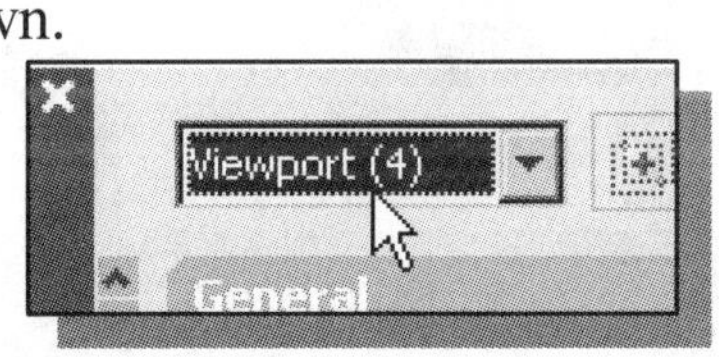

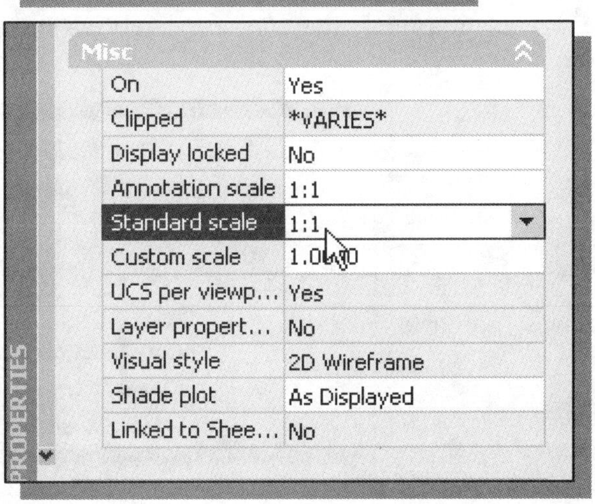

9. Pick the ***Standard scale*** property in the *Misc* list as shown.

10. Select **1:1** to set the scale to one to one. This will set all displayed views to *full scale*.

11. Move the cursor inside the graphics window, and hit the [Esc] key once to deselect the 4 viewports.

Locking the Base View

1. Select the **lower left viewport** by clicking on one of the viewport borders.

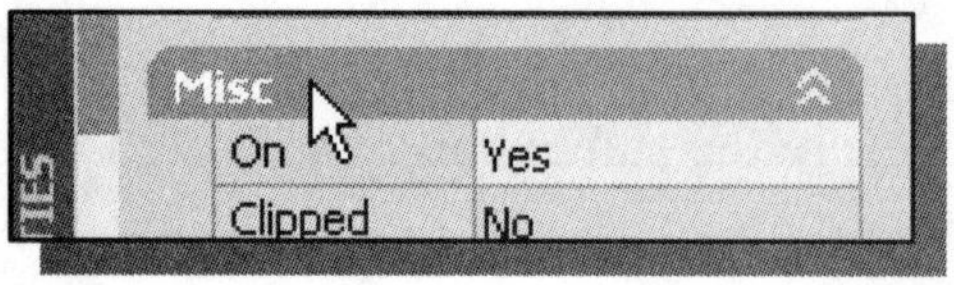

2. Find the **Misc** tab in the Properties Palette as shown.

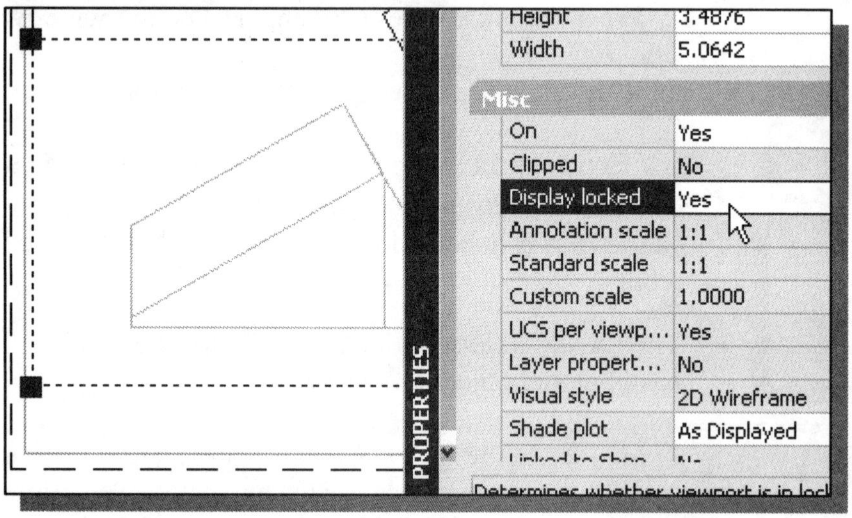

3. Pick ***Display Locked*** option in the *Property* lists.

4. Set the option to **Yes** as shown.

5. Close the *Properties* window by clicking on the [**X**].

- By setting the *lock* option, the displayed view is locked at its current location. We will use this view as the base view.

Aligning the 2D Views

- We will create two construction lines to assist the alignments of the 2D views.

1. Confirm that the *paper space* is active. Click on the *MODEL* button if it is not set to the *paper space*.

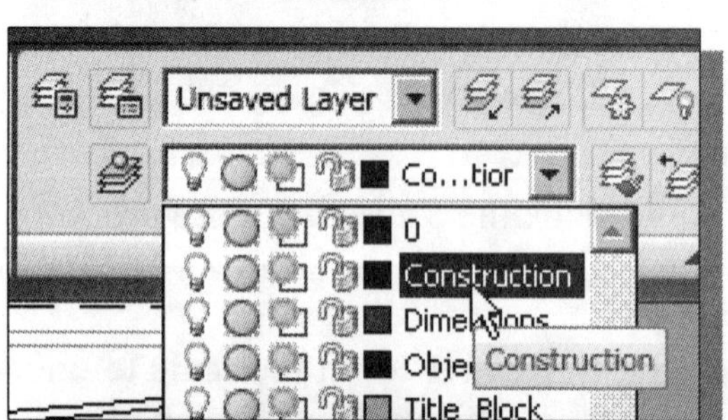

2. Switch ***ON*** and set the ***Construction*** layer as the *Current Layer* as shown.

3. Click **Construction Line** in the *Draw* toolbar as shown.

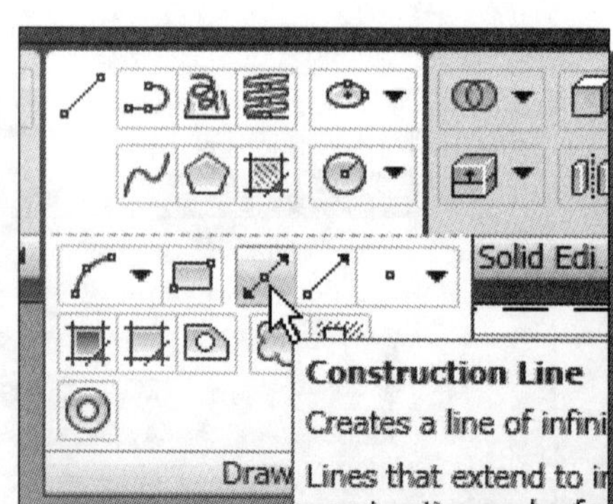

4. On your own, create two lines aligned to the upper left corner of the front view as shown. (Hint: turn ***ON*** the *OSNAP* and *OTRACK* options to help the constructions.)

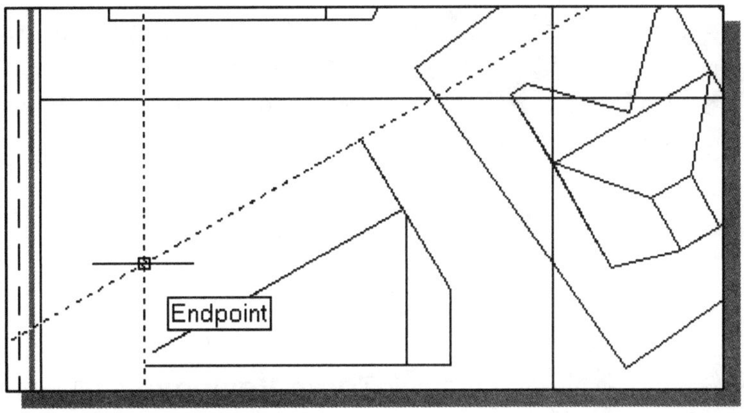

5. Double-click inside the upper left viewport to activate the viewport.

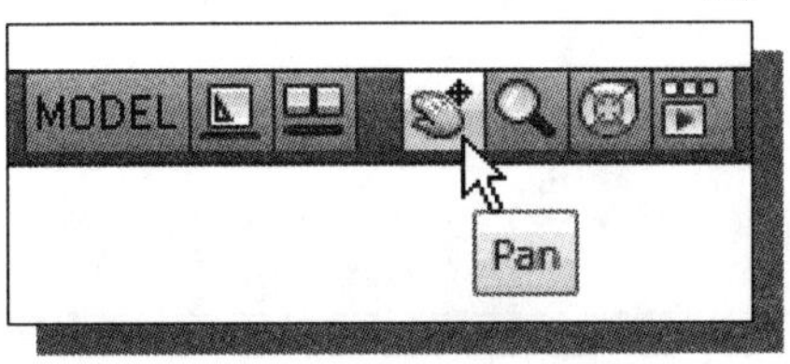

6. Activate the **Pan Realtime** command in the *Status* toolbar as shown.

7. On your own, reposition the displayed top view so that it is aligned vertically to the front view. Use the vertical construction line to assist the alignment.

8. Repeat the above steps and reposition the *Auxiliary* view so that it is aligned to the front view as shown in the below figure.

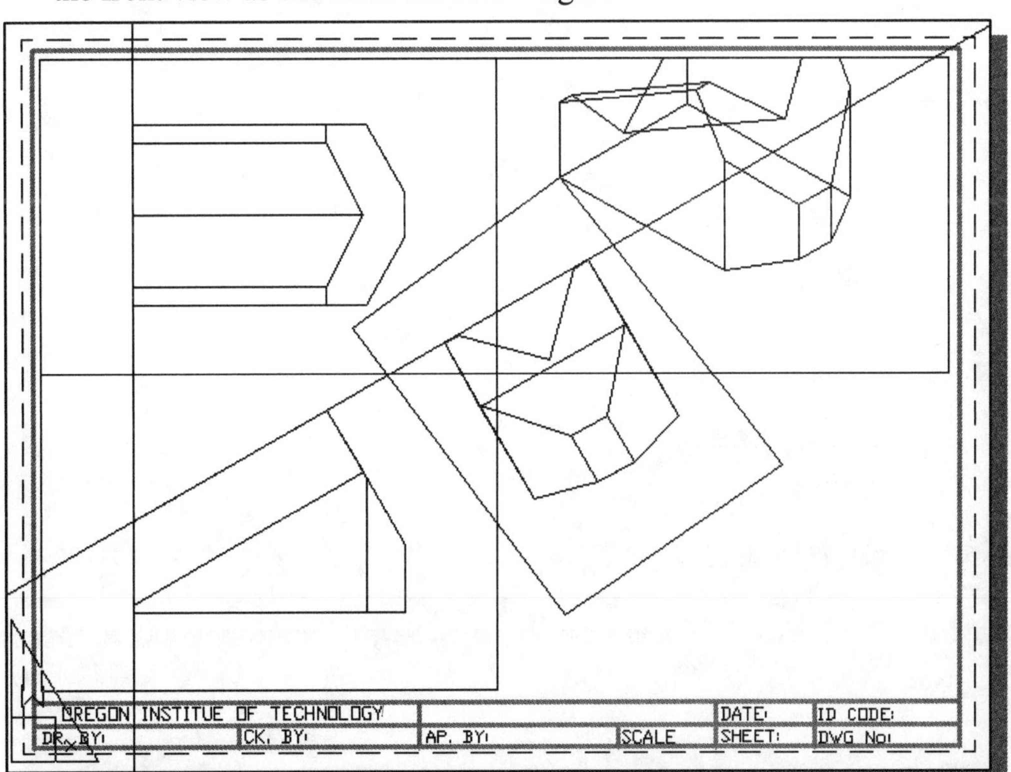

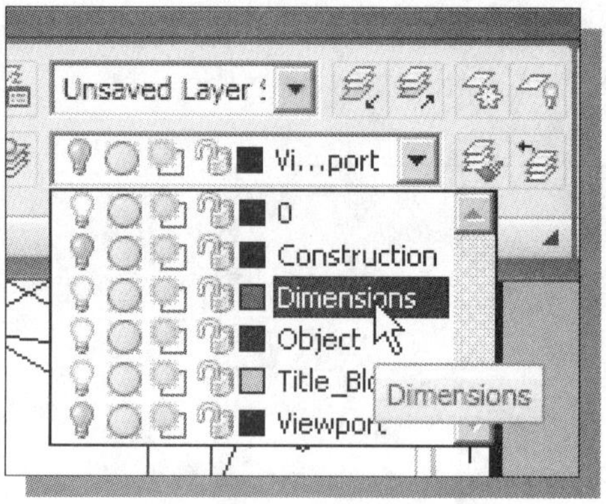

9. Turn ***OFF*** layer *Viewport* and layer *Construction* and set the **Dimension** layer as the active layer, in the *Layer Control* box as shown.

- Note that the viewport borders and the two construction lines are switched off since they are placed in the layer *Viewport*.

10. Double-click on the inside of the isometric view and note the upper right viewport is activated.

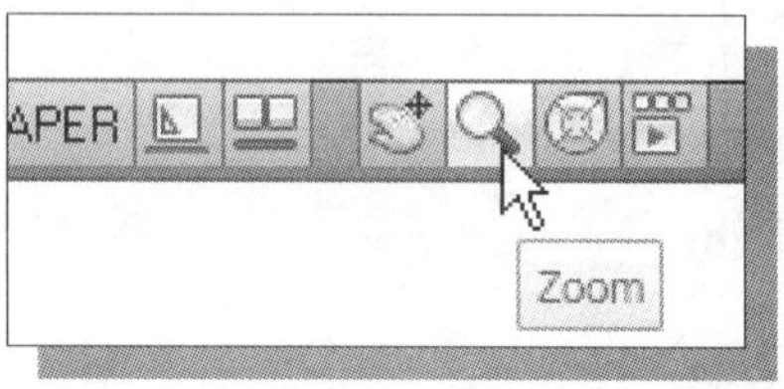

11. Click **Zoom Realtime** in the *Standard* toolbar as shown.

12. On your own, resize and reposition the isometric view so that it does not overlap with the *Auxiliary* view.

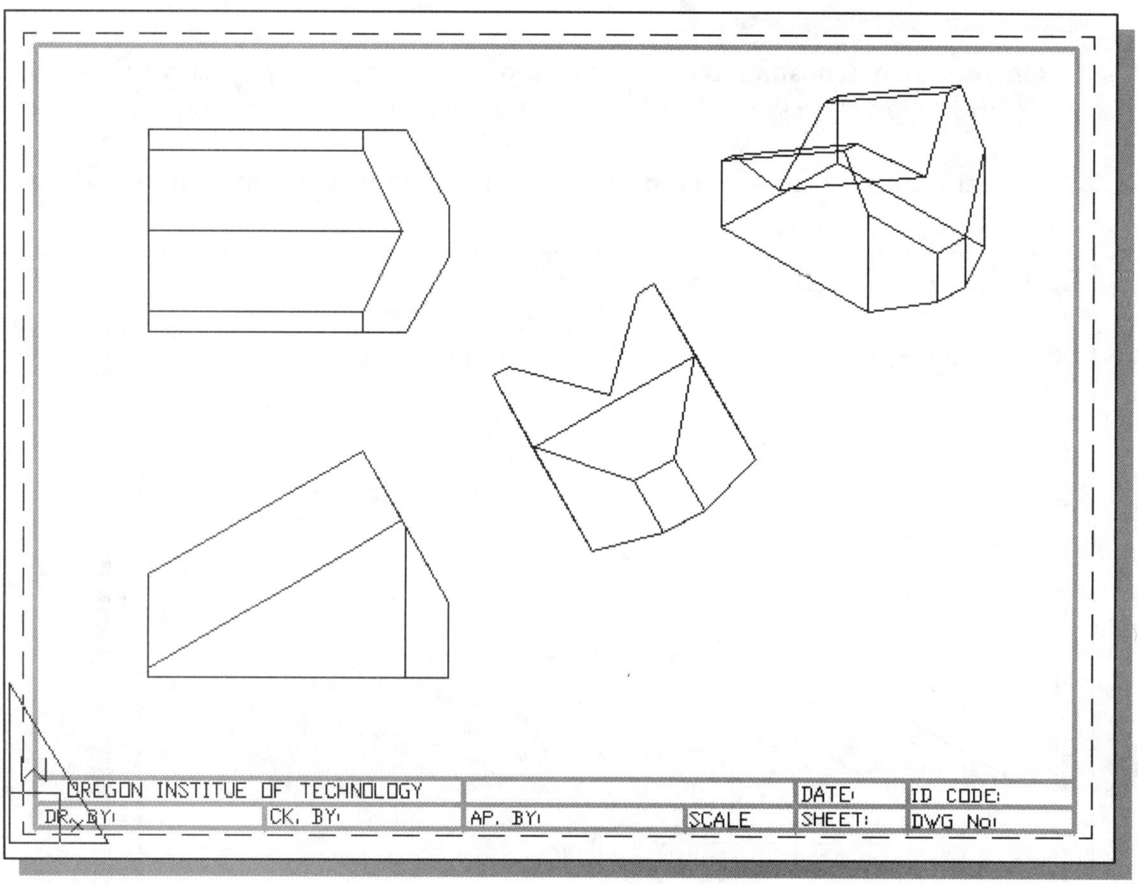

Creating 2D Projected Entities – SOLPROF

- The views created so far are still 3D in nature. This prevents us from setting color or linetype for individual edges, so that hidden features can be described correctly based on engineering drafting standards. To overcome this problem, we will generate 2D entities from the established viewports. We can then use layer controls to set color and linetype options, which allows us to distinguish visible and hidden objects in individual views.

1. Double-click inside the **lower left viewport** to activate the viewport.

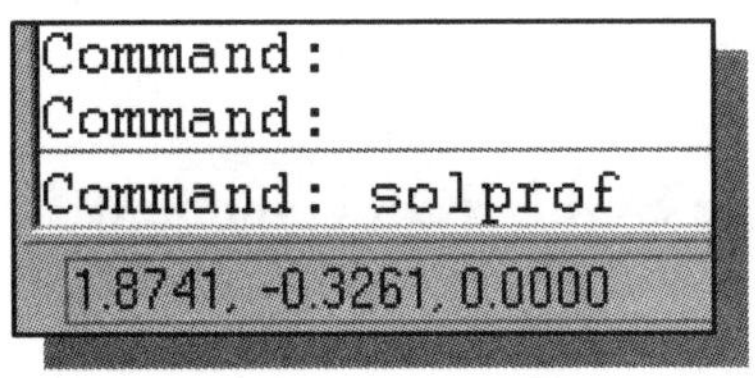

2. At the *command prompt*, enter: **solprof** **[ENTER]**

3. In the command prompt area, the message "*Select objects:*" is displayed. Pick the **solid model** inside the active viewport.

4. Inside the active viewport, **right-mouse-click** once to accept the selection.

5. In the command prompt area, the message "*Display hidden profile lines on separate layer? [Yes/No] <Y>:*" is displayed. Enter: **Y** **[ENTER]**

6. In the command prompt area, the message "*Project profile lines onto a plane? [Yes/No] <Y>:*" is displayed. Enter: **Y** **[ENTER]**

7. In the command prompt area, the message "*Delete tangential edges? [Yes/No] <Y>:*" is displayed. Enter: **Y** **[ENTER]**

- The display in the layout appears to be the same before the SOLPROF command was executed. Projected 2D entities (profile lines) are created in the view direction of the viewport.

8. Pick the **Model** tab to switch back to the 3D *model space*.

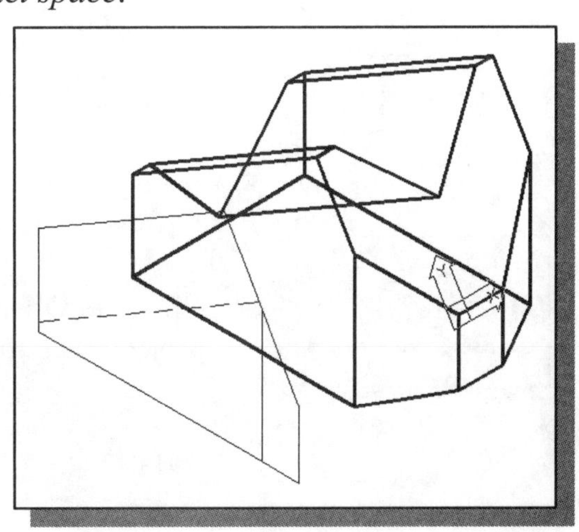

- The projected 2D entities appear in *model space*. Note that the locations of the projected entities might be at a different location on your screen than is displayed in the figure.

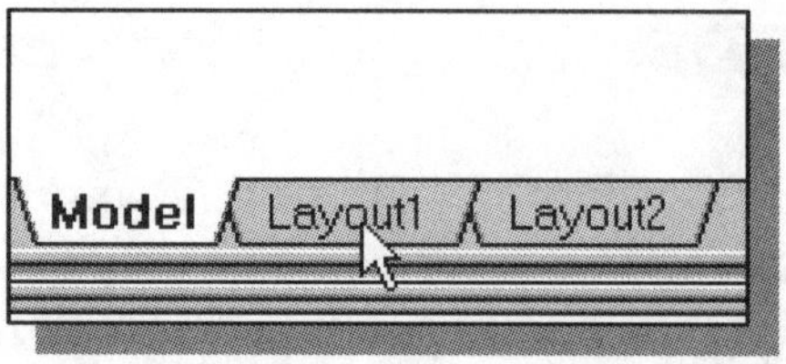

9. Pick the **Layout1** tab to switch back to the two-dimensional *paper space*.

10. Click on the **Layer Properties** icon in the *Layers* toolbar.

- Note that two additional layers are created by the SOLPROF command. The *PV-xx* layer is for the projected visible lines and *PH-xx* layer is for the projected hidden lines.

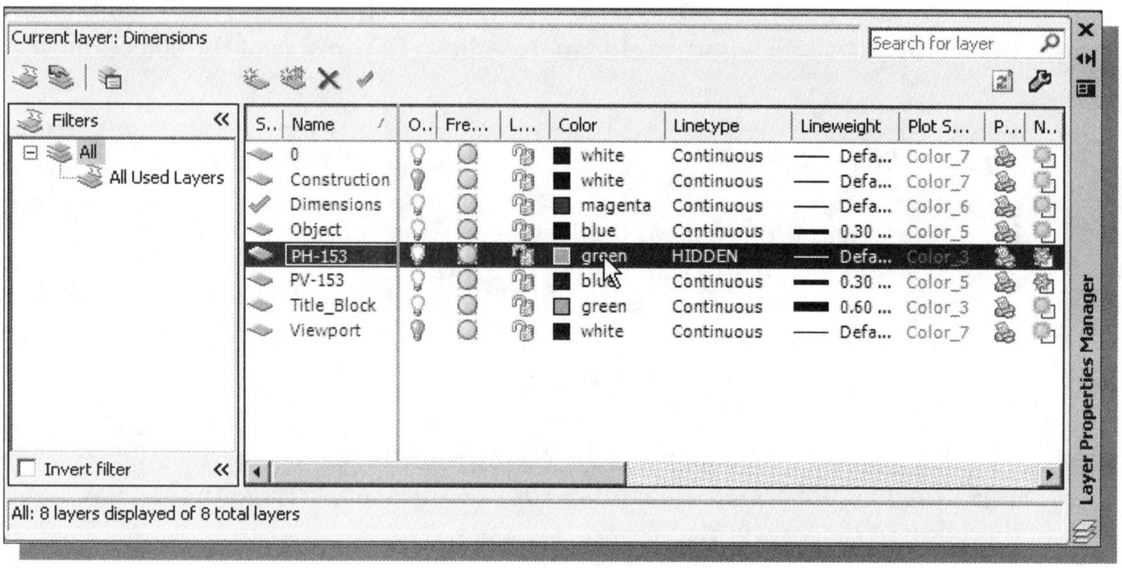

11. On your own, change the two layers to the following settings:

Layer	***Color***	***LineType***	***Lineweight***	***PlotStyle***
PH-xx	**Green**	**HIDDEN**	**Default**	**Normal**
PV-xx	**Blue**	**Continuous**	**0.3mm**	**Normal**

12. On your own, ***Freeze*** the layer *Object* to remove the solid object from the display.

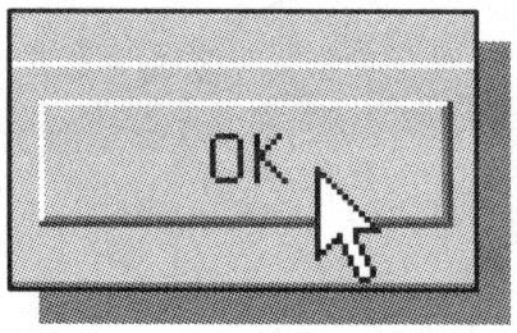

13. Click the **OK** button to accept the settings. (Note that only the projected entities are displayed.)

14. On your own, ***Thaw*** the *Object* layer and repeat the above steps to generate 2D projected entities for the other three views.

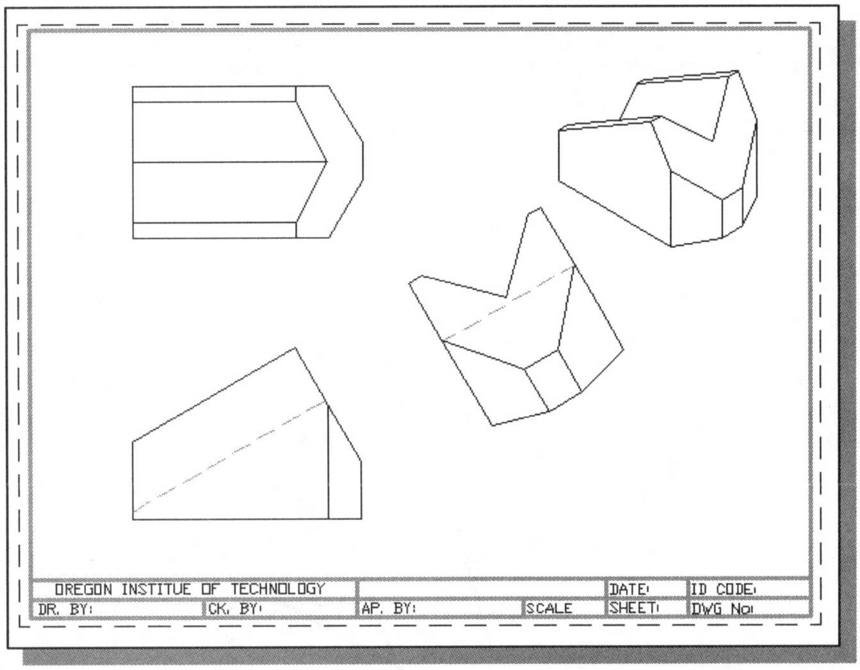

Completing the 2D Drawing

- Dimensions and notes can be placed in the *model space* or the *paper space*. From a design/modeling perspective, it is generally agreed that the dimensions should be placed in the 2D *paper space*.

1. Confirm the active mode is set to ***paper space*** as shown in the *Status Bar* area.

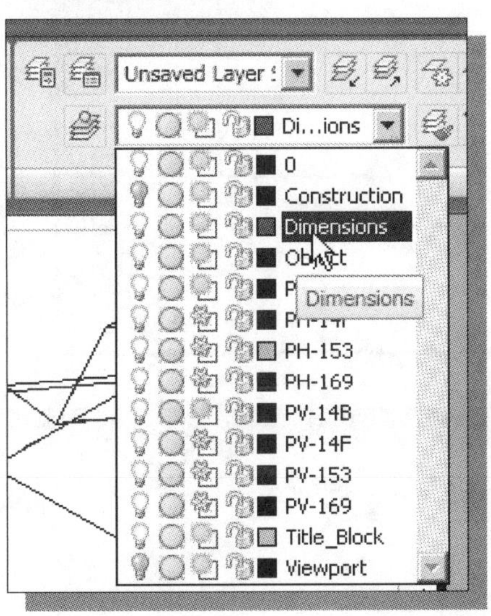

2. On your own, set layer ***Dimensions*** as the *Current Layer* in the *Layer Properties* box as shown.

3. Move the cursor to the *Standard* toolbar area and right-mouse-click on any icon in the *Standard* toolbar to display the option list.

4. Select **Toolbar → AutoCAD →Dimension** to display the *Dimension* toolbar on the screen.

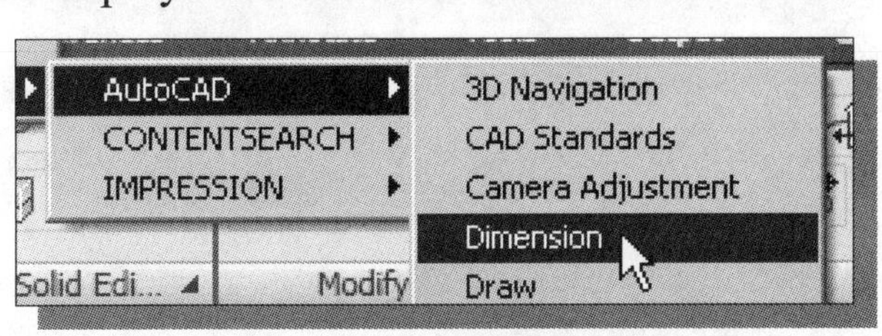

5. On your own, create the necessary dimensions and complete the 2D drawing as shown.

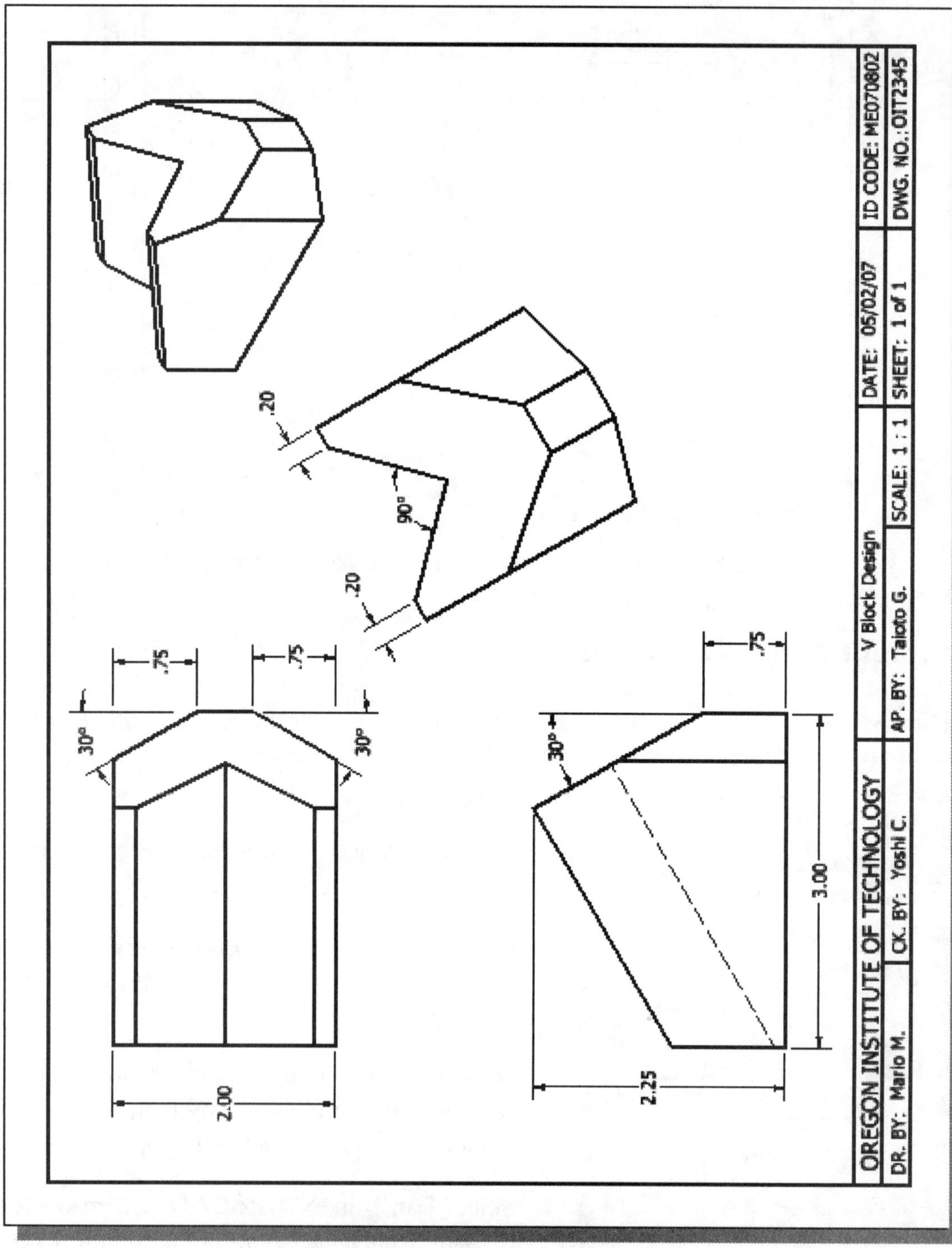

Questions:

1. What is an auxiliary view and why would it be important?

2. List and describe the types 2D views used in the lesson.

3. Why and when should you use the **SOLPROF** command?

4. What is the difference between *model space* and *paper space* in AutoCAD?

5. Why and when should you use the **DVIEW** command?

6. Identify the following commands:

(a)

(b)

(c)

(d)

Exercises: Create the following solid models and generate multiview drawings from the 3D models. (All dimensions are in inches.)

1.

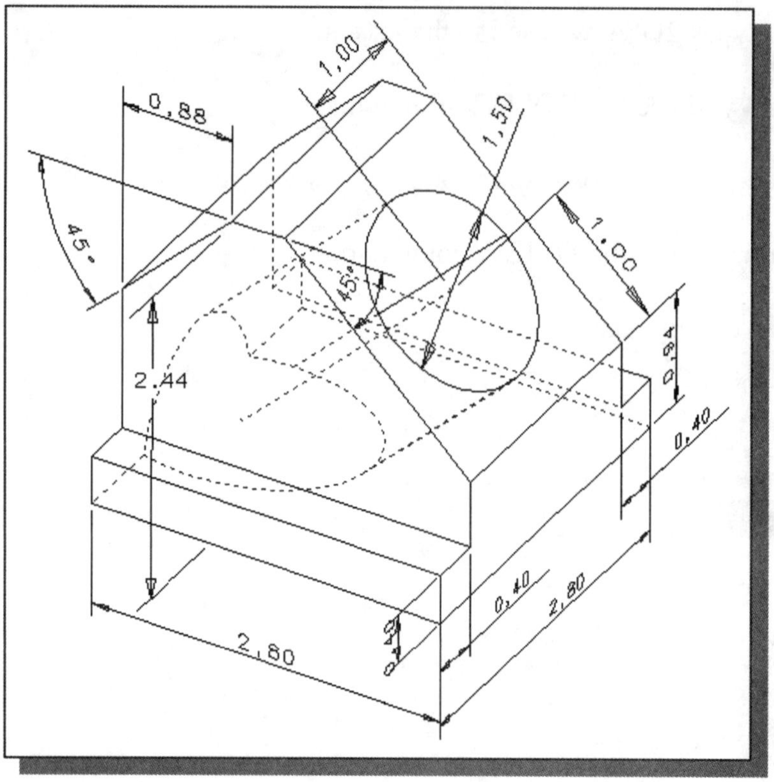

2.

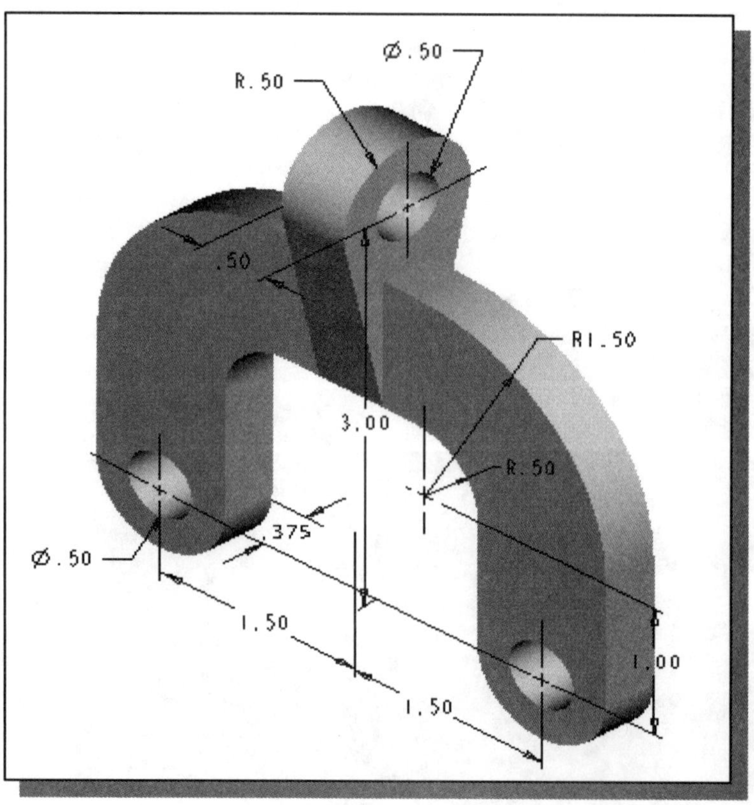

3.

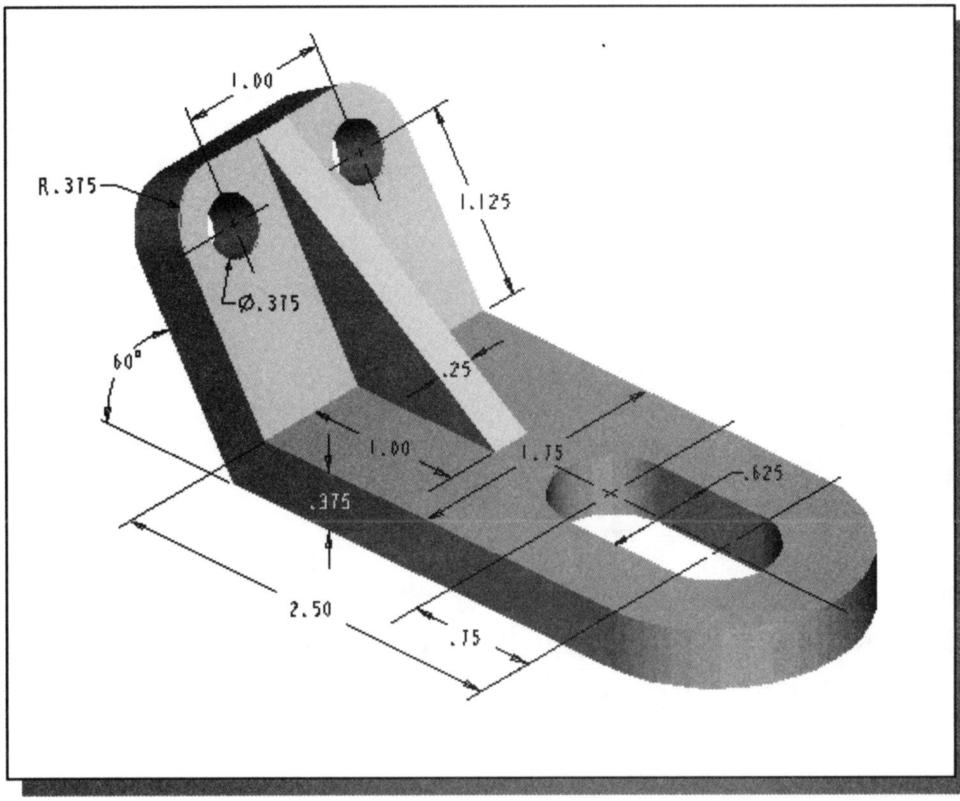

NOTES:

Chapter 9
Symmetrical Features in Designs

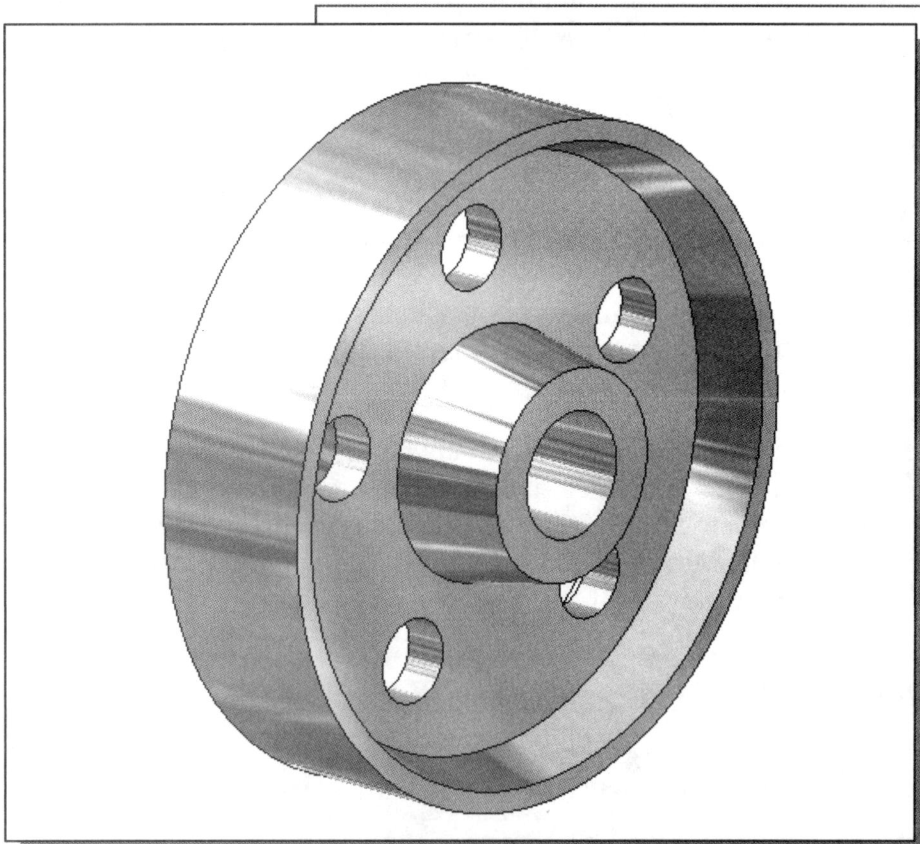

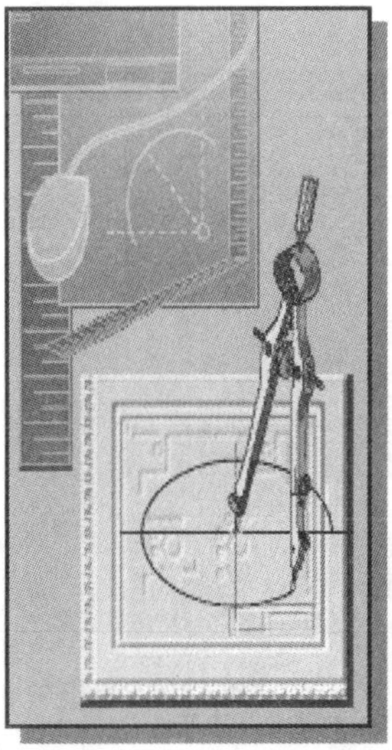

Learning Objectives

- Create Revolved Features
- Use the Mirror Part Command
- Understand and Create Construction Geometry
- Create Combined Parts
- Create and Modify Feature Arrays
- Understand the Importance of Identifying Symmetrical Features in Designs

Introduction

In solid modeling, it is important to identify and determine the features that exist in the design. *Modern solid modeling systems* enable us to build complex designs by working on smaller and simpler units. This approach simplifies the modeling process and allows us to concentrate on the characteristics of the design. Symmetry is an important characteristic that is often seen in designs. Symmetrical features can be easily accomplished by the assortments of tools that are available in feature-based modeling systems, such as AutoCAD.

The modeling technique of extruding two-dimensional sketches along a straight line to form three-dimensional features, as illustrated in the previous chapters, is an effective way to construct solid models. For designs that involve cylindrical shapes, shapes that are symmetrical about an axis, revolving two-dimensional sketches about an axis can form the needed three-dimensional features. In solid modeling, this type of feature is called a **revolved feature**.

In AutoCAD, besides using the **Revolve** command to create revolved features, several options are also available to handle symmetrical features. For example, we can create multiple identical copies of symmetrical features with the **Array** command, or create mirror images of models using the **Mirror** command. In this chapter, the construction and modeling techniques of these more advanced features are illustrated.

A Revolved Design: *Pulley*

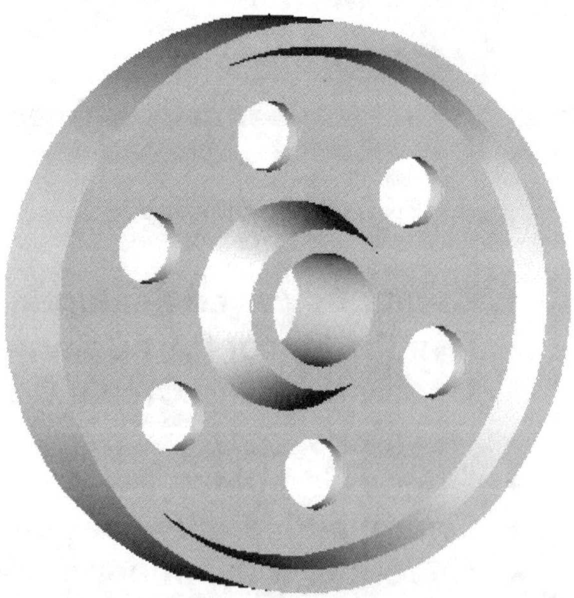

❖ Based on your knowledge of AutoCAD, how many features would you use to create the design? Which feature would you choose as the starting point for creating the model? Identify the symmetrical features in the design and consider other possibilities in creating the design. You are encouraged to create the model on your own prior to following through the tutorial.

Modeling Strategy – A Revolved Design

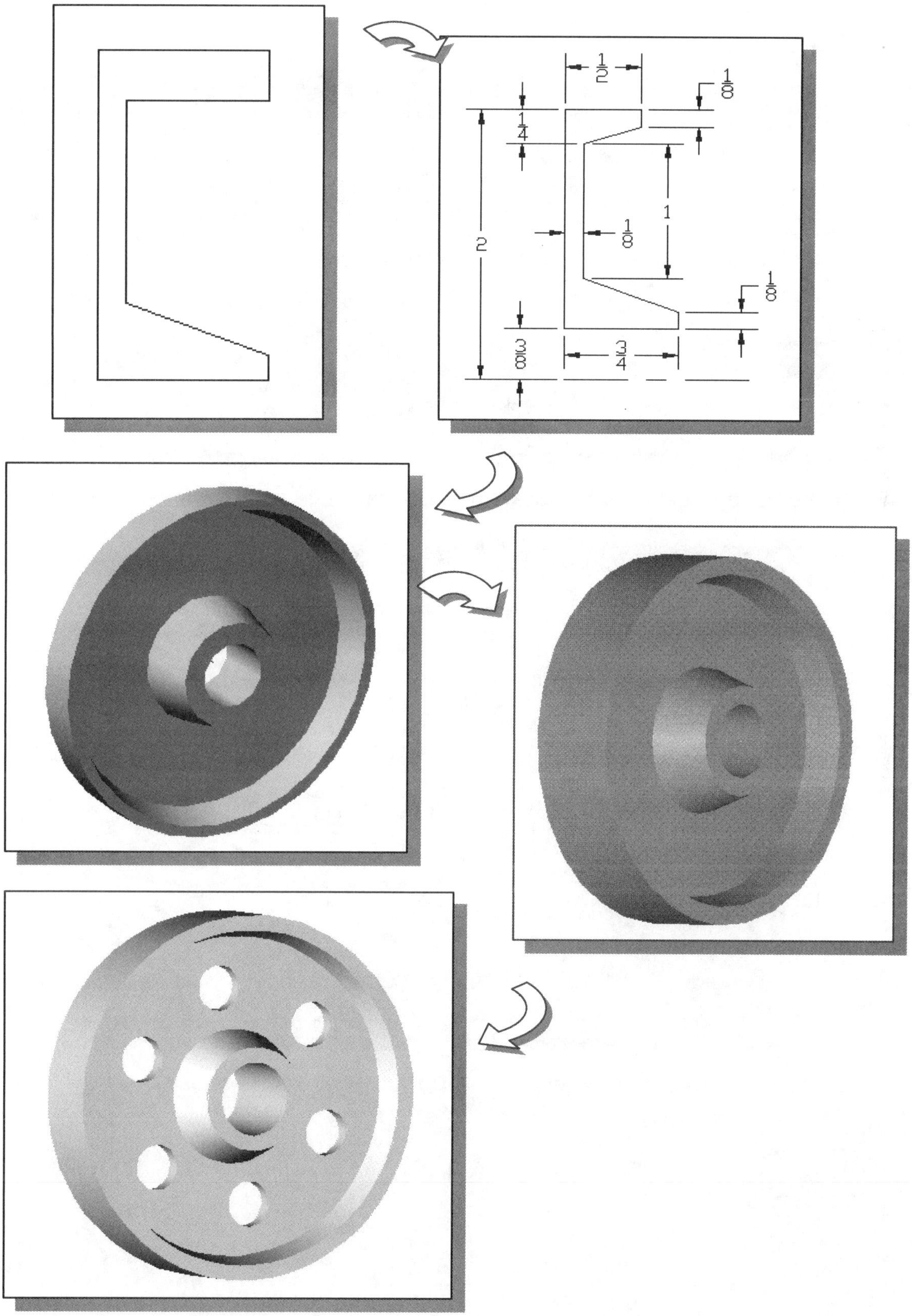

Starting Up AutoCAD® 2009

1. Select the **AutoCAD 2009** option on the *Program* menu or select the **AutoCAD 2009** icon on the *Desktop*.

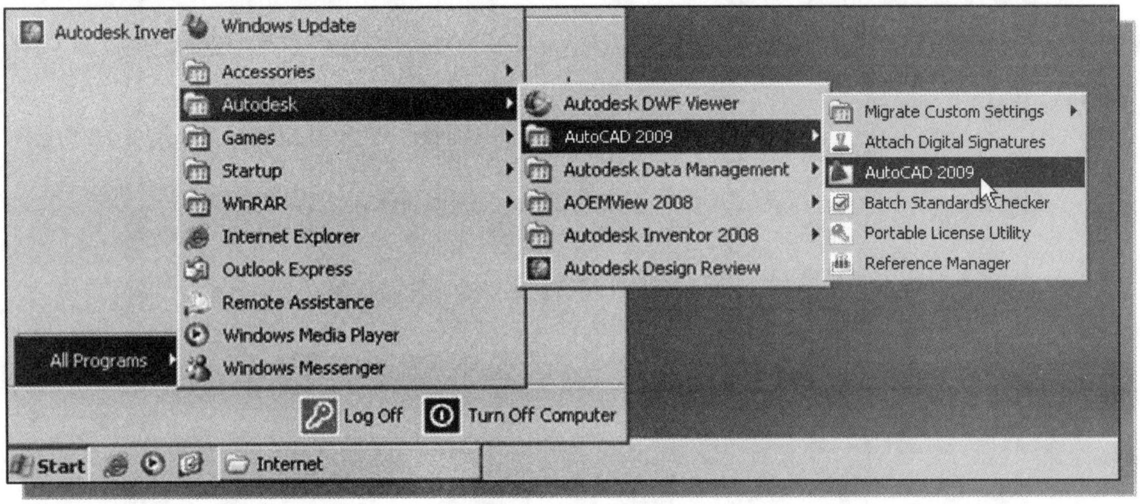

2. In the startup window, select **Start from Scratch**, as shown in the figure below.

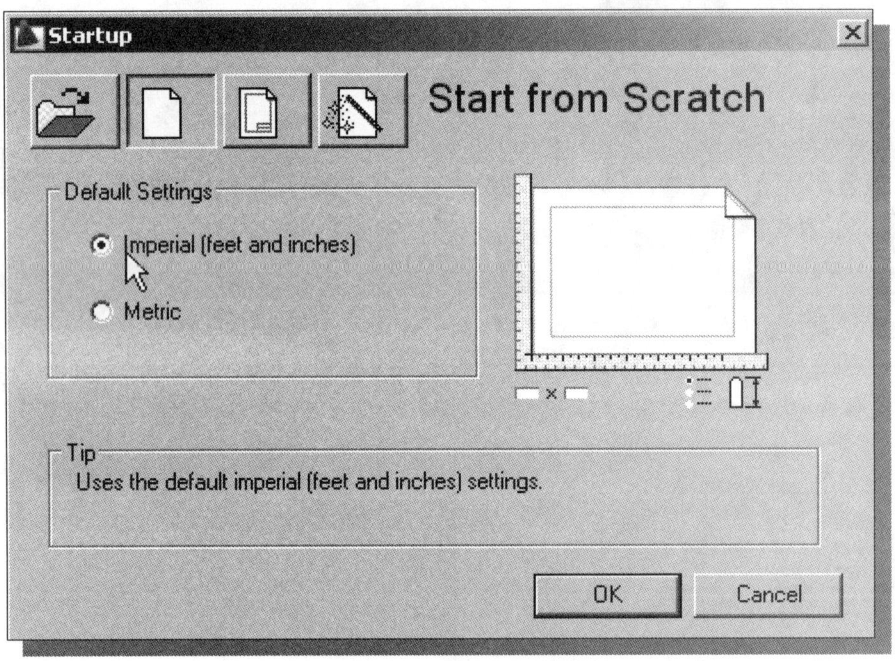

3. In the *Default Settings* section, pick **Imperial (feet and inches)** as the drawing units.

4. Pick **OK** in the startup dialog box to accept the selected settings.

Layers Setup

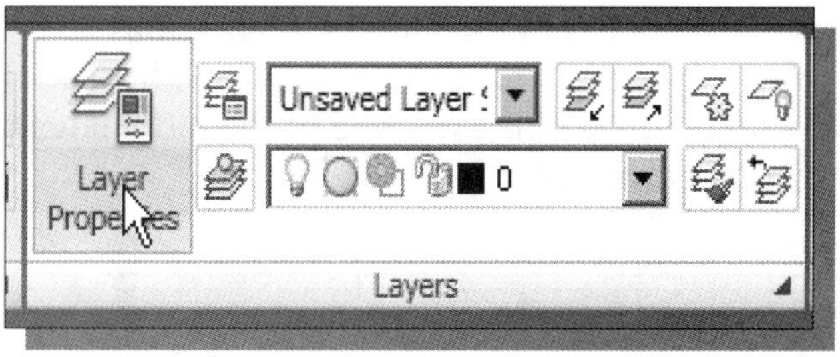

1. Pick **Layer Properties Manager** in the *Object Properties* toolbar.

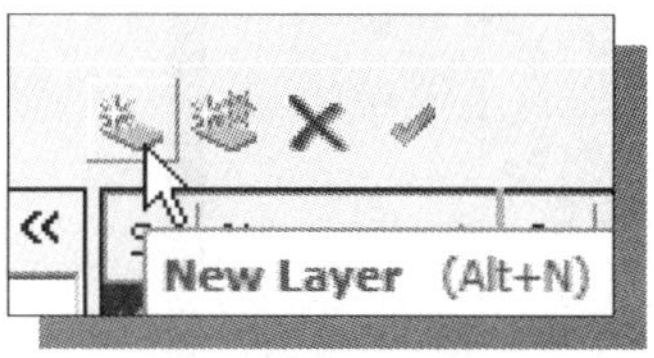

2. Click on the **New** button to create new layers.

3. Create **three new layers** with the following settings:

Layer	*Color*	*LineType*	*LineWeight*
Center_lines	**Red**	**Center**	**Default**
Dimensions	**Megenta**	**Continuous**	**Default**
Object_lines	**Cyan**	**Continuous**	**0.30mm**

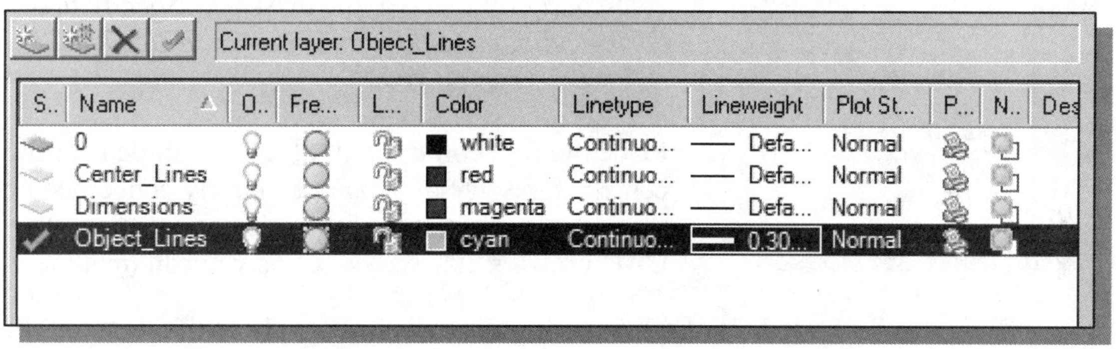

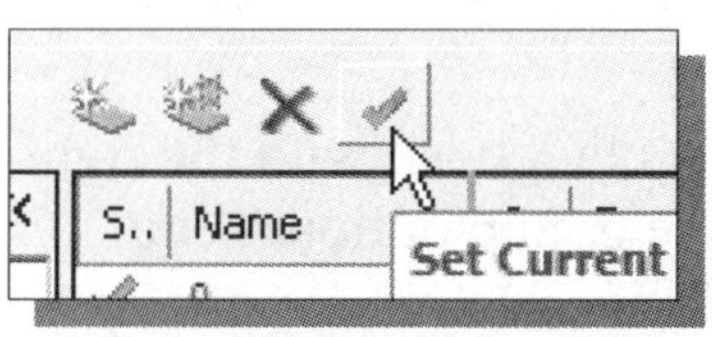

4. Highlight the layer ***Object_lines*** in the list of layers.

5. Click on the **Current** button to set layer ***Object_lines*** as the *Current Layer*.

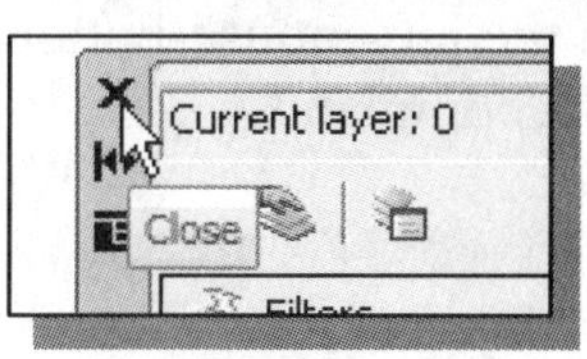

6. Click on the **Close** button to accept the settings and exit the *Layer Properties Manager* dialog box.

7. In the *Status Bar* area, reset the options and turn ***ON*** the *Polar, Object Snap, Object Snap Tracking, Dynamic Input* and *Line Weight* options.

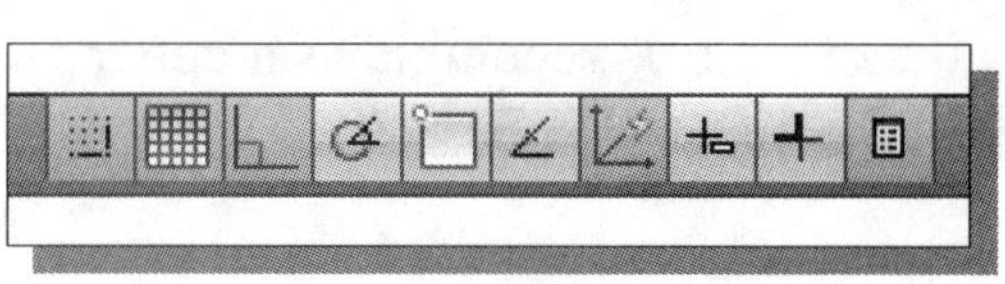

Setting Up a 2D Sketch for the Revolved Feature

- Note that the *Pulley* design is symmetrical about a horizontal axis as well as a vertical axis, which allows us to simplify the 2D sketch as shown below. Instead of creating the 2D sketch by the Line command, we will use some of the more advanced editing options available with the Region command.

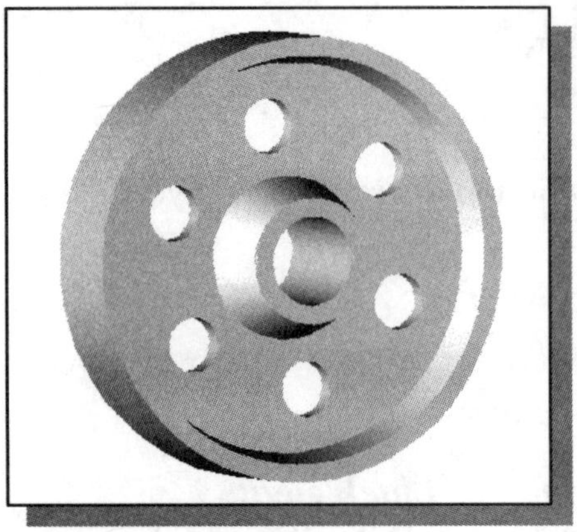

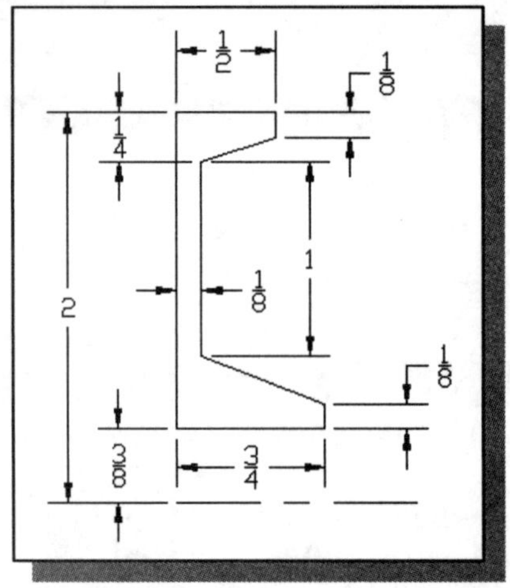

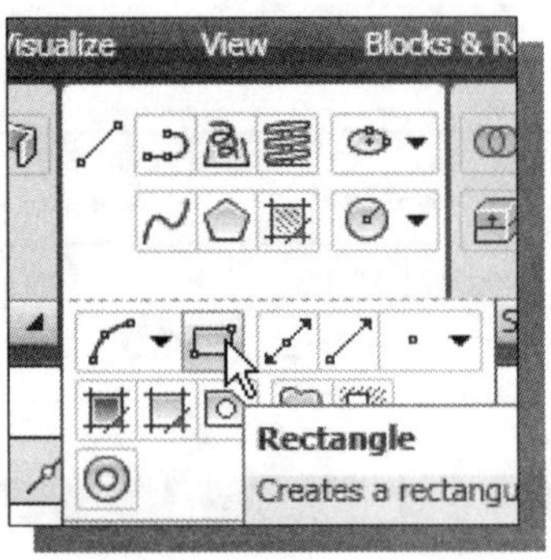

1. Select the **Rectangle** icon in the *Draw* toolbar. In the command prompt area, the message "*Specify first corner point or [Chamfer/Elevation/Fillet/Thickness /Width]:*" is displayed.

2. Place the first corner point of the rectangle near the center of the screen. Do not be overly concerned about the actual coordinates of the selected location; the CAD drawing space is as big as you can imagine.

3. We will create a 0.75″ × 1.625″ rectangle for the main body of the sketch. Enter **@0.75,1.625 [ENTER]**.

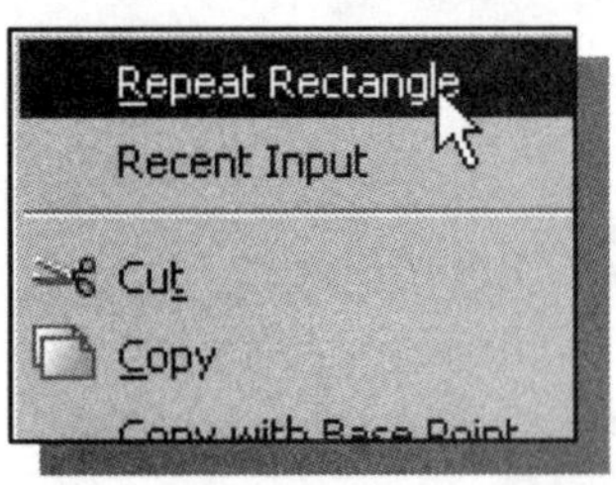

4. Inside the graphics window, click once with the right-mouse-button to bring up the popup option menu.

5. Pick **Repeat Rectangle**, with the left-mouse-button, in the popup menu to repeat the last command.

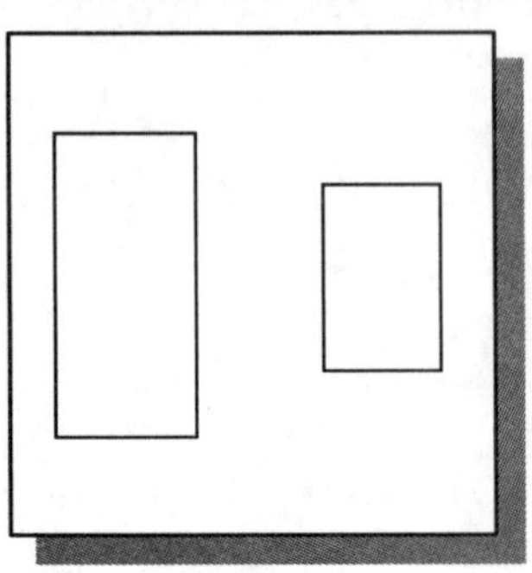

6. Place the first corner point of the rectangle toward the right side of the previous rectangle.

7. We will create a 0.625″ × 1.0″ rectangle as a cutter sketch. Enter **@0.625,1.0 [ENTER]**.

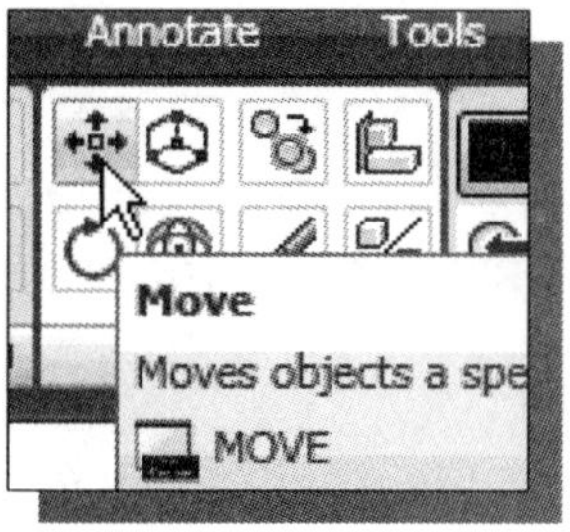

8. Select the **Move** icon in the *Modify* toolbar.

9. In the command prompt area, the message "*Select Objects:*" is displayed. Pick the cutter rectangle, the **smaller rectangle**, to move.

10. Inside the graphics window, **right-mouse-click** to accept the selection.

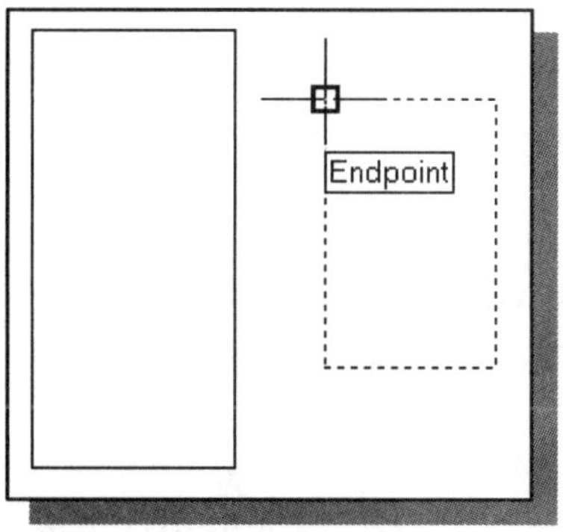

11. In the command prompt area, the message "*Specify base point or displacement:*" is displayed. Pick the upper left corner of the smaller rectangle as shown.

12. Inside the graphics window, hold down the [**SHIFT**] key and **right-mouse-click** once to bring up the *Object Snap* shortcut menu.

13. Select the **From** option in popup window.

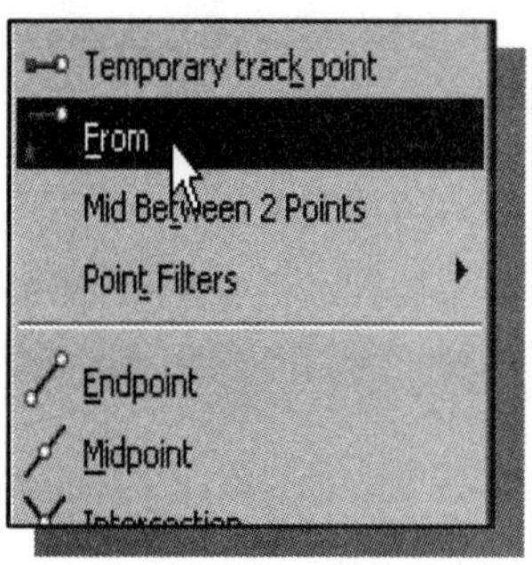

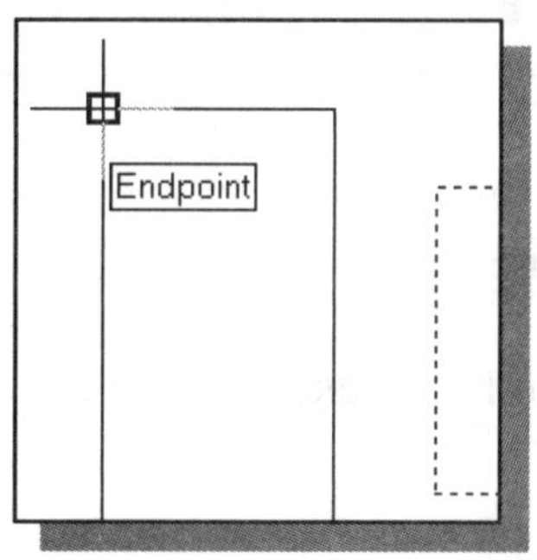

14. Pick the upper left corner of the larger rectangle as shown.

15. In the command prompt area, the message "*Specify base point or displacement: _from Base point: <Offset>:*" is displayed. Enter: **@0.125,-0.25** [**ENTER**].

16. Pre-select the **smaller rectangle** to activate the grip-editing function.

17. Pick the **lower right grip point** displayed along the right vertical edge.

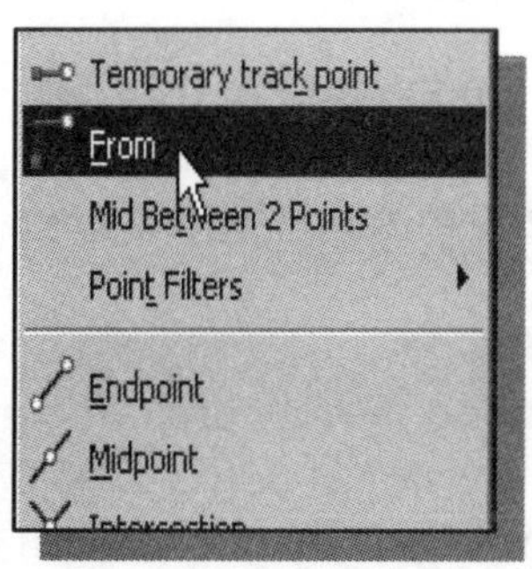

18. Inside the graphics window, hold down the [**SHIFT**] key and **right-mouse-click** once to bring up the *Object Snap* shortcut menu.

19. Select the **From** option in popup window.

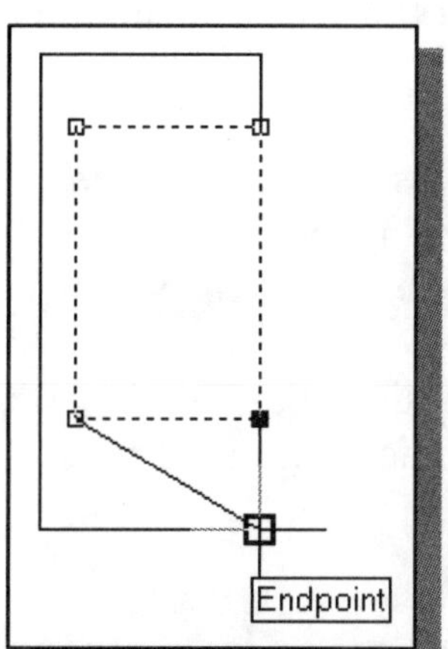

20. Pick the lower right corner of the larger rectangle.

21. At the command prompt: **@0,0.125** [**ENTER**]

22. Press the [**Esc**] key once to deselect any selected entities.

Perform 2D Boolean Operations

- AutoCAD's 2D regions are special types of filled polygons. We can create composite 2D regions by applying *Boolean operations* to subtract, find the intersection, or combine two or more regions.

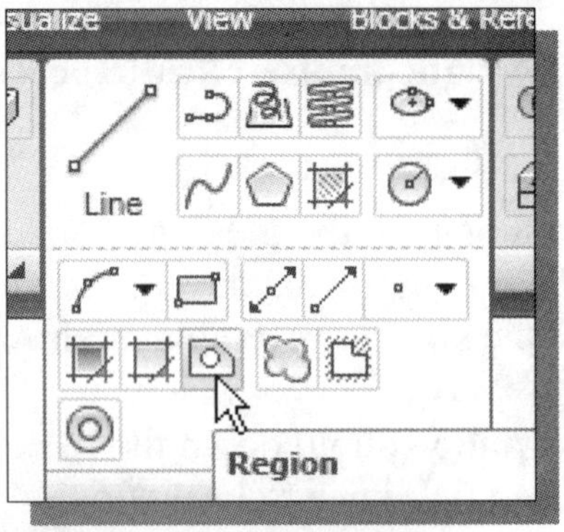

1. Select the **Region** command icon in the *Draw* toolbar.

2. In the command prompt area, the message "*Select objects:*" is displayed. Select the **polygon** we just edited.

3. Inside the graphics window, **right-mouse-click** to accept the selection and create a region.

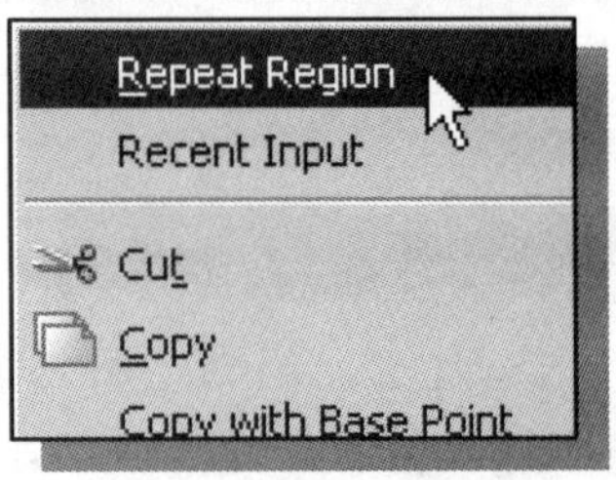

4. Inside the graphics window, click once with the right-mouse-button to bring up the popup option menu.

5. Pick **Repeat Region**, with the left-mouse-button, in the popup menu to repeat the last command.

6. In the command prompt area, the message "*Select objects:*" is displayed. Select the rectangle by clicking on one of the edges.

7. Inside the graphics window, right-mouse-click to accept the selection and create a region.

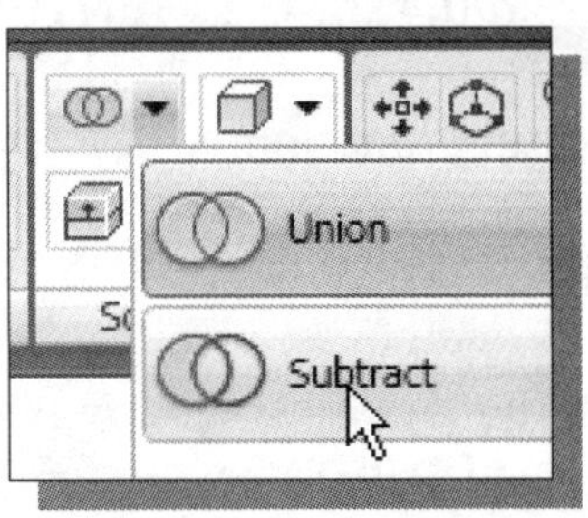

8. In the *Modeling* toolbar, click on the **Subtract** icon. In the command prompt area, the message "*_subtract Select solids and regions to subtract from ... Select Objects:*" is displayed.

9. Pick the **rectangle** by clicking on one of the edges.

10. Inside the graphics window, right-mouse-click to accept the selection and proceed with the Subtract command.

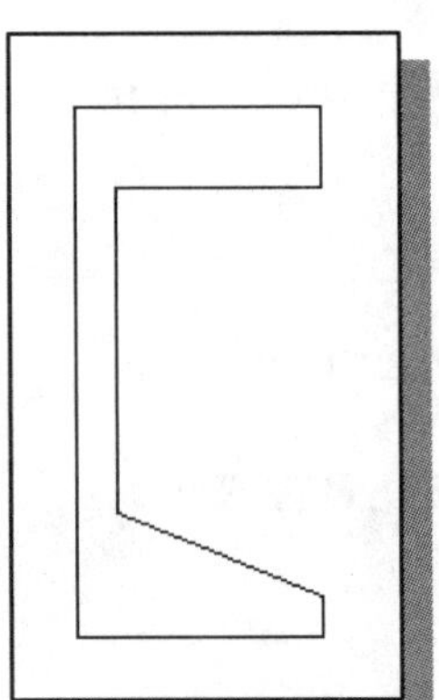

11. In the command prompt area, the message "*Select solids and regions to subtract ... Select Objects:*" is displayed. Pick the four-sided **polygon** by clicking on one of the edges.

12. Inside the graphics window, right-mouse-click to accept the selection and proceed with the Subtract command. The completed 2D sketch is as shown.

- AutoCAD's region is a special type of geometric entity. It was developed based on the CSG solid modeling approach and is valuable in the sense that it provides a different method to construct complex geometric shapes. In many cases, the Boolean operations are more efficient than creating geometry by entering point-to-point coordinates.

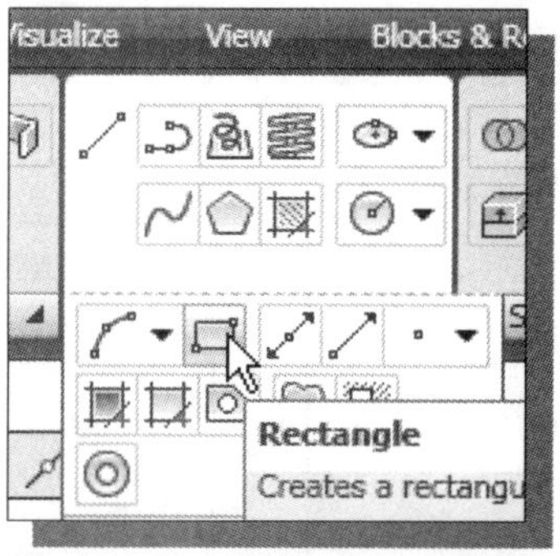

13. Select the **Rectangle** icon in the *Draw* toolbar.

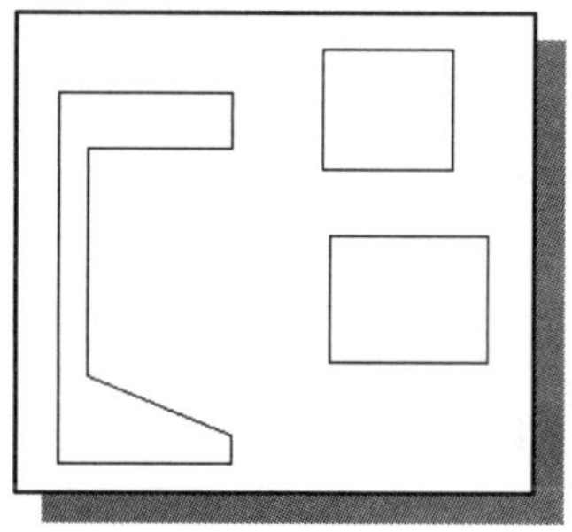

14. On your own, create two arbitrary rectangles roughly positioned as shown. We will use these two rectangles to shape the upper regions of the design.

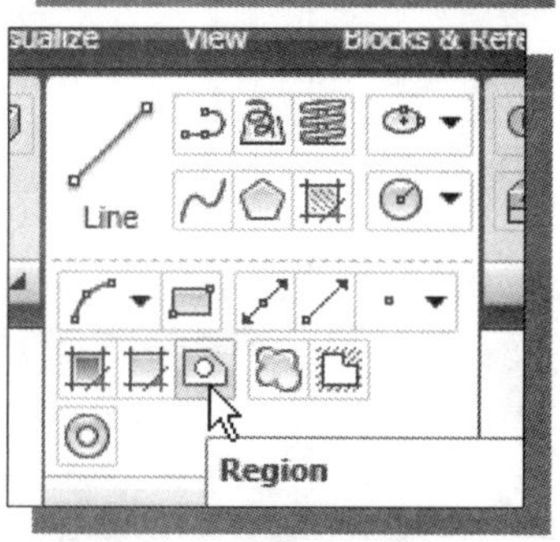

15. On your own, convert the two rectangles into **two regions**.

16. Select the **Move** icon in the *Modify* toolbar.

17. In the command prompt area, the message "*Select Objects:*" is displayed. Pick **one of the rectangles** to move.

18. Inside the graphics window, **right-mouse-click** to accept the selection.

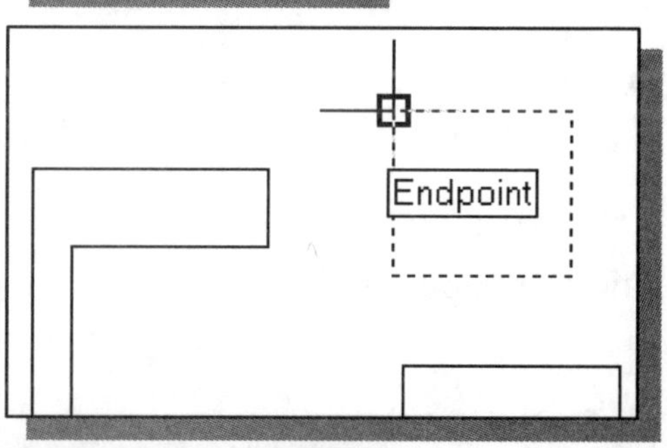

19. In the command prompt area, the message "*Specify base point or displacement:*" is displayed. Pick the **upper left corner** of the selected rectangle as shown.

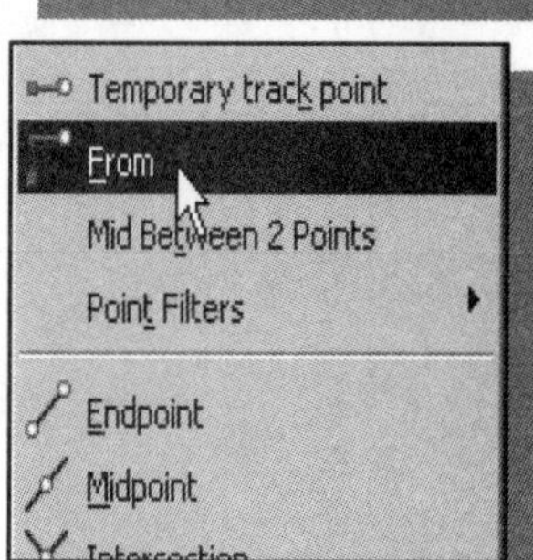

20. Inside the graphics window, hold down the [**SHIFT**] key and **right-mouse-click** once to bring up the *Object Snap* shortcut menu.

21. Select the **From** option in popup window.

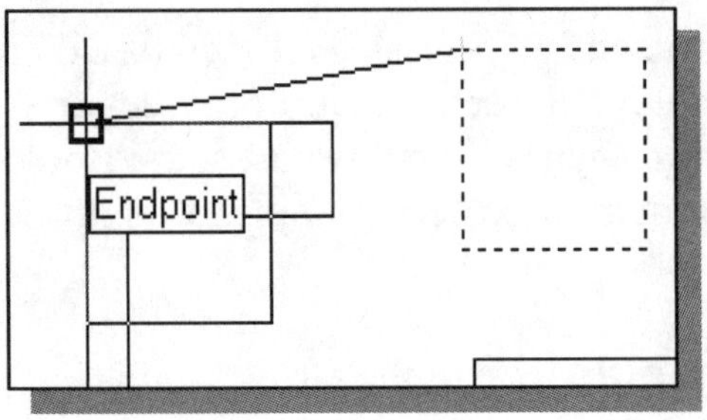

22. Pick the upper left corner of the larger rectangle as shown.

23. In the command prompt area, the message "*Specify base point or displacement: _from Base point: <Offset>:*" is displayed.
Enter: **@0.5,0.0 [ENTER]**

24. On your own, perform the **Boolean Subtract** operation and create the 2D sketch as shown.

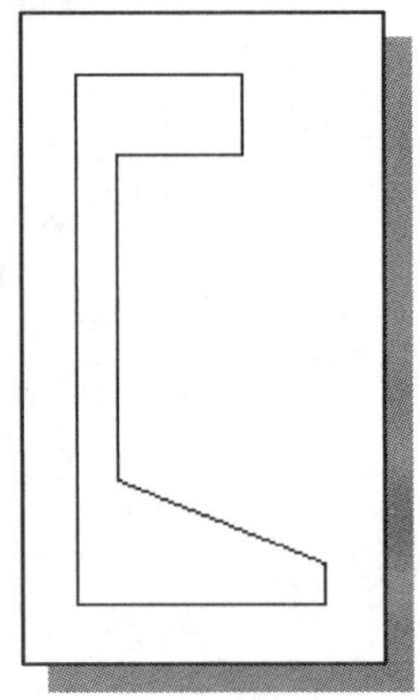

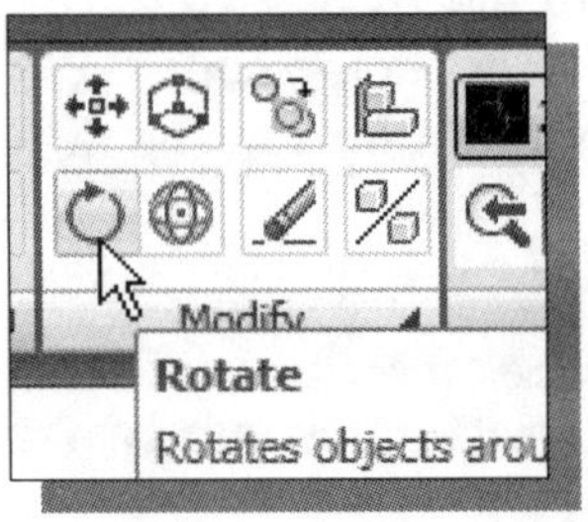

25. Select the **Rotate** icon in the *Modify* toolbar.

26. In the command prompt area, the message "*Select Objects:*" is displayed. Pick the rectangle to rotate.

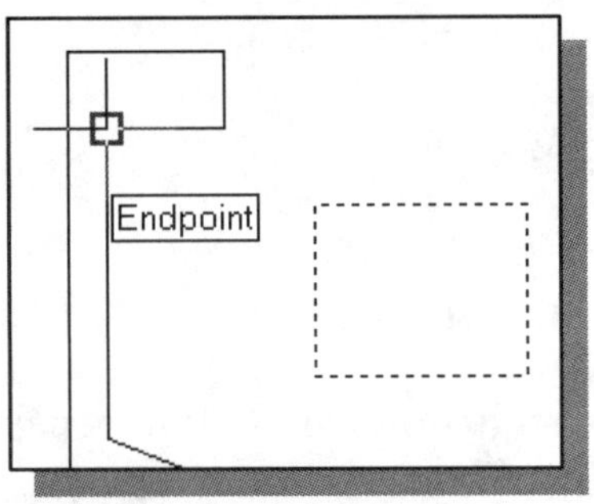

27. Inside the graphics window, right-mouse-click to accept the selection.

28. In the command prompt area, the message "*Specify base point or displacement:*" is displayed. Pick the **inside corner** of the 2D sketch as shown.

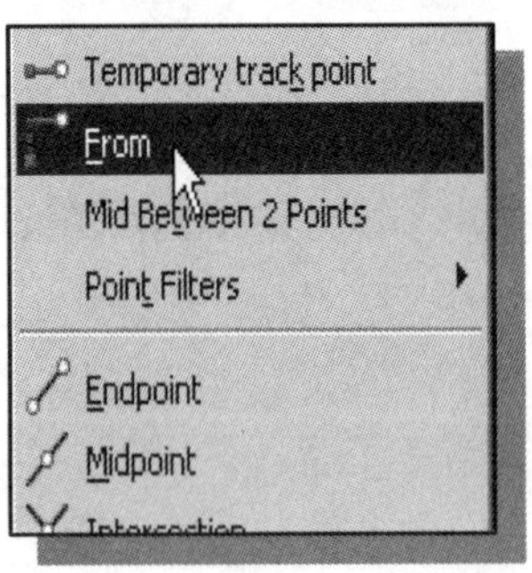

29. Inside the graphics window, hold down the [**SHIFT**] key and **right-mouse-click** once to bring up the *Object Snap* shortcut menu.

30. Select the **From** option in popup window.

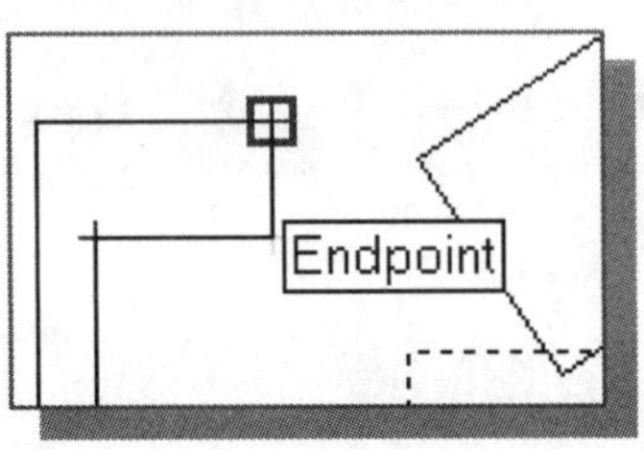

31. Pick the upper right corner of the 2D sketch as shown.

32. At the command prompt: **@0,-0.125 [ENTER]**

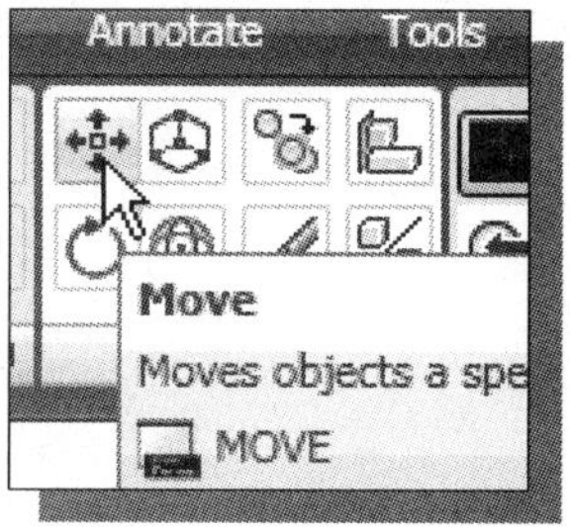

33. Select the **Move** icon in the *Modify* toolbar.

34. In the command prompt area, the message "*Select Objects:*" is displayed. Pick the rotated rectangle to move.

35. Inside the graphics window, right-mouse-click to accept the selection.

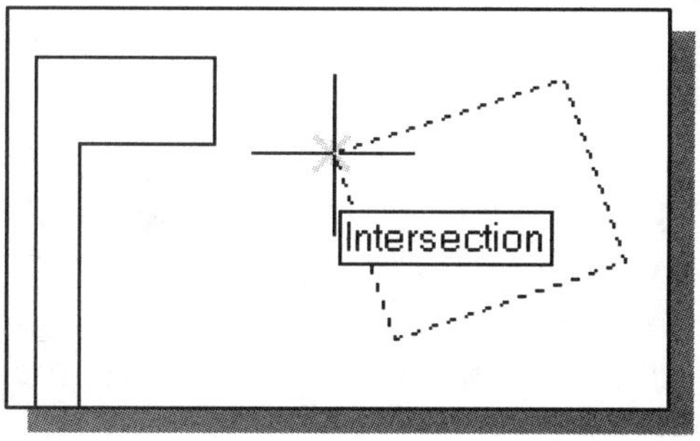

36. In the command prompt area, the message "*Specify base point or displacement:*" is displayed. Pick the upper left corner of the selected rectangle as shown.

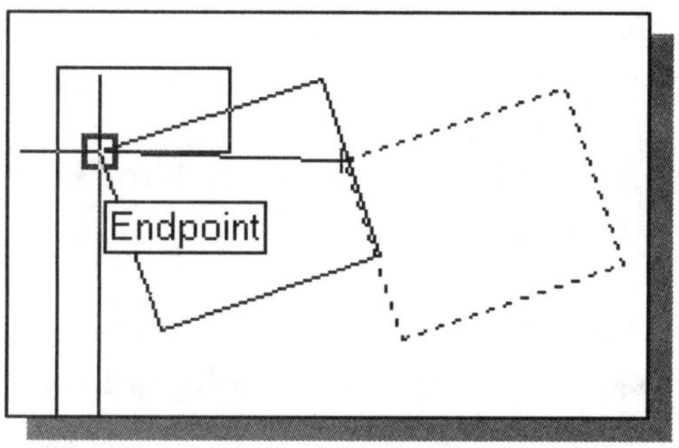

37. In the command prompt area, the message "*Specify base point or displacement:*" is displayed. Pick the inside corner of the 2D sketch as shown.

38. On your own, perform the **Boolean Subtract** operation and complete the 2D sketch as shown.

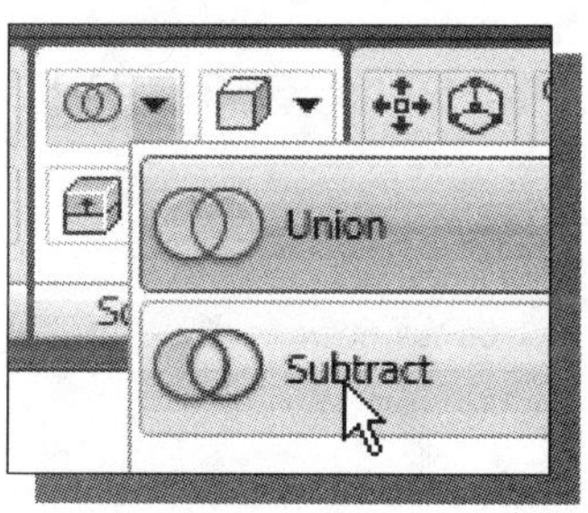

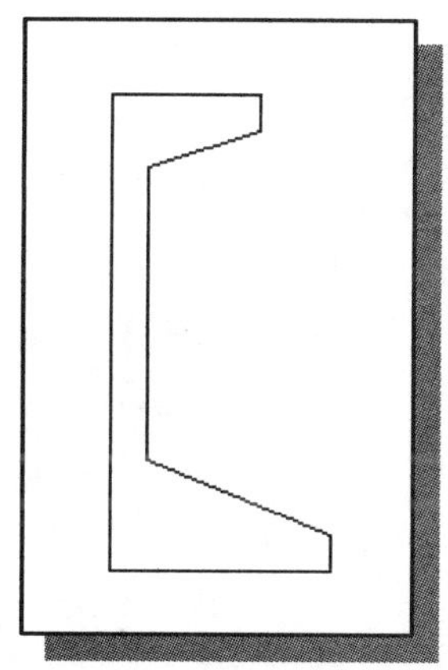

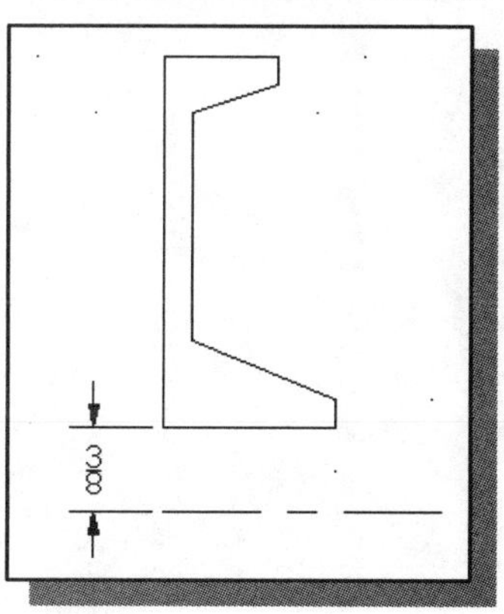

39. On your own, create a line that is 3/8 below the 2D sketch as shown. This line will be used as the axis of rotation for the revolved feature. Trim the line so that the **left endpoint is aligned to the left edge of the 2D sketch**.

Creating the Revolved Feature

1. Select **Revolve** in the *Modeling* toolbar as shown.

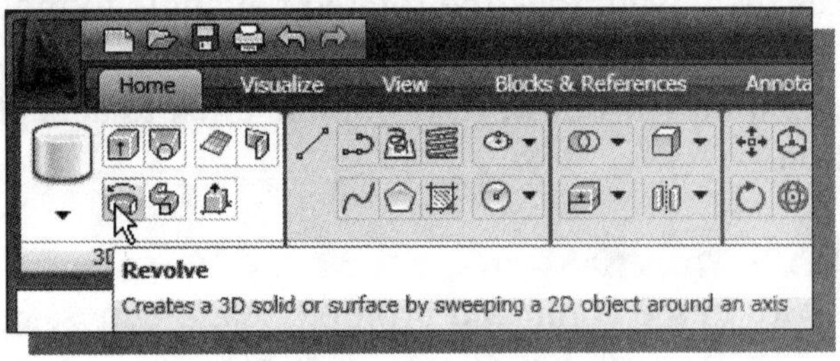

2. In the command prompt area, the message "*Select objects:*" is displayed. Select the 2D region by clicking on any of the displayed segments.

3. Inside the graphics window, right-mouse-click to accept the selection and proceed with the **Revolve** command.

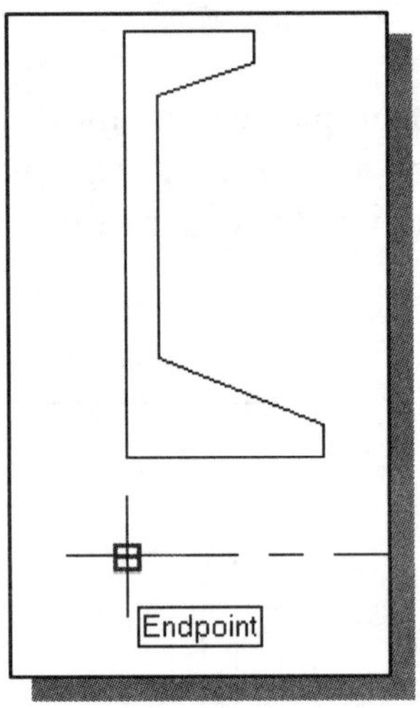

4. In the command prompt area, the message "*Define axis by [Object/X (axis)/Y (axis)}]:*" is displayed. Pick the **left endpoint of the centerline** as shown.

5. In the command prompt area, the message "*Specify endpoint of axis:*" is displayed. Pick the **right endpoint of the centerline**.

6. In the command prompt area, the message "*Specify angle of revolution <360>:*" is displayed. Enter: **360.0 [ENTER]**

- The revolved part is created as shown.

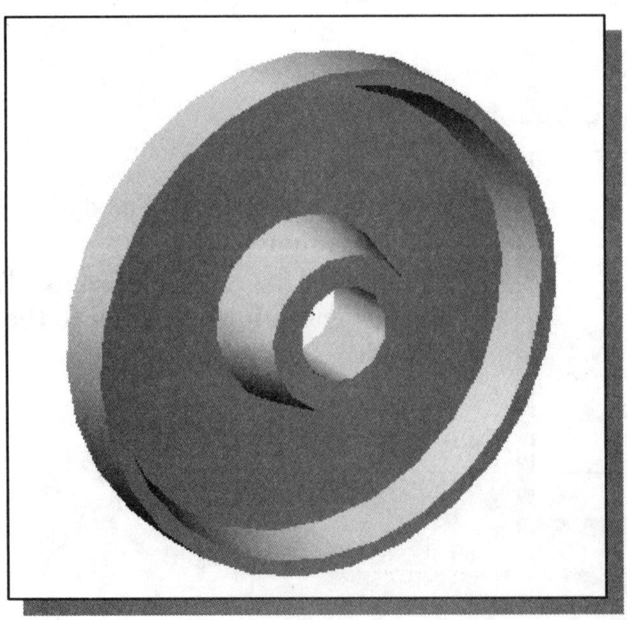

Mirroring Part

- In AutoCAD, we can mirror a 2D sketch or a 3D part about a line or a specified surface. We can define the line by selecting existing points or by picking locations on the screen. We can physically flip the part about a reference plane or create a new mirrored part.

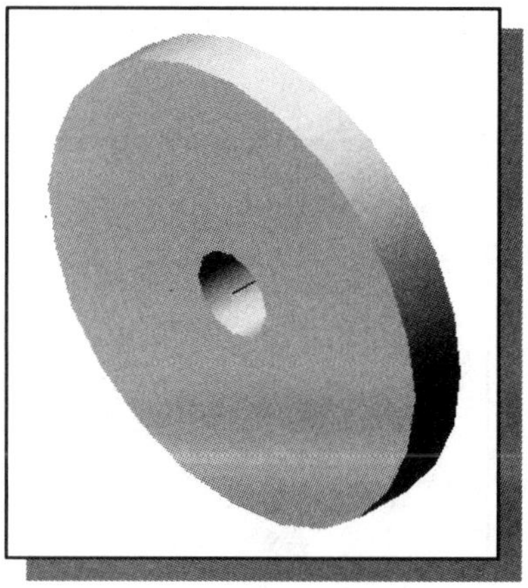

1. On your own, change the display to **SW Isometric View** and use the **Free Orbit** command to display the flat face of the solid model as shown.

2. In the *Modify* toolbar, select **[3D Mirror]**

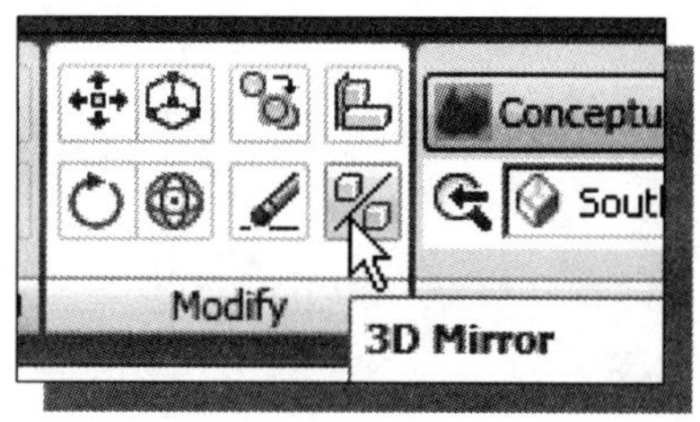

3. In the command prompt area, the message "*Select objects:*" is displayed. Select any edge of the 3D model.

4. Inside the graphics window, **right-mouse-click** to accept the selection.

5. In the command prompt area, the message "*Specify first point of mirror plane (3 points) or [Object/Last/Zaxis/View/XY/YZ/ZX/3points] <3points>:*" is displayed. Choose the YZ plane by entering: **YZ [ENTER]**

6. In the command prompt area, the message "*Select point on YZ plane <0,0,0>:*" is displayed. Pick the **left endpoint of the centerline**.

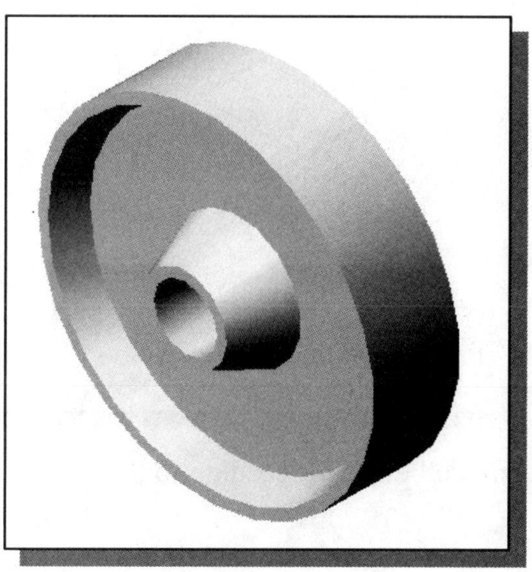

7. In the command prompt area, the message "*Delete source objects? [Yes/No] <N>:*" is displayed. Inside the graphics window, right-mouse-click to bring up the option menu and select **No** to create a new part.

Combining Parts

- We have created two separate parts with the **Mirror 3D** command. We will combine the two parts into a single part using the CSG *Boolean operations*.

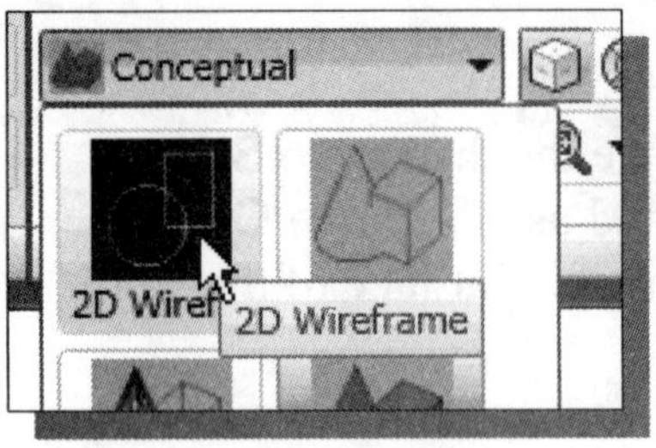

1. Select **2D Wireframe** by left-clicking once on the icon in the *Visual Styles* toolbar.

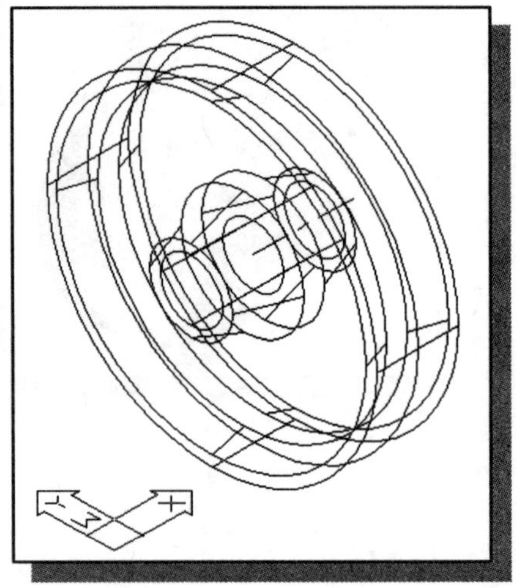

- Note the edges separating the two parts displayed on the screen.

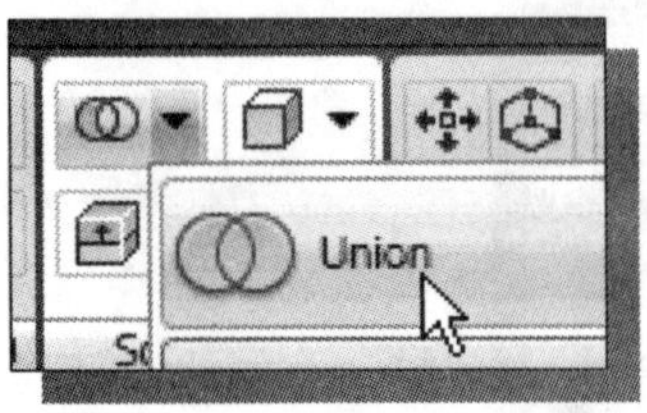

2. Pick **Union** in the *Modeling* toolbar as shown.

3. In the command prompt area, the message "*Select Objects:*" is displayed. Pick the two parts.

4. Inside the graphics window, right-mouse-click to accept the selection and proceed with the Union command to combine the two parts into a single part.

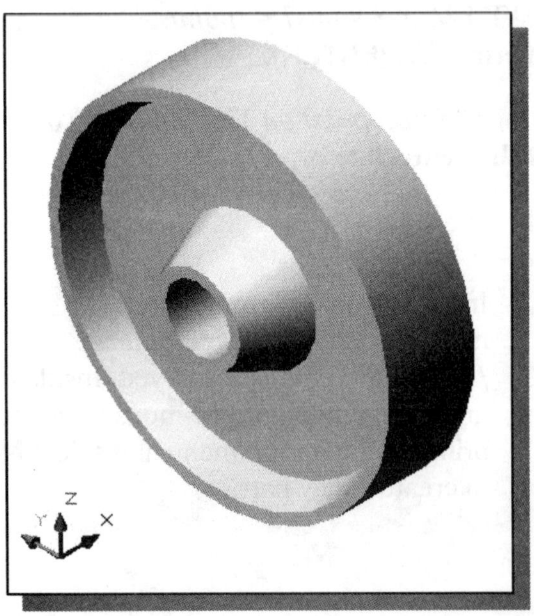

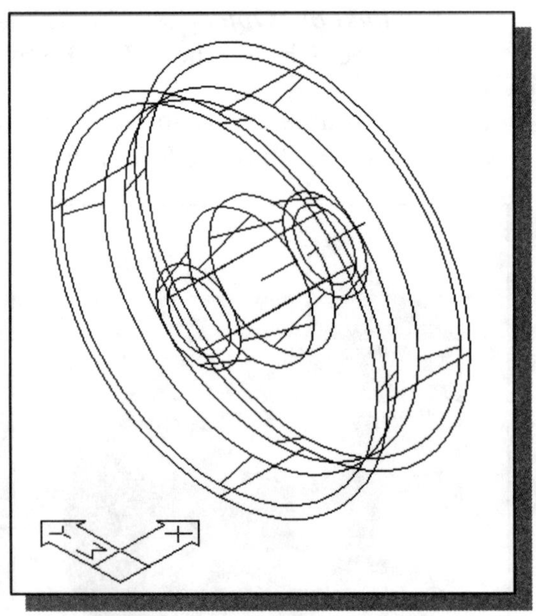

- Reset the display to **2D Wireframe** mode before proceeding to the next section.

3D Array

- In AutoCAD, existing 2D and/or 3D features can be easily duplicated. The **Array** command allows us to create both rectangular and polar arrays of features.

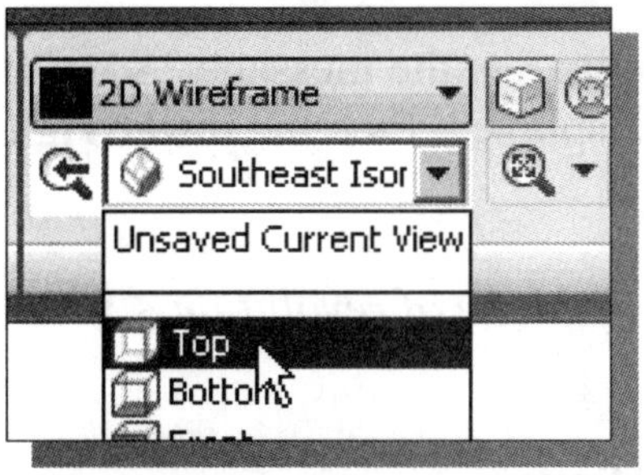

1. In the *View* toolbar, select the **Top View** option to reset the display.

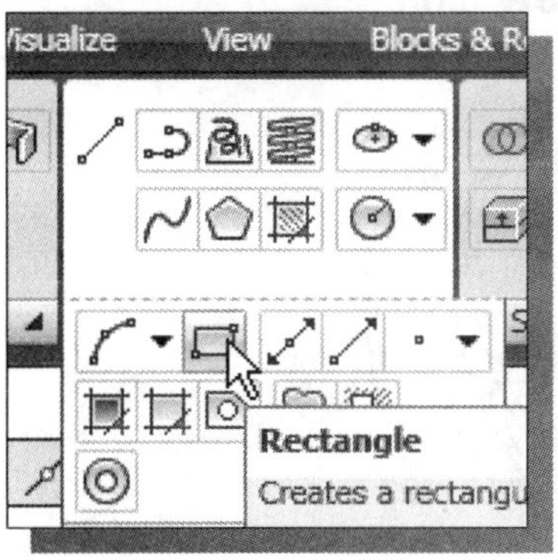

2. Select the **Rectangle** icon in the *Draw* toolbar.

3. On your own, create a rectangle that is **1.0″ × .25″** toward the right side of the solid model.

4. On your own, convert the rectangle into a ***region***.

   - The rectangle will be used to create a cylindrical solid model. The cylinder will be used to generate a polar array using the Array command.

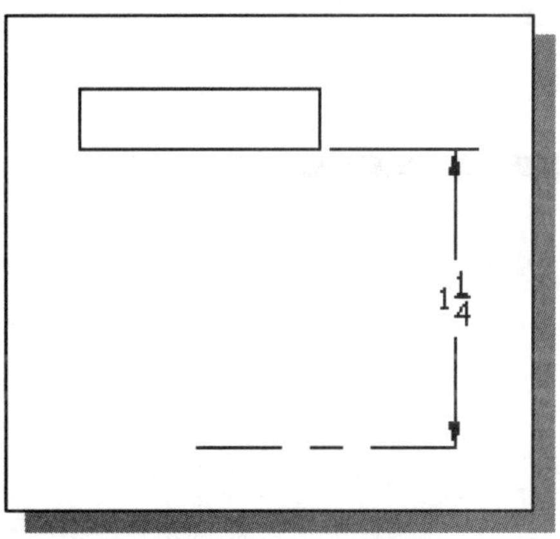

5. On your own, create a centerline that is **1¼″** below the rectangle with the **left endpoint aligned to the center of the rectangle** as shown.

   - The centerline will be used as the axis of rotation to create the *polar array*.

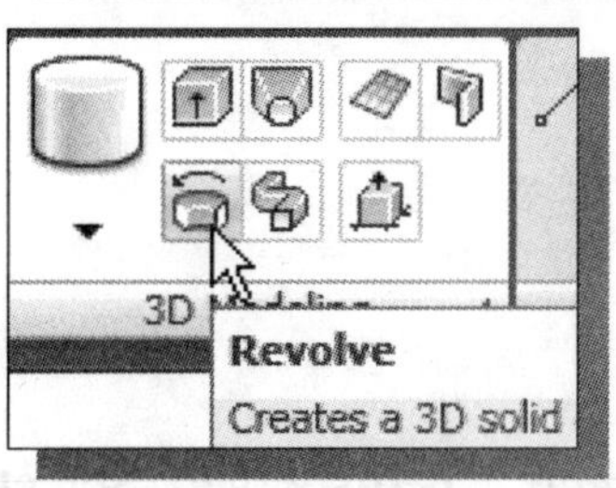

6. Select **Revolve** in the *Modeling* toolbar as shown.

7. In the command prompt area, the message "*Select objects:*" is displayed. Select the **rectangular region** by clicking on any of the displayed segments.

8. Inside the graphics window, **right-mouse-click** to accept the selection and proceed with the Revolve command.

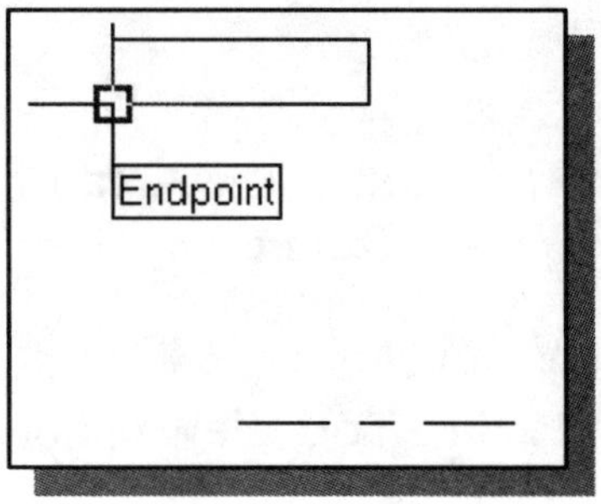

9. In the command prompt area, the message "*Define axis by [Object/X (axis)/Y (axis)}]:*" is displayed. Pick the **lower left corner** of the region as shown.

10. In the command prompt area, the message "*Specify endpoint of axis:*" is displayed. Pick the **lower right corner** of the region.

11. In the command prompt area, the message "*Specify angle of revolution <360>:*" is displayed. Enter: **360.0 [ENTER]**

12. In the *View* toolbar, click on the **SE Isometric View** icon.

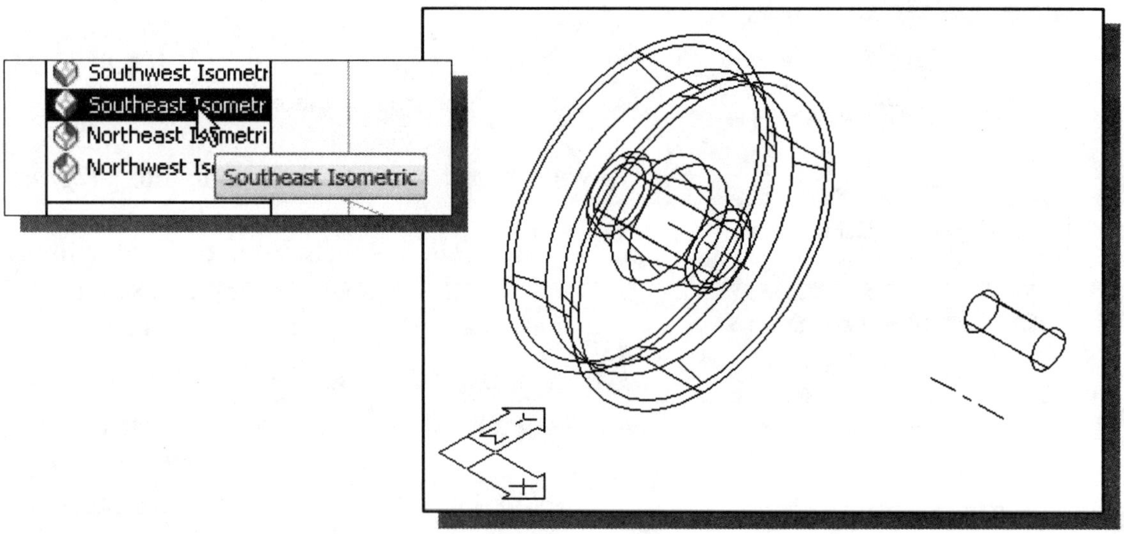

13. In the *Modify* toolbar, select **[3D Array]**.

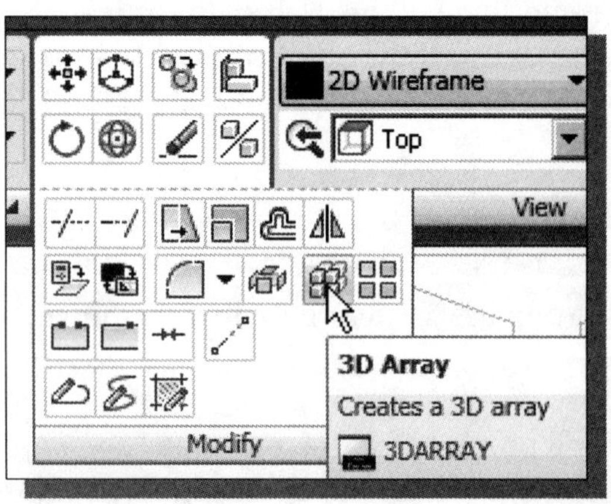

14. In the command prompt area, the message "*Select objects:*" is displayed. Select the **small cylinder** by clicking on any edge of the cylinder.

15. Inside the graphics window, **right-mouse-click** to accept the selection.

16. In the command prompt area, the message "*Enter the type of array [Rectangular/Polar] <R>:*" is displayed. Choose the *Polar* option by entering: **P [ENTER]**

17. In the command prompt area, the message "*Enter the number of items in the array:*" is displayed. We will create 6 items by entering: **6 [ENTER]**

18. In the command prompt area, the message "*Specify the angle to fill (+=ccw, -=cw) <360>:*" is displayed. Enter: **360 [ENTER]**

19. In the command prompt area, the message "*Rotate arrayed objects?[Yes/No] <Y>:*" is displayed. Enter: **N [ENTER]**

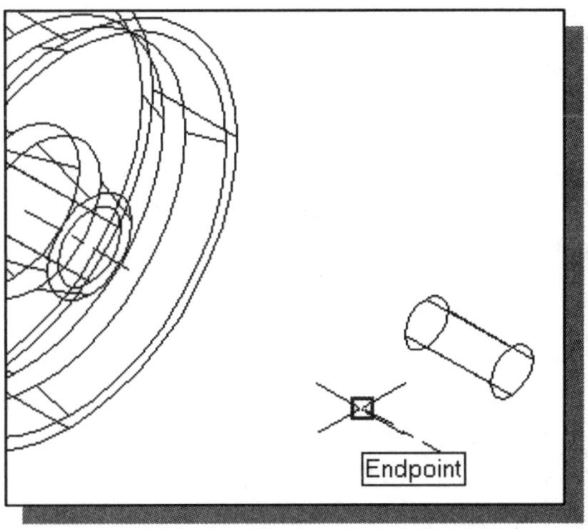

20. In the command prompt area, the message "*Specify center point of array:*" is displayed. Pick the **left endpoint of the centerline** as shown.

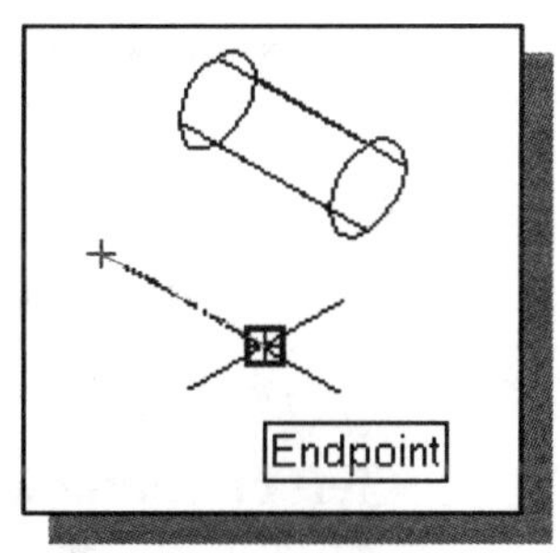

21. In the command prompt area, the message "*Specify second point on axis of rotation:*" is displayed. Pick the right endpoint of the centerline as shown.

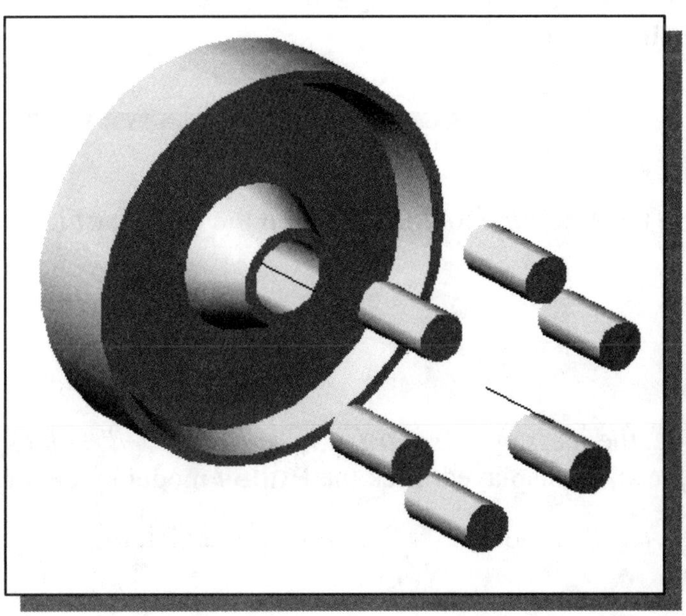

Position and Perform the Cut

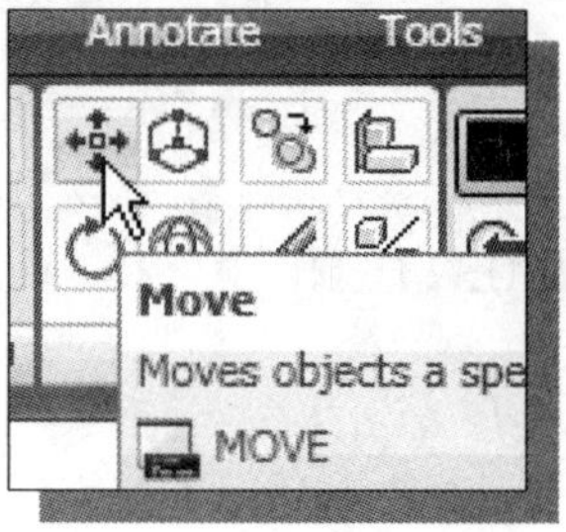

1. Select the **Move** icon in the *Modify* toolbar.

2. In the command prompt area, the message "*Select Objects:*" is displayed. Pick the **six cylinders** we just created.

3. Inside the graphics window, **right-mouse-click** to accept the selection.

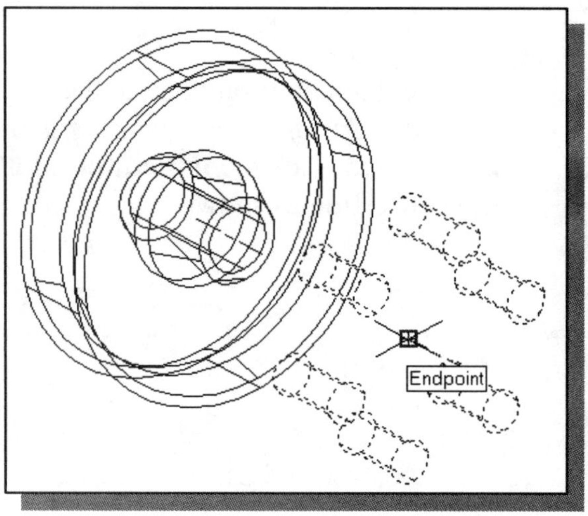

4. In the command prompt area, the message "*Specify base point or displacement:*" is displayed. Pick the **left endpoint the polar array centerline** as shown.

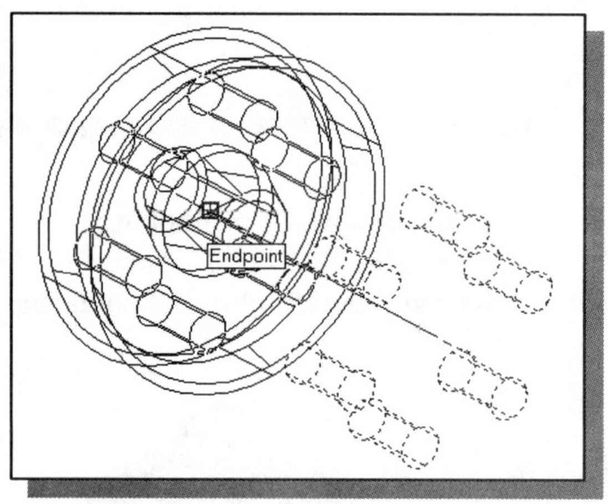

5. In the command prompt area, the message "*Specify base point or displacement:*" is displayed. Pick the **left endpoint of the centerline** of the *Pulley* as shown.

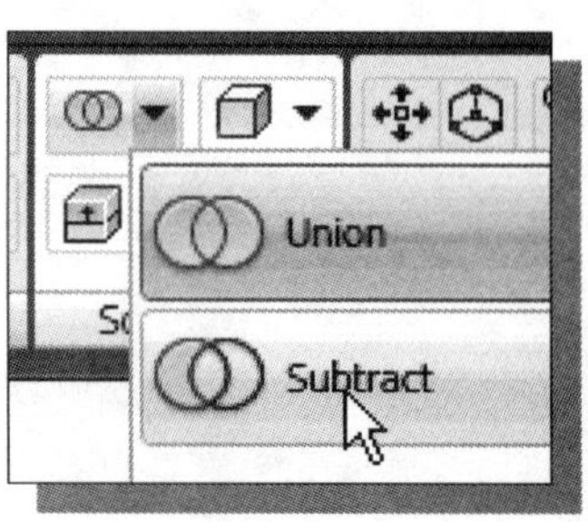

6. In the *Modeling* toolbar, click on the **Subtract** icon.

7. In the command prompt area, the message "*_subtract Select solids and regions to subtract from ... Select Objects:*" is displayed. Pick the **Pulley** model by clicking on one of the edges.

8. Inside the graphics window, **right-mouse-click** to accept the selection and proceed with the Subtract command.

9. In the command prompt area, the message "*Select solids and regions to subtract .. Select Objects:*" is displayed.

10. Pick the **six cylinder** blocks by clicking on their circular edges.

11. Inside the graphics window, right-mouse-click to accept the selection and proceed with the Subtract command.

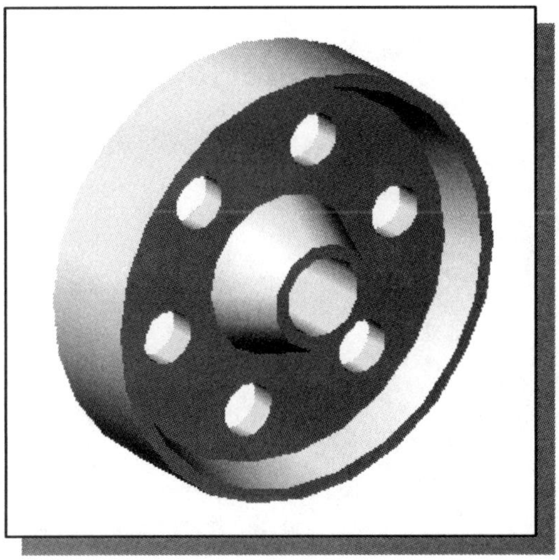

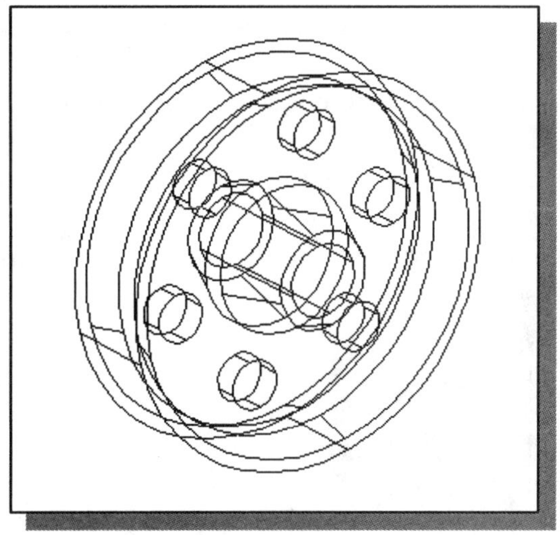

- On your own, create the 2D drawing from the 3D model as shown.

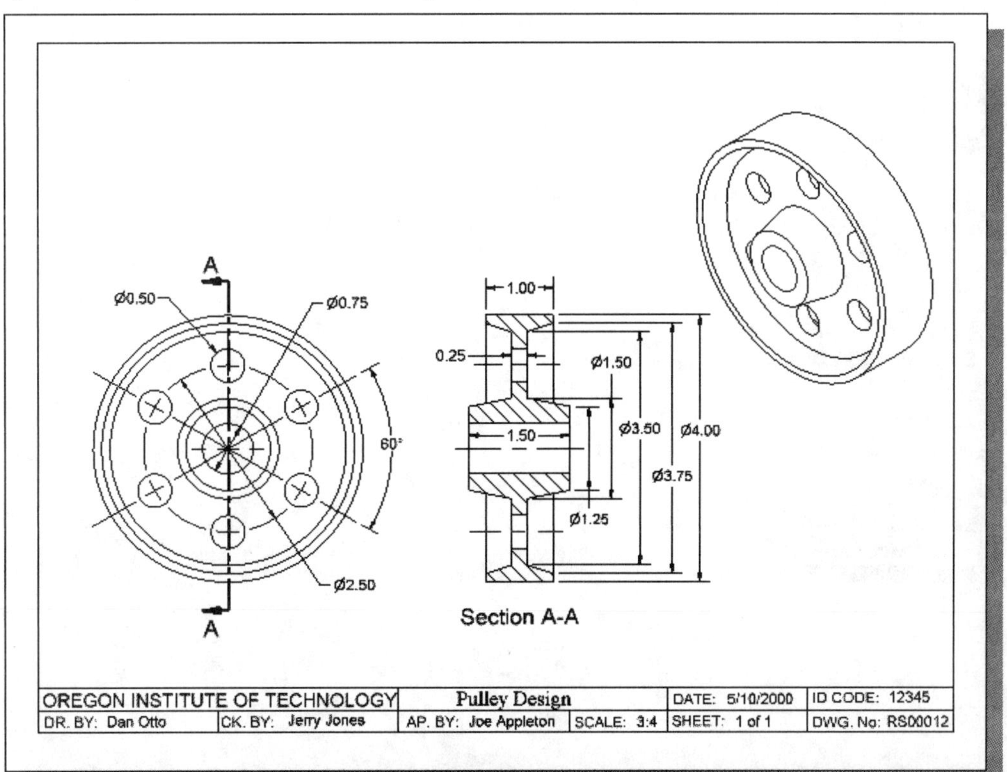

Questions:

1. List the different symmetrical features created in the *Pulley* design.
2. What are the advantages of using *regions*?
3. Describe the steps required in using the **Mirror Part** command.
4. Why is it important to identify symmetrical features in designs?
5. When and why should we use the **Array** option?
6. What is the difference between *Rectangular Array* and *Polar Array*?
7. When and why should you use the **Revolve** command in AutoCAD?
8. Identify and describe the following commands:

(a)

(b)

(c)

(d)

Exercises:

1.

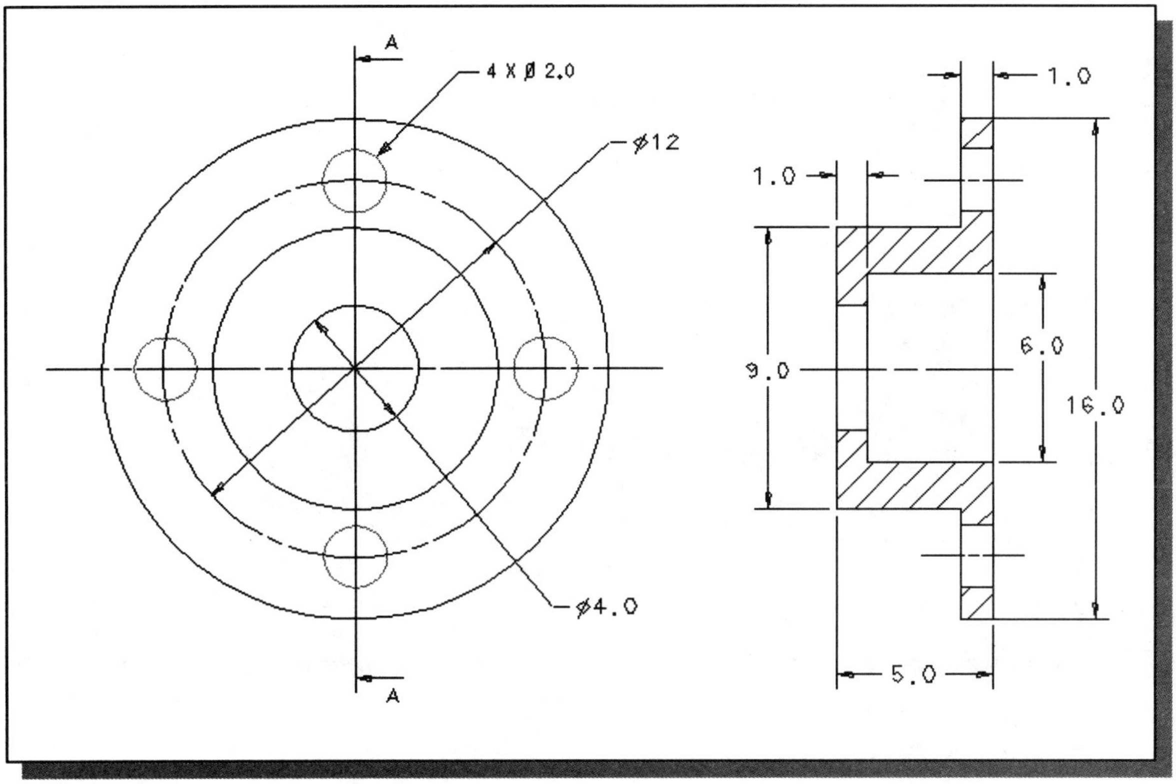

2. Plate thickness : 0.25 inch

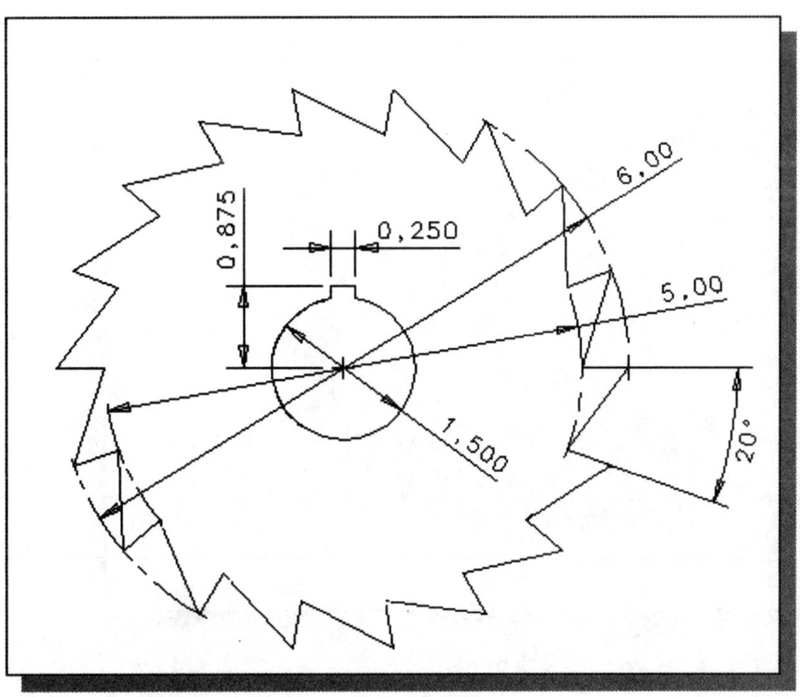

3.

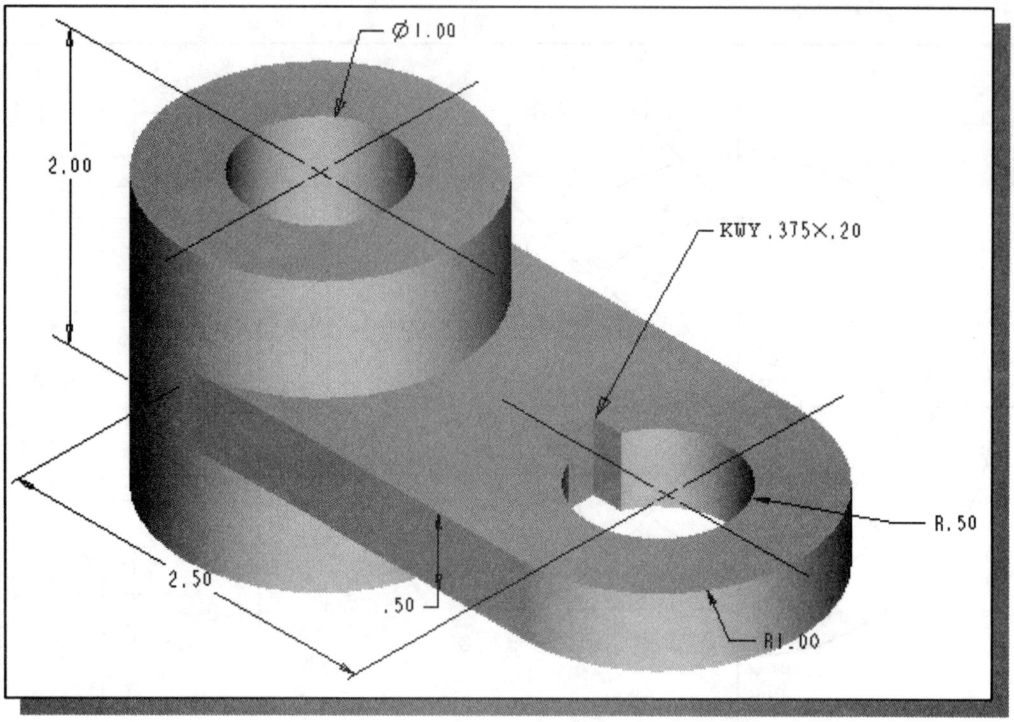
Ø1.00
2.00
KWY .375X.20
R.50
2.50
.50
R1.00

4.

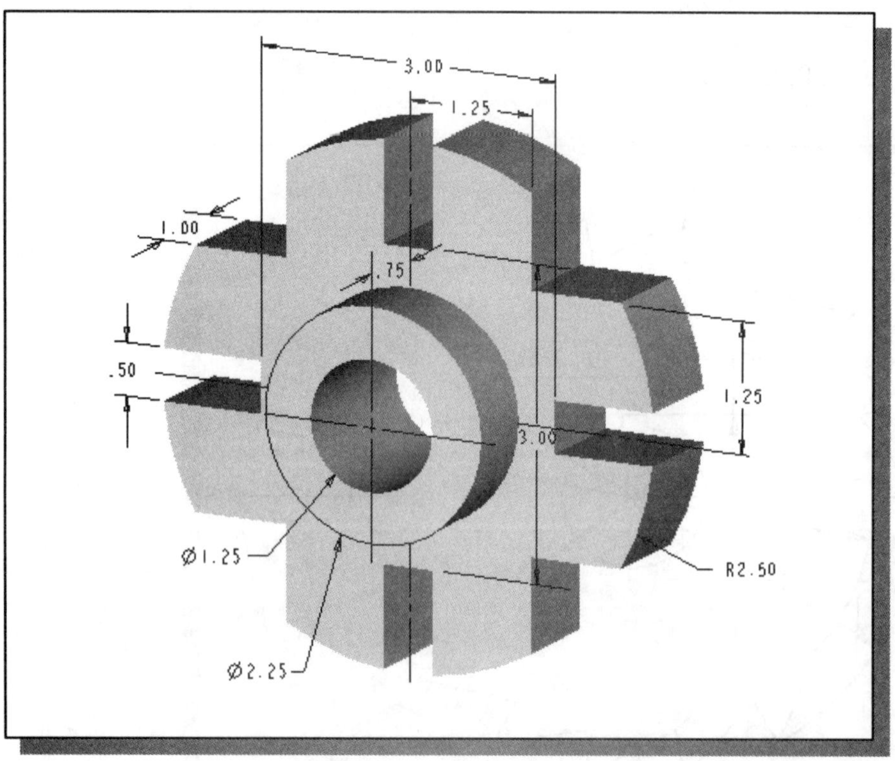
3.00
1.25
1.00
.75
.50
1.25
3.00
Ø1.25
R2.50
Ø2.25

5.

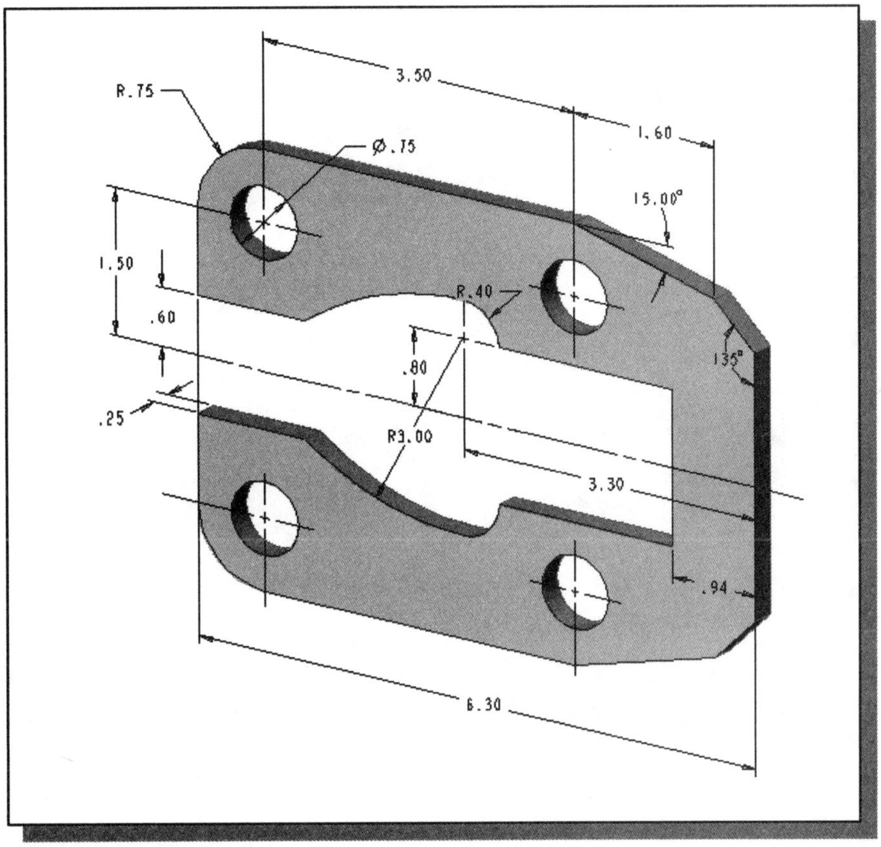

6. Plate thickness: 0.25

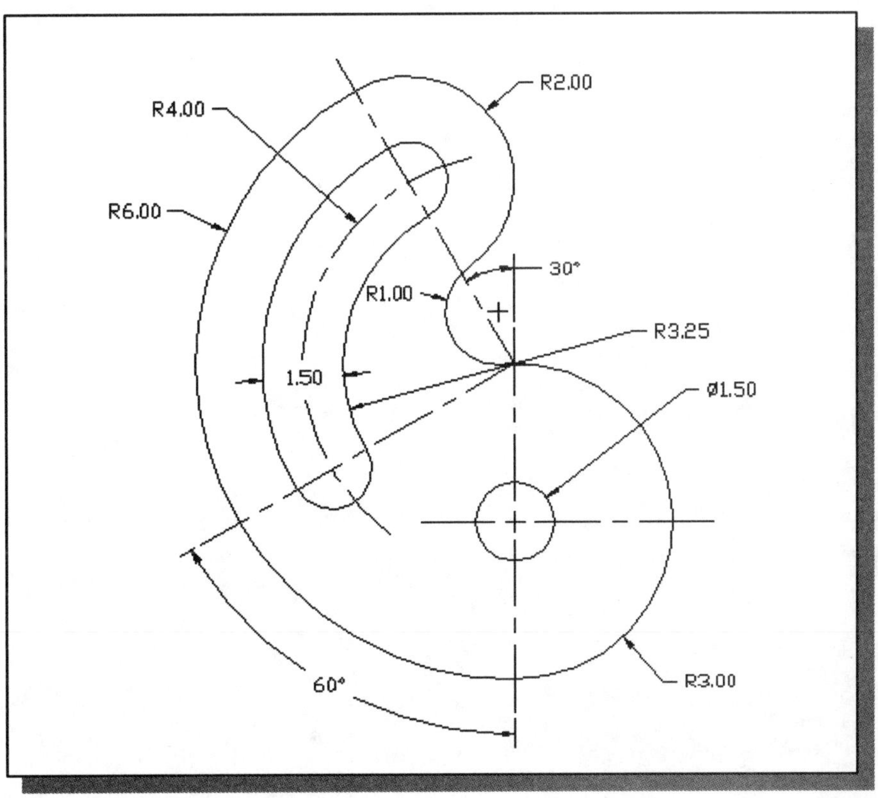

NOTES:

Chapter 10
Advanced Modeling Tools & Techniques

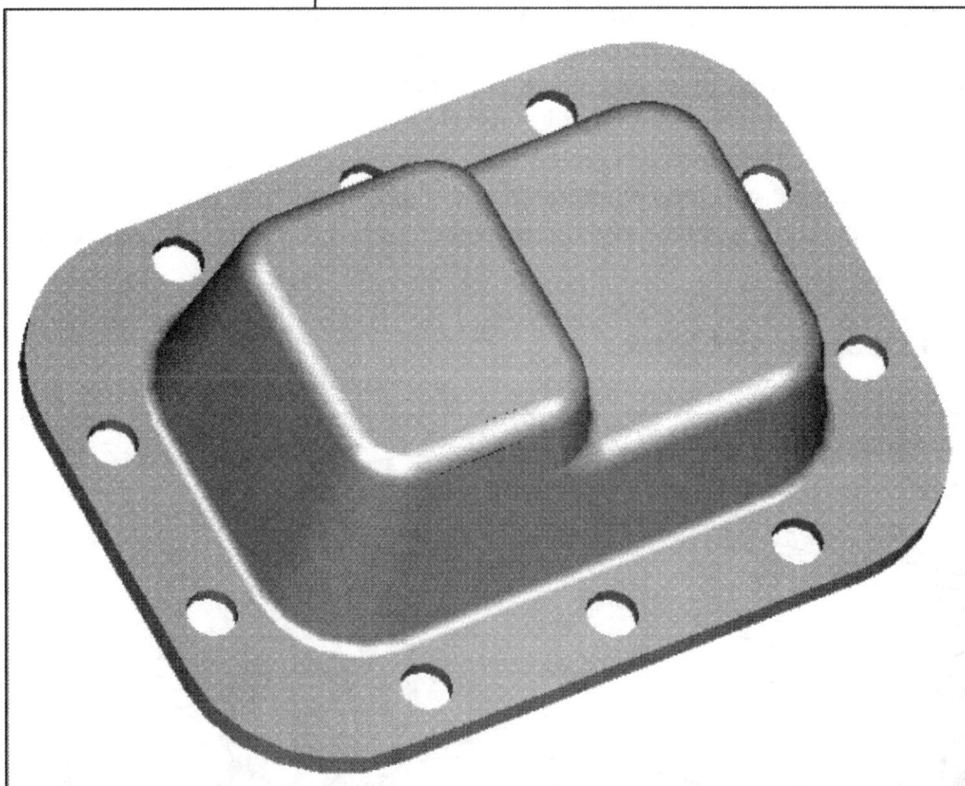

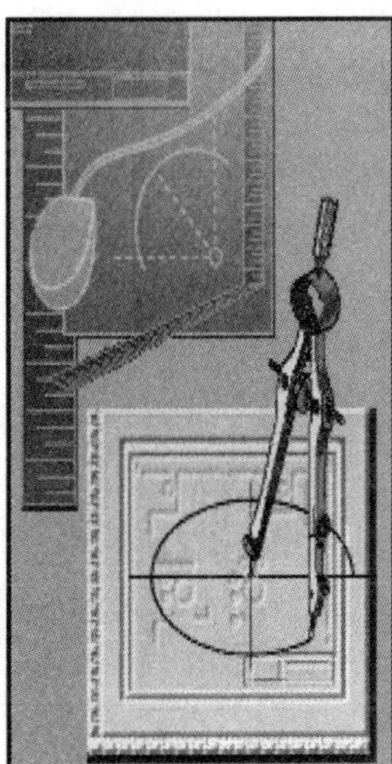

Learning Objectives

- Using More Advanced Solid Modeling Construction Tools
- Create Draft Angle Features
- Use the 3D Rounds & Fillets Command
- Create Rectangular Patterns
- Use the Shell Command
- Use the Copy Faces Command
- Using the DUCS option

Introduction

AutoCAD provides an assortment of three-dimensional construction tools to make the creation of solid models easier and more efficient. In this chapter, we will examine the procedures to create the *Draft Angle* feature, the *Shell* feature and also for creating three-dimensional *Rounds* and *Fillets* along edges of a solid model. These features are common characteristics of molded parts. The three-dimensional **Fillets** and the **Shell** commands will usually create complex three-dimensional spatial curves and surfaces. These commands are more sensitive to the associated geometric entities. For this reason, the *3D Fillets* and the *Shell* features are typically created last, after all associated solid features are created. In this chapter, we will also examine the new tools available in AutoCAD 2009 for referencing to existing surfaces and the enhancement of the Grip editing tools.

A Thin-walled Design: *Oil Sink*

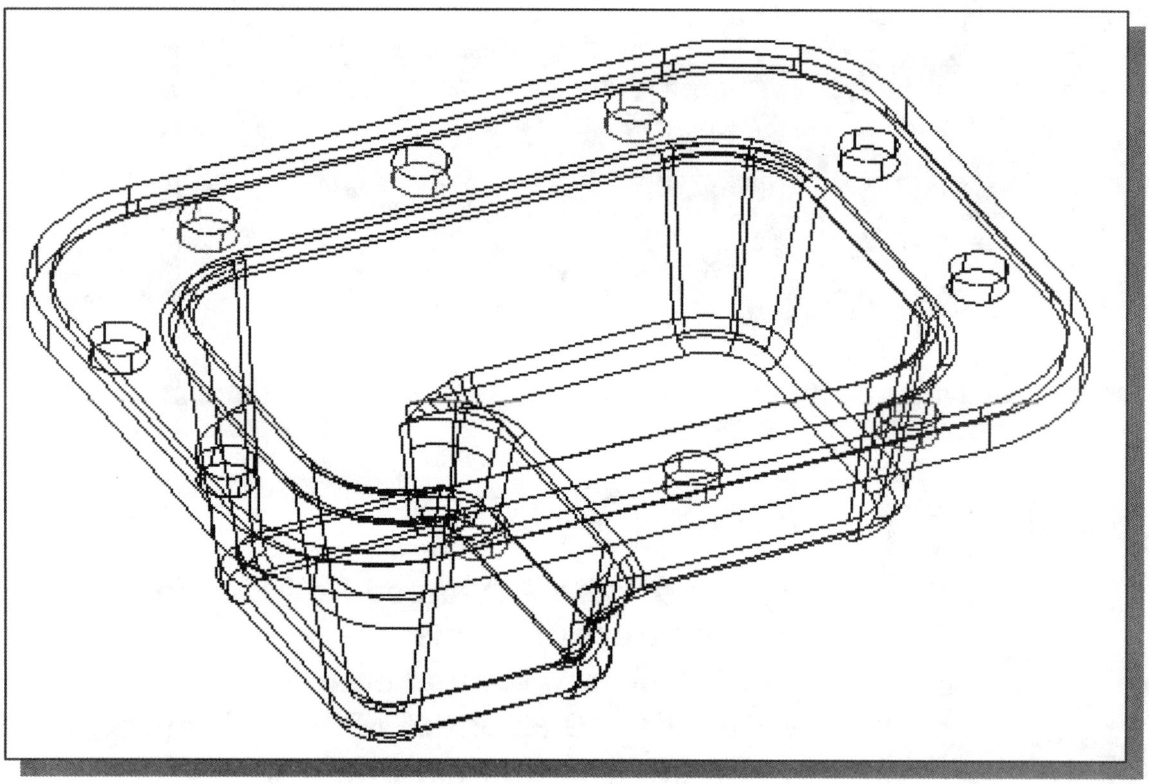

❖ Based on your knowledge of AutoCAD so far, how many features would you use to create the design? Which feature would you choose as the starting point in creating the model? What are the more difficult features involved in the design? What is your choice in arranging the order of the features? Take a few minutes to consider these questions and do preliminary planning by sketching on a piece of paper. You are also encouraged to create the design on your own prior to following through the tutorial.

Modeling Strategy

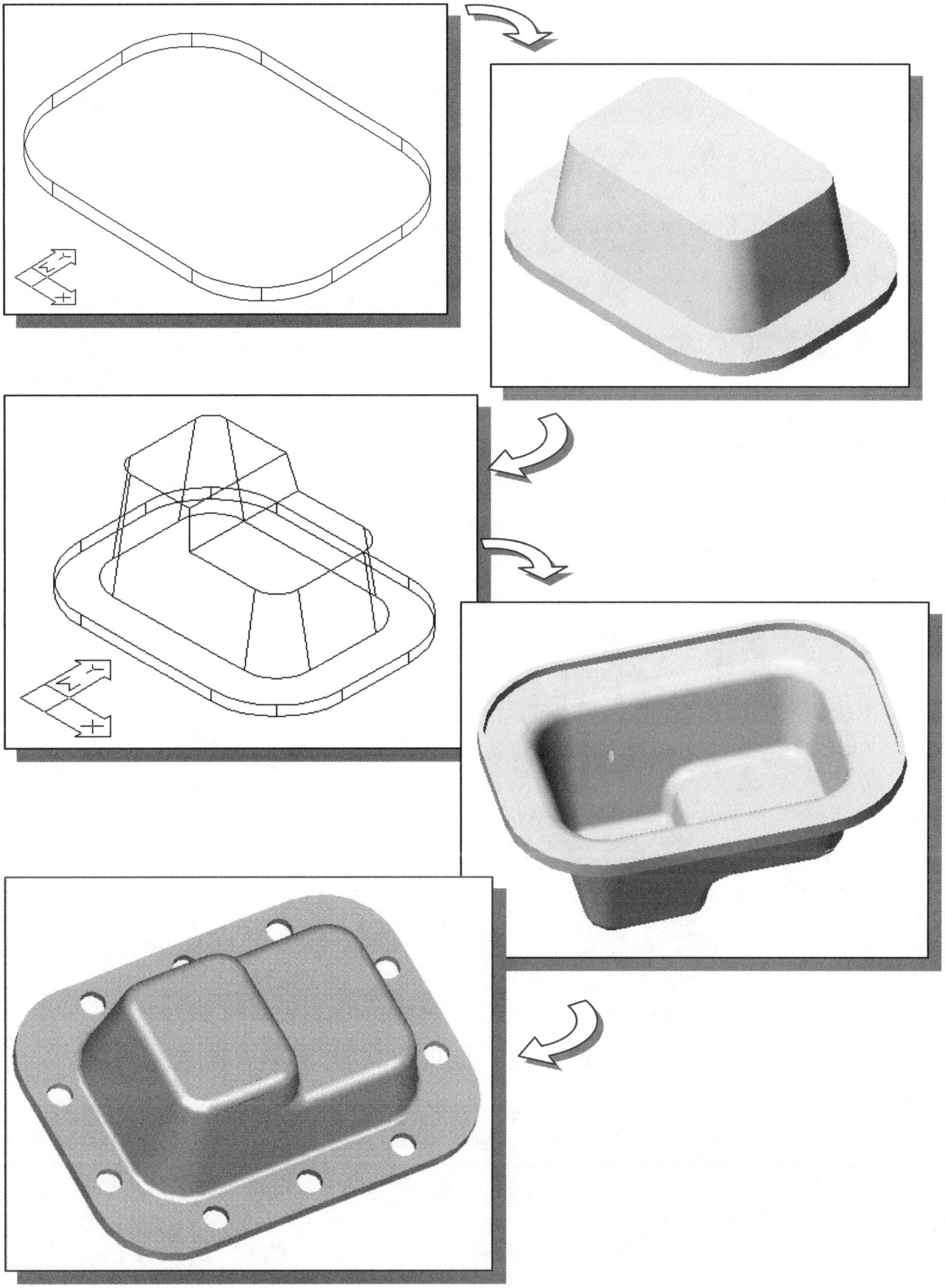

Starting Up AutoCAD® 2009

1. Select the **AutoCAD 2009** option on the *Program* menu or select the **AutoCAD 2009** icon on the *Desktop*.

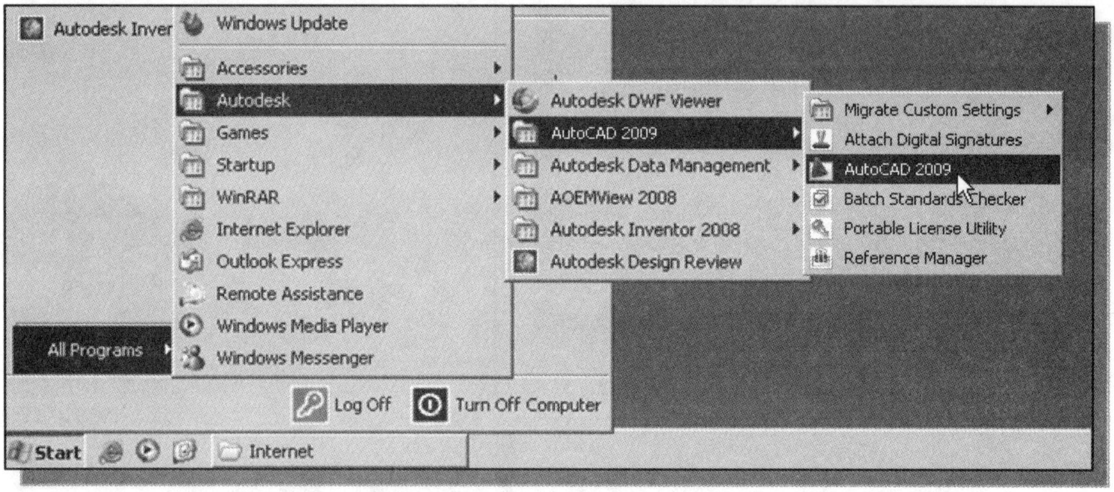

2. In the *Startup* window, select **Start from Scratch**, as shown in the figure below.

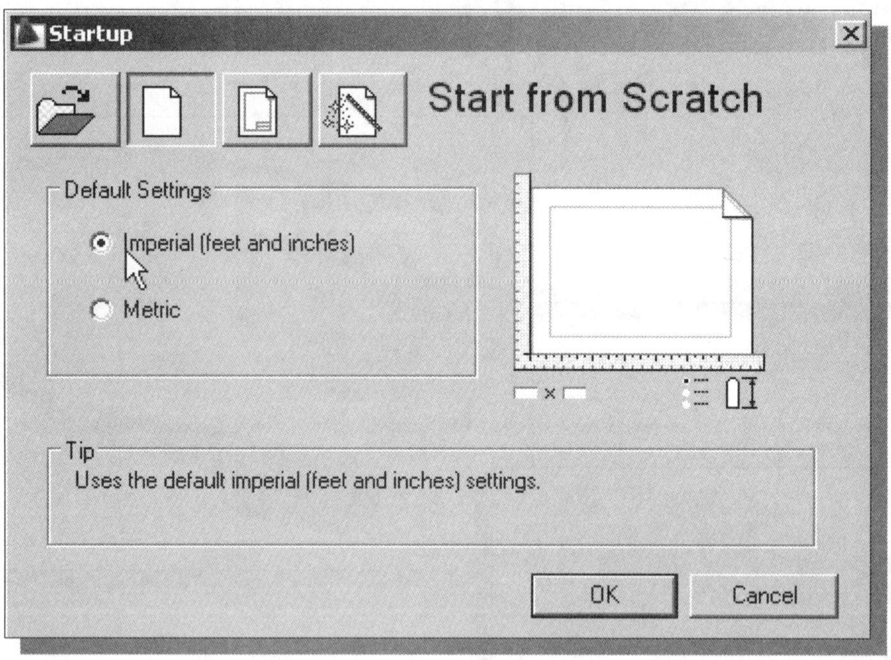

3. In the *Default Settings* section, pick **Imperial (feet and inches)** as the drawing units.

4. Pick **OK** in the *Startup* dialog box to accept the selected settings.

Layers Setup

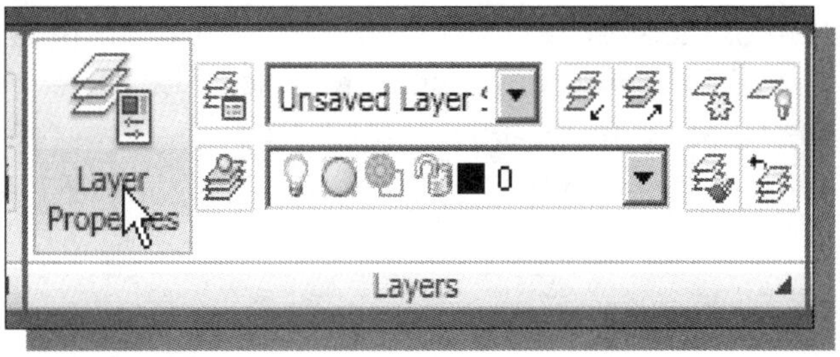

1. Click **Layer Properties Manager** in the *Object Properties* toolbar.

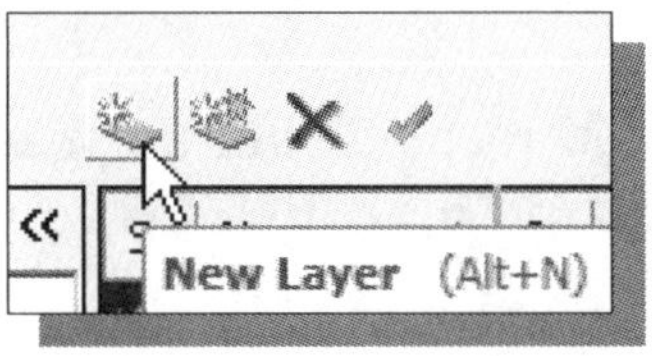

2. Click on the **New** button to create new layers.

3. Create **three new layers** with the following settings:

Layer	***Color***	***LineType***	***LineWeight***
Center_lines	**Red**	**Center**	**Default**
Dimensions	**Magenta**	**Continuous**	**Default**
Object_lines	**Cyan**	**Continuous**	**Default**

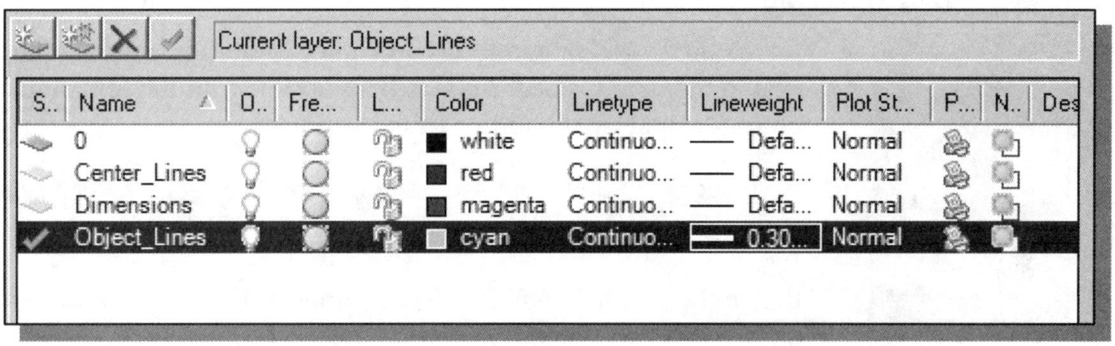

4. Highlight the layer ***Object_lines*** in the list of layers.

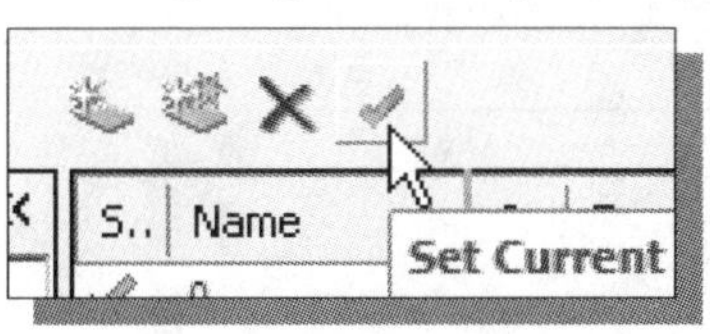

5. Click on the **Current** button to set layer ***Object_lines*** as the *Current Layer*.

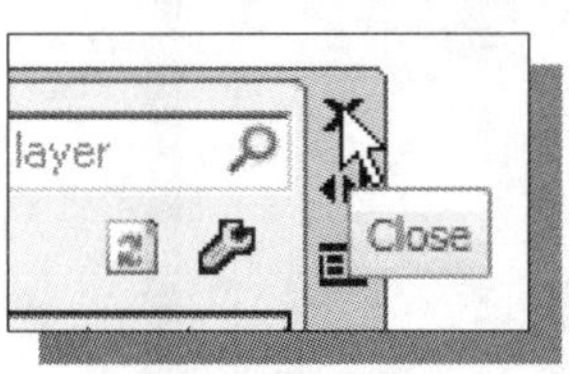

6. Click on the **Close** button to accept the settings and exit the *Layer Properties Manager* dialog box.

7. In the *Status Bar* area, reset the options and turn ***ON*** the *Polar, Object Snap, Object Snap Tracking, Dynamic Input* and *Line Weight* options.

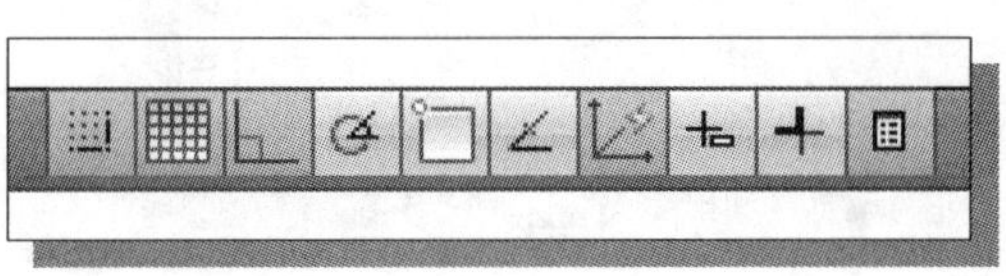

The First Extruded Feature

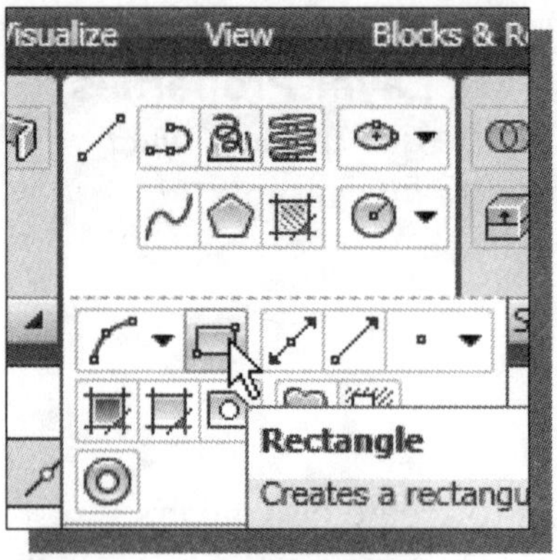

1. Select the **Rectangle** icon in the *Draw* toolbar. In the command prompt area, the message "*Specify first corner point or [Chamfer/Elevation/Fillet/Thickness/Width]:*" is displayed.

2. Place the first corner point of the rectangle near the lower left corner of the screen.

3. We will create a 16″ x 12″ rectangle for the main body of the sketch. Enter **@16,12 [ENTER]**.

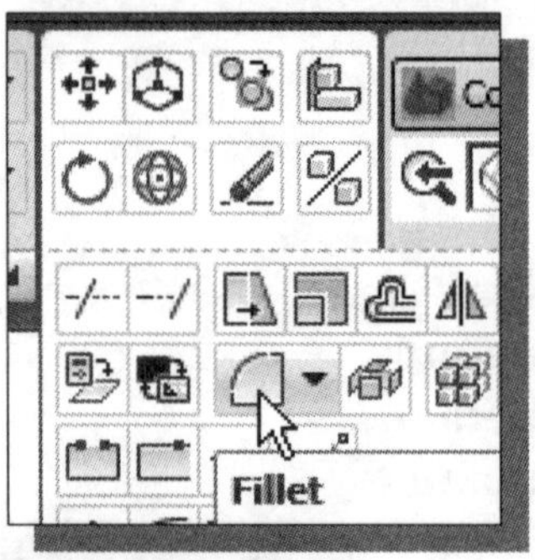

4. Select the **Fillet** command icon in the *Modify* toolbar. In the command prompt area, the message "*Select first object or [Polyline/Radius/Trim]:*" is displayed.

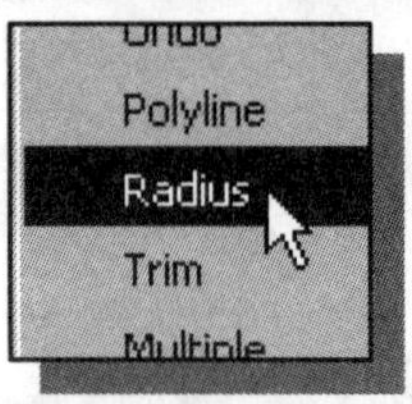

5. Inside the graphics window, right-mouse-click to activate the option menu and select the **Radius** option with the left-mouse-button to specify the radius of the fillet.

6. In the command prompt area, the message "*Specify fillet radius:*" is displayed. *Specify fillet radius:* **4.0 [ENTER]**

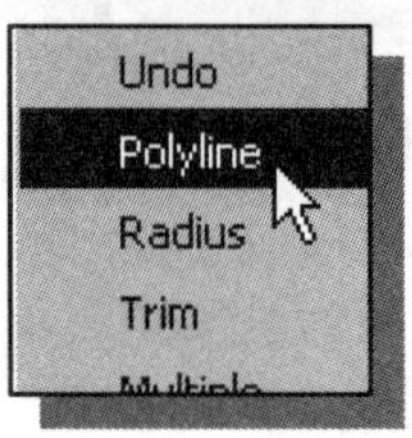

7. Inside the graphics window, right-mouse-click to activate the option menu and select the **Polyline** option.

8. Pick the rectangle to create **four rounded corners**.

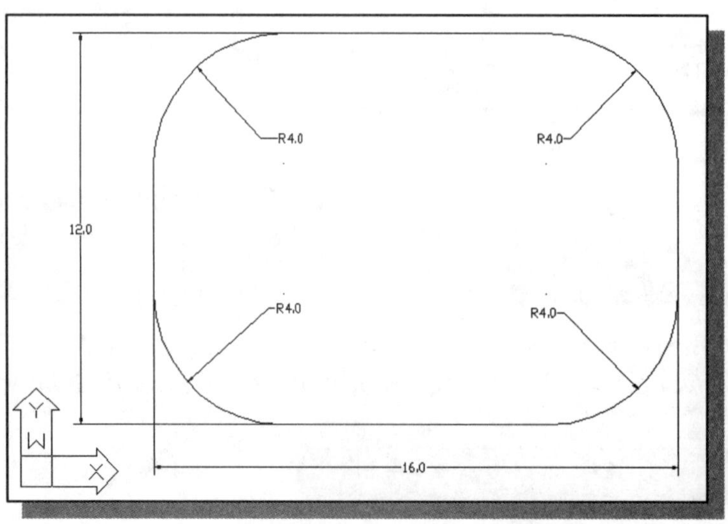

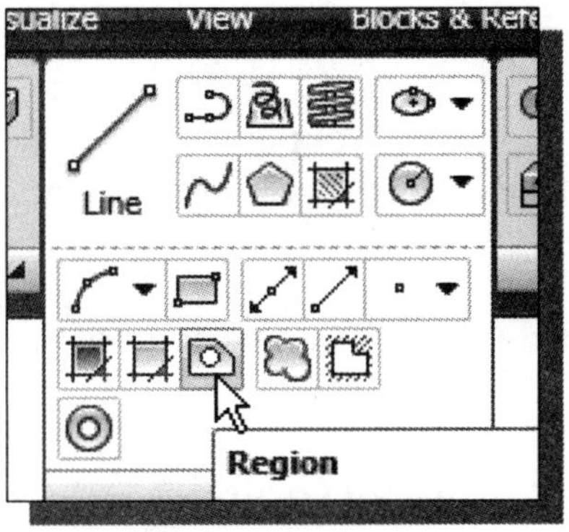

9. Select the **Region** command icon in the *Draw* toolbar.

10. In the command prompt area, the message "*Select objects:*" is displayed. Select the **polyline** by clicking on any segments of the 2D sketch.

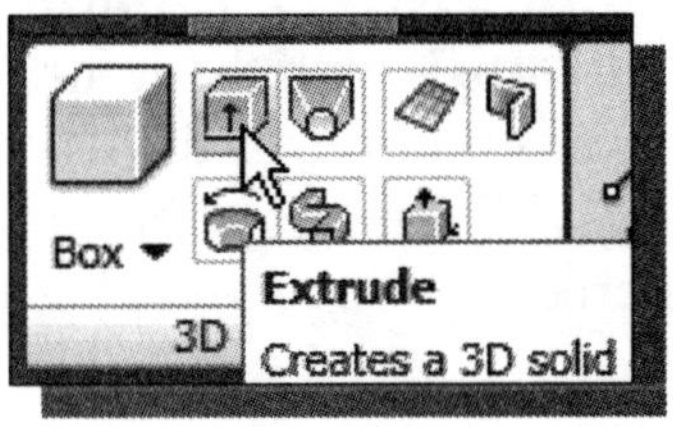

11. Select **Extrude** in the *Modeling* toolbar as shown.

12. In the command prompt area, the message "*Select objects:*" is displayed. Select the region by clicking on any of the displayed segments.

13. Inside the graphics window, **right-mouse-click** to accept the selection and proceed with the **Extrude** command.

14. In the command prompt area, the message "*Specify height of extrusion or [Direction/Path/Taper Angle]:*" is displayed. Enter: **0.625 [ENTER]**

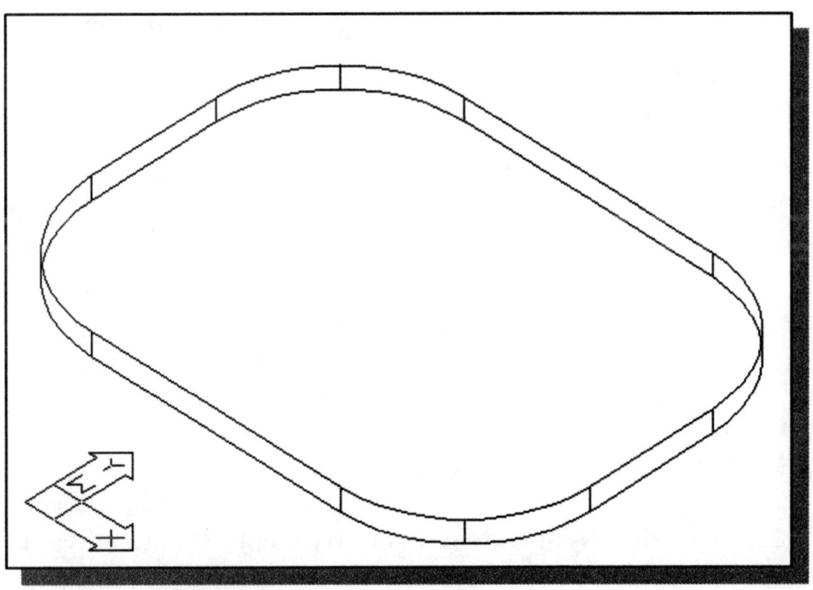

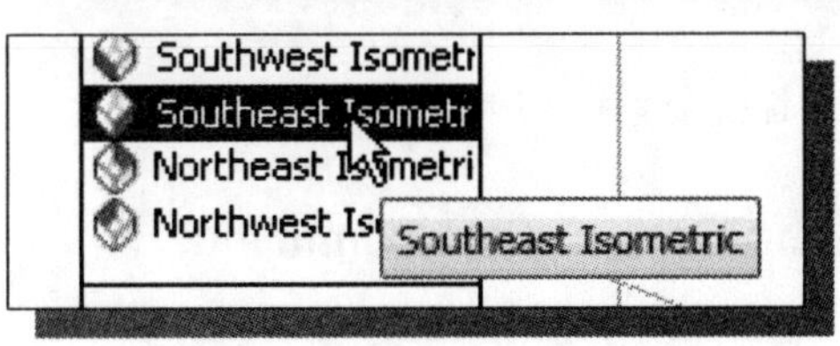

15. Set the display to **SE Isometric** as shown.

Create an Offset Geometry from an Extracted Surface

- In AutoCAD, several options are available to create geometry from existing solid features. We will use the Copy Faces command to assist constructing geometry from the existing surfaces.

1. Move the cursor to the *Standard* toolbar area and right-click on any icon of the *Standard* toolbar to display the option list.

2. Select **[Toolbar] → [AutoCAD] → [Solids Editing]**, with the left-mouse-button, to display the *Solid Editing* toolbar on the screen.

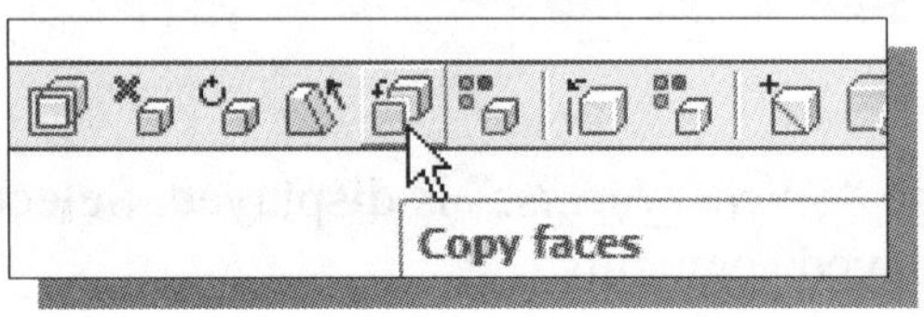

3. Click on the **Copy Faces** icon to activate the command.

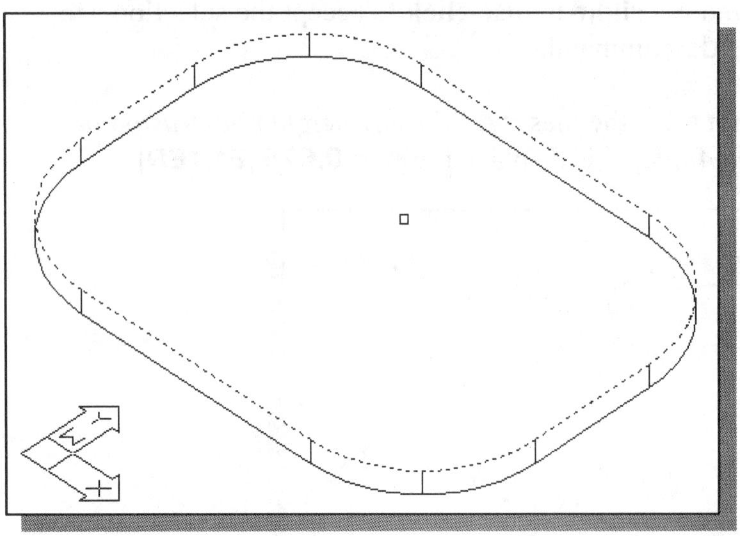

4. In the command prompt area, the message "*Select faces or [Undo/ Remove/ All]:*" is displayed. Pick the **upper surface** by clicking on the inside of the surface as shown.

5. Inside the graphics window, **right-mouse-click** to bring up the option menu and select **Enter** to accept the selection.

6. In the command prompt area, the message "*Specify a base point or displacement:*" is displayed. Enter: **20,0 [ENTER]**

7. Inside the graphics window, **right-mouse-click** to accept the entered values.

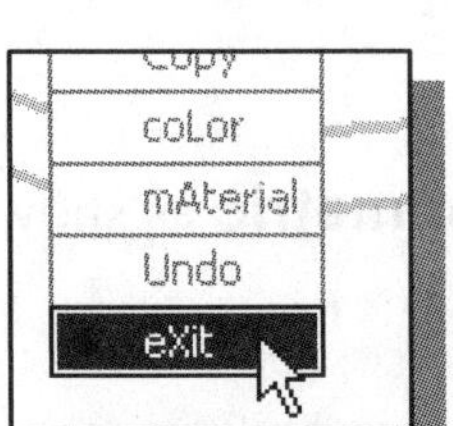

8. In the option menu and select **Exit**.

9. Select **Exit** again to end the Copy Faces command.

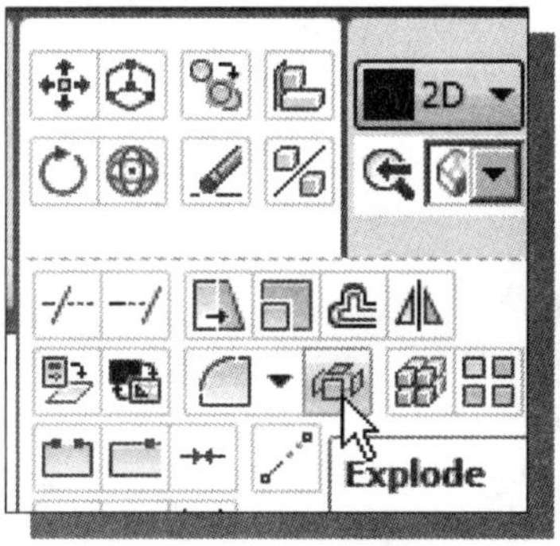

10. Select the **Explode** command icon in the *Modify* toolbar. In the command prompt area, the message "*Select objects:*" is displayed.

11. Pick the *surface* we just created.

12. Inside the graphics window, **right-mouse-click** to end the **Explode** command.

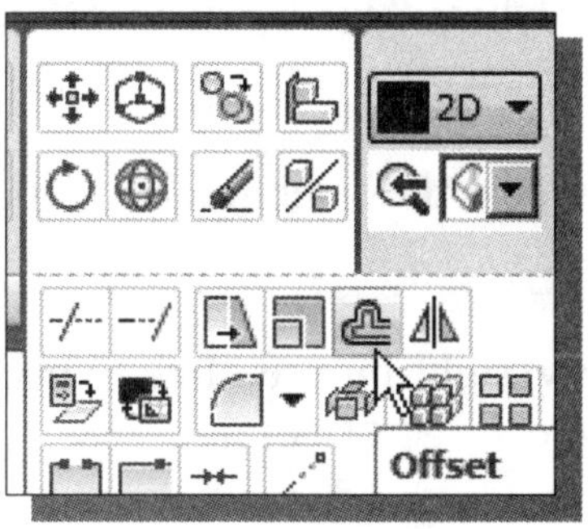

13. Select the **Offset** command icon in the *Modify* toolbar. In the command prompt area, the message "*Specify offset distance or [Through]:*" is displayed.
Specify offset distance or [Through]: **2.0 [ENTER]**

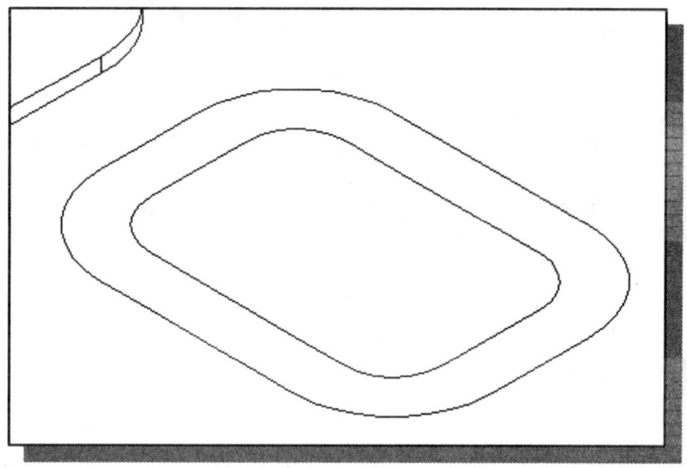

14. On your own, create a set of entities on the **inside** of the exploded surface as shown.

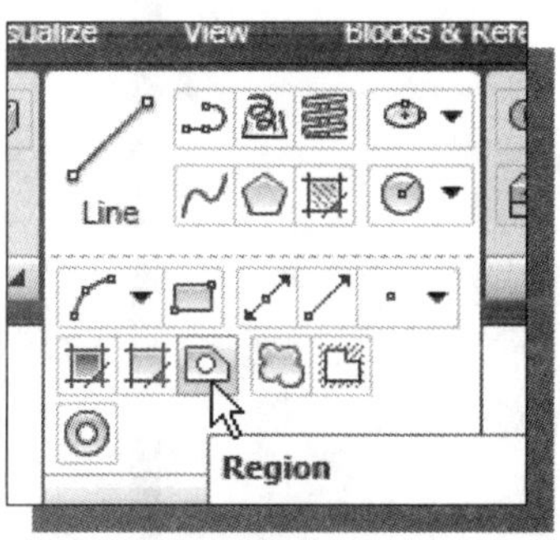

15. Select the **Region** command icon in the *Draw* toolbar.

16. In the command prompt area, the message "*Select objects:*" is displayed. Select the **entities** we just created with the Offset command (the objects inside of the *copy*).

17. Inside the graphics window, **right-mouse-click** to accept the selection and create a region.

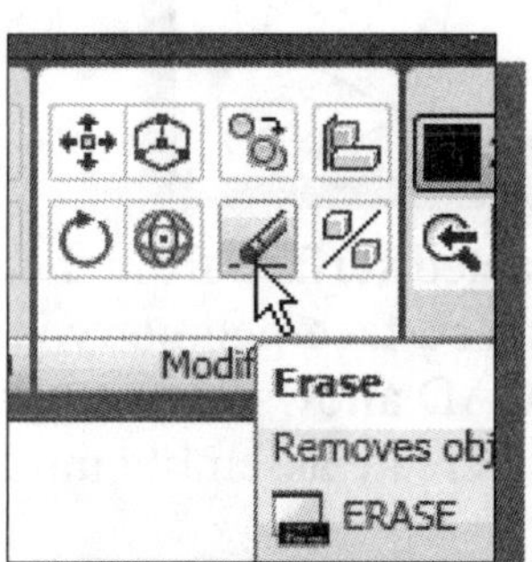

18. Select the **Erase** command icon in the *Modify* toolbar.

19. In the command prompt area, the message "*Select objects:*" is displayed. Select the **outer loop entities** that were created with the Copy Faces command.

20. Inside the graphics window, **right-mouse-click** to accept the selection and end the Erase command.

Extrude with Draft Angle

1. Select **Extrude** in the *Modeling* toolbar as shown.

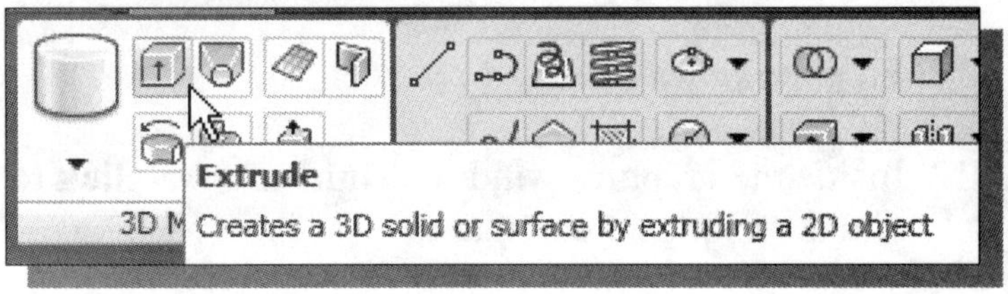

2. In the command prompt area, the message "*Select objects:*" is displayed. Select the 2D region by clicking on any of the displayed segments.

3. Inside the graphics window, right-mouse-click to accept the selection and proceed with the **Extrude** command.

4. Inside the graphics window, right-mouse-click to bring up the option menu and select **Taper Angle**.

5. In the command prompt area, the message "*Specify angle of taper for extrusion <0>:*" is displayed. Enter: **10.0 [ENTER]**

6. In the command prompt area, the message "*Specify height of extrusion or [Direction/Path/Taper Angle]:*" is displayed. Enter: **4.0 [ENTER]**

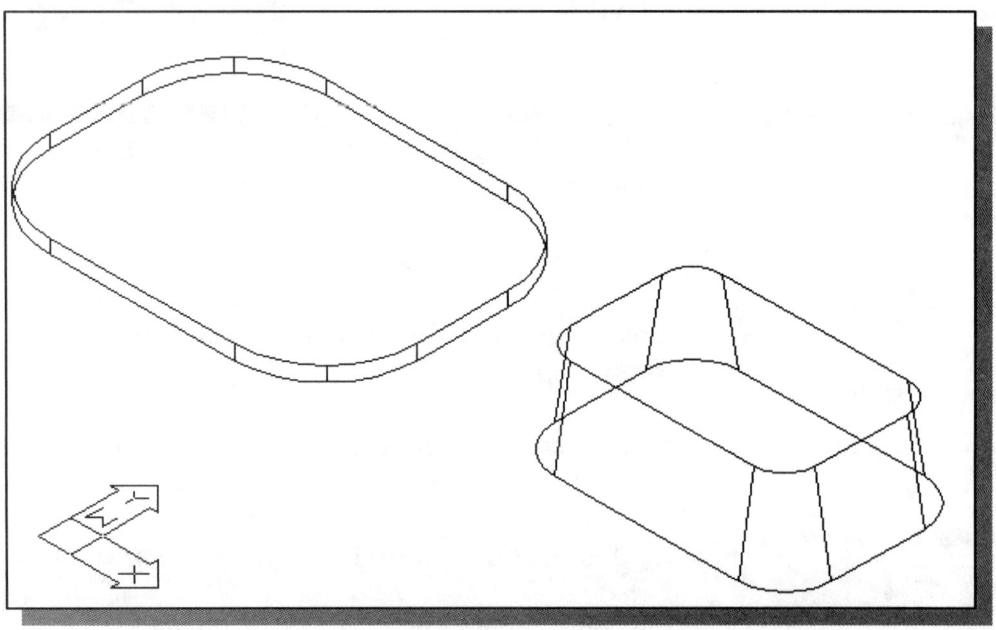

- Note that the second part is created by extruding an extracted surface from the first solid model. The ability to extract and re-use existing surface-geometry is an important aspect of solid modeling. Also note that AutoCAD allows us to create multiple parts in a single drawing file, which allows us to create assembly models under the same deign environment.

Aligning the Parts

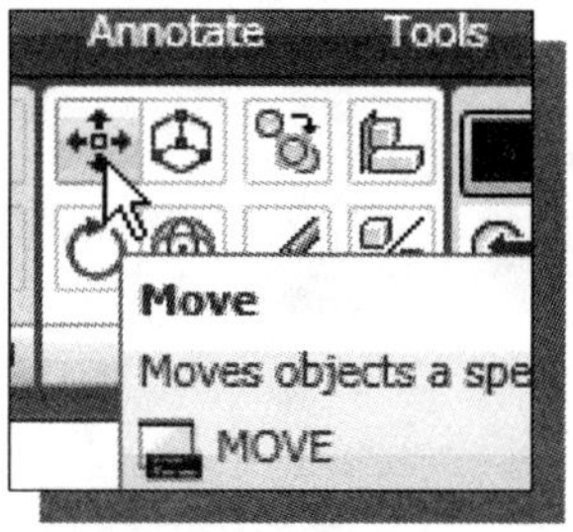

1. Select the **Move** icon in the *Draw* toolbar.

2. In the command prompt area, the message "*Select Objects:*" is displayed. Pick the *second part* we just created.

3. Inside the graphics window, right-mouse-click to accept the selection.

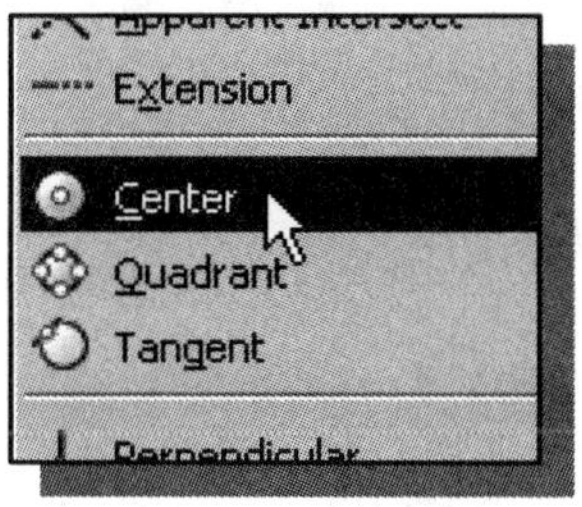

4. Inside the graphics window, hold down the [**SHIFT**] key and **right-mouse-click** once to bring up the *Object Snap* shortcut menu.

5. Select the **Center** option in popup window.

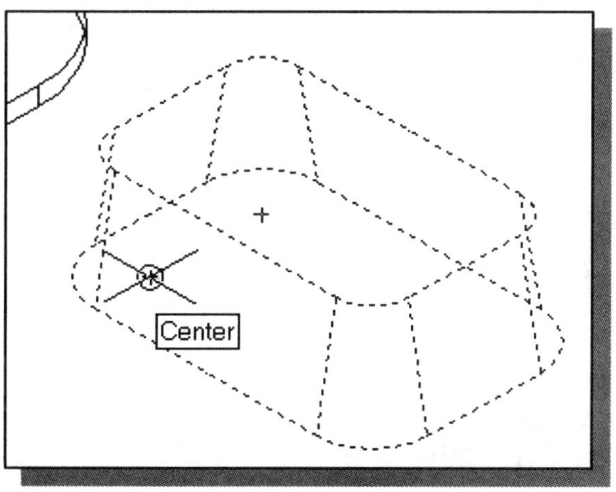

6. Pick the center of the bottom left arc as shown in the figure.

7. Inside the graphics window, hold down the [**SHIFT**] key and **right-mouse-click** once to bring up the *Object Snap* shortcut menu.

8. Select the **Center** option in popup window.

9. Pick the corresponding center point on the **top surface** of the solid model as shown.

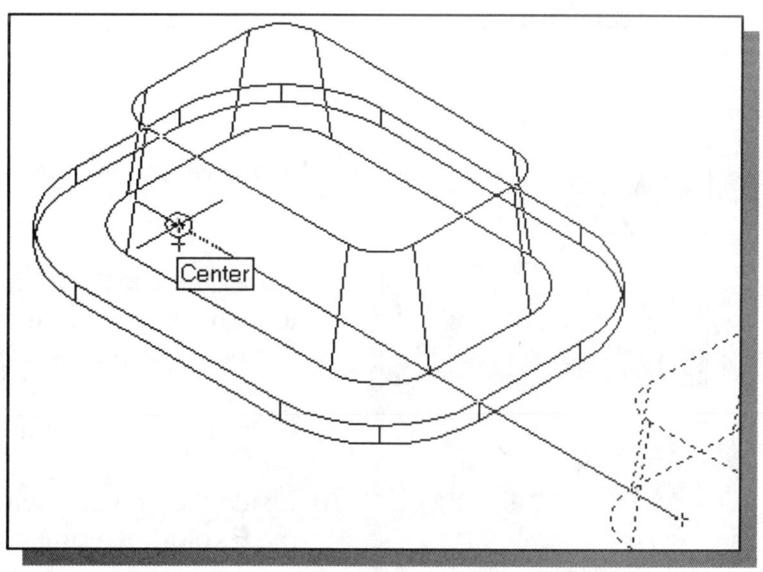

Create another Extracted Surface

1. Click on the **Copy Faces** icon to activate the command.

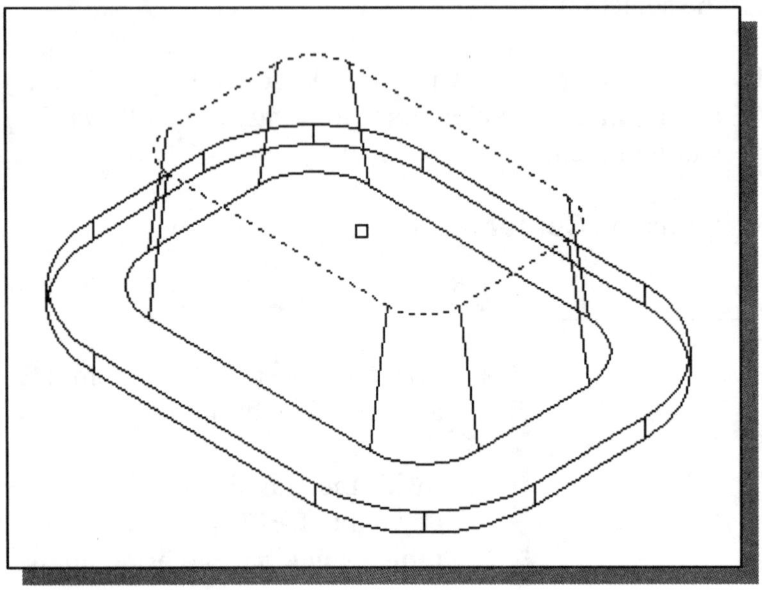

2. In the command prompt area, the message "*Select faces or [Undo/ Remove/ All]:*" is displayed. Pick the top surface of the tapered part by clicking on the inside of the surface as shown.

3. Inside the graphics window, right-mouse-click to bring up the option menu and select **Enter** to accept the selection.

4. In the command prompt area, the message "*Specify a base point or displacement:*" is displayed. Enter: **20,0 [ENTER]**

5. Inside the graphics window, right-mouse-click to accept the entered values.

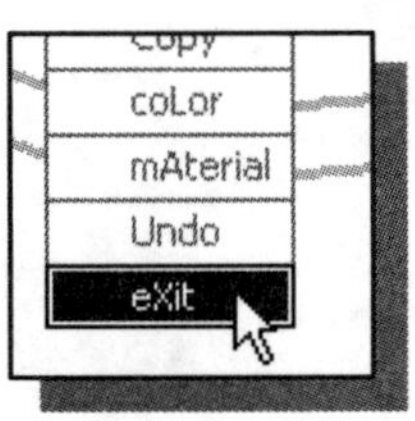

6. Select **eXit** in the option menu.

7. Select **eXit** in the option menu again to end the Copy Faces command.

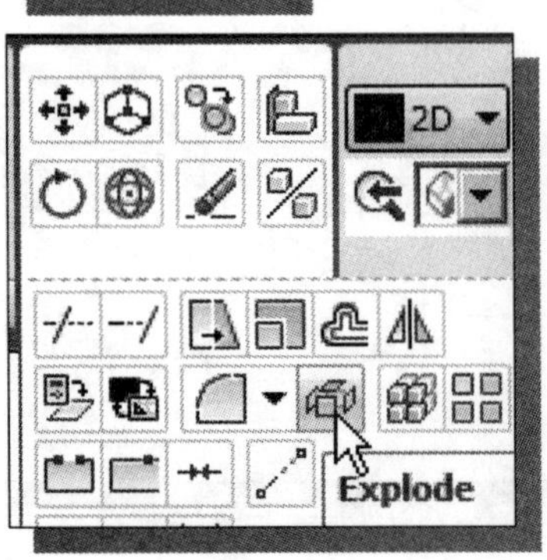

8. Select the **Explode** command icon in the *Modify* toolbar. In the command prompt area, the message "*Select objects:*" is displayed.

9. Pick the *surface* we just created.

10. Inside the graphics window, right-mouse-click to end the Explode command.

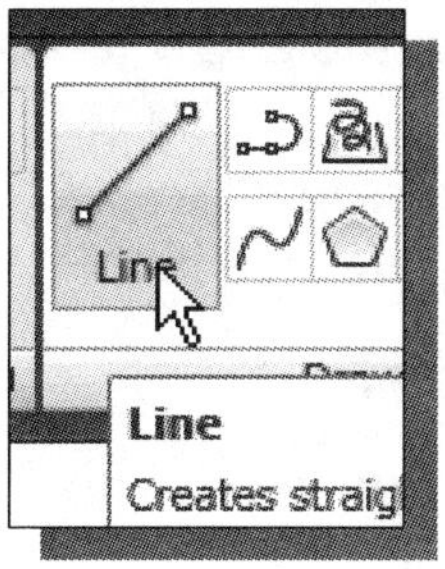

11. Select the **Line** command icon in the *Draw* toolbar.

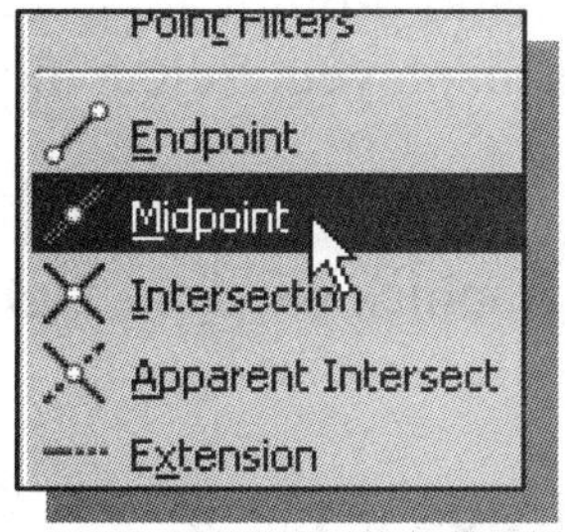

12. Inside the graphics window, hold down the [**SHIFT**] key and **right-mouse-click** once to bring up the *Object Snap* shortcut menu.

13. Select the **Midpoint** option in popup window.

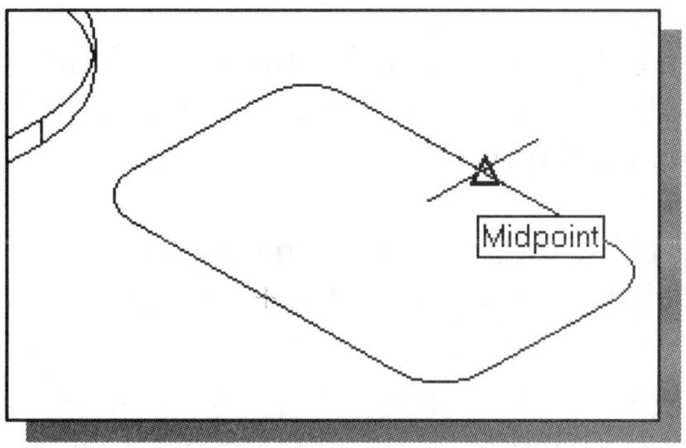

14. In the command prompt area, the message "*_line Specify first point:*" is displayed. Pick the line segment on the extracted surface as shown.

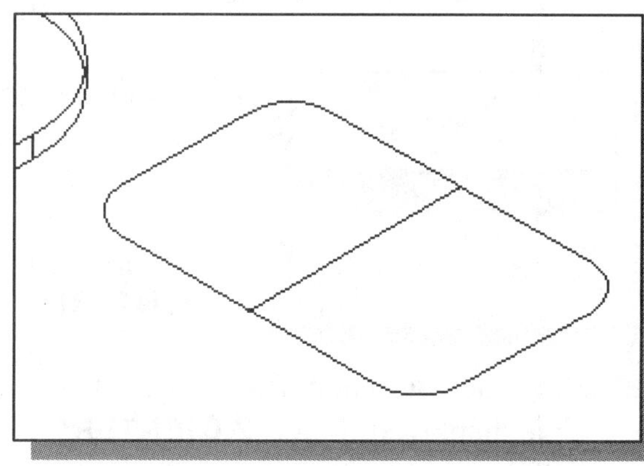

15. On your own, repeat the ***Midpoint SNAP*** option and create a line as shown.

16. Inside the graphics window, right-mouse-click once and select **Enter** to end the Line command.

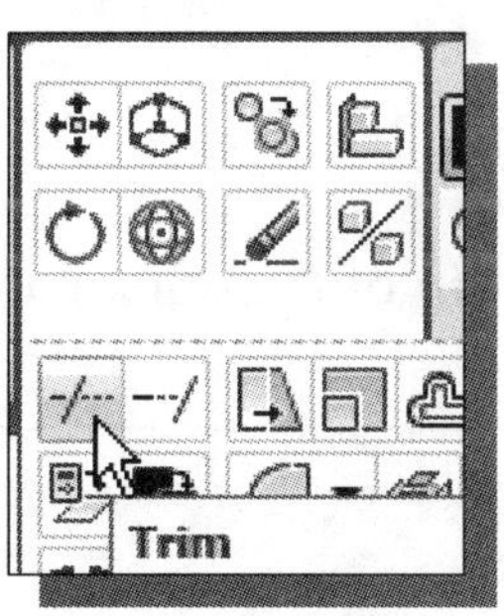

17. Select the **Trim** command icon in the *Modify* toolbar.

18. In the command prompt area, the message "*Select boundary edges... Select objects:*" is displayed. Pick the **line** across the center of the 2D sketch.

19. Inside the graphics window, **right-mouse-click** to proceed with the Trim command.

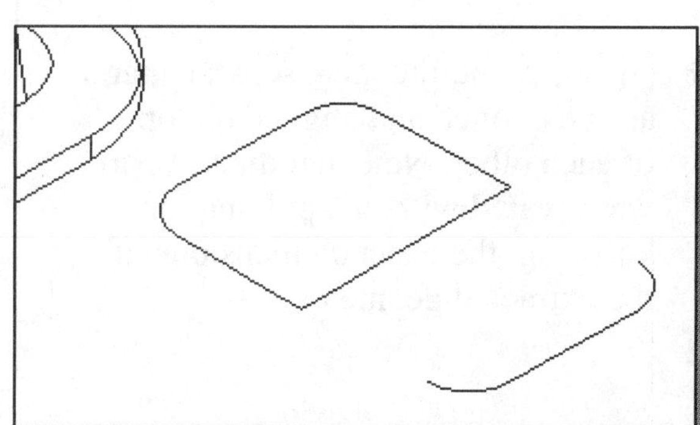

20. The message "*Select object to trim or shift-select object to extend or [Project/ Edge/ Undo]:*" is displayed in the command prompt area. Trim the two lines of the exploded geometry as shown.

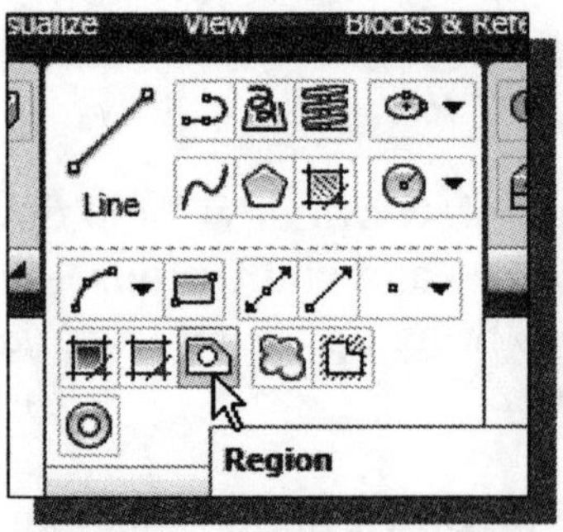

21. Select the **Region** command icon in the *Draw* toolbar.

22. In the command prompt area, the message "*Select objects:*" is displayed. Select the entities we just modified.

23. Inside the graphics window, **right-mouse-click** to accept the selection and create a region.

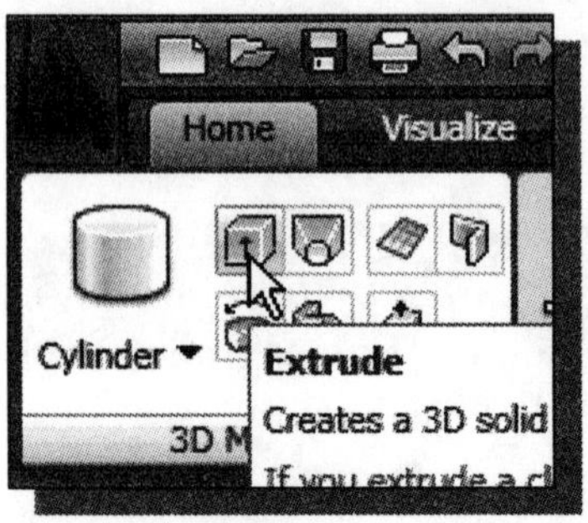

24. Select **Extrude** in the *3D Modeling* toolbar as shown.

25. In the command prompt area, the message "*Select objects:*" is displayed. Select the 2D region by clicking on any of the displayed segments.

26. Inside the graphics window, right-mouse-click to accept the selection and proceed with the Extrude command.

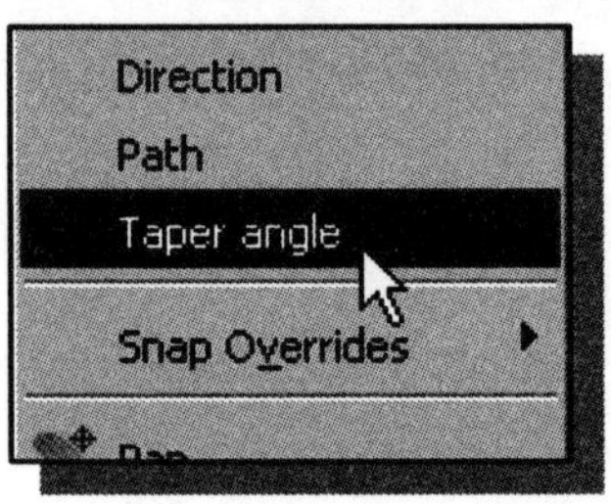

27. Inside the graphics window, right-mouse-click to bring up the option menu and select Taper Angle.

28. In the command prompt area, the message "*Specify angle of taper for extrusion <0>:*" is displayed. Enter: **10.0 [ENTER]**

29. In the command prompt area, the message "*Specify height of extrusion or [path]:*" is displayed. Enter: **2.0 [ENTER]**

30. Select the **Move** icon in the *Modify* toolbar.

31. On your own, reposition the part on **top** of the other parts as shown.

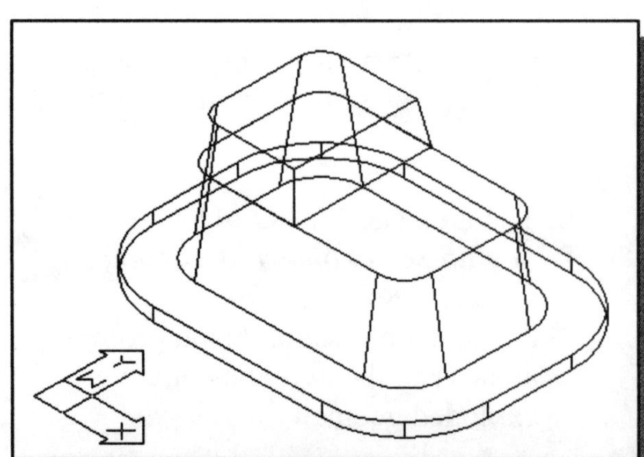

- At this point, the three separate parts are positioned and aligned on top of each other. Note that the last part was created without applying, or knowing, the exact diemensions of the extracted geometry.

Combining Parts – Boolean UNION

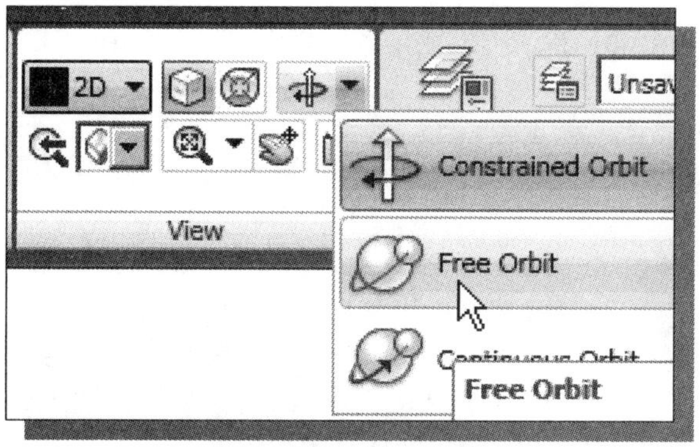

1. Select **Free Orbit** in the *View* toolbar.
   [Orbit] → [Free Orbit]

2. On your own, rotate the created models in 3D space and confirm the three parts are positioned on top of each other.

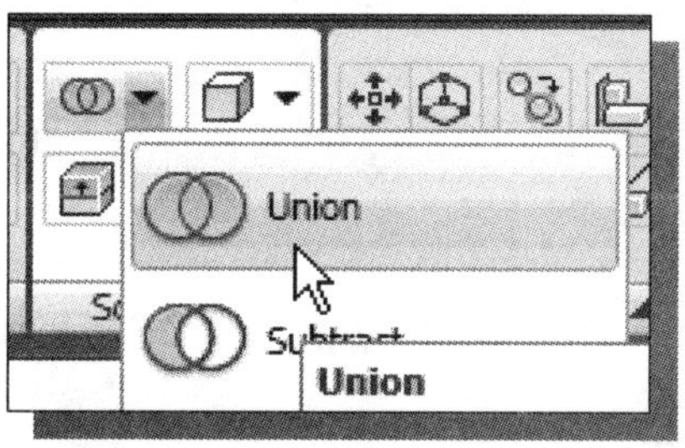

3. In the *Solid Editing* toolbar, click on the **Union** icon. In the command prompt area, the message "*Select Objects:*" is displayed.

4. Pick all the solid models by clicking on their edges.

5. Inside the graphics window, **right-mouse-click** to accept the selection and proceed with the Union command.

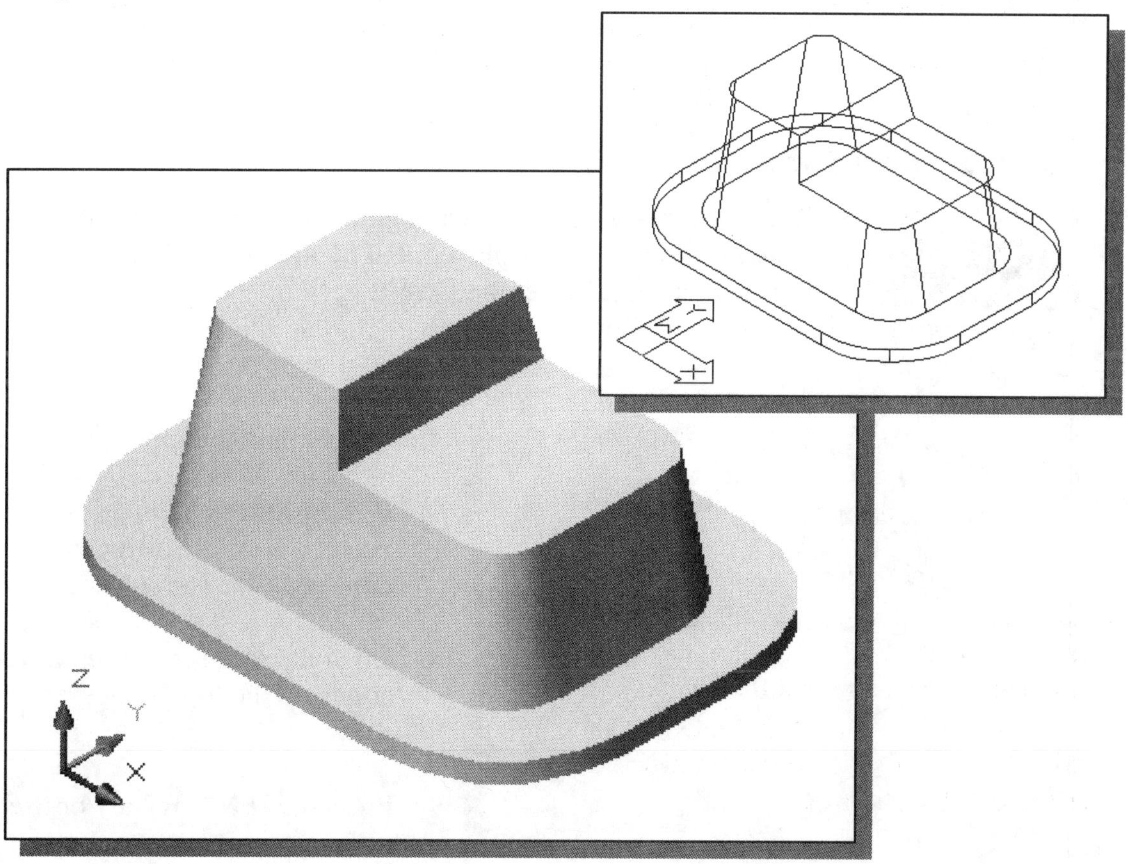

Creating 3D Rounds and Fillets

- In **AutoCAD® 2009**, the same **Fillet** command can be applied to both 2D and 3D designs.

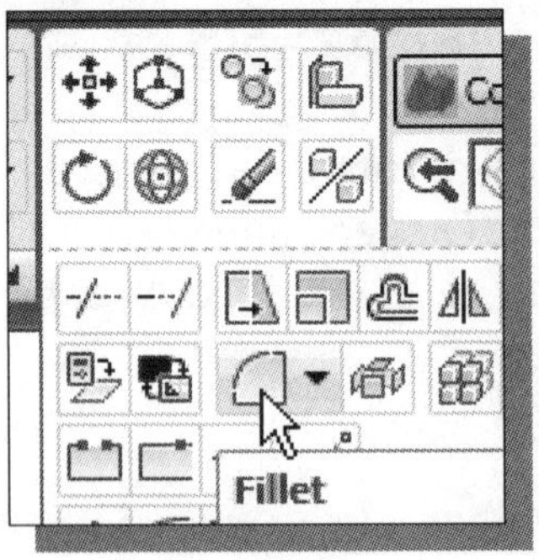

1. Select the **Fillet** command icon in the *Modify* toolbar.

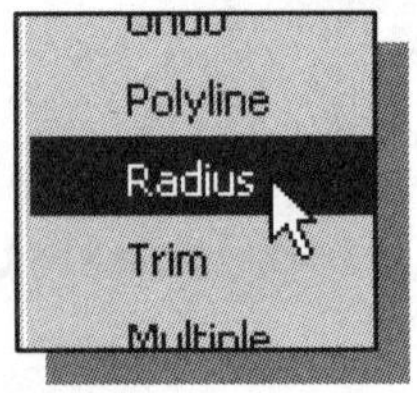

2. Inside the graphics window, right-mouse-click to activate the option menu and select the **Radius** option with the left-mouse-button to specify the radius of the fillet.

3. In the command prompt area, the message "*Specify fillet radius:*" is displayed.
   Specify fillet radius: **0.75 [ENTER]**

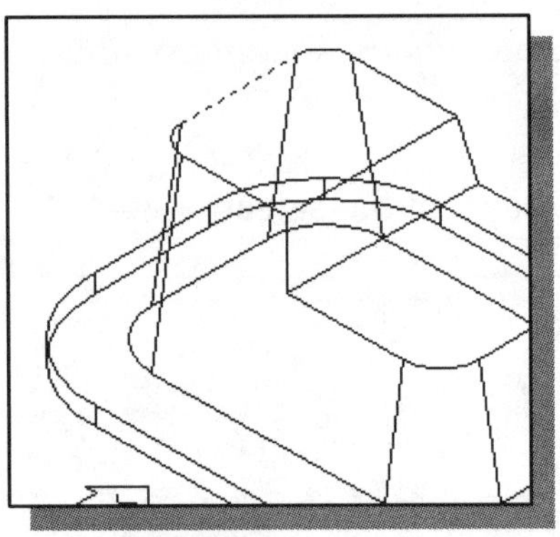

4. Pick the **top back edge** as shown.

5. In the command prompt area, the message "*Enter fillet radius <0.75>:*" is displayed. **Right-mouse-click** to accept the displayed value.

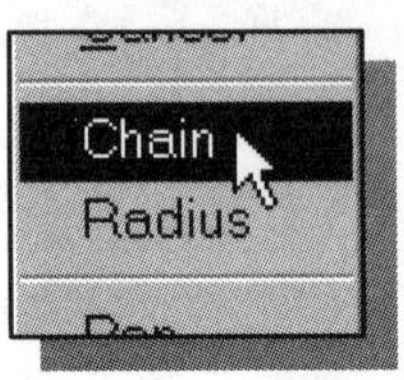

6. In the command prompt area, the message "*Select an edge or [Chain/Radius]:*" is displayed. **Right-mouse-click** to activate the option menu and select the **Chain** option.

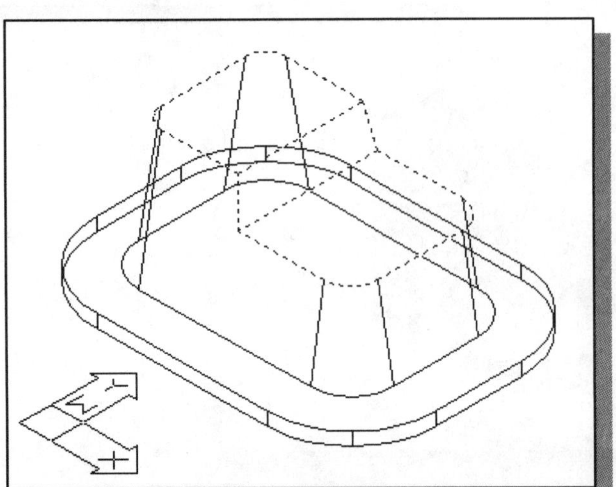

7. In the command prompt area, the message "*Select an edge or [Chain/Radius]:*" is displayed. Select one of the **adjacent curves** on the top surface.

8. On your own, select the **adjacent edges** on the top surfaces as shown in the figure.

9. Press the **[ENTER]** key or use the right-mouse-button and select **Enter** to accept the selection.

- The **Fillet** command can be used to create complex 3D curves and surfaces as shown in this example.

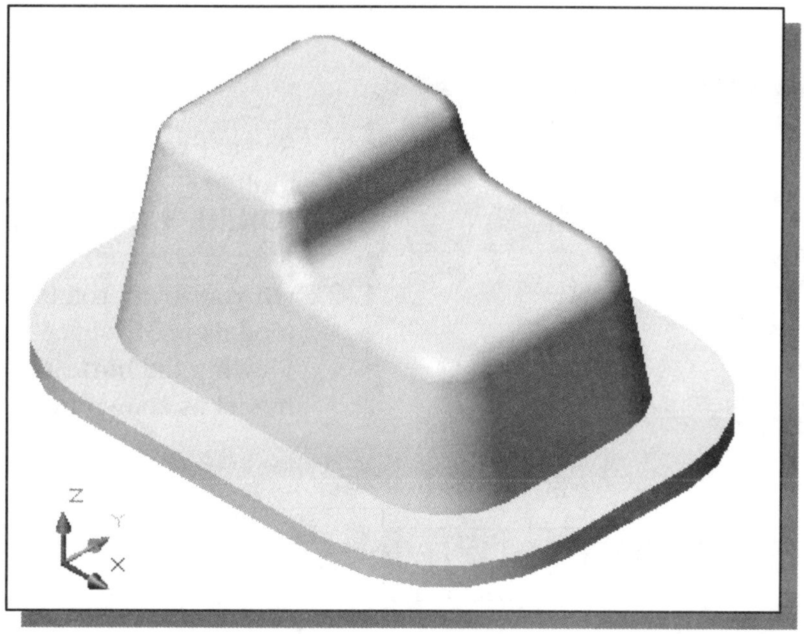

- On your own, create a *chained fillet* of **0.5 radius** at the bottom edges as shown.

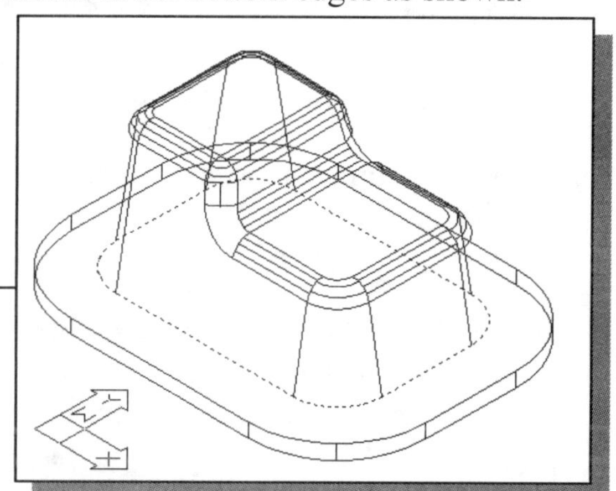

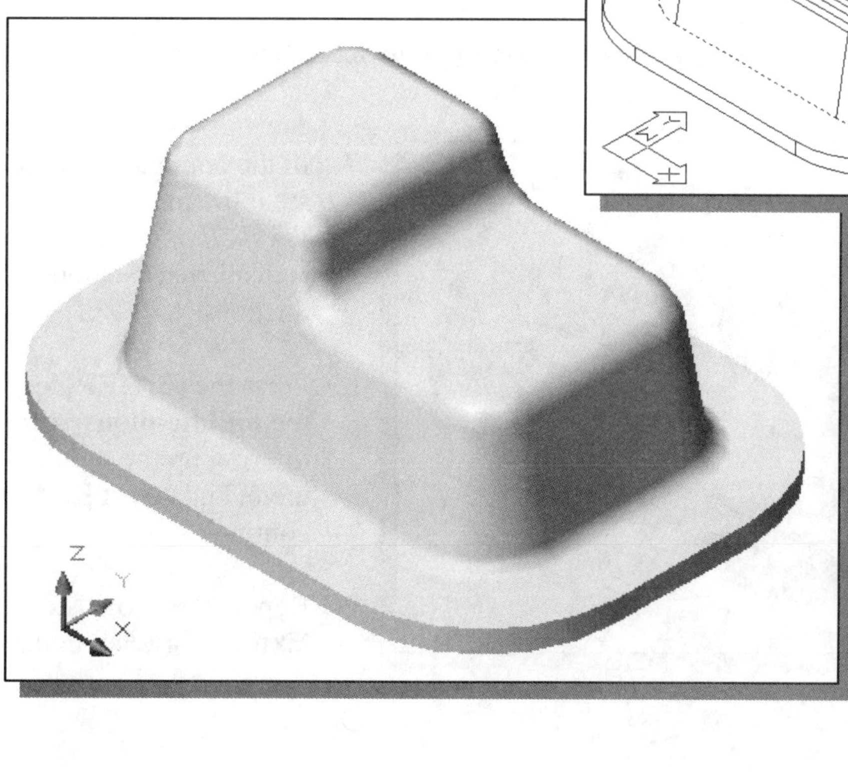

Creating a Shell Feature

- The **Shell** command can be used to create new faces by offsetting existing ones inside or outside of their original positions.

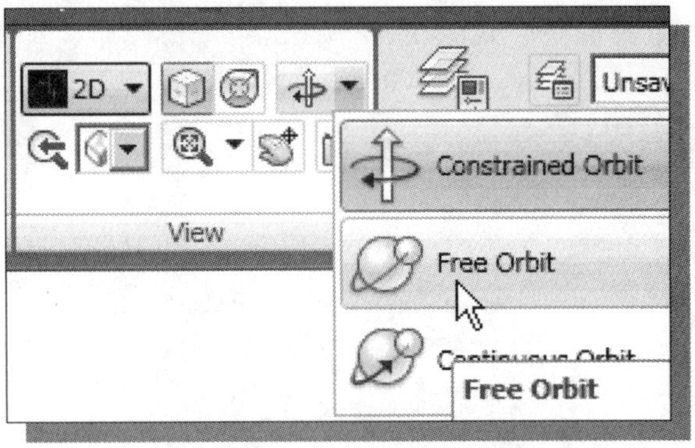

1. Select **Free Orbit** in the *View* toolbar.
   [Orbit] → [Free Orbit]

2. On your own, rotate the created models in 3D space so that we are viewing the **bottom flat face** of the model as shown in the figure below.

3. Choose **Shell** in the *Solid Editing* toolbar.

4. The message "*Select a 3D solid:*" is displayed in the command prompt area. Pick any surface of the 3D solid. Note the entire solid is selected.

5. In the command prompt area, the message "*Remove faces or [Undo /Add /All]:*" is displayed. Select the **top flat side** (as oriented in the figure below) of the *Oil Sink* model. (AutoCAD will remove this surface before creating the shell feature.)

6. Inside the graphics window, **right-mouse-click** to accept the selection and proceed with the Shell command.

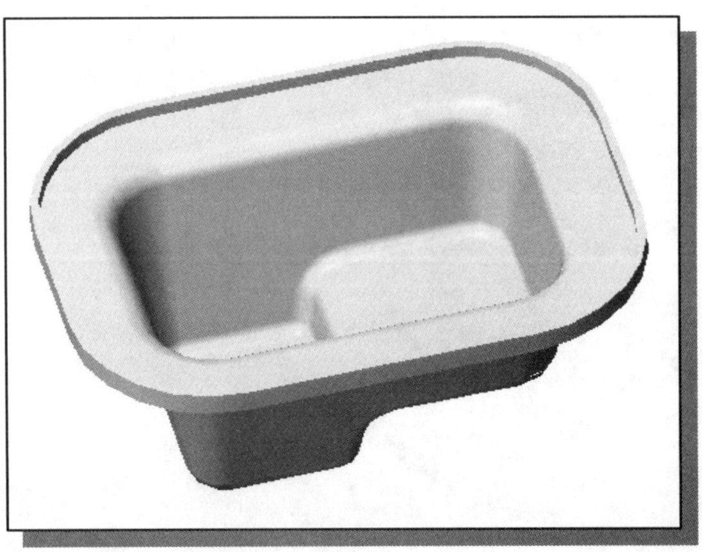

7. In the command prompt area, the message "*Enter the shell offset distance:*" is displayed. Set the thickness to **0.25**.

8. Press the [**ENTER**] key or the **middle-mouse-button** to bring up the option menu and select **Exit** to continue.

9. Repeat the above step and **Exit** the Shell command.

Creating a Rectangular Array Cut Feature

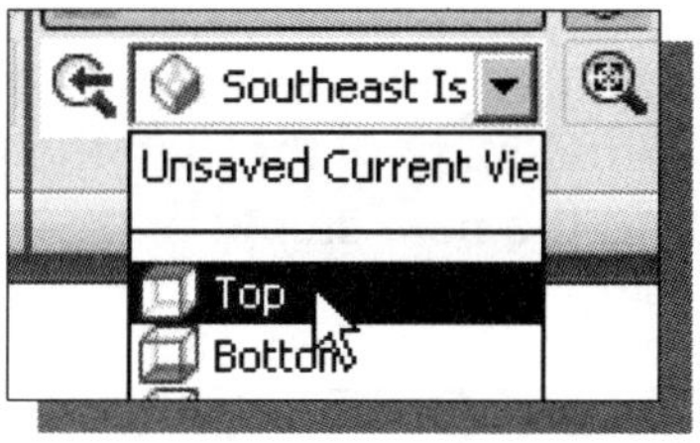

1. In the *View* toolbar, select the **Top View** option to reset the display to the XY plane of the coordinate system.

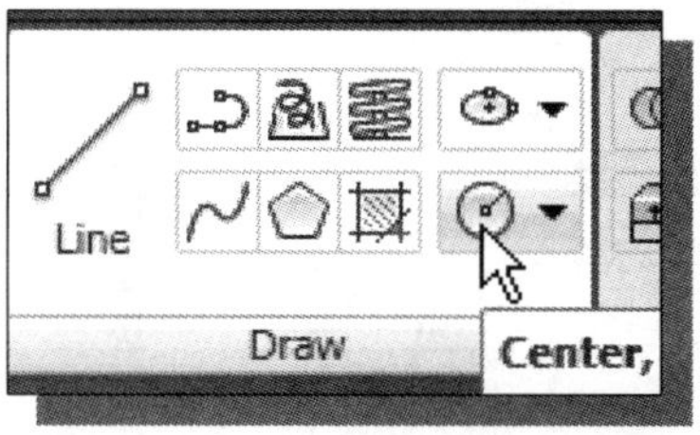

2. Select the **Circle** icon in the *Draw* toolbar.

3. On your own, create a circle (diameter **0.75**) that is toward the right side of the solid model. Note that, in AutoCAD, ***circles*** are created as valid ***regions***.

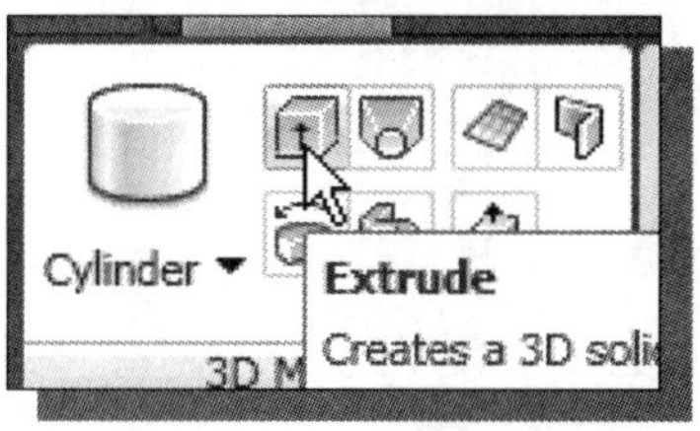

4. On your own, extrude the region into a **1″** high cylinder. (Taper angle set to **0**.)

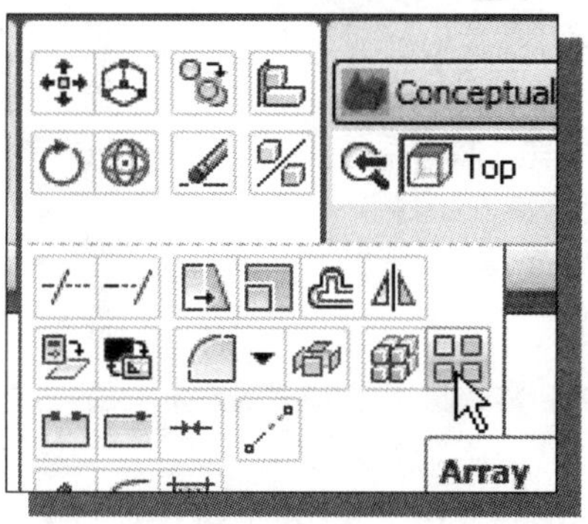

5. Select **Array** in the *Modify* toolbar as shown.

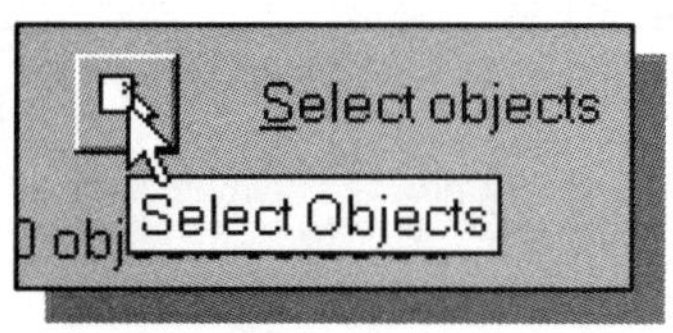

6. Click on the **Select Objects** button.

7. Select the **cylinder**.

8. Inside the graphics window, **right-mouse-click** to accept the selection and return to the Array command.

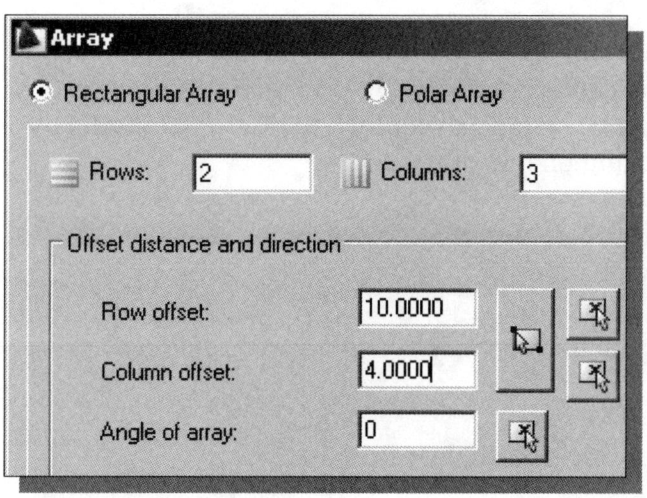

9. In the *Array* window, fill in the items as shown: ***Rectangular array***, **2 *Rows*** with **10″ *Row offset*** and **3 *Columns*** with **4″ *Column offset***.

10. Click on the **OK** button to accept the settings.

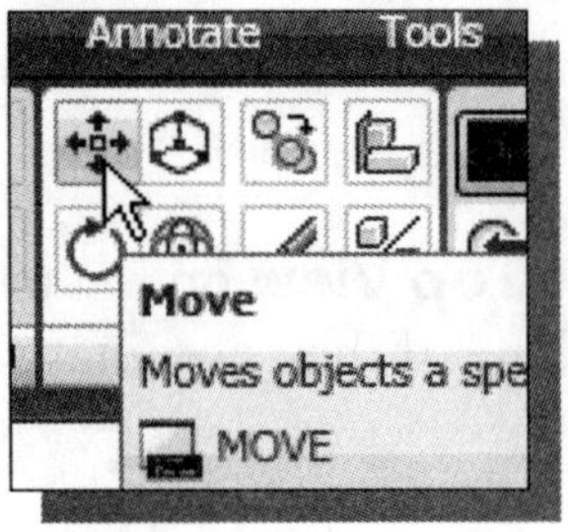

11. Select the **Move** icon in the *Draw* toolbar.

12. On your own, reposition the six cylinders as shown in the figure below. Make sure the cylinders pass through the ***Oil Pan*** model before proceeding to the next step.

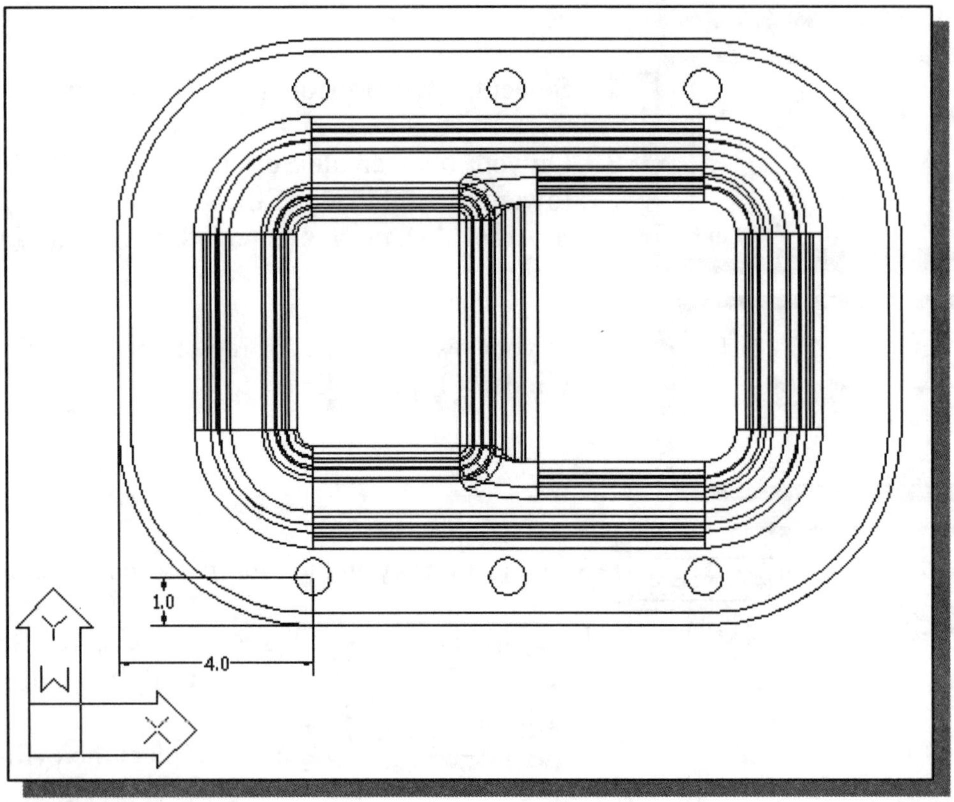

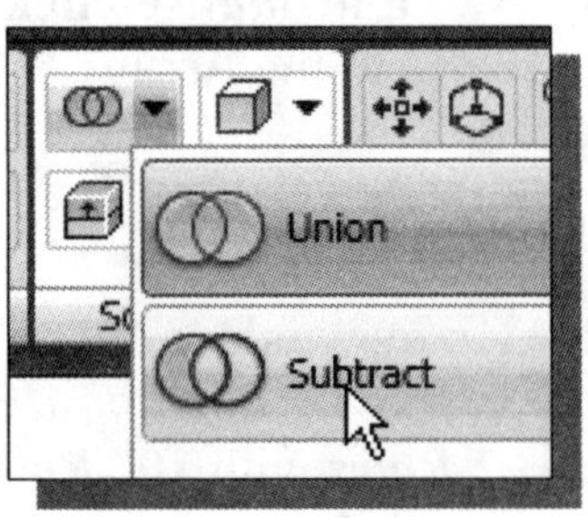

13. In the *Solid Editing* toolbar, click on the **Subtract** icon.

14. In the command prompt area, the message "*_subtract Select solids and regions to subtract from .. Select Objects:*" is displayed. Pick the ***Oil Pan* model** by clicking on one of the edges.

15. Inside the graphics window, **right-mouse-click** to accept the selection and proceed with the Subtract command.

16. In the command prompt area, the message "*Select solids and regions to subtract .. Select Objects:*" is displayed.

17. Pick all **six cylinder blocks** by clicking on the circular edges.

18. Inside the graphics window, right-mouse-click to accept the selection and proceed with the **Subtract** command.

Creating Another Rectangular Array Cut Feature

1. On your own, repeat the above steps and create another rectangular array as shown (circular hole: diameter **0.75**, ***Rectangular array***, **2** ***Rows*** with **4″** ***Row offset*** and **2** ***Columns*** with **14″** ***Column offset***.)

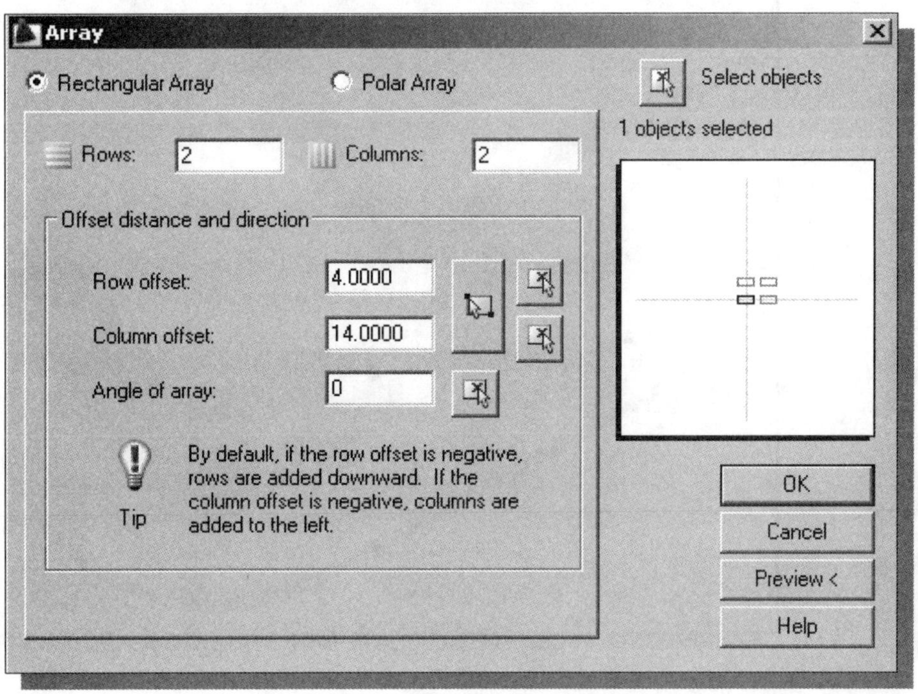

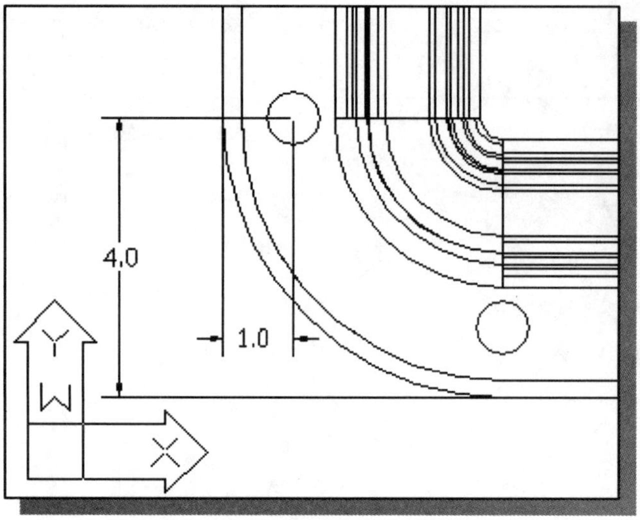

2. On your own, reposition the rectangular array so that the lower left cylinder is located at 4.0 inches away from the bottom edge of the base feature and 1.0 inch away from the left edge of the *Oil Pan* model.

3. Complete the model with the **Subtract** command.

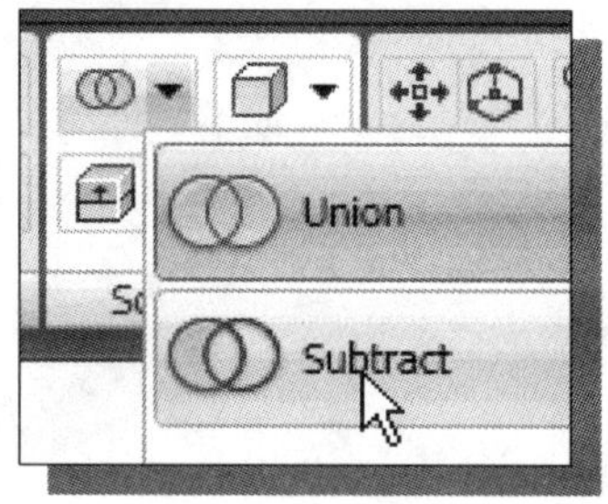

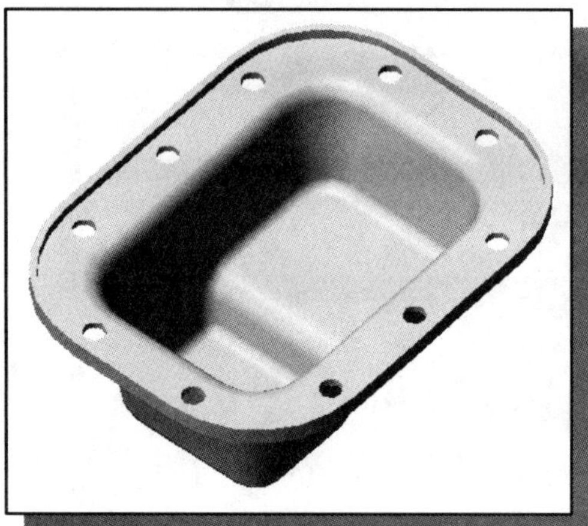

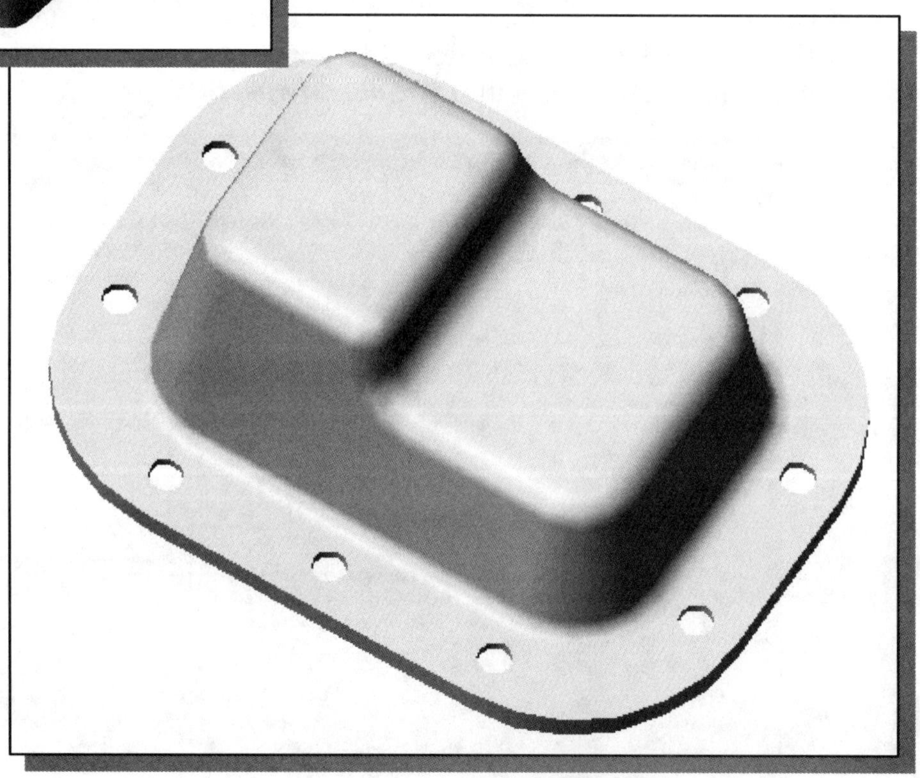

Making a Design Change

❖ Engineering designs usually go through many revisions and changes before they go into production. In AutoCAD 2009, an assortment of 3D tools has been implemented to handle design changes more quickly. In this section, two different approaches to perfrom simple design change are illustrated: (1) Modify with the Grip Editing tools. (2) Creating with Dynamic UCS.

Grip Editing Approach: One of the main 3D editing enhancements in AutoCAD 2009 is the Grip Editing Tools. We can now use grips to manipulate original solid primitive forms that were used to make up ***composite solids***. **Composite solids** are solids created from two or more individual solids through any of the *Boolean* commands: **UNION**, **SUBTRACT**, and **INTERSECT**. To select an individual form of a composite solid, press and hold the **CTRL** key while selecting. We will change one of the hole diameter from 0.75 to 1.0 using this approach.

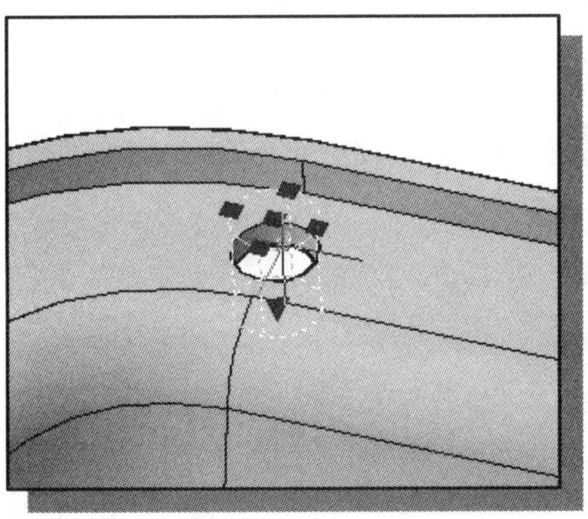

1. Select one of the hole features by pressing down the **CTRL** key and clicking on the cylindrical surface as shown.

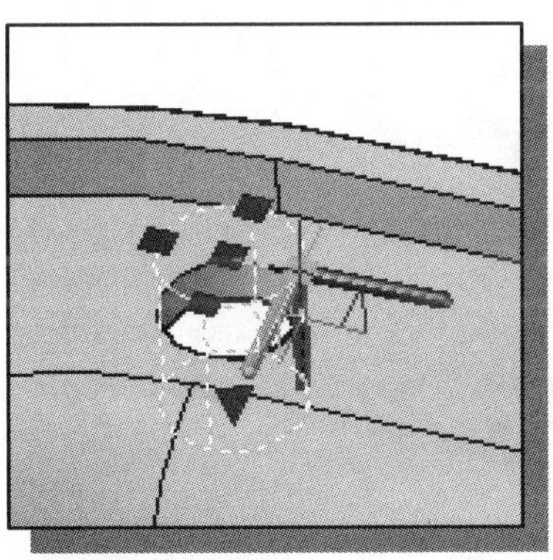

2. Move the cursor on top of one of the square grips and notice the grip axes appeared on top of the grip point.

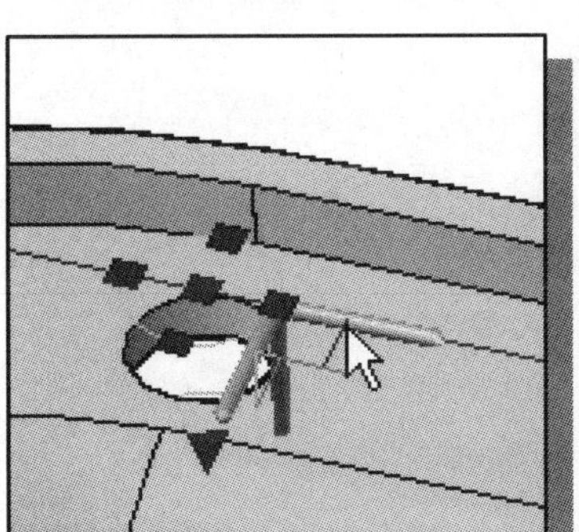

3. Click on the grip axis that is parallel to the longer edges of the oil pan. This will activate the constrained move along the selected axis.

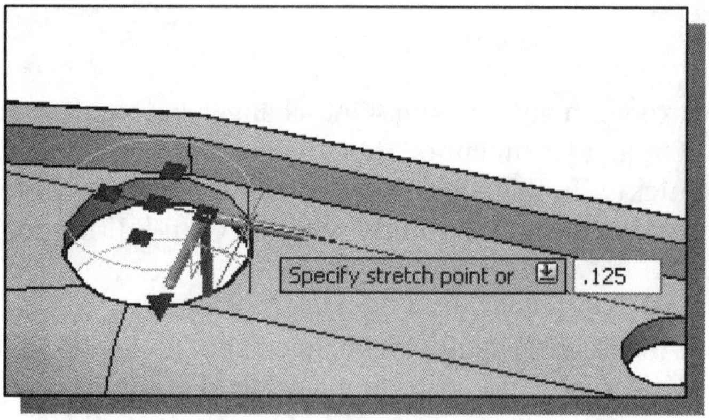

4. In the command prompt area, the message "*Specify stretch point or [Base point/Undo/eXit]:*" is displayed. Enter: **0.125 [Enter]**

5. On your own, use the **[Tools] → [Inquiry] → [Distance]** command to confirm the design change has been performed correctly.

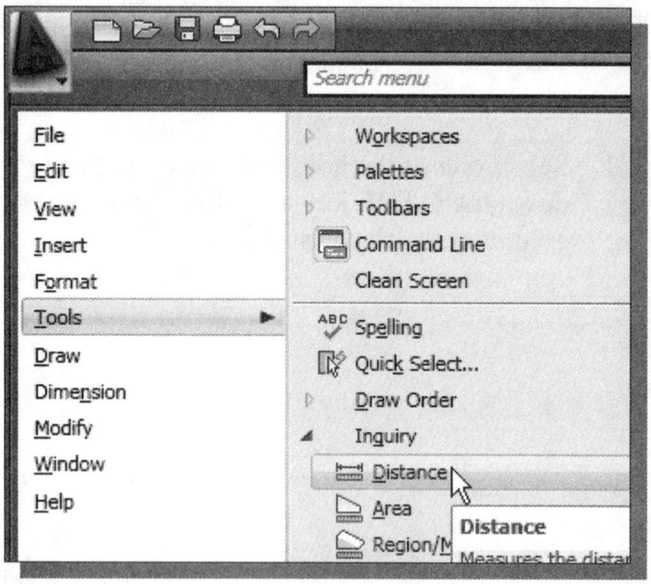

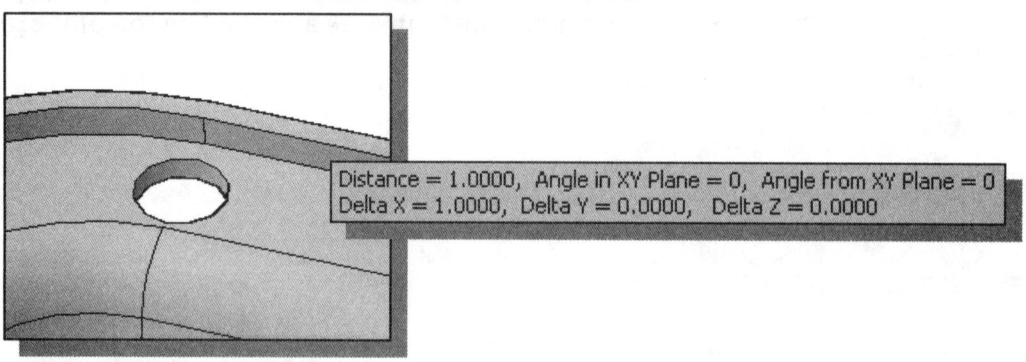

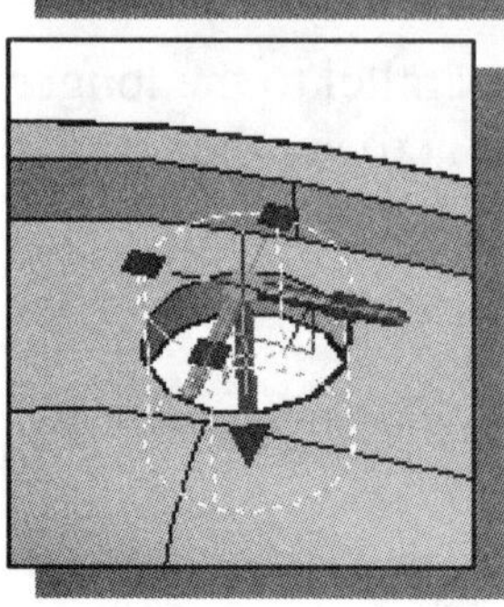

- On your own, experiment with modifying the different grip points available on the cylinder. Pay more attentions to the square center grip point and the triangle grip point.

Dynamic UCS Approach: In AutoCAD 2007, a new UCS tool (the **Dynamic UCS** option) was introduced, which allow quick alignment of UCS to existing surfaces. The dynamic UCS can be used to create objects on a planar face of a 3D solid without manually changing the UCS orientation. During a command, the dynamic UCS temporarily aligns the XY plane of the UCS to a planar face of a 3D solid when you move the cursor over the face. When the dynamic UCS is active, specified points, and drawing tools, such as polar tracking and the grid, are all measured relative to the temporary UCS established by the dynamic UCS. In this section, we will add an additional cylindrical solid feature on the inside wall using this approach.

1. In the *Status Bar* area, activate the *Dynamic UCS* option by clicking on the **DUCS** option button as shown.

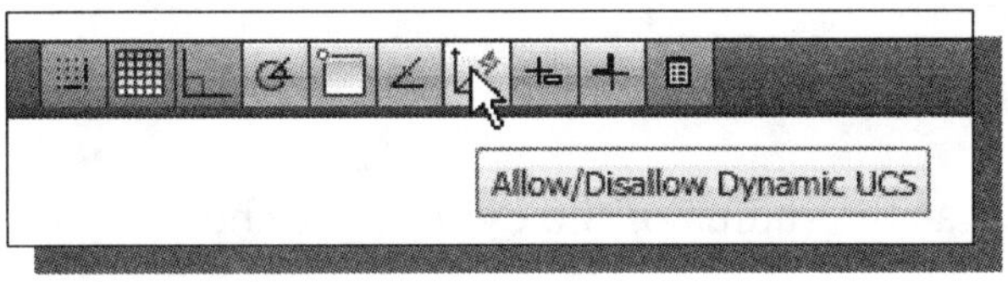

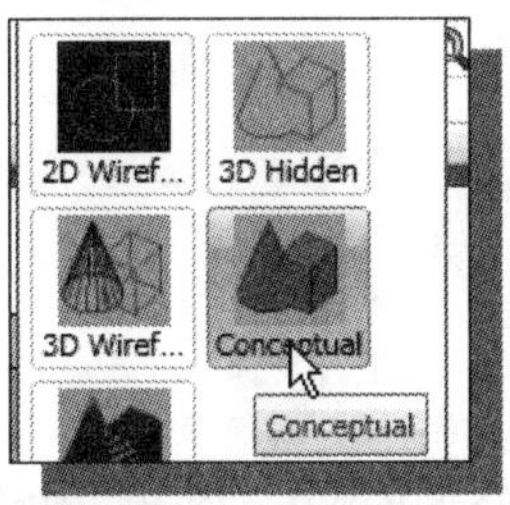

2. Set the display option to **Conceptual Visual Style** by clicking on the icon in the *Visual Styles* toolbar as shown.

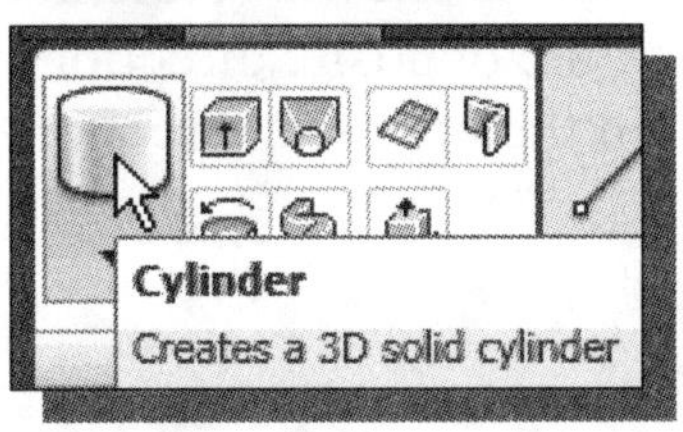

3. Click on the **cylinder** icon to activate the create cylinder command.

4. Move the cursor on top of any planar surface and notice the displayed dashed edges signifying the alignment of the XY plane of the temporarily UCS to the surface.

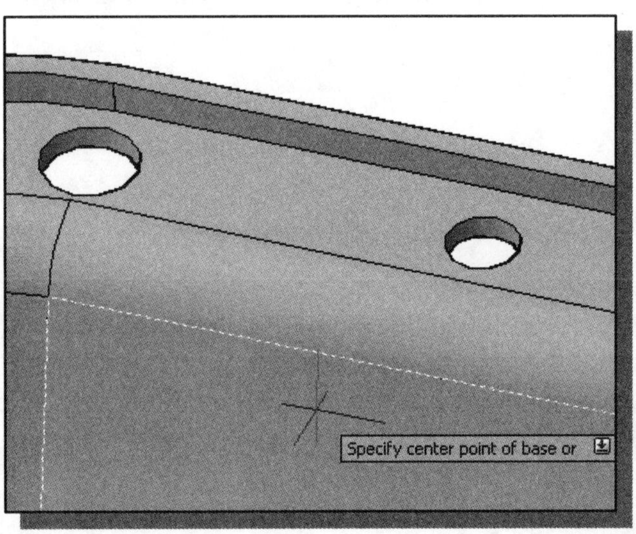

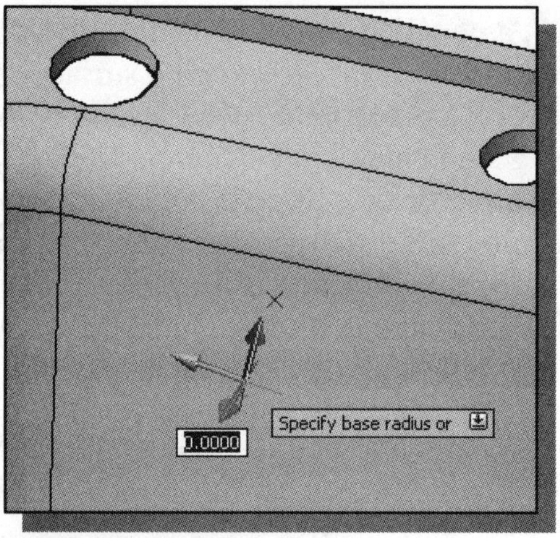

5. Pick an arbitrary location on the surface to use as the center point of the cylinder. Note the display of the alignment of the temporarily UCS.

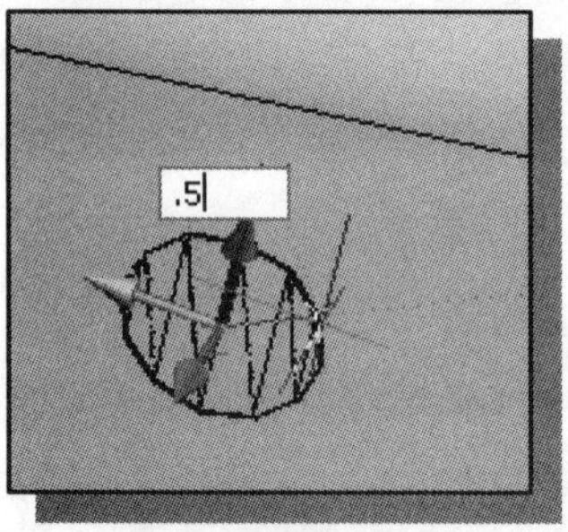

6. Enter **0.5** as the radius of the cylinder as shown.

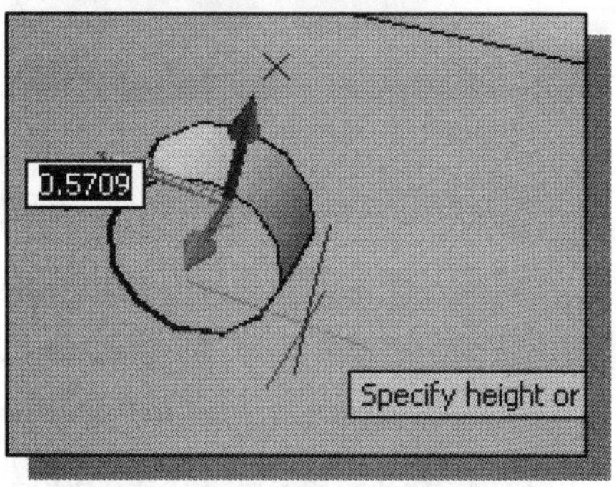

7. Move the cursor forward and observe the preview of an extrusion as shown. (Note that moving the cursor in the opposite direction will create an extrusion in the opposite direction.)

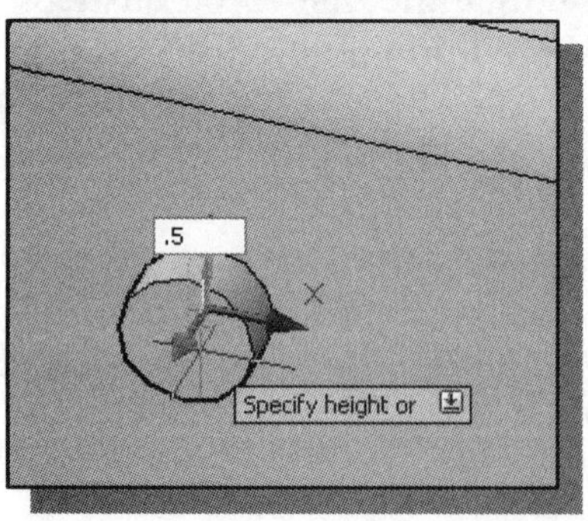

8. Enter **0.5** as the height of the cylinder as shown.

- Note that we have successfully placed a cylinder on the inclined surface. We can now move the cylinder to any desired location and join the cylinder to the main body. The Dynamic UCS approach reduced the tedious work of orienting the UCS prior to creating the necessary solid feature. In the next chapter, we will examine the use of Dynamic UCS as a powerful design tool.

Questions:

1. Describe the method used in the tutorial to create *Draft Angle* features in AutoCAD.
2. List and describe the differences between *Cut with a Pattern* and *Cut Each One Individually*.
3. Which command is used to create 3D rounded corners in AutoCAD?
4. What elements are required to define a *Rectangular Array* in AutoCAD?
5. How do we create a thin-walled part in AutoCAD? What elements are required to perform the operation?
6. Identify the following commands:

(a)

(b)

(c)

(d)

Exercises:

1. Dimensions are in inches.

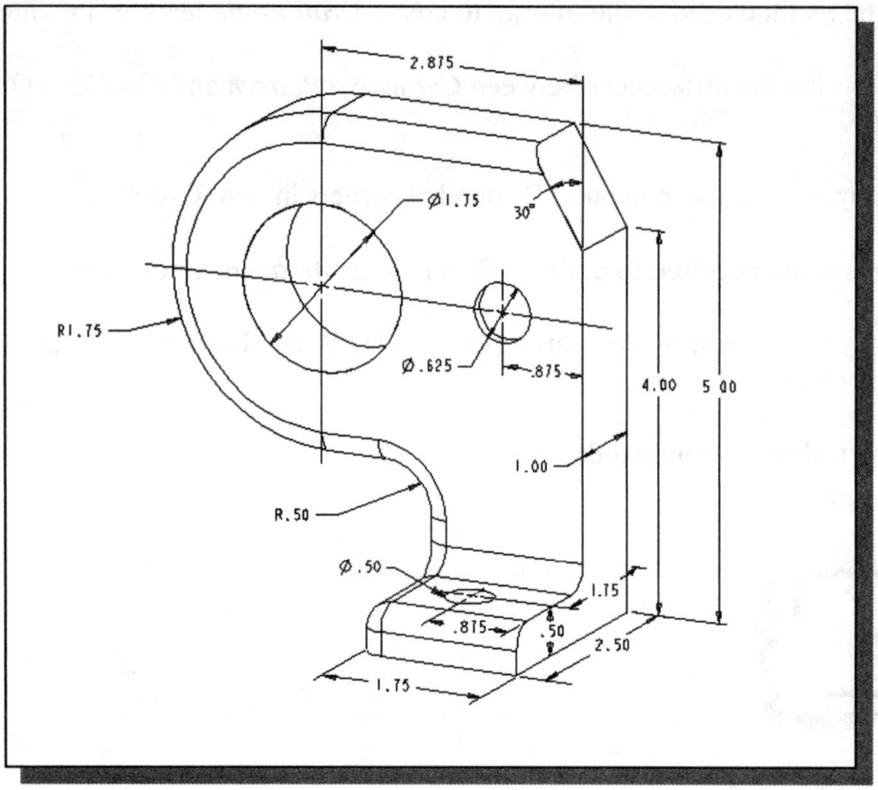

2. Dimensions are in millimeters.

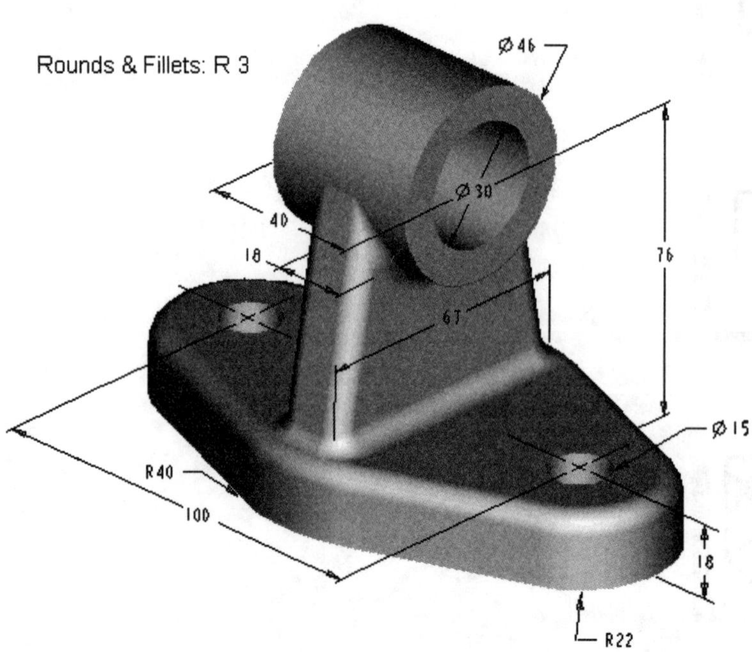

Chapter 11
Conceptual Design Tools & Techniques

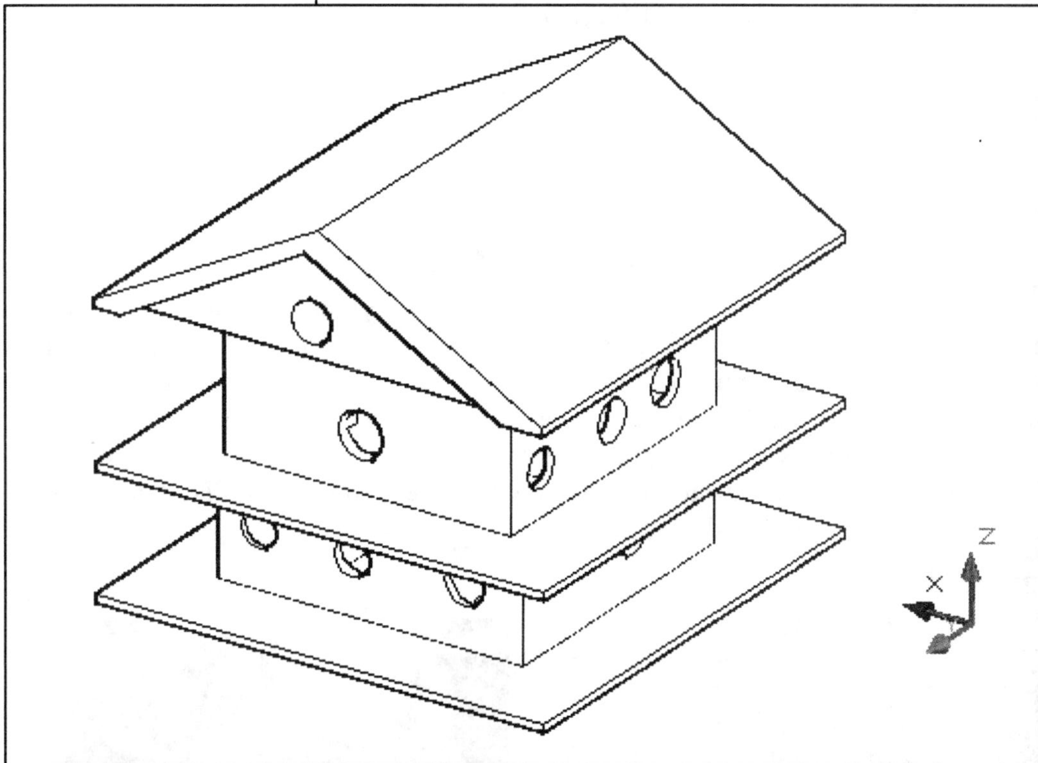

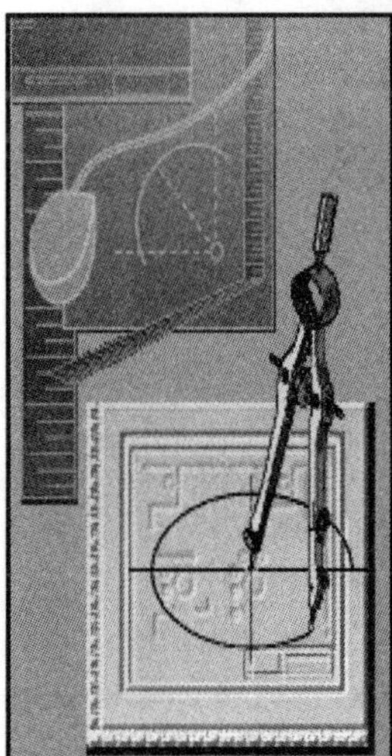

Learning Objectives

- **Using the Conceptual Modeling Construction Tools**
- **Use the Dynamic UCS option**
- **Use the Press/Pull Command**
- **Create Rectangular Patterns**
- **Use the Shell Command**
- **Use the Copy Faces Command**

Introduction

Engineering design is the ability to create and transform ideas and concepts into a product definition that meet the desired objective. The general procedure for the design of a new product, or improving an existing product, involves the following six stages:

1. **Develop and identify the desired objectives.**
2. **Conceptual design stage – Concepts and Ideas of possible solutions.**
3. **Computer Modeling and Engineering analysis of components**
4. **Prototypes and testing.**
5. **Refine and finalize the design.**
6. **Working drawings of the finalized design.**

It is during the **conceptual design** stage, the first drawings, known as **conceptual drawings**, are usually created. The conceptual drawings are typically done in the form of freehand sketches showing the original ideas and concepts of possible solutions to the set objectives. From these conceptual drawings, engineering analyses are performed to improve and confirm the suitability of the proposed design. Working from the sketches and the results of the analyses, the design department then creates prototypes or performs computer simulations to further refine the design. Once the design is finalized, a set of detailed drawings of the proposed design.

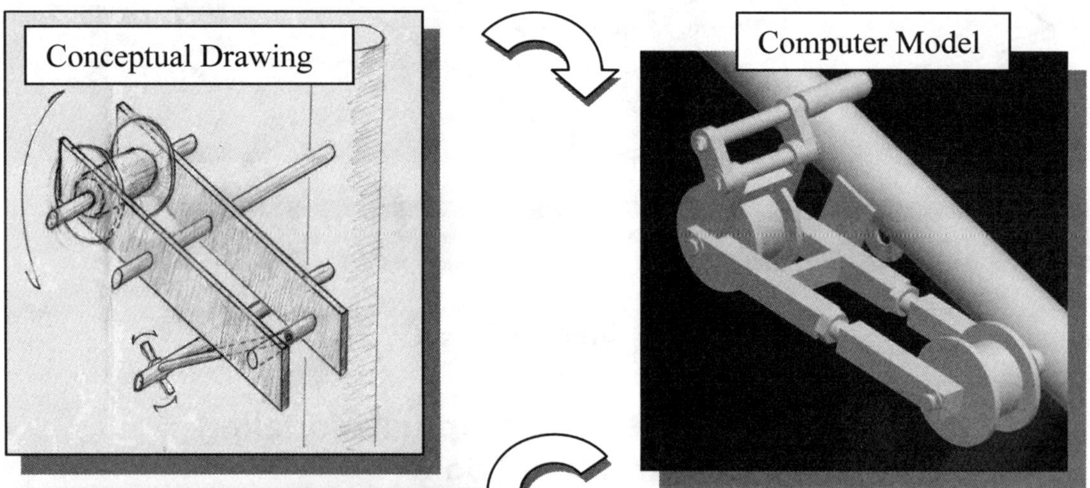

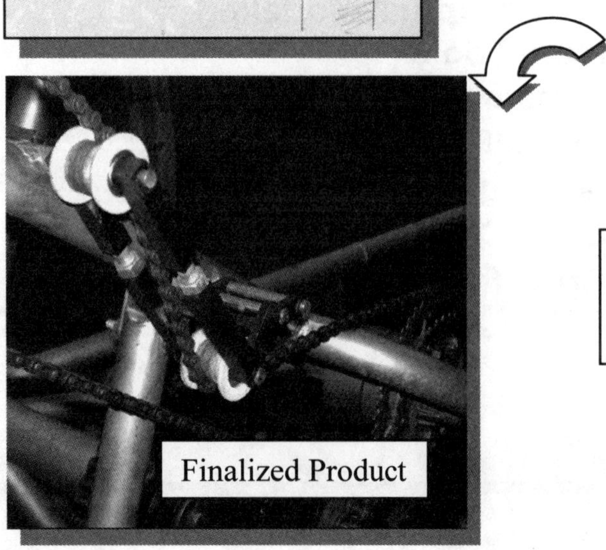

Courtesy of *Wes Fullenwider*,
2006 MET Senior Project
Oregon Institute of Technology

During the **conceptual design** stage of the design process, the main emphasis is typically placed on the conceptualization of problems and solutions. Also, very little emphasis is placed on the finer details, only a few rough estimates of the actual sizes are considered, of the design during the conceptual design stage.

The initial conceptual drawings and sketches represent the idea or essence of what the designer is trying to communicate. Getting the conceptual design correct at the beginning avoids the risk of costly redesign further down the line. Think about how expensive it would be to add a second bathroom once all the plumbing has been done.

One of the main enhancements of AutoCAD 2007 was the introduction of the 3D conceptual modeling tools, which allow the users to very quickly create 3D conceptual models. With the 3D conceptual computer models, the ideas and concepts of a design can be further examined and options explored. The introduction of the 3D conceptual modeling tools has made AutoCAD not just a drafting tool, but a very powerful design tool.

In this chapter, we will use a relative simple design to illustrate the conceptual modeling tools that are available in AutoCAD 2009.

A Bird-House Design

In this tutorial, we will create a 3D conceptual model of a birdhouse design, based on the rough sketches shown below. Note that detailed dimensions are not of great concerns during the conceptual design phase, only rough sizes are noted. This approach is also known as the **shape before size** design philosophy, where the primary concern is the shapes and forms of the design.

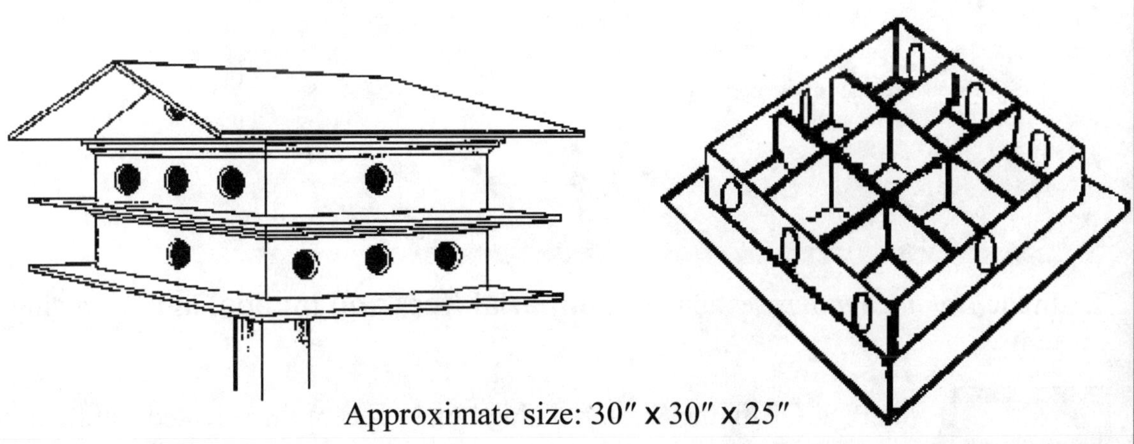

Approximate size: 30″ x 30″ x 25″

Starting Up AutoCAD® 2009

1. Select the **AutoCAD 2009** option on the *Program* menu or select the **AutoCAD 2009** icon on the *Desktop*.

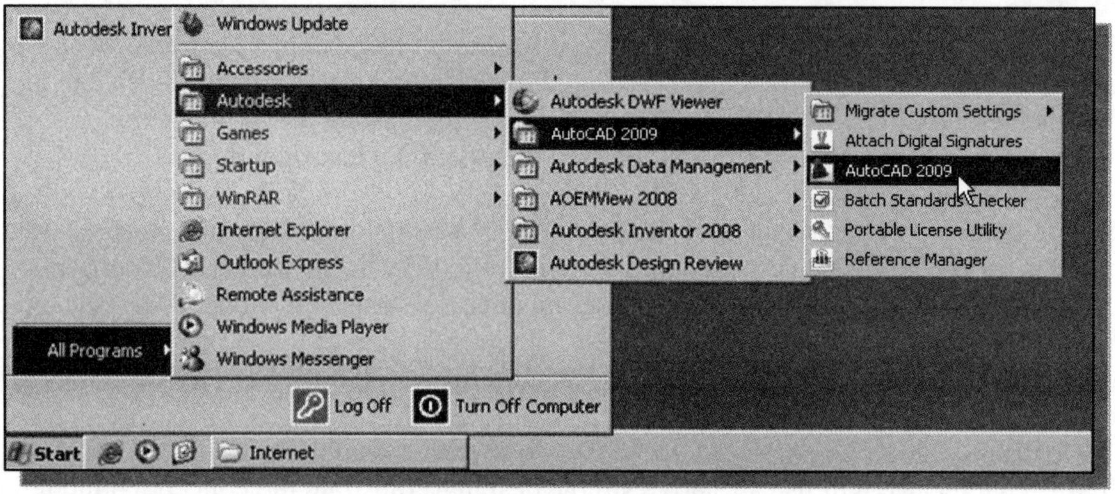

2. In the *Startup* window, select **Start from Scratch**, as shown in the figure below.

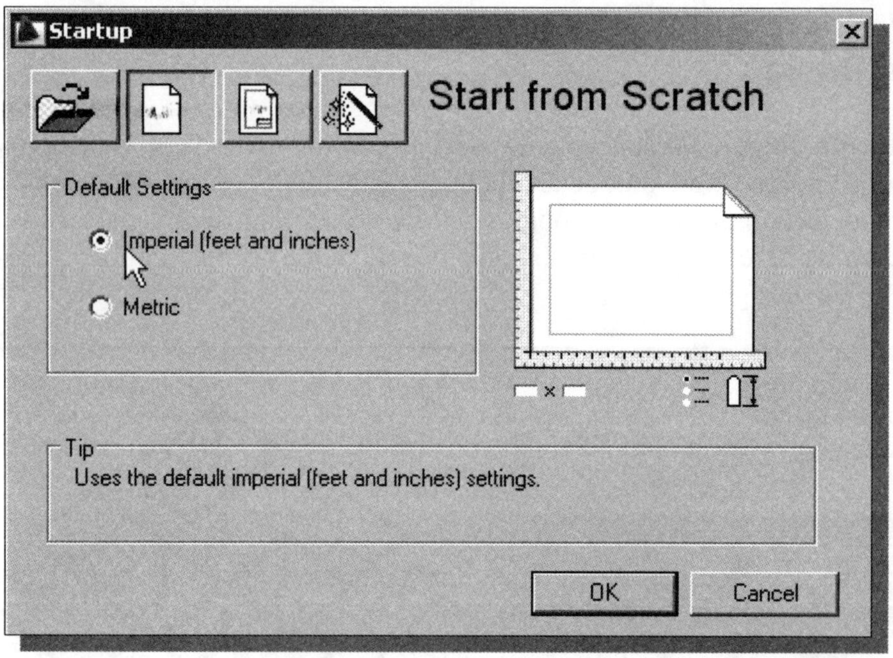

3. In the *Default Settings* section, pick **Imperial (feet and inches)** as the drawing units.

4. Pick **OK** in the *Startup* dialog box to accept the selected settings.

Layers Setup

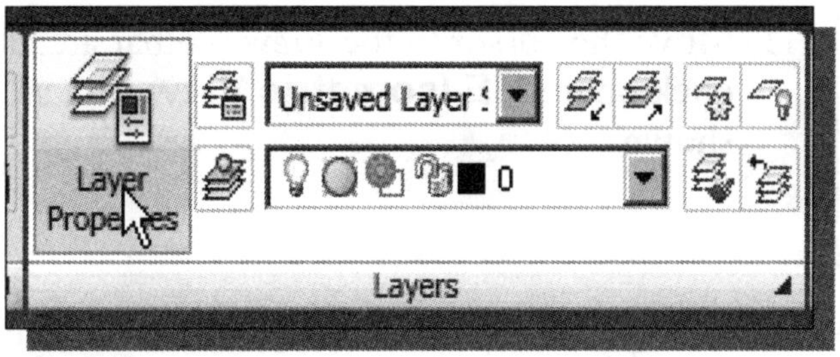

1. Pick **Layer Properties Manager** in the *Object Properties* toolbar.

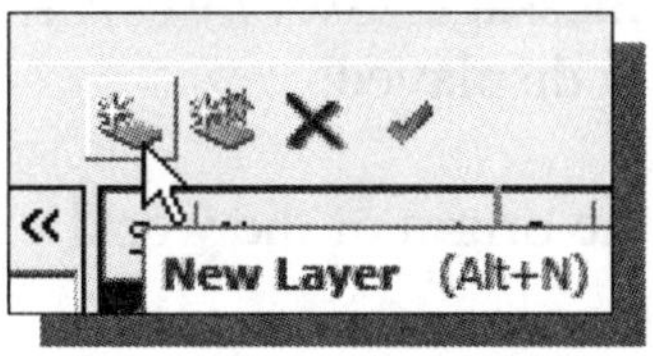

2. Click on the **New** button to create new layers.

3. Create **two new layers** with the following settings:

Layer	*Color*	*LineType*	*LineWeight*
Base	**Cyan**	**Continuous**	**Default**
Roof	**Blue**	**Continuous**	**Default**

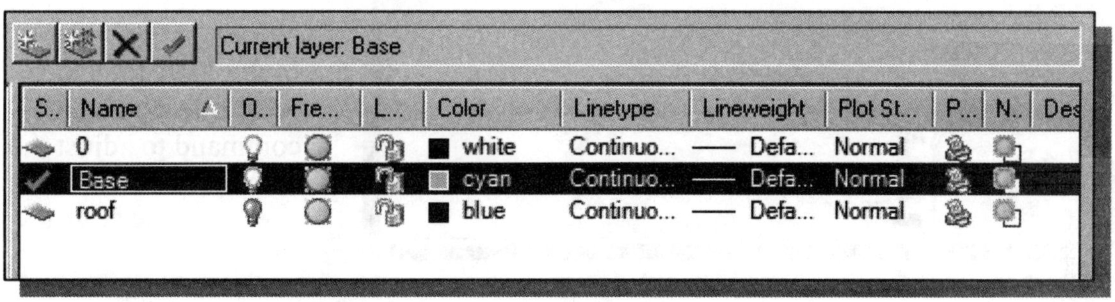

4. Highlight the layer ***Base*** in the list of layers.

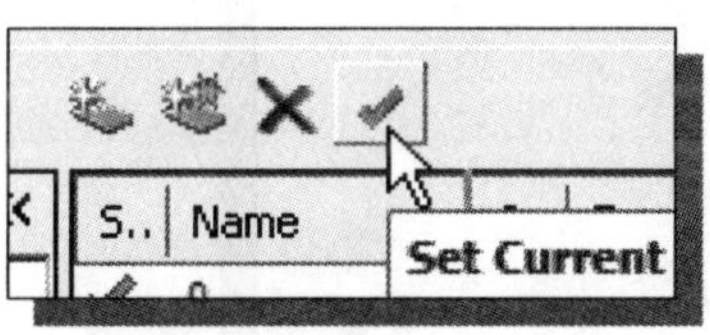

5. Click on the **Current** button to set layer ***Base*** as the *Current Layer*.

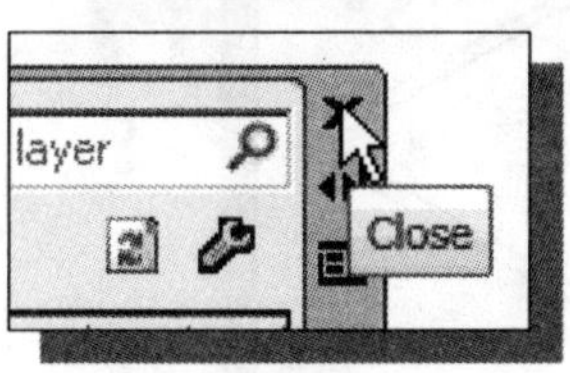

6. Click on the **Close** button to accept the settings and exit the *Layer Properties Manager* dialog box.

7. In the *Status Bar* area, reset the options and turn ***ON*** the *Polar, Object Snap, Object Snap Tracking, Dynamic Input* and *Line Weight* options.

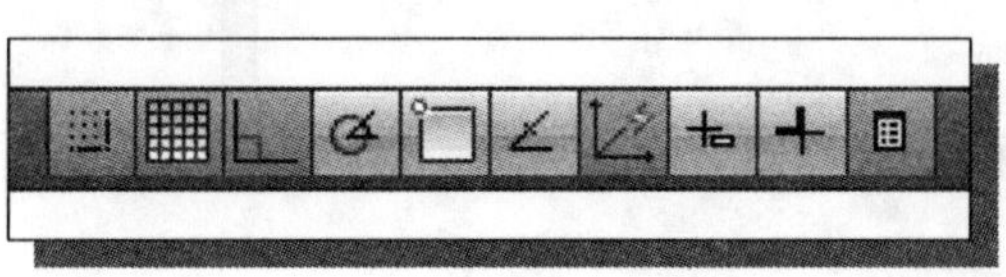

The Base Plate

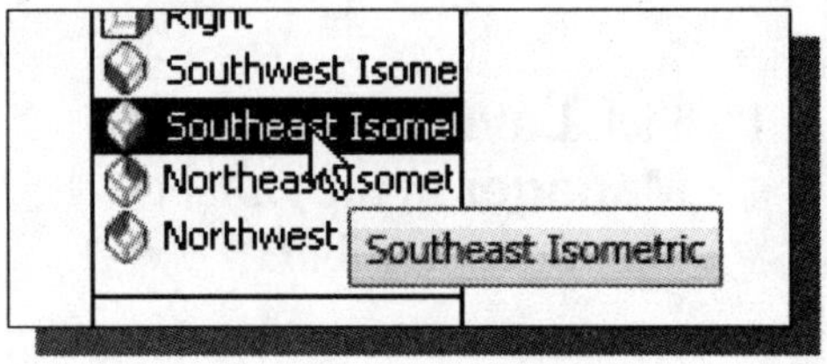

1. Move the cursor to the *View* toolbar area and click on the **SE Isometric View** icon as shown.

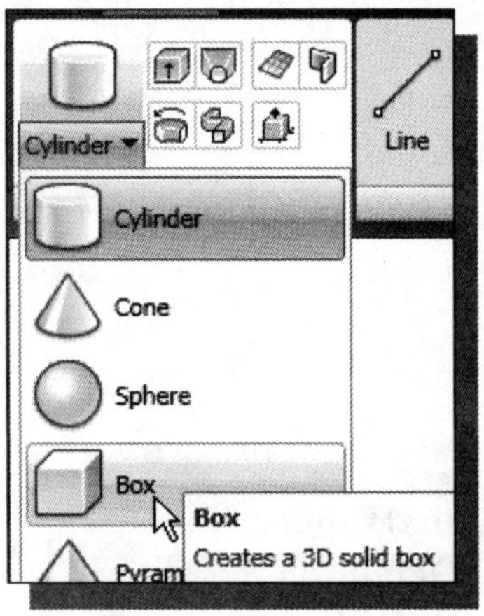

2. In the *Modeling* toolbar, click on the **Box** icon. In the command prompt area, the message "*Specify corner of box or [Center] <0,0,0>:*" is displayed.

3. Pick a location that is near the origin of the world coordinate system.

4. In the command prompt area, the message "*Specify corner or [Cube/Length]:*" is displayed. Enter: **@30,30 [ENTER]**.

5. For the height of the box, enter **0.5 [ENTER]**.

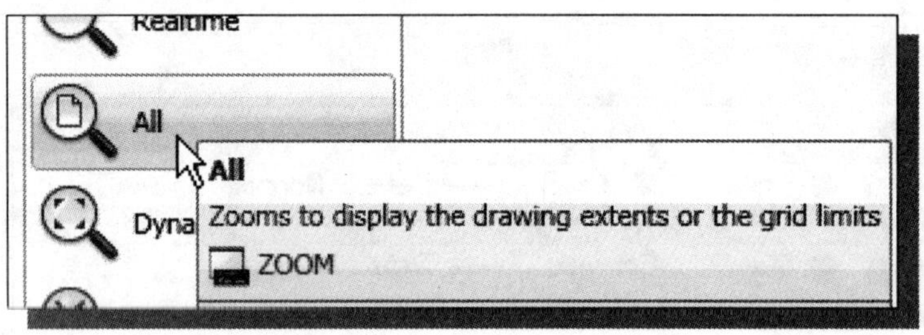

6. In the *View* toolbar, select the **Zoom All** command to adjust the display.

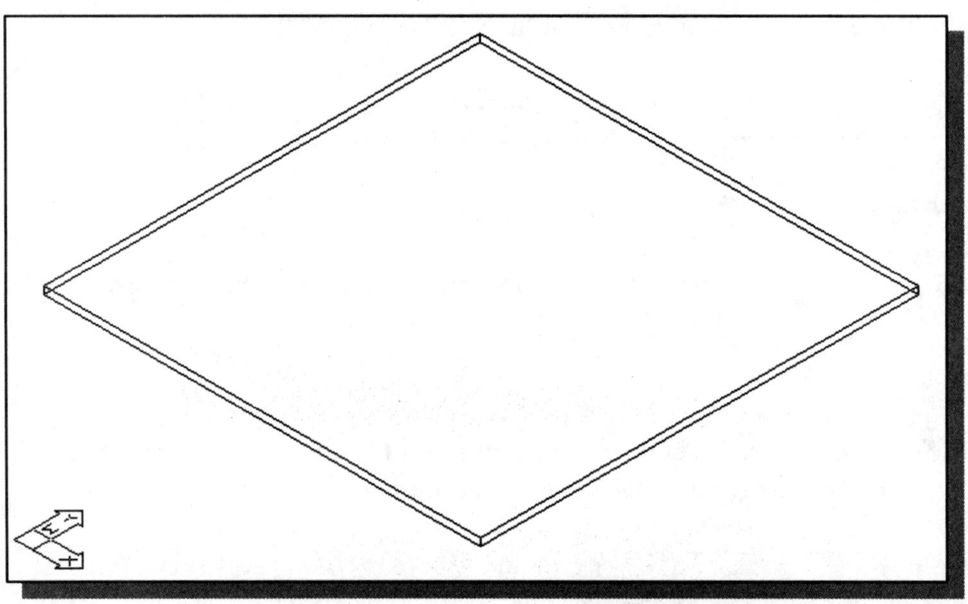

Create the 1st floor inside compartments

- In AutoCAD, the **Dynamic UCS** option can be used to quickly align UCS to existing surfaces. The dynamic UCS can be used to create objects on a planar face of a 3D solid without manually changing the UCS orientation.

1. Activate the *Dynamic UCS* option, by clicking on the **associated** icon in the *Status* toolbar as shown.

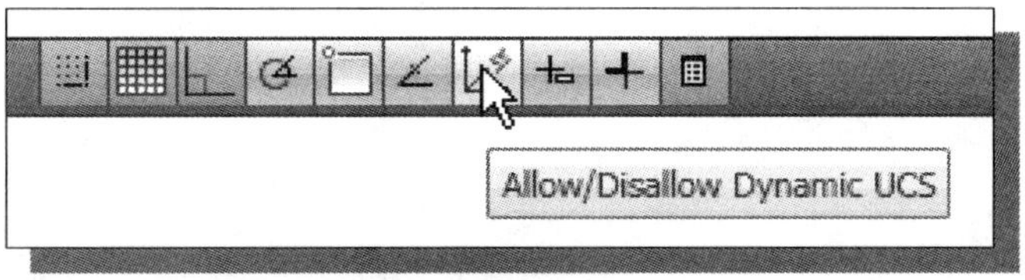

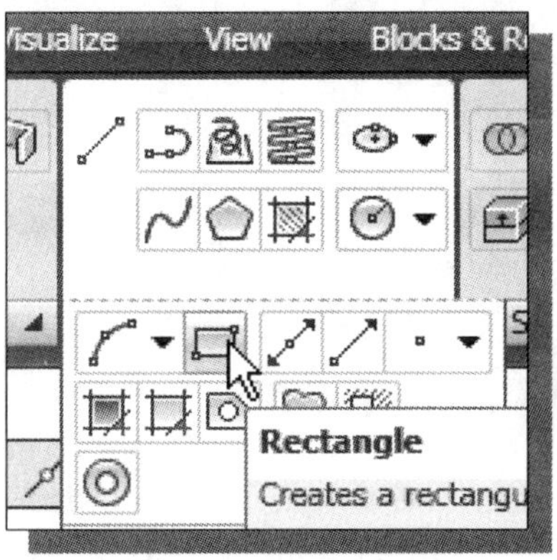

2. Select the **Rectangle** icon in the *Draw* toolbar. In the command prompt area, the message "*Specify first corner point or [Chamfer/Elevation/Fillet/Thickness/Width]:*" is displayed.

3. Move the cursor on the top plan of the 3D base and noticed the dynamic UCS option automatically aligns the UCS to the top plan as shown in the figure.

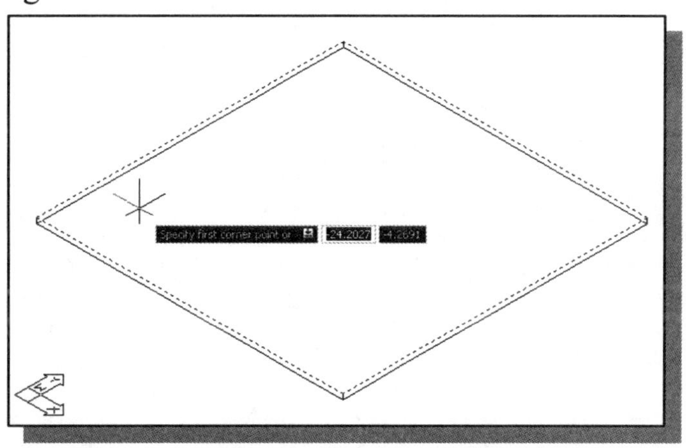

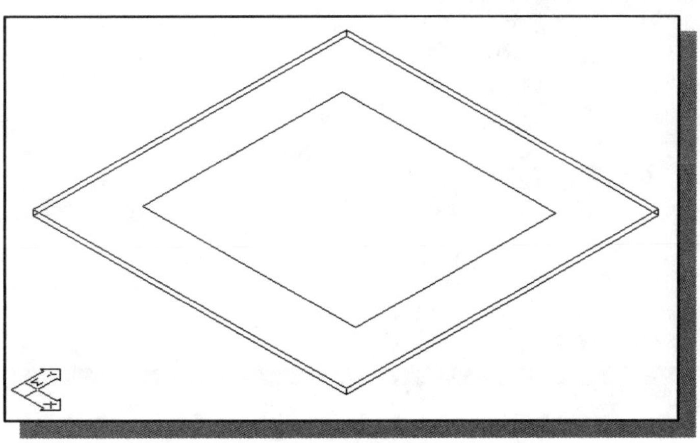

4. On your own, create a rectangle that is about 2/3 in size of the base as shown.

5. On your own, repeat the above steps and create four additional rectangle as shown in the below figure. Do not be overly concerned with the actual sizes and dimensions of the sketch; the main goal is "fast and loose" for conceptual models.

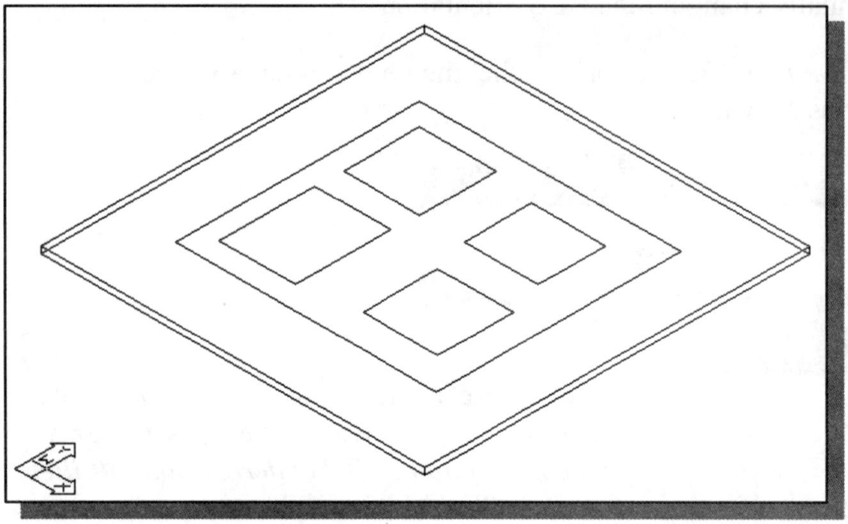

Create a Solid Feature Using the Press/Pull command

- The **Press/Pull** command allows us to press or pull bounded areas. The bounded area must be bounded by coplanar lines or edges. This command can be activated through the icon panel or by pressing and holding CTRL + ALT, and then picking the area.

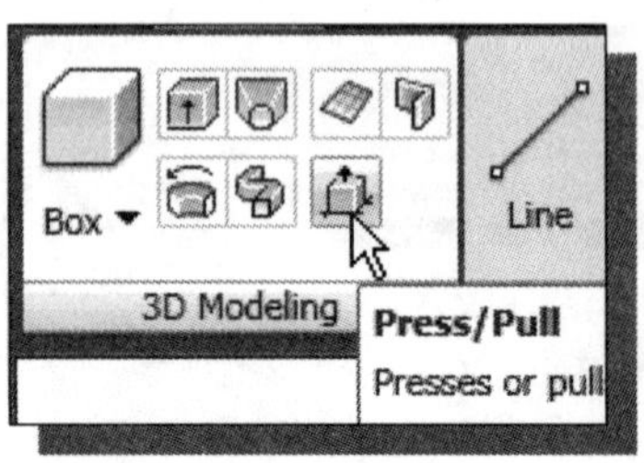

1. Select **Press/Pull** in the *Modeling* toolbar as shown.

2. In the command prompt area, the message "*Click inside the bounded are to press or pull:*" is displayed. Move the cursor near the center of the 2D sketch and noticed the dashed lines indicating the selected area.

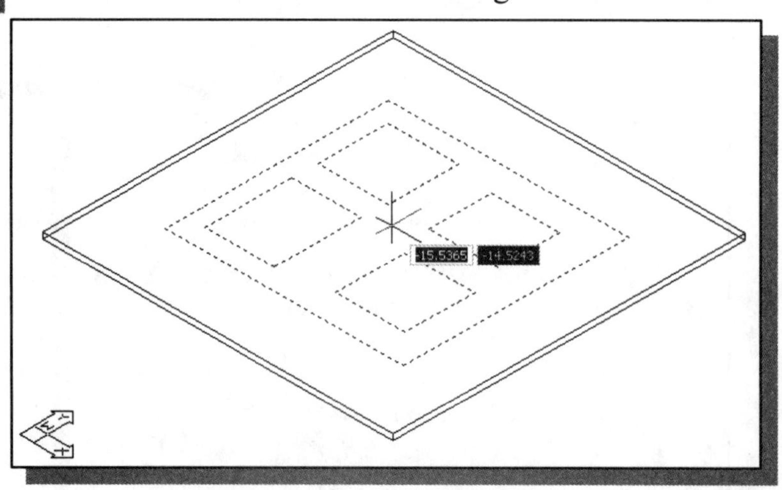

3. Inside the graphics window, press down the left-mouse-click and pull the selection upward as shown.

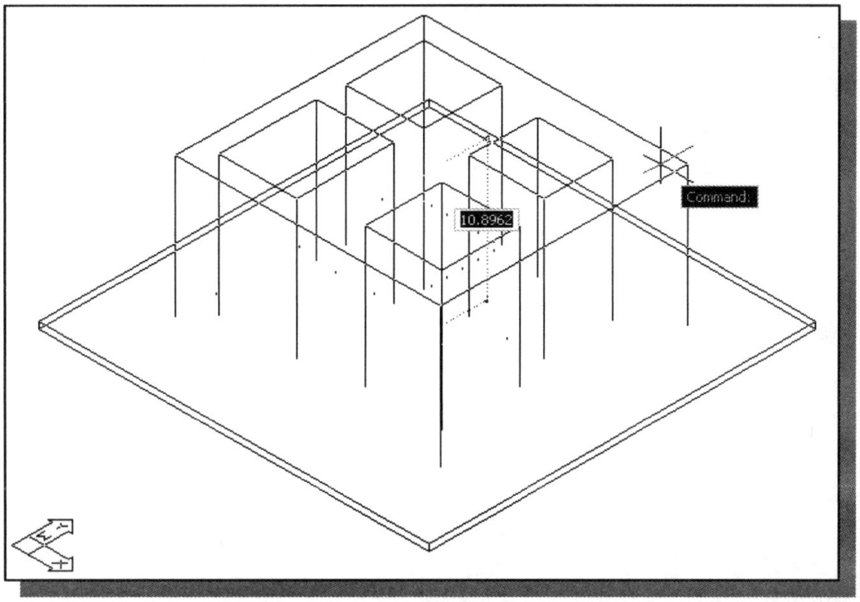

4. Inside the graphics window, left-mouse-click once to create the solid feature.

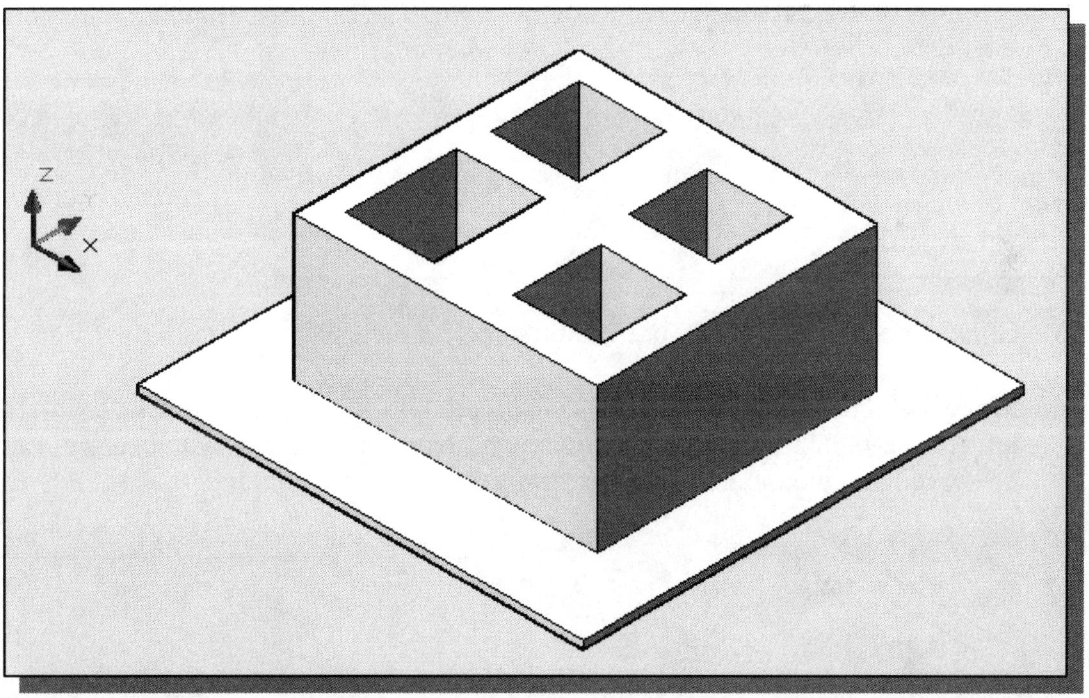

- Note that the solid feature created with the Press/Pull command automatically joins the feature to the existing solid model. The Press/Pull command allows us the ability to create solids from 2D geometry. Note that this is a totally different approach than the **Region** command. This new approach was first introduced by the @Last Software Co. (now part of Google) in their SketchUp software.

Using the Press/Pull Command as an Editing Tool

- The **Press/Pull** command can also be used as an editing tool. This command enables us to quickly resize any of the existing solid features.

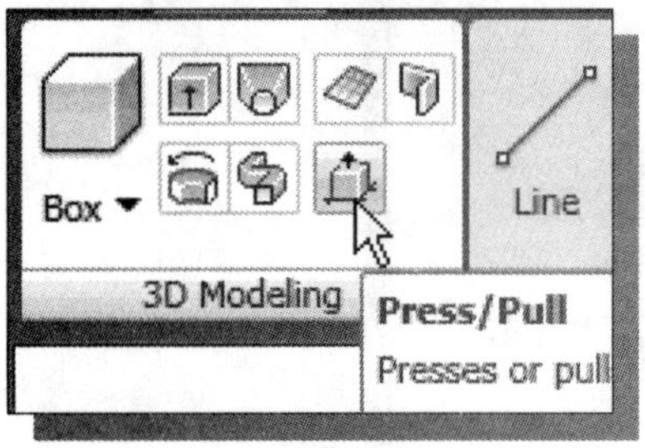

1. Select **Press/Pull** in the *Modeling* toolbar as shown.

2. Move the cursor on top of the inside vertical wall of the lower-left compartment, note the dashed lines indicating the currently selectable area.

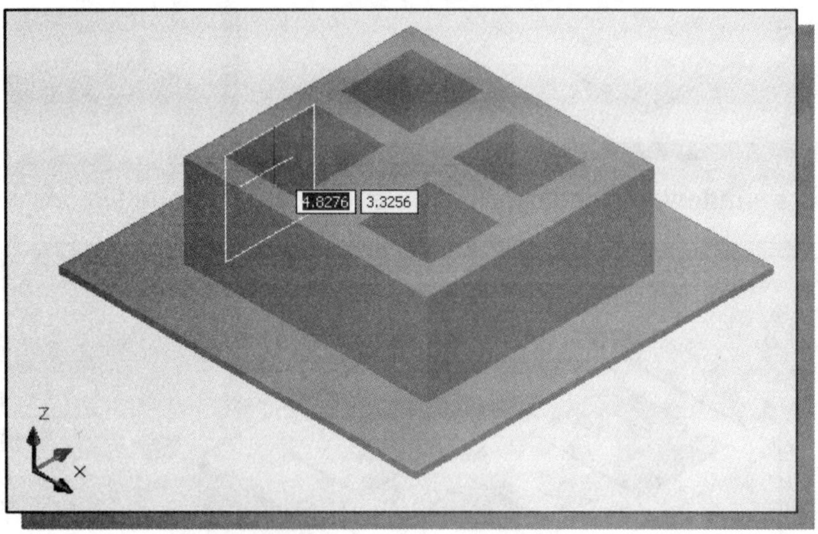

3. Click once with the left-mouse-button to select the surface.

4. Move the cursor and notice the selected surface is being adjusted. Click with the left-mouse-button to accept the adjustment. Note that the individual surface can be moved and the model resized with the Press/Pull command.

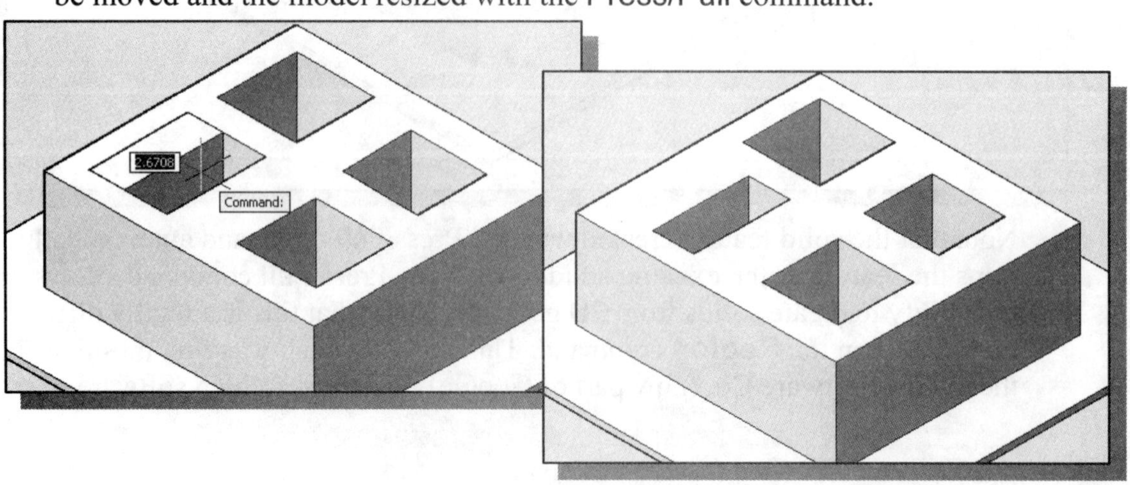

Create Another Cut feature

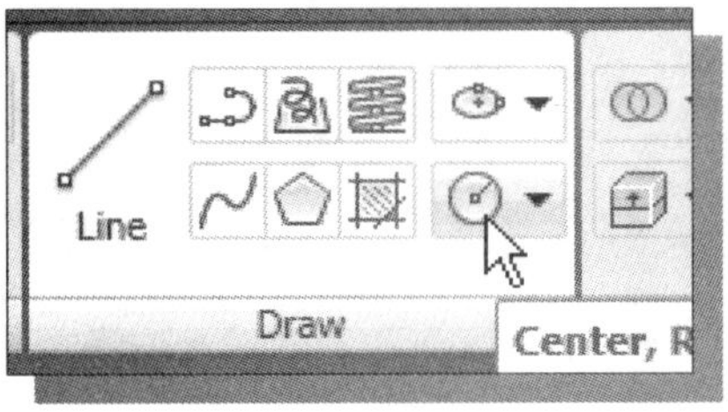

1. In the *Draw* toolbar, click on the **Circle** icon to activate the circle command. In the command prompt area, the message "*Specify center point for circle or [3P/2P/Ttr]:*" is displayed.

2. Move the cursor on the front plan of the 3D base and noticed the dynamic UCS option automatically aligns the UCS to the front plan as shown.

3. Pick a location to place the center point so that it is aligned to the center of the square opening.

4. Create a circle that is about half of the width of the square opening as shown in the below figure.

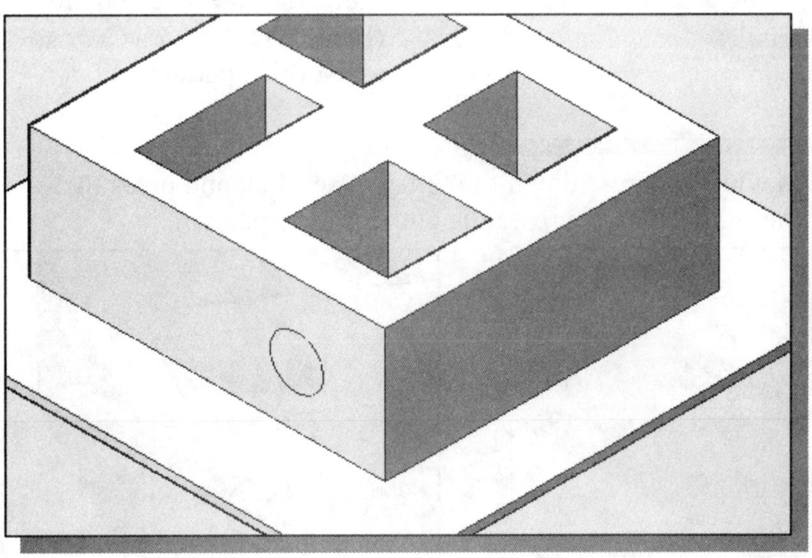

5. Inside the graphics window, select the circle by clicking once with the left-mouse-click. Notice that the 2D grip editing tool is also available for us to quickly adjust the size and location of the sketched 2D geometry.

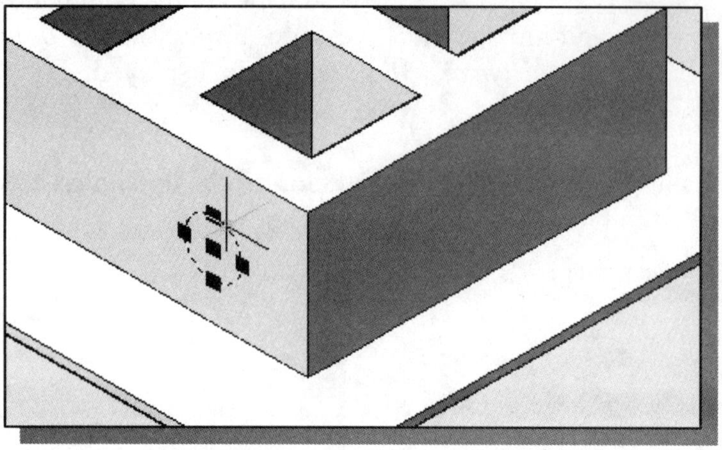

6. Press the [**Esc**] key once to deselect any entities.

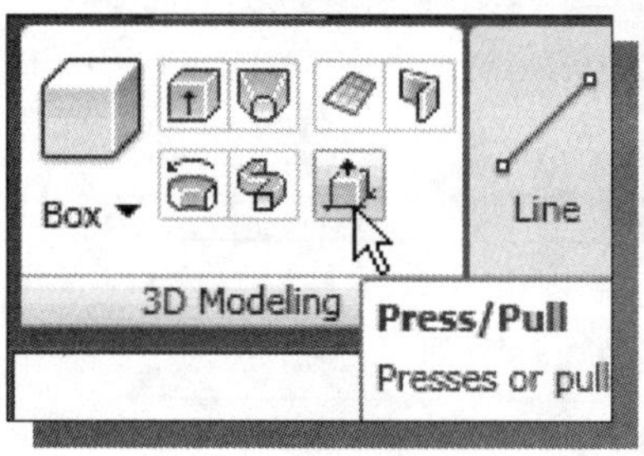

7. Select **Press/Pull** in the *Modeling* toolbar as shown. In the command prompt area, the message "*Click inside the bounded are to press or pull:*" is displayed.

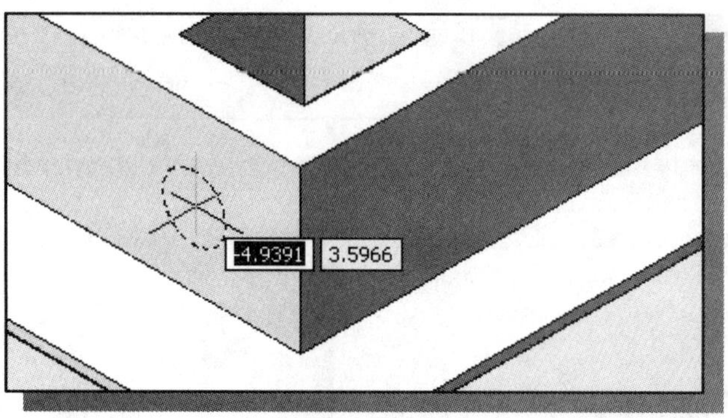

8. Move the cursor near the center of the circle we just created and noticed the dashed lines indicating the selected area. (Hint: Use the *ViewCube* to assist this operation.)

9. Inside the graphics window, press down the left-mouse-click and press the selection toward the right side and create the cut feature as shown.

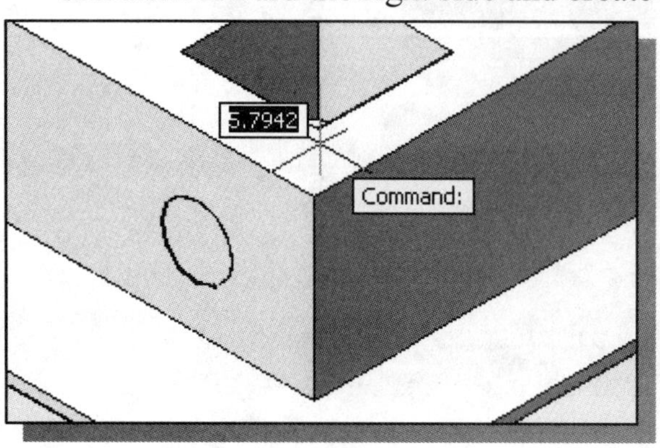

Adjusting the Compartments

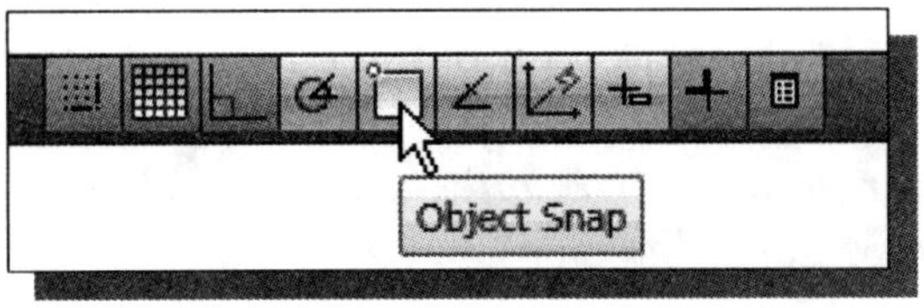

1. Deactivate the *Object Snap* option, by clicking on the **associated** icon in the *Status* toolbar as shown.

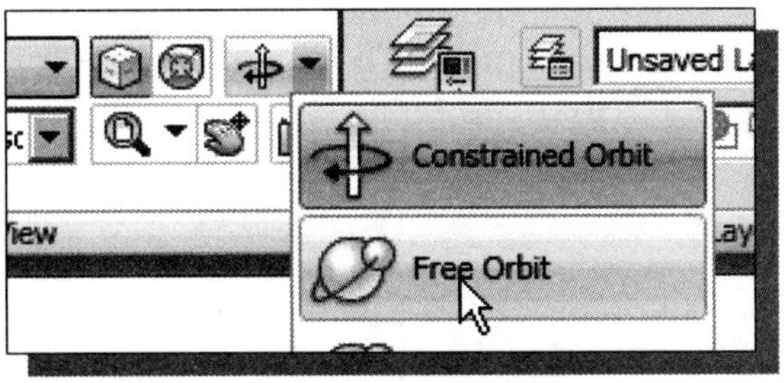

2. On your own, use the **Free Orbit** option to view the current 3D solid model.

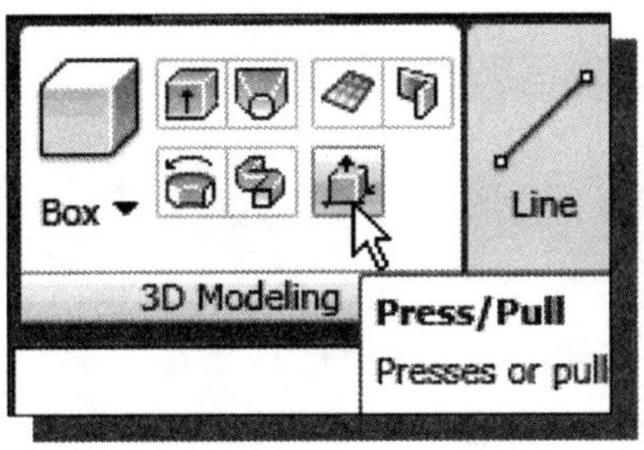

3. Select **Press/Pull** in the *Modeling* toolbar as shown. In the command prompt area, the message "*Click inside the bounded are to press or pull:*" is displayed.

4. On your own, adjust the compartments so that we can add additional compartments, in between the existing ones, as shown in the blow figure.

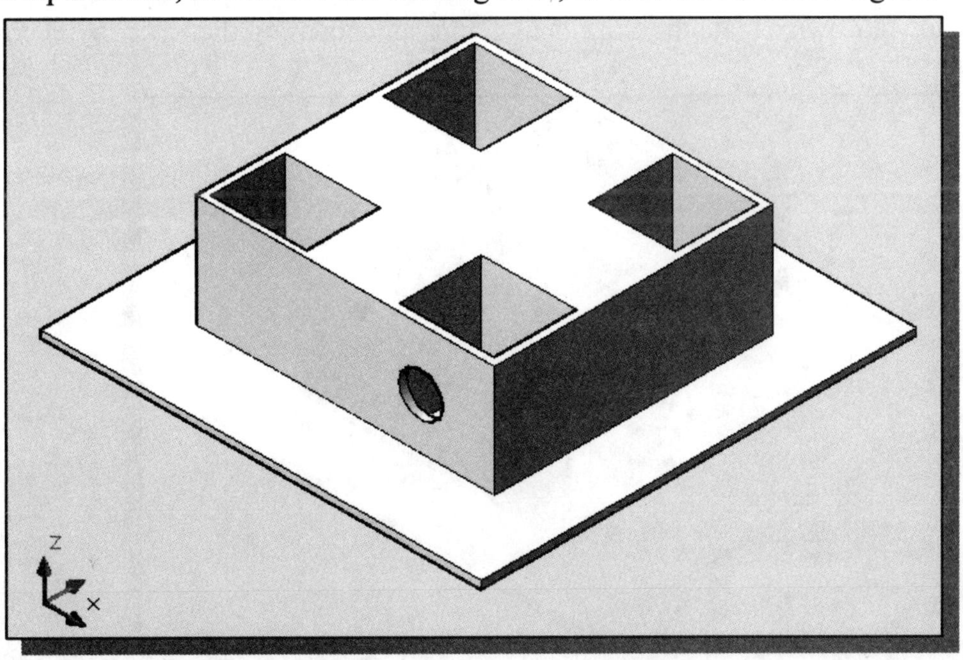

- The Press/Pull command enables us to perform fast and loose adjustments of existing surfaces, which conforms to the basic concept of conceptual design.

Adding Additional Compartments

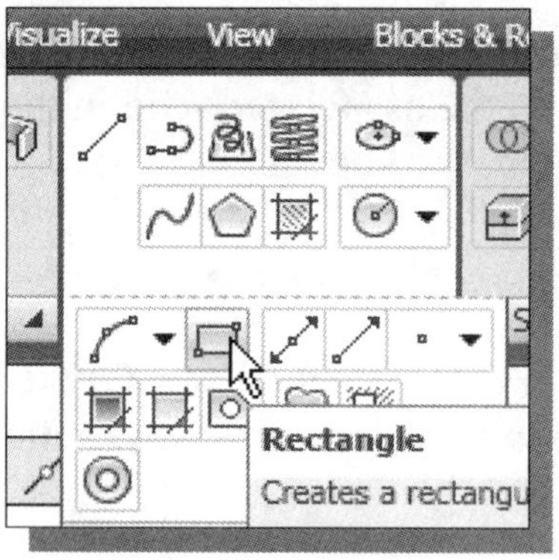

1. Select the **Rectangle** icon in the *Draw* toolbar. In the command prompt area, the message "*Specify first corner point or [Chamfer/Elevation/Fillet/ Thickness/Width]:*" is displayed.

2. Move the cursor on the top plan of the 3D base and noticed the dynamic UCS option automatically aligns the UCS to the top plan.

3. On your own, create the four additional rectangles as shown in the below figure.

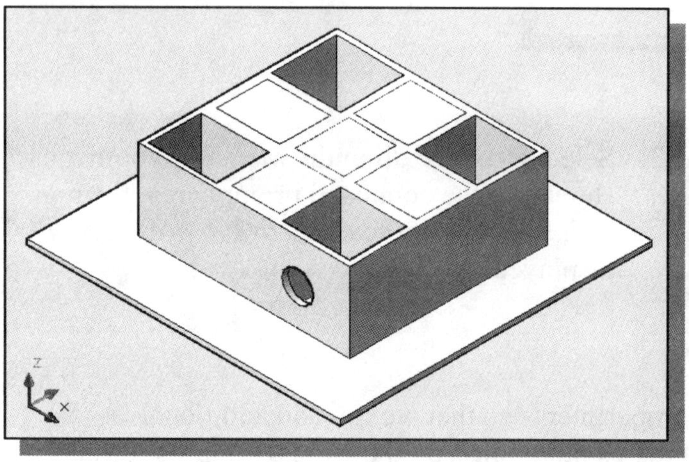

4. On your own, create the additional compartments using the **Press/Pull** command.

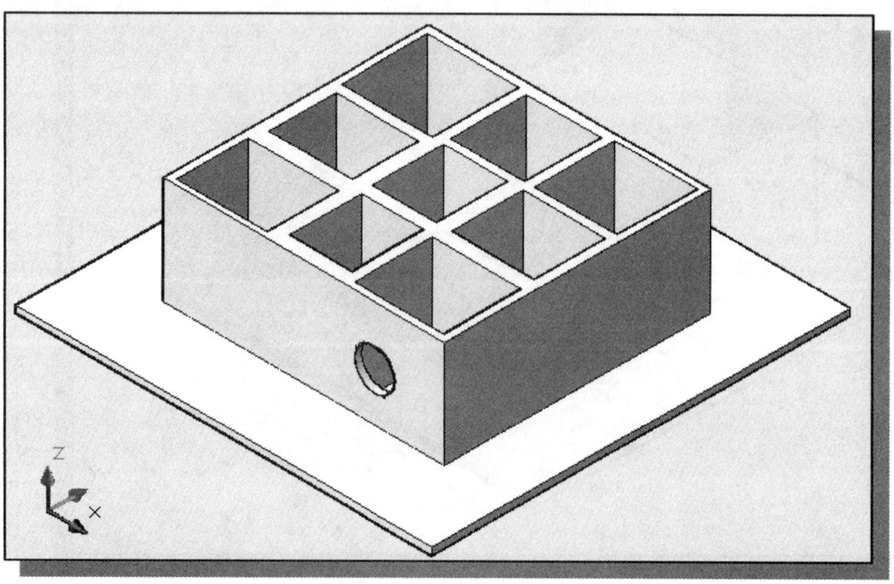

Creating the Doors

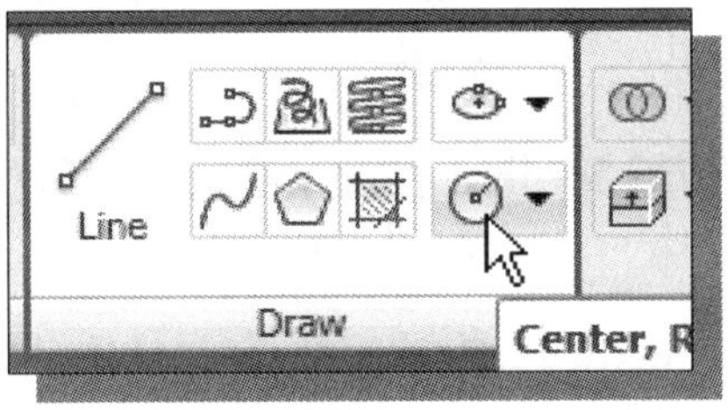

1. Click on the **Circle** icon to activate the circle command. In the command prompt area, the message "*Specify center point for circle or [3P/2P/Ttr]:*" is displayed.

2. Move the cursor on the front plan of the 3D base and noticed the dynamic UCS option automatically aligns the UCS to the front plan as shown.

3. On your own, create the additional circles as shown in the below figure.

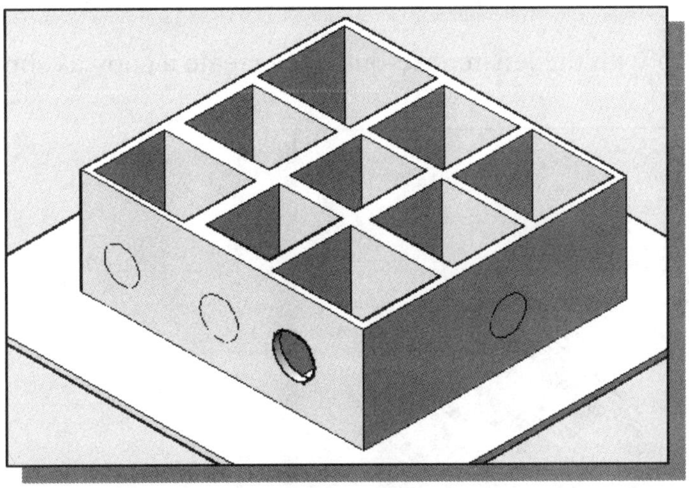

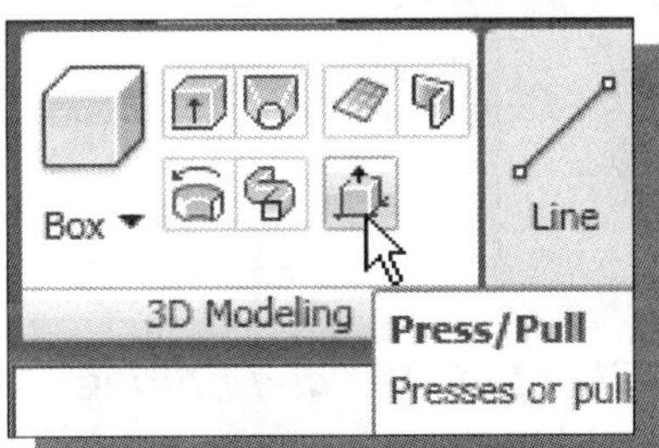

4. On your own, use the **Press/Pull** command and create the doors as shown in the below figure.

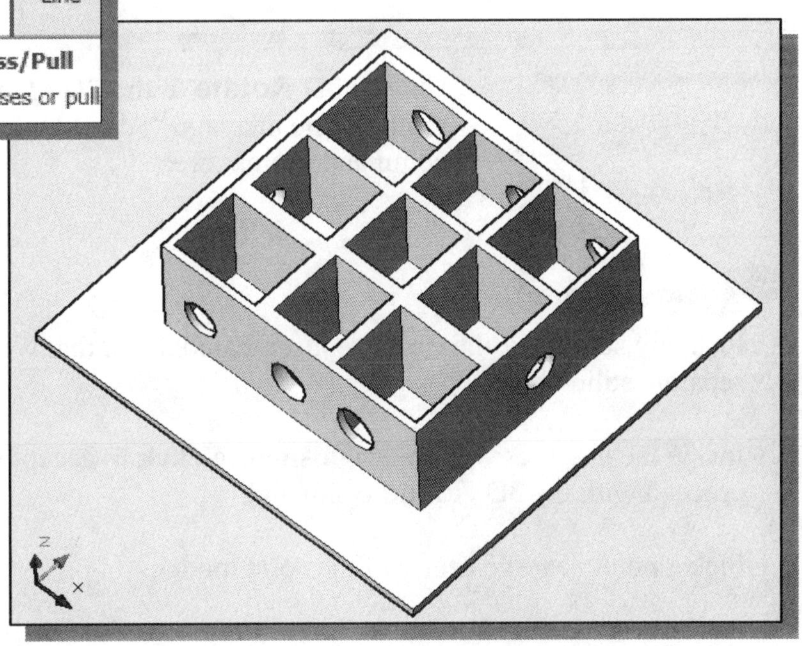

Creating the 2nd Floor

- We will next create the 2nd floor of the birdhouse, we will do this by simply making a copy of the 1st floor model.

1. Choose **Copy** in the *Modify* toolbar. The message "*Select Objects:*" is displayed in the command prompt area.

2. Pick any surface of the 3D solid. Note the entire solid is selected.

3. Inside the graphics window, **right-mouse-click** to accept the selection and proceed with the Copy command.

4. On your own, drag and drop with the left-mouse-button to create a copy as shown.

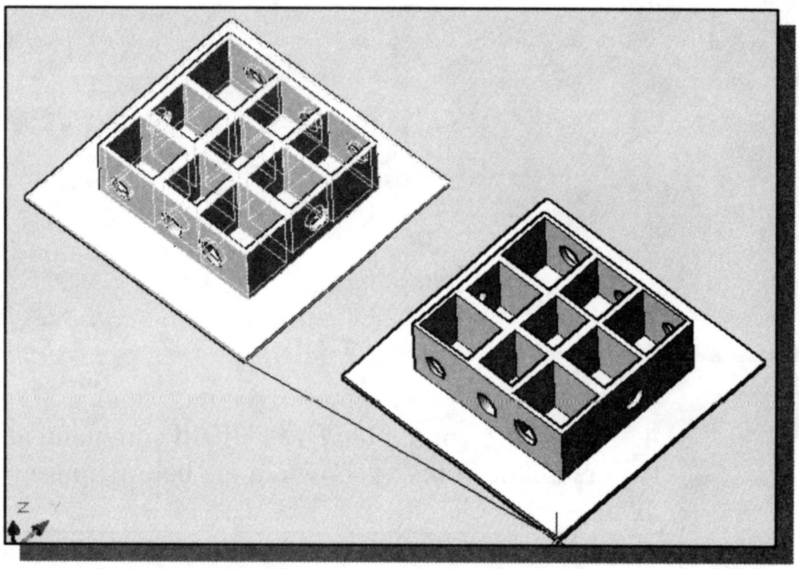

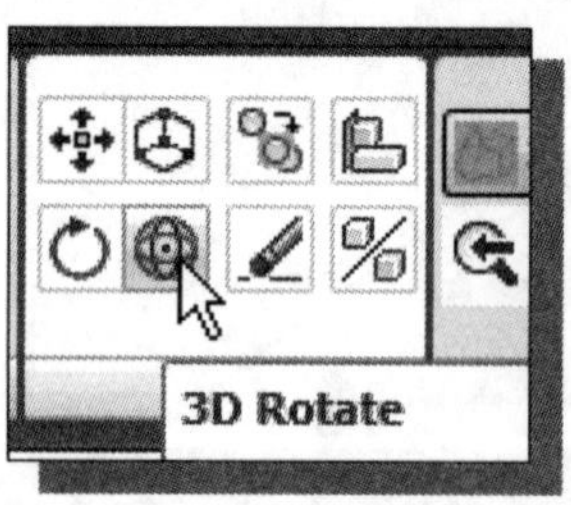

5. Choose **3D Rotate** in the *3D Modeling and Editing* toolbar. The message "*Select Objects:*" is displayed in the command prompt area.

6. Pick any surface of the copy we just created. Note that we currently have two separate solid objects.

7. Inside the graphics window, **right-mouse-click** to accept the selection and proceed with the 3D Rotate command.

8. Pick a point near the center of the solid model.

9. Select the **horizontal ring** that is associated with the **Z** rotation axis as shown.

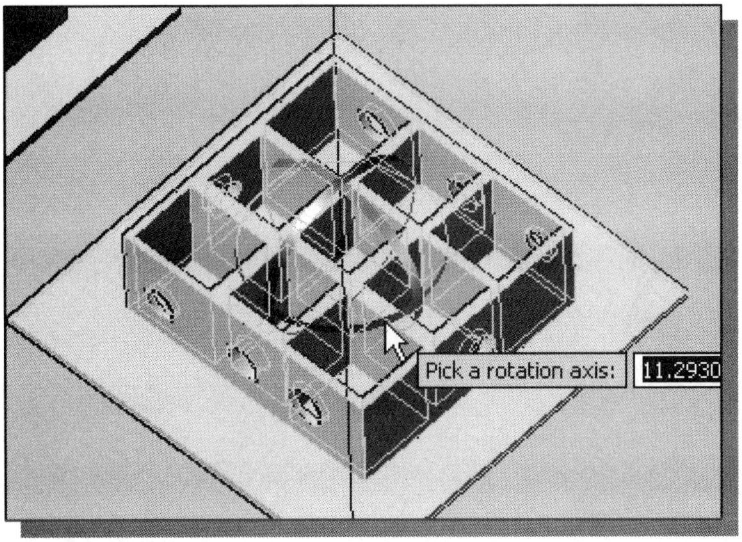

10. We will rotate the model 90 degrees about the Z-axis. Enter **90** as the rotation angle as shown.

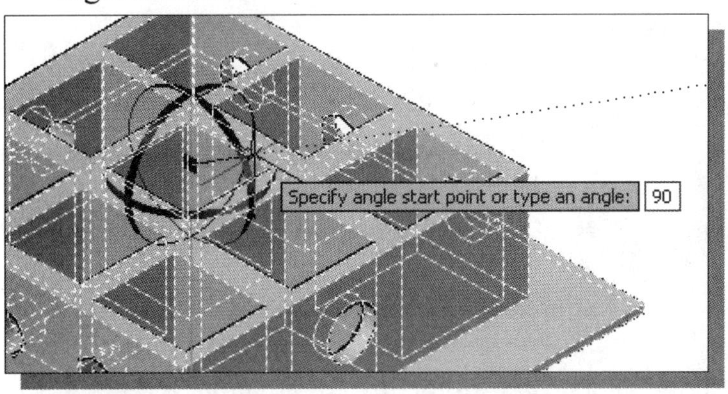

11. The 2nd floor is now rotated 90 degrees; note that all of the AutoCAD solid modeling tools are also available for conceptual modeling.

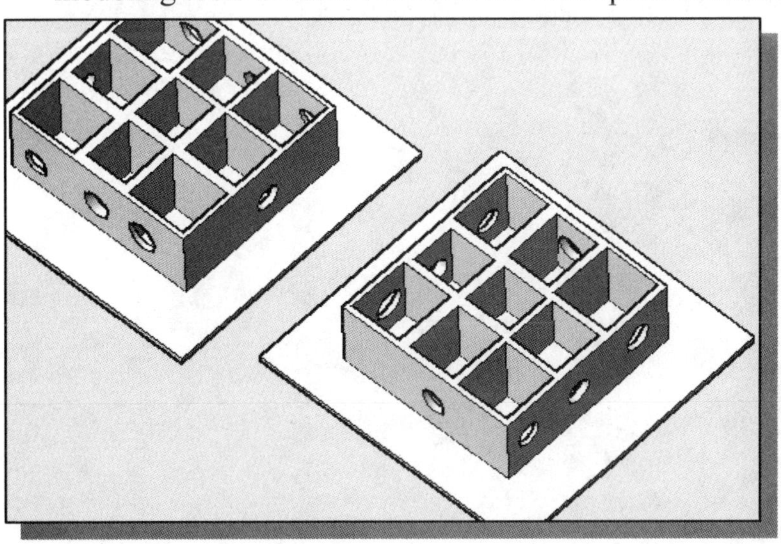

Repositioning the 2nd Floor

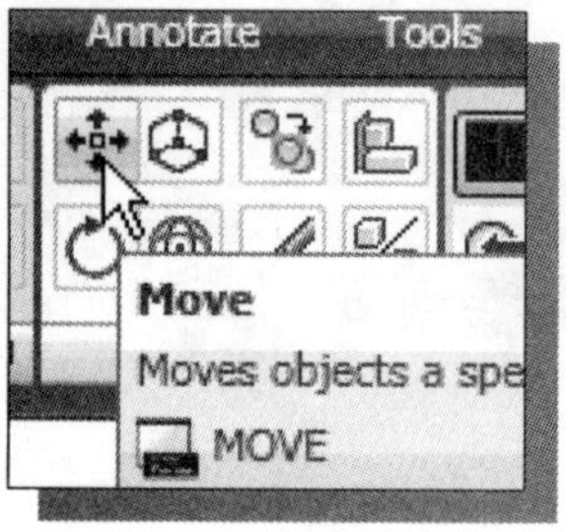

1. Click on the **Move** icon in the *Modify* toolbar. The message "*Select Objects:*" is displayed in the command prompt area.

2. Pick any surface of the 2nd floor model we just rotated.

3. Inside the graphics window, **right-mouse-click** to accept the selection and proceed with the Move command.

4. On your own, switch on the ***Object Snap Tracking*** and the ***Object Snap*** options as shown in the below figure.

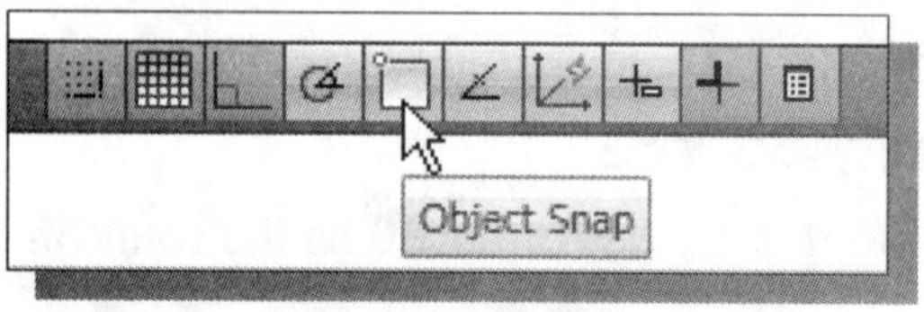

5. Select the lower left corner of the 2nd floor model as the **base point**, as shown in the figure.

6. Align the new location to the intersection of the lower and upper left corners of the 1st floor model as shown in the below figure. (Hint: Pause at the two reference corners and observed the dashed lines showing alignments.)

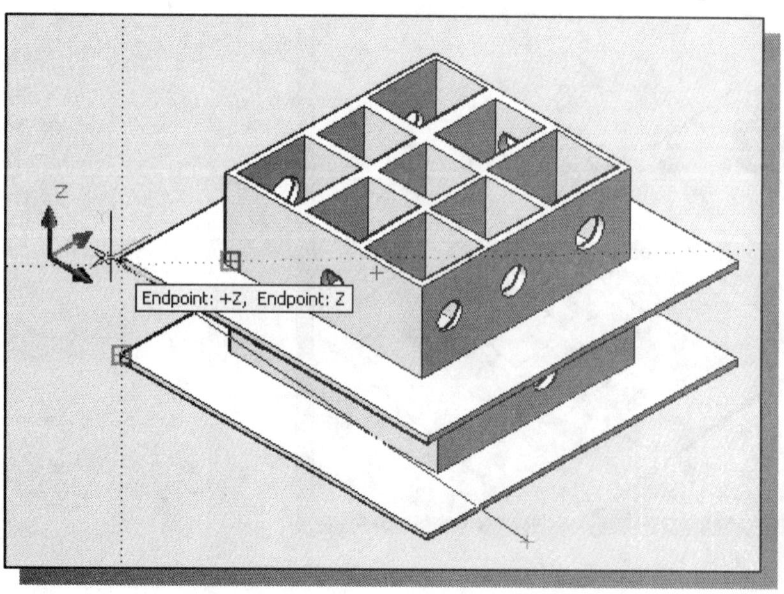

Modeling the Roof Section with the Press/Pull command

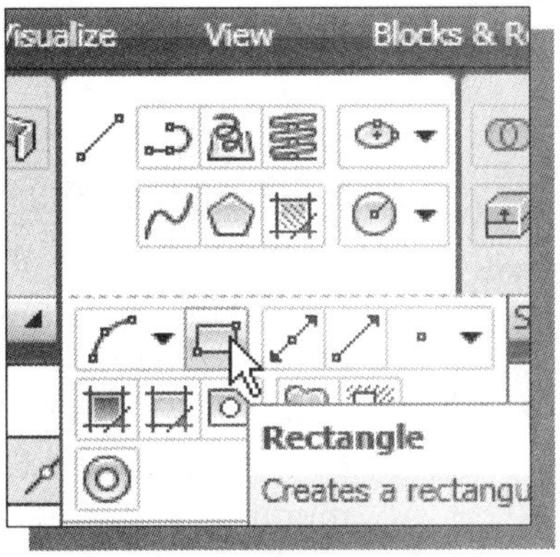

1. Select the **Rectangle** icon in the *Draw* toolbar. In the command prompt area, the message "*Specify first corner point or [Chamfer/Elevation/Fillet/ Thickness/Width]:*" is displayed.

2. Place the first corner point of the rectangle to the right side of the current 3D model.

3. We will create a rectangle that is the same size as the base of the model. Enter **@30,30** [**ENTER**].

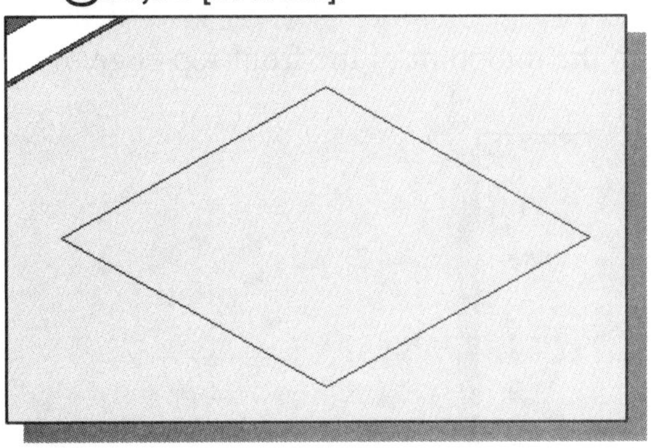

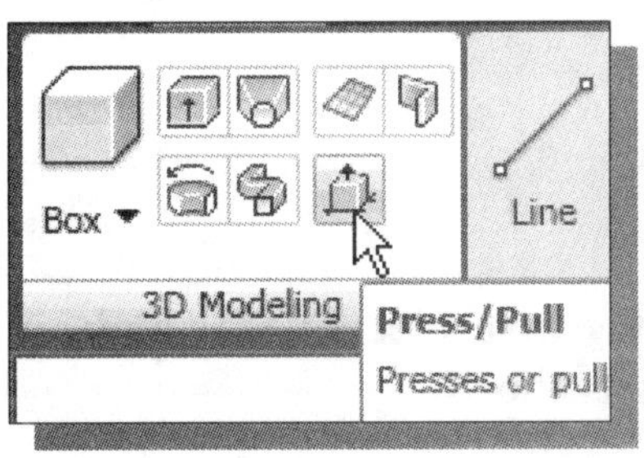

4. Pick the **Press/Pull** icon in the *Solid Editing* toolbar as shown in the figure.

5. Pick a location inside the rectangle we just created.

6. Move the cursor upward and enter **.5** as the height value as shown in the below figure.

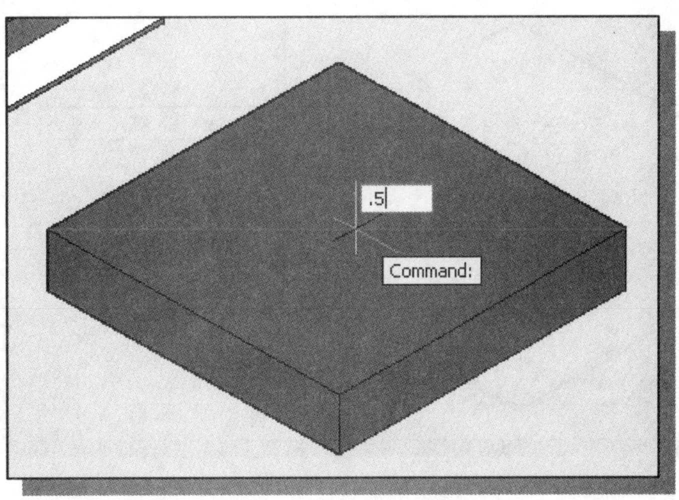

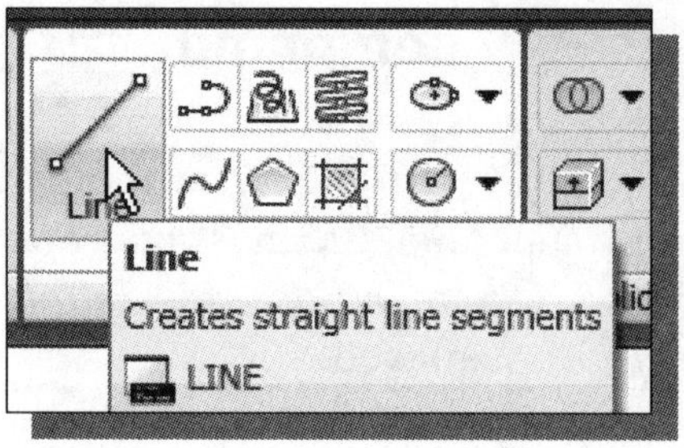

7. Select the **Line** icon in the *Draw* toolbar. In the command prompt area, the message "*_line Specify first point:*" is displayed.

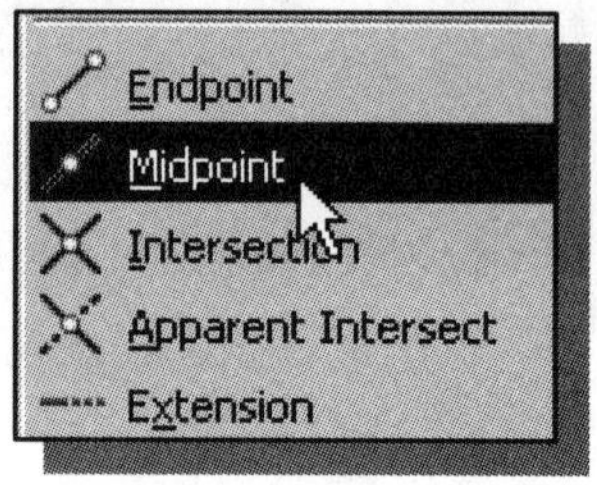

8. Inside the graphics window, hold down the **[SHIFT]** key and **right-mouse-click** once to bring up the *Object Snap* shortcut menu.

9. Select the **Midpoint** option in popup window.

10. Place the first endpoint by snapping to the midpoint of the front-top edge of new model as shown.

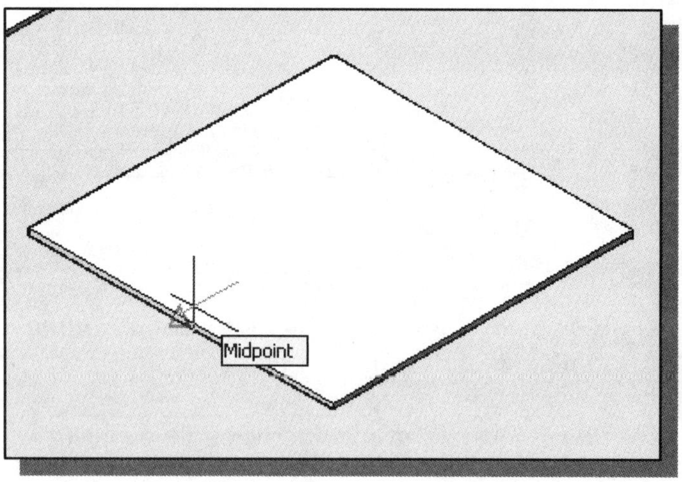

11. Complete the line by making it perpendicular to the first selected edge and extended beyond the top of the rectangular block as shown.

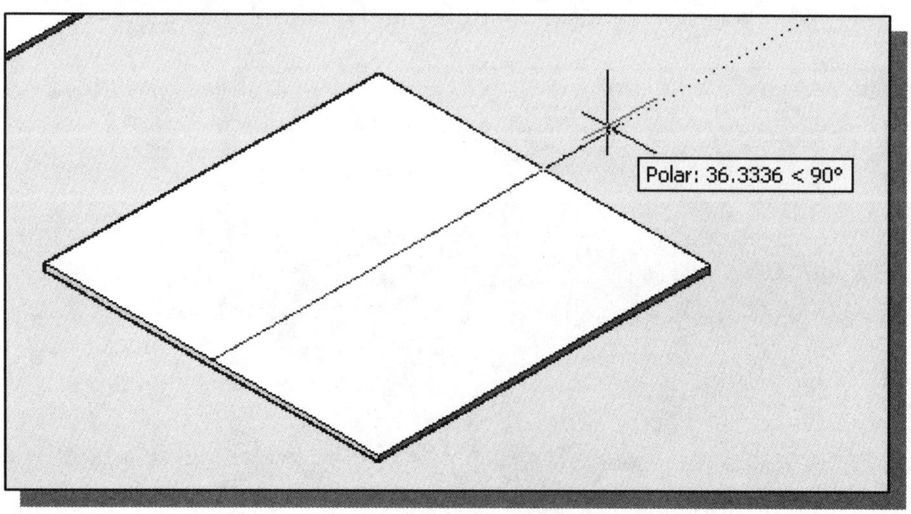

Using the Imprint Command

- In AutoCAD, the appearance of a surface on a 3-D solid can be adjusted by imprinting the surface with an object that intersects with it. Imprinting combines the object with the surface, creating a new edge.

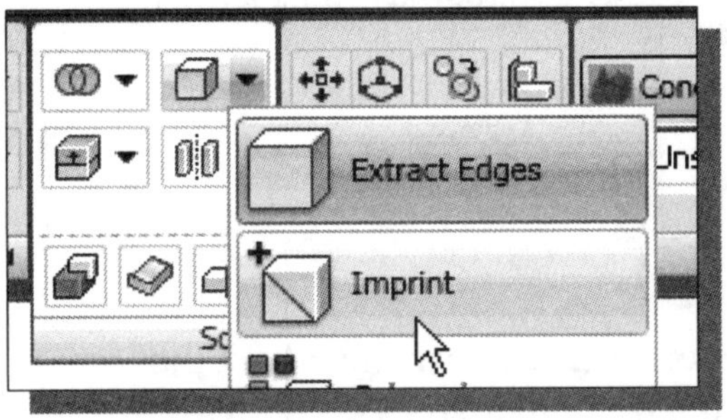

1. In the *Solid Editing* toolbar, click on the **Imprint** icon. In the command prompt area, the message "*Select a 3D Object:*" is displayed.

2. Select the **rectangular block** as the solid object to be adjusted.

3. In the command prompt area, the message "*Select an object to imprint:*" is displayed. Select the **line** we just created.

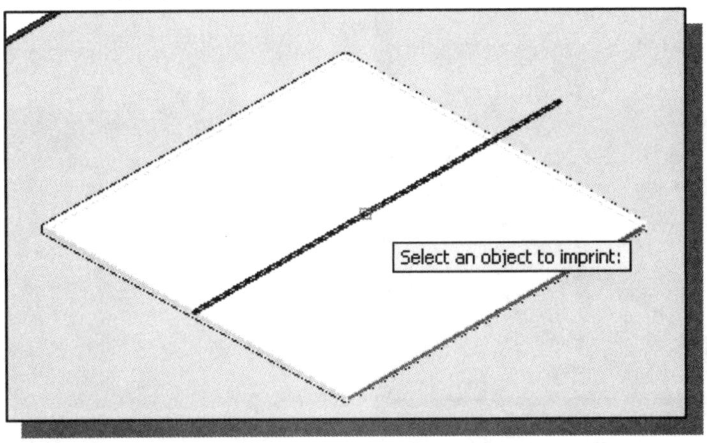

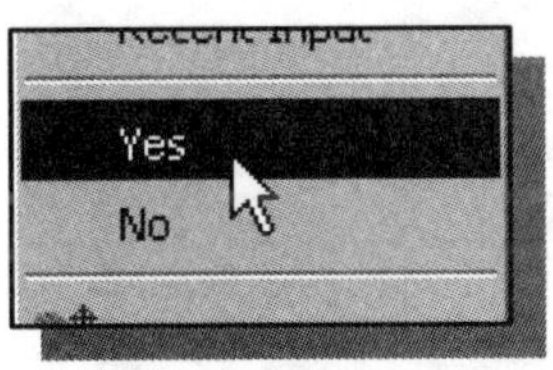

4. In the command prompt area, the message "*Delete the source object [Yes/No]:*" is displayed. Click once with the **right-mouse-click** to bring up the option menu and select **Yes** as shown.

5. In the command prompt area, the message "*Select an object to imprint:*" is displayed. Click once with the **right-mouse-button** to **end** the **Imprint** command.

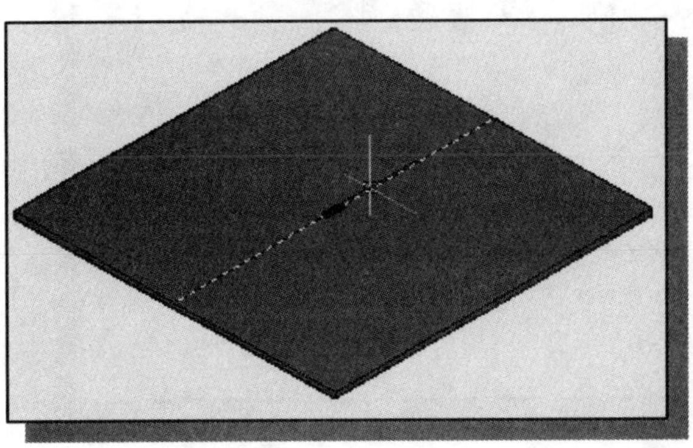

6. Press down the [**CTRL**] key and move the cursor on top of the imprinted line we just created. Note that the two surfaces are also selectable, move the cursor around to cycle through the possible selections. Select the **line** when it is highlighted as shown.

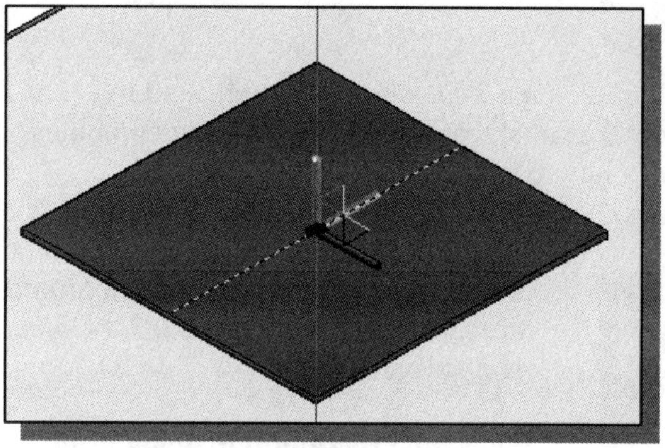

7. Move the cursor on top of the blue grip point near the center. Select the **vertical axis** when it is displayed as shown.

8. Move the cursor **upward** to pull the center edge upward and adjust the rectangular shape of the solid model into a triangular shape as shown.

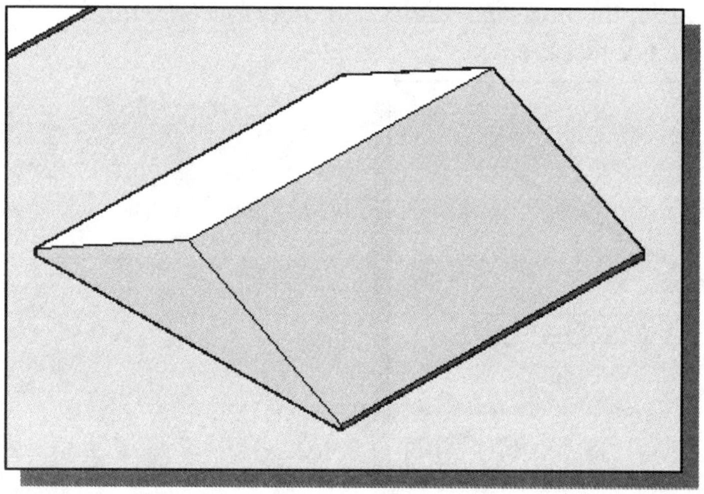

9. On your own, create a triangle aligned to the triangular surface of the roof as shown in the figure.

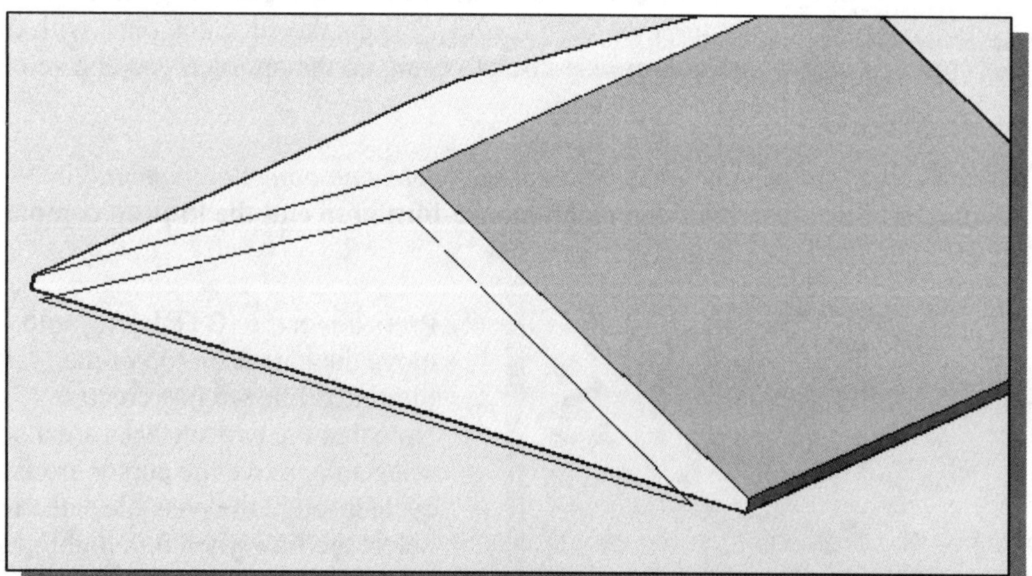

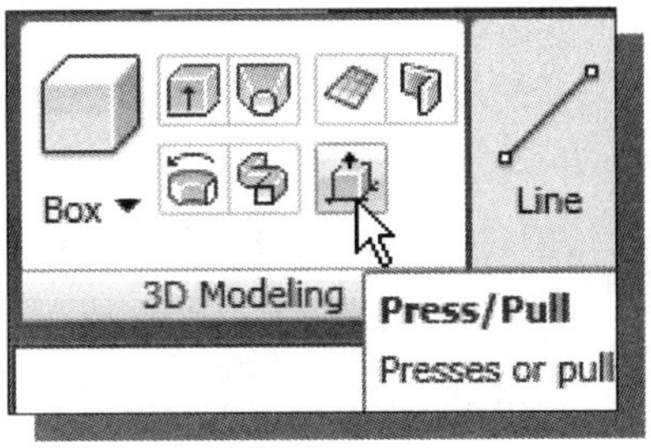

10. Pick the **Press/Pull** icon in the *Solid Editing* toolbar as shown in the figure.

11. Pick a location inside the triangle we just created.

12. On your own, create a cut feature on the roof section as shown in the figure.

13. On your own, position the roof section on top of the 2nd floor model to complete the conceptual model of the birdhouse design as shown.

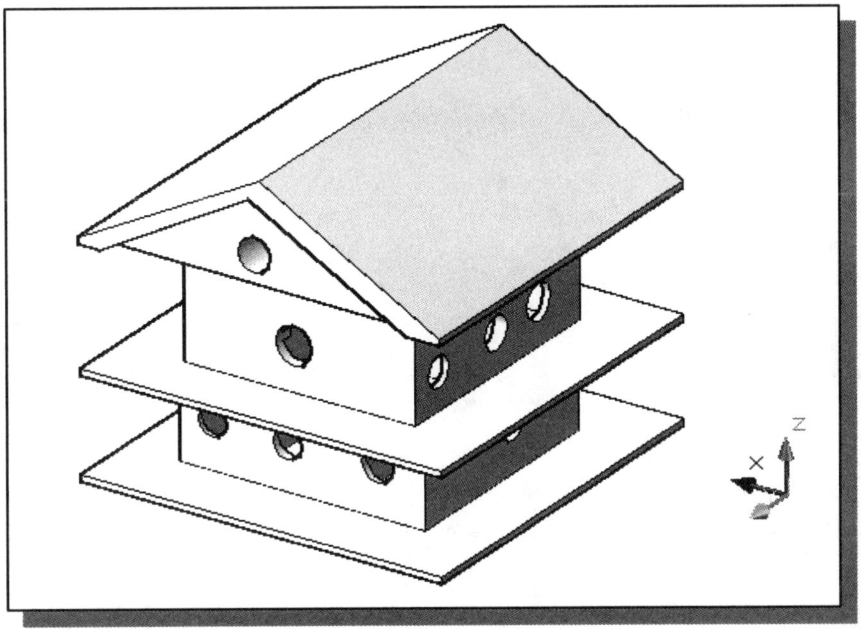

Conclusion

Design includes all activities involved from the original concept to the finished product. Design is the process by which products are created and modified. For many years designers sought ways to describe and analyze three-dimensional designs without building physical models. With the advancements in computer technology, the creation of computer solid models on computers offers a wide range of benefits. Solid models are easier to interpret and can be easily altered. Solid models can also be analyzed using finite element analysis software, and simulation of real-life loads can be applied to the models and the results graphically displayed.

Throughout this text, various modeling techniques have been presented. Mastering these techniques will enable you to create intelligent and flexible solid models. The goal is to make use of the tools provided by AutoCAD and to successfully create solid models of the product. In many instances, only a single approach to the modeling tasks was presented; you are encouraged to repeat all of the chapters and develop different ways of thinking in accomplishing the same tasks. We have only scratched the surface of AutoCAD's functionality. The more time you spend using the system, the easier it will be to perform solid modeling with AutoCAD.

Questions:

1. Describe the general stages involved in an engineering design procedure.

2. What is the purpose of creating a *Conceptual Model*?

3. What are the main differences between a conceptual drawing and a detail drawing?

4. Which command can be used to quickly resize a 3D model in AutoCAD?

5. How do we alter an existing surface AutoCAD? What elements are required to perform the operation?

6. Identify the following commands:

(a)

(b)

(c)

(d)

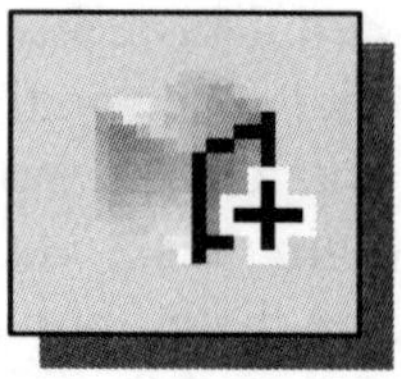

Exercises:

Create conceptual sketches and conceptual models of the following design projects:

1. **A better mousetrap.**
2. **A four-legged walking robot.**
3. **A rocket launcher.**
4. **A vehicle powered by birthday candles.**
5. **A hand-launched glider aircraft.**
6. **A Catapult for water balloons.**
7. **A vehicle to carry an egg safely down an inclined surface into a wall.**
8. **A vehicle to be powered solely by a hamster.**
9. **A rubber band powered all-terrain vehicle.**

Leveling Assembly
(Create a set of detail and assembly drawings. All dimensions are in mm.)

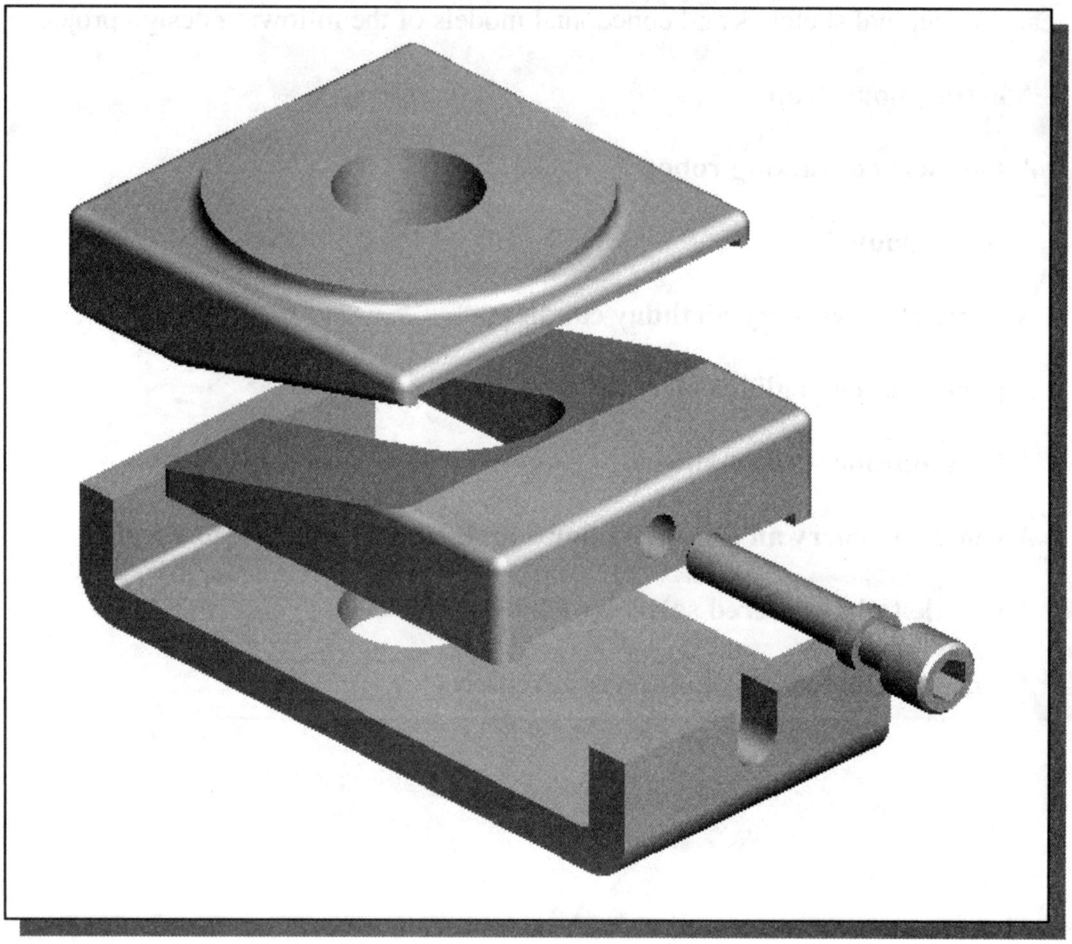

(a) Base Plate

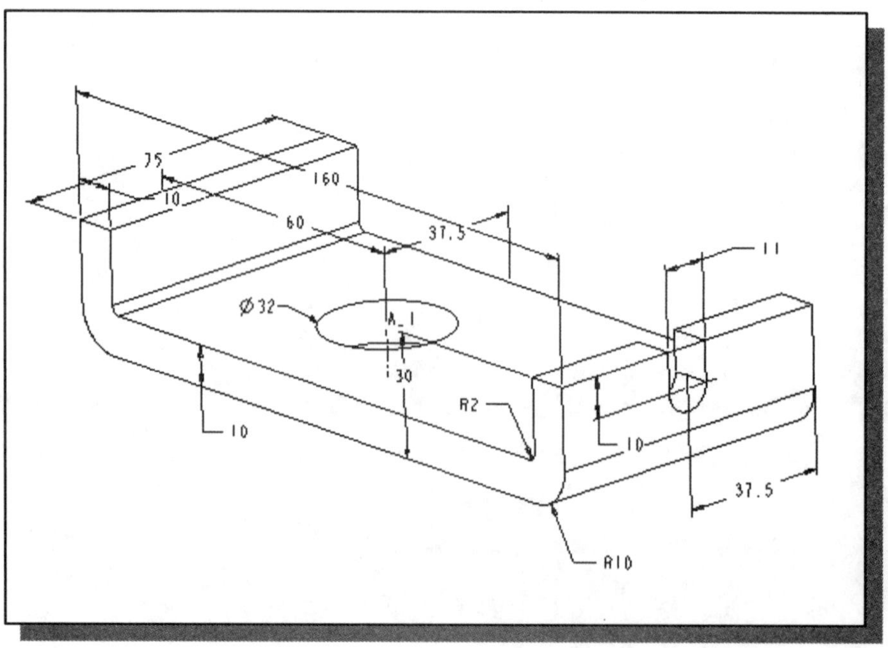

(b) **Sliding Block** (Rounds & Fillets: R3)

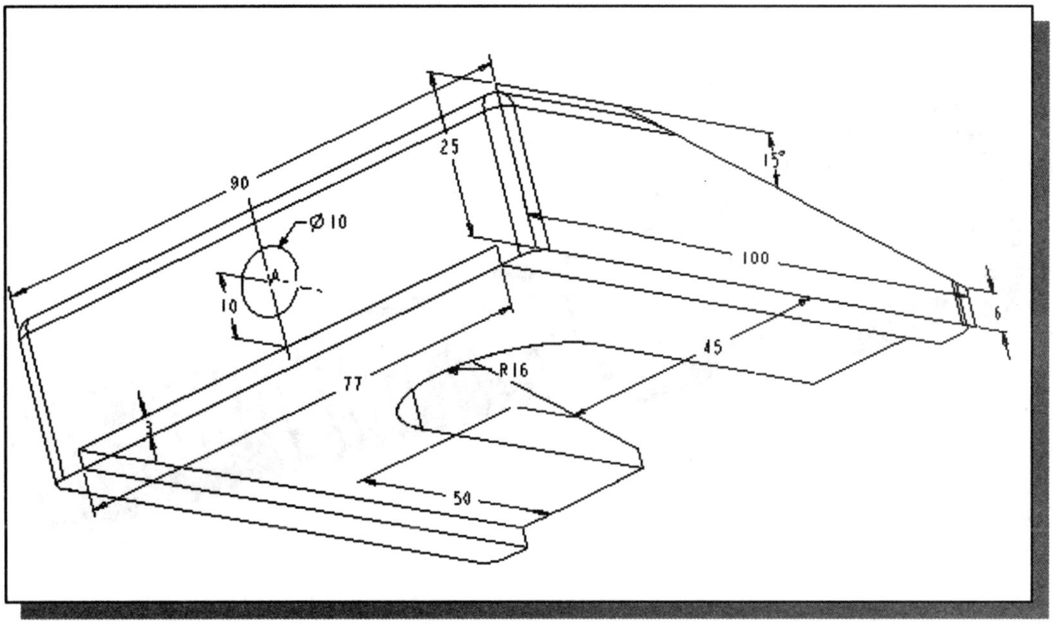

(c) **Lifting Block** (Rounds & Fillets: R3)

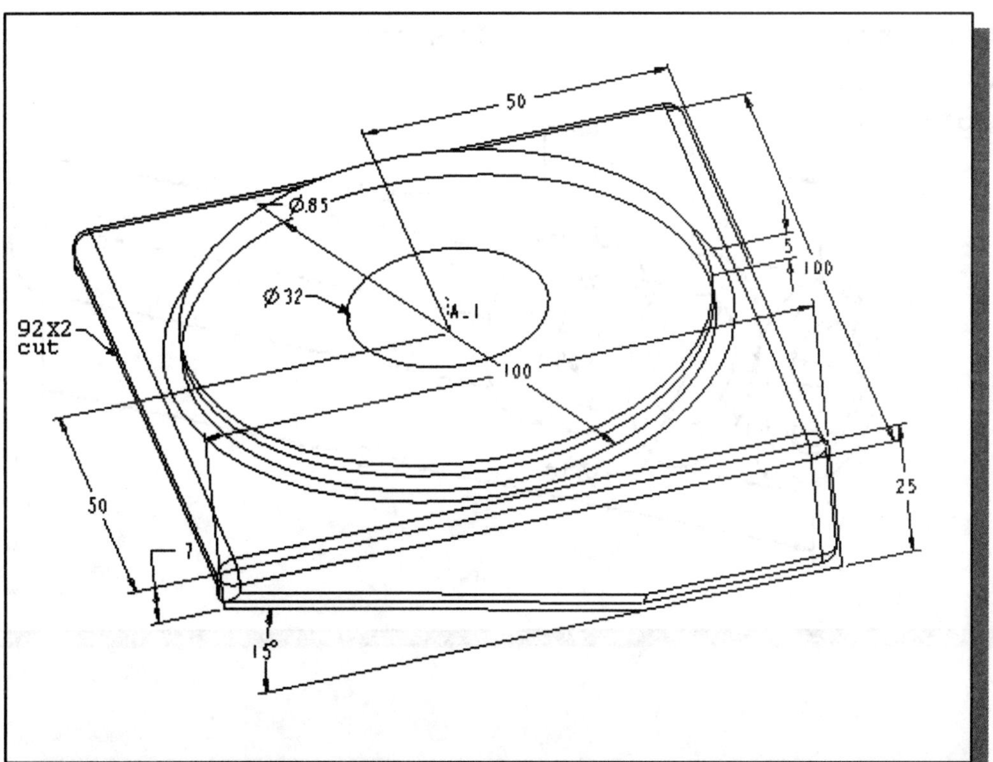

(d) **Adjusting Screw** (M10 × 1.5)

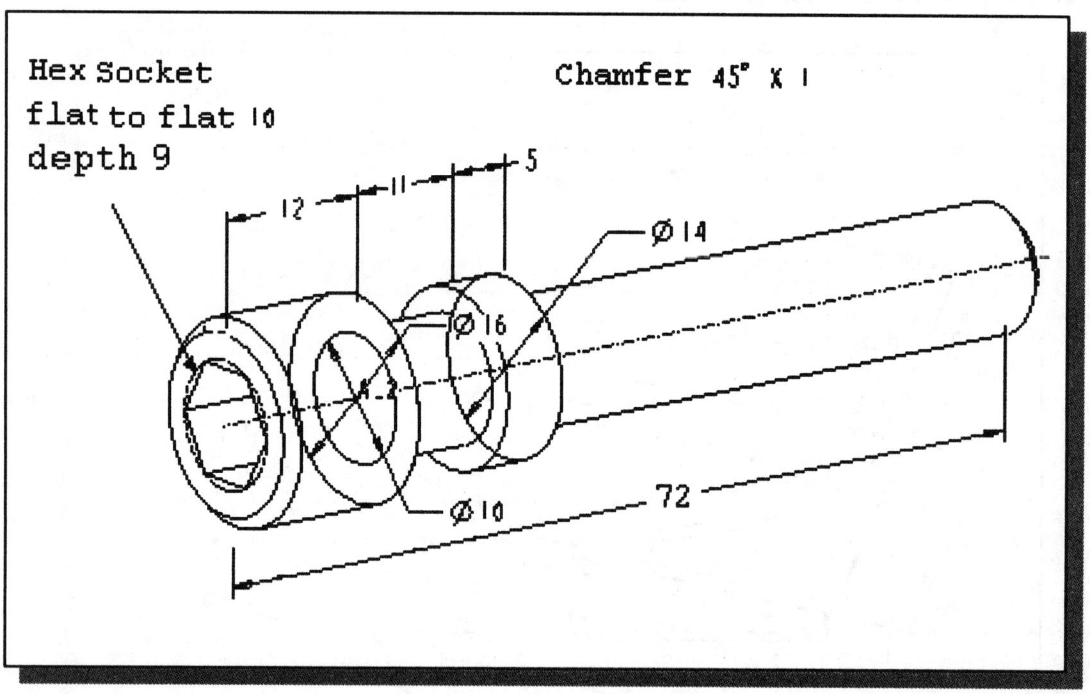

INDEX

W

X

Y

Z

NOTES

NOTES

NOTES

NOTES

NOTES

NOTES